TEACHER PREP

MERRILL
PRENTICE HALL

Teacher Preparation Classroom

See a demo at
www.prenhall.com/teacherprep/demo

Your Class. Their Careers. Our Future. Will your students be prepared?

We invite you to explore our new, innovative and engaging website and all that it has to offer you, your course, and tomorrow's educators! Preview this site today at www.prenhall.com/teacherprep/demo. Just click on "go" on the login page to begin your exploration.

Organized around the major courses pre-service teachers take, the Teacher Preparation site provides media, student/teacher artifacts, strategies, research articles, and other resources to equip your students with the quality tools needed to excel in their courses and prepare them for their first classroom.

This ultimate online education resource will provide you and your students access to:

Online Video Library. More than 250 video clips—each tied to a course topic and framed by learning goals and Praxis-type questions— capture real teachers and students working in real classrooms.

Student and Teacher Artifacts. More than 200 student and teacher classroom artifacts— each tied to a course topic and framed by learning goals and application questions— provide a wealth of materials and experiences to help your students observe children's developmental learning.

Lesson Plan Builder. Step-by-step guidelines and lesson plan examples support students as they learn to build high-quality lesson plans.

Articles and Readings. Over 500 articles from ASCD's renowned journal *Educational Leadership* are available. The site also includes Research Navigator, a searchable database of additional educational journals.

Strategies and Lessons. Over 500 research-supported instructional strategies appropriate for a wide range of grade levels and content areas.

Licensure and Career Tools. Resources devoted to helping your students pass their licensure exam; learn standards, law, and public policies; plan a teaching portfolio; and succeed in their first year of teaching.

Access Code previously been used?
Students:
- To purchase or renew an access code, go to *www.prenhall.com/teacherprep* and click on the "Register for Teacher Prep" button.

Instructors:
- Email *Merrill.marketing@pearsoned.com* and provide the following information:
  - Name and Affiliation
  - Author/Title/Edition of Merrill text

Upon ordering *Teacher Prep* for their students, instructors will be given a lifetime *Teacher Prep* Access Code.

Special Education for Today's Teachers

An Introduction

Michael S. Rosenberg

Johns Hopkins University

David L. Westling

Western Carolina University

James McLeskey

University of Florida

PEARSON

Merrill
Prentice Hall

Upper Saddle River, New Jersey
Columbus, Ohio

Library of Congress Cataloging in Publication Data

Rosenberg, Michael S.
   Special education for today's teachers : an introduction / Michael S. Rosenberg, David L. Westling, James McLeskey.
      p. cm.
   Includes bibliographical references and indexes.
   Contents: Pt. 1. Becoming a professional: what are the foundations of special education? — pt. 2. Teaching effectively in the classroom: what can you expect? — pt. 3. Meeting the multiple needs of students with exceptionalities: what is effective practice? — pt. 4. A successful career: growing in your profession.
   ISBN 0-13-118560-8 (pbk.)
      1. Children with disabilities—Education—United States. 2. Special education—Study and teaching—United States. 3. Special education teachers—United States I. Westling, David L. II. McLeskey, James, III. Title.

LC4031.R678 2008
371.9'0973—dc22   2006052534

Vice President and Executive Publisher: Jeffery W. Johnston
Executive Editor: Ann Castel Davis
Editorial Assistant: Penny Burleson
Development Editor: Heather Doyle Fraser
Production Editor: Sheryl Glicker Langner
Design Coordinator: Diane C. Lorenzo
Cover Design: Candace Rowley
Cover Image: Corbis
Photo Coordinator: Valerie Schultz
Production Manager: Laura Messerly
Director of Marketing: David Gesell
Marketing Manager: Autumn Purdy
Marketing Coordinator: Brian Mounts

This book was set in Garamond and Legacy Sans by Carlisle Publishing Services. It was printed and bound by Courier Kendallville, Inc. The cover was printed by Phoenix Color Corp.

Photo Credits: Photo credits can be found on p. xxiii.

Pearson Education Ltd.
Pearson Education Singapore Pte. Ltd.
Pearson Education Canada, Ltd.
Pearson Education–Japan

Pearson Education Australia Pty. Limited
Pearson Education North Asia Ltd.
Pearson Educación de Mexico, S.A. de C.V.
Pearson Education Malaysia Pte. Ltd.

10 9 8 7 6 5 4 3 2 1
ISBN-13: 978-0-13-118560-9
ISBN-10: 0-13-118560-8

To Irene and Daniel—So Much! Again and Always.
-MSR

To Wendy, Jen, Jess, & Mere—Thanks for your love and support.
-DLW

To Nancy, Gaby, and Robby, your support was priceless!
-JLM

Preface

Recent landmark legislation (No Child Left Behind and the Individuals with Disabilities Education Improvement Act of 2004) requires that all teachers be highly qualified, a designation that for the first time is actually specified by federal statute. As a result, the ways in which our teacher workforce is being prepared are changing significantly. In this changing environment, we have tried to create a text that addresses the needs of all people interested in the profession of teaching, whether they are traditional special education students, traditional general education students, or alternative certification students.

During the writing of this text, one question has remained in the forefront of our minds: "Regardless of who you are, are you prepared to serve and teach all students?" With this question guiding our writing, we have crafted a succinct and approachable text in which the information and research-based, practical strategies are presented in a realistic manner. We provide the most valuable information regarding each disability area so that all who read this book can acquire a working knowledge of the characteristics and learning needs of students who have exceptionalities. This book serves as a foundations of special education text and a recruitment text that will:

- Provide basic foundational knowledge of special education (chapters 1–5),
- Provide a broad view of effective practices in the classroom while also examining the defining characteristics of disabilities (chapters 6–15), and
- Provide an understanding of and a commitment to professionalism and the issues that underlie the field of special education (chapters 1 and 16).

Additionally, as you look at the table of contents and examine not only the chapter content but also the pedagogical features that support the narrative, you will notice the strong focus on professionalism, instructional application, and reflection. These three themes drive this text and our thinking on key issues related to education in general, and special education in particular.

My Profession, My Story: Monique Green

Monique Green has experienced the rewards and frustrations associated with providing a free appropriate education to students with disabilities. As a beginning teacher in an inner-city urban school district, Monique was disappointed to find that students with special needs were treated as if they could not learn and were not considered part of the neighborhood school community. For the most part, the strong educational and due process requirements of the Individuals with Disabilities Education Act (IDEA), as well as Monique's advocacy, ensured that students received books, supplies, and services. However, the laws, rules, and regulations that provide due process rights to students with disabilities can also provide challenges and frustrations. Currently, Monique is facing a difficult case in which parents and advocates believe that a student with a history of frequent violent outbursts is best served by being included in the general school environment. Monique and her team believe that the student would be better

Monique Green did not set out to be a special educator. She completed her degree in communications from American University and was following news reports of her local urban school district's inability to bridge the achievement gap, retain qualified teachers, or be in compliance with the requirements of federal special education laws. However, what most impacted Monique was a visit to her former middle school. She was flabbergasted and appalled at how things had deteriorated; there was little discipline and little instruction being provided for students, and those with special needs were contained rather than educated. This was a pivotal moment: After this visit, Monique applied to the District of Columbia Teaching Fellows (DCTF) program, a preparation program sponsored by the school district and George Washington University. The students deserved more than they were receiving.

Although her first year of teaching was quite difficult, Monique survived. DCTF provided a solid

My Profession, My Story

Each chapter begins with a story of a teacher. Some have found their way to education through traditional routes and others have come by way of different life experiences, but all are engaged in teaching students in today's diverse classrooms. These stories focus on the backgrounds of the teachers, how they came to the profession, their dispositions and characteristics, and how all of this relates to their teaching and classroom experiences. Periodically throughout the chapters, these teachers are brought back into the discussion to further elaborate on chapter content. Additionally, five of these teachers are featured on the DVD-ROM that accompanies the book.

DVD-ROM: Professionalism Component

The five teachers highlighted on the DVD-ROM discuss various issues of professionalism and how these issues factor into their daily practice in the classroom. Each discussion is punctuated with classroom footage to provide context and additional insight. Throughout the book readers will notice margin notes directing them to the DVD-ROM for a video discussion related to professionalism and the chapter content from the teacher's point of view.

Site Visit: Effective Practices in Action

EFFICACY OF SYSTEMATIC, COMPREHENSIVE, SCHOOLWIDE BEHAVIOR-MANAGEMENT PROGRAMS

The implementation of systematic, comprehensive behavior-management systems is a prime example of an evidence-based intervention that is a suggested practice for our nation's schools and classrooms. In fact, both *Early Warning, Timely Response: A Guide to Safe Schools* (Dwyer, Osher, & Warger, 1998) and *Safeguarding Our Children: An Action Guide* (Dwyer & Osher, 2000), two federally funded guides for violence prevention in schools, strongly recommend that schools build a supportive schoolwide foundation to meet the behavioral needs of all students. This is done in large part to the positive outcomes reported by program developers in large numbers of project schools. Three of the more prominent schoolwide positive behavior support (PBS) models are Effective Behavioral Supports (Lewis & Sugai, 1999), PAR (Rosenberg & Jackman, 2003), and Unified Discipline (White et al., 2001). Data from more than 500 schools nationwide (Sugai & Horner, 2002) indicate that the application of PBS decreases the frequency of office referral between 40 and 60% as well as improves the quality of the referrals seen by administrators. Moreover, as the climate of the school improves, teachers spend more time teaching and students experience corresponding academic gains. The effects of the intervention maintain for 5 to 7 years in those settings where validated practices are adopted. Office referrals in more than 25 PAR program (Rosenberg & Jackman, 2000) schools decreased from 3 to 77% In one middle school, tracked for a 4-year period, suspensions fell from 285 to 5; and climate measures reflected increases in staff morale, instructional time, and quality of collaborative relationships among teachers, administrators, and parents. Comparing the effects of the Effective Behavior Support Program in seven elementary schools over 2 years with the remaining 28 schools in a school district, Nelson, Martella, and Marchand-Martella (2002) found that the intervention schools experienced declines in suspensions, emergency removals, and office referrals while the other schools had increases in these areas. Moreover, academic achievement was superior in the intervention schools, and those students who required targeted or specialized treatments improved on measures of social competence. Finally, the teachers in the intervention schools were supportive of the initiative and believed that the program was easy to apply and beneficial to students. Clearly, no matter what the program is called, comprehensive schoolwide approaches to behavior management are a viable means of creating positive learning environments for all students.

Site Visit: Effective Practices in Action

Throughout the book (chapters 3–15) we highlight programs where educators are engaging in effective, research-based practices for the classroom. These features list the goals of the featured program, define and describe the program, identify the skill areas that the program addresses, and then show the outcomes for the program as supported by research. It is our hope that these snapshots encourage readers to investigate the myriad opportunities for continuing education and entice readers to nurture themselves as lifelong learners in the profession of teaching.

Chapter 16—Continuing a Successful Career: Professionalism, Collaborative Support, and Professional Development

All special education teachers—regardless of the manner in which they are prepared—require certain general skills to succeed in their work. Although it lies beyond the scope of this text—or a course in which it is used—to develop them, novice teachers and teacher education students must be made aware early in their programs of the importance of communication, collaboration, and commitment to ongoing professional development. The text concludes with a discussion of how readers can continue their own professional development and personal growth as they progress through their training, and later in their careers, in special education.

Addressing the Professional Standards and PRAXIS Correlation Matrix

Following the summary of each chapter we have included the CEC Core Knowledge Standards that best reflect the content covered in the chapter. Additionally, there are three appendices in the text that connect to the standards. Appendix A shows the correlation of the Coverage of Content Areas for PRAXIS II® Test to the core content in the text, chapter by chapter. Appendix B is a complete listing of the CEC Knowledge and Skill Standards Common Core highlighted at the ends of chapters. Appendix C is the CEC Code of Ethics and Standards for Professional Practice referred to in chapter 16. Readers can use these guides to make sure they are aware of the standards set for the profession and can also use them when they are studying for their licensure and PRAXIS™ exams.

A Focus on Instructional Application

Highly Effective Instructional Strategies

In each of the categorical chapters (6–15) we highlight a particularly effective instructional strategy as it relates to the chapter content. We introduce the strategy with an in-depth discussion, and then present the strategy in a step-by-step manner so that the beginning teacher can easily understand the steps necessary to incorporate the strategy into classroom teaching. Additionally, readers can go to the Teacher Prep website (see discussion on page xi) to explore other situations, classrooms, artifacts, and strategies that connect to and enhance the content presented in the feature.

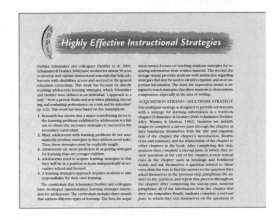

Can You Help Me with This Student?

This feature (chapters 2–15) examines a scenario or case where a teacher is facing a difficult or challenging situation with a student. A bulleted step-by-step list of supports and then a section on more information (readings that reinforce the discussion) follows the scenario. Finally, "extend and apply" activities encourage readers to think beyond the stated situation and put themselves in the place of the teacher. Additionally, readers can go to the Teacher Prep website (see discussion on page xi) to explore other situations, classrooms, artifacts, and strategies that connect to and enhance the content presented in the feature.

Technology for Access

Technology is a huge part of today's teaching. This feature gives snapshots throughout the text of different technologies that enable students with exceptionalities to better access the general education curriculum.

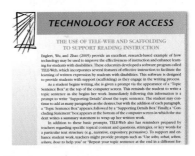

DVD-ROM: Classroom Application Component

As discussed on page viii, five of the teachers highlighted in each chapter are also depicted on the DVD-ROM that accompanies the book. In addition to covering the topic of professionalism, we also show all of the individuals teaching in their classrooms and using strategies that are helpful for all students—but particularly those with the specific exceptionalities highlighted in the accompanying chapter. Throughout the book readers will notice margin notes directing them to the DVD-ROM to see a particular strategy in action.

Chapter 5: Teaching, Learning, and Behavior Management

Teaching, learning and behavior management are inherently linked in every lesson or unit that the teacher plans. In order to provide readers with the best understanding possible of these underlying principles, we have devoted an entire chapter to this subject.

> "One of the most rewarding experiences I had was watching a student come out of Character Counts, learn to read, and enter a regular class on grade level and complete the pupil progression plan. Another was to have a student whom I taught go on to enter high school and become the student-body president after leaving a center for severely emotionally disturbed students."
>
> Veteran teacher Suzy Ann Clary Wilson from Gainesville, Florida, on some of the positive experiences she has had as a special education teacher for 30 years

Chapter 1—Teaching Students with Special Educational Needs: Finding Your Role

Chapter 1 encapsulates what it means to be a teacher in today's classroom and discusses what your role will be—whatever path you choose in education. It requires you to really think about and reflect upon the choices you will be making regarding your career and if you have the dispositions and attitudes necessary to become a successful teacher in general, or a special education teacher in particular.

Reflect Upon Focus Questions

These focus questions at the beginning of each chapter orient the reader to chapter content and serve as not only an advance organizer, but also as items for reflection. Additionally, each question aligns with a major section of the chapter and connects to the chapter summary.

Reflective Exercise #1
How do current issues involving bioethics (e.g., stem-cell therapy, genetic mapping) remind some people of the dark days of eugenics? Can you think of similarities and differences between these situations?

Reflective Exercise Margin Notes

These margin notes (all chapters) engage readers in thought-provoking reflective exercises that extend the content of the narrative and allow readers to really examine their beliefs about and perceptions of special education.

DVD-ROM: Reflection Component and Students to Students

In addition to discussing professionalism and showing classroom strategies, all of the five teachers featured on the DVD-ROM also reflect on what brought them to the profession, pivotal aspects of their teaching careers, their opinions of current issues in the field, and advice for beginning teachers. Additionally, the final component on the DVD-ROM is called *Students to Students*. In this section of the DVD-ROM, college students at various levels in their education comment on some of the *Reflective Exercises* presented in the text. Throughout the book readers will notice margin notes directing them to the DVD-ROM for the teacher's point of view on a variety of topics.

Multimedia Supplementary Materials: Experience the Classroom

We have created an instructor and student support package that is both comprehensive and easy to use. Our package includes access to the Teacher Preparation Classroom website, a DVD-ROM packaged in the back of the text, a Companion Website, an Instructor's Manual with Test Items, a computerized test bank and assessment software (Test Gen), and a PowerPoint Lecture Presentation.

Teacher Preparation Website and Access Code

To enhance your experience with the content presented in each chapter, we have integrated the Teacher Prep website into two features of this text: *Can You Help Me with This Student?* and *Highly Effective Instructional Strategies* (see page ix). Organized around the major courses pre-service teachers take and built around the principles of learning, the site offers authentic content, sound pedagogy, and inquiry material that help prepare students as they progress through their educational career. (An access code is included with this book.)

With the Teacher Prep website as part of your course, you have access to:

- *Online Video Library:* More than 250 video clips framed by learning goals and Praxis-type questions.
- *Student and Teacher Artifacts:* More than 200 student and teacher classroom artifacts framed by learning goals and application questions.
- *Lesson Plan Builder:* Step-by-step guidelines and lesson plan examples to support students as they learn to build high-quality lesson plans
- *Research Articles:* Over 500 articles from ASCD's renowned journal *Educational Leadership* and a searchable database of additional educational journals.
- *Teaching Strategies:* Over 500 research-supported instructional strategies across grade levels and content areas.
- *Licensure and Career Tools:* Resources devoted to helping students pass their licensure exam, learn standards, law, and public policies, plan a teaching portfolio, and survive their first year of teaching.

DVD-ROM to Accompany *Special Education for Today's Teachers: An Introduction*

The DVD-ROM that accompanies this text focuses on five teachers that are featured in the *My Profession, My Story* pieces that open each chapter in the book. Each teacher discusses topics of professionalism and also reflects on areas of his or her career, including how each came to the profession and what it takes to be a successful and effective teacher in today's classroom. These discussion clips are interspersed with video footage of the teacher working with students in the classroom to serve as concrete examples for the discussions. Additionally we have specific classroom application clips for each teacher that show highly effective instructional strategies in action. In the *Students to Students* component of the DVD-ROM, a group of college students discusses some of the Reflective Exercises that are featured in the margins of the text. All of the clips on the DVD-ROM have accompanying commentary from the authors of this text and questions for reflection to better aid in viewer comprehension.

Companion Website

The Companion Website (CW) located at **http://www.prenhall.com/rosenberg** is designed to complement this text, and is integrated into the textbook via margin notes at the end of each chapter. Identified by the Companion Website logo, these notes direct readers to online materials that will assist in reviewing chapter content, doing research online, and accessing related materials and professional resources.

The CW includes a wealth of resources for both professors and students. Instructors can access other online materials by going to the Instructor Resource Center at **http://www.prenhall.com.** Here you will be prompted to login or register for an access code (see Instructor Resource Center section below for more information).

The student portion of the website helps students gauge their understanding of chapter content through the use of online chapter reviews, resources, DVD-ROM activities, discussion questions, and interactive self-assessments (multiple choice, and short answer/essay).

Instructor's Manual with Test Items and TestGen Software

The Instructor's Manual (also available online at the Instructor's Resource Center, described below, at **www.prenhall.com**) includes numerous recommendations for presenting and extending text content. It is organized by chapter and contains chapter objectives, chapter summaries, presentation outlines, discussion questions, application and DVD-ROM activities, homework assignments, and test items. The test item bank contains over 600 questions. These multiple-choice, short answer, and essay questions can be used to assess students' recognition, recall, and synthesis of factual content and conceptual issues from each chapter.

The computerized version of these test items (TestGen) is available in both Windows and Macintosh format, along with assessment software allowing professors to create and customize exams and track student progress.

PowerPoint Lecture Presentation

The lecture presentation—available in PowerPoint slide format at the Instructor Resource Center, described below, at **www.prenhall.com**—highlights key concepts and summarizes content from the text.

Instructor Resource Center

The Instructor Resource Center at **www.prenhall.com** has a variety of print and media resources available in downloadable, digital format—all in one location. As a registered faculty member, you can access and download pass-code protected resource files, course management content, and other premium online content directly to your computer.

Digital resources available for *Special Education for Today's Teachers: An Introduction* include text-specific PowerPoint Lectures and an online version of the Instructor's Manual with Test Items.

To access these items online, go to **www.prenhall.com,** click on the Instructor Support button, and then go to the Download Supplements section. Here you will be able to log in or complete a one-time registration for a user name and password. If you have any questions regarding this process or the materials available online, please contact your local Merrill/Prentice Hall sales representative.

Acknowledgments

Throughout this text we stress the importance of professionalism, reflection, and application. In particular, we emphasize repeatedly the value of collaboration and teamwork when educating students with disabilities and learning differences. We have seen first-hand how teams of committed and creative educators have positive and long-lasting effects on the lives of children and adolescents. Developing a comprehensive textbook to reach a variety of readers interested in teaching students with disabilities successfully is no different. At every stage of this project we were awed by the creativity, knowledge, and accessibility displayed by friends and colleagues, old and new, and we consider ourselves extremely fortunate to have had their enthusiastic support and cooperation.

First, we wish to recognize the Herculean efforts of the professionals at Merrill/Prentice Hall. Along with Executive Editor Jeff Johnston, former Acquisitions Editor Allyson Sharp provided much needed initial momentum for our entry into this project. Ann Davis "picked us up" from Allyson, and with her keen eye for what works in the real world of textbook development, made sure that we stayed *on message* with minimal tilting at windmills. Our many inquiries to the offices in Columbus were addressed cheerfully and expediently in editorial by Kathy Burk and Penny Burleson and in marketing by Autumn Purdy. Val Schultz and Carol Sykes in the photo editing department did a great job of ensuring that we had excellent images to supplement our text, and Dawn Potter copyedited our manuscript with skill, grace, and speed. Carl Harris' video expertise resulted in a wonderful DVD-ROM of featured teachers and preservice teachers. We are also appreciative of efforts of Tammy Feil, who developed the extensive student and instructor ancillaries that complement the text. Finally, we are grateful for the creative coordination of Sheryl Langner, Senior Production Editor, who made sure that all the pieces of this project fit together in an attractive and logical fashion.

Special thanks to our lifeline at Merrill/Prentice Hall, Senior Development Editor Heather Doyle Fraser. Heather's unparalleled editorial and organizational skills are exceeded only by her grace, charm, and diplomacy. There were times when we dreaded the additional work associated with one of her calls. However, Heather's gifts of task analysis, keeping mercurial authors on task, and providing constructive feedback with encouragement made the iterative process of rewriting both energizing and productive.

We wish to recognize Dorene Ross, Margaret Kamman, and Maria Coady of the University of Florida, who co-wrote chapter 3; Sunil Misra of Johns Hopkins University who contributed to chapter 10; Jennifer Howell of the Utah Schools for the Deaf and the Blind, who wrote chapter 13; and also Eric Jones of Bowling Green State University and W. Thomas Southern of Miami University of Ohio who co-wrote chapter 15. Thank you for your time, effort, and expertise in carefully writing and revising these chapters to meet our needs and those of our reviewers.

We owe a great debt to the many teachers and students who agreed to be featured in the text and DVD-ROM. Our cadre of featured master teachers gave of their time liberally and shared with candor their views of what it takes to succeed in today's schools. Specifically we are indebted to Carol Sprague, Amanda Adimoolah, Robert Hessels, Bobby Biddle, Suzy Clary Wilson, Kathy Blossfield, Bill Addison, Meridith Taylor-Strout, Kim Thomas, Kathleen Lance Morgan, Pam Mims, Ryan Hess, Shannon Hunt, Julie Lenner, and Monique Green. Graduate students at Johns Hopkins University also shared their views as to why they are pursuing careers in special education. For their time and expert opinions we thank Melissa Geraci, Jacqueline LeVine, Shana Alter, Annaleese Boyd, Tonette Campbell, Jacqueline Cantara, Howard Caplan, Joyce Chapman, Sharie DeGross, Michael Ensslen, Catherine Kalafut, Dawn McCrea, Nina McQueen, and John Sancandi.

The staff at all three of our universities assisted with tasks large and small. At Johns Hopkins we are appreciative of the efforts of Pam Griner and Juliana Blyth. Sharon Lampkin did a great job of organizing permissions. Sunil Misra graciously assisted in the development of the glossary as well as serving as an extraordinary research associate. We also thank Chad Kramer for providing his dissertation results as one of our features.

At Western Carolina University we appreciate the advice and comments of our colleagues who provided feedback on various concepts, ideas, and chapter drafts. Most notably we appreciate the help of Karena Cooper-Duffy, Bill Ogletree, and David Shapiro for their strong input on chapter content; and to Marissa Ray, Ken Prohn, and Kelly Kelley for their assistance and various forms of support that contributed both directly and indirectly to this work. At the University of Florida we'd like to thank Shaira Rivas-Otero, Vicki Tucker, Michell York, and Penny Cox for their support in a range of activities, big and small, as well as for picking up the slack when deadlines approached.

Numerous drafts of chapters were sent out for review and we are indebted to the many teacher educators who took the time to provide extensive and highly constructive feedback. Specifically we would like to thank Ellyn Arwood, University of Portland; Barbara A. Beakley, Millersville University; Alicia Broderick, California State University, Long Beach; Albert M. Bugaj, University of Wisconsin, Marinette; Mike Cass, Sul Ross State University; Karen B. Clark, Indiana University, South Bend; Greg Conderman, Northern Illinois University; Helen T. Dainty, Tennessee Technological University; Beverly Doyle, Creighton University; Sheila Drake, Mid America Nazarene University; Linda K. Elksnin, The Citadel; Mary Bailey Estes, University of North Texas; Ruth A. Falco, Portland State University; Cecil Fore III, University of Georgia; Billie L. Friedland, Delaware State University; Blanche Glimps, Tennessee State University; Holly Hoffman, Central Michigan University; Jack Hourcade, Boise State University; Kathryn A. Lund, Arizona State University; Angela S. McIntosh, San Diego State University; Martha J. Meyer, Butler University; Mark P. Mostert, Regent University; Rita Mulholland, California State University, Chico; Linda H. Parrish, Texas A & M University; Alec Peck, Boston College; Rebecca Peters, Aquinas College; Eve A. Puhalla, West Chester University; and Marcee M. Steele, University of North Carolina, Wilmington.

We are especially grateful for initial work contributed by Paul Sindelar. Paul helped us to conceptualize and think through the themes and organization of this text.

Finally, each of us is blessed with the love and support of our families—wives Irene, Wendy, and Nancy; children Daniel, Jennifer, Jessica, Meredith, Gaby, and Robby; and grandchildren Hayden and Riley.

MSR

DLW

JLM

www.prenhall.com/rosenberg

Brief Contents

www.prenhall.com/rosenberg

Contents

Contents

www.prenhall.com/rosenberg

Photo Credits

PART I

BECOMING A PROFESSIONAL: What Are the Foundations of Special Education?

TEACHING STUDENTS WITH SPECIAL EDUCATIONAL NEEDS: *FINDING YOUR ROLE*

1

SPECIAL EDUCATION TODAY: *AN UNFINISHED HISTORY*

2

1 Teaching Students with Special Educational Needs:

Finding Your Role

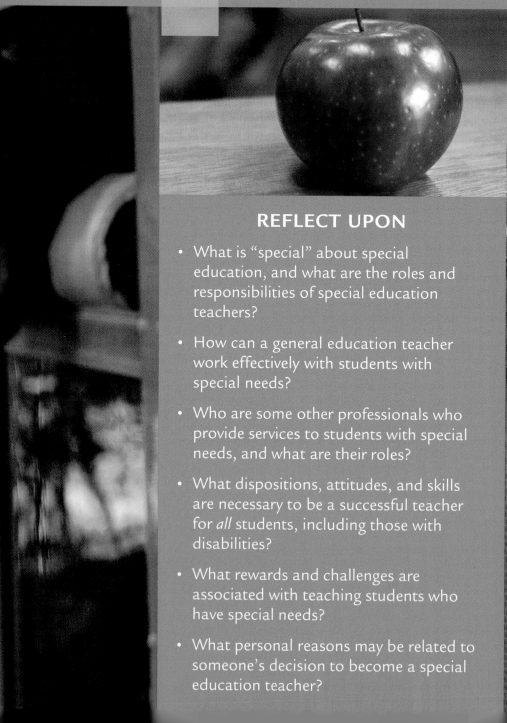

REFLECT UPON

- What is "special" about special education, and what are the roles and responsibilities of special education teachers?

- How can a general education teacher work effectively with students with special needs?

- Who are some other professionals who provide services to students with special needs, and what are their roles?

- What dispositions, attitudes, and skills are necessary to be a successful teacher for *all* students, including those with disabilities?

- What rewards and challenges are associated with teaching students who have special needs?

- What personal reasons may be related to someone's decision to become a special education teacher?

Michael S. Rosenberg

"Before entering the field, special education struck me as merely teaching basic skills in small segregated classrooms, giving kids as much time as they needed to complete tasks, and speaking slowly with a louder voice. In college, I learned that effective special education is much more. I observed first hand how specialized supports, creative accommodations, and caring professionals contribute to important academic and behavioral student outcomes. I was taken by the thought that, with the right training, I could impact the lives of others."

James McLeskey

"I never planned to become a teacher. However, I couldn't find a job in my chosen profession and stumbled into a teaching position with students who were labeled with mild and moderate intellectual disabilities. My classroom was in a Quonset hut on a dusty, remote corner of the campus of a modern vocational high school. On the first day of class, I had no idea what to expect. I arrived early and was greeted by one of my students, Henry. I was struck by how "normal" Henry was—much more like me than he was different. From that day on, special education has been a challenge as I've learned new things almost every day. It's also been the most enjoyable and rewarding career I could imagine."

"When I went to college, I really had no idea what I was going to do. At some point I decided to be a high school English teacher, but that didn't work out. Then I found my way into special education. Honestly, I never would have thought about it as a career, but I have to tell you, it's been great in so many ways."

David Westling

You may already know what you would like to do, or maybe you're still trying to decide.

It is often interesting to learn about how people arrived at their current positions and the path they traveled to get there. One of the oldest icebreakers goes something like this: "So why did you decide to become a nurse?" or "When did you first think about being a fire fighter?" As a reader who is in all likelihood enrolled in an introductory course in special education, you may be on the road to your future. Maybe you intend to become a special education teacher or work in a related area that provides services to students with special needs, such as speech/language pathology or physical therapy. On the other hand, you may be in this course because you are planning to become a general education teacher at the elementary, middle school, or high school level, and this course is a required part of your program. Some readers might even be already employed as teachers and need the course to earn a teaching license or certificate. Perhaps you have not yet decided what you want to do and are here to find out more about your options.

Our goal is to provide you with useful information regardless of where you are now or where you are heading. Obviously, we will speak most often to future special education teachers, but we also hope that those preparing to be general educators and other professionals will hear and learn from what we present.

Whether you will be a special education teacher, a general education teacher, or a person who supports students with special needs in other ways, two broad factors will influence what you do and how well you succeed. The first is the personal characteristics and traits that have unfolded in you up to this point in your life. These are the sum of your inherited features and what you have learned that makes you the individual you are. The second factor is the knowledge and skills you have yet to acquire through different learning opportunities. This is where our text becomes important. We hope that we can begin to provide you with useful and valid information so that no matter what career path you follow, the interactions, instruction, and other services you ultimately share with students who have special needs will have positive outcomes for them and for you.

In this chapter we will give you a personal introduction to the field of special education. To do this we will focus on a number of key topics that we believe are essential for any teacher or other professional who wants to work effectively with students with special needs. Let's begin now by discussing what *special education* means and the key people who work in this unique field.

Reflective Exercise #1
Special education means different things to different people. What words, phrases, characterizations, thoughts, and emotions come to mind when you hear the term? Would you characterize your responses as positive, neutral, or negative? **To hear students like you discuss this topic, go to the Students to Students module on the DVD and click on Clip 1: Perceptions of Spec. Ed.**

WHAT IS "SPECIAL" ABOUT SPECIAL EDUCATION?

Special education is a term that often evokes emotion and passion. The nature and content of reactions vary, however, depending on who is responding. For the parent-advocate who has a teenager with a severe disability, special education represents a hard-fought civil rights victory for access to a free and appropriate education. For the school board member, special education usually involves concern about finances and the expenses associated with delivering supplemental services as required by federal law. To the 10th-grade science teacher, special education is the "inclusion section" of biology in which several students with learning and behavioral disabilities need content enhancements to participate in the required textbook and laboratory activities.

And for the third-grade student with a hearing impairment, special education is the mechanism through which she is able to acquire a phonic ear, an assistive device that helps her participate in class activities with her friends and classmates.

A special education teacher, if asked, is likely to tell you that special education means providing different kinds of supports that are meant to make students' lives better. The special education teacher provides some of these supports, and other professionals provide others. The special educator is primarily responsible for designing and implementing instruction and evaluating how well students are learning. Most effective special educators are concerned about how a student performs not only in school but also in the home, the community, and, later in life, in the workplace (Heward, 2003).

Special education means different things to different people. It means providing different kinds of supports.

Students with special needs face learning challenges. Therefore, to be effective, special education must be more precise, intensive, structured, and tightly controlled than general education. Moreover, the curriculum of special education often must augment the curricula of general education by using strategies, content enhancements, and assistive technology devices that facilitate the acquisition of knowledge and skills (Kauffman & Hallahan, 2005). This is what we mean when we say that special education is special (see Table 1.1).

Students who receive special education services often need more than instruction, and a special education teacher sometimes has to go a little beyond a teacher's typical duties. Although they are teachers, special educators often accept added tasks necessary for improving quality-of-life conditions for students with special needs. This may involve activities such as helping a student become a member of a school club or a team, working with community mental health personnel to improve out-of-school services, or learning about a new assistive technology device that could help a student learn to read or communicate. This, too, is what is special about special education.

THE ROLES OF SPECIAL EDUCATION TEACHERS

According to the U.S. Department of Education (2005), more than 416,000 special education teachers provide instruction to almost 6.5 million students with disabilities between the ages of 3 and 21. Although we cannot claim to know all of these teachers, we know a good number of them. One thing we have noticed is that many have taken different and sometimes unusual avenues to get to where they are. Some have had siblings or family members with disabilities, some were tutors or "best buddies" in high school, and some came into the field simply because someone they trusted suggested it. We have also seen people become special educators after making a leap from other careers, including some former military personnel, nurses, business executives, and ministers!

"One of the most rewarding experiences I had was watching a student come out of Character Counts, learn to read, and enter a regular class on grade level and complete the pupil progression plan. Another was to have a student whom I taught go on to enter high school and become the student-body president after leaving a center for severely emotionally disturbed students."

Veteran teacher Suzy Ann Clary Wilson from Gainesville, Florida, on some of the positive experiences she has had as a special education teacher for 30 years

TABLE 1.1

WHAT MAKES SPECIAL EDUCATION "SPECIAL"?

The following nine dimensions are often considered to be distinguishing characteristics of special education (Kauffman & Hallahan, 2005).

Dimension	Special Education
Pacing	Special education requires that the pacing of instruction match an individual student's ability to learn what is taught.
Intensity	Special education often involves adjusting the intensity of instruction by altering the amount of time devoted to direct instruction and practice as well as the complexity of steps used to teach multifaceted concepts and operations.
Relentlessness	Rather than adhering to a fixed instructional timetable, special education requires the tenacity and perseverance to try a variety of approaches when students have difficulty acquiring critical elements of the curriculum.
Structure	Special education provides students with disabilities with learning conditions that are more direct, organized, explicit, and predictable than what is often required by nondisabled students.
Reinforcement	Students with disabilities often require high rates of positive and sometimes tangible reinforcers to facilitate the early acquisition of skills and behaviors.
Pupil-teacher ratio	Because special education requires more increased structure as well as intensive and relentless instruction, smaller ratios between teachers and students are often necessary for success.
Curriculum	Although the general education curriculum is appropriate for most students with disabilities, many require specialized supports and accommodations to access the material; other students with more severe disabilities require specialized instruction in basic life skills, alternative communication skills, and social skills.
Monitoring/ assessment	Special education law requires that specific procedures be followed in documenting student progress; frequent assessments of performance ensure that the methods chosen for instruction are working for the individual student.
Collaboration	Special education requires the input and participation of all stakeholders in the lives of students with disabilities.

Source: From James M. Kauffman, Daniel P. Hallahan. Special Education: What It Is and Why We Need It. Published by Allyn and Bacon, Boston, MA. Copyright © by Pearson Education. Adapted by permission of the publisher.

FIGURE 1.1

THE FUTURE SPECIAL EDUCATOR'S MOTIVATION SCALE

Rate each of these reasons for why you believe you may want to become a special education teacher. Use the following rating scale:

1 = Strongly disagree
2 = Disagree
3 = Somewhat disagree
4 = Agree and disagree
5 = Somewhat agree
6 = Agree
7 = Strongly agree

1. I am drawn by the opportunity to have smaller class sizes.	1	2	3	4	5	6	**(7)**
2. I look forward to the challenge of teaching difficult students.	1	2	3	4	5	**(6)**	7
3. I like the idea of the possibility of extra pay.	1	2	3	4	5	6	**(7)**
4. I have an interest in specific disabilities (e.g., autism, Down syndrome).	1	2	3	4	5	**(6)**	7
5. I know that special education has good job availability and offers various opportunities.	1	2	3	4	5	**(6)**	7
6. I am excited by the opportunity to witness student improvement in knowledge, skills, or behavior.	1	2	3	4	5	6	**(7)**
7. I have a high level of regard for people with disabilities.	1	2	3	4	5	6	**(7)**
8. My personal characteristics fit well with the special educator's job (e.g., I am very patient or not easily stressed).	1	2	3	4	5	**(6)**	7
9. I have a friend or family member with a disability.	1	2	3	4	**(5)**	6	7
10. I have worked or volunteered with students with disabilities before and found it to be extremely rewarding.	1	2	3	**(4)**	5	6	7

If you talk to veteran special educators, chances are you won't find them or their lives trivial or routine. Throughout your professional development, you will meet special education teachers and other professionals supporting students with special needs; and as you will see, many have very interesting stories about how they got to where they are and what they do now that they are there.

What's your story? Maybe you are currently attempting to determine the correct career choice for yourself. If you are, we have a short questionnaire for you. In Figure 1.1 you will find a brief questionnaire titled "The Future Special Educator's Motivation Scale." Copy this survey from the text and then complete it. If you wish, compare your responses with your classmates', and maybe even ask your instructor if members of the class can discuss their views about the items on the survey. At the end of the chapter we will return to the survey questions, tell you how we interpret the outcomes, and encourage you to reflect on the reasons you want to be a special education teacher.

"Becoming a special education teacher was not something that I planned early in my life or even early in my career. My academic career was uneventful, but my teaching career quickly took a new direction as I practiced my craft. I quickly realized that, within any given classroom, students had a wide range of skills and abilities both academically and behaviorally, and I didn't have the knowledge to meet their needs and work with struggling readers. Thankfully, I met a teacher who became my mentor and encouraged me to become a special education teacher."

Carol Sprague, an elementary special education teacher in Thomas County, Georgia

TABLE 1.2

PUBLIC SCHOOL DISABILITY CATEGORIES

Disability	Definition
Autism (Chapter 10)	*Autism* is a developmental disability significantly affecting verbal and nonverbal communication and social interaction, generally evident before age 3, that adversely affects a child's educational performance. Other characteristics often associated with autism are engagement in repetitive activities and stereotyped movements, resistance to environmental change or change in daily routines, and unusual responses to sensory experiences. The term does not apply if a child's educational performance is adversely affected primarily because the child has an emotional disturbance. A child who manifests the characteristics of autism after age 3 could be diagnosed as having autism if the criteria in this paragraph are satisfied.
Deaf-blindness (Chapter 13)	*Deaf-blindness* means concomitant hearing and visual impairments, the combination of which causes such severe communication and other developmental and educational needs that they cannot be accommodated in special education programs solely for children with deafness or children with blindness.
Deafness (Chapter 13)	*Deafness* is a hearing impairment so severe that the child is impaired in processing linguistic information through hearing, with or without amplification, and that adversely affects a child's educational performance.
Emotional disturbance (Chapter 7)	*Emotional disturbance* is a condition exhibiting one or more of the following characteristics over a long period of time and to a marked degree that adversely affects a child's educational performance: 1. An inability to learn that cannot be explained by intellectual, sensory, or health factors 2. An inability to build or maintain satisfactory interpersonal relationships with peers and teachers 3. Inappropriate types of behavior or feelings under normal circumstances 4. A general pervasive mood of unhappiness or depression 5. A tendency to develop physical symptoms or fears associated with personal or school problems The term includes schizophrenia. The term does not apply to children who are socially maladjusted, unless it is determined that they have an emotional disturbance.
Hearing impairment (Chapter 13)	*Hearing impairment,* whether permanent or fluctuating, adversely affects a child's educational performance but is not included under the definition of deafness.
Mental retardation (Chapters 8, 12)	*Mental retardation* means significantly subaverage general intellectual functioning, existing concurrently with deficits in adaptive behavior and manifested during the developmental period, that adversely affects a child's educational performance.
Multiple disabilities (Chapter 12)	*Multiple disabilities* are concomitant impairments (e.g., mental retardation–blindness, mental retardation–orthopedic impairment), the combination of which causes such severe educational needs that they cannot be accommodated in special education programs solely for one of the impairments. The term does not include deaf-blindness.

Reflective Exercise #2

Have you been closely acquainted with a special education teacher? How did this individual enter the field? In a typical fashion or by a more nontraditional route?

WHO DO SPECIAL EDUCATION TEACHERS TEACH? WHERE DO THEY TEACH?

In Chapters 6 through 15 of this textbook we will introduce you to students with special needs and many of the special education and related services they receive. Federal law requires that these students be placed into different disability categories. As a point of reference for our present discussion, Table 1.2 presents the disability categories. More detailed discussions of these students appear in the chapters noted in the table.

Orthopedic impairment (Chapter 14)	*Orthopedic impairment* means a severe structural impairment that adversely affects a child's educational performance. The term includes impairments caused by congenital anomaly (e.g., clubfoot, absence of some member), impairments caused by disease (e.g., poliomyelitis, bone tuberculosis), and impairments from other causes (e.g., cerebral palsy, amputations, and fractures or burns that cause contractures).
Other health impairment (Chapter 14; see Chapter 9 for ADHD)	*Other health impairment* means having limited strength, vitality, or alertness, including a heightened alertness to environmental stimuli, that results in limited alertness with respect to the educational environment, that 1. Is due to chronic or acute health problems such as asthma, attention deficit disorder or attention deficit hyperactivity disorder, diabetes, epilepsy, a heart condition, hemophilia, lead poisoning, leukemia, nephritis, rheumatic fever, and sickle cell anemia; and 2. Adversely affects a child's educational performance.
Specific learning disability (Chapter 6)	*Specific learning disability,* in general, means a disorder in one or more of the basic psychological processes involved in understanding or using language, spoken or written, which may manifest itself in the imperfect ability to listen, think, speak, read, write, spell, or do mathematical calculations. The term includes such conditions as perceptual disabilities, brain injury, minimal brain dysfunction, dyslexia, and developmental aphasia. It does not include a learning problem that is primarily the result of visual, hearing, or motor disabilities; of mental retardation; of emotional disturbance; or of environmental, cultural, or economic disadvantage.
Speech or language impairment (Chapter 11)	*Speech or language impairment* means a communication disorder, such as stuttering, impaired articulation, a language impairment, or a voice impairment that adversely affects a child's educational performance.
Traumatic brain injury (Chapter 14)	*Traumatic brain injury* means an acquired injury to the brain caused by an external physical force, resulting in total or partial functional disability or psychosocial impairment, or both, that adversely affects a child's educational performance. The term applies to open or closed head injuries resulting in impairments in one or more areas, such as cognition; language; memory; attention; reasoning; abstract thinking; judgment; problem solving; sensory, perceptual, and motor abilities; psychosocial behavior; physical functions; information processing; and speech. The term does not apply to brain injuries that are congenital or degenerative or to brain injuries induced by birth trauma.
Visual impairment including blindness (Chapter 13)	*Visual impairment including blindness* means an impairment in vision that, even with correction, adversely affects a child's educational performance. The term includes both partial sight and blindness.

Source: Adapted slightly from Regulations to IDEA 97, 20 U.S.C. 1401(3)(A) and (B); 1401(26); §300.7.

Given the range of student needs, public schools usually provide special education and related services in various settings, and the special educators working in these settings have different roles and responsibilities. Figure 1.2 shows the full range of settings, or the "continuum of services." *For the most part,* special educators teach in one of three types of settings: as co-teachers with general education teachers in general education classrooms, in resource rooms, or in self-contained special classrooms (in either general education or special schools).

FIGURE 1.2

THE CONTINUUM OF SERVICES IN SPECIAL EDUCATION

- The general education classroom, with supplementary aids and services (such as special education teacher or paraeducator support)
- A part-time special class or a resource room for part of the day, with the student spending the remainder of the day in the general education classroom or in activities with students who do not have disabilities
- A full-time, self-contained special class within the regular school, with no or only a few opportunities to be integrated into other classes or settings
- A full-time, self-contained special class in a separate special school that serves only students with disabilities
- A residential placement in a state-operated or private residential school
- Instructional services in the student's home or a hospital

CO-TEACHING IN THE GENERAL EDUCATION CLASSROOM

Many students with special needs spend a significant amount of time in the general education classroom, as the diagram in Figure 1.3 shows. To serve these students, special education teachers work as co-teachers in inclusive general education classrooms with their colleagues in elementary or secondary education.

When working in these classrooms, special educators typically provide instruction and support for students of various backgrounds and with different needs. Most of these students participate in the general curriculum with students without disabil-

FIGURE 1.3

PERCENT OF TIME THAT STUDENTS WITH DISABILITIES SPEND IN AND OUT OF THE GENERAL EDUCATION CLASSROOM

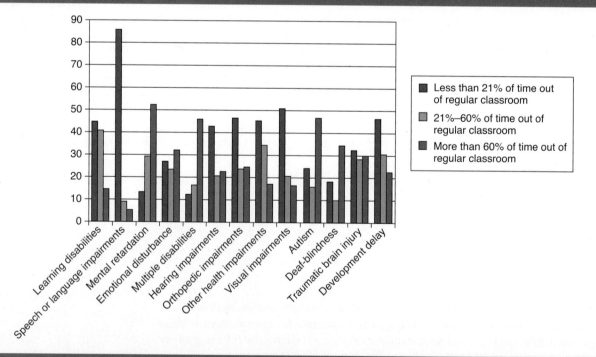

Source: Developed from U.S. Department of Education (2003). *Twenty-fifth annual report to Congress on the implementation of the Individuals with Disabilities Education Act.* Washington, DC: Author.

www.prenhall.com/rosenberg

ities. Although most students with disabilities in the general education classroom are likely to have high-incidence or mild disabilities (including **learning disabilities**, **emotional disturbance/behavior disorders**, or **mild intellectual disabilities**), others may have more severe or low-incidence disabilities: they may fall on the **autism spectrum**; have **moderate, severe, or profound intellectual disabilities**; or perhaps have **multiple disabilities** (see Figure 1.3).

As a co-teacher, the special educator will plan with the general education teacher to make sure that students with special needs are able to participate meaningfully in the general curriculum. The special educator will also help students work toward achieving any other **individualized education program (IEP)** goals. In classrooms where the special educator and the general education teacher both work for the entire day, their roles are often indistinguishable to the students because both teach all of the students at different times.

The special education teacher and the general education teacher must plan together so that students with special needs can participate meaningfully.

Sometimes the special education co-teacher will not be in the general education classroom full time. In this case, he or she may co-teach for shorter periods and serve as a consultant to the classroom teacher (and often to the **paraeducator**) so that students with disabilities may continue to receive services when the special educator is not there. Under this arrangement, the special educator will consult with the general education teacher and the paraeducator to support students when they are in the general education classroom. He or she also may serve students directly in a resource room or a part-time special class.

TEACHING IN A RESOURCE ROOM

Resource rooms are separate, part-time, special classrooms where students with disabilities go to improve their academic skills or to get supports to assist them in achieving the knowledge and skills required by the general curriculum. Although they may spend the majority of their time in the general education classroom, some students with disabilities report to the resource room to receive intensive, small-group instruction on topics or subjects that they find especially difficult. They might also work to improve their study skills and their organizational and test-taking skills, develop better problem-solving skills, or learn to use other strategies that will help them be successful in the general education classroom. The resource room teacher usually works with students one on one or in small groups. He or she may also double as a co-teacher and work closely with the general education teacher as just described.

Working as a resource room teacher is one of the most common jobs of special educators because most students in special education attend resource rooms for at least part of the day. Like other special education teachers, this person will provide direct instruction and also meet with parents and other professionals, assess students' academic skills, develop IEPs, and plan instruction.

"Visiting one of the schools that I once attended, I was flabbergasted at how badly things had deteriorated. There was little authority and order, and students with learning needs were being ignored. After seeing this, I decided to apply to the District of Columbia Teaching Fellows Program to become a special education teacher."

Monique Green, on why she decided to become a special education teacher for students with learning disabilities

TEACHING IN A SELF-CONTAINED SPECIAL CLASSROOM

Some special educators teach in self-contained classrooms in elementary, middle, or high schools or in separate **special schools**. Usually students with more severe intellectual, behavioral, physical, or sensory disabilities are placed in special classes, although it isn't uncommon for some of them to be served in general education classrooms as well.

There are important distinctions between teaching in a self-contained special class and working as a co-teacher or a resource room teacher. The special class teacher has more direct contact with the students and more responsibility for instruction in all curricular areas, and he or she works with the same students for the entire day. Also, self-contained special classes generally have fewer students, typically between 7 and 12. Often one or more paraeducators assists the teacher in self-contained settings, depending on the nature of the students' needs. This can be an important factor because it means the teacher must know how to work effectively with the paraeducators just as he or she works effectively with the students.

OTHER DUTIES OF SPECIAL EDUCATORS

A teacher's classroom time fills most of the day, but teachers also have other responsibilities. Virtually all public school educators must perform a variety of noninstructional duties. These vary but usually include tasks such as monitoring students outside of the classroom (in the hallways and the cafeteria or when waiting for the bus), sponsoring student organizations, attending open houses and school meetings with parents, going to faculty meetings, and participating on school committees. In addition, if you are a special education teacher, you have to attend IEP and other meetings, write teaching plans for individuals and groups, attend staff development sessions, conduct end-of-year assessments, and meet with parents at certain times throughout the year. Teachers sometimes complain about the meetings and paperwork, but unfortunately they are part of the job. In Chapter 16 we discuss some of these noninstructional duties and how you can manage your time and energy to address them effectively.

THE GENERAL EDUCATION TEACHER'S CONTRIBUTION TO STUDENTS WITH SPECIAL NEEDS

As you saw in Figure 1.3, many students with special needs spend some, if not most, of their time in the general education classroom. Their success depends a great deal on how well the general education teacher can collaborate with the special educator to deliver an appropriate educational program.

THE RESPONSIBILITIES OF THE GENERAL EDUCATION TEACHER

General education teachers have the primary responsibility for teaching specific subject matter to their students from the time they are in kindergarten until they complete high school. General educators are prepared to teach students who have "typical" abilities. For the most part, their students can acquire information efficiently through verbal and written instruction and through other kinds of learning experiences. Among their varied responsibilities, general education teachers must plan lessons, prepare materials, organize instructional activities, and use instructional media and materials to teach specific content.

THE GENERAL EDUCATION TEACHER
AND THE INCLUSIVE CLASSROOM

When students with special needs require alternative forms of instruction or have learning goals that fall outside of the norm, general education teachers often require support to find ways to instruct them and incorporate them into the general classroom and the general curriculum. As you will learn in Chapter 2, federal law now requires that, to the maximum extent possible, all students have an opportunity to be in, and learn in, normalized school environments.

The practice of including students with disabilities in general education classrooms and encouraging their participation in the general curriculum, although often the preferred option, places the general education teacher in a critical role. For this reason, a general education teacher often must serve on IEP teams and work closely with the special education teacher so that students with special needs can be accommodated. Although we can't expect that general education teachers will have the preparation or the breadth or depth of knowledge about students with disabilities that a special educator should have, it is fair to expect that the general education teacher can *share* in the responsibility for providing instruction to students with disabilities in general education classrooms.

"I strongly believe that every child can learn and . . . I think kids want to belong and be with their peers. . . . I think it's important for kids to be around all kinds of kids."

Shannon Hunt, second-grade teacher in Asheville, North Carolina, on why she likes to have children with special needs in her general education classroom

CREATING A POSITIVE INCLUSIVE CLASSROOM

As much as formal preparation, an open mind and a willingness to collaborate are required for a classroom teacher to be successful in teaching students with disabilities in the general education classroom. The teacher not only needs to help students with disabilities feel that they belong with their nondisabled peers but also needs to be a catalyst for acceptance. Most important, special education teachers and general education teachers must learn to plan, teach, and problem-solve collaboratively (Janney, Snell, Beers, & Raynes, 1995).

Reflective Exercise #4

If you plan to be a general education teacher, what types of support do you think you would need to successfully include students with disabilities?

The teacher should be a catalyst for acceptance.

Many general educators support inclusion. Research shows that if teachers have enough time for collaborative planning, receive necessary instruction in teaching students with disabilities, have adequate assistance from special education teachers and paraeducators, are provided with adequate material resources, and have reduced class sizes, they are more likely to have positive attitudes about including students with disabilities (Scruggs & Mastropieri, 1996).

OTHER INDIVIDUALS WHO WORK WITH STUDENTS WITH SPECIAL NEEDS

Besides special education teachers and general education teachers, a significant number of other professionals provides direct or indirect services to students with special needs.

RELATED-SERVICES PROFESSIONALS

Federal law requires that "related services" be provided to students in special education to the extent that these services are necessary to help them benefit from other school services (see Chapter 2). For example, if a student needs physical therapy to participate in learning activities, then physical therapy must be provided. The result of this legal requirement is that public schools employ many professionals besides teachers to serve students with special needs.

According to data from the U.S. Department of Education (2005), U.S. public schools employ approximately 17,800 social workers, about 37,600 speech/language pathologists, more than 6,300 physical therapists, and nearly 13,000 occupational therapists to work with students with disabilities. Additionally, educational administrators, counselors, rehabilitation specialists, and school psychologists play significant roles in the education of students with special needs (U.S. Department of Education, 2005). While we can't fully describe all of these professionals, Table 1.3 lists and briefly describes the roles of some who commonly work with students with special needs. One very important professional is the speech/language pathologist (SLP). As we've noted, school districts employ a significant number of SLPs to address the speech and language needs of students with special needs. Kathleen Lance Morgan is one of these professionals. (See Chapter 11 for a discussion of these students with speech and language disorders.)

PARAEDUCATORS

As a special educator, a general education teacher, or another professional who works with students who have special needs, you are likely to find that paraeducators (also referred to as paraprofessionals, teacher assistants, or teacher aides) also play a major role in the education of these students. Although paraeducators often work closely with teachers in self-contained special classes, more of them are now working with students with disabilities in general education classrooms (Giangreco & Doyle, 2002; Giangreco, Edelman, Broer, & Doyle, 2001).

Paraeducators may perform many duties similar to those carried out by teachers, including instructional and noninstructional activities. The primary differences between teachers and their assistants are (1) teachers must hold at least a four-year degree from a college or university, whereas paraeducators need two years of college or the equivalent; (2) teachers are the primary planners and decision makers responsible for developing instructional programs, whereas paraeducators may play a role in the delivery of instruction; and (3) teachers are held accountable for students' learning, whereas paraeducators may be held accountable for assisting teachers. In Figure 1.4 we list some duties that are appropriate for paraeducators. Such duties should always be carried out under the direction and supervision of the teacher.

"At first I wanted to pursue being a pediatrician; I knew I wanted to work with children . . . and then my dad said, 'Well, why don't you think about being a speech pathologist?' And I decided that indeed was what I wanted to pursue, to work with children, to make a difference."

Kathleen Lance Morgan, on why she became a speech/language pathologist

Reflective Exercise #5
What has been your experience with different professionals who have worked with students with disabilities? What did they do? Did they like their jobs? What aspects of these jobs do you think you would like or dislike?

TABLE 1.3

OTHER PROFESSIONALS WHO WORK WITH STUDENTS WITH DISABILITIES

Professional	Role
School psychologists	The primary role of the school psychologist is to conduct assessments to determine the present level of cognitive, academic, social-emotional, and adaptive behavioral functioning of students with disabilities.
Physical and occupational therapists (PTs and OTs)	The PT evaluates, plans, and develops interventions to improve posture and balance; to prevent bodily misformations; and to improve walking ability and other gross-motor skills. The PT works primarily with students who have severe disabilities. The OT has knowledge and skills similar to the PT's but has an orientation toward purposeful activities or tasks such as the use of fine-motor skills related to daily living activities.
Speech/language pathologists (SLPs)	The SLP evaluates a student's speech and language abilities and develops appropriate goals in this area if necessary. SLPs also may work with students with more severe disabilities to develop alternate or augmentative communication systems.
Social workers	Social workers address many issues that occur outside of the school. They may deal with family matters and will often make home visits to help resolve conflicts or improve parent-child interactions. They also can arrange for other service agency support.
School guidance counselors	Guidance counselors can help provide direction for academic or behavioral improvements. They will work one on one with students or with groups.
Art, music, and recreational therapists	Professionals in these areas use their particular specialties to help improve students' functioning in different ways, such as improving their communication or social skills.

FIGURE 1.4

DUTIES APPROPRIATE FOR PARAEDUCATORS

- Supervise individuals and small groups
- Provide individual assistance to students when necessary
- Help prepare materials and arrange the classroom
- Be responsible for keeping the classroom neat and orderly
- Assist in preparing materials, bulletin boards, adaptive equipment, classroom furniture, etc.
- Collect student performance data
- Help implement positive behavioral support plans
- Intervene in medical emergencies and contact an appropriate individual for emergency medical services
- Engage in clerical tasks that free teachers to spend more instructional time with students

Source: Adapted from Giangreco, Broer, & Edelman, 1999; Giangreco & Doyle, 2002; Westling & Fox, 2004.

BEING A GOOD TEACHER OF ALL STUDENTS

What does it take to be a good teacher? How about a good special education teacher? What personal qualities are important? What areas of knowledge and sets of skills must be learned? As you have seen, special education teachers can work in different types of settings, each with different sets of responsibilities. Furthermore, you know that general education teachers and other professionals also play important roles in the education of students with special needs. Previously, we asked you to complete our survey (in Figure 1.1) to express some of the reasons why you thought you might like to pursue a career in special education. At this time, we would like to share what we consider to be some important attributes and characteristics for *all* teachers who wish to be effective for *all* of their students.

DEVELOPING AND MAINTAINING APPROPRIATE DISPOSITIONS

To be most effective as a teacher, you should have a *disposition* that values the nature of human differences and recognizes the importance of being a good teacher for *all* students. Teacher dispositions are just as important as having appropriate content knowledge and pedagogical skills. Many public school students have challenges that test the skills of the best teachers. But if you plan to be a professional educator, you must accept that you have a responsibility to teach all students regardless of their different challenges or special needs.

Organizations concerned with the preparation and continued success of teachers recognize the importance of appropriate teacher dispositions. The National Council for the Accreditation of Teacher Education (2002) states that future teachers should "reflect the dispositions expected of professional educators" and should "recognize when their own dispositions may need to be adjusted" (p. 16). The council further writes, "Regardless of whether they [future teachers] live in areas with great diversity, candidates must develop knowledge of diversity in the United States and the world, [and] dispositions that respect and value differences, and skills for working in diverse settings" (p. 31).

The Interstate New Teacher Assessment and Support Consortium (1992), a program of the Council of Chief State School Officers, has voiced a similar position:

> The teacher believes that all children can learn at high levels and persists in helping all children achieve success. The teacher appreciates and values human diversity, shows respect for students' varied talents and perspectives, and is committed to the pursuit of "individually configured excellence." The teacher respects students as individuals with differing personal and family backgrounds and various skills, talents, and interests. The teacher is sensitive to community and cultural norms. The teacher makes students feel valued for their potential as people, and helps them learn to value each other. (pp. 18–19)

As you can see, having an appropriate disposition to be a teacher means having an outlook that maintains that all students are important and should be valued as members of the learning community. Without a disposition of this nature, the quality of a teacher is likely to be diminished. This is especially true if you want to teach students with special needs.

TEACHER ATTITUDES THAT MATTER

Teachers sometimes are frustrated because certain students don't have positive attitudes toward learning. But teachers themselves should reflect on their own attitudes to see how they might influence their teaching. Here we examine some critical attitudes that are necessary for an effective teacher. As you read, you should see how the dispositions just discussed are necessary for these attitudes to flourish.

Reflective Exercise #6
Before you read ahead, what do you think are necessary attitudes for being an effective teacher? **To hear students like you discuss this topic, to to the Students to Students module on the DVD and click on Clip 4: Attitudes & Dispositions.**

www.prenhall.com/rosenberg

Caring, Fairness, and Respect

Caring, fairness, and respect are not just good qualities for teachers to have; they are essential. A teacher who cares about his or her students is more likely to have a positive impact. Bell (2003) suggests that, for schools to be successful with all students, teachers must both be instructionally effective and show caring and patience for their students: "You can be the reason some kid gets up and comes to school when his life is tough. You can be the reason some student 'keeps on keeping on' even though her parents are telling her she can't succeed. You can inspire your at-risk students" (p. 34). In an interesting study, Langer (2000) compared students in demographically similar schools who were considered to be at risk for failure. She wanted to know why some teachers' students were succeeding while others were not. Although Langer found several important differences, one of the most important was that the teachers of the more successful students showed signs that they cared about the students and about the students' success.

Fairness and respect are also important attitudes for teachers. Fairness means that teachers provide the instruction and support that individual students need without bias. Respect means that a teacher interacts with students in ways that acknowledge their humanity and strengths. Teachers who are fair and who show respect will monitor their own behavior to make sure that their interactions do not fluctuate as a function of a person's background or personal characteristics. Stronge (2002) reports that students feel most strongly about the following:

- They expect teachers to treat them as people.
- They view effective teachers as those who do not ridicule students nor allow them to be embarrassed in front of their peers.
- They believe effective teachers are fair with regard to gender, race, and ethnicity.
- They see teachers who are consistent and allow students to have input into the classroom as fair and respectful.
- They believe effective teachers offer all students opportunities to participate and to succeed.

> "The students need a lot of attention, and I try to remind them that when they come to school, it's okay to be a student. They don't have to be the bigger brother or the mama or the daddy in their household, so they should relax and let's try to have a real positive day and learn as much as they can. I remind them that they can learn something new every day."
>
> Veteran teacher Suzy Ann Clary Wilson

Reflective Exercise #7
From a student perspective, how have you been affected by the care, fairness, and respect of a teacher? Describe some positive and negative experiences.

Enthusiasm, Motivation, and Dedication to Teaching

Experience suggests that students' interest in what is being taught is affected by the teacher's interest. Teachers who are excited about what they are doing tend to increase the excitement and interest of their students (Brophy, 1998; Stronge, 2002). For example, in one study researchers found that when teachers exhibited more enthusiasm during instruction of students with learning disabilities, their students learned more and exhibited fewer behavior problems (Brigham, Scruggs, & Mastropieri, 1992). Teachers can show enthusiasm in different ways. Look at some characteristics of enthusiastic teachers in Figure 1.5 and see if you can suggest others.

If you are enthusiastic about teaching, you will probably also be motivated to be an effective teacher. Your enthusiasm and motivation can have two positive outcomes. First, you can be sustained through challenging times; and second, you can have a positive impact on your students by improving their motivation and interest in what is being taught.

If you are a person who is dedicated to teaching, you will have interest in both your students' learning and your own. You will always be searching for better ways to teach and more effective ways to get your students to learn. You will take courses, participate actively in professional development sessions, and attend professional

FIGURE 1.5

SIGNS OF A TEACHER'S ENTHUSIASM

- Uses humor and appears to enjoy the subject
- Relates personal experiences to students about the topic
- Shows excitement when discussing the topic
- Is animated when presenting the lesson
- Maintains an active pace when covering the topic

Reflective Exercise #8
How important are a teacher's enthusiasm, motivation, and dedication? How would you rate your own? Is it possible to be an effective teacher without these characteristics?

A high level of personal teaching efficacy will better ensure your success as a teacher.

Reflective Exercise #9
Although you are planning to be a teacher, how much confidence do you have in yourself about teaching students in a classroom? Have you had any successful experience in teaching someone to do something? How did this make you feel?

conferences. You will also collaborate with other professionals, share and receive ideas, and often volunteer to contribute to needs in the school or community. This is what it means to be dedicated to teaching.

Teacher Expectations and Personal Teaching Efficacy

Finally, a necessary and important attitude of effective teachers is the belief that they can have a positive impact on students, *regardless* of the nature or degree of the students' needs. Your view of your potential for success as a teacher is known as your "personal teaching efficacy." Teachers with high levels of personal teaching efficacy believe that they can positively influence student achievement and motivation (Bandura, 1977; Rotter, 1966; Tschannen-Moran, Woolfolk Hoy, & Hoy, 1998). Research has shown that teacher efficacy correlates positively with student achievement, teachers' willingness to implement innovations, less teacher stress, less negative affect in teaching, and teachers' willingness to stay in the field (Carlson, Lee, & Schroll, 2004; Ross, 1994; Soto & Goetz, 1998; Tschannen-Moran et al., 1998).

A teacher with a high level of personal teaching efficacy will feel that she or he can be successful regardless of students' abilities or backgrounds. If you have a high level of personal teacher efficacy, you will view the success of students as a factor related to your own knowledge, teaching ability, and creativity, even when students are having difficulty succeeding.

USING EVIDENCED-BASED TEACHING APPROACHES

While we cannot underestimate the importance of appropriate dispositions and attitudes for teachers, we also need to state quite frankly that these are not enough. Successful teaching requires using the most effective teaching practices. This is especially true when the student has learning difficulties or special needs.

Teachers will often cite a number of reasons for teaching the way they do or for using a particular instructional method. But are all methods equal? Not really. Some instructional procedures will be more effective, while others will be less. To be most effective, therefore, teachers must seek and use **evidenced-based** instructional approaches whenever possible. Evidenced-based methods are those that are supported by scientific research and have been shown to demonstrate a relatively high degree of success in terms of student learning outcomes.

Although evidenced-based practices have been promoted for many years in other professions (e.g., medicine), they are a new concept in much of education, including special education. In our field, we have only recently begun to think about what we mean by scientifically based evidence and what is suitable to drive what schools and teachers do (Odom et al., 2005).

To be a successful teacher, you must learn about the most effective ways to teach and promote children's learning. Although research cannot claim to produce the only effective ways to teach, for much of what we do, we can find evidence that is either supportive or critical of our methods. Obviously finding this evidence is an ongoing process, one that should be a part of your development as a professional. We will help you begin by discussing evidenced-based methods for teaching and improving social behavior in Chapter 5 and then continue this discussion in the chapters that address specific disabilities.

FINDING YOUR PROFESSIONAL ROLE: WHY SHOULD YOU BE A TEACHER? WHY A SPECIAL EDUCATION TEACHER?

We hope that you can see that being a good teacher requires both personal characteristics and learned knowledge and skills. Do you have these characteristics? Should you continue on this path to becoming a teacher? These are questions you should reflect upon and address with much candor. As you do so, you need to consider the rewards and challenges of teaching. Here we will specifically consider these with regard to being a special education teacher.

"I loved it. It just felt really good and right."

Kathy Blossfield, preschool special education teacher from Asheville, North Carolina, on how she felt when she first worked with children with disabilities at a summer camp

THE REWARDS OF BEING A SPECIAL EDUCATION TEACHER

Many experienced teachers will tell you that teaching students with special needs can be very rewarding. What we have noted over the years is that many ordinary people become special education teachers, but most do it for reasons that are not so ordinary. Here are some reasons why some teachers we have known like their work as special education teachers.

Recognizing Potential and Seeing Progress

Many teachers receive positive reinforcement for their work when they see their students' progress. They say things like "It's wonderful to see them grow," and "It is rewarding to know that you are having a positive effect."

For some people, having a role in the improvement of others is extremely rewarding: helping them learn something, showing them how to perform a new skill, finding a way for them to overcome some boundary. Certainly, with the great diversity of students with special needs, significant student outcomes can mean achievement in a number of different areas. From improved behavior, to better academic skills, to something as simple and basic as learning to feed yourself or put on your pants: these are the essential sources of reinforcement for many special educators.

Taking on Challenges

Some people are challenged by games played on a field and some by difficult business pursuits. But for many teachers, their day-to-day challenges stimulate their efforts. They wish to do more, to do better, to improve their understanding of their students, to find more successful ways to teach. They wish to get their students to learn despite their shortcomings and to help their students find happy, successful lives despite the odds. Students with special needs form a very heterogeneous group. Even within a particular disability category, such as autism, you will rarely find two individuals who are the same. Many teachers of students with special needs love these differences and know that they will constantly be challenged to find a way to work effectively with their students. They will say they find particular students "fascinating" and enjoy trying to figure out "what makes them tick." So for many special education teachers, a significant part of why they do what they do is simply because they like the challenges that it presents.

Special education teachers are valued by society.

Reflective Exercise #10
If you think you want to be a special education teacher, which of these factors might motivate you?

Achieving Respect, Admiration, and Gratitude

Many people achieve respect by holding influential positions in industry or government. Others do so by giving large amounts of money to important causes. Still other people achieve respect by the nature of the work they do. Special educators fall into this category. Like nurses, paramedics, fire fighters, and police officers, special education teachers realize that most of society values and respects the work they do. And knowing they are doing good work is enough to keep them doing it.

THE CHALLENGES OF BEING A SPECIAL EDUCATION TEACHER

On the other side of the coin, as you probably realize, being a special education teacher presents some challenging conditions. You should be aware of these challenges so that you will be well prepared to deal with them. Here are some difficulties that are often reported and some ideas for countering them.

Common Problems for New Special Education Teachers

Several studies have reported the unique difficulties faced by new special education teachers. The following are often mentioned (Billingsley & Tomchin, 1992; Busch, Pederson, Espin, & Weissenburger, 2001; Kilgore & Griffin, 1998; Kilgore, Griffin, Otis-Wilborn, & Winn, 2003; Mastropieri, 2001):

- Role ambiguity brought about by unclear or mixed directives from different people
- Students' difficult behavioral and academic problems and little progress in improvement
- Class sizes or case loads that are too large
- Insufficient curriculum resources or materials
- Inadequate time for planning and collaboration
- Inadequate support from administrators
- Too little time and too many demands, including meetings and paperwork

Kilgore and her associates (2003) interviewed and observed 36 new special educators over a two-year period to learn about their problems and what helped them deal with those issues. They found that teachers reported many of the problems just listed, such as having several content areas to teach to students at different ability levels and sometimes not having enough time or resources. According to Kilgore et al., "in many respects, these novice teachers had curricular responsibilities exceeding their general education peers, yet they struggled to find curricular resources to assist them in developing appropriate materials for their students" (p. 46). The new teachers also reported having insufficient opportunities for planning. One teacher pointed out that, unlike the students of general educators, none of her students went to "specials" (music, P.E.) at the same time. This meant that she was never completely without students and thus never had sufficient time to plan.

Fortunately, along with these challenges, Kilgore and her colleagues reported several sources of support for many new teachers. Very often the new special educators said that other, more experienced colleagues, including both special and general educators, provided them with needed information, materials, and guidance. Veteran teachers were often good models for planning and teaching and gave valuable advice about the operations of the school and curriculum development. Many others were also helpful. When principals supported the teachers, the teachers really liked it. One

FIGURE 1.6

WAYS SCHOOLS CAN EFFECTIVELY SUPPORT NEW TEACHERS

- Offer an induction program attuned to the specific needs of new teachers that allows a great deal of input from them
- Understand the experiential limitations of new teachers and give them assignments that include fewer students, adequate resources, and a limited number of academic preparations per day
- Have structures that allow and promote ongoing collaboration between teachers and administrators
- Have an open school culture that helps teachers maintain a healthy attitude toward their job and profession

Source: Adapted from Kilgore, Griffin, Otis-Wilborn, & Winn, 2003.

teacher said, "As a first year teacher, it's been really nice to know that I could walk into my principal's office and talk with her like a tenured teacher" (p. 45).

Figure 1.6 lists some other ways that schools can be supportive, especially of new teachers.

Unfortunately, for some teachers, the problems just described are not limited to the beginning years, and ultimately they can take a heavy toll. Studies have often found high levels of stress and burnout among special educators (Wisniewski & Gargiulo, 1997). In some cases, the teachers may leave the job or the profession; in others, they may continue to work but not very effectively.

Many of the conditions we mentioned in the previous section have been found to correlate with high levels of stress and burnout. Teachers who experience these feelings often feel that they have little control over these conditions and that there is little they can do to improve them. Unfortunately, stress and burnout are often linked to ineffective teaching practices and a poor sense of personal teaching efficacy.

Still, you should not think that these conditions are inevitable. Gersten, Keating, Yovanoff, and Harniss (2001) propose that the solution to many of the problems that special educators face is to improve teachers' working conditions and the overall job design. Gersten and his colleagues recommend the following:

- Greater support from principals, other teachers, and central office administrators
- More relevant professional development opportunities
- Assistance for sorting through dissonant directives
- Help in prioritizing and solving problems
- Allowing teachers more opportunities to engage in meaningful and substantive conversations with colleagues and administrators

YOUR REFLECTIONS ON TEACHING STUDENTS WITH SPECIAL NEEDS

We hope that at this point you have started to develop a picture of the professional lives of teachers and other professionals regarding their work with students with special needs. We have discussed special education and what makes it "special" and have described some of responsibilities of special education teachers. We have also discussed the importance of general educators who teach in inclusive classrooms and some of the other professionals who provide related services. Additionally we have presented conditions and personal factors that many believe are necessary to be a good teacher as well as the rewards and challenges associated with teaching students with special needs.

So where are we now? Where are you?

Before you continue with this textbook and your course, reflect on your part. Do you believe that providing an important service to others will lead to personal satisfaction? If so, then teaching may well be the right choice for you. Do you think that there is value in helping to form the lives of young people, improving the quality of our society, or experiencing a lifetime of self-growth? If so, then you probably have identified a good reason to be a teacher (Kauchak, Eggen, & Carter, 2002).

What about being a *special education* teacher? Is this what you think you should do? Let's return to "The Future Special Educator's Motivation Scale" that we presented in Figure 1.1 and consider your responses to it. We developed this self-assessment to help you evaluate your reasons for becoming a special educator. Using the rating system provided, you could rate the importance of each item as it relates to your becoming a special education teacher. Why not look at your responses now and consider the meaning of your answers.

If you had relatively high ratings on items 1, 3, 5, and 8, a choice of special education as a career *might* be related to personal comfort and convenience. On the other hand, if your ratings on items 4, 7, and 9 were high, you probably have a particularly high regard for the idea of providing support to individuals with disabilities. Finally, if you marked items 2, 6, and 10 high, then you are probably a person who will enjoy the challenges and benefits often associated with the work of a special education teacher. While any of these factors might lead you to want to become a special education teacher, which do you think are more likely to predict your happiness in the field of special education?

Reflective Exercise #11
How did you answer on "The Future Special Educator's Motivation Scale"? Do you still think you should be a special education teacher?

For more information about topics covered in this chapter, go to the Web Links module in Chapter 1 of the Companion Website at www.prenhall. com/rosenberg.

SUMMARY

Many special education teachers enter the field for different reasons, and many people have different perspectives about what special education means. But special education teachers, general education teachers, and many other professionals make significant contributions to the lives of students with special needs.

Why Special Education Is "Special" and the Roles and Responsibilities of Special Education Teachers

- Special education is often seen as providing instruction that is more precise, intense, structured, and controlled than instruction provided through general education. Teachers must often use different strategies and tactics to promote learning in students with special needs.
- Most special education teachers will work as co-teachers in general education classrooms, resource rooms, or part-time special classes, or separate self-contained classes for students with special needs.

The Role of the General Education Teacher with Students with Special Needs

- Most students with special needs are taught in regular education classrooms for at least a part of the instructional day. The general education teacher thus plays an important role in their education.
- The general education teacher's willingness to collaborate with special education teachers will be

one of the most important factors leading to a student's success in the general education classroom.

Other Professionals Who Provide Services to Students with Special Needs and Their Roles

- Related-services professionals in public schools commonly include speech/language pathologists (SLPs) and physical and occupational therapists (PTs and OTs).
- Additional key professionals include school psychologists, administrators, social workers, and various other therapists.
- Paraeducators also play an important role in educating students with special needs.

Dispositions, Attitudes, and Skills Necessary to Be a Successful Teacher

- Critical attitudes include acceptance, caring, fairness, and respect for all students.
- Teachers should also be enthusiastic and motivated and maintain a high level of dedication.
- Teachers should believe in their ability to be successful—that is, should have a high level of personal teaching efficacy.
- Teachers should know and use evidenced-based teaching methods.

www.prenhall.com/rosenberg

Rewards and Challenges of Teaching Students with Special Needs

- Some of the rewards of teaching students with special needs include the opportunity to see progress; accepting challenges that others would not; and achieving the respect, admiration, and gratitude of many members of society.
- Challenges include difficult assignments, possible stress, and burnout.

Personal Reasons for Becoming a Special Education Teacher

- Here are some good reasons for deciding to become a special education teacher: personal experiences, looking for an interesting and challenging job, and realizing that the job matches your personality.

 **ADDRESSING THE PROFESSIONAL STANDARDS**

Council for Exceptional Children (CEC) Knowledge Standards addressed in the chapter:

CC1K1, CC1K3, CC1K5, CC1K9, GC1K1, GC1K4, GC1K5, CC1S1, CC5K4, CC6K2, CC7K5, CC9K1-CC9K4, CC10K4

Appendix B: CEC Knowledge and Skill Standards Common Core has a full listing of the standards referenced here.

students with disabilities and the importance of legal protections afforded to those with learning and behavioral disabilities. A mentor also helped by providing feedback on Monique's instruction and behavior management techniques. The reality of working with challenging students became apparent on her first day in the classroom. When one of her students could not find his pencil, he decided to toss a chair across the room! Monique considered this a welcome to the real world of teaching students with extreme behaviors—a crash course in what is not provided in the textbooks.

For Monique, the greatest rewards of teaching are exposing students to new things (she took her students to the opera) and seeing her students light up when they realize that they can be successful in the classroom (Wow, Ms. Green, I'm really not stupid!). Still, there are frustrations. Although she is organized, she does not seem to have enough time to document all of the information required by the school district. Moreover, many transfer students come from other schools with little information, requiring intensive assessments for instruction. Monique believes that her organizational skills, creativity, and persistence allow her to develop systems that track student progress. Most important, Monique loves her students and sees herself as a change agent.

For those thinking of becoming a teacher, Monique emphasizes the need to understand that, regardless of observed deficits and disabilities, parents are sending us their beloved children. In addition to being an educator, we become therapist, friend, advocate, mediator, and sometimes magician for the family. To meet these multiple roles, teachers must be aware of current practices and stay organized, flexible, and caring.

To meet Monique Green, hear her views on the issues addressed in this chapter, and see her teaching in the classroom, go to the Ms. Green module on the DVD-ROM and view the video clips.

Special education is a profession shaped by a rich social history, landmark legislation, past and current political events, as well as the courageous actions of parents, teachers, and advocates. As you prepare to teach students with disabilities, you will undoubtedly formulate your own view, or **conceptual framework,** of special education. Such thinking allows you to develop a well-articulated and coherent vision of what you hope to accomplish with the students in your classroom. You are able to go beyond the immediacy of daily professional activities and reflect on why certain practices—due process and least restrictive environment, for example—are essential to student success. Developing your own conceptual framework is neither quick nor easy; a personal view of special education requires knowledge, experience, and opportunities for reflection. Specifically, why do we prepare individual educational plans and use specialized methods for students with disabilities? Why were they considered necessary? How did schools and society treat students with disabilities and their families before civil rights advocates fought for due process of law? What social and civil actions prompted the right to education, **deinstitutionalization,** and inclusion movements?

Having an awareness of the social history of our field is essential in the development of professional competence and, more important, one's personal commitment to the field. Unfortunately, most teachers have little time to reflect on these topics. On any given day, they are faced with numerous immediate and practical concerns, such as managing problem behavior, instructing a struggling reader, or engaging a reluctant parent in a home-school partnership. Since these matters often demand decisive and

FAQ Sheet

UNFINISHED HISTORY

Why should we be aware of the social history of special education?	Knowledge of our history sheds perspective on current issues, helps us understand the changing cultural contexts of schools, and decreases the possibility that we hold on to policies and procedures that don't work.
What will tomorrow's historians identify as today's key issues?	Prevailing issues occupying center stage in special education include service-delivery alternatives, ensuring that every student with a disability is provided with an appropriate education, and the overrepresentation in special education of students from certain racial and ethnic groups.
What are the major components of NCLB?	Five principles form the core of the NCLB legislation: • Strong accountability for results • Increased flexibility and local control of schools • Teaching methods based on scientific research • Expanded options for parents • Highly qualified teachers
What are the major components of IDEA 2004?	The major requirements of IDEA include • Nondiscriminatory identification, assessment, and evaluation • Least restrictive environment • Individualized educational plans • Procedural safeguards
What other relevant legislation influences the education of students with disabilities?	Section 504 of the Rehabilitation Act of 1973 provides protections for those with disabilities who do not fit the definitions under IDEA. The Americans with Disabilities Act (ADA) is civil rights legislation that prohibits discrimination and requires accessibility to buildings and their physical facilities.

immediate responses, it is easy to understand why teachers pay little attention to the history of our policies, procedures, and methods of service delivery. For a quick introduction to special education's unfinished history, consult the FAQ Sheet.

SPECIAL EDUCATION STORIES: THE SOCIAL HISTORIES OF OUR FIELD

Consider the value of knowing the social history of special education. First, knowledge of our history provides new or different perspectives on current issues and challenges (Smith, 1998). Being aware of how individuals with disabilities were warehoused into isolated, overcrowded facilities provides insight about the motivation of those who advocate for full inclusion. Second, the history of special education parallels the histories of public education, psychology, medicine, law, and politics (Kauffman, 1981). By examining the development of our field, we are able to understand the changing cultural context of our schools and society. Third, knowledge of history increases the application of effective classroom interventions and professional practices. In contrast, educators who are unaware of what has been successful in special education have a tendency to jump quickly on bandwagons, adopt reconstituted fads, and cling to empirically baseless interventions (Kauffman, 1981; Mostert & Crockett, 2000). Finally, a historical view of special education allows for a more complete understanding of the people and social circumstances associated with precedent-setting events.

Historically, the people involved in social and educational change revealed complexity, courage, and humanity in the ways they addressed challenges and dilemmas (Smith, 2004). Understanding their circumstances, motives, and feelings deepens our appreciation of their accomplishments and motivates us to continue our important work. Many of these histories inspire and provide direction; others, unfortunately, are frightening and signal the need for caution and reexamination of our present-day ethics and values (see Figure 2.1).

BEYOND CRUELTY AND NEGLECT: TIMES OF RECOGNITION, CHARITY, AND EDUCATION (1500–1900)

Before 1500, individuals with disabilities, if they were fortunate enough to survive infancy and early childhood, had lives filled with a mixture of brutality, hardship, derision, and neglect (Safford & Safford, 1996). Most physical and mental exceptionalities were viewed as divine or satanic messages: Those with disabilities and/or their families were being punished for secret sins, and their afflictions could not be altered through human or "earthbound" intervention. With the exception of individuals who were blind—who many believed were compensated with special powers—those with physical or mental differences were feared and treated as inferior beings. What would it take to change misunderstandings and ill treatment of those with disabilities? We examine three stories of people who advanced the quality of life for individuals with disabilities.

Pedro Ponce de Leon: Teaching Deaf Adolescents

One of the earliest known efforts to truly educate persons with disabilities took place in Spain toward the end of the 16th century (Winzer, 1998). Pedro Ponce de Leon, a Benedictine monk, instructed wealthy boys who were deaf. Financial concerns motivated de Leon's efforts: The sons of the wealthy nobility needed to read in order to qualify for their inheritance and property ownership. However, such activities were revolutionary in that they challenged Plato's and Aristotle's prevailing views that, without speech and hearing, people could not learn. Even more courageous, de Leon broke with the prevailing church view that people who were born deaf could not have faith because they could not hear the word of God. De Leon used a rather direct method for teaching his students. He would point to an object, write the written characters, and then have his students link specific hand configurations to each letter of the alphabet (Deaf Culture Information, 2005).

Itard and the Wild Boy of Aveyon

A wild "man-animal" found in the forests of France in 1799 was a curiosity to the citizens of Europe. Considered an "incurable idiot," he was a dirty, inarticulate young boy of approximately 11 years of age who trotted and grunted like the beasts of the field. Incapable of attending to or perceiving heat and cold, he spent much of his time rocking back and forth like an animal in the wild and took great pleasure in only the basic biological functions of eating, sleeping, and sheltering himself from the unwanted attentions of others.

www.prenhall.com/rosenberg

FIGURE 2.1

HISTORICAL OVERVIEW OF SPECIAL EDUCATION

Beyond Cruelty and Neglect (up to 1900)

1590 Pedro Ponce de Leon teaches deaf young men, linking hand configurations to letters of the alphabet.

1799 Jean-Marc-Gaspard Itard works with Victor, the Wild Boy of Aveyon.

1817 Thomas Gallaudet opens the American Asylum for the Education of the Deaf and the Dumb.

1832 Samuel Howe opens the New England Asylum for the Blind.

1841 Dorothea Dix begins her work on behalf of people with disabilities incarcerated in jails and poorhouses.

1848 The first residential institution for people with mental retardation is founded by Samuel Gridley Howe at the Perkins Institution in Boston.

1860 Simon Pollak demonstrates the use of braille at the Missouri School for the Blind.

1869 The first wheelchair patent is registered with the U.S. Patent Office.

Edouard Sequin founds the Association of Medical Officers of American Institutions for Idiots and Feebleminded Persons. It is later renamed the American Association on Mental Retardation.

Steps Forward and Back (Early 20th Century)

1903 Helen Keller, the first deaf-blind person to enroll in college, publishes her autobiography, *The Story of My Life*.

1906 Elizabeth Farrell institutes a program of ungraded classes as an alternative to institutionalization.

1912 Building on Galton's view of eugenics, Henry H. Goddard publishes *The Kallikak Family*, a book linking disability with immorality and alleging that both are tied to genetics.

1922 The Council for Exceptional Children (CEC) is founded.

1924 The Commonwealth of Virginia legalizes sterilization of the feebleminded, insane, depressed, and mentally handicapped.

1927 Franklin Roosevelt co-founds the Warm Springs Foundation at Warms Springs, Georgia. The facility for polio survivors becomes a model rehabilitation and peer-counseling program.

1943 Congress passes the Vocational Rehabilitation Amendments, known as the LaFollette-Barden Act, adding physical rehabilitation to the goals of federally funded vocational rehabilitation programs.

1949 The United Cerebral Palsy Organization is founded.

Civil Rights and Access (1950–1990)

1950 The Association for Retarded Children, now called the ARC, is founded.

1954 The *Brown v. Board of Education* court ruling ends the separate but equal philosophy.

1961 President Kennedy appoints a special President's Panel on Mental Retardation to investigate the status of people with mental retardation and develop programs and reforms for its improvement.

1963 The Association for Children with Learning Disabilities is founded.

President Kennedy, in an address to Congress, calls for a reduction "over a number of years and by hundreds of thousands, [in the number] of persons confined" to residential institutions.

1964 The Civil Rights Act, a model for subsequent disability rights legislation, is passed.

1966 *Christmas in Purgatory*, by Burton Blatt and Fred Kaplan, is published, documenting the appalling conditions at state institutions for people with developmental disabilities.

1969 Swedish educator Bengt Nirge coins the term *normalization*.

1972 Wolf Wolfensberger popularizes the term *normalization* in the United States.

PARC and *Mills* rulings guarantee the right to education of all children with disabilities.

1973 Section 504 of the Rehabilitation Act is passed. It prevents discrimination based upon disability.

1975 The Education for All Handicapped Children Act, later renamed the Individuals with Disabilities Education Act (IDEA), is passed.

1984 *Rowley v. Hendrick Hudson School District* ruling declares that schools must provide services that students require to benefit from education.

1986 The reauthorization of IDEA mandates services for preschoolers with disabilities and requires that individualized family service plans (IFSPs) be developed for each student receiving services.

1990 The Americans with Disabilities Act (ADA) is passed. The reauthorization of IDEA mandates that transition be addressed for adolescents in special education.

1997 Reauthorization of IDEA requires that students with disabilities be included in state- and district-wide assessments and that IEPs address access to the general education curricula.

2002 The No Child Left Behind Act (NCLB) is passed. It mandates accountability for results, methods based on scientific research, expanded parent options, and highly qualified teachers in every classroom.

2004 The most recent reauthorization of IDEA is passed, emphasizing the need to reduce burdensome paperwork and improve methods used to identify students with learning disabilities.

Source: Adapted from Cimera, 2003; Rehabilitation Research and Training Center, 2002.

Jean-Marc-Gaspard Itard believed that the behaviors of Victor, the Wild Boy of Aveyon, could be changed.

Jean-Marc-Gaspard Itard claimed that the boy's aberrant behavior was the result of a severe lack of social contact with other human beings. Consequently, Itard believed the boy's behaviors could be changed. Similar to the current-day educators who develop individual educational plans (IEPs), Itard generated five goals related to the mental and moral education of the young boy (see Figure 2.2). Victor (the boy's given name) benefited significantly from Itard's efforts. Although not completely "cured," he developed into an affectionate young man who, despite his inability to develop speech, could appreciate relationships with those who cared for him and understand what was said to him. Beyond the positive changes in Victor, Itard's efforts are significant because the methods used to educate the boy signaled to the world that a specific set of procedures to improve the behaviors of those believed to be untreatable actually existed (Humphrey, 1962).

Laura Bridgeman and Samuel Gridley Howe

Consider the observations of Charles Dickens upon meeting 13-year-old Laura Bridgeman during a tour of the United States in 1842:

> I sat down . . . before a girl, blind, deaf, and dumb; destitute of smell; and nearly so of taste: before a fair young creature with every human faculty and hope, and power of goodness and affection inclosed [sic] within her frame, and but one sense—the sense of touch. . . . Her face was radiant with intelligence and pleasure. Her hair, braided by her own hands, was bound about a head, whose intellectual capacity and development were beautifully expressed in its graceful outline, and its broad open brow.

At age 2, Laura Bridgeman was stricken with scarlet fever that left her deaf and blind. At 7 years of age, Laura attended the Perkins Institution for the Blind in Boston, where she had the rare good fortune to be taught by the founder, Samuel Gridley Howe. A teacher of the blind, Howe believed that special instructional techniques could allow students with visual impairments to learn as much as those with sight. For Laura, Howe developed a system that used raised letters that spelled out words that corresponded to common objects. Building on her ability to distinguish among

FIGURE 2.2

ITARD'S "IEP" GOALS FOR VICTOR	
Goal 1	To interest him in social life by rendering it more pleasant to him than the one he was then leading, and above all more like the life which he had just left.
Goal 2	To awaken his nervous sensibility by the most energetic stimulation, and occasionally by intense emotion.
Goal 3	To extend the range of his ideas by giving him new needs and by increasing his social contacts.
Goal 4	To lead him to the use of speech by inducing the exercise of imitation through the imperious law of necessity.
Goal 5	To make him exercise the simplest mental operations upon the objects of his physical needs over a period of time afterwards inducing the application of these mental processes to the objects of instruction.

Source: Adapted from Itard, 1962.

www.prenhall.com/rosenberg

shapes, Howe taught Laura the relationship between words and objects, and ultimately Laura acquired a manual alphabet that allowed her to communicate with others. Laura's desire to learn was legendary, and Howe's methodology was widely disseminated and applied to children with multiple disabilities. Interestingly, his work had a dramatic effect on Anne Sullivan, the well-known teacher and "miracle worker," who employed many of Howe's techniques in her work with Helen Keller.

STEPS BACK, STEPS FORWARD: EARLY 20TH CENTURY

The optimism exemplified by the efforts of de Leon, Itard, and Howe did not extend to all individuals with disabilities, nor were they maintained over time. Although professional organizations were founded to address the needs of individuals with sensory and orthopedic disabilities, those with intellectual deficits received little or poor attention. Two stories reflect the events of this period.

Goddard and Eugenics

Can humanity be improved through scientifically controlled reproduction? Should government have a say in whose DNA is most worthy of procreation? Unfortunately, **eugenics,** or the science of human improvement by better breeding (Davenport, 1910), dominated much of the social thinking in the early 20th century. For those with cognitive disabilities, this meant subjecting them to segregation and sterilization to keep them from reproducing and polluting the good genetic stock (Kauffman, 1981). Such thinking is not new: In ancient Greece, Plato advocated selective reproduction. In the mid-19th century, Sir Francis Galton, using the theories of his cousin, Charles Darwin, asserted that society could not be saved from mediocrity unless the less intelligent stopped outreproducing those with greater intelligence. However, Henry Goddard's case study, "The Kallikak Family: A Study in the Heredity of Feeble-Mindedness," claimed it was *scientific fact* that mental disabilities and criminality were based on heredity. Consistent with this "science," Goddard and other eugenicists advocated reproduction restrictions among criminals, prostitutes, and those with undesirable social behaviors and said that a mental age of 12 should be the minimum level for people who were permitted to have children. Responding to such calls, nearly every state segregated people with cognitive disabilities in institutions, and 32 states enacted compulsory sterilization laws. Approximately 60,000 people in the United States were sterilized (Larson, 2002).

Elizabeth Farrell and Ungraded Classes

During the popular eugenics movement, many reform-minded educators provided needed services to students who differed from the mainstream population. Recall that the beginning of the 20th century was a time of great immigration to our nation, and cities were home to many poor families who had not acquired the language or culture of their new surroundings. Not surprisingly, the new science of intelligence testing identified a disproportionate share of children from immigrant families, along with other "idiots" and "cripples," as defective. In 1899, Elizabeth Farrell got her start as a teacher of these "misfits" on New York's Lower East Side, an area of high immigrant concentration. Based on her success with these challenging students, Farrell was appointed in 1906 as head of the city's newly formed Department of Ungraded Classes.

Farrell's goals for these classes differed from those held by many of the leading educators of the times. Rather than viewing her classrooms as mere holding centers, Farrell believed that attendance in the classes could awaken the constructive, acquisitive, and initiative instincts in the child (Hendrick & Macmillan, 1989; Safford & Safford, 1996). With activity being the major theme, Farrell's curriculum emphasized motor skills and allowed for increased emphases on socialization and self-expression. Farrell collected follow-up data on many of her "defective" students. Rather than being institutionalized in wholesale fashion, 54.8% were employed, and 8.8% were not working but were considered able. The most compelling outcome: Only 4% of Farrell's former students were in institutions (Safford & Safford, 1996).

Reflective Exercise #1
How do current issues involving bioethics (e.g., stem-cell therapy, genetic mapping) remind some people of the dark days of eugenics? Can you think of similarities and differences between these situations?

CIVIL RIGHTS AND ACCESS (1950–1990)

The **civil rights movement** of the mid-20th century had a monumental effect on the lives of many members of disenfranchised groups, including individuals with disabilities. As was the case with young African American schoolchildren, advocates for those with disabilities used the schools as a prominent battleground in efforts to achieve equal rights and due process of law. In fact, many of the original decisions rectifying the exclusion and segregation of students based on race were expanded to include students with disabilities (Murdick, Gartin, & Crabtree, 2002). Characterized as "a quiet revolution," parents and civil rights advocates took on state governments and large school districts to ensure that students with disabilities had access to resources necessary to meet their individualized needs (Weintraub & Abeson, 1976). Moreover, people in the public eye who had children with disabilities—celebrities like Roy Rogers and political families like the Kennedys—lobbied stridently for services and legal rights. Later in this chapter we describe the important judicial decisions and landmark legislation that contributed to the institutionalization of special education procedures and due process protections we see today. Here we focus on stories of individuals who brought the plight of students with disabilities to the forefront of our national consciousness.

Blatt and Rivera: Dignity and Disability Rights

Burton Blatt was a prolific writer and distinguished educator at Syracuse University who founded the Center on Human Policy in 1967; Geraldo Rivera was a young reporter beginning his broadcasting career at WABC television in New York City in 1972. Both men, from very different walks of life, share the distinction of having brought the horrors of institutional life for those with disabilities to the general public. Through photographic essays, textbooks, and a novel (e.g., *Christmas in Purgatory* [1966], *Exodus from Pandemonium* [1970], *Revolt of the Idiots* [1976]) Blatt exposed the inhumane conditions, pain, and drudgery inflicted on those in institutions. Using a hidden camera, Blatt and his collaborator, Fred Kaplan, took photos that made the American public aware of the cruelty and neglect that was hidden from view. Blatt's work contributed to a growing call for the deinstitutionalization of those with disabilities and the development of community-centered residential facilities to actually habilitate those disabilities (Herr, 1995).

However, it took the power of television to bring the horrors of institutional life fully into America's homes. In early 1972, Geraldo Rivera, along with a cameraman, was able to sneak into the Willowbrook State School, an institution located on New York City's Staten Island. The facility housed 6,000 residents of varying disabilities and levels of intelligence. Rivera shared the following with his viewers:

> The ward residents, who were children, slept on wooden benches and straight back chairs in the dark cold ward. Some had no clothes. One was drinking water like a dog from an open toilet. The odors were foul beyond description. (Rivera, 2004)

The initial reports of the Willowbrook tragedy resulted in an explosion of public outrage. A number of organizations filed suit against the state for violation of the

Burton Blatt's photographic essays exposed the inhumane conditions inflicted on those in institutions.

Through television, Geraldo Rivera brought the horrors of institutional life into America's living rooms.

civil rights of the children, and Willowbrook was eventually shut down (Goode, 1998). One of the more compelling images was that of Bernard Carabello, an 18-year resident of the facility who had cerebral palsy but not mental retardation, as he was finally being moved out of the institution. This and the many horrific images presented by Blatt and Rivera spurred a generation of family members and advocates to use the courts (and the court of public opinion) to fight for appropriate, inclusive, and community-based educational and rehabilitative services.

Sam Kirk: Recognizing Learning Disabilities

In 1963, Sam Kirk recognized an entirely new group of students with special needs whose characteristics had previously been misunderstood and misdiagnosed: students with learning disabilities (LD) (Chalfant, 1998; Gallagher, 1998). A prolific academic (he established the Institute for Research at the University of Illinois in 1951 and wrote extensively on numerous topics in special education), Kirk was extremely active in the formulation of some of the first federal public policies involving students with exceptionalities. For example, after Kirk had served on the Presidential Committee on Mental Retardation in the early 1960s, President Kennedy named him the first director of the Division of Handicapped Children and Youth in the U.S. Office of Education. He was involved in strengthening professional organizations such as the Council for Exceptional Children (CEC) and instrumental in assisting in the formation of parent organizations advocating for the education of children with mental retardation and learning disabilities.

Kirk created formal mechanisms for identifying and assessing LD and developed the diagnostic-prescriptive approach to teaching, a process that links diagnosis and remediation of learning difficulties. His conceptualization of **intraindividual differences,** the variability of strengths and weaknesses within a student, is generally regarded as the hallmark of LD and serves as the basis for discerning learning disabilities from other types of cognitive and psychological difficulties and disabilities (Minskoff, 1998). Without Kirk's groundbreaking scholarship and advocacy, large numbers of students with specific learning disabilities would either remain unserved or receive an education that fails to respond to their needs.

TOMORROW'S HISTORY: INCLUSION, ACCOUNTABILITY, AND OVERREPRESENTATION

What will the historians of tomorrow identify as the key issues that faced special education today? We believe that three of the field's current issues—service delivery, assurances that an appropriate education is being provided to every student with a disability, and the overrepresentation of students from certain racial and ethnic groups in special education—reflect our era. For example, in their history of the inclusion movement, Fuchs and Fuchs (1994) assert that vocal "inclusionists" advocate dismantling the continuum of placements and refashioning general education classes to accommodate all children. Although it will take years to fully assess the impact of such policies on student outcomes, it is clear that inclusive philosophies are driving a number of historic special education reforms.

Similarly, while there is little argument about the need for accountability in the delivery of instruction to students with special education needs, we are only in the initial stages of developing valid and reliable methods for making appropriate test accommodations. As you will see in later sections of this chapter, federal legislation (e.g., No Child Left Behind) requires all students to pass state tests or alternate assessments (Thurlow, Elliott, & Ysseldyke, 2003). Finally, future historians of special education will note how this generation of leaders addressed issues associated with the overrepresentation of certain minority groups in special education. As we fully describe in Chapter 3, it is likely that two interacting areas will continue to be investigated: (1) the role of demographic, social, and economic factors and (2) school processes (e.g., referral and assessment systems) that are insensitive to cultural and linguistic differences (Coutinho & Oswald, 2000).

Reflective Exercise #2
Investigative journalism played a key role in the attainment of civil rights and educational services for individuals with disabilities. Today, our ever-present media have focused on a number of controversial special education issues. Can you identify these issues and comment on the impact of the media on them?

Reflective Exercise #3
We have identified three current issues surrounding the delivery of special education. What issues do you believe historians 30 years in the future will focus on?

FEDERAL LEGISLATION

Two major legislative acts, the **Individuals with Disabilities Education Improvement Act of 2004 (IDEA 2004)** and the **No Child Left Behind Act (NCLB)** of 2001, shape how teachers do their jobs. Although each of these important pieces of legislation has evolved in different ways and serves different purposes, policymakers have worked to align both into a coherent educational policy framework that benefits students with and without disabilities. In our discussions of IDEA 2004 and NCLB, we consider the historical developments that led to their passage, describe the major components of the legislation, and conclude with a discussion of how these laws impact the professional lives of teachers.

INDIVIDUALS WITH DISABILITIES EDUCATION IMPROVEMENT ACT (IDEA 2004)

The Individuals with Disabilities Education Improvement Act of 2004 (IDEA 2004), the most recent iteration of the landmark Education of All Handicapped Children Act (EAHCA) of 1975, is arguably the most significant piece of legislation supporting the education and treatment of children and youth with disabilities. Figure 2.3 provides a quick introduction to IDEA 2004.

Legal Basis for IDEA 2004

To hear Monique Green and her colleague discuss their views of IDEA, go to the Ms. Green module on the DVD-ROM and click on clip 6: IDEA.

Approximately 40 years ago, there was no guarantee that a child with a disability could get a free appropriate public education. Consider these data from 1970: Approximately 1 million children between the ages of 7 and 17 were not enrolled in school. Their absence from school was not a family choice. Instead, school officials decided, often arbitrarily, that such children were beyond their responsibility (Abeson, Bolick, & Hass, 1976). Highly restrictive institutions that provided little more than food, clothing, and shelter were homes for approximately 200,000 individuals with significant disabilities. Schools

FIGURE 2.3

SELECTED QUICK FACTS: IDEA 2004

Free Appropriate Public Education (FAPE)

All children regardless of severity of disability can learn and are entitled to a free appropriate public education.

Special education and related services are provided at public expense in conformity with an IEP.

Nondiscriminatory Assessment

All testing and evaluation used to identify and assess students with disabilities are not to be racially or culturally discriminatory.

Evaluations requiring tests are to be in the child's native language or appropriate mode of communication and must be validated and administered by trained personnel.

Least Restrictive Environment (LRE)

The preferred placement for students with disabilities is the general education classroom. When success in the general education classroom cannot be achieved even with significant alterations, alternatives on the continuum of placements are to be considered.

Individualized Educational Program (IEP)

An IEP is to be developed for each student with a disability and include (1) current levels of performance, (2) annual goals, (3) extent of participation in general education programs, (4) beginning dates and anticipated duration of service, and (5) evaluation methods.

Participants in IEP planning are to include at least one special and general educator, a representative of the local education agency, an evaluation specialist, related-service specialists, and parents.

Parent Participation

Written permission is needed for all testing, evaluation, and changes in services.

Parents actively participate in IEP development and annual reviews.

Procedural Safeguards

Adequate notice is provided for meetings.

Disagreements can be settled through mediation and due process hearings.

www.prenhall.com/rosenberg

in our nation educated only one in five children with disabilities, and many states had laws that explicitly excluded students with certain types of disabilities.

Obviously, there have been many changes in educational policy, which now guarantee students with disabilities a free and appropriate public education. Significant **legislation** (laws and their accompanying interpretive regulations) have resulted in explicit rights for students with disabilities and their families as well as a range of responsibilities for professionals who work in schools and treatment centers. IDEA 2004 updates and amends earlier landmark legislation that served as the legal basis for the education of those with disabilities (Education of All Handicapped Children Act [EAHCA] of 1975; the 1983 and 1986 EAHCA amendments; and the Individuals with Disabilities Education Act [IDEA] of 1990, 1992, and 1997). Keep in mind that legislation is temporary, fluid, and subject to the influence of political pressure. For example, much of the legislation involving students with disabilities in schools has resulted from the tireless efforts of parents and disability-rights advocates who lobbied Congress for equal rights, due process, and educational equality for all learners. Figure 2.4 lists and describes earlier legislation that has had an impact on our current IDEA.

The due process rights afforded to students with disabilities and their families are, in large part, the result of grassroot parent activism and advocacy.

In addition to evolving legislation, **litigation** (legal cases in which a judge or a jury interprets the law in situational disputes) influenced the initial passage and prompted improvements in the provisions of IDEA 2004. Following are the legal principles that have had the most influence in the development of special education law. After reading them, review the cases in Table 2.1 and try to identify the principles that the courts used in making their decisions.

- **Due process.** The due process clauses of both the 5th and 14th Amendments require that laws be applied to all with sufficient safeguards. For students with disabilities, this means fair and specific procedures related to assessment, identification, and placement of children in special education (Turnbull, Stowe, & Huerta, 2007).
- **Equal protection.** The equal protection clause of the 14th Amendment forbids states from denying anyone equal protection of the laws without justification. Therefore, states must provide the same rights and benefits (e.g., opportunities to have qualified teachers, go on field trips, and participate in extracurricular activities) to students with disabilities as to those without disabilities.
- **Zero reject.** No child with a disability can be excluded from school, and all school agencies are to follow a policy of zero reject.
- **Free and appropriate education (FAPE).** Individual students must be provided with a full range of appropriate direct and related educational services at no cost to students or their families.
- **Least restrictive environment (LRE).** Services are to be delivered in settings that best meet the needs of the student and are closest to the typical general education setting.
- **Nondiscriminatory assessment.** Biased evaluation instruments and/or procedures constitute a denial of equal access to education. Students can be harmed by assessments that wrongly label them and mistakenly place them in environments that deprive them of opportunities for advancement. Moreover, stigmatizing labels resulting from misclassification can set in motion a host of problematic occurrences such as lowered expectations and isolation from peers.

To learn more about IDEA 2004, go to the Getting Your License & Beginning Your Career section on the Teacher Prep Website, click on Law & Public Policies, and then IDEA 2004.

FIGURE 2.4

EVOLUTION OF IDEA 2004 LEGISLATION

- **P.L. 83-531, Cooperative Research Act (1954),** involved cooperative research in education, including students with mental retardation.
- **P.L. 88-164, Mental Retardation Facilities and Community Mental Health Center's Construction Act (1963),** brought together into one unit expanded teacher-training programs and a new research program for the education of students with disabilities.
- **P.L. 88-164, Research and Demonstration Projects in Education of Handicapped Students Act (1964),** made grants to state and local agencies to educate students with handicaps and provided funds for construction, equipment, and operation of facilities for research and training of research personnel.
- **P.L. 89-313, Elementary and Secondary Education Act Amendments (1965),** encouraged programs to educate students with disabilities who were residing in institutions and similar state-operated or -supported residential facilities.
- **P.L. 89-750, Title VI, Education for Handicapped Students (1966),** allowed grants to states through the Elementary and Secondary Education Act (ESEA) for special-needs students.
- **P.L. 90-538, Handicapped Students' Early Education Assistance Act (1968),** was developed exclusively for students with disabilities to establish experimental preschool and early education programs for special-needs students.
- **P.L. 92-424, Economic Opportunity Amendments (1972),** mandated that a minimum of 10% of the enrollment slots in Head Start programs be made available to students with disabilities.
- **P.L. 93-112, 504, 29 U.S.C. 794, Rehabilitation Act (1973),** specified that no handicapped individual in the United States shall, solely by reason of his or her handicap, be excluded from the participation in, be denied the benefits of, or be subjected to discrimination under any program or activity receiving federal financial assistance.
- **P.L. 93-380, Education Amendments (1974),** increased monies available to public agencies for the education of students with special needs and protected the confidentiality of school records, provided procedures to challenge questionable information contained in the records (Buckley Amendment), and required states to locate and serve all students with disabilities.
- **P.L. 94-142, Education for All Handicapped Children Act (1975),** the precursor to IDEA 2004, often referred to as the Bill of Rights for students with disabilities, guaranteed the availability of a "free appropriate education," "due process," and "individualized educational plans" to all students with disabilities.
- **P.L. 98-199, Parent Training and Information Centers (1983),** entailed the training and provision of information to parents and volunteers.
- **P.L. 99-457, Education for All Handicapped Students Act Amendments (1986),** extended the mandate from P.L. 94-142 to include special education and related services beginning at age 3 and created a discretionary early intervention program to serve students from birth through age 2.
- **P.L. 101-476, Individuals with Disabilities Education Act (1990),** further amended the provisions of P.L. 94-142 and P.L. 99-487, renamed the act IDEA, and mandated that the IEP include a statement of transition services.
- **P.L. 101-336, Americans with Disabilities Act (1990),** prohibited discrimination based on disabilities in the areas of employment, public services, transportation, public accommodations, and telecommunications.
- **P.L. 101-392, Carl D. Perkins Vocational and Technology Education Act (1990),** provided resources for improving educational skills needed in a technologically advanced society, guaranteeing full vocational educational opportunities for all special populations.
- **P.L. 103-239, School to Work Opportunities Act (1994),** encouraged partnership models between school- and employment-based sites at the local level by encouraging schools and employment-site personnel to plan, implement, and evaluate integrated school- and work-based learning. It encouraged interagency agreements; technical assistance; and services to employers, educators, case managers, and others.
- **P.L. 102-476, Individuals with Disabilities Education Act: IDEA (1990), amended in 1997 as P.L. 105-17,** established a number of new provisions designed to improve outcomes for students with disabilities. Provisions inherent in the reauthorized law (IDEA 1997) include requirements that students with disabilities be included in state- and district-wide assessments, that students' IEPs address the issue of access to general education curricula, and that states establish performance goals and indicators for students with disabilities.

Source: Adapted from Rosenberg, Michael S.; O'Shea, Lawrence J.; O'Shea, Dorothy J., Student Teacher to Master Teacher: A Practical Guide for Educating Students with Special Needs, 4th edition, © 2006. Electronically reproduced by permission of Pearson Education, Inc., Upper Saddle River, New Jersey.

From Law to Classroom: Major Components of IDEA 2004

Undoubtedly, IDEA 2004 and its preceding litigation and legislation guide how we view, approach, educate, and evaluate students with disabilities. All of us—special educators, general educators, related-service providers, administrators, and paraprofessionals—participate in the implementation of its mandates, regardless of the setting or type of school we work in. In many respects, the components of IDEA 2004 form a core of competencies reflecting what all teachers should know and be able to do when teaching students with disabilities in their classrooms (Rosenberg et al., 2006).

Nondiscriminatory Identification, Assessment, and Evaluation. A major component of the original IDEA legislation was literally to locate the large number of children with disabilities who were unserved when the law passed in 1975. IDEA 2004 continues these

www.prenhall.com/rosenberg

TABLE 2.1

COURT CASES INFLUENCING THE DEVELOPMENT OF IDEA 2004

Case/Date	Context and Findings
Brown v. Board of Education of Topeka, Kansas (1954)	Consolidating cases from four states (Kansas, South Carolina, Virginia, and Delaware), the U.S. Supreme Court ruled that African American students who were required to attend segregated schools were not receiving an equal education. The "separate but equal" doctrine was struck down.
Hobson v. Hansen (1967)	The system used to place a disproportionate number of African American students into the lower tracks of the Washington, DC, school system was invalidated. Special classes were allowed as long as testing and retesting procedures were frequent and rigorous.
Diane v. State Board of Education (1970)	California was ordered to correct biases in assessment procedures used with culturally and linguistically diverse students.
Mills v. Board of Education (1972)	Students with disabilities are to have access to a free appropriate public education and due process regardless of the school district's financial status.
PARC v. the Commonwealth of Pennsylvania (1972)	In a consent degree agreement, the Commonwealth of Pennsylvania assured the court that a free appropriate education would be provided to all students and that there would be no exclusion of students with mental retardation.
Wyatt v. Stickney (1972)	Institutionalized students with mental retardation had a constitutional right to treatment.
Armstrong v. Kline (1979)	The 180-day school year violates some children's rights to a free appropriate education, and the state must supply instruction to meet individualized needs without limitation.
Larry P. v. Riles (1972, 1984)	Use of IQ tests as a measure for placing African American students in special education was determined to be discriminatory.
Board of Education v. Rowley (1982)	The requirement to provide an appropriate education does not mean that a school must provide the "best" education or one to maximize student potential. A program must be individualized and enable a student to benefit from an education.
Jose P. v Ambach (1984)	To increase delivery of services in a timely fashion, no more than 30 days should elapse between referral and evaluation.
Daniel R. R. v. State Board of Education (1989)	Although a program need not be modified beyond recognition, the general education curriculum must be modified for a student who requires accommodations and supports. The student with disabilities need not be expected to learn at the same rate as other students in the class, and schools are to consider broader educational benefits when considering mainstreaming.
Schaffer v. Weist, Montgomery County Schools (2005)	Parents who demand better special education programs for their children have the burden of proof in their challenges with the school districts.

Child Find activities and mandates school systems to identify those who could benefit from early intervention. The law requires that schools and community agencies evaluate students to determine if there is the presence of a disability and, if so, to identify the full spectrum of educational services needed for the student to have success in school or preschool settings. When conducting such evaluations, the law requires that educators

1. Employ testing materials and procedures in the student's primary language or mode of communication

class in which few direct supports are necessary. Moreover, placements for students will change based upon their academic and behavioral performance. The settings you will work in will depend on the needs of the students and could, and often will, vary in the course of your workday.

Individualized Educational Plans (IEPs). IDEA 2004 requires that each student identified as having a disability receive an **individualized educational plan (IEP),** a document that informs and guides the delivery of instruction and related services. Requirements for the development of an IEP are quite specific in terms of information included and the individuals who develop the plan. Six categories of information are required:

1. The student's current levels of academic and functional performance, with particular emphasis on how the student's disability affects participation and progress in the general education curriculum
2. Measurable annual goals related to meeting the student's needs resulting from the disability and enabling progress in the general education curriculum or, when necessary, short-term objectives for those students who participate in alternative assessments
3. A description of how the student's progress toward meeting annual goals is measured, how often progress is reported, and to whom it is reported (e.g., periodic reports to parents)
4. A statement of special education and related services and supplementary aids and services, based on research to the extent practicable, provided for or on behalf of the student
5. The extent, if any, to which the student will not participate with nondisabled students in the general education environment
6. The projected date for the beginning of services and the anticipated frequency, location, and duration of those services and modifications

The IEP team will also address postsecondary transition issues for students turning 16 (or younger, if deemed necessary by the team). Consequently, the IEP must include measurable goals and corresponding services based upon appropriate transition assessments. Finally, as the student approaches the state's legal age, the IEP must include a statement that the student has been informed of his or her rights in regard to IDEA 2004. (Developing IEPs is discussed in Chapter 4.)

Because the IEP is the focal point for planning, coordinating, and evaluating education services, successful development and implementation requires input from a number of informed stakeholders. IDEA 2004 requires that the IEP team include

*   At least one general education teacher of the student (if he or she is, or is planning to, participate in general education activities)
*   At least one special educator of the student
*   A school district representative who is knowledgeable about available service-delivery options and programs as well as the general education curriculum and related-service availability
*   An evaluation specialist who can interpret the instructional implications of assessments
*   Other specialists who can provide important information, such as related-service providers, transportation specialists, physicians, lawyers, and advocates
*   Parents, guardians, surrogate parents, and, when appropriate, the student

To reduce some of the logistical burdens on IEP meeting participants, IDEA 2004 excuses a team member from attending if that member's area is not being discussed or if there is agreement that written input is acceptable.

Procedural Safeguards. Before 1975 and the passing of the first IDEA, parents of students with disabilities, when not ignored, were often viewed as adversaries, subject to unpredictable, paternalistic, and jargon-saturated treatment from school personnel (Johnson, 1976). IDEA 2004 requires that schools ensure that parents (or guardians or surrogates) have the opportunity to participate in every decision related to the iden-

Reflective Exercise #4
In spite of all of the effort involved in developing IEPs, their use during classroom instruction is limited. Can you think of ways to make IEPs user-friendly?

www.prenhall.com/rosenberg

tification, assessment, and placement of their child. In addition to providing adequate notice for meetings and scheduling them at a mutually agreed-on time and place, school district personnel are to notify parents when considering changes in educational programming or related services.

What happens if parents believe that their rights have been violated or if there is disagreement regarding the development of their child's IEP? An initial step is *mediation*, a voluntary process in which a qualified, impartial facilitator works with the parties to come to resolution. If mediation does not satisfy the parties, IDEA 2004 mandates the convening of a due process hearing. These hearings allow injured or dissenting parties to question decisions and actions. Parties also have the right to appeal due process hearing decisions in federal court if they remain unsatisfied. IDEA 2004 urges states to strengthen their mediation procedures in the belief that structured opportunities for purposeful discussion between parties can reduce the need for protracted and costly legal activities associated with due process hearings and appeals.

Suspensions and Expulsions. When it comes to suspending, changing the placement, or expelling a student for violations of school rules, IDEA 2004 protections are prominent and somewhat controversial. Most people agree that legally correct and educationally relevant consequences must be delivered fairly regardless of disability status (Rosenberg et al., 2006). For those inappropriate behaviors deemed not a manifestation (i.e., caused by or related substantially to the disability or a failure to implement IEP procedures) of the student's special needs, schools can apply disciplinary actions in the same manner as they do for students without disabilities (as long as special education services continue). However, schools cannot remove a student with a disability from his or her current placement for more than 10 days if it is determined that the problem behaviors are a function of the disability. After a number of debates during the reauthorization process (i.e., on the difficulty of determining whether specific behaviors are a result of a disability; the safety of other students in school), IDEA 2004 provided schools with the authority to consider unique circumstances on a case-by-case basis to change a student's placement for violations such as (1) bringing a dangerous weapon to school, (2) selling or possessing illegal drugs, and (3) inflicting serious bodily injury on another person while at school or at a school function. In such cases, the school district may unilaterally place a student in an interim alternative placement for up to 45 school days.

Confidentiality and Access to Information. Student information, including the results of all assessments and reports, is confidential. In fact, IDEA 2004 requires that one official in each school district assume responsibility for ensuring confidentiality of school records and ensuring that those who have contact with student records are trained in records-management procedures. Parents by law have the right to inspect and review all information on their child, and it is not unusual for them to request an explanation regarding the information in the records.

Services to Infants, Toddlers, and Preschoolers. Historically, many states did not provide services to infants, toddlers, and preschoolers with disabilities. It was not until 1986, and an early reauthorization of IDEA, that preschool special education services were mandated for children ages 3 to 5 and incentives were provided to states encouraging the development of programs for infants, toddlers, and their families. Preschoolers are afforded the same services and protections available to school-aged children. Since infants and toddlers with disabilities often require medical, psychological, and human service interventions, as do members of the entire family, the federal government has encouraged the development of statewide, multidisciplinary, interagency programs by offering increased grant support.

IDEA Outcomes and Improvements

Recall that, before 1975, large numbers of students with disabilities received minimal services, often in highly restrictive, segregated settings. As a result of IDEA, most of today's children and youth with disabilities are educated in their neighborhood

Reflective Exercise #5
Consider the issues of equity involved in having different standards for suspension and expulsion. Is manifestation of a disability justification for having differing disciplinary consequences? How should we address the breaking of school rules by students with disabilities?

schools in general education classrooms with their nondisabled peers. Moreover, postschool employment rates for people with disabilities, although not where they should be, are twice those of older adults with similar profiles who did not have the rights and protections of the law. Even more heartening are the numbers of students with disabilities who attend college; compared to 1978, the number of first-year college students with disabilities has more than tripled (U.S. Department of Education, n.d.). IDEA also supports the development of quality model programs in the areas of early childhood special education, culturally relevant instructional methods, parent training, and teacher development as well as improved protocols for promoting transition to the world of work and strategies for assisting students to acquire content-rich curricula.

Even with these considerable accomplishments, advocates continue to identify aspects of the law that require improvement. Influenced by a presidential commission report, changes in the most recent reauthorization of IDEA were particularly significant. Two key themes that emerged from the report centered on the burdensome paperwork and administrative duties required to comply with the legal requirements of IDEA and the methods used to identify students with learning disabilities. In trying to reduce administrative and paperwork burdens, IDEA 2004

- No longer requires short-term objectives on students' IEPs except for those who take alternate assessments in place of the state's standardized assessment program
- Authorizes pilot projects in up to 15 states to develop multiyear IEPS, not to exceed 3 years
- Creates a 15-state paperwork demonstration program that allows states to test methods of reducing administrative reporting requirements without affecting applicable civil rights requirements

The new bill also addresses the controversial aptitude-achievement discrepancy method of identifying learning disabilities (see Chapter 6). No longer is a local education agency required to consider if there is a discrepancy between achievement and intellectual ability. Instead, the district can use a process that considers the child's response to scientific, research-based methods, an identification method known as *response to intervention (RTI).*

NO CHILD LEFT BEHIND

The No Child Left Behind Act (NCLB) of 2001 is a comprehensive federal initiative designed to improve the educational performance of *all* students. Although it is a reauthorization of earlier Elementary and Secondary Education Acts (ESEA), NCLB represents a major expansion of the federal government's role in public education. Rather than merely providing financial assistance to states in their efforts to set standards and improve student achievement, the act explicitly mandates compliance to high standards and sanctions states and schools that fail to meet set criteria (Hardman & Muldur, 2004; Yell & Drasgow, 2005). Figure 2.5 offers a quick introduction to NCLB.

With governance of schools the purview of individual states, the federal government cannot enact laws that mandate uniform policies and procedures. Nonetheless, it influences schools powerfully by invoking other provisions of the U.S. Constitution. Just imagine for a moment how different our schools would be if the Constitution did not protect our rights as citizens. In *Brown v. Board of Education* (1954), the landmark case that struck down racial segregation in public schools, the Supreme Court used the 14th Amendment to rule that separation between groups prevented equal educational opportunities. Without such federal intervention, states would have had the option of continuing the practice of "separate but equal." As with IDEA, the 14th Amendment and *Brown* were significant factors in legal decisions associated with the provision of a free, appropriate public education to students with disabilities.

In enacting NCLB, Congress was asserting that states were not doing enough to ensure that all students were performing adequately in school. Many students, once

Reflective Exercise #6
Consider the major accomplishments of IDEA since its original enactment in 1975. Has the law fulfilled its mission of providing a free appropriate education to all students? What can improve the act?

Reflective Exercise #7
Federal government involvement in education is a hot political issue. Do you believe that federal agencies and national policymakers should influence the policies of neighborhood schools? If so, under what circumstances do you believe that states and local governments should object to such influence?

FIGURE 2.5

SELECTED QUICK FACTS: THE NO CHILD LEFT BEHIND (NCLB) ACT OF 2001

Accountability for Results
- Creation of state assessments to measure what children know and learn
- Annual report cards on school performance allowing parents to know about the quality of the children's schools, the qualifications of teachers, and progress in key subjects
- Statewide performance reports disaggregated according to race, gender, and other relevant criteria to assess closing of achievement gap

Expanding Options for Parents
- Parents with children in failing schools allowed to transfer child to a better-performing public or charter school
- Title I funds available for supplemental educational programs (e.g., tutoring, after-school services, summer school) for children in failing schools
- Expanded federal support for charter schools

Strengthening Teacher Quality
- A highly qualified teacher in every public school classroom by 2005

---

again, were being denied equal opportunities for success. NCLB requires states to reduce the disparity in performance between those groups of students who typically achieve and those students who have had difficulties meeting standards, often due to economic disadvantage, linguistic differences, or disability status.

Major Components of NCLB

NCLB legislation is based on five core principles: (1) strong accountability for results; (2) expanded flexibility and local control of schools; (3) an emphasis on teaching methods based on scientific research; (4) expanded options for parents, particularly those whose children attend low-performing schools; and (5) highly qualified teachers.

Strong Accountability for Results. Among educators, the letters of the alphabet that most closely follow NCLB are AYP. AYP refers to **adequate yearly progress,** the minimum standard, or benchmark, expected of every student and school (see Figure 2.6). NCLB makes it very clear that states must develop clearly defined goals, or proficiency standards, and then assess if individual students and schools meet these targets. Comparing student performance data to the standards allows parents to know how their child is doing at school. In turn, policymakers and school leaders are able to assess how individual schools and school districts are performing in relation to state standards. In addition to measures of performance for all students across schools and districts, states are required to parse out, or disaggregate, data for specific groups of students, including those who are economically disadvantaged, members of varying culturally and linguistically diverse groups, and students with disabilities. Schools that meet their AYP goals receive positive public acknowledgement of effort. Those that do not meet their goals for two years running are deemed in need of improvement.

What about students with disabilities? Historically, students with disabilities were excluded, both formally and informally, from school and district assessments, perpetuating low expectations throughout their educational careers. Although many have welcomed inclusion, questions remain regarding the appropriateness of including students with severe cognitive disabilities in overall determinations of school effectiveness. To address this concern, NCLB allows school districts and states to exempt 1% of all students from the usual assessments. This 1% represents about 9% of those with disabilities and includes those with the most severe disabilities. Responding to concerns voiced by state and local officials, the U.S. Department of Education allows additional flexibility: an additional 2%, those identified as being in need of modified standards and assessments, can be assessed through alternative measures rather than the usual tests.

Expanded Flexibility and Local Control. NCLB recognizes that local officials have greater sensitivity to the needs of neighborhood schools than do federal administrators

Reflective Exercise #8
Critics of NCLB have asserted that the rhetoric of the act is admirable but in some cases unreasonable. For example, is it realistic to expect that *all* students will be able to meet state-mandated proficiency levels?

Reflective Exercise #9
The transferring and consolidation of funds between and among programs can be controversial. What are the potential advantages and disadvantages associated with this flexibility? Why might advocates for students with disabilities be concern by this practice?

FIGURE 2.7

PROMOTING DIGNITY: USING PERSON-FIRST LANGUAGE

Do the words we use to describe people affect them and influence how they are perceived and treated by others? Or are protestations to employ more sensitive language in our descriptions of people with differences and disabilities merely a "touchy-feely" fad or an exercise in political correctness? According to Snow (2006), the words we use to describe people are powerful; and the inappropriate use of old, inaccurate, and medically based descriptors remains the largest obstacle facing individuals with disabilities. In fact, when we use descriptors based on medical or educational diagnoses (e.g., Dave is mentally retarded, Sue is autistic), we marginalize that person and fail to recognize that she is much more than her disability.

Treating persons with disabilities with dignity involves recognizing that they are, first and foremost, people. Like most of us, they assume varied and overlapping roles—parents, sons, daughters, friends, colleagues, co-workers, entertainers, researchers, and, yes, sometimes even irritating store clerks. Consequently, the guiding principle when referring to individuals with disabilities is to recognize individuals as whole human beings. The American Psychological Association (2003) suggests avoiding language that (1) implies that the person as a whole is disabled, (2) equates persons with their disability, (3) implies negative overtones, and (4) is regarded as a slur. Such language implies that individuals with disabilities do not have the capacity or right to express themselves as resourceful and contributing members of society.

The APA recommends that the following guidelines be used when referring to individuals with disabilities.

- *Put people first.* Avoid the implication that the person as a whole is disabled.
  No: learning disabled student
  Yes: student with learning disability
- *Use emotionally neutral descriptors.* Avoid expressions that suggest helplessness and negativity.
  No: afflicted with cerebral palsy
  Yes: youngster with cerebral palsy
- *Emphasize abilities instead of limitations.* Employ positive statements that reflect functioning.
  No: confined to homebound instruction
  Yes: student taught at home
- *Focus on capacity to express control.* Use language that reflects on the person's ability to express goals and self-determine services and supports.
  No: placement decisions
  Yes: discussions of appropriate service delivery
- *Reflect the person as a resource rather than a burden or a problem.* Language should reflect that service delivery involves inclusion and supports rather than solving a problem.
  No: problem of autism
  Yes: challenges faced by students with autism

SUMMARY

Special education has been influenced by historical events, significant litigation, landmark legislation, and the courageous actions of advocates, teachers, and parents.

Social History: Individuals and Events Shaping Current Practices

- Although 1500 to 1900 is a period that can be characterized as "beyond cruelty and neglect," the stories of Pedro Ponce de Leon, Jean-Marc-Gaspard Itard, Laura Bridgeman, and Samuel Gridley Howe illustrate how the typical maltreatment of some with disabilities was beginning to change.
- During the early 20th century, the work of Henry Goddard and other eugenicists represented fear and contempt for those with disabilities. At the same time, advocates such as Elizabeth Farrell developed

curricula that helped students with disabilities obtain employment.

- Between 1950 and 1990, a period characterized by the fight for civil rights, there were significant efforts to ensure that students with disabilities had access to appropriate educational services and treatment.

IDEA 2004

- IDEA 2004, the most recent iteration of the landmark EAHCA of 1975, is the most significant legislative effort supporting the education of students with disabilities.
- IDEA, a confluence of significant legal decisions and principles, ensures that all students, regardless of their disability, receive a free appropriate education in the least restrictive environment.
- Because of IDEA, the majority of children with disabilities are educated in their neighborhood schools and, to a large extent, in general education classrooms.

No Child Left Behind (NCLB)

- No Child Left Behind is a comprehensive federal initiative designed to improve the educational performance of *all* students.
- NCLB mandates compliance to high standards and sanctions states and schools that fail to meet set criteria.

- The major components of NCLB—strong accountability for results, expanded flexibility, scientifically based teaching methods, expanded options for parents, and highly qualified teacher requirements—are having a substantial impact on how all students are being educated.
- Students and their families have procedural due process protections and are assured of receiving a nondiscriminatory assessment of strengths and weaknesses.
- An individualized educational plan containing current levels of functioning, annual goals, special education and related services, projected dates, and the extent of participation in the general education environment guides instructional efforts.

Section 504 and the ADA

- These significant pieces of legislation provide protections for those with disabilities who do not match the definitions provided under the IDEA statutes.
- Section 504 considers a child with a disability if he or she functions as disabled.
- ADA expands protections to prohibit discrimination in employment and public accommodations.

 Council for Exceptional Children **ADDRESSING THE PROFESSIONAL STANDARDS**

Council for Exceptional Children (CEC) knowledge standards addressed in the chapter:

CC1K1, CC1K2, CC1K6, CC1K8, GC1K3, GC1K4, GC1K5, CC9S8,

Appendix B: CEC Knowledge and Skill Standards Common Core has a full listing of the standards listed here.

All too often, the diversity of the teaching force does not match the diversity of students.

employ experienced, qualified, knowledgeable, effective teachers (Carey, 2004b). Children in high-poverty schools are almost twice as likely as other children (20% versus 11%) to have novice teachers (Carey, 2004b). This lack of highly qualified teachers is likely to be even more extreme for special education teachers in high-poverty schools (Tyler, Yzquierdo, Lopez-Reyna, & Flippin, 2004).

The featured teacher in this chapter, Suzy Clary Wilson, expressed concern about the fact that students in her school are almost exclusively poor and non–European American and noted the impact of lack of resources on their educational opportunities. Non–European American students also are less likely than European American children to have access to other resources that are linked with increased achievement. "In predominantly minority schools, which most students of color attend, schools are large (on average, more than twice as large as predominantly White schools. . .); on average, class sizes are 15 percent larger overall (80 percent larger for non-special education classes); [and] curriculum offerings and materials are lower in quality" (Darling-Hammond, 1998, p. 30).

THE DEMOGRAPHIC DIVIDE BETWEEN TEACHERS AND STUDENTS

Another factor that contributes to the achievement gap is the lack of teachers from culturally and linguistically diverse backgrounds. According to data collected by the National Education Association (2003), the teaching workforce in the United States is largely European American (86%), female (more than 75%), and middle-aged (median age of 46). Furthermore, the proportion of African American teachers has declined from 8% to 6% since the 1990–1991 school year.

The increasing diversity of the school population, coupled with the homogeneity of the teaching workforce, creates a demographic divide in many schools. According to a 2003 National Commission on Teaching and America's Future report, individuals of African American, Hispanic and Latino, Asian, and American Indian/Alaska Native descent make up 14% of K–12 teachers, while 36% of the students are from these backgrounds. In the nation's largest urban schools, students from diverse backgrounds make up 69% of the population, while only 35% of their teachers are from similar backgrounds (National Education Association, 2003).

We do not mean to suggest that teachers from the majority culture cannot successfully teach students with disabilities from diverse backgrounds. This is certainly not the case. However, it is important that the teacher workforce include at least a reasonable proportion of teachers who share the cultural and language experiences of their students. These teachers can serve as a rich resource for other teachers and ensure that the diverse backgrounds of students are used to enrich the lives of everyone in the school (Tyler et al., 2004). In the next section, we discuss how all teachers can bridge the demographic divide by learning about a child's background and experiences, and how these cultural experiences influence student behavior in school.

THE ROLE OF CULTURE IN EXPLAINING DIFFERENTIAL OUTCOMES

Clearly there are significant differences in the educational outcomes for students who vary by class, race, and home language. Factors such as access to resources; the demographic divide between teachers and students; and factors such as access to high-

www.prenhall.com/rosenberg

quality teachers, the nature of family support, and societal racism all help to explain why these discrepancies exist. However, we are not suggesting that these factors predetermine educational outcomes. There are children within and across these groups who achieve amazing success. For example, *And Still We Rise* (Corwin, 2001) documents the outcomes for 12 gifted high school students living in the Watts neighborhood of Los Angeles. Despite what most of us would consider overwhelming odds (i.e., poverty, second-language background, gang culture, teenage pregnancy, homelessness), most succeed and move toward promising futures.

Additionally, it is important to emphasize that children are not defined by any one factor. Each student has a complex history that encompasses varied factors such as social class, race, language, family structure, medical history, school history, ability, and disability. For example, the school experience and probable educational outcomes for a middle-class European American student with a moderate learning disability will not be the same as those of a student with a similar disability who is from a poor migrant family and is an English-language learner. Yet there is great variability in the educational outcomes within groups as well. Think about how the experiences of the second child just described might be different if the teacher came from a second-language background, had knowledge of the student's home culture, and/or had watched a family member overcome a learning disability. The connections (or lack of connections) between children and their teachers often facilitate or impede academic success.

One might think that the more points of difference between the children and the teacher, the more difficult it is for children to succeed. In many cases this is true. However, more significant than the number of differences is how teachers perceive difference. While human variation falls along a continuum (Baglieri & Knopf, 2004), the human tendency is to perceive difference as dividing people and behavior into two groups, "normal" and "abnormal." We tend to perceive those most like us as "normal" and those who differ from us in significant ways as "abnormal." For most of us, these perceptions are implicit feelings rather than explicit decisions. Try a little experiment to help you think about your perceptions of "normal" and how hard it is to alter one's perceptions.

Cross your arms across your chest in the way that you habitually cross them (in the akimbo position). Notice which hand is on top. Now cross your arms so that the *other* hand is on top. Many of our students find this so "abnormal" that it takes several tries to cross their arms in the nonhabitual way, but there is nothing inherently "normal" about having one's left (or right) hand on top. Yet even when you *know* that there is nothing abnormal about the new position, it feels weird; and without deliberate intention, you will habitually return your arms to their accustomed position.

In school, teachers often define "normal" students as those who come prepared to behave in particular ways and to handle a specific type of academic structure. For example, "normal" students might be those who

- Are able to sit and listen for extended periods of time
- Complete pencil-and-paper tasks with minimal assistance
- Take turns speaking in class, use standard grammar
- Are deferential to adults
- Look teachers in the eye when reprimanded
- Ask questions when they don't understand
- Use a logical sequential communication style
- Have parents who help them with homework and attend school events

If you are a European American, middle-class female who has spoken English from birth, these characteristics of appropriate behavior and activity probably seem "normal." Yet each of those characteristics is outside the norm for one or more cultural groups. This can mean that the teacher perceives actions that fall within the norms for children's cultures as "abnormal."

Although few teachers talk about children or their families as abnormal, teachers' lack of familiarity and/or comfort with the norms of other cultures and backgrounds can lead to the following kinds of perceptions about students or families:

- He just has no idea of appropriate behavior. He is out of his seat *all* the time and talks constantly when the teacher or other children are talking.
- Those parents just don't care. They never return my phone calls, never come to parent conferences, and don't even sign the student's planner.
- I had to keep saying to her, "Look at me. Look at me." These children just don't respect teachers. Their parents have taught them no respect.

When a teacher's implicit evaluation of a student leads to the conclusion that the child's academic or social behavior is outside the norm of appropriate behavior, the teacher may make well-intended decisions that are unlikely to enhance the child's educational success.

One example of the influence of culture concerns the decision to refer a child for possible special education placement. This is an inferential decision. That is, the teacher makes a decision to refer the student because he or she believes that the student's academic or social behavior is so far outside the expectations for "normal" behavior that special services are warranted.

Notice the word *believes* in the previous sentence because teachers' beliefs are influenced by their cultural expectations. Consider these facts. A review of studies on race and special education placement revealed that school districts with predominantly European American populations enrolled a higher percentage of students from diverse backgrounds in special education than did districts with higher percentages of students from non–European American backgrounds (Fletcher & Navarrete, 2003). In addition, districts with a greater percentage of teachers from non–European American backgrounds enrolled lower percentages of students from diverse backgrounds in special education. These findings suggest that students who fall outside the norms of behavior expected by European American, middle-class teachers are at greater risk for being referred to special education.

WHAT IS CULTURE AND WHY IS IT SO IMPORTANT?

Culture is a concept that helps teachers understand the implicit evaluations they make and the reasons behind some of the behaviors of students that "seem" atypical or abnormal. The construct of culture includes the values, beliefs, and behaviors associated with a particular group of people.

Nieto (2004) defines culture as "the values; traditions; social and political relationships; and worldview created, shared, and transformed by a group of people bound together by a common history, geographic location, language, social class and/or religion" (p. 436). As this definition suggests, culture is dynamic, or changing, and is socially constructed by those who participate in it. Culture has also been referred to as an invisible web of shared meanings (Geertz, 1973). Because culture is invisible, it can be very difficult to perceive the defining characteristics of one's own culture (Greenfield, Raeff, & Quiroz, 1996). In addition, the invisible rules (or norms) of culture, including behaviors, values, and beliefs that guide human interaction, may be confusing to people when they attempt to participate in a different culture. You may have seen the sitcom *Phil of the Future* or the older show *Third Rock from the Sun.* In both shows, characters from another time period or planet are often puzzled by people's "normal" actions that fall outside their own realm of experience or understanding. The sitcoms use the generally invisible norms of social interaction to create humor.

Cultural Norms and School: Some Examples

Some societies are considered *individualist* in their culture and communication style, while others are *collectivist.* According to Gudykunst and Kim (2003), **individualist cultures** emphasize individual achievement and initiative and promote self-realization. Students in individualist cultures are motivated by individual recognition. For example, the teacher might create a public display of achievement by hanging individual student work on the wall with stars and stickers for accomplished work. Or a teacher might praise individual students for good behavior and refer to an individual as a "model" student. Some examples of individualist cultures include Australia, France, Ireland, Israel, Italy, Norway, Switzerland, and the United States (Gudykunst & Kim, 2003).

The emphasis in **collectivist cultures** is on the collective and not the individual. In a collectivist culture, working for the common good is more highly valued than individual achievement. Students from collectivist cultures may prefer to work in groups rather than independently, and each member's contribution is "successful" only to the degree that it enhances the whole group. Individuals from collectivist cultures may not be motivated by individual praise and displays of accomplishment; instead, they are motivated by group productivity and accomplishment (Trumbull, Rothstein-Fisch, & Greenfield, 2000). Examples of collectivist cultures include Brazil, China, Egypt, Greece, India, Korea, Mexico, Pakistan, Thailand, and Venezuela (Gudykunst & Kim, 2003). Although cultural groups have tendencies toward individualism or collectivism, it is important to note that individualism and collectivism fall along a continuum, that all cultures have both individual and collective traits, and that individuals within cultures differ with regard to these traits.

The Impact of Culture on Education

Cultural tendencies impact the way children participate in education. Table 3.1 describes different expectations about "normal" school behavior for students from individualist and collectivist cultures. As you review this information, take a moment to think about how teachers who lack knowledge about culture might interpret the behavior of a child from a collectivist culture. These differences may cause educators to inaccurately judge students from some cultures as poorly behaved or disrespectful. In addition, because cultural differences are hard to perceive, students may find themselves reprimanded by teachers but fail to understand what they did that caused concern.

TABLE 3.1

INDIVIDUALIST AND COLLECTIVIST CULTURAL PERSPECTIVES ON EDUCATION	
Individualist Perspective	**Collectivist Perspective**
Students work independently; helping others may be cheating.	Students work with peers and provide assistance when needed.
Students engage in discussion and argument to learn to think critically.	Students are quiet and respectful in class in order to learn more efficiently.
Property belongs to individuals, and others must ask to borrow it.	Property is communal.
Teacher manages the school environment indirectly and encourages student self-control.	Teacher is the primary authority, but peers guide each other's behavior.
Parents are integral to child's academic progress and participate actively.	Parents yield to teacher's expertise to provide academic instruction and guidance.

Source: Adapted from Individualist and Collectivist Perspectives on Education, from the Diversity Kit (2002). Providence, R.I.: The Education Alliance.

The influence of culture on beliefs about education, the value of education, and participation styles cannot be overestimated. Many Asian students, for example, tend to be quiet in class, and making eye contact with teachers is considered inappropriate for many of these children (Bennett, 2003). In contrast, most European American children are taught to value active classroom discussion and to look teachers directly in the eye to show respect, while their teachers view students' participation as a sign of engagement and competence.

Another contrast involves the role of Hispanic parents in education. Parents from some Hispanic cultures tend to regard teachers as experts and will often defer educational decision making to them (Valdés, 1996). In contrast, European American parents are often more actively involved in their children's classrooms, are visible in the classrooms, or volunteer and assist teachers. These cultural differences in value and belief may cause educators to make inaccurate judgments regarding the value that non–European American families place on education. While it is important to keep in mind that different cultural groups *tend* to follow particular language and interaction styles, there is tremendous variability within cultural groups (Gutiérrez & Rogoff, 2003). Thus, educators need to understand individual histories and ideologies regarding education and learning as well as the cultural patterns and beliefs of groups. Let's look at a couple of cases to examine in more detail how culture impacts educational interactions.

UNDERSTANDING CULTURE THROUGH THE LENS OF RACE, CLASS, AND STUDENT BEHAVIOR

To illustrate the significance of culture, let's consider the case of a fourth-grade African American male student identified with an emotional/behavior disorder. Deshawn, who has been retained twice, is 2 years older and appreciably larger than most of his classmates. His academic work is significantly below grade level, and he has difficulty controlling his anger in school. Marks (2005) describes an incident involving this child with Ms. Lucy Payton (pseudonyms are used for this teacher and student), an African American teacher at the same school where our featured teacher in this chapter, Suzy Clary Wilson, teaches.

Reflective Exercise #2
What would be a professional response to this situation? What would you say to Deshawn? What would you do? And how would you want the teacher to respond if Deshawn were *your* child?

> At the end of the day students were given 20 minutes of free time to read or catch up on writing and [Deshawn] who was having a difficult day wanted to leave school early. He was hovering around the classroom door holding his backpack and looked like a caged tiger walking back and forth. This was a management problem waiting to explode. (Marks, 2005, p. 85)

Before we talk about how Ms. Payton responded, let's look at what often happened with Deshawn and another teacher in the school. Confronted by Nancy Whitford, a young European American, middle-class teacher, Deshawn often responded by talking back, getting angry, or having an explosive outburst. Ms. Whitford viewed him as a continual behavior problem and expressed frustration at his disrespect, anger, and inappropriate behavior.

Although Deshawn was not a model student for Lucy Payton, his anger seldom erupted in her class. Watch how she handled the situation just described:

> "Come over here baby. Come and talk to your mama." The student walked over to Ms. Payton, kicking his backpack. Ms. Payton asked in a quiet voice, "What are you doing?" He responded that he wanted to go home. "Baby we got 20 more minutes of school. You can't stand there for 20 minutes. Go find something to do. Hang in there then you can go and do whatever you want. Just hang in there with me." (Marks, 2005, p. 85)

At this point, Deshawn joined Ms. Payton and a small group of students in an activity at her desk. Marks (2005) explained that rather than creating a power struggle by ordering compliance (as Nancy Whitford might have done), Lucy Payton used her relationship with the student to support and guide him to resolve his problem. The

www.prenhall.com/rosenberg

differences between Deshawn's behavior and success in these two classrooms suggest the importance of a teacher's knowledge of culture and acceptance of difference in addressing a student's needs.

Deshawn's behavior with these two teachers is influenced by his relationship with each teacher and by the way each teacher perceives him and his actions. Teachers' responses to any student's behavior are grounded in their culturally derived judgments about the behavior. If the behavior is judged as inappropriate the teacher then makes a determination about how severe (or how far outside the realm of "normal") the infraction is. These judgments are informed by cultural assumptions. Consequently, teachers may inappropriately judge culturally defined actions as resistant.

For example, talking loudly, a not uncommon African American cultural characteristic, is often misinterpreted by European American teachers as defiance (Thompson, 2004). In the current case, Nancy Whitford interprets Deshawn's resistance as defiance. Within her cultural definitions of student and teacher, the teacher has authority by virtue of her position; therefore, students should comply with teacher requests. Her response to perceived defiance is a stronger and ultimately punitive insistence on compliance. This response escalates problems with Deshawn and other students with similar behavior.

Lucy Payton, who shares many elements of Deshawn's racial and social class background, recognizes that African American children and adults who live in poverty often distrust authority because they believe systems like school are inherently unfair (Payne, 2003). She interprets his resistance as an expression of discontent or disconnection and recognizes that, as an overage, low-achieving fourth grader, Deshawn's strongest desire is to escape. Rather than assert her authority, she grounds her response in her relationship with him, drawing on their shared culture as a way to connect. Then, drawing on her knowledge of culturally responsive classroom management, she provides both structure and choice, insisting on appropriate behavior but avoiding a power struggle and preserving Deshawn's autonomy and self-respect in the process (Brown, 2004; Payne, 2003).

Note that these teachers have the same goal: to return Deshawn to his seat and engage him in productive activity. However, the teachers' judgments about the student lead to different responses and different results. Viewing a behavior as a manifestation of defiance often leads to conflict and disruption of the learning environment. Understanding the possible cultural sources of student resistance requires that teachers look at their own and their students' behavior in new ways. It is important to note, however, that the ability to attend to cultural differences does not require that the teacher share the same culture as the student (Bondy, Ross, Gallingane, & Hambacher, 2006).

UNDERSTANDING CULTURE THROUGH THE LENS OF LANGUAGE AND DISABILITY

Let's explore another set of cultural factors as we consider the experiences of Carlos, a 7-year-old, second-grade boy who has been living in the United States for 10 months. His family speaks only Spanish in the home, and both parents are literate in Spanish.

Upon his arrival in the United States, Carlos was enrolled in the local elementary school and participated in a general education classroom with English-language learner (ELL) support provided in a separate classroom setting. Berta, his mother, has been increasingly concerned about Carlos's performance in school. She receives notes from the general education teacher

Students bring many language backgrounds to the classroom.

HOW CULTURE MEDIATES SCHOOL EXPERIENCE

Looking at school achievement through different cultural lenses demonstrates the ways in which teacher and student behaviors are mediated by their culturally derived values, experiences, and beliefs (Garcia, Perez, & Ortiz, 2000). The challenge for teachers is that students vary in so many ways. The examples we provided describe just a few of these variations and suggest the complex interaction of factors. However, there are many more to think about. Consider just a few of the ways in which students' or families' norms may contradict European American norms:

- Parents from some cultures believe that actively interacting with the school communicates distrust of and disrespect for educators (Epstein, 2001).
- Students from a culture of poverty may enter school with little experience in using a formal language register (the language of school). At home they may use a predominantly informal register that relies on a 400- to 800-word vocabulary and depends on nonverbal interactions to assist in conveying meaning (Payne, 2003).
- Students from a culture of poverty may have little experience with "school-task" questions in which students are expected to answer test-type questions to which the teacher already knows the answer (Heath, 1982).

In addition to describing the many ways in which children vary—by race, ability, disability, birth language—we have talked about the fact that students vary simultaneously across many factors. Two areas of cultural difference are so significant that they warrant special attention. One is the issue of poverty, and the second is the interface between culture and parental expectations.

The Significance of Poverty

We are highlighting poverty because, as our featured teacher Suzy Clary Wilson noted, lack of economic resources limits the ability of parents and children to accommodate other influences. Poverty impacts access to medical care, prenatal care, high-quality preschool, therapy, tutors, after-school and summer enrichment programs, stable housing, and sufficient quantities of healthy food. And as we've noted, it often limits access to good schools and certified teachers. In this way poverty diminishes the opportunities for success. Consider just a few of the ways in which poverty undermines achievement.

The rate of asthma is significantly higher for children from lower-class backgrounds than for those from the middle or upper classes (Rothstein, 2002). Children from high-poverty backgrounds are less likely to receive treatment for asthma, which impacts sleep patterns, ability to be attentive in school, and school attendance. Each of these factors in turn influences achievement. In addition to asthma, children from non–European American and low-income backgrounds experience high levels of untreated problems with vision, hearing, and oral health. Research suggests that attention to these problems might impact school achievement more quickly and more substantially than changes in teaching practice (Rothstein, 2002).

Data from other sources reveal that the life circumstances of children living in poverty mean they begin school behind and never catch up (Books, 2004). These findings are not intended to dismiss the significant role that schools play in creating opportunities for children. Powerful education can alter the life circumstances for children in poverty (e.g., Corwin, 2001). However, decreasing the achievement gap requires much more than changes in pedagogy, monitoring student performance on standardized tests, and making sure each student has a high-quality teacher as suggested by the national policy guiding the No Child Left Behind Act (NCLB). Solving the achievement gap requires social policy that directly tackles the challenges of poverty rather than suggesting that schools alone can solve the problem.

Students from diverse backgrounds who have disabilities often struggle to meet the academic expectations that state and local education agencies place on schools. These expectations have changed several times in most states over the past few years as a result of state legislation and the passage of the federal NCLB and IDEA 2004. Figure 3.3 provides an example of the special challenge that high-stakes testing and changing expectations present for these students.

Reflective Exercise #3
High-stakes testing requires that states balance the need for high standards with equitable treatment of all students. What issues do states face in achieving this balance? For example, what issues arise if states have different expectations for certain groups of students (e.g., lower expectations for students with disabilities or students who are English-language learners)?

www.prenhall.com/rosenberg

FIGURE 3.3

THE SPECIAL CHALLENGE OF HIGH-STAKES TESTING

With the passage of the No Child Left Behind Act in 2001, many states began to implement high school exit exams. By 2006, 25 states had or were phasing in mandatory exit exams (Center on Education Policy, 2006). These exams are intended to make the high school diploma "mean something," ensuring that the recipient has a certain level of knowledge and skills that are needed to succeed in a job and other aspects of daily life (Bhanpuri & Sexton, 2006). Thus, students face high stakes when they take the exam, as graduation from high school with a regular diploma is contingent on achieving a certain score.

Most professionals recognize that high-stakes tests in general, and high school exit exams in particular, can be a very good thing for students who historically have not achieved at a high level (including students with disabilities, English-language learners, and students from non–European American backgrounds who live in poverty) (Johnson & Thurlow, 2003; O'Neil, 2001; Ysseldyke, Dennison, & Nelson, 2004). For example, these tests are intended to

- Ensure high expectations for all students
- Hold schools accountable for the achievement of all students (e.g., before NCLB, most states did not hold local schools accountable for the achievement of students with disabilities)
- Ensure that all students participate in the general education curriculum
- Reduce differences among groups of students (e.g., students with disabilities and those who do not have disabilities)
- Improve instruction to better meet the needs of students who do not do well on high-stakes exams
- Serve as a catalyst for school improvement in settings where students do not achieve at appropriate levels

In spite of these positive intended outcomes, controversy has emerged regarding the use of high-stakes tests. Critics fear that they will increase the dropout rate, reduce the number of students who receive a regular diploma, and lower student self-esteem due to repeated failure on exit exams (Johnson & Thurlow, 2003). Some also contend that a single test should not be the basis for making a high-stakes educational decision and that alternative assessments should be available (O'Neil, 2001). Perhaps the greatest concern raised by critics is that schools will not have the resources to provide remedial support for students who do not make adequate progress toward achievement goals (Center on Education Policy, 2004).

Alternatives for exit exams are beginning to emerge in some states, in part as a result of high failure rates for certain groups of students, including students with disabilities, English-language learners, and students from non–European American backgrounds (Bhanpuri & Sexton, 2006). These alternatives include waivers or exemptions (e.g., for students with disabilities based on IEP goals), substitute tests, and alternate diplomas (Center on Education Policy, 2004). Critics fear that these alternatives will result in lowered expectations for students. Moreover, individual accountability is crucial if students are to be held to high standards (O'Neil, 2001). If students are "issued diplomas regardless of performance, their degrees may be tainted with a stigma and their achievements discounted" (pp. 187–188).

Culture, Parent Expectations, and Disability

Cultural values and beliefs influence how people view disability (Wilder, Taylor Dyches, Obiakor, & Algozzine, 2004). Some Hispanic mothers, for example, may view caring for a child with a severe disability as a form of devotion, while others may view this as a curse or a result of a *mal ojo*, or evil eye, based on their spiritual practices. Linguistic differences also affect a cultural group's understanding of disability. For example, there is no word for autism in some Asian languages (Wilder et al., 2004). The lack of vocabulary to describe a disability may indicate a different cultural idea or value related to the disability itself.

Correa and Tulbert (1993) outline several cultural tendencies that educators should consider that may provide a better understanding of how to work effectively with Hispanic families. First, many Hispanic families are large, extended units. The broad social network of families provides a sizable source of information for educators. This network may include the *compadres,* or godparents, of Hispanic children as well as grandparents, aunts, and uncles.

Second, many Hispanic parents place high value on respect for individuals and the family as well as affection for children. As such, family members, including extended family members, may provide emotional and economic support for each other. This corresponds to collectivist notions of culture discussed earlier. As a result, Hispanic children tend to work well in cooperative groups, and educators who appear impartial or objective in working with children may be perceived as uncaring (Correa & Tulbert, 1993).

Third, for many, Hispanic notions of being *bien educado,* or well educated, often include both academic achievement and appropriate behaviors such as respect toward adults and the family (Escamilla & Coady, 2001). As a result, parental expectations of children may not align with educator expectations about the importance of attaining high test scores and grades.

This is just one example of the range of beliefs and perspectives that different cultural groups have regarding disability. It is also important to keep in mind that within groups there is tremendous variation in beliefs (i.e., not all Hispanic families have the same beliefs regarding disability). As Correa and Tulbert (1993) suggest, "cultural profiles of ethnic groups will be effective [for professionals only if they] can affirm that the cultural pattern does indeed exist within the individual family" (p. 256). Thus, it is very important for a teacher to know her students, learn about students' lives outside of school, and understand an individual family's cultural perspectives about medicine and disability. This information is crucial in guiding interactions with parents.

Given that children vary in many ways both within and across cultures and that the problems of poverty are pervasive and beyond teachers' control, you may be feeling overwhelmed and somewhat discouraged about your capacity to make a difference. We want to be clear that schools and teachers play a critical role and vary in their capacity to make a difference. In fact, it is clear that teachers who accept the responsibility to make a difference with *every* child have a powerful impact on achievement. This difference is magnified when teachers and administrators in entire schools accept this mission (Bempechat, 1998; Corbett, Wilson, & Williams, 2002; Irvine, 2002; Ladson-Billings, 1994).

WHAT CAN TEACHERS DO? GUIDELINES FOR CULTURALLY RESPONSIVE TEACHING

The remainder of this chapter draws on the literature about **culturally responsive teaching** and **culturally responsive classroom management** to suggest guiding principles for teachers of students with disabilities from diverse backgrounds. This information is intended to complement and extend upon the information regarding specific pedagogy for students with disabilities that is provided in other chapters in this text. Used in combination, these guidelines and pedagogical information will better equip you to address the needs of all of your children, regardless of their background.

WHAT IS THE GOAL?

Although improving children's achievement-test scores is important, raising scores is too limited a goal. The real goal is to help children develop their capacity to be resilient; that is, we want to enhance children's strengths in order to support their capacity and motivation to learn and their beliefs that they are capable. **Resilience** has been defined as the "capacity for or outcome of successful adaptation despite challenging or threatening circumstances" (Masten, Best, & Garmezy, 1990, p. 425). Resilience is not the result of innate abilities but is a capacity available to all children that is bolstered by supportive factors (Bempechat, 1998; Benard, 2004).

The goal, then, is to assess the strengths children bring to school and build on them by tailoring instruction toward their strengths while building capacity in weaker areas. In this way teachers help students believe in themselves, their futures, and their capacity to succeed.

Reflective Exercise #4
Research has revealed that students' beliefs in their capacity to succeed were stronger predictors of success in school than IQ or achievement test scores (Bempechat, 1998). How would you as a teacher ensure that students in your class believe in their capacity to succeed?

www.prenhall.com/rosenberg

Teachers and the school environment are critical protective factors for fostering resilience. For example, it is critically important that teachers believe in students' strengths and resilience. Imagine how a teacher who believes each student has strengths that must be enhanced and cultural and learning differences that must be accommodated might approach instruction differently from a teacher who perceives that students have cultural and learning deficiencies that must be remediated. How we think about disabilities and cultural differences becomes very important. Consider the example in Figure 3.4 regarding different ways in which we think about disabilities.

Reflective Exercise #5
How do you think about disabilities? Which of the two models (medical and interactional) better characterizes your perspective? Discuss with another member of class your perspective on these models and whether how we think about disabilities is important.

FIGURE 3.4

HOW WE THINK ABOUT DISABILITIES: DOES IT MAKE A DIFFERENCE?

Historically, disabilities have been defined much like diseases, from a medical perspective. The words that were used (and continue to be used by some) reflected this perspective. Individuals were "diagnosed" with disabilities (much like diseases), and "treatments" were sought to fix or cure the diagnosed deficiency. The assumption was made that the disability resided within the person (again, like a disease), and external factors had little influence on the disability. This view of disability is commonly referred to as the *medical model* (Hahn, 1985; Kavale & Forness, 1995; Sleeter, 1995).

In reaction to the medical model, leaders in the field of disability studies have advocated for an interactional model (Hahn, 1985; Sleeter, 1995). They argue that disability originates from the interaction between the individual and society and that the remedy for disability-related problems is a change in these interactions (Hahn, 1985). This may seem to be a relatively trivial change, but consider the following differences in how people think about disabilities using these models.

Medical Model	Interactional Model
Disability is a deficiency.	Disability is a difference.
A disability is negative.	A disability is neutral.
A disability resides within a person.	A disability results from the relationship (or the interaction) between a person and society.
The professional is the expert.	An expert can be the person with the disability, an advocate, or anyone who changes the social relationship.

Obviously, the medical model views disability from a negative perspective and places the responsibility (and, in some cases, blame) for the disability on the person with the "deficiency." In contrast, the interactional model views disability not as a deficiency to be fixed but as a difference that creates challenges to be addressed. The interactional model does not ignore the disability or the challenges that a person with a disability will face. Rather, the disability is no longer perceived in a negative light but is viewed from a neutral or positive perspective, and the influence that society has on a disability, for good or bad, is recognized.

To illustrate, for most of the 20th century, most persons with disabilities that limited their mobility lacked access to many buildings because most buildings were not designed to be accessible (a societal decision). This lack of access was produced by a lack of convenient parking, the use of steps rather than ramps for entering buildings, heavy doors that required much arm strength to open rather than automatic doors, restrooms that were not accessible, and lack of elevators to access different floors of a building, among other things.

During the last 25 years of the 20th century, society made a decision (with the passage of Section 504 of the Rehabilitation Act and the Americans with Disabilities Act) that persons with disabilities that reduced their mobility should have access to buildings. Thus, newly constructed buildings were required to be accessible (e.g., with designated parking spaces, ramps, automatic doors, elevators, accessible restrooms), greatly enhancing the independent access to these settings.

Available information regarding culturally responsive pedagogy and classroom management suggests several guidelines for effective practice. Culturally responsive teachers are simultaneously curious about culture and introspective. They know that culture impacts people's perceptions, knowledge, and interactions and that the impact of cultural assumptions is often implicit. They strive to learn more about who they are, what they believe, and how their beliefs and experiences influence their perceptions of and interactions with students and their families.

Become a Student of Culture and Difference

No teacher, and certainly no novice teacher, will possess comprehensive knowledge about all of the possible cultures, languages, disabilities, and economic influences on learning that one might encounter. While knowledge is important, a teacher's underlying curiosity about culture and difference is more important (Banks et al., 2005). A teacher who is culturally curious recognizes that all people are influenced by their background, culture, and experience. Tatum (1997) noted that many of the European American college students she teaches believe they have no culture, whereas her students from diverse backgrounds easily identify cultural influences in their lives.

While one is inevitably influenced by one's culture, the pervasiveness of the dominant (European American, heterosexual, middle class) culture can make it invisible to those who have grown up inside that culture. Think back to how you answered the first question on the demographic questionnaire at the beginning of the chapter. If you are white, middle class, monolingual, and of European descent, and you omitted these characteristics, your answers suggest that parts of your culture are invisible to you.

The culturally responsive teacher actively strives to see alternative perspectives. One strategy is to critically examine the impact of your differences from others. Our students find it helpful to start this process by thinking about how experiences are different for men and women, for people who are thin and heavy, or for those who are heterosexual and non-heterosexual. Understanding how these differences influence our perspectives helps make us more open to a broader range of differences. In this chapter you have learned about some of the ways that people from various cultures

While no teacher is familiar with all cultures, we all benefit from learning about the cultural experiences of others.

www.prenhall.com/rosenberg

view parenting, teachers, authority, social interaction, and disability. Our hope is that this has made you curious about other perspectives.

Develop a Vision of Students Who Succeed

Culturally responsive teachers, like Suzy Clary Wilson, recognize the impact of poverty but accept no excuses when students fail to learn. Yet many teachers attribute poor academic performance to the student, particularly if the student's background is different from their own. Although teachers probably do not want to believe they have low expectations, in fact, teachers who excuse students' failures because they are poor, live in foster care, are second-language learners, or have a disability have low expectations. As noted, these students do, in fact, have challenges that impact their success. It would be unrealistic to suggest that all students, despite the challenges they face, will achieve to the same level within schools as currently constituted. Nevertheless, culturally responsive teachers *must* believe they can reach every child and work to accomplish this goal, even knowing that occasionally they will not be fully successful. To give up, particularly on the basis of characteristics in the child's background, ensures that certain groups of children will continue to fail.

One strategy for developing this vision is to seek out examples of students whose background and experience are different from the norm but who succeed in school. We can read about teachers who are successful in reaching all children. Examples of such books include *There Are No Shortcuts* (Esquith, 2004), *Educating Esme* (Codell, 2001), and *White Teacher* (Paley, 2000). Other books provide examples of students who succeed: *And Still We Rise* (Corwin, 2001) and *Learning Outside the Lines* (Mooney & Cole, 2000). Additionally, all school systems have teachers whose success with students is legendary. Visiting these teachers' classrooms will help you see what successful teaching looks like and give you experiences that help you believe success is possible. If others can do it, so can you. Effective teaching for *all* children is not magic, and it is not a bag of pedagogical skills (though you certainly will need to develop many skills!). Effective teaching for *all* children is the constant pursuit of the mission to help all children succeed. The first step is to develop the belief that success is possible and a picture of what success looks like.

Learn Not to Judge

Remember that the way we have grown up and experienced life defines "normal" for each of us. Working effectively with students from diverse backgrounds requires us to constantly question our reactions to students and their families and to check the human tendency to judge different as "abnormal." This is easy to say but very difficult to do. Recall how weird it felt to cross your arms in an abnormal way. Even though you know (a cognitive reaction) that there is nothing abnormal about putting the opposite hand on top, it still feels weird (an affective reaction). How will you know when cultural difference may be a factor in your interactions with students?

Learning not to judge requires that you analyze your affective reactions. Consider the example of Nancy Whitford presented earlier in the chapter. If Ms. Whitford analyzed her classroom interactions, she would notice that many of her management challenges come from African American boys who resist her and become confrontational when she reprimands them. This should be a clue that her instructional and management style may conflict with the cultural expectations of these students.

It is important to stress that neither Nancy Whitford's expectations nor her students' resistance are unreasonable. Unfortunately, Ms. Whitford's response is to judge, to believe that the students are not motivated to learn. This judgment precludes her from solving the problem because her perception of deficiency leads her to blame the students. Nancy Whitford would be more likely to solve the problem if she recognized that the students' responses are reasonable, patterned behavior linked to their culture and experiences. If Ms. Whitford perceived that the problems might be based in culture, she would be better able to address their

FIGURE 3.5

UNDERSTANDING THE PERSPECTIVES OF PARENTS

In *Learning Outside the Lines* (Mooney & Cole, 2000), Jonathan, a young man who has coped with a reading disability throughout his academic life, tells the story of his second-grade year when he struggled in spelling and reading. His mother often kept him out of school on Friday, which was spelling-test day. Can you think of two ways to explain this mother's decision?

One explanation is that the mother did not care about her son's academic future and did not understand how important school attendance is. A child with a disability needs school even more than others and cannot afford to miss even one day. This mother kept her son out often. Her behavior was irresponsible and unjustifiable.

The explanation that Jonathan provides is that school and particularly spelling-test day was so challenging for him during that year that his mother was struggling to preserve his sense of himself as a valuable, capable person. By taking him out of school on a high-stress day, a day when failure was inevitable, she believed she was saving him and making future success more likely because she knew that, if he saw himself as a failure, he would eventually stop trying.

needs. Ms. Payton has few classroom management problems with these same boys because she addresses their needs by incorporating more collaborative activity, more movement, more opportunity for performance, and a greater level and variety of verbal participation.

Learning not to judge and constantly questioning our reactions to parents is also important. We all tend to judge parents based on our experiences and background, which at times can result in misperceptions. Consider the example in Figure 3.5, which addresses a parent's reaction to her son's disability.

COMMUNICATE CARE TO ALL STUDENTS AND FAMILIES

> My guess is that when schools focus on what really matters in life, the cognitive ends we now pursue so painfully and artificially will be achieved somewhat more naturally. . . . It is obvious that children will work harder and do things—even odd things like fractions—for people they love and trust (Noddings, 1988, p. 32).

Teachers who care about children communicate in varied ways that they believe in them and expect them to succeed (Benard, 2004). The concept of care means more than loving children. Suzy Clary Wilson clearly cares about her children, yet former students describe her as "tough." Teachers who care treat children with respect, require them to treat others with respect, perceive them as capable, and accept them unconditionally, even as they help them change undesirable behavior (Benard, 2004). Obviously, communicating care requires acknowledging and valuing other cultures and developing a nonjudgmental stance as suggested in the previous section. In this section we talk about strategies to help you know, understand, and value the particular children you will teach each year.

Learn About Students, Their Backgrounds, and Their Experiences

Culturally responsive teachers must really *know* their students in order to teach them. Here is a story from one of this chapter's authors. It describes an experience from her first year of teaching.

> Alton and Barry challenged me daily. They were quick to get angry and fight and demonstrated little interest in any academic activities. I remember an evening conversation with my mother. I began railing against the behavior of these two "troublemakers." I wondered how I was to teach when they wouldn't cooperate and when no punishment I devised seemed to affect them. I can still hear the words my mother used when she responded because that conversation helped shape the teacher I became. "Honey," she said, "those boys are not out to get you. Whatever they say and do is, to them, the most appropriate response to the situation as they perceive it. Your job is to see things as they see things. Then you'll know what to do."

To see other veteran teachers discuss communicating care, to to the Ms. Biddle module on the DVD-ROM and click on clip 6: Relationships.

Long before our profession began to talk about such things, this mother was teaching her daughter the foundational principle of culturally responsive teaching. To teach students, we must know them, know how they perceive the world, know their language, know their family traditions and customs, know their interests, know their dreams, know their learning strategies, and know what they care about (Banks et al., 2005).

There are no magic strategies for learning about students and their families. The process is as simple, and as complicated, as spending time with them. Culturally responsive teachers spend time in children's communities, visit homes, interact with families, and attend relevant cultural and family-oriented activities. Even those who live outside the community in which they teach find ways to become part of the community. Parents know them and see them in the community, and the teachers know families well enough to know the cultural and experiential resources in students' homes. This has been called knowing the "funds of knowledge" within students' homes (Gonzalez, Moll, & Amanti, 2005).

In addition to learning more about children's homes and communities, it is important to develop specific knowledge about children through questionnaires (for students grades 3 and up), informal conversations with students and parents, observation, and analysis of students' work. Moreover, it is important to become a student of children's culture. What are their favorite television shows? Movies? Music? Video games? Where do they go and what do they do after school? What significant events have happened in the community? The more you know about the children, the greater your capacity to link schoolwork to their culture and experience.

Establish an Ethos of Care in the Classroom

Research on classrooms that support students' motivation to achieve (Patrick, Turner, Meyer, & Midgley, 2003; Weinstein, 2002), on classrooms that scaffold student resilience (Benard, 2004), and on culturally responsive classroom management (Brown, 2004; Bondy et al., 2006) suggests guidelines for establishing an ethos of care in the classroom.

Create a Sense of Community in the Classroom. Culturally responsive teachers bring themselves into the classroom and enable students to do the same. The teachers share their families, their interests, and their lives with the students and use structures like class meetings to enable students to know one another. They communicate that respect for others is highly valued by respecting and listening to students and teaching students to respect and listen to one another.

To see a beginning teacher discuss community in her classroom, go to the Ms. Adimoolah module on the DVD-ROM and click on clip 6: Diversity & Community and clip 5: Inclusion.

These classrooms are the opposite of a "collection of strangers," a description that unfortunately fits many American classrooms. You may have experienced a classroom setting where much of the year goes by and you still do not know the names of everyone in the room. When students are strangers, it is impossible to create a network of caring peers who support one another through learning challenges. In addition, classroom-management problems escalate when students do not know one another.

Teach Classroom Rules, Routines, and Procedures Explicitly. Culturally responsive teachers *never* assume that students know what is expected. They teach the behaviors they expect students to demonstrate. In fact, explicitly teaching rules and procedures is a long established principle of effective classroom management (Emmer, Everton, & Anderson, 1980; Evertson, Emmer, Sanford, & Clements, 1983). Nevertheless, many teachers neglect this important step. These teachers either assume students know the rules and procedures or believe that stating the rule is sufficient instruction. Then the teachers implement an escalating sequence of consequences and punishments. The result is the development of a negative, often punitive, classroom environment where many fail to thrive.

The following principle may help you: Assume that students will behave appropriately if they know and remember what the teacher expects. Culturally responsive elementary classroom teachers teach their expectations using multiple strategies (Bondy et al., 2006). They state their expectations, provide models and demonstrations, provide

Reflective Exercise #6

How can it be so difficult for students to remember a simple rule like raising one's hand to speak? What if in a child's family multiple people often speak simultaneously? Can you think of other classroom rules that might differ from a student's cultural experiences?

To see a veteran teacher discuss student success, go the the Ms. Biddle module on the DVD-ROM and click on clip 2: Responsibility for Learning.

humorous negative examples, require student restatement of expectations, provide opportunities for practice with feedback, repeat instruction as necessary, and remind students of and reinforce appropriate behavior.

Protect the Classroom Community Through Teacher Insistence. A key difference between teachers who establish environments that support achievement motivation and those who do not is that effective teachers strategically and respectfully insist that students abide by rules and procedures and that they respect one another and the teacher (Patrick et al., 2003). That is, the teachers do not let students continue behavior that fails to meet the teachers' expectations. Yet in their "insistence," they always preserved the respectful and caring connection to each student.

All teachers want their students to abide by classroom rules. Some, in trying to be fair, give students "chances" that send inconsistent messages to students. Others do not know how to insist respectfully and become punitive and threatening. Both kinds of teachers undermine the expectation that students must be respectful of one another—the former by allowing disrespectful behavior, and the latter by treating students disrespectfully. In both cases, students learn more by observing their teachers than through statements about desired behavior.

Have High Expectations for Student Achievement

Never Give Up on a Child. Culturally responsive teachers take to heart the adage "If at first you don't succeed, try, try again!" and they teach it to their students. These teachers view student learning as a puzzle that they are constantly striving to solve (Banks et al., 2005; Corbett et al., 2002). They do not blame students or families if students are not succeeding. They accept responsibility for student learning and look for other ways to accomplish the goal. These are teachers who simply refuse to believe there is any child who cannot be reached. They actively communicate this belief to students. The teachers may end the year without succeeding with a student, but they never stop searching for another way.

Provide Explicit Instruction Linked to Meaningful Activity. Culturally responsive teachers provide a challenging curriculum that stresses critical thinking, respects children's curiosity, poses challenging problems for them to solve, and equips them with the skills and knowledge to be successful. These teachers provide the explicit instruction students need to succeed and opportunities for meaningful use of their learning (Banks et al., 2005; Delpit, 1995). Explicit instruction is sometimes misunderstood as a drill of low-cognitive-level skills. While explicit instruction includes this kind of drill, it involves a great deal more. In determining whether they are providing clear, explicit instruction that is meaningful to students, teachers should ask themselves the following questions:

- Have I clearly defined my goals in terms of performance or product and all the skills and competencies students need to succeed?
- Do I know which subskills and competencies students have mastered?
- Have I modeled all necessary skills and competencies?
- Have I provided sufficient opportunities for students to practice skills and competencies with feedback?
- Have I provided authentic opportunities for students to use newly acquired skills and competencies?

The last question on this list is critically important to culturally responsive teaching and, unfortunately, often is neglected. Imagine joining a soccer team where you do practice drills every day but never play a game. Not only would you lose interest in practice, but also your mastery of the skills would be shallow because you would not understand the context of their use. This is unfortunately the case in many classrooms where students practice skills and concepts, are tested on them, and then move on to

www.prenhall.com/rosenberg

the next set of skills and concepts. As in the soccer example, the result is that they lose interest in participating in practice and their learning is shallow.

Insist on Completion and Quality. Culturally responsive teachers do not allow students to do less than their best (Corbett et al., 2002). They insist that students complete and revise their work until it meets the standard. In a study of urban middle school students' perspectives about effective teachers, students valued teachers who "nudged and cajoled" them into doing their work (Wilson & Corbett, 2001). Others have made the same point in stressing that important learning inevitably involves struggle (e.g., Weinstein, 2002). Effective teachers not only convey that the struggle is important but insist that students persist in working through barriers and support them until they succeed. Teachers who provide this support encourage students to try, refuse to allow students to get by with incomplete or sloppy work, give them opportunities to make up work, provide after-school tutoring, make work relevant to students' lives, and reteach using varied strategies until everyone understands (Wilson & Corbett, 2001).

USE CULTURALLY RELEVANT CURRICULUM

Obviously, culturally relevant curriculum must be culturally specific. In this section we provide examples drawn primarily from literature on culturally relevant practice for low-income African American children and youth.

Tailor Curriculum Materials to the Students and the Context

The school curriculum is not culturally neutral. The curriculum as represented in texts, in national and state standards, and in the lived experience of most teachers is a reflection of the dominant culture. Hollins (1996) explains that the school curriculum "promotes its own (a) cultural values, practices and perceptions; (b) psychological, social, economic, and political needs; and (c) elevated status within the larger society" (p. 82).

The established curriculum reflects a Eurocentric view of the world. For example, texts will mention the names of a small, often repeated group of African American men and women who fought for freedom, voting rights, and economic equity in the United States (e.g., Rosa Parks; Martin Luther King, Jr.; Harriet Tubman), but the detail devoted to this struggle for freedom receives far less attention in our history than the struggle of our revolutionary period. And even in reporting our early history, few of us learn about men like James Armistead, a slave who was freed for his surveillance efforts during the struggles of that time (Selig, 2005). Few of us know that African Americans fought in every major battle during the Revolutionary War and most were returned to slavery at its conclusion.

Culturally responsive teachers know that children need to see themselves in the curriculum. If the faces in the textbook are predominantly European American, children learn that history and scientific achievement are the work of European Americans. In addition, the fiction and nonfiction students read needs to be culturally relevant so that they see their lives and cultures reflected in the characters, setting, and plot of the story. To be effective, teachers need "wide ranging knowledge of subject matter content, so that they can construct a curriculum that includes multiple representations addressing the prior experiences of different groups of students" (Banks et al., 2005, p. 251).

One important way to connect culturally and linguistically diverse students to the school context is to use children's literature that reflects their cultural background and life experiences. When students see themselves in their books, they enjoy reading and make a connection to literature. Students build vocabulary and language skills that assist them academically. Moreover, using children's literature representing different cultural groups in the classroom is a way for students and the

Reflective Exercise #7
Do you think that a teacher who gives a student an *F* when he or she fails to complete an assignment or performs poorly rates low in professionalism because the teacher has low expectations? Why or why not?

Reflective Exercise #8
Take a minute to list as many famous European Americans as you can; then list as many famous African Americans as you can (no sports or entertainment figures). Assume that the difference in your lists is *not* because African Americans never did anything of historical significance. What does this mean?

Reflective Exercise #9

You have a student with a physical disability who is included in a general education classroom. The student uses a voice-activated computer for writing activities. A student in your class has complained that this student receives preferential treatment and that all students should be treated equally. How would you respond? Discuss your response with a peer in your class.

 To link to websites that support and extend the content of this chapter, go to the Web Links module in Chapter 3 on the Companion Website, www.prenhall.com/rosenberg.

Ensure That Students Understand What Equity Means. According to *The New Oxford American Dictionary* (Jewell & Abate, 2001), *equal* refers to "being the same in quantity, size, degree, or value" (p. 573). In contrast, *equitable* refers to being "fair and impartial" (p. 574). Equity is sometimes a difficult concept for students to grasp. Many come into a classroom with the perspective that *fair* means treating everyone exactly the same (e.g., providing the same, or *equal,* instruction for everyone). As we have emphasized throughout this chapter, treating everyone equally is not always fair or equitable and does not result in effective instructional practices or desired educational outcomes. This is especially the case for students from diverse backgrounds and students with disabilities but is true for other students as well.

This chapter has provided many examples of the need to adapt classroom practices based on student characteristics and needs. We will provide similar suggestions in each chapter that addresses specific disabilities. These suggestions are built upon the assumption that equitable treatment of students is giving them what they need, not treating all students the same.

It is important that teachers discuss this distinction with their students and help them understand why some students need different types of support and instruction to be successful.

SUMMARY

As teachers enter classrooms each year, they are faced with an increasingly diverse range of students. All too often the backgrounds of these students differ significantly from the background of the teacher, creating a demographic divide. In this chapter, we addressed this demographic divide and described strategies that may be used to meet the needs of students from diverse backgrounds.

How Are the Demographics of Public School Students Changing?

- The demographics of public school students are rapidly changing in terms of race, language, poverty, and disability as classrooms across the United States become more diverse.
- Within the next 20 years, more than one-half of all students will be non–European American, and 40% will not have English as their first language.

What Is the Demographic Divide and Why Does It Matter?

- The demographic divide describes the disparity between the demographics of teachers and students. Students from diverse backgrounds make up 36% of the school population, while 14% of teachers are from similar backgrounds.
- This demographic divide contributes to an achievement gap that exists for many students from diverse backgrounds, demonstrating that schools are not consistently successful in teaching non–European American students, children in poverty, English-language learners, and students with disabilities.

How Can We Explain the Significant Discrepancies in Educational Outcomes for Children Who Vary by Race, Culture, Socioeconomic Status, Language, and Learning Differences?

- The demographic divide is at least partially responsible for this discrepancy.
- The lowest-performing schools (primarily schools with a high percentage of students from non–European American backgrounds who are living in poverty) typically have lower-per-pupil expenditures, fewer highly qualified teachers, and lower-quality curriculum and materials.
- The demographic divide and fewer resources do not destine a student to failure. Many students within and across these groups are achieving substantial success.
- By exploring these cases, we can better learn how to help children with complex histories succeed in the classroom and cross the border of language, culture, and disability.

What Do Successful Teachers Believe and Do to Enhance the Educational Futures of All Children?

- Culturally responsive teaching is designed to foster resilience in students, improve student outcomes, and enhance the educational futures of children.
- Culturally responsive teachers are those who
  - Examine themselves and the role that culture plays in their perceptions
  - Adopt an attitude of inquiry about culture and difference

- Create a vision of non–European American, non–middle-class English-language learners and students with disabilities who succeed
- Communicate care to all students and families
- Commit to learning about students, their backgrounds, and their experiences

- Create a classroom centered on care
- Teach classroom rules, routines, and procedures explicitly
- Have high expectations for student achievement
- Incorporate culturally relevant curriculum

 **ADDRESSING THE PROFESSIONAL STANDARDS**

Council for Exceptional Children (CEC) Knowledge Standards addressed in the chapter

CC1K7, CC1K8, CC1K9, CC1K10, CC2K3, CC2K4, EC2K4, CC3K3, CC3K4, CC3K5, CC5K7, CC5K8, CC5K9, CC5K10, CC6K1, CC6K2, CC6K3, CC9K1, CC10K4

Appendix B: CEC Knowledge and Skill Standards Common Core has a full listing of the standards referenced here been prepared to do. Instead of working with small groups of kids in a resource room on reading and math skills, she found herself in a self-contained special class with kids who had very serious emotional and behavioral problems. She was at a loss and was herself rapidly becoming emotionally drained. "The classroom was totally, totally different. I was very frustrated. I cried every day on the way home for over a half a year. I really questioned whether or not I had made the right choice."

How was Kathy able to hang on to become a great special educator? Three keys led to her success. First, she couldn't quit. There was no noble reason for this. She owed money, had adopted a child with special needs, and needed a job. Although she wasn't getting rich, being a teacher paid fairly well, and she knew what it was like to scrape by on low-paying jobs. Second, she was supported by her fellow teachers. They helped her develop lessons and gave her ideas for working with her students. Third, she found support through a special project called the Teacher Support Program at Western Carolina University. A faculty member involved in this program came to her school, helped her reorganize her classroom, and provided her with reading material and instructions on how to implement positive behavior support practices. Because of this contact, Kathy returned to graduate school part time and, after another several years of schooling, finished her master's degree.

Kathy can't imagine doing anything else now. After 11 years as a teacher, she knows the tough side of special education, but she also knows that it can be a great area to work in. She feels bad for other teachers whose working conditions aren't as good as hers; but as for herself, she couldn't ask for a situation that suits her better.

To see two other teachers whose path to special education was an indirect one, go to the Ms. Green and Ms. Biddle modules on the DVD-ROM and click on clip 1: Life Experiences.

Many students are identified as having disabilities after experiencing academic or social problems in school.

From Kathy Blossfield's story you can learn two important lessons: one about yourselves and one about the students you may teach. First, finding your best niche may not come easily or quickly, but it may nevertheless come. Second, there are many different types of students served in the field of special education, and some may have the exact characteristics and needs that fit with your skills and abilities. Our purpose in this chapter is to discuss the procedures by which these students are identified to receive special education services.

Suppose you took a position as a special education teacher of middle school students who were classified as having learning special needs. Or if you are a general education teacher (for example, a sixth-grade social studies teacher), imagine that you had a student who was said to have mild intellectual disabilities. When do you think these students would have been identified as having these conditions? What procedures were necessary to decide on these classifications?

FAQ Sheet

IDENTIFICATION AND PLANNING

What are Part C services, and whom are they for?	States may offer Part C services for children with special needs under age 3 and their families. States may apply for federal funds to offer these services. The services are named after the part of the law (IDEA 2004) that describes them.
What is an individualized family service plan (IFSP)?	An IFSP is the document used to plan the services for infants and toddlers served by Part C services. The plan can include services for the child and the family.
At what age does a child become eligible for special education services?	When a child is 3 years old, he or she has the right to a free appropriate public education under IDEA 2004 if eligibility requirements are met. This right continues until the child turns 21.
What are early intervening services?	Early intervening services are intensive interventions provided to students having difficulties in general education who have not yet been referred to special education. The purpose of these services is to try to keep children from being placed in special education unless absolutely necessary.
What is response to intervention (RTI)?	RTI is a new approach to determine if students who are in early intervening services primarily for academic skill improvement should be placed in special education. Students who do not respond adequately to more intense levels of intervention would be more likely candidates for special education. RTI may be used in lieu of traditional evaluations for determining if a child should be classified as learning disabled.
What is an individualized education plan (IEP)?	An IEP is a document that lists the educational goals for students with special needs, the special education and related services the student is to receive, the placement of the student, and other important information. The IEP is developed and approved by the IEP team, which includes professionals and the student's parents.
What is a 504 plan?	A 504 plan is developed for students who under Section 504 of the Rehabilitation Act are considered to be people with a disability but who under IDEA 2004 do not qualify for special education services. Students who qualify under 504 have the right to plans that specify any accommodations or adaptations that they need to participate in school activities.
What is a statement of transition services?	When a student with special needs turns 16, the IEP must include a statement about transition from school to adult life. It will include the preparation that will occur in high school to meet various needs in adulthood such as postsecondary education, employment, or residential living.

Reflective Exercise #1
What kinds of emotions would you expect parents to have if they thought their child might have special needs? What would your reaction be if you were a parent? **To hear students like you discuss this topic, go to the Students to Students module on the DVD-ROM and click on clip 3: Parents & Families.**

For students like these, who are often described as having "mild disabilities," and for most students who receive special education services, their classifications probably occurred during the early elementary years. It is very likely that they were identified as students with special needs after they experienced problems with their academic work or their social behavior. When they were much younger, it was probably not possible for professionals to recognize any apparent symptoms that would suggest a disability; and for the most part, their early development was probably more typical than atypical.

On the other hand, students with more severe disabilities (like autism, severe intellectual disabilities, or multiple disabilities) are usually recognized as having special needs earlier in life, even when they are infants or toddlers. These children generally exhibit serious medical needs or have very uncommon developmental characteristics that lead their parents to seek professional services. You saw that Kathy Blossfield was teaching in a preschool program. The children she supports in their fully inclusive classrooms were identified earlier rather than later because their conditions were identified at a young age.

The process of how children become eligible for special education services is important and complex. In this chapter we examine these procedures for the two groups of students just mentioned: those who can be identified early in life, and those who are not identified until the school years. We also discuss the formal planning procedures and documents necessary for serving these students as well as the tests and assessment procedures that are used. We summarize many of the important features of identification and planning in the "FAQ Sheet."

IDENTIFYING AND PLANNING FOR CHILDREN WITH SPECIAL NEEDS BEFORE THE SCHOOL YEARS

IDEA 2004, the federal law that governs special education in public schools, requires that states identify children with special needs who are between the ages of 3 and 21 years and, if they meet the eligibility requirements, provide them with a "free appropriate public education." Some children will show evidence of special needs, or conditions related to special needs, very early in life, many before they are 3 years old, some even at birth. These children and their families may receive special services even when they are still infants or toddlers, and states can apply to the federal government for grants to assist them in providing these services.

IDENTIFYING INFANTS AND TODDLERS WITH SPECIAL NEEDS

According to federal legislation, an "infant or toddler with a disability" is a child under 3 years of age who needs early intervention services because he or she "is experiencing developmental delays" in one or more areas, including "cognitive development, physical development, communication development, social or emotional development, and adaptive development," or "has a diagnosed physical or mental condition that has a high probability of resulting in developmental delay." If individual states decide, this term can also include "at-risk infants and toddlers" (IDEA 2004, Part C, Sec. 632).

To help identify and serve children with special needs, states must use a **child find** system. Under IDEA 2004, Congress required that states' child find systems focus especially on identifying infants and toddlers who may have special needs who reside in foster care, those living with homeless families, those who are wards of the state, and those who have been exposed to domestic violence and abuse (U.S. Department of Education, 2005).

The child find system operates as a public awareness program that distributes information about early intervention and preschool programs through the media, doctors' offices, health service agencies, and other public agencies. Also, many states have birth-defect surveillance programs that identify newborns with characteristics such as **chromosomal anomalies** (e.g., **Down syndrome**) or **musculoskeletal disorders** (e.g., limb abnormalities) so early intervention programs can begin as soon as possible (Farel, Meyer, Hicken, & Edmonds, 2003). Under IDEA 2004, the early intervention lead service agency must especially target parents of children who are born prematurely or with other "physical risk factors associated with learning or developmental complications" in order to provide them with information about early intervention services (U.S. Department of Education, 2005).

Because individual states (not the federal government) must decide which children under age 3 will be eligible for Part C services (so-called because of the section of the law in which they are located), there is great deal of variability from state to state in the number and characteristics of infants and toddlers who are actually identified (Shackelford, 2006; Wolery & Bailey, 2002).

Parents and professionals are most likely to identify infants or toddlers who either have clear characteristics of specific syndromes or are showing significant evidence of delay in key developmental areas. Once children are identified, after an initial referral, agencies can begin to provide services if assessments by skilled clinicians show that a child is truly experiencing a delay. The clinicians will conduct their evaluations using **developmental assessments** to determine how much of a delay is occurring in different areas. States use different criteria in determining a significant delay, but typically they include a substantial delay in one area (e.g., a 50% delay from the norm) or a significant, but less serious, delay in more than one area (e.g., a 25% delay in two or more areas) (McLean, 2004).

PLANNING FOR INFANTS AND TODDLERS WITH SPECIAL NEEDS AND THEIR FAMILIES

Federal law provides financial support for states that choose to offer special services to infants or toddlers with special needs. If a state offers the service, it must designate a lead agency (usually the health and human services agency) to operate the program. To provide appropriate services, agencies must develop a written **individualized family service plan** (IFSP). The IFSP states the types of services provided to the infant or toddler and the child's family. Because of the young age of the child, the law recognizes that services for the child should not be separated from the needs of the parents and family members, so the IFSP addresses not only the child's needs but how to support the family to help meet these needs. Services for an infant or toddler are often provided in the family's home, but the child may also be served in a special center. A change in the most recent version of the law (IDEA 2004) requires that services be "based on scientifically based research" and include "preliteracy and language skills, as developmentally appropriate for the child" (U.S. Department of Education, 2005).

When professionals prepare an IFSP, they must involve the parents and other family members. Also, friends or advocates of the child and family can participate in the process if the parents so desire. A service coordinator who is identified by the public agency providing the services oversees the design and implementation of the IFSP. Other professionals will also help write the IFSP if they have conducted evaluations of the child and/or will provide services to the child or the family. The IFSP itself is a rather extensive document that must include several key components (See Figure 4.1).

Professionals must involve parents in developing the Individualized Family Service Plan.

FIGURE 4.1

REQUIRED COMPONENTS OF THE INDIVIDUALIZED FAMILY SERVICE PLAN

1. Information about the child's status, including physical health, cognitive development, communication development, social-emotional development, and adaptive development
2. Family information (if the family agrees to provide it) about family needs, resources, and priorities related to the development of the child
3. The type of early intervention services to be provided "based on peer-reviewed research to the extent possible," the natural environments in which they will be provided, how often they will be provided, and who will provide them (IDEA 2004, Sec. 636 [d] [4])
4. A statement of measurable results or outcomes, including preliteracy and language skills, as developmentally appropriate for the child
5. Other services that will be provided, such as medical services
6. The dates on which services will be provided and the duration of services
7. The name of the service coordinator who will be responsible for implementing the IFSP and coordinating all of the services to be provided
8. A description of appropriate transition services to help the child and the family when it is time for the child to move from the early interventions program into a preschool program

IDENTIFYING PRESCHOOLERS WITH SPECIAL NEEDS

Beginning when a child with an eligible disability is 3 years old and until he or she reaches age 21, the child has the legal right to special education and any necessary related services. As we have described, agencies *may have been* providing services to children from the time they were infants. When the children turn 3, however, this is no longer an option; public schools must provide services. *If* the child *has* been in a Part C program, the law requires a smooth transition between the early intervention program and the preschool program.

In general, professionals often find it difficult to accurately determine if a young child has a disability unless, as we have said, the child shows clear physical characteristics or indicators that suggest a disability. These characteristics are usually associated with conditions such as cerebral palsy, visual disabilities, hearing impairments, severe intellectual disabilities, or multiple disabilities. Aside from such indicators, professionals must rely on developmental lags and behavioral characteristics that might suggest that the child has a condition such as autism or an intellectual disability. The younger the child is and the less pronounced the developmental lag, the more challenging it is to make a definitive determination. This is primarily because there is the chance that the child will outgrow the delay. But because we don't know if this is going to occur, and we *do* know that the earlier we can intervene when a child has a disability, the better, then the accuracy of early identification is always a critical issue. For an example of this dilemma, examine the information that we provide about a child who may have a disability in "Can You Help Me with This Student?" What do you think? Does this child have a disability? How would you have reacted if you were the child's preschool teacher?

Part C services for infants and toddlers might not include children such as Jeremy, simply because when such a child is younger, professionals cannot always reliably determine that he or she has special needs. As the child gets a little older, however, the needs become more apparent, and he or she is likely to be served in a preschool program. Children who are good candidates for preschool programs will show risks primarily in two areas: communication delays and challenging behaviors. There are also certain sociocultural factors that suggest a child may be at risk for later delays.

Communication Delays

Lagging communication is the most prevalent symptom of developmental delays. However, if there is no other readily observable condition, often these children will not be recognized until they are 2 to 3 years old (Wetherby, Goldstein, Cleary, Allen, & Kublin, 2003). Recently, some **prelinguistic communication** characteristics have

88   www.prenhall.com/rosenberg

Can You Help Me with This Student?

Near Jeremy's first birthday, his mom started to worry about him. What concerned her was that Jeremy was becoming less and less interested in her and the other members of the family and spent longer amounts of time engaged with the same toy, a stuffed beagle puppy. He was also using his few words less and less often and not in ways you might expect. Sometimes when she began to change his diaper, he would arch his back and contort his face and scream, "Cook, cook!" Jeremy's pediatrician said it was too early to worry about anything and that Jeremy was probably going through a phase that he would outgrow. Now that Jeremy was 18 months old, nothing had improved. At his nursery school, while the other toddlers followed each other around from one interesting activity to another, Jeremy often crouched against the wall, holding and smelling his stuffed beagle. His preschool teacher, Melissa, had never had a child like Jeremy, and she didn't want to overreact. But she was beginning to agree with Jeremy's mom. She, too, thought something might be wrong despite the fact that he was physically one of the most attractive and able children in the toddler room. Melissa and Charlotte, the director of the preschool, decided to talk to Jeremy's mom. They said they did not want to overreact, but here is what they recommended:

- Contact the state developmental special needs office and ask for a developmental assessment. Be sure to ask for a speech/language specialist who can evaluate language skills.
- Get your pediatrician to refer Jeremy to a pediatric neurologist for an examination. Someone with experience with developmental delays is preferrable.

- Try different ways to get Jeremy to respond and interact with you and other family members. Spend as much time with him each day as possible, prompting him to make eye contact, look at different items with you, and repeat names of items.
- Search the Internet for information about autism spectrum disorders and parent groups that you can contact.
- Be confident that the teachers at school were encouraging Jeremy to become actively involved and inviting the other children to play with him and talk to him.

For more information about young children with autism, consult the following resources:

Wetherby, A. M., Woods, J., Allen, L., Cleary, J., Dickinson, H., & Lord, C. (2004). Early indicators of autism spectrum disorders in the second year of life. *Journal of Autism and Developmental Disorders, 34,* 473–493.

Prizant, B. M., Wetherby, A. M., Rubin, E., & Laurent, A. C. (2003). The SCERTS Model A transactional, family-centered approach to enhancing communication and socioemotional abilities of children with autism spectrum disorder. *Infants and Young Children, 16,* 296–316.

EXTEND AND APPLY

- Do you believe Melissa and Charlotte took the right action? Would you have done something else?
- What are some natural ways you might try to get a young child with autism more engaged with his peers? Are there some things you might say to the peers to encourage them to play with and talk to Jeremy?

Activity: Go to the Video Classroom section of the Teacher Prep website, click on Special Education and then module 10: Autism. Watch videos 1 and 2 and answer the accompanying questions. Think about how early intervention on Jeremy's behalf could make a difference.

---

been shown to be associated with later language abilities. For example, before children can use words, they typically regulate communication by using eye gaze, affect, gestures, and vocalizations. A lack of these prelinguistic characteristics may predict later language delays, and such language delays are characteristic of children with **autism spectrum disorders,** which includes **autism** and related disorders such as **Asperger's syndrome** (Wetherby et al., 2003; see Chapter 9). Predictors such as the conditions listed in Figure 4.2, which can be seen very early, even during the infant and toddler years, could suggest a problem in the development of communication skills. At least such conditions would call for a formal assessment by a skilled developmental psychologist or speech/language pathologist.

Challenging Behavior

In addition to early language delays, inappropriate and uncommon behavior in young children, such as acts of aggression or ongoing disruptive behavior, may signal long-term

> **Reflective Exercise #2**
> Do the indicators of communication problems in Figure 4.2 suggest to you that Jeremy, the child described in the box feature, may have a disability? What do you think would be the best way to communicate with a parent if you suspect a child has a special need?

FIGURE 4.2

INDICATORS OF COMMUNICATION PROBLEMS

- No babbling by 12 months, no single words by 16 months, or no two-word spontaneous utterances by 24 months
- Failure to respond when name is called by familiar person
- No engagement in joint attention
- Limited gestures by 12 months
- No imitation of another's facial or body movements
- Apparent lack of emotional concern for others, such as when another person is accidentally hurt
- Limited interest in toys, playing, and pretending; focusing more on specific items and actions (e.g., twirling a string)
- Loss of language or social skills at any age

Source: Adapted from Kasari & Wong, 2002; Woods & Wetherby, 2003.

behavioral problems (Drotar, 2002). **Self-injurious behaviors (SIBs)** such as head banging, self-scratching, or self-biting are also very troubling. Sometimes such behaviors appear as a part of normal development but then disappear. When they do not, however, concern about severe developmental delays may be warranted. SIBs are often associated with specific developmental disability syndromes, including **Cornelia de Lange, Fragile X, Lesch-Nyhan, Smith-Magenis,** and **5p** (or **cri-du-chat**) (MacLean & Symons, 2002).

Sociocultural Factors

Certain sociocultural factors can place children at risk for later cognitive, academic, and behavioral difficulties in school. These factors can even affect children who physically and behaviorally appear to be developing normally. The impact of sociocultural factors have been identified in studies going back for a half-century or more (Uzgiris, 1970), and children exposed to these conditions may be identified in the first 15 months of life based on some of these factors. For example, La Paro, Olsen, and Pianta (2002) found that children under the age of 16 months who were from poor homes in which parents provided little stimulation, whose mothers lacked sensitivity, and who exhibited behavior problems early in life were well below average in language development and intellectual development at 36 months of age. The authors noted that, when such children are young, they often are not identified or are not eligible for special services, even though it is likely that they will later end up in special education. During their early years they may have speech and language problems or difficulty in learning basic concepts (e.g., numbers, alphabet, days of the week, colors, shapes), and they may be restless and easily distracted. Sometimes these children might have trouble interacting with their peers or could have difficulty in following directions or routines, and their fine-motor skills may be slow to develop (Schwab Foundation for Learning, 1999).

PLANNING FOR PRESCHOOLERS WITH SPECIAL NEEDS

Reflective Exercise #3
Why do you think parents of children with special needs would elect to keep their child in an early intervention program instead of transferring him or her to a preschool program at the age of 3? What do you think you might do if you were a parent in this situation?

Under IDEA 2004, if a child has been in a Part C program, states may develop a plan that allows parents to keep their child in this program, if they wish, until he or she reaches kindergarten age. Parents can choose this option instead of transferring the child into a preschool program, which would be the typical placement for children who are 3 to 4 years old (U.S. Department of Education, 2005). If parents choose this option, the IFSP continues as the planning document for the child until he or she reaches kindergarten age. Even if a Part C child transfers to a preschool program at age 3, the IFSP developed when he or she was enrolled in a Part C program may still serve as the child's IEP until the next IEP is developed.

When children like Jeremy, who most likely were not served in a Part C program, begin preschool, public school officials will create an individualized educational plan

www.prenhall.com/rosenberg

(IEP) for them. The IEP will specify the services for the child, just as it does for school-age students. (We discuss IEPs in detail in the next section of this chapter.)

Public schools may use early childhood or early childhood special education settings to serve preschool-age children with identified disabilities and may offer either full- or part-time services. The schools will often use the designation "child with a disability" when referring to a preschooler with special needs instead of placing the child in a specific disability category. They may use this classification until the child is 9 years old.

General early childhood education settings are used to serve more than a third of the preschool-age children with special needs (U.S. Department of Education, 2003). This allows them the opportunity to model the communication and social skills of children who have no special needs. But mixing young children with and without special needs can present challenges. Sometimes the children with special needs, especially those with communication or behavioral challenges, are not well accepted by their young peers; and many times early childhood teachers lack the skills necessary to help them improve their behavior and increase their acceptance. In "Site Visit" box feature, we describe the Asheville City Schools Preschool Program that has worked to improve its preschool program for all children, including those identified as having autism or falling on the autism spectrum. This is where Kathy Blossfield, whom you met at the beginning of this chapter, works.

Research has shown that preschool programs for children with special needs, such as the one in the box feature, are very effective. According to Salisbury and Smith (1993), these programs "(1) ameliorate, and in some cases, prevent developmental problems; (2) result in fewer children being retained in later grades; (3) reduce educational costs to school programs; and (4) improve the quality of parent, child, and family relationships" (p. 1). These authors also report that the most effective preschool programs include the following characteristics:

- Encourage the involvement of parents to reinforce critical skills in natural contexts
- Occur early in the child's life
- Operate from a more structured and systematic instructional base
- Prescriptively address each child's assessed needs
- Include normally developing children as models

IDENTIFYING STUDENTS WITH SPECIAL NEEDS DURING THE SCHOOL YEARS

As we have said, most students with special needs are not recognized as requiring special education and related services until they are in elementary school. In this section we provide a detailed look at the process by which these children are identified and how they are served during the school years. As we present this information, keep in mind that while federal laws apply to all school districts and schools in the United States, state and local laws may also be applied, and they may vary. Therefore, as a new teacher, whether in special education or general education, you should familiarize yourself with local policies that address referral and placement procedures for students with special needs.

IDENTIFICATION THROUGH PARENTS, TEACHERS, AND SCREENING

During the early elementary school years, school officials might recognize a child as a possible candidate for special education services in different ways. In many cases, parents may feel their child is having difficulty and discuss this issue with the teacher. This discussion might lead to a formal evaluation that may confirm that the child is eligible for special education services. Even without input from a parent, the teacher may recognize that the child is having learning or behavioral difficulties and request a formal evaluation. If this occurs, the school notifies the parents to ask for their consent to allow the evaluation process to begin.

Reflective Exercise #4
Do you think more preschool programs for children with special needs should be inclusive? What are the advantages of having children with and without special needs together at a young age?

Site Visit:
Effective Practices in Action

THE ASHEVILLE CITY SCHOOLS
PRESCHOOL PROGRAM

When a visitor comes in to the Asheville (North Carolina) City Schools Preschool Program, it's hard to tell it is a program that serves 3- to 5-year-old children with special needs. Unless you take a close look, you will not see that there are children of all ability levels in the school. Some are on or above developmental expectations for their age level, and some are below. There are children who are considered to be autistic or on the autism spectrum and some with identifiable syndromes of intellectual disabilities, such as Down syndrome, and some who have delays but who have not been diagnosed. But for the most part, the children at the ACS Preschool are about as typical as the ones you might find at any preschool.

Of the 62 children in the school, 16 have identifiable special needs with IEPs developed for their teachers to follow. A typical classroom has 16 children, and about four have a disability. In each classroom you will find an environment created for children. There are toys, games, and big books; stuff for pretending to dress, cook, and work; bright lights and pretty posters on the walls; and plenty of small pieces of furniture and boxes full of odds and ends that offer a never-ending supply of things for learning and development.

All of these things you would expect to find in any preschool. But if you look carefully, there are some other things too. The carpeted group-time area is outlined with masking tape to help kids know where to sit. There is a big bean-bag chair that is soft and comfortable if someone needs to take a break before becoming too upset to cope. There are pictures and drawings used to help some of the kids remember what they should be doing and when they should do it. Some classrooms have good behavior charts and displays showing how good the boys and girls have been. Most important, you will see Kathy Blossfield, the special education teacher, coming in from time to time to work collaboratively with the classroom teacher. Kathy doesn't pull out the children with special needs but works with them—as well as the other children—right in the classroom.

The children with special needs at the ACS Preschool will benefit from their experiences here for many years to come. And so will the children without special needs. But the program didn't happen because of magic. There was a lot of hard work and a strong commitment made by many people. Here are some of the key aspects of what made the program successful:

- Administrative personnel have a strong commitment to the philosophy of inclusion for preschool children.
- The necessary personnel are dedicated to making the program work. Not only is there a full-time special education teacher (Kathy Blossfield) working with all of the teachers, but there are two teaching assistants in each classroom.
- The teachers and their assistants have been given ongoing support and training for working with the children who have special needs. A lot of attention has been given to the prevention of behavior problems and the use of positive behavior supports to address them when they occur.
- There is a great deal of collaboration among the professionals and paraprofessionals who work in the school, with the parents and families, and with other agencies that serve the children.

Success at the ACS Preschool did not come overnight, but with work and dedication it has thrived.

Additionally, most school districts use **screening tests** to find children who might have special needs. These screenings look for academic or learning problems, behavioral problems, or sensory or physical needs of young children. It is important to note that large-scale screening procedures are only intended to help identify students who *potentially* have special needs. The testing instruments used for screenings do not possess the technical qualities that would allow a definitive determination to be made about a student's eligibility for special services. For this to occur, only an individual evaluation procedure can be used.

EARLY INTERVENING SERVICES

Historically, regardless of the source of concern about the child—parental worry, teacher observation, or a screening process—most school districts would not refer a child experiencing academic or behavioral difficulties for an initial eligibility evaluation until after attempting a **prereferral intervention.** The child would continue in the general education classroom while this special effort was undertaken to address academic or behavioral needs.

Prereferral interventions have never been required under federal law, and they still are not; but over the years many states have required their school districts to use them, and most of the other states have strongly recommended them to their school districts (Buck, Polloway, Smith-Thomas, & Cook, 2003). Under IDEA 2004, school districts may use a portion of their federal special education funds (up to 15%) to "develop and implement coordinated, **early intervening services** . . . for students in kindergarten through grade 12 (with a particular emphasis on students in kindergarten through grade three) who have *not* been identified as needing special education or related services but who *need* additional academic and behavioral support to succeed in a general education environment" (U.S. Department of Education, 2005, italics added). This means that the U.S. Department of Education would like school districts to successfully serve students in general education rather than identify them as eligible for special education services.

Aligned with this new option is the relatively new practice of using **response to intervention (RTI)** as a basis for decision making about placing many children in special education. RTI is a process whereby the decision to place a child in special education is made based on how well he or she does or does not improve after different levels of intervention have been attempted instead of basing the decision on formal tests (Fuchs, Mock, Morgan, & Young, 2003; also see Chapter 6 on identifying students with learning disabilities).

When a child is identified as needing prereferral or early intervening services, this is not technically a special education placement. Nevertheless, most state and local policies require that schools notify parents as soon as they recognize a possible problem. At this stage school administrators usually will invite the parents to provide information and participate in planning the intervention as well as ask them to provide support at home.

As we have noted, prereferral interventions have been used for many years. One of the most common models is the teacher assistance teams approach (Chalfant, Pysh, & Moultrie, 1979). Teacher assistance teams (or TATs, known also as prereferral assistance teams, child study teams, or general education assistance teams) are comprised of professionals such as teachers, administrators, and specialists (e.g., a school psychologist or a special educator) who collaborate to come up with tactics that will help the general education teacher increase the student's success in the general education classroom. Often a structured, collaborative, problem-solving, team approach is used to create successful intervention strategies (Bangert & Cooch, 2001; Fuchs et al., 2003). The prereferral intervention is usually tried for a specific amount of time and then evaluated. It can include modifications in different areas such as changes in the curriculum, instructional procedures, classroom management, or the classroom environment (Mastropieri & Scruggs, 2000).

The early intervening option expands and enhances the traditional prereferral practice, placing greater emphasis on trying to find effective interventions to keep students in general education. Using the RTI approach, schools are likely to follow a practice such as this (Fuchs et al., 2003):

Reflective Exercise #5
Prereferral interventions and early intervening services seem to make a lot of sense, and many school districts use these approaches. What do you perceive to be the pros and cons of these practices?

1. Students receive generally effective instruction from their classroom teacher.
2. Their progress is monitored.
3. If they are not successful, additional or different support is provided in the general education program.
4. Their progress continues to be monitored.
5. If they still do not succeed, they may be evaluated for special education services or assigned to receive these services.

REFERRAL OF STUDENTS FOR INITIAL EVALUATION AND PLACEMENT

It is difficult to say exactly how successful prereferral or early intervening programs are, but we do know that many children who might be considered as candidates for special education can be successfully maintained in the general education classroom through effective interventions (Fuchs et al., 2003; Sindelar, Griffin, Smith, & Watanabe, 1992). On the other hand, if the child's problems are too challenging, if the general education classroom intervention is not effective, or if there *is* no prereferral intervention, sooner or later a decision will be made to refer the child so that he or she can be evaluated for special education services. When this occurs, school districts must follow procedural guidelines required in IDEA 2004.

Submission of a Written Referral Form

Notwithstanding prereferral or early intervening actions, the formal path for a school-age child into special education usually begins when the classroom teacher or another school employee submits an official referral for evaluation. This form expresses concern about the student's academic or behavioral performance in school. Through it, the teacher asks that the child be evaluated to determine eligibility for special education. Parents or other interested persons may also submit such a request to the school.

Usually the referral is sent to a designated individual in the school such as the school counselor or an assistant principal, and this person then forwards the referral to the central district administrative office. A placement specialist at the administrative office will usually arrange a schedule for conducting the necessary evaluations.

Reflective Exercise #6
When it originated, IDEA was considered to be a strong "parents' rights" law. How important do you think it is for parents to consent to have their child evaluated for special education services, and how much effort do you believe school districts should make to get this consent? **To hear students like you discuss this topic, go to the Students to Students module on the DVD-ROM and click on clip 3: Parents & Families.**

If parents have not yet been involved in a prereferral or early intervening process or have not yet been notified that their child is having difficulty, federal law requires that they be notified when a referral is submitted, *except* under the following circumstances (U.S. Department of Education, 2005):

- Despite reasonable efforts to do so, the agency cannot discover the whereabouts of the parent of the child.
- The rights of the parents of the child have been terminated in accordance with state law.
- The rights of the parent to make educational decisions have been subrogated by a judge in accordance with state law, and consent for an initial evaluation has been given by an individual appointed by the judge to represent the child.

Most school districts will offer to meet with parents in order to make sure that they understand their child's status and the procedures involved in evaluating the child. Although rare, at this point, some parents may disagree with the school's desire to evaluate their child for special education placement and not provide the required permission. When this happens, schools have the option to pursue the evaluation through due process or mediation procedures or to not proceed with the evaluation.

Initial Evaluation

When a referral is submitted, relevant information about the child such as screening-test results, performance or behavioral records developed by the teacher, and the results of any prereferral or early intervening efforts will accompany it. The placement

www.prenhall.com/rosenberg

specialist will review all of the available information and will recommend any additional testing. IDEA 2004 requires that for the initial evaluation and any subsequent evaluation

- the individualized education program (IEP) team and other qualified professionals, as appropriate, shall review existing evaluation data on the child . . .
- and, on the basis of that review, and input from the child's parents, identify what additional data, if any, are needed to determine:
  ○ Whether the child is a child with a disability,
  ○ The educational needs of the child, or, in the case of a reevaluation of a child, whether the child continues to have such a disability and such educational needs; and
  ○ The present levels of academic achievement and related developmental needs of the child. (IDEA 2004, Sec. 614[c][1][b])

Any necessary additional evaluations will then be scheduled and carried out. Remember that, before the schools can carry out any of these evaluations, generally parental consent must be received. On the other hand, if a parent feels that an evaluation should be conducted but the school disagrees, the parents may initiate an evaluation, and the results must be considered by the school district. Likewise, if the school district conducts an evaluation and the parents disagree with the results, the parents have the right to have an independent evaluation conducted.

Assuming parents and the school district agree that the child should be evaluated and considered for special education, then the school district has 60 days to conduct a "full and individual initial evaluation" before providing the child with special education or related services. Most school districts employ school psychologists or educational diagnosticians to administer tests, conduct observations, and interview key people such as the student's teacher and parents in order to gather necessary evaluative information.

An important change in IDEA 2004 from earlier versions of the law affected the way in which students may be determined to have learning special needs. Whereas in the past states have identified students with learning special needs based on a significant difference between their presumed ability (defined usually by an IQ score) and their academic performance (based on a standardized academic assessment), IDEA 2004 no longer requires use of this discrepancy model. Now when determining whether or not a child has a specific learning disability, a school district "shall not be required to take into consideration whether a child has a severe discrepancy between achievement and intellectual ability" and instead "may use a process that determines if the child responds to scientific, research-based intervention as a part of the evaluation procedures" (IDEA 2004, Sec. 614[b][a][b]). In other words, under IDEA 2004, how well a child responds to a research-based intervention (i.e., a high-quality RTI program during an early intervening period) is more important when determining if a child has a learning disability than exhibiting the traditional ability-performance discrepancy. In some states and school districts, this change may eliminate much of the formal assessment procedures used to determine if a student should be considered to have a learning disability.

Determining Eligibility and Developing an Initial IEP

After the placement specialist has collected all relevant test results and other data, including the student's RTI performance if it is available, school district personnel will call a meeting to consider the information and make a decision about whether the child is to be considered "a child with a disability" and, if so, what disability the child has. Assuming the student is considered to be eligible for special education, an initial IEP will be developed.

Reflective Exercise #7
The use of RTI to determine who should be a student with a learning disability is a major shift in thinking in the field of special education. It might portend important changes in future populations of students classified as having learning special needs. What is your opinion of this change? Will it be helpful? Who will support it, and who will oppose it?

Schools must provide a full and individual initial evaluation before initiating services.

A group of professionals from the school district, the child's parents, and other advocates or professionals who are invited by the parents will attend the meeting. These persons will form the **IEP team** for the student. According to IDEA 2004, the IEP team must include the following:

- The parents of a child with a disability
- At least one general education teacher if the child is, or might be, participating in the general education program
- At least one special education teacher or, where appropriate, at least one special education provider
- A representative of the local education agency (generally school district) who is
  - Qualified to provide or supervise the provision of specially designed instruction to meet the unique needs of children with special needs
  - Knowledgeable about the general education curriculum
  - Knowledgeable about the availability of resources of the local education agency
- An individual who can interpret the instructional implications of evaluation results (this person may be one of those already listed)
- Other individuals who have knowledge or special expertise regarding the child, including related-services personnel (if desired by the parents or the school district)
- Whenever appropriate, the child with the disability

At this initial meeting, the school must have a written copy of the evaluation report to give to the parents, but parents and their supporters may also present information they believe is relevant. If they do, the committee will have to give this information due consideration. The law requires that, to determine the student's eligibility for special education, the school district must consider information coming from multiple sources, including tests (except with regard to identifying students with learning special needs through an RTI process as previously explained), parent input, and teacher recommendations.

Ultimately the committee must decide if the child meets the criteria for a specific disability and, if so, which one. The categorical special needs specified by federal law for use in public schools were listed and defined in Table 1.2 in Chapter 1. When making the placement decision, the committee will consider the definitions and criteria for each disability recognized under IDEA 2004 as shown previously in that figure.

There are three factors that would make the child *ineligible* to receive special education services. One is if his or her inadequate performance in school is due to poor instruction in reading or math. Another is if the learning problems are related to inadequate English proficiency. The third is if the child clearly does not meet any of the requirements to be considered as having a disability.

Reflective Exercise #8

When you look at the special needs categories in Figure 1.3, do they all look different to you? Do you suppose that sometimes IEP teams have difficulty in determining the disability of a student? Are there other factors they might consider besides specific evaluation criteria?

The IEP team must consider information from various sources.

If the child is found to be eligible for special education, the team must develop an IEP, and implement it as soon as possible. Subsequently, the IEP must be reviewed and updated as necessary, at least on an annual basis, and must be in place at the beginning of each school year. More about the IEP is discussed in the following section.

PLANNING FOR STUDENTS WITH SPECIAL NEEDS DURING THE SCHOOL YEARS

Since 1977, the IEP has been the central document devoted to specifying the nature of special education services for students with special needs. Additionally, other key documents specify the nature of services that a school district can provide to a student. We examine these in the following sections.

INDIVIDUALIZED EDUCATION PROGRAM

The actual content of an IEP is very clearly spelled out in the law. Although different school districts may use different forms and formats when creating an IEP, the minimum content cannot vary. The initial IEP and all subsequent IEPs must include the following parts:

1. *A statement of the child's present level of educational achievement and functional performance.* The IEP must contain information about the student's educational skills and how they affect his or her performance in the general curriculum. For preschool children, this information must tell how the disability affects the child's ability to participate in age-appropriate activities.

2. *A statement of measurable annual goals and, for students evaluated through alternate assessments, benchmarks or short-term objectives.* These goals must be related to meeting the child's needs that result from his or her disability in order to enable the child to be involved and progress in the general curriculum or, for a preschool child, to participate in appropriate activities. The goals must also address each of the child's other educational needs that result from his or her disability. IDEA 2004 eliminated the need for short-term objectives for most students with special needs, requiring them only for students who must be evaluated through alternate assessments (primarily students with more severe special needs).

3. *A statement of the special education and related services and supplementary aids and services to be provided to the child.* This part of the IEP must also include a statement of the program modifications or supports for school personnel that will be provided for the child so that he or she can advance appropriately toward attaining annual goals, participate and progress in the general curriculum, and participate in extracurricular and other nonacademic activities with children with and without special needs. The services provided must be based on "peer-reviewed research to the extent practicable" (IDEA 2004, Sec. 614[d][1][a]).

4. *An explanation of the extent, if any, to which the child will not participate with nondisabled children in the general education classroom and in other school activities.* The assumption is that a child with a disability *will* be included in the general education classroom, participate in the general curriculum, and in other ways be involved in school activities. To the extent that this does not occur, an explanation must be included on the IEP.

5. *A statement about the child's participation in state- or district-wide assessments of student achievement.* This statement must include any individual modifications in the administration of state- or district-wide assessments that are needed in order for the child to participate in the assessment. If the IEP team determines that the child will not participate in a particular state- or district-wide assessment, the IEP must state why that assessment is not appropriate for the child and how the child will be assessed.

6. *The projected dates for beginning services and modifications.* These dates refer to services described in item 3 and their anticipated frequency, location, and duration.

Reflective Exercise #9
The IEP is a complex document that requires a lot of time from teachers and administrators. Under the most recent law, short-term objectives were eliminated for most students. Do you think other parts of the IEP should be eliminated? Do you think the entire IEP should be eliminated? Think about this as you read the following sections.

7. *A statement of how the child's progress toward the annual goals described in item 2 will be measured and how the child's parents will be regularly informed.* Parents of children with special needs must be informed of their children's progress at least as often as other parents are informed of their children's progress. The progress reports must tell parents about a child's progress toward his or her annual goals and the extent to which that progress is sufficient to enable the child to achieve the goals by the end of the year.

504 PLANS

Any student who is eligible to receive special education services will have an IEP. However, you will encounter other students with special needs who are *not* eligible for special education services but who may still require accommodations in school. Often these students will have what are referred to as 504 plans.

Section 504 of the Rehabilitation Act protects the rights of persons with special needs when served by public agencies that receive funds from the federal government. Section 504 is not an education law per se but a civil rights act like the American with Disabilities Act (ADA) of 1990. Under Section 504, individuals with special needs, who are otherwise qualified, cannot be excluded from activities or services that are available to all others.

Because public schools receive federal funds, they must comply with Section 504. However, because a disability is more broadly defined under the Rehabilitation Act, many students in public schools that are not in special education may still be considered to have a mental or physical disability that "substantially limits a major life activity." For example, a student who has asthma may not need special education services because her school performance may be adequate. However, she may still qualify for supports and services under Section 504. Therefore, Section 504 covers all students with special needs, including those receiving services under IDEA and those who qualify according to the Rehabilitation Act (U.S. Department of Education, Office for Civil Rights, n.d.). If a student with a disability has an IEP, it will meet the requirement for an intervention plan under both IDEA and Section 504. However, if the student is not in special education but is eligible for services under Section 504, then a 504 plan is required. For the most part, Section 504 plans affect the development of accommodations for students in general education.

TRANSITION SERVICES STATEMENT

For students who are adolescents and approaching adulthood, the law says the IEP must include a statement of transition services. According to IDEA 2004, *transition services* means a "coordinated set of activities" that

- Is "results-oriented" in that it focuses on "improving the academic and functional achievement" of a student and facilitates "movement from school to post-school activities"
- May include postsecondary education, vocational education, integrated employment (including supported employment), continuing and adult education, adult services, independent living, or community participation
- Is based on individual needs that consider the student's strengths, preferences, and interests
- Includes instruction, related services, community experiences, the development of employment and other postschool adult living objectives, and, when appropriate, acquisition of daily living skills and functional vocational evaluation (IDEA 2004, Sec. 602[34])

Transition services for each student with a disability must begin at age 16. These services are indicated in the IEP

Transition services must begin by age 16.

Can You Help Me with This Student?

Jeffrey is 17 years old, handsome, and a really nice guy. For the most part he has done well in school, notwithstanding the fact that he only reads on about a fourth-grade level. Jeffrey is classified as having a learning disability. His measured intelligence is within 1 or 2 points of being average, he is quite able to take care of himself, and he makes average grades in most of his subjects thanks to the support of his special education teacher. He has not thought about college (his mom and dad never went) but assumed he would probably get a job after high school in the nearby furniture factory or maybe drive a truck. After talking to his dad, though, he doesn't know if this is going to be possible. The furniture factory announced that it was closing, and the price of fuel is making trucking less and less profitable. So Jeffrey's been thinking more about the community college. He doesn't know what he will study, and he's not sure how he'll do, but he can't think of many other options. Last week Jeffrey started talking to Mrs. Staley, his resource room teacher who helps him with his general education classroom subjects. She said that actually she, his mom and dad, and other people who were on his IEP team were supposed to be developing a transition plan for his future, so now might be a good time to get serious about it. Here's what she told Jeffrey they should do before the next IEP meeting:

- Think about possible options, including the community college but also other job ideas. There may be things besides factory work and truck driving that are appealing.
- Find out about a vocational interest inventory that Jeffrey might take to help him think about an initial career direction.

- Talk to the coordinator of disability services at the community college and find out about the supports the school offers and some possible areas of study that might be interesting.
- Think about what additional courses in high school might be helpful for whatever direction is decided.

For more information about transition planning and postsecondary education for students with learning disabilities, consult the following:

Trainor, A. A. (2005). Self-determination perceptions and behaviors of diverse students with LD during the transition planning process. *Journal of Learning Disabilities, 38,* 233–249.

Hitchings, W. E., Luzzo, D. A., Ristow, R., Horvath, M., Retish, P., & Tanners, A. (2001). The career development needs of college students with learning disabilities: In their own words. *Learning Disabilities Research & Practice, 16,* 8–17.

EXTEND AND APPLY

- Do you believe Mrs. Staley is being helpful to Jeffrey? What else would you have done?
- You might find it helpful and interesting to look at support services offered in nearby colleges and universities for students with learning disabilities. More and more of these students are participating in postsecondary education like other students.

Activity: Go to the Student and Teacher Artifacts section of the Teacher Prep website, click on Special Education and then module 18: Transitions. View artifacts 1 and 2 and answer the accompanying questions. Think about how resources like these might help Jeffrey.

by a statement of measurable postsecondary goals. The goals must be based on assessments that can report the student's skills in areas of training, education, employment, and, when appropriate, independent living skills. To help the student reach the goals, the IEP must include a statement of transition services, including courses of study (such as participation in advanced-placement courses or a vocational education program), and a statement of the interagency responsibilities or any needed links.

You might consider transition planning to be one of the most important parts of the IEP. When the student is 21 years old, he or she is no longer entitled to a "free appropriate special education." Thus, preparation for adult life is a critical issue. Take a look at the student we describe in the "Can You Help Me with This Student?" box feature. Can you make any recommendations for this student's transition plan?

PARENT PARTICIPATION IN PLANNING

As we have discussed, parents have the right to approve the initial evaluation of their child and attend the meeting where eligibility will be determined and an initial IEP developed. They also have a right to express their opinions about the placement of their child as a special education student and about all other components of the IEP. Schools are required to do all that is possible to facilitate parents' attendance and participation in meetings, including having meetings at a place and time when the parents can attend and providing an interpreter if a parent speaks a foreign language or is deaf. If parents' physical attendance is not possible, the law allows telephone or video conferences. IDEA 2004 allows for IEP team members to *not* attend IEP meetings under two circumstances: (1) if the parents and school district agree that a team member need not attend because his or her area of expertise will not be discussed or (2) if the parents and the school district agree that input from a particular team member may be made in writing.

After the IEP has been written and signed by members of the IEP team, school officials must give the parents a copy. Since they are supposed to be members of the team, ideally parents will have full knowledge of the contents of the IEP, will have agreed to it, and will also have agreed to the placement decision that is required as part of the IEP. However, suppose that parents *do not agree* to have special education services provided for their child. What then? Under IDEA 2004, the school district may not provide these services and may not appeal through due process procedures to require the child to participate in special education. The law clearly states: "If the parent of a child for whom an agency is seeking consent to provide special education and related services refuses to consent to services . . . the LEA [local education agency] shall not provide special education and related services to the child by utilizing the [due process] procedures" (614[a][1][D][i][II], [ii][II]). Further, the law states that "If the parent of such child refuses to consent to the receipt of special education and related services, or if the parent fails to respond to a request to provide such consent":

- The LEA shall not be considered to be in violation of the requirement to make available a free appropriate public education (FAPE) to the child for the failure to provide such child with the special education and related services for which the LEA requests such consent; and
- The LEA shall not be required to convene an individualized education program (IEP) meeting or develop an IEP under this section for the child for the special education and related services for which the LEA requests such consent. (IDEA 2004, Sec. 614[a][1][d])

Notwithstanding this condition of the law, it is important for teachers and other school personnel to know that parental agreement to the initial evaluation and their acceptance of the results of the evaluation *does not* mean that the parents have agreed to a specific special education placement for their child (such as a special classroom or special school). This requires a separate consent. As we saw in Chapter 1, the law requires a continuum of placements in special education, and parents have the right to express their opinion about the placement they desire for their child and to argue their case through the due process procedures outlined in the law.

PLACEMENT IN SPECIAL EDUCATION

Once the IEP has been completed and signed, an eligible student may begin to receive services. The most significant ingredients of the IEP will be the goals the student will work on and the type of placement where the student is served. Because a high priority is placed on the child's participation in the general curriculum and education with students without special needs, the law requires that the student be placed in the **least restrictive environment (LRE)** in which his or her unique needs can be effectively served. The LRE for any child is the placement on the continuum of services that is as close as possible to the general education classroom. This means that if the general education classroom, with adequate supports and accommodations, meets the student's needs, then according to the law that is the appropriate place for service delivery. If the student is not placed in the general education classroom, then the setting in which the student can be successful that is closest to it on the continuum should be used. For example, a student would not be placed in a separate special school if placement in a special class in the general education school would serve his needs just as well.

REEVALUATIONS AND UPDATING THE IEP

Neither the student's placement in special education nor the student's special education goals are static. So after the student is placed and begins to receive services and supports, subsequent reevaluations for eligibility and meetings for updating the IEP may be necessary.

According to IDEA 2004, school districts should conduct reevaluations if the student's academic or functional progress seems to have been sufficient to warrant a reevaluation or if the parents or a teacher request a reevaluation. However, schools are not required to conduct reevaluations more than once a year unless the school district and the parent both agree that it is necessary. On the other hand, schools must conduct reevaluations at least every 3 years unless the district and the parents agree that it is not necessary to do so to establish the eligibility of the student.

At least once a year, or more often if the parents or the school feels it is necessary, an IEP meeting must be held so that the student's progress toward his or her annual goals and participation in the general curriculum can be reviewed. If necessary, the IEP may be revised at this meeting to change the goals; include any recent evaluation results or any relevant information provided by the parents; change the services, supports, or placement; or make any other relevant changes.

Schools must make a good-faith effort to help students with special needs achieve their goals and objectives and to provide them with the services and supports that will help them to do so. But the law does not allow the school district or any individual, including the teacher, to be held accountable if the student's annual goals are not achieved. Sometimes teachers believe that, if students do not achieve a particular goal, they might be sued or in some other way faulted. As a result, teachers may not set goals or standards high enough to maximize the student's growth. But teachers are only expected to do their best, and this knowledge should influence them to work as hard as possible so that all of their students do as well as possible.

Reflective Exercise #10
Reevaluations and meetings to update IEPs are time-consuming and costly. Do you believe they are worth the time and effort? Do you think they should occur more or less often?

TESTING AND EVALUATION PROCEDURES

Testing is a significant aspect of special education. As you have seen, schools must evaluate students to determine if they are eligible for special education and sometimes reevaluate them to decide if they should continue to receive services. Additionally, evaluation is important for planning to meet students' needs. Further, if students *without* special needs are participating in mandatory end-of-the-year assessments, students *with* special needs are also required to be assessed. So it is important that teachers be aware of the tests that are part of special education.

NORM-REFERENCED AND CRITERION TESTS

Teachers and evaluators use tests that are either **norm-referenced** or **criterion-referenced.** A norm-referenced test is one that interprets the results for a particular student by comparing them to the results generated by a representative sample of students during the **standardization process.** For example, if you give a student a norm-referenced reading test, you can determine how well she did by comparing her score to the average as determined by the standardization sample. Intelligence tests, developmental assessments, and many academic achievement tests are norm-referenced.

Criterion-referenced tests are not intended to allow a comparison between a student and representative sample but to determine if the student can perform a skill to a predetermined criterion level. For example, if the criterion of interest is to read 80% of the words on a sight-word reading list, then you could give a criterion-referenced test to determine if the criterion had been met. Whereas norm-referenced tests are commercially produced, criterion-referenced tests can be created by a teacher, a school, or a school district.

Unfortunately we do not have space here to discuss how tests are created or their important properties such as reliability and validity. If you are interested, however, good explanations about tests can be found in Venn (2007), Overton (2006), or online from the Buros Institute of Mental Measurements (http://www.unl.edu/buros/).

TYPES OF TESTS USED IN SPECIAL EDUCATION

In your teaching career, you are certain to encounter various types of tests used with students with special needs. To introduce you to some relevant ones, we will briefly explain the following types:

- Developmental assessments
- Screening tests
- Individual intelligence tests
- Individual academic achievement tests
- Adaptive behavior scales
- Behavior rating scales
- Curriculum-based assessments
- End-of-grade, end-of-course, and alternate assessments

Developmental Assessments

Developmental assessments are norm-referenced scales designed to assess the development of infants, toddlers, and preschoolers in key areas. These areas include fine- and gross-motor, communication and language, social, cognitive, and self-help skills. If a very young child is thought to be experiencing delays, and especially if the child is going to be served in an infant-toddler program, professionals will use developmental assessment scales to identify strengths and weaknesses. The scales are administered through direct observations of the young child and parent questionnaires. From the results of the assessment, the evaluator can determine how delayed or advanced the child is in the key areas just mentioned.

There are numerous developmental assessment scales. Two that are often used are Developmental Indicators for the Assessment of Learning (3rd ed.)(DIAL-3) (Mardell-Czudnowski & Goldenberg, 1998) and the Denver Developmental Screening Test II (Frankenburg et al., 1990).

Screening Tests

As we have said, schools often use screening tests to help find children who might be below the norm in different areas. Screening instruments are very easy to administer, contain relatively few items, and can be completed in a relatively brief time, often requiring only a few minutes per child. They may be pencil-and-paper tests, rating scales or checklists used to document certain behaviors, or direct observations of skills or abilities. Their purpose is to alert the school to a *potential* problem so that more in-depth assessments can be conducted.

Undoubtedly you are familiar with Snellen charts, which schools use to screen for visual acuity. Examples of other relevant screening tests include the Pre-Kindergarten Screen (Webster & Matthews, 2000) designed to identify possible pre-academic weaknesses in 4- and 5-year-olds; the Iowa Test of Basic Skills (Hoover, Dunbar, & Frisbie, 2001) to quickly test basic academic skills with groups of students; the Revised Behavior Problem Checklist (Quay & Peterson, 1993) used to identify children at risk for behavior problems; and the Kaufman Brief Intelligence Test (2nd ed.) (KBIT-2) (Kaufman & Kaufman, 2004), intended to provide a quick estimate of verbal and nonverbal intelligence.

www.prenhall.com/rosenberg

Individual Intelligence Tests

Although intelligence has been discussed and debated for many years, most experts agree that it can be defined as a capacity for abstract thinking, mental reasoning, good judgment, and sound decision making. Most important, intelligence—at least as measured by most intelligence tests—generally correlates with one's potential to learn academic skills. For this reason, individual tests of intelligence have almost always been used when students have been considered for special education. The outcome of this norm-referenced test will help to determine if the student's learning problems are associated with general subaverage intellectual abilities or if other factors, such as specific learning disabilities or emotional disturbance, may be related to the problem. As we saw in Figure 1.3, the diagnosis of mental retardation (or intellectual disabilities) requires a significantly low level of measured intelligence whereas learning special needs and emotional disturbance assume an average or above-average level of intelligence.

Only a psychologist or diagnostician trained and certified in the administration of specific intelligence tests, often called IQ (intelligence quotient) tests, can administer them. This is because, in order for the test to be considered reliable and valid, it must be administered and scored in a very precise manner.

Most intelligence tests report an overall or general IQ score as well as subscores in areas such as verbal skills, motor performance, and visual reasoning. Intelligence tests commonly used in the public schools are the Wechsler Intelligence Scale for Children (3rd ed.) (WISC-III) (Wechsler, 1991), the Stanford-Binet Intelligence Scale (4th ed.) (Thorndike, Hagen, & Sattler, 1986), and the Woodcock-Johnson III Tests of Cognitive Abilities (WJ III) (Woodcock, McGrew, & Mather, 2001).

Individual Academic Achievement Tests

Most students in special education, and those referred for special education consideration, will be weak in one or more academic areas. In order to determine most precisely which academic areas are of concern, a psychologist or educational evaluator will administer at least one broad ranging, multiple-skill academic achievement test to the child. The results of the test will tell how the child stands in key academic skills such as reading, written expression, arithmetic, general information, and specific school subjects.

Traditionally, professionals have used norm-referenced academic achievement tests for formal evaluations to help determine a student's special education eligibility, placement, and IEP goals. These tests will also be useful for documenting the academic progress of students over a long period of time.

Unlike the administration of intelligence tests, which requires the evaluator to receive specific clinical training, teachers can usually administer academic achievement tests. When they do, they must carefully follow administration guidelines. Like most special education teachers, you are likely to take at least one course on special education assessment. During this course you will probably learn how to administer and interpret at least one academic achievement test. Tests that you may have the chance to learn about include the Peabody Individual Achievement Test—Revised/Normative Update (PIAT-R/NU) (Markwardt, 1998), the Kaufman Test of Educational Achievement/Normative Update (K-TEA/NU) (Kaufman & Kaufman, 1998), and the Wechsler Individual Achievement Test, Second Edition (WIAT-II) (Wechsler, 2001).

Adaptive Behavior Scales

A student with mental retardation (or intellectual disabilities) must exhibit a deficit in adaptive behavior (see Figure 1.3). Adaptive behavior skills are those that are especially useful for daily functioning. Typical items on adaptive behavior scales include daily living skills; community participation skills; and functioning in specific ability areas such as demonstrating appropriate social behaviors, communication, motor abilities, and applying basic academic skills.

A teacher or another person can assess a person's adaptive behavior skills by using a commercially produced adaptive behavior scale. You do not need formal training to use an adaptive behavior scale, although it is very important that each scale be carefully reviewed before use. Using the scale requires an evaluator to rate each item using the scale's specific rating system. The evaluator must either be very familiar with the student (e.g., a teacher, parent, or caregiver) or interview someone who is knowledgeable about the student's ability.

Among the most commonly used scales are the second edition of the AAMR Adaptive Behavior Scales (ABS), including the Residential-Community versions (ABS-RC:2) (Nihira, Leland, & Lambert, 1993) and the School version (ABS-S:2) (Lambert, Nihira, & Leland, 1993). Other useful scales are the Vineland Adaptive Behavior Scales (2nd ed.) (Vineland-II) (Sparrow, Cicchetti, & Balla, 2005) and the Scales of Independent Behavior—Revised (Bruininks, Woodcock, Weatherman, & Hill, 1996).

Behavior Rating Scales

Inappropriate behavior is a reason why many children are referred to special education. To determine and document the extent of behavioral difficulties, evaluators will often use behavior rating scales. These scales present a list of various challenging behaviors, sometimes clustered into subcategories, and the rater uses a rating scale (such as a 1-to-5-point scale) to indicate how frequent or intense the behavior is.

Like adaptive behavior scales, a parent or a teacher may complete the scale or an evaluator can obtain the relevant information from someone else who knows the child. After rating different behaviors, the evaluator can then calculate summary scores; and because the scales are norm-referenced, the scores for the child can be used to determine his or her behavioral status compared to others.

Rating scales that are frequently used in schools are the Devereux Behavior Rating Scale—School Form (Naglieri, LeBuffe, & Pfeiffer, 1993) and the Social Skills Rating System (Gresham & Elliot, 1990).

Curriculum-Based Assessment

A school psychologist or teacher can use the norm-referenced tests we have discussed thus far for documenting a student's status at a particular time, but these tests have drawbacks. They are commercially produced and therefore costly, they sample a student's ability across an array of skills but do not hone in on more specific skills, and they report the student's status in comparison to others when often it is more important to know how a student's skills are developing in a relatively brief period of time. For these reasons, teachers often use curriculum-based assessments.

Curriculum-based assessments are often made by the teacher to determine the student's skill level in specific curriculum areas at a certain point in time. For example, if a student has an IEP goal to learn to read on the fifth-grade level, the teacher is not likely to regularly administer a standardized reading test to see if the goal is being achieved. Instead, the teacher might ask the student to read aloud two or three times a week from a fifth-grade reader and answer comprehension questions abut the material. At each session, the teacher would record and chart the number of words read correctly, the number misread, and the number of comprehension questions answered. By using this form of curriculum-based assessment, the teacher could determine if the student was making progress toward the goal.

Curriculum-based assessment provides a viable approach for evaluating how well a student responds to intervention (Fuchs et al., 2003). For this reason, teachers are likely to use it very often when evaluating students who are participating in early intervening activities. By using the curriculum-based assessment, teachers and other professionals will be able to determine if a particular intervention is succeeding.

End-of-Grade, End-of-Course, and Alternate Assessments

As you know from Chapter 2, the purpose of the No Child Left Behind Act (NCLB) was to close the achievement gap between students with high and low levels of performance. Schools are required to demonstrate adequate yearly progress for all students or make significant changes in the way schools are run. In order to show if schools are

To see how a special education teacher monitors her students' reading fluency weekly, go to the Ms. Sprague module on the DVD-ROM and click on clip 9: Progress Monitoring.

making adequate progress, students are tested at the end of each grade. Currently, this testing applies to children between the third and eighth grades.

Besides NCLB, many states also have educational accountability laws that operate in a similar way. In North Carolina, for example, the ABCs of Public Education is designed to provide for school accountability, emphasizing development of skills in the basic subject areas and allowing as much local decision making as possible (Public Schools of North Carolina State Board of Education, 2004).

Students in special education are not exempt from these tests; in fact, IDEA 2004 requires their participation. If students with special needs are unable to participate in the general education mandated assessment, there are two possibilities. First, they may take the test with accommodations that allow them to participate. Second, they may participate through an alternate assessment procedure. Most students with academic special needs and with sensory or physical impairments are provided with accommodations, whereas students with more severe intellectual special needs are evaluated using an alternate assessment. In either case, the student's IEP must indicate how the end-of-grade or end-of-course test is to be given (Browder & Spooner, 2003).

Reflective Exercise #11
Considering your possible role as a professional working with students with special needs, which of the described tests or testing procedures would be most useful for you? Why? What do you like or dislike about the different tests?

 To link to websites that support and extend the content of this chapter, go to the Web Links module in Chapter 4 of the Companion Website, www.prenhall.com/ rosenberg.

SUMMARY

Effective special education practices begin with identification and planning. Sometimes this will begin when children are very young and sometimes not until they reach the early school years.

Identification and Planning for Infants and Toddlers and Their Families

- Some children will show signs of special needs very early in life, even as infants or toddlers. Most of these children will have recognizable physical or sensory disabilities and will experience cognitive, physical, communicative, and/or adaptive delays.
- Professionals will document these delays using developmental assessments. Sometimes states will also serve infants or toddlers who are considered at risk for delays, even if the delays have not yet occurred.
- Individualized family service plans (IFSPs) are the planning tools used with infants and toddlers with special needs and their families. Parents participate in constructing these plans, and a planning coordinator oversees their implementation.

Special Needs Characteristics of Preschool-Age Children and the Plans Used to Provide Services

- Preschool personnel recognize many children with special needs because of their delays in language or because they are exhibiting uncommon challenging behavior.
- Sometimes children will also exhibit risk factors because of harsh environmental conditions.
- When a preschool-age child is suspected of having a special need, an educational evaluator will conduct assessments to determine if the child is eligible for special education services.
- Preschoolers who receive special education services may have these services directed by the IFSP if one was developed for them as participants in a Part C program or by an individualized education program (IEP).

Initial Recognition of School-Age Students Possibly Needing Special Education Services and Following Procedures

- Initial recognition of students with special needs during the school years usually occurs because of academic or behavioral challenges.
- Screening tests or parent or teacher concerns can be the impetus for initiating movement toward special education services.
- Most of the time, prereferral or early intervening strategies will be used in the general education classroom before referral for special education eligibility evaluation.
- If a student does not succeed in a prereferral or early intervening program, school personnel will make a referral for evaluation to determine if the student is eligible for special education services.
- If the results of the evaluation indicate the student is eligible, an IEP will be developed by the IEP team, and the student will receive special education services.
- The student must be reevaluated for eligibility no more than once a year and at least every 3 years unless the school district and the parents agree that there is no need for an evaluation to maintain eligibility.

Content of an IEP, Members of the IEP Team, and Other Special Plans

- The IEP includes the special education goals for the student, the placement, how the student will participate in the general curriculum, and other critical information. When a student with special needs reaches age 16, the IEP must include a statement of transition needs.
- Schools must have an IEP when a student begins special education, and an IEP must exist as long as the student continues to receive special education services.
- The IEP team will generally update the IEP at least once a year.
- The IEP team includes professionals, the student's parents, and, when appropriate, the student.
- Some students who are not eligible for special education services will still have needs that require accommodations.

- Under Section 504 of the Rehabilitation Act, schools must provide these accommodations.
- Section 504 plans are similar to IEPs, but they focus primarily on supports necessary for students in general education settings.

Tests Used to Identify and Plan for Students with Special Needs

- Tests are used to determine if a child is eligible for special education and for planning appropriate educational programs.
- Types of tests used for these purposes include developmental assessments; screening tests; individual intelligence tests; individual academic achievement tests; adaptive behavior scales; behavior rating scales; curriculum-based assessments; and end-of-grade, end-of-course, and alternate assessments.

 Council for Exceptional Children **ADDRESSING THE PROFESSIONAL STANDARDS**

Council for Exceptional Children (CEC) Knowledge Standards addressed in the chapter:

CC1K5, CC1K6, CC1K7, GC1K1, GC1K5, GC2K3, CC8K1-5, GC8K1-4

Appendix B: CEC Knowledge and Skill Standards Common Core has a full listing of the standards referenced here.

(and other needs). Digital textbooks contain multiple representations (e.g., image, text, video) of content and can transform one medium to another (e.g., text-to-speech or speech-to-text) or modify the characteristics of a presentation (e.g., size and color of text, loudness of the sound) (Hitchcock et al., 2002).

These modifications have the potential to benefit all students, particularly those whose primary language is not English, those who have difficulty maintaining attention to materials for long periods of time, students who have reading difficulties, persons who lack the motor skills to write or type, or those with intellectual disabilities. Merely a decade ago, universal design for learning was the distant, far-fetched dream of a few instructional technology experts. However, given the dramatic and awe-inspiring improvements in technology that have occurred during the past decade, universal design is a reality that will soon be a mainstay of most curriculum materials.

Technology plays a critical role in classroom-based universal design accommodations.

PLANNING PYRAMIDS

Many teachers use grade-level textbooks that align with state content standards as their primary planning tool for instruction. These textbooks meet the majority of students' instructional needs in a relatively straightforward fashion. However, instruction based largely on textbooks is often too difficult for students who do not read well, lack subject-specific knowledge of vocabulary, lack background knowledge regarding the content, or have disabilities that limit their access to the material (Schumm, 1999).

One way teachers can plan instruction to meet the diverse needs of all students in a classroom is by using *planning pyramids* (Schumm, 1999; Schumm, Vaughn, & Leavell, 1994; Vaughn, Bos, & Schumm, 2007). Built on the concept of "degrees of learning," planning pyramids help teachers analyze both the content and instructional practices as they plan lessons or units of instruction. Similar to Bloom's taxonomy, the fundamental idea is that while "all students are capable of learning, not all students will learn all the content covered" (Vaughn et al., 2007, p. 190). Key concepts and skills to be learned for the specific lesson are first identified and then categorized based on three levels of learning:

1. Content all students will learn (the base of the pyramid)
2. Content that most (but not all) students will learn (the middle of the pyramid)
3. Content that a few students will learn (the top of the pyramid)

Figure 5.2 illustrates a sample middle school science pyramid lesson plan addressing weathering and erosion. The base of the pyramid includes content important for all students to learn, such as the forces that change the earth's crust. At the next level is content that most but not all students will learn, including how humans cause weathering. Finally, the top of the pyramid includes content that only a few students will learn, including how the earth looked during the Ice Age. In addition to planning content, the unit planning form prompts decisions regarding materials and resources; instructional strategies and adaptations; and evaluation/products to meet the needs of all students. Keep in mind that students are not slotted permanently into one part of the pyramid and that the amount of content a student will learn will vary over time and across content and lessons.

www.prenhall.com/rosenberg

FIGURE 5.2

THE PLANNING PYRAMID UNIT PLANNING FORM

UNIT PLANNING FORM		Date: _Sept. 1 – 30_ Class Period: _1:30 – 2:30_

Date: _Sept. 1 – 30_   **Class Period:** _1:30 – 2:30_
Unit Title: _Weathering and Erosion_

What some students will learn.	• How Earth looked during Ice Age • Disasters caused by sudden changes • Geographic examples of slow and fast changes
What most students will learn.	• Compare and contrast weathering and erosion • How humans cause physical and chemical weathering • Basic types of rocks
What ALL students should learn.	• Basic components of Earth's surface • Forces that change crust are weathering and erosion

Materials/Resources:
Guest speaker on volcanoes
Video: erosion and weathering
Rock samples
Library books — disasters, volcanoes, etc.
Colored transparencies for lectures

Instructional Strategies/Adaptations:
Concept maps
Cooperative learning groups to learn material in textbook
Audiotape of chapter
Study buddies to prepare for quizzes and tests

Evaluation/Products:
Weekly quiz
Unit test
Learning logs (daily record of "What I learned")
Vocabulary flash

Source: Vaughn, S., Bos, C., & Schumm, J. (2007). Teaching students who are exceptional, diverse, and at-risk in the general education classroom (4th ed.), p. 218. Boston: Allyn & Bacon.

ADAPTING CURRICULUM AND INSTRUCTION

To facilitate student participation in the general education curriculum, teachers can choose among nine types of instructional adaptations (see Table 5.1). The most frequently used tend to be the more obvious—adaptations in size (e.g., the number of items that a student is expected to complete) and time (e.g., time allocated for completing a task). However, creative teachers consider variable ways to (1) adjust the difficulty level of lessons, (2) structure how students participate and provide responses, (3) provide support, and (4) recognize an individual student's success in large-group lessons. As you review the nine types of adaptations, keep in mind that some are intended for use with all students. Others are intended for students who may not learn the same content as others but who may learn adapted or alternative content (Cole et al., 2000).

Reflective Exercise #2
How can you justify the fairness of using adaptations for some students and not others? How could you determine which adaptations are best for individual students?

DELIVERING INSTRUCTION

Until this point, we have focused on _what_ students are taught; we now address _how_ students are taught effectively. In general, the majority of students, approximately 50 to 80%, seem to easily learn required content in their general education classrooms. The remaining students do not learn this content easily as they move from one grade level to the next. These students may or may not be identified as having a disability. Nonetheless, they share a struggle to learn academic content and to pass state-mandated accountability tests. These students require teachers, like Bobby Biddle, who recognize that there are alternative approaches to teaching and use evidenced-based techniques and methods for systematically teaching well-defined content.

TABLE 5.1

NINE TYPES OF ADAPTATIONS

Adaptation	Definition	Example
Input	The instructional strategies used to facilitate student learning	Use of videos, computer programs, field trips, and visual aids to support active learning
Output	The ways learners can demonstrate understanding and knowledge	Students write a song, tell a story, design a poster or brochure, perform an experiment
Size	The length or portion of an assignment, demonstration, or performance learners are expected to complete	Reduce the length of report to be written or spoken, reduce the number of references needed, reduce the number of problems to be solved
Time	The flexible time needed for student learning	Individualize a timeline for project completion, allow more time for test taking
Difficulty	The varied skill levels, conceptual levels, and processes involved in learning	Provide calculators, tier the assignment so that the outcome is the same but with varying degrees of concreteness and complexity
Level of support	The amount of assistance to the learner	Students work in cooperative groups or with peer buddies, mentors, cross-age tutors, or paraeducators
Degree of participation	The extent to which the learner is actively involved in the tasks	In a student-written, -directed, and -acted play, a student may play a part that has more physical action rather than has numerous lines to memorize
Modified goals	The adapted outcome expectations within the context of a general education curriculum	In a written language activity, a student may focus more on writing some letters and copying words rather than composing whole sentences or paragraphs
Substitute curriculum	Significantly differentiated instruction and materials to meet a learner's identified goals	In a foreign language class, a student may develop a play or script that uses both authentic language and cultural knowledge of a designated time period rather than reading paragraphs or directions

Source: Adapted from Cole et al., (2000). Adapting curriculum and instruction in inclusive classrooms: A teachers' desk reference (2nd ed., p. 39). Bloomington, IN: Indiana Institute on Disability and Community.

APPROACHES TO TEACHING

Since the passage of the first IDEA in 1975, special education has been dominated by one approach to instruction: a behavioral approach. The behavioral approach emphasizes explicitly identifying content or objectives and systematically teaching this content to students. This approach has been the foundation for numerous instructional practices that have been effective for students with disabilities. Arguably the most common behavioral

www.prenhall.com/rosenberg

method, **Direct Instruction (DI)** has explicit guidelines as to what a teacher does to begin a lesson, present information during the lesson, guide student practice after instruction, correct student work and provide feedback, plan and carry out student seatwork, and follow up the lesson (Carnine, Silbert, Kame'enui, & Tarver, 2003; Rosenshine & Stevens, 1986). Chapter 8 contains detailed information regarding Direct Instruction.

The behavioral approach to instruction is most effective when teaching students fundamental types of information (e.g., basic skills such as vocabulary or math facts). However, it not always sufficient to meet many of the higher-order needs of students with learning problems or disabilities. In such cases a cognitive approach to instruction is necessary. Cognitive approaches view students as active, strategic learners who are able to solve problems when provided with appropriate supports and accommodations. Specific teaching methods within this approach are not as explicitly structured as those found within the behavioral approach. However, common instructional techniques include (1) comparing and contrasting, (2) concept formation and exemplar selection, (3) informed guessing, and (4) development of specific problem-solving sequences.

Keep in mind that these approaches to teaching are not mutually exclusive. Effective instruction is often a blend of techniques and methods. A widely applied example of a successful combination of the cognitive and behavioral approaches is the **strategies intervention model (SIM),** conceptualized and developed at the University of Kansas Center for Learning. The cognitive component of the model focuses on the teaching of learning strategies—techniques, rules, and generalizations that guide students in the acquisition, integration, storage, and retrieval of curriculum content (Rogan, 2000). Behavioral principles are used to directly teach the strategies through an explicit instructional sequence. Specifically, using a structured series of learning activities, targeted strategies are described, modeled, rehearsed, practiced, and, if successful, generalized to other areas of instructional content (Deshler & Schumaker, 2006). We have an in-depth discussion on SIM in Chapter 6.

SYSTEMATIC TEACHING

How do effective teachers deliver instruction? What do teachers need to know to deliver instruction to diverse and sometimes challenging groups of students? We focus on five elements of effective teaching: grouping for instruction, presenting content, providing opportunities for practice, monitoring student progress, and using technology to support instruction.

Grouping for Instruction

How were you grouped for instruction during your years in school? You may remember instances of small-group work and working in collaborative teams. However, it is more likely you will recall a teacher at the front of the room providing instruction to all students in your class. There are advantages to this type of large-group instruction: Information is quickly and efficiently conveyed to a large number of students, and many students learn this information and can respond correctly to questions on a test when asked about the content. Still, there are many students who cannot learn academic content in whole groups and require some instruction that uses alternative grouping arrangements. We focus on three alternative grouping strategies that are designed to allow teachers to provide more focused instruction to students who struggle when faced with whole-class instruction.

Ability grouping allows teachers to focus on students' common learning characteristics and instructional needs. When used judiciously, this type of instructional arrangement can be highly effective, allowing struggling learners to benefit from the intensive and targeted instruction they need to make adequate academic progress. Unfortunately, the overuse of ability grouping can be detrimental academically and socially, with low-performing students spending most of their school day separated, and eventually alienated, from high-achieving peers (Freeman & Alkin, 2000; Good & Brophy, 2003; Oakes, 1992; Reutzel, 2003; Salend & Duhaney, 1999).

Mixed ability grouping is an approach in which small groups of students (usually three to six) work in cooperative groups to learn and to ensure that others on their team learn as well (Slavin, 1995). Validated by years of research (e.g., Good & Brophy, 2003;

Reflective Exercise #3
Think back to your days as an elementary and secondary student. What content were you taught using a behavioral approach? A cognitive approach? Which of these approaches were most effective for you?

To see how Bobby Biddle uses cooperative grouping in her classroom, go to the Ms. Biddle module on the DVD-ROM and click on clip 8: Cooperative Groups.

Johnson, Johnson, & Holubec, 1993; Slavin, 1995), cooperative learning groups vary widely in type yet share some common beneficial characteristics (Putnam, 1998):

- *Positive interdependence.* The accomplishment of the group goal depends on heterogeneous, diverse group members working together *and* each individual attaining his or her goal.
- *Individual accountability.* All students are held individually accountable for their own learning as well as for their contributions to the group.
- *Cooperative skills.* Students practice social and cooperative skills that are commonly used in group activities, such as sharing materials, turn taking, helping one another, and encouraging others.
- *Student reflection and goal setting.* At the end of a cooperative activity, students evaluate how the group functioned and whether the group's goals were met.

Individual tutoring is generally recognized as the optimal instructional method for meeting the needs of students who are struggling academically (Pinnell, Lyons, De-Ford, Bryk, & Seltzer, 1994; Slavin et al., 1994; Spear-Swerling & Sternberg, 1996; Vaughn, Gersten, & Chard, 2000) Of course, the drawback to this method is that it is very labor-intensive and expensive. To reduce costs, some schools have rearranged the school day to allow teachers to provide tutoring just before or after school. Others have trained tutors (e.g., parent volunteers, teacher education students from local universities) to work with students during or after school hours.

Peer-tutoring programs, widely used and cost-effective, often focus on afterschool tutoring in subject areas for middle or high school students or tutoring in basic skills areas (e.g., reading and math) for elementary students. These programs use same-age peers or cross-age arrangements, typically older students tutoring younger students. Interestingly, well-designed tutoring programs result in improved educational outcomes for both the tutor and the tutee who is struggling to learn academic content (Elbaum, Vaughn, Hughes, & Moody, 1999; Fuchs, Fuchs, & Burish, 2000; Mathes, Howard, Babyak, & Allen, 2000; Vaughn et al., 2000).

Presenting Content

The effective presentation of new content typically begins with an overview, or **advance organizer,** of the activities students will do and how they fit contextually with previous and future lessons and units. Once this initial review is completed, instruction on new content begins with an explicit demonstration of target concepts, facts, skills, or principles. Lecturing is a primary way of presenting information in content classes. However, effective teachers often introduce demonstrations from students and frequently check for student understanding by providing opportunities to respond (e.g., unison and individual responding). To engage students during instruction, it is critical that teachers question students in ways that match the specific goals of the lesson for the individual student (Rosenberg, O'Shea, & O'Shea, 2006). For example, depending on the goal of the lesson for the student, questions range from factual knowledge and comprehension to higher-order demands such as application, analysis, integration, and evaluation of information. Equally important is how teachers provide feedback to students. Effective teachers typically respond to students' correct answers with statements that paraphrase or elaborate on the content. When responses are incorrect, teachers provide additional cues and corrective feedback.

Well-designed peer tutoring activities result in improved outcomes for those who both give and receive assistance.

www.prenhall.com/rosenberg

Opportunities for Practice

Guided practice is characterized by closely supervised activities in which the teacher uses prompts, cues, and feedback to shape fluent student performance. However, as students begin to acquire the content of a lesson, teachers begin to fade their level of prompts and focus on fast, accurate, and fluent responding. Keep in mind that, in many lessons, the shift from presenting content to guided practice is often indistinguishable; the most important factor is that students have numerous opportunities to practice the content of the lesson. Examples of effective guided practice activities include unison responding (groups of students responding to a single request simultaneously), having several students solving a problem on the board, and having groups of students working together cooperatively to illustrate a specific concept or operation (Rosenberg et al., 2006).

Independent practice follows success with guided practice, when students are ready to work toward greater fluency through activities such as seatwork and homework. Although independent practice can be addressed through instructional games and cooperative learning activities, seatwork is the most frequently used form of independent practice; students spend as much as 70% of their day in such activities. Consequently, it is essential that independent seatwork be prepared in effective ways. According to Gaffney (1987), successful teachers

- Develop and assign independent seatwork activities that are age-appropriate, attractive, organized, and directly related to the goals and objectives of their lessons
- Preface seatwork with instructions that are clear and succinct
- Design seatwork with multiple stimulus and response formats
- Ensure that the activities can be completed with a high degree of success and that provisions are made for students to check the accuracy of their responses

Once students demonstrate proficiency with specific concepts and operations, independent practice activities can be given as homework assignments. Like seatwork, homework is most helpful when teachers adhere to certain guidelines (Cooper, 2001; Marzano, Pickering, & Pollock, 2001). However, when assigning homework, keep in mind that for younger students homework is a method to foster positive attitudes toward school and to develop desirable work habits; for older students the main goal is to provide additional practice opportunities to reinforce skills acquired in class. Consequently, homework should not be used to punish students or to replace school-based instruction (see Figure 5.3).

FIGURE 5.3

HOMEWORK: GUIDELINES FOR TEACHERS TO ENSURE EFFECTIVE PRACTICE

1. The amount of homework should differ based on the student's grade level.
   Grades 1–3: three or four assignments per week, lasting 10–30 minutes each
   Grades 4–6: three or four assignments per week, lasting 40–60 minutes each
   Middle school: four or five assignments per week, lasting 70–90 minutes each
   High school: four or five assignments per week, lasting 100–120 minutes each
2. Homework for students with disabilities should be similar to homework completed by others.
3. The purpose of homework should be clear to students and their parents:
   Practice information already learned
   Elaborate on information already learned
   Prepare to learn new information
4. Homework should be work that the student can complete independently and include both mandatory and voluntary assignments.
5. The role of the parent in homework is to create a positive home environment for completing homework.
6. Feedback should be provided for all homework that is completed.

Source: Adapted from Cooper, 2001; Cooper & Nye, 1994; Marzano et al., 2001.

Child doing homework at home: Rather than punish students or replace instruction, homework should be used to foster desirable work habits and reinforce skills.

Monitoring Student Performance

When teachers monitor student academic progress and make changes in instruction based on this progress (or lack of progress), student academic achievement improves (Deno, 2003; Fuchs, 2004). Teachers monitor their students by directly observing them performing academically (e.g., reading orally, completing math problems, conducting a science experiment), administering quizzes and exams, and analyzing independent assignments and homework. Teachers also receive summative, long-term feedback from standardized tests. Unfortunately, many teachers do not have readily available information to monitor the effectiveness of instruction on a daily or weekly basis, data needed to make decisions about changes in instruction (e.g., reteaching a basic skill or concept).

A system of classroom assessment called **Curriculum-Based Measurement (CBM)** can help address this shortcoming (Deno, 1985, 2003; Fuchs, 2004). CBM is a simple, easy-to-use approach for assessing student progress in academic content areas over time. Compared to other procedures that monitor student progress, CBM has the following advantages (Deno, 2003; Fuchs, 2004):

- It allows teachers to select skills measured based on the curriculum being taught.
- It is quick and efficient, taking 1–3 minutes.
- It is used to plan student instruction (e.g., identifying specific skill deficits to reteach).
- It compares the progress of students as needed.

A number of studies have demonstrated the value of CBM. Since teachers assess student performance as students are acquiring skills, instructional methods can be modified to facilitate better academic achievement (Overton, 2006).

USING TECHNOLOGY TO SUPPORT INSTRUCTION

Technology continues to greatly influence the way instruction is delivered at all levels of education. Two types of technology are commonly used in educational setting: instructional technology and assistive technology. **Instructional technology (IT)** is hardware- and software-designed to enhance teaching and learning in your current courses (Edyburn, 2000). IT is so pervasive (applications of Blackboard, PowerPoint presentations, etc.), that some teachers view it as distracting, overwhelming, and a "solution in search of a problem." To avoid such a situation, teachers should evaluate each piece of hardware or software, keeping the following questions in mind (Edyburn, 2000; Higgins, Boone, & Williams, 2000):

1. Is the IT easy to use and based on the principles of effective teaching?
2. Has research been conducted to support the effectiveness of the instructional technology?
3. Does the IT address the objectives that guide your instruction and address the needs of students at different skill levels?
4. Is the IT accessible for students with different types of disabilities (e.g., cognitive, sensory, physical)?

Assistive technology (AT) refers to "any item, piece of equipment, or product system, whether acquired commercially off the shelf, modified, or customized, that is used to increase, maintain, or improve the functional capabilities of a child with a disability" (IDEA, 2004, Sec. 620[1]). Recall that IDEA requires that assistive technology be considered when planning IEPs for students with disabilities. AT devices used to enhance the performance of students with disabilities include communication boards for persons with limited mobility and devices that translate written words into tactile symbols for persons who read braille (Edyburn, 2002; Westling & Fox, 2005). (Features on how technology is applied to the education of students with specific disabilities appear in later chapters.)

MANAGING STUDENT BEHAVIOR

If interesting, well-planned, evidenced-based lessons are to reach students, they must be complemented by efficient and positive strategies for managing student behavior. Consider the following scenario illustrating the importance of classroom management. You are teaching a very interesting lesson on the characteristics of American society that contributed to the birth of rap and hip-hop music. You observe that most of the 10th graders are engaged in the lesson. Why not? You spent more than 3 hours preparing the lesson, carefully selecting a series of recordings by musicians who have influenced generations of adolescents. Moreover, you have tied the music to a timeline of significant historical events ranging from civil rights marches to demonstrations against the persistent poverty in urban centers such as Los Angeles and Detroit. Most of the students are truly motivated by the lesson. Still, as he has for several weeks, Sammy Tisch has refused to settle down and attend to the lesson. Even when he chooses to participate in the discussion, he does so in a most inappropriate fashion. He tries to upstage his classmates by ridiculing their opinions, acting like the class clown, and denigrating aspects of your teaching. Although he has no definitive opinions of his own, Sammy disrupts the flow of class by frequently talking out of turn and using suggestive and sometimes profane language. Even more significant, he has yet to hand in an acceptable assignment.

In one form or another, situations like this one occur in classrooms. Consequently, teachers' level of anxiety and concern about behavior management, particularly if they are beginning teachers, is quite high. In polls of teacher attitudes toward the public schools, 65% of the teachers responding indicated that the lack of discipline is a very or fairly serious problem in their local school. In a national survey of public school teachers, 41% noted that student misbehavior interfered with their teaching and that they had to interrupt instruction an average of 10.33 times per week (Langdon, 1999; NCES, 2002). This need not be the case: Along with teaching students to understand curriculum, teachers can minimize classroom disruptions by managing and directing the complex interrelationships among structure, expectations, and student behaviors.

Fortunately, most school and classroom misbehavior is related to a few well-defined factors, including inattention to task, crowd control issues during transitions, getting work accomplished in a timely fashion, and students trying to be cool by testing the limits (Jones & Jones, 2004; Kottler, 2002). Common misbehaviors include tardiness, disrespect, being unprepared, talking, calling out, and mild, infrequent varieties of verbal and physical acting out. Many of these behaviors can be prevented

Reflective Exercise #4
Discipline and behavior-management issues tend to elicit considerable anxiety among beginning teachers. Think of a teacher you have observed who managed the classroom in a calm, positive, and effective manner. Do you have dispositions that will help you manage student behavior in your classroom?

Behavior management is a major anxiety-producing concern for many beginning teachers.

FIGURE 5.6

GOTTA HAVE IT CARD

Have you got IT? - No?
Well, here's how to get IT?
Why? Because you Gotta

Students will be rewarded for a variety of behaviors on a school-wide basis through the "Gotta Have It Cards":

- Get your Gotta Have It Card from your homeroom teacher.
- Immediately write your full name and homeroom on the back of the card to make it valid.
- Students are responsible for holding onto their cards and presenting them on request. (Stay alert for teachers asking for the Gotta Have It Card throughout your school day.)
- Collect teacher stamps by showing all teachers how well you follow the rules.
- Once your card is filled it can be deposited in drawing containers or used to purchase admission to a variety of activities that will be announced.

Examples of behaviors that the Gotta Have It Card may be used for:

Hallway behaviors: - Teachers recognizing compliance with rules during hallway movement will stamp the card of students and verbally acknowledge the behavior.

Attendance: - Monthly, homeroom teachers will stamp the cards of students who have had perfect attendance for that month.

Uniform compliance: - Teachers tracking compliance of wearing the school uniform daily will stamp cards on Fridays to indicate compliance for an entire week. Attendance is necessary.

Source: Adapted from Deer Park Middle School. (1998) PAR manual.

Don't mistake the presence of a hierarchy as a requirement that every step be used every time a student acts out. The hierarchy is a guide for teachers and allows for a graduated response to behavior.

Crisis Management. The most frightening part of a crisis situation is that the student involved appears to have little or no control over his or her behavior. Consequently, surface management techniques and consequences have little or no effect. When a crisis occurs, the teacher's initial task is to help get the student through the crisis in a safe, nonthreatening, and nonpunitive fashion and maintain the safety of others. When dealing with the crisis, you should not exceed your level of expertise. Note that crisis intervention is different from crisis management in that it requires a series of actions from counselors, psychologists, and certified crisis personnel. Nonetheless, all teachers should know how to manage a crisis situation. The ideal course of action is for each school to develop a crisis response team of four or five people trained in both verbal intervention techniques and safe, nonaversive methods of physical restraint (Johns & Carr, 1995). However, you may be in a school without a proper functioning team. When required to manage crisis situations, do the following (Albert, 2003; Johns & Carr, 1995; Jones & Jones, 2004):

- Remain calm and send someone for assistance.
- Guard against body language and punitive, confrontational verbalizations that can escalate the situation.
- Be aware of the safety needs of other students.
- Have a plan for reentry after the crisis.

www.prenhall.com/rosenberg

FIGURE 5.7

HALLEY BROCHURE

Halley School Rules STARS	Positive Behavior Recognition	Hierarchy of Consequences
Succeed Stay on task. Try your best and put forth your best effort. Be prepared for class. **T**hink Think safety first. Think of how others feel. Think of yourself. Think before you act. **A**ttitude Follow directions the first time they are given. Use appropriate language and tone. Be on time. Build up, no put-downs. **R**espect Respect each other's space, feelings, and property. Show respect for adults. Respect yourself. Take responsibility for your own actions. **S**oar Set goals. Go beyond expectations. Reach for the stars.	• Smiles • Stickers • Happy Notes • Star Bookmarks • Character awards • Specialist awards • Bus awards • Cafeteria awards • Happy phone call home • Special privileges • Lunch with an adult • Special treats • Tokens • Games or activities • Each teacher has developed a specific plan to reward positive behavior in his/her classroom. Be sure to ask your teacher about the reward program in your child's classroom.	• Non-Verbal Cues • General Classroom Reminders • Student Specific Warning • Time-out in Classroom • Time-out in Another Classroom • Parent Contact • After-School Detention • Guidance Referral • Office Referral* • CT Button* * Parents may be notified at any level depending on the severity of the situation or problem. * Some inappropriate student behavior may warrant immediate use of more severe consequences.

Source: Adapted from Willam Halley Elementary School. (2001) Brochure.

Promoting Access to the Plan. Once a comprehensive behavior-management plan is conceptualized, you will want to disseminate it to students, their families, administrators, and related-service providers. Some schoolwide teams and individual teachers create full-sized manuals that articulate rather completely the major components (mission statement, rules, procedures, consequences) of the management plan. Others have developed user-friendly brochures that highlight the major components of the plan. Figure 5.7 provides an example of a brochure produced by the teachers of William Halley Elementary School as part of their participation in the PAR project at Johns Hopkins University (Rosenberg & Jackman, 2003).

TARGETED AND WRAPAROUND INTERVENTIONS

All schools have students who do not respond to even the most well-designed inclusive management plans. In fact, inclusive comprehensive management plans are effective for approximately 85% of students and are not designed to significantly improve the behavior of students who exhibit extreme, frequent, and persistent patterns of problem behavior (Taylor-Greene et al., 1997). To address the needs of these students, teachers and school personnel use targeted interventions and wraparound interventions. **Targeted interventions** are powerful, school-based actions directed toward the chronic, repetitive, and pervasive problem behaviors of individual students (Walker et al., 1995). These interventions are typically dynamic, simultaneously strengthening appropriate behavior as they weaken the presenting challenging behaviors.

Wrap-around interventions are even more intensive, typically requiring the structured, coordinated, and integrated efforts of a team of professionals (Eber, Sugai, Smith, & Scott, 2002). How are targeted and wraparound interventions designed? The most direct method is to complete a three-stage process that includes (1) conducting functional behavioral assessments (FBA), (2) developing behavior intervention plans (BIPs), and (3) evaluating the effectiveness of intervention. Specific applications of these processes are illustrated throughout the categorical chapters of this text, and details on conducting an FBA appear in Chapter 7.

When developing interventions to address the needs of students who exhibit extreme problem behavior, remember that you are not alone. Typically, a team of specialists from human service backgrounds will be convened to develop a comprehensive intervention. Within any number of schools there are administrators, behavior specialists, counselors, social workers, psychologists, and behavior-support teams that implement specialized programs of outreach and intervention. For example, it is not unusual for counseling and guidance personnel to deliver family-support interventions or for school psychologists to have social-skills training groups and short-term individual therapy sessions for high-need students. Outside the school, students can be "wrapped around" by services from physicians, mental health service providers, family-preservation personnel, and state protective-service officers, juvenile justice personnel, and even law-enforcement officers.

Keep in mind that services should be grounded in values that emphasize family empowerment, cultural competence, flexibility, and the strengths of the child and family. As a teacher involved in this team process, you must embrace families as full partners in the intervention process and stay involved with the range of service providers both within and outside the school system. (Descriptions of wraparound programs for students with emotional and behavioral disorders are detailed in Chapter 7.)

COMMUNICATING INSTRUCTION AND BEHAVIOR MANAGEMENT

Arguably, the most important consideration in teaching and managing student behavior is the manner in which teachers interact with students and colleagues. In many cases, it is not just what teachers say but the manner in which they communicate. To be productive instructional leaders, teachers need to be models of appropriate behavior and to communicate goals, requests, and intentions directly and efficiently. Most important, to be effective, teachers must convey to their students that they truly care about them.

DEVELOPING AUTHENTIC RELATIONSHIPS

To see Bobby Biddle and her principal discuss the concepts of caring and building relationships, go to the Ms. Biddle module on the DVD-ROM and click on clip 2: Responsibility for Learning and clip 6: Relationships.

Mr. Andrew Del Priori, known as Mr. Del to both students and adults at the local middle school, teaches one of the most difficult math classes, Introduction to Algebra, to students with a wide range of abilities. He has the reputation of having high expectations for all students and for being a strict but fair evaluator. His students report that he runs a tight, structured classroom in which instructional time is valued with ferocity. Mr. Del is one of the most popular teachers in the school. Students congregate in his room before and after school, and many consult with him when facing confusing situations in their academic and personal lives. What is it about Mr. Del that makes him so attractive to students? Why do they confide in him when faced with problems? Students who know Mr. Del trust him and believe he cares about them as both developing young people and advanced math students. Mr. Del projects openness and concern and appears to really enjoy interacting with students (even the ones considered challenging).

How does a teacher begin to develop authentic relationships with students? First, you should realize that relationship building is more evolution than revolution. Relationships with students take time to develop and are influenced by the many brief contacts and interactions that you have with students every day. Small investments of teacher energy such as greeting students at the start of the day, expressing appreciation for their efforts, recognizing special talents, taking an interest in aspects of their activities and personal lives, and predicting success in assignments will enhance the development of productive relationships (Koenig, 2000). As exchanges accumulate, students assess teacher credibility, seeing if what they do corresponds with what is said. Second, authentic relationships are based on listening to students rather than just reacting to them. As observed by Postman and Weingartner (1969) in their classic text *Teaching As a Subversive Activity,* listening is the only way to learn what students view as relevant and the one true way to validate if what they say deserves attention, even if it is not always on target. Finally, developing children and adolescents often choose to express themselves through a variety of creative ways, including dress, speech, demeanor, and belief systems. Relationships grow when teachers accept students for who they are, encourage them to maintain their individuality, and make continued attempts to understand the world from their point of view.

CIVILITY AND RESPECT

Effective teachers demonstrate civility and respect in interactions with students and exhibit genuine concern for their individual welfare. When we speak of civility, we mean being cognizant that all our actions have consequences for others and anticipating what those consequences may be (Forni, 2002). By respect we are referring to one's basic human right to be acknowledged and treated with dignity. Teachers model civility and respect by engaging in many of the behaviors that maximize effective interpersonal communication, including (1) a vocal tone that conveys patience and understanding and uses a minimum of judgmental language; (2) focused active listening with accompanying eye contact; and (3) regular private interactions that convey a desire to know students and their individual opinions and concerns (Kauffman Mostert, Trent, & Hallahan, 2002; Rosenberg et al., 2006).

It is important to treat students with respect even when you are frustrated by their academic performance or disappointed by their behaviors. Although this is often difficult, you should emphasize that their problematic behaviors are the focus of disapproval, not the students themselves. Keep in mind that up to 90% of what we communicate is transmitted in ways other than the actual words we use. Nonverbal communication, facial gestures and body language, and the rate, pitch, and volume of speech often reflect values and acceptance of students. Although unintended, actions as simple as diverting one's eyes, stepping back, looking at one's watch, or speaking quickly send negative signals to students seeking our approval.

CREDIBILITY, DEPENDABILITY, AND ASSERTIVENESS

Credibility with students develops when (1) verbal behavior—what teachers say—coincides consistently with what they actually do and (2) when students perceive that their teachers are prepared and doing all they can to meet responsibilities in the classroom (Rosenberg et al., 2006). Credibility will not develop if teachers break their own rules and standards (e.g., socializing with other teachers during "sacred" reading instruction time), choose not to follow inconvenient schoolwide procedures, or are inconsistent in enforcement of a behavior-management plan. Finally, it is important that we realize that conveying authority need not involve threat, intimidation, or intrusiveness. In fact, confrontational styles of communication do little to promote credibility and dependability. Strong leaders convey their authority with tact, subtlety, diplomacy, and even humor. Consider these interpersonal communication guidelines (Curwin & Mendler, 1999; Westling & Koorland, 1988):

- Use positive, calm, controlled, and defined statements when requesting student attention and compliance.
- Be confident, self-assured, and consistent; speak without hostility when delivering consequences.
- Be firm, use a soft voice, and avoid arguing with students.

Reflective Exercise #8
Think of a situation when another person's nonverbal communication appeared in sharp contrast to the words being expressed. How did this situation make you feel? What were your thoughts regarding the honesty and integrity of that individual?

- Let students know that their concerns will be addressed in a timely, caring, and constructive manner.
- Don't embarrass a student in front of peers.

BEING PROFESSIONAL: KEEP THINGS IN PERSPECTIVE

Even with the best of plans and communication strategies, events are going to happen that are frustrating, unfair, and sometimes infuriating. Things will not always go as planned; and like all aspects of life, there will be individuals, both students and colleagues, who appear disillusioned and manipulative. In fact, some of your most challenging situations associated with teaching and behavior management may be people and events peripheral to student misbehavior. For example, teachers may have heated disagreements with colleagues regarding the correct way to meet the academic needs of a student, administrators may fail to support disciplinary actions adequately, and parents may fight well-intentioned efforts to improve a student's academic performance or turn a pattern of inappropriate behavior around.

What can you do to respond in a professional manner? First, be patient, keep things in perspective, and be aware of the big picture. Schools are microcosms of society, and events do not always go as planned or desired. Don't take it personally. Second, remain diplomatic and consider the perspective of the individual causing the disagreement or even the *function* of that person's actions. For example, think about the frustrations experienced by the parent of a student who is repeatedly in trouble at school or the pressures on an administrator who must sort through multiple sources of information related to a disciplinary infraction.

Third, remain poised and try to settle conflicts in ways that are in the best interests of the student. Keep in mind that how you comport yourself during difficult and stressful circumstances is a public display of your competence. Furthermore, your successful navigation through delicate circumstances is a model of behavior for students. Finally, reflect on your own role in the situation. Consider what actions you are taking that may be contributing to the conflict. As Kottler (2002) has aptly observed, we are the primary authors of our own life stories, and we must determine what we are doing to either produce or maintain our disagreements with others.

To link to websites that support and extend the content of this chapter, go to the Web Links module in Chapter 5 of the Companion Website at www.prenhall.com/rosenberg.

SUMMARY

A teacher's major responsibility is to deliver effective instruction in a safe and orderly classroom. To meet this challenge, you must know what to teach, how to apply evidenced-based instructional techniques, and how to choose and implement strategies for managing student behavior.

General Education Curriculum and Tools Used to Adapt Instruction

- State governments are increasing their influence over the development of the curriculum—i.e., the content taught in local schools.
- Most students with disabilities are expected to participate and make progress in some aspects of the general education curriculum.
- Effective teachers use different strategies and tools to adapt curriculum and instruction, including

taxonomies, universal design for learning, planning pyramids, and instructional accommodations.

Major Approaches to Instruction and Systematic Teaching

- Three common approaches for delivering instruction are behavioral, cognitive, and a combination of the two.
- The behavioral approach is most useful for teaching basic skills; cognitive and combined approaches such as the Strategies Intervention Model (SIM) are useful for teaching problem solving and higher-order content.
- Effective teachers make use of evidence-based practices in the areas of instructional grouping, presenting content, providing opportunities for practice, monitoring student progress, and using technology to support instruction.

Systematic, Proactive, and Positive Behavior Management

- Well-planned, supportive lessons will fail if behavior-management concerns are neglected; fortunately, most student misbehavior can be addressed by focusing on inattention to task, crowd control, and general testing of limits.
- Effective teachers make use of three tiers of behavior management:
  - Inclusive classroom management practices focus on the prevention of problem behaviors, including the careful design of the physical environment, the quality of instruction, and the clarity of the management plan.
  - Targeted intervention plans are made available for those students who do not respond positively to the universal interventions.
  - Wraparound interventions are for students whose severe and intractable behaviors require community and interagency intervention.

- Well-designed management plans include five elements: a mission statement; rules, procedures, and supports; consequences for appropriate and inappropriate behavior; a crisis plan; and a document that presents the plan.

Effectively Communicating Instruction and Behavior Management

- Of equal importance to the technical aspects of instruction and behavior management is the manner in which we communicate to students, colleagues, and families.
- Strategies that contribute to effective communication include the development of authentic relationships, civility and respect, conveying appropriate expectations, cultural sensitivity, and maintaining credibility and dependability.
- Keep things in perspective and realize that, even with the best of plans, problems occur. How one behaves during stressful situations is a public display of competence.

 **Council for Exceptional Children** ADDRESSING THE PROFESSIONAL STANDARDS

Council for Exceptional Children (CEC) Knowledge Standards addressed in the chapter:

CC5K1, CC5K2, CC5K3, CC5K4, CC5K6, CC5S10, CC5S13, CC7K1, CC7K3

Appendix B: CEC Knowledge and Skill Standards Common Core has a full listing of the standards referenced here.

PART III

MEETING THE MULTIPLE NEEDS OF STUDENTS WITH EXCEPTIONALITIES: *What Is Effective Practice?*

LEARNING DISABILITIES

6

EMOTIONAL AND BEHAVIORAL DISABILITIES

7

MILD INTELLECTUAL DISABILITIES

8

ATTENTION DEFICIT HYPERACTIVITY DISORDERS

9

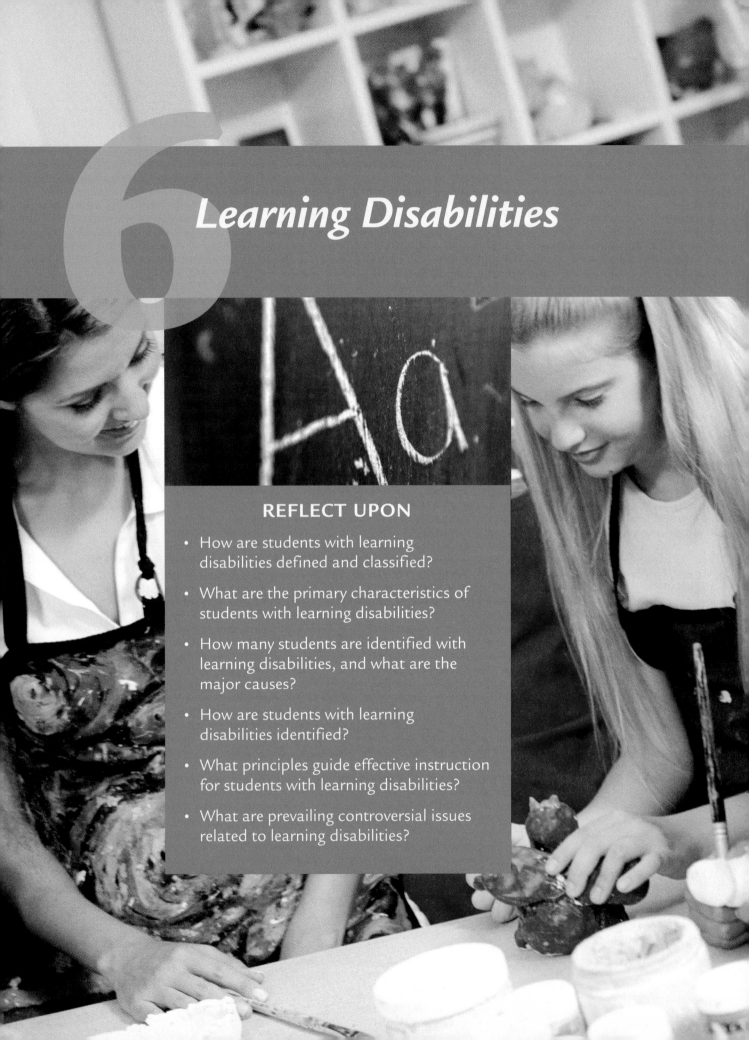

Learning Disabilities

6

REFLECT UPON

- How are students with learning disabilities defined and classified?

- What are the primary characteristics of students with learning disabilities?

- How many students are identified with learning disabilities, and what are the major causes?

- How are students with learning disabilities identified?

- What principles guide effective instruction for students with learning disabilities?

- What are prevailing controversial issues related to learning disabilities?

My Profession, My Story: Carol Sprague

Carol Sprague began teaching after completing an undergraduate degree in elementary education. She loved school as a child, always knew she wanted to be a teacher, and has never questioned her decision to become a teacher. She entered teaching because every day is different and a challenge. Teaching for Carol Sprague is not a job but a career.

Carol has taught at both elementary and secondary levels, as both a general and special education teacher. Many of her assignments have been in inclusive settings. For several years Carol has taught in an inclusive elementary classroom.

A typical day in Carol Sprague's classroom begins with a morning meeting in which students share things that have happened to them, learn to know and appreciate one another socially, and get excited about learning. Throughout the day, she strives to connect academic content across the curriculum and make this information applicable to the students' lives. She asks questions to make these connections as well as to encourage students to think deeply and learn about small things in their lives. Carol goes on to note that learning is more fun for students and the teacher and stu-

dents retain more information if learning is made real for them.

Carol describes her greatest successes as a teacher in relation to individual students. She describes several students, some of whom had learning disabilities, who made significant progress in learning to read during their time in her class and learned to feel successful and confident as readers when they left her class. Interestingly, when asked about the positive impact she has had on her students, she emphasizes the classroom climate and sense of community she has worked to develop. She notes that when she develops a good classroom climate, all students, including low, middle, and high achievers, are supported and make progress in learning the academic content.

An effective teacher for students with learning disabilities, from Carol's perspective, is a teacher who views students as individuals and takes responsibility for each student's learning. She emphasizes

that a lack of academic progress should *never* be viewed as the student's fault. Rather, an effective teacher closely monitors student progress, reflects on her practice, examines what could have been done differently, and adapts instruction until the student does make progress. Carol notes that a large part of meeting students' needs relates to how the teacher organizes instruction. Small groups, cooperative groups, peer tutoring, and related activities provide more individualized instruction that focuses on the specific skills the student needs.

A final quality of an effective teacher that Carol emphasizes relates to the need to understand what children need to learn and monitor their progress as they learn this content. She notes that state standards have been quite helpful in that teachers know what students need to learn and when. She states that an effective teacher systematically monitors student progress toward learning content, especially students who are struggling, and organizes her class to ensure that all students reach benchmarks.

While Carol loves to teach, some aspects of teaching nonetheless frustrate her. Two major sources of frustration are paperwork and giving students grades. She makes every attempt to limit paperwork that doesn't support student learning but has little control over it. However, she does have control over student grades. From her perspective, teachers vary greatly in the criteria they use for grading students, emphasizing some combination of effort, mastery of material, and progress related to others. She recently developed a new report card at her school to ensure that grades were used to support students and clearly communicate with parents. Carol emphasizes that grading should be fair to all students, which means that grading should vary depending on the student's needs.

Carol notes that certain characteristics have helped her continue to improve as a teacher, including the fact that she works hard and doesn't give up easily. She also emphasizes the need for all teachers to continue to learn throughout their educational career. She emphatically states that most "sit and get" professional development has not been useful for her. The source of the most beneficial learning for Carol has come from a network of friends who are also teachers. They meet frequently to discuss teaching issues and how to improve as a teacher. She also notes that she benefited from teaching in a school with a well-developed learning community. This school supported continual teacher learning by providing retreats, time for teachers to plan together, book studies, and so forth.

Carol's advice to a beginning teacher is to view teaching as a career, not just a job. She also encourages new teachers to "find a way to feed yourself and continually learn. The best way to do this is to surround yourself with other teachers who share a similar philosophy, who will challenge and feed off each other."

To learn more about Carol Sprague and to see her in action in the classroom, go to the Ms. Sprague module of the DVD-ROM.

If you think back on your school experience, you will probably remember students who seemed typical on the playground or when you interacted with them socially. However, in the classroom these students struggled greatly to learn academic content in reading or mathematics, resulting in a high level of frustration for both student and teacher. In this chapter, we consider a group of students who, by virtue of their disability, struggle in school and require special supports to make **adequate yearly progress (AYP)** academically, as mandated by NCLB. These students are identified with a learning disability (LD).

Students with learning disabilities are often perplexing to parents and teachers because they have difficulty in some academic areas but not others. This uneven pattern of development is a primary characteristic of these students. Moreover, students with learning disabilities are sometimes said to have a *specific* learning disability because they tend to struggle to learn academic content in one or two specific academic areas and have strengths in other areas (Torgesen, 2002).

What sets these students apart from others in general education classrooms who struggle to learn academic content is that they often continue to struggle, even when given highly effective, intensive instruction, and are typically the lowest of the low achievers in general education classrooms (Fuchs, Fuchs, Mathes, Lipsey, & Roberts, 2002). These students need a highly effective teacher, much like our featured teacher in this chapter, Carol Sprague. Carol's persistence, never-give-up attitude, use of varied grouping strategies, and application of effective instructional strategies are all vital if the needs of students with learning disabilities are to be met and these students are to make adequate yearly progress in core academic areas.

Students with learning disabilities often continue to struggle in certain academic areas, even when given highly effective, intensive instruction.

Reflective Exercise #1
Did you have a student in your classes when you were in school who struggled to learn academic content in a specific content area? How did the student react to these academic struggles? How did you and other students react?

DEFINITIONS AND CLASSIFICATION CRITERIA FOR LEARNING DISABILITIES

DEFINITION OF STUDENTS WITH LEARNING DISABILITIES

For at least the past 40 years, students with learning disabilities have perplexed educators, parents, and researchers. These students, at least superficially, do not seem to differ from their typical peers yet struggle to learn academic content in particular academic areas. Since the passage of the original Individuals with Disabilities Education Act in 1975, children with learning disabilities have been defined and identified based on "unexpectedly" low achievement (Fletcher, Morris, & Lyon, 2003). That is, their measured level of intelligence suggests that they should learn academic content with little difficulty; but for some unexplained reason, they do not readily learn this information.

As we noted in Chapter 4, the most widely accepted definition for learning disabilities has been provided by the U.S. Department of Education in the regulations for P.L. 94–142, the Individuals with Disabilities Education Act:

> A) In general—The term "specific learning disability" means a disorder in one or more of the basic psychological processes involved in understanding or in using language, spoken or written, which disorder may manifest itself in the imperfect ability to listen, think, speak, read, write, spell, or do mathematical calculations.
> B) Disorders included—Such term includes such conditions as perceptual disabilities, brain injury, minimal brain dysfunction, **dyslexia,** and **developmental aphasia.**
> C) Disorders not included—Such term does not include a learning problem that is primarily the result of visual, hearing, or motor disabilities, of mental retardation, of emotional disturbance, or of environmental, cultural, or economic disadvantage. (IDEA 2004, H.R. 1350, Sec. 602 [30])

FAQ Sheet

STUDENTS WITH LEARNING DISABILITIES

Who are they?	• Students with learning disabilities have an intelligence level in the normal range (i.e., above the cutoff for intellectual disabilities) and unexpectedly low achievement in one or more academic areas, most often in reading. • Students with learning disabilities have also been labeled with terms such as dyslexia (reading disability), **dysgraphia** (handwriting or written expression disability), **dyscalculia** (math disability).
What are typical characteristics?	• Low achievement • Inattention/distractibility • Information-processing deficits • Social-skills deficits • Poor motivation • A heterogeneous category
What are the demographics?	• 5.24% of students ages 6 to 17 (approximately 2.58 million) have been identified with learning disabilities. • Approximately 45% of all school-age students with disabilities have a learning disability. • The percentage of the school-age population identified with learning disabilities increased by approximately 14% between 1990 and 2004. • 90% of students identified with learning disabilities have reading problems. • Approximately 75% are male.
Where are students educated?	• 51% of students identified with learning disabilities spend most of the school day in general education classrooms. • The proportion of students with learning disabilities who are educated in highly segregated separate settings declined by approximately 42% between 1990 and 2003.
How are students identified and assessed for intervention?	• Primary criteria for identification are a severe discrepancy between expected and actual achievement levels and exclusion of students who have other disabilities and those who have not had adequate opportunities to learn. • A test of intelligence is used to determine expected achievement level, while a standardized achievement test is used to determine actual achievement level. These tests are compared to determine if a severe discrepancy exists between expected and actual achievement levels. • Curriculum-based measures are used to determine current academic level in classroom curriculum as well as to monitor student progress.
What are the outcomes?	• Reading problems tend to become more severe as students with learning disabilities move through school. • Learning disabilities tend to persist into adulthood. • Many adults with learning disabilities have difficulty finding good employment, living independently, and finding satisfaction in life.

There are four primary components of this definition. First, learning disability is defined as low academic achievement in one or more of several academic areas. Second, it is assumed that these academic problems exist because of some form of psychological processing disorder, which causes a student to have difficulty in acquiring academic knowledge and skills in certain areas. For example, many students with

www.prenhall.com/rosenberg

learning disabilities who have difficulty learning to read have trouble using sound-symbol correspondences to sound out words they have not previously seen, which is referred to as a **phonological processing** problem (Torgesen, 2002).

Third, learning disability is considered to be synonymous with several labels that have been used in the past (perceptual disabilities, brain injury, minimal brain dysfunction) or terms that are presently used by some educators (dyslexia, developmental aphasia). Finally, students with other disabilities (e.g., mental retardation, visual impairment) or who have learning problems because of environmental factors (e.g., living in poverty) are excluded from being identified with a learning disability. This so-called **exclusion clause** is included in the definition to ensure that the primary reason the student has difficulty progressing academically relates to a learning disability and not to another type of disability or to environmental conditions (e.g., poor teaching).

The federal definition of learning disabilities was a model to states in the late 1970s as they developed definitions and identification criteria of their own. In spite of most states' widespread acceptance of the federal definition of learning disability (Ahearn, 2003), there has been much controversy regarding how the definition should be used to identify students with learning disabilities (MacMillan & Siperstein, 2002). This has resulted in significant differences across states in the identification rates for these students and practices that have been characterized as "confusing, unfair, and logically inconsistent" (Gresham, 2002, p. 467). To illustrate, data from the U.S. Department of Education (2006a) reveal that, in 2005–2006, 5.24% of students in the United States were identified with learning disabilities. However, across states, the identification rate varied from 2.18 to 7.66%, with the result that some states (i.e., Iowa, Oklahoma, Rhode Island, District of Columbia) identified twice as many students with learning disabilities as did other states (i.e., Georgia, Kentucky, Louisiana).

In addition to inconsistent identification of students with learning disabilities, another controversial aspect of this category is that students often must fail before they can be identified with a learning disability. This wait-to-fail approach to identification has led to frustration for many educators and parents and a desire to develop an approach to learning disability identification that allows the use of more preventive measures (Ahearn, 2003). These concerns regarding the learning disability definition and identification criteria were significant factors that led to the inclusion of a response-to-intervention approach to identifying students with learning disabilities in IDEA 2004. This approach to identification will be described in more detail in the following section, which addresses classification criteria for identifying students with learning disabilities.

Reflective Exercise #2
Have you been in a class with a student with a learning disability? How did the teacher react to this student's academic difficulty? How did the teacher support the student?

CLASSIFICATION CRITERIA FOR LEARNING DISABILITIES

The passage of IDEA 2004 resulted in significant changes in the criteria and related procedures that may be used to identify students with learning disabilities. In this section, we initially address criteria that are currently used to identify students with learning disabilities in most states. This is followed by a discussion of the changes in classification criteria that were included in IDEA 2004 and how these changes may influence identification criteria in the near future. Finally, we describe an alternative approach to the identification of students with learning disabilities that is allowed by changes in IDEA 2004.

Identification Criteria

Four criteria are frequently used to identify students with learning disabilities. The most widely used criterion is a **severe discrepancy** between how well the student is achieving in an academic area and how well the student is expected to achieve based on ability. (Ability is typically determined by using an intelligence test.) Thus, a student in the fifth grade who has an average level of intelligence (i.e., a measured IQ of 100) and is reading on a second-grade level (as measured by a standardized achievement test) would have a severe discrepancy between expected and actual achievement levels and would most likely meet this severe discrepancy criterion.

viewed as a psychiatric condition requiring clinical intervention, teachers are, arguably, in the best position to identify symptoms since they see students in many social and academic situations.

What does one look for to detect depression in students, and how do we determine risk factors from the moody and emotional behaviors typical of developing children and adolescents? Wright-Strawderman and Lindsay (1996) suggest that teachers be aware of students who manifest extreme and persistent affective disturbances such as a depressed mood, low self-esteem, withdrawal, emotional mood swings, and negative expressions about the future. Teachers should also be aware of significant changes in social behavior and academic performance. Students with depression often have difficulty forming and maintaining relationships with others, and they give little attention to social problem solving. In the academic area, teachers may see changes in energy, with assignments not being completed and increased levels of distractibility. Obviously, any suspicion of suicidal behavior should be addressed immediately.

OTHER BEHAVIORS

Attention Deficits

Students who are inattentive go to great lengths to avoid tasks that require sustained mental effort and concentration, have difficulty staying in their seats, and act hurriedly and unsystematically with little regard for consequences. Seemingly impatient, they blurt out comments, talk out of turn, have short-term memory gaps, and interrupt others excessively (Henley, Ramsey, & Algozzine, 2006; Schworm & Birnbaum, 1989). It is easy to understand how such patterns of behavior, when frequent, intense, and sustained, can be viewed as a behavior disorder. Keep in mind that for some students, attention deficits are severe enough to be considered indications of attention deficit hyperactivity disorder (ADHD). We discuss fully the essential features of ADHD in Chapter 9.

Social Skills Problems

When we speak of social skills deficits, we are referring to shortcomings in social competence. Although it often means different things to different people, social competence is best viewed as a set of interpersonal behaviors that parents, teachers, and students consider important for success. Recent data indicate that students with EBD have consistently and significantly lower social skills than peers with and without disabilities (Wagner, Kutash, Duchnowski, Epstein, & Sumi, 2005). According to Gresham and colleagues (e.g., Gresham, 1988; Gresham, Sugai, & Horner, 2001), there are three types of social skills deficits: skills deficits, performance deficits, and fluency deficits. Students with skills deficits have not acquired the knowledge or skills required to perform the social behavior. In contrast, students with performance deficits have the social skills in their repertoire but, for one reason or another, do not exhibit those behaviors consistently. Either the student does not have the opportunity to perform the behavior, or he or she makes an active decision not to perform the behavior because of particular circumstances (e.g., not motivated to do so, considerable secondary gain in misbehavior, etc.). Finally, fluency deficits are the result of inadequate exposure to models of social skills and/or too few opportunities to rehearse or practice appropriate behaviors.

Being aware of the different types of social skills deficits helps teachers select or design interventions. For example, it would not be effective to teach social skills or behaviors to students who already have them in their repertoires but who actively choose not to use them. It would be better to consider an approach designed to increase the performance of that skill. Similarly, an intervention to increase performance would have limited utility with a student who had not acquired the targeted social skill.

Reflective Exercise #3
What do we mean when we say someone has good social skills? How are such skills learned? Can you think of reasons why some students fail to acquire and perform acceptable social skills?

COGNITIVE AND LEARNING CHARACTERISTICS

In addition to significant problems with social-emotional and behavioral functioning, students with EBD tend to have IQ scores in the low average range, with scores represented disproportionately in the mild developmental disability range. Relatively few students tend to fall in the upper ranges, and verbal subtest scores tend to be higher than performance scores (Kauffman, 2001; Mattison, 2004). Similarly, when compared to the academic profiles of typically developing peers, students with EBD present moderate to severe academic difficulties in multiple areas that do not improve over time. Reports on the academic characteristics of students with EBD (Lane, 2004; Wagner et al., 2005) indicate that they earn lower grades and fail their courses more often than do students in any other disability group. Consequently, they are retained in grade at more than twice the rate (16%) of their general education peers. Dropout rates for students with EBD are a tragic 58.6%, more than three times that of their peers (Osher, Morrison, & Bailey, 2003; Wagner & Blackorby, 1996) (see Figure 7.2).

The presence of academic deficits among students with EBD is not surprising. The students engage in behaviors incompatible with learning—not attending to instruction, disrupting class repeatedly and aggressively, responding impulsively—that ultimately result in academic underachievement. In some cases, students act out to mask their inability to complete difficult tasks. There has also been speculation that the academic deficits of some students with EBD may be the result of concomitant learning disabilities (LD). Although the precise prevalence of concomitance is uncertain, studies of students with EBD have found that between 38 and 75% were also identified as having LD (Mattison, 2004; Rock, Fessler, & Church, 1997).

FIGURE 7.2

STUDENT VOICES: THE CHALLENGES OF HIGH SCHOOL COMPLETION

Why do so many students with EBD fail to complete their high school education? Unfortunately, we know more about the number of students with EBD who leave school than we do about the reasons that precipitate such a devastating decision. To shed some light on the issue, Kortering, Braziel, and Tompkins (2002) surveyed students with EBD to learn why school completion is challenging. In one-on-one interviews with 33 high school students who received special education services, researchers solicited opinions regarding (1) the best and worst parts of school, (2) changes that would help them and others stay in school, and (3) the characteristics of teachers who had helped them learn. What follows is a synthesis of their responses:

- Best classes were those that allowed physical activity, provided vocational tasks (e.g., auto mechanics), and socialization.
- Worst situations were difficult and boring classes as well as frequent negative encounters with teachers.
- Students recognize the importance of education in making a successful transition to adulthood and believe they need more academic supports to acquire high-level content material and strategies for getting along with teachers and peers.
- Students respond best to those teachers who remain positive and who provide individual help, encouragement, and curricular accommodations.

What do we learn from these responses? Clearly, students with EBD have distinct preferences for specific classroom environments and teacher behaviors as well as equally strong feelings about those practices they find aversive. The authors of the study suggest that alterations in the ways we design programs and the manner in which we interact with students would impact rates of school completion.

PREVALENCE, COURSE, AND CAUSAL FACTORS

PREVALENCE

The prevalence, or frequency of occurrence, of students with EBD is less than 1% (0.73%) of the school-age population (U.S. Department of Education, 2004). This represents approximately 473,000 students, 8.2% of all students identified as having a disability. Although this low rate of occurrence has been stable for three decades, many believe that the percentage of students who need services (3–6%) far surpasses the number who actually receive them.

Issues surrounding the prevalence of students with EBD are complex and controversial. Although there is agreement that students with EBD remain underidentified and underserved, there is great concern that certain groups of students are overrepresented. For example, compared to white students, African Americans are approximately 1.7 times more likely to be identified. Native Americans are also overrepresented, while Asian/Pacific Islander and Hispanic students are underrepresented (Coutinho, Oswald, & Forness, 2002). Compounding these racial differences are data indicating that identification rates vary by state and local school district. African American students are twice as likely to be identified as white students in 29 states. Locally, African American students were likely to be overidentified in districts in which they had minority status and underidentified in those districts in which they were a majority (Osher et al., 2004). Keep in mind that disproportional representation is probably the result of many factors (e.g., poverty and family status) and that these factors are not equally distributed across ethnic groups. Consequently, we must be cautious that efforts to achieve equal identification rates do not overlook the need for necessary interventions (Coutinho et al., 2002).

Analyzing several large national databases of students with disabilities in schools, Wagner et al. (2005) found additional demographic data regarding students with EBD:

- More than three fourths of those classified as EBD are boys.
- Students with EBD are more likely than other students to live in households with several risk factors, including poverty, living in a single-parent household, living with an unemployed head of household, and having a peer with a disability.
- Students with EBD are more likely than other students to change schools often.

COURSE OF DISABILITY

The outcomes for students with EBD continue to be among the most dismal of any disability group. Consider the results of several key longitudinal studies summarized by Henderson and Bradley (2004). Although identified later than students with other disabilities, approximately three-quarters of students with EBD get suspended or expelled from school compared with 32.7% of students with disabilities and 22% of students in the general population. This typically leads to excessive involvement with the justice system, with more than a third (34.8%) of students with EBD being arrested during their school years. Among those who drop out, 70% are arrested within 3 years of leaving school.

Unfortunately, things do not get better over time. Over their lifetimes, people with EBD experience high unemployment and occupational adjustment problems. Approximately one half of students with EBD are unemployed 3 to 5 years after leaving school, and only 40% of those with EBD live independently (Corbett, Clark, & Blank, 2002; Wagner, Blackorby, Cameto, Hebbeler, & Newman, 1993). The antisocial behavior from childhood and adolescence remains debilitating and durable. Students with EBD face mental health challenges and incarceration at higher rates than that of any other population, with drug abuse and addiction contributing greatly to these problems (Bullis, 2001; Wagner et al., 1993). Unfortunately, as the problems of individuals with EBD multiply, there are few fiscal and community resources available for treatment (Quinn & Poirier, 2004).

CAUSAL FACTORS

What causes students with EBD to behave in such extreme and disparate ways? Why is one student so active, aggressive, and oppositional and another so anxious, withdrawn, and socially phobic? Are these behaviors a function of heredity, the symptoms of biochemical anomalies, or the result of traumatic events in the past? These are just some of the questions that naturally arise when teachers work with students with EBD. Because the complex behavioral patterns of EBD are a function of interrelated, interacting factors rather than singular events, it is difficult if not impossible to identify definitive causes of the disability. For our purposes, it is more productive to consider the range of influences that may contribute to the cause and maintenance of the disorder (Kauffman, 2001) and then focus on what can be modified.

Biophysical Influences

While a range of possible biophysical factors may influence behavior problems, they are tied together by one common theme: EBD is considered a manifestation of some underlying physiologic disturbance, disease, or disorder. Consider the three major types of biophysical causal factors. *Biochemical abnormalities* refers to disruptions of the body's central nervous system or metabolism. **Brain injury** and *neurological dysfunction* are indications of specific injury or damage to the brain or central nervous system, resulting in improper functioning. *Genetic transmission* refers to the role of heredity in the development of problem behaviors.

Historically, because medical-model explanations fall outside our areas of expertise, special educators have de-emphasized their relevance. In fact, it has been suggested that biophysical explanations of EBD actually create negative expectations for students and are a convenient excuse for why some interventions do not work. For example, you may hear a colleague say, "Of course, I can't get Brad to stop yelling out; he has been diagnosed with brain and central nervous system damage."

How should we view biophysical factors associated with EBD? Obviously, as educators, we must recognize that our responsibility to teach students does not end with the identification of a biophysical causal factor or the prescription of a medical intervention (Kauffman, 2001). However, this does not mean ignoring biophysical factors. Recent advances in the study of psychiatric medications with children have been significant enough to suggest that screening for biophysically based psychiatric problems should be part of educators' assessment and planning repertoire (Konopasek & Forness, 2004).

Psychodynamic Influences

Psychodynamic explanations of EBD center on disturbances among the components of an individual's personality structure. According to the classic work of Redl and Wineman (1957), some children with EBD have underdeveloped or deficient internal, or intrapsychic, structures (e.g., ego, id, superego), making them unable to control their impulses. Others have delinquent structures in which elements of the personality develop adequately but are used to rationalize misconduct. These and other psychodynamic theories provide a structure to understand actions and emotions. However, there is little empirical evidence to support their hypotheses, and they arguably have little utility for classroom teachers.

Familial and Home Influences

In the classic Russian novel *Anna Karenina,* Tolstoy observes that all happy families resemble each other, yet each unhappy family is unhappy in its own way. Clearly, family structure and dynamics influence attitudes, emotions, behaviors, and, to some degree, our happiness. But how much do such factors contribute to the development of EBD? According to Kauffman (2001), most family factors predispose or increase risk but do not alone account for EBD. For example, factors like physical and psychological abuse increase substantially the risk that children will learn from their childhood experiences and view violence as appropriate responses to daily events. Such maltreatment also increases the risk of acquiring many of the characteristics associated with EBD, such as aggression, rule breaking, and depression. However, risk is not synonymous with inevitability. Many children are resilient and remain psychologically healthy even in the most abusive of situations (Feldman, 2000).

Family structural factors such as being a member of a single-parent family or a blended family do not by themselves influence the development of behavior problems. However, when the level of stress increases in the family unit, typical parenting practices are disrupted, and behavior in the home may become inconsistent and unpredictable. Such events can result in an inability to meet the basic psychological needs of children, resulting in behaviors reflective of inadequacy and low self-worth. Household stress can also increase the rate of coercive interactions among family members, with all members of the home engaging in high rates of negative, aggressive, and aversive attempts at control. Not surprisingly, children and adolescents from such environments are at high risk for developing many of the antisocial behaviors associated with EBD (Walker, Severson, & Feil, 1995).

Societal/Environmental Influences

Several radical psychologists of the 1960s, such as R. D. Laing (1967) and Thomas Scheff (1966), asserted that disturbed behavior is a natural reaction to the mad world around us. Moreover, those who do not develop disturbed patterns of behavior are the ones who are truly deviant. Although this is an extreme proposition, let's consider the possibility that the development of emotional and behavior problems is influenced by social and environmental events. First, there are many (e.g., Walker et al., 1996) who contend that our society is caught up in an epidemic of violence—acts including road rage, mean-spirited bullying, sexual harassment, and the use of weapons to settle disagreements—and that this violence is spilling over into the daily lives of our children. Correspondingly, aggressive, antisocial, impulsive, and destructive acts are increasingly typical of students in our schools and classrooms. Second, children with EBD are more likely to live in dilapidated and crowded areas in which they experience extreme rates of poverty, violence, and crime. These types of environments provide far too few positive exemplars of adaptive behavior and contribute to feelings of fear, stress, helplessness, and alienation (Cullinan, 2002).

Third, there is the constant barrage of media influencing the behavior of children and adolescents. In addition to high rates of television viewing, with estimates as high as 35 hours per week for many children, the quality of what is viewed has been linked to social and emotional difficulties. For example, violent programs, some with as many as 20 violent acts per hour, can make children afraid, worried, or suspicious and may increase aggressive behavior. Moreover, television often portrays sexual behavior and the use of alcohol, cigarettes, or drugs in inviting terms (Kidsource, 2000).

Some students, particularly those with multiple risk factors, will react negatively to the disorder and incivility of overcrowded and underresourced schools.

School Influences

Can schools, the social institutions charged with the education and emotional development of young people, contribute to the onset and maintenance of EBD? Unfortunately, the answer is yes, but the extent of the influence often depends on the characteristics of individual students. First, there are some students, particularly those with multiple risk factors, who react negatively to the overcrowding, disorder, vandalism, and incivility found in far too many large, impersonal, comprehensive schools. Clearly these climate factors contribute additional risks to those who enter with vulnerabilities.

www.prenhall.com/rosenberg

Second, although inadvertent, some teachers contribute to risk by being insensitive to students' individuality, providing inadequate instruction, being inconsistent in behavior management, failing to teach and model appropriate social skills, as well as having unreasonable expectations for their students (Kauffman, 2001; Mayer, 2001; Sprague & Walker, 2005). When having lower expectations, teachers treat students differently by staying physically and psychologically distant, assigning less challenging assignments, and providing fewer indications that success is possible to attain. A **self-fulfilling prophecy** occurs, and students behave in ways that meet rather than exceed their teachers' low expectations. With exceedingly high, unreasonable expectations, students become frustrated and depressed because they are unable to meet the standards set by their teachers. Not surprisingly, inappropriate behaviors such as class disruptions, immaturity, and aggression increase when students are given tasks that are too far outside their threshold for success.

Reflective Exercise #4
Now that you have reviewed the range of causal influences associated with EBD, comment on how useful knowledge of such factors would be in your planning of classroom-based interventions.

IDENTIFICATION AND ASSESSMENT

As with the variety of theoretical orientations and classification systems, there are a number of methods for identification and assessment of EBD. Regardless of methods used, the process typically follows a three-step approach: screening, identification, and instructional/behavioral planning.

SCREENING

When screening for EBD, you are determining if a student has the broad set of characteristics suggesting risk for the disability. If the screening is positive, more intensive assessment is necessary to determine the actual presence or absence of the disability. Most teachers, through their daily interactions and observations, informally screen for behavioral difficulties on a regular basis. When inappropriate behavior patterns such as hostility, aggression, and disruptions persist over time and escalate, students are typically referred for a more in-depth examination. Although this informal screening appears practical and straightforward, recognize that it has several shortcomings. First, students who exhibit externalizing and disruptive behaviors are overrepresented, and those with internalizing problems are rarely recognized. Second, teachers vary greatly in their tolerance levels for certain externalizing behaviors. Specifically, teachers with low tolerance levels will likely refer large numbers of students, while those with high tolerance levels will identify few students and actually fail to identify a significant proportion of students at risk (Rosenberg et al., 2004).

To address these limitations, formalize the screening process. One approach is to actively rank students on categories of functioning such as appropriate classroom behavior, social competence, and withdrawal. Those ranked at the problematic extreme ends of the distributions would be considered for additional evaluation. A second, more structured, approach is to use commercially prepared systems of screening such as the Systematic Screening for Behavior Disorders (SSBD) (Walker & Severson, 1992) and the Early Screening Profile (ESP) (Walker, Severson, & Feil, 1995). Both the SSBD and the ESP are multistep screening systems (see Figure 7.3) designed for students between the ages of 3 and 11. Teachers initially rank every student in their classes in terms of their internalizing and externalizing behaviors. The top three students on each list proceed to the second step in which their behaviors are analyzed against typical classroom behavioral standards and expectations. Those who exceed normative criteria proceed to the third step where direct observations are conducted during instruction and independent work periods.

IDENTIFICATION

Those students screened as possibly having EBD are referred to multidisciplinary or child study teams for more intensive evaluation. This evaluation is conducted to determine if there is a disability and, if so, the intensity of special education services

FIGURE 7.3

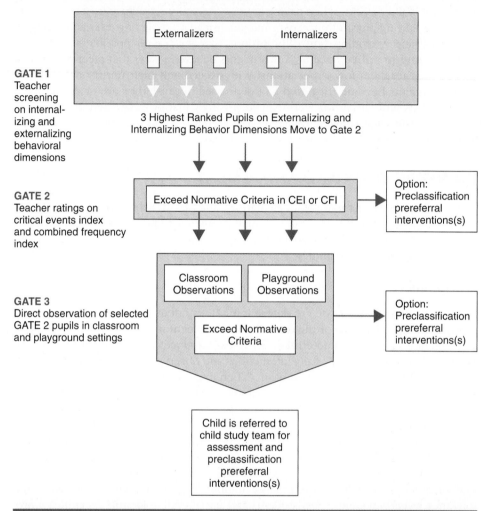

MULTIPLE-STEP SCREENING SYSTEM

Pool of Students in Classroom

GATE 1
Teacher screening on internalizing and externalizing behavioral dimensions

Externalizers   Internalizers

3 Highest Ranked Pupils on Externalizing and Internalizing Behavior Dimensions Move to Gate 2

GATE 2
Teacher ratings on critical events index and combined frequency index

Exceed Normative Criteria in CEI or CFI

Option: Preclassification prereferral interventions(s)

GATE 3
Direct observation of selected GATE 2 pupils in classroom and playground settings

Classroom Observations   Playground Observations

Exceed Normative Criteria

Option: Preclassification prereferral interventions(s)

Child is referred to child study team for assessment and preclassification prereferral interventions(s)

Source: Walker, H. M., Severson, H., Stiller, B., Williams, G., Haring, N., Shinn, M., & Todis, B. (1988). Systematic screening of pupils in the elementary age range at risk for behavior disorders: Development and trial testing of a multiple gating model. *Remedial and Special Education, 9,* 8–14.

necessary for academic and social success. Two types of assessment methods are most often used: behaviorally based methods and personality-oriented methods.

Behaviorally Oriented Methods

Direct measurement using behavior rating scales is the most common method for identifying EBD. Behavior rating scales are relatively easy to administer, can be used repeatedly across settings and sources (teachers, parents, and students), and serve as efficient summaries of different types of behaviors (Elliott & Busse, 2004). Among the more frequently used checklists are the Child Behavior Checklist (CBCL) (Achenbach & Rescorla, 2001), the Walker Problem Behavior Identification Checklist (Walker, 1983), the Behavioral and Emotional Rating Scale (BERS) (Epstein & Sharma, 1998), and the Social Skills Rating System (SSRS) (Gresham & Elliott, 1990).

To illustrate the essential components of behavior rating scales, consider the CBCL, regarded as the most comprehensive and technically sound. There are two forms of the CBCL, one for ages 1.5–5 and one for ages 6–18. In both forms, parents, guardians, or close family members consider 118 problem behaviors and rate how true each item is for their child (see Figure 7.4 for sample items). There are also 20 com-

www.prenhall.com/rosenberg

FIGURE 7.4

ITEMS FROM CBCL

Please print. Be sure to answer all items.

Below is a list of items that describe children and youths. For each item that describes your child **now** or **within the past 6 months,** please circle the **2** if the item is **very true or often true** of your child. Circle the **1** if the item is **somewhat or sometimes true** of your child. If the item is **not true** of your child, circle **0.** Please answer all items as well as you can, even if some do not seem to apply to your child.

0 = Not True (as far as you know) 1 = Somewhat or Sometimes True 2 = Very True or Often True

0 1 2	1. Acts too young for his/her age		0 1 2	32. Feels he/she has to be perfect
0 1 2	2. Drinks alcohol without parents' approval (describe): _____		0 1 2	33. Feels or complains that no one loves him/her
			0 1 2	34. Feels others are out to get him/her
0 1 2	3. Argues a lot			
0 1 2	4. Fails to finish things he/she starts		0 1 2	35. Feels worthless or inferior
0 1 2	5. There is very little he/she enjoys		0 1 2	36. Gets hurt a lot, accident prone
0 1 2	6. Bowel movements outside toilet		0 1 2	37. Gets in many fights
0 1 2	7. Bragging, boasting		0 1 2	38. Gets teased a lot
0 1 2	8. Can't concentrate, can't pay attention for long		0 1 2	39. Hangs around with others who get in trouble
0 1 2	9. Can't get his/her mind off certain thoughts; obsessions (describe): _____		0 1 2	40. Hears sound or voices that aren't there (describe): _____
			0 1 2	41. Impulsive or acts without thinking

Source: Achenbach, T. M., & Rescorla, L. A. (2001). *Manual for the ASEBA school-age forms and profiles.* Burlington: University of Vermont, Research Center for Children, Youth, and Families.

petence items covering the child's activities, social relations, and school performance. The CBCL results in normative comparisons on the broad dimensions of externalizing and internalizing behaviors as well as on several specific factors such as aggression, delinquency, and anxiety/depression.

Personality-Oriented Methods

Although less frequently used in education settings, personality-oriented methods remain prevalent among clinicians who work with children and adolescents. When measuring a personality, the goal is to capture how an individual thinks, behaves, and feels across situations and over periods of time. There are two major categories of personality measurement: objective and projective (Cullinan, 2002). Objective instruments, such as the Piers-Harris Self-Concept Scale (Piers & Harris, 1984) present items in a standard fashion, use a protocol for scoring, and employ normative data to determine the presence of a disability. Projective measures, such as the Rorschach Ink-Blot test (Rorschach, 1932) require that individuals interpret or project meaning onto ambiguous pictures, images, or statements. Interpretations of responses are believed to reveal an individual's innermost thoughts, feelings, needs, and motives. These methods can yield interesting information about students. However, be aware that the technical adequacy of these instruments, particularly in the areas of validity and reliability, is questionable. For example, the self-report nature of certain test items makes them susceptible to demand or social desirability effects: Students may wish to please or shock an examiner. Also, the heavy reliance on subjective clinical judgment in the scoring of the projective tests limits the consistency of test-result interpretations.

INSTRUCTIONAL/BEHAVIORAL PLANNING

The measurement of student performance for instructional and behavioral planning is arguably the most important aspect of the assessment process. Following the determination of EBD, this process involves the identification of instructional and behavioral problems as well as the generation of a plan to address them. The most effective

Highly Effective Instructional Strategies

THE FUNCTIONAL BEHAVIORAL ASSESSMENT (FBA)

The logic behind conducting an FBA is that much of an individual's behavior is supported by the environment, occurs within a particular context, and serves a specific purpose. Specifically, we all behave in ways to satisfy needs or achieve desired outcomes. In most situations appropriate methods are used to get what is wanted. However, some students, particularly those with EBD, use extreme, inappropriate methods to reach their goals. Students who employ disruptive and unproductive behaviors typically require guidance in seeking alternative ways, or *replacement behaviors,* to address their legitimate social and academic needs. The planning for this type of intervention requires the development of an FBA.

FBAs are most useful when you consider the following. First, behaviors, both appropriate and inappropriate, are learned and can be reduced (Chandler & Dahlquist, 2002). Second, all behaviors are purposeful. There is a reason why the individual is engaging in a behavior. Since many behaviors arise from and are maintained by environmental factors, FBAs allow us to determine those factors that influence an individual's behaviors.

Third, multiple behaviors can serve one function; and correspondingly, one behavior can serve multiple functions. For example, a student may sit for 5 or 10 minutes; begin to fidget, doodle, get up to sharpen a pencil, and talk with others on the way back to the table; and openly defy attempts to redirect him to his assignment. These multiple behaviors may have one purpose: to escape difficult or confusing work. One behavior can also have multiple purposes: A student may loudly defy a teacher's attempts to have her complete an assignment, which may result in a referral to the office. The purpose of student's behavior may be to escape difficult work and gain an opportunity to chat with other students and even staff about pleasant topics. Finally, an FBA is most effective when members of a team collaborate in assessing the behavior, planning the intervention, and evaluating the treatment.

Effective FBAs can be developed by following a user-friendly, six-step process (Center for Effective Collaboration and Practice, 1998; McConnell, Hilvitz, & Cox, 1998; Ryan, Halsey, & Matthews, 2003; Shippen, Simpson, & Crites, 2003):

- *Step 1: Describe and verify the seriousness of the problem.* Judge the significance of the behavior problem by considering (a) if the student's behavior differs significantly from classmates, (b) whether the behavior is

Reflective Exercise # 5
Although most agree they provide a wealth of information about behavior, FBAs are not used with great frequency. What factors contribute to their limited use by teachers? What can be done to increase their use?

and comprehensive method for instructional/behavioral planning is a functional behavioral analysis (FBA). As described in the "Highly Effective Instructional Strategies" feature, the FBA allows us to identify many of the events, activities, and situations associated with a student's problem behaviors and, more important, to make environmental adjustments that can alter the frequency of such behaviors. FBAs provide essential information to establish relevant instructional and behavioral goals and to test interventions that are hypothesized to facilitate the achievement of those goals. Clearly, awareness of setting events, antecedents, and consequences help identify the functions of the problem behaviors and assist in the development of effective and efficient intervention plans (Gable, Hendrickson, & Van Acker, 2001).

EDUCATIONAL PRACTICES

Several **evidence-based educational practices** are recommended for addressing the instructional and behavioral needs of students with EBD. We begin with the controversial area of service delivery and then focus on several of the more common interventions and techniques that, regardless of setting, are successful in improving academic and social/behavioral performance.

SERVICE DELIVERY

Students with EBD are educated in restrictive settings more often than any other students with disabilities. In fact, approximately one third of all students with EBD between the ages of 6 and 21 spend more than 60% of their time outside of general chronic and a threat to others, and (c) if the behavior is an excess or deficiency rather than a cultural difference.

- *Step 2: Refine the definition of the problem behavior.* Narrow the defining characteristics of the problem behavior by noting (a) the times when the behavior occurs, (b) where the behavior occurs and who is present, (c) the conditions (e.g., during large-group instruction, during unstructured time) in which the behavior occurs, (d) events and conditions that occur both before and after the behavior, and (e) common setting events (e.g., when late to school, after missing breakfast).

- *Step 3: Collect information on the environment, setting demands, and possible functions of the problem behavior.* Employ multiple methods to collect information on the behavior and the student, including review of records and academic products interviews with parents and relevant school personnel, and direct observations. Describe the environment, the time, and what is expected of the student. Characterize the behavior by function—getting something such as attention, revenge or avoiding something such as difficult assignments or interactions with certain peers—or whether the problem is a skill deficit (not knowing how to behave) or a performance deficit (knowing how to behave but not performing it under specific conditions).

- *Step 4: Analyze the information.* Synthesize the data collected, focusing on the sequence of observed behaviors.

- *Step 5: Generate hypothesis statement and plan for replacement behaviors.* Develop a concise summary of information, focusing on factors surrounding the student's behavior and including both the antecedents and consequences. The hypothesis is a best guess as to why the behavior is occurring.

- *Step 6: Develop, implement, and evaluate intervention plan.* Develop an intervention plan that includes positive behavior-change strategies, program modifications, and behavior supports necessary to address the problem behavior. Remember that the plan should directly address replacement behaviors, those functionally equivalent actions that allow students to meet their needs but in a more socially acceptable manner. Implement the plan with fidelity and collect data consistently on the targeted behavior in order to evaluate the efficacy of your intervention plan.

Keep in mind that an FBA is a process rather than a fixed, single set of procedures, forms, and instruments. In fact, it is best if all possible sources of information are considered. By relying on both formal assessment techniques and indirect information-gathering strategies (e.g., interviews with students and parents, rating scales) teachers have a higher probability of getting at those conditions that both trigger and sustain a student's challenging behaviors (Fox & Gable, 2004).

TEACHER PREP

MERRILL
PRENTICE HALL

Activity: Go to the Video Classroom section of the Teacher Prep website, click on Special Education and then module 7: Emotional and Behavioral Disorders. Watch video 1 and answer the following questions. Think about how you might use the concepts of an FBA with young children.

education classes in their neighborhood schools, 11.1% are served in separate day treatment facilities like the one Bill Addison teaches in, and 1.4% are educated in their homes or in hospitals (Henderson & Bradley, 2004).

What are the implications of these data? Educators continue to debate how best to deliver the variety of special services needed by students with EBD. The debate is the result of the tension between the desire to provide essential services and the need to maintain these students in the least restrictive environment. As we have noted elsewhere in this text, the rationale for inclusive education is compelling. All children, even those with challenging behaviors, should garner the benefits of inclusive programming (e.g., attending one's neighborhood school, interacting with appropriate peer role models, participating in shared content-rich educational experiences). Unfortunately, the intense needs of many students with EBD make such programming challenging if not unrealistic. Teachers often believe they lack the expertise and skills to address the extreme behaviors of these students. Moreover, it has been argued (e.g., Kauffman, Bantz,

Techniques that can facilitate the inclusion of students with EBD include cooperative learning and peer tutoring.

Reflective Exercise #6
Students with EBD present many behaviors that general education teachers feel unprepared to manage. How do you feel about students with extreme problem behaviors being included with the general population of students? **To hear students like you discuss this topic, go to the Students to Students module on the DVD-ROM and click on clip 6: EBD.**

& McCullough, 2002) that education provided in separate settings more effectively addresses the intensive needs of some students with EBD (e.g., support, individualization, and monitoring) than does education delivered in the typical environment. The consensus in the field is that students with EBD require individually tailored programs that make use of the full continuum of placement and service options.

There are a series of activities that can maximize efforts to support students with EBD in less restrictive classroom environments. From a schoolwide perspective, co-teaching by general and special education teachers, adult mentors and peer facilitators, flexibility in training, integration of socials skills instruction into curriculum, and opportunities for out-of-school activities have facilitated the inclusion of students with challenging behaviors. Specific in-class curricular techniques that are effective tools for inclusion include **self-management,** cooperative learning, peer tutoring, and problem-solving training (Guetzloe, 1999; Shapiro, Miller, Sawka, Gardill, & Handler, 1999).

EARLY INTERVENTION

There is almost universal agreement that early childhood is the most opportune time to intervene in the challenging behaviors associated with EBD (Kendziora, 2004). Although many developing young children exhibit episodic troublesome behaviors, approximately 4 to 6% of preschool-age children have serious emotional and behavioral issues that require immediate and intensive action. Consider what happens without intervention. Left unserved, young children with EBD attend, participate, and learn less than their peers and have difficulty being accepted by both classmates and teachers. Not unexpectedly, their difficulties stabilize or escalate, and they are frequently held back in early grades (Raver & Knitze, 2002).

For early intervention efforts to succeed, young children with EBD must be provided with environments that teach and actively support prosocial behaviors. Consequently, programs typically focus on two areas: (1) center-based programs address the child's acquisition of cognitive skills required for appropriate social behavior and (2) home-based programs provide families with strategies to promote and maintain appropriate behavior. Reviews of center-based, home-based, and combined alternatives indicate that five factors affect program outcomes (Kendziora, 2004; Ramey & Ramey, 1998):

Home-based early intervention programs provide families with the skills and support to develop and maintain their child's appropriate behavior during key developmental stages.

- *Developmental timing.* Programs started early in a child's development result in the most benefit.
- *Program intensity.* Programs with higher concentrations of home and center contact time produce larger positive developmental outcomes than do less intensive alternatives.
- *Direct delivery of instruction.* For acquisition of cognitive skills, direct instruction to the child is more effective than indirect methods of instruction (e.g., teaching parents to provide social skills instruction).
- *Breadth of program.* Programs that include a wide range of services (e.g., education, health, social services) are more effective than alternatives with a narrow focus.
- *Maintenance of outcomes.* Without environmental supports, program benefits are lost.

Three factors limit the success of early intervention for students with EBD (Conroy, Hendrickson, & Hester, 2004; Kendziora, 2004). First, there is no universal, systematic screening program to identify those who would benefit from early intervention

Site Visit:
Effective Practices in Action

FIRST STEPS TO SUCCESS

First Steps to Success is a collaborative, highly structured school and home early intervention program that focuses on the prevention and remediation of emerging antisocial behavior patterns among kindergarten students at risk for falling behind age-grade peers. Developed by Hill Walker and colleagues (1998) at the University of Oregon, the program is designed to help young children develop friendships, respond appropriately to adult expectations, and experience success at school. A secondary goal of the program is to divert students who are already showing antisocial behaviors from developing EBD.

The program consists of three interrelated components. First, children in kindergarten are screened and identified for indications of antisocial behavior patterns. The second component, the School Intervention Module, is a 30-day, consultant-based intervention designed to directly teach academic readiness and social skills. Performance criteria for each day must be met, or the activities for that day are repeated. During the initial days of the program the consultant models behavior-change techniques, gradually fading their direction as the teacher acquires the skills. Components of the program include awarding praise and points consistent with program guidelines and communicating with parents regarding student performance. Following intervention, points are faded, and students are rewarded primarily with praise and expressions of approval.

In the third component—home intervention—consultants make weekly home visits to teach parents and caregivers how to maximize their child's chances for success in school. Over the course of 6 weeks, parents use lesson plans, games, and structured activities to address six skill areas:

- Communication and sharing in school
- Cooperation
- Limits setting
- Problem solving
- Friendship making
- Development of confidence

Do the outcomes required of First Steps to Success merit the intensity of effort required of parents, teachers, and consultants? Reviewing the available research, Conroy et al. (2004) concluded that there is ample empirical evidence to support the use of the program. Perhaps the most impressive outcomes of the program are that positive results attained by students maintain over time and teachers are likely to continue using elements of the program in their instructional routines.

programs. Who gets selected for services is often a function of highly variable eligibility criteria of community social service programs or the clinical judgment of health care professionals. Second, the majority of students identified for early intervention tend to be children with externalizing behavior problems. Although large numbers of students suffer from internalizing problems such as anxiety and depression, manifestations of these problems tend not to bother others and remain largely ignored. Finally, because young girls tend to exhibit fewer externalizing behavior problems, they tend to be underrepresented in early intervention programs. However, in later years, a higher proportion does act out, in part because of internalizing problems developed in early childhood. Arguably, early intervention efforts could have altered the development of these behaviors.

ACADEMIC AND SOCIAL/BEHAVIORAL INTERVENTIONS

Although the selection of specific interventions should be driven by the results of an individual student's FBA, certain practices have a history of effectiveness for students with EBD. Several common interventions for both academic and social/behavioral deficits are highlighted here.

Academic Interventions

With extreme social and emotional behaviors being the defining characteristics of the disability, it is not surprising that little attention is paid to the academic needs of students with EBD. This lack of attention is prevalent in classrooms—some teachers in self-contained EBD settings devote only 30% of the school day to instruction—as well as in many teacher preparation programs (Wehby, Lane, & Falk, 2003). Comprehensive reviews of academic interventions (e.g., Coleman & Vaughn, 2000; Lane, 2004; Pierce, Reid, & Epstein, 2004) indicate that both teachers and peers can contribute to efforts that improve the academic performance. Specific teacher-based actions, typically guided by the results of an FBA, include consideration of task difficulty, instructional modifications, learning strategies, providing choices, and content enhancements. Peer-mediated approaches include structured tutoring programs in which higher-performing readers are paired with their lower-performing classmates to supplement reading instruction.

Consider how these techniques come together in the classroom. Employing the results of a functional assessment, Penno, Frank, and Wacker (2000) applied several accommodations that resulted in both improved academic productivity and reduced behavior problems among several students who exhibited severe and chronic behavior problems. Among the accommodations employed for the adolescent boys during their reading and math assignments were (1) working with a peer tutor, (2) shortened work assignments, (3) self-monitoring worksheets, and (4) completing assignments on the computer. Before the application of the academic supports, the students' high rates of inappropriate behavior were due to a desire to escape from difficult academic tasks. By making assignments less aversive to the students and easier to accomplish, discernible changes in academic performance and classroom behavior were observed.

Social/Behavioral Interventions

Behavioral Techniques. The most common approaches for addressing the social/behavioral needs of students with EBD involve the simultaneous strengthening and reducing of targeted behaviors through the use of behavioral techniques. Techniques exclusively intended to reduce or eliminate challenging behaviors are often ineffectual because they fail to strengthen appropriate replacement behaviors. To avoid this situation, behavioral interventions are typically dynamic, simultaneously strengthening appropriate behavior as they weaken the challenging behaviors.

The **token economy** is the behavioral technique that best manages the gamut of behaviors associated with EBD as well as incorporates the range of techniques used to increase and decrease behavior. The fact that more than 90% of teachers of students with EBD use some form of token economy is testament to its acceptance and efficacy (Rosenberg et al., 2004). The classic study by O'Leary and Becker (1967) illustrates why these procedures are replicated in many of our classrooms today. In their study, tokens were awarded for intervals of time in which students acted appropriately (i.e., did not disrupt classroom activities); inappropriate behaviors were ignored. Disruptive behaviors decreased from a baseline of 76% of the time intervals to 10% of the intervals following introduction of the token economy.

Can You Help Me with This Student?

IMPROVING RATES OF PARTICIPATION AND ACADEMIC SUCCESS

Ms. LoDucca could sense that Taquon, a 12-year-old student with EBD in her sixth-grade math class, was going to have another bad day. When she assigned independent seatwork, Taquon was again engaging in a series of disruptive and oppositional behaviors. After taking a quick look at the fraction problems, he tried to engage his neighbor, Corey, in an argument over which basketball team would win the NBA championship. When directed to return to work, Taquon swore under his breath and began to doodle on his worksheet. After a few moments, Taquon put his head on the desk and screamed for all to hear that he was "on strike," refusing to do any work involving fractions. Although on strike, Taquon continued to speak out loudly and inappropriately. Ms. LoDucca was at a loss; during the past few weeks, she had assigned Taquon to the time-out area, withheld recess, and sent him to the office with a disciplinary referral. None of this seemed to get him back on task.

This situation represents an unfortunate yet familiar scene in classrooms serving students with EBD. One accommodation that has demonstrated considerable promise in addressing these problems is offering students choice-making opportunities. Here is how the technique is implemented:

- The student who is not participating is provided with two or more options regarding the completion of an assignment, allowed to independently select an option, and then provided with that option.
- Choices are provided either before or during the task. Students like Taquon may be provided with the opportunity to decide when they will begin their assignment, if they will require any mini-breaks during the assignment, the number and order of problems to be completed, and under what kind of conditions they would like to complete the task (e.g., type of writing utensil, color of paper, area of room to move desk).
- Teachers reinforce that choice making allows the student to see that positive outcomes are possible when they honor their choices.

Providing students with choices has benefits. First and foremost, the available research indicates that it increases academic achievement and reduces inappropriate behaviors. Second, the use of the technique improves the classroom climate with enhanced teacher-to-student and student-to-student relationships. Finally, the technique allows students with EBD to assert decision-making power in the classroom, a process that increases the motivation to succeed.

For more information on applying choice making to academic activities, consult the following resource prepared by Jolivette and colleagues.

Jolivette, K., McCormick, K. M., & Lingo, A. S. (2004). Embedding choices into the daily routines of young children with behavior problems: Eight reasons to build social competence. *Beyond Behavior, 13*(3), 21–26.

EXTEND AND APPLY

- Why does choice making improve student participation in class activities?
- In general, having the opportunity to make choices provides predictability, consistency, and, most important, a sense of control over behavior. Unfortunately, students like Taquon do not always see relationships between their actions and environmental events. Can you think of other student behaviors that can be improved through choice-making opportunities?
- What types of choices would be appropriate to present to students in those situations?

Activity: Go to the Video Classroom section of the Teacher Prep website, click on Classroom Management, and then module 5: Maintaining Appropriate Student Behavior. Watch video 1 and answer the accompanying questions. Think about how the teacher in the video is providing his students with choices in this situation.

In some circumstances, token economies are complemented by a *levels system,* a structure in which students progress through varying token or point-based systems as their behavior changes. As the student moves to a higher level, expected behaviors and responsibilities typically increase in difficulty and/or demand; correspondingly, potential privileges also increase. In many settings for students with EBD, progression through levels continues until the behaviors suggest that movement to a less restrictive environment is warranted.

Teaching Self-Control.   The ultimate goal of any intervention is for a student to regulate his or her own behavior independently. How do we move students to such levels of independence? Self-control is one technique that has demonstrated positive outcomes, allowing students with EBD to assume larger roles in their behavior change efforts. Most self-control programs consist of three components: self-assessment, goal setting, and self-determination of reinforcement (Polsgrove & Smith, 2004). In self-assessment, a student reflects on his or her own behavior and recognizes that the behavior of interest is inadequate or inappropriate. The student then recognizes the behaviors required, sets goals, and selects strategies that help regulate behavior. Finally, through the process of self-determination, the student evaluates his or her performance and considers the nature and scope of reinforcement that should be received for performance of the target behavior.

TECHNOLOGY FOR ACCESS

USING PALM PILOTS TO HELP STUDENTS SELF-MONITOR

Many adolescents with EBD have difficulty finding success during their academic careers and after they leave school. Many of these difficulties have been linked to a lack of self-control rather than a lack of vocational knowledge or cognitive ability. One strategy that has been successful in improving social behaviors is self-monitoring. Unfortunately, many students with EBD are resistant to intrusive behavior interventions that make them appear different from their peers; others find it particularly difficult to reflect on their own behavior using traditional pen-and-paper methods.

The use of handheld computers shows promise in supporting self-monitoring for such students. During a 12-week intervention, Kramer (2004) taught eight adolescent males with EBD to monitor their behavior using handheld computers such as Palm Pilots. The handheld computers were programmed to sound a signal every 10 minutes that would prompt students to answer if they were performing five prosocial behaviors, including respecting peers and following directions. The devices were included in one class and gradually introduced into a total of three classes over the length of the study. By the end of the intervention phase, all of the participants were two to four times more likely to demonstrate the targeted behaviors. An unexpected benefit was that, after the 3rd week of the study, social behaviors increased in classes where the handheld devices were not present. This trend intensified over the duration of the study; and by the study's conclusion, the social skills demonstrated in the intervention and nonintervention classes were nearly equal. Additionally, the students were able to maintain the positive behavior change in all classes as the use of the handheld devices was faded and eventually discontinued.

Why did the students improve in such dramatic fashion? For the most part, the use of the handheld devices reduced the resistance to behavior-change interventions common among students with EBD. All of the participants reported that they enjoyed using the handheld computers and preferred it to being verbally reminded by staff members, suggesting that the intervention device was considered socially appropriate by the students. The students' feedback and improvement in social skills performance suggest that the infusion of technology into self-monitoring is a potentially powerful method to increase student participation and appropriate behavior.

Note: Charles Kramer contributed to this feature.

Social Skills Instruction.   Since large numbers of students with EBD have social skills deficits, logic dictates that direct instruction in behaviors associated with social competence should be a priority. Social skills instruction activities typically include (1) identification of social skills needing improvement, (2) modeling and explaining the identified skills, (3) providing opportunities for practice while being coached, (4) delivering feedback and reinforcement during practice, and (5) identifying real situations where the skills can be applied (Kavale, Mathur, & Mostert, 2004).

How do we actually teach social skills? Many teachers look first to commercially prepared social skills curricula. Two of the more popular treatment packages are AC-CEPTS (A Children's Curriculum for Effective Peer and Teacher Skills) (Walker et al., 1983) and the Skillstreaming series (Goldstein & McGinnis, 1997; McGinnis & Goldstein, 1997). In both programs specific skills are clustered in groups or domains (e.g., dealing with feelings, friendship-making skills, coping skills), and instructional sequences for teaching the skills are provided. It is extremely useful to know what to look for when selecting a social skills curriculum. Sugai and colleagues (Carter & Sugai, 1989; Sugai & Lewis, 1996) suggest that a program should include instructional components such as direct instruction, modeling, coaching, reinforcement, and positive practice. Moreover, one should ensure that the program includes assessment instruments and has the flexibility to address the needs of individual students as well as small groups. Finally, one should consider the level of training needed to administer the program, the cost of the program, and the emphasis placed on generalization and maintenance of program outcomes.

Teachers who design their own methods and activities for teaching social skills often make use of instruction in replacement behaviors (also known as the teaching of alternative behaviors). **Replacement behaviors** are a series of actions that achieve the same intent as the problem behaviors (Neel & Cessna, 1990). Determining what behaviors to replace is very similar to conducting an FBA. We first determine the intent or functions of the inappropriate behaviors and then focus our instructional efforts on teaching appropriate ways to achieve the desired outcomes. Subsequent instruction focuses on when and under what conditions students are to perform the replacement behaviors (Meadows & Stevens, 2004).

Life-Space Interview.   The **life-space interview (LSI)** is a technique used when students with EBD are in crisis or in response to severe acting out and violent behaviors. Originally developed as a therapeutic tool to aid in the rehabilitation of students in residential treatment programs, LSI is based on the assumption that verbal mediation following an extreme behavioral event can result in enduring behavioral change. Consider the logic of the approach. When students with EBD are in crisis or engaged in intense emotional acting-out situations, their perception of reality is distorted, and they are in need of emotional support. At such times, the usual impenetrable defensive barriers to behavioral change are weakened, and the student is unusually open to intervention. At such times therapeutic actions can accomplish two major goals: Emotional First Aid on the Spot (EFAS) and Clinical Exploitation of Life Events (CELE) (Redl & Wineman, 1957). Specific activities associated with each of these goals are highlighted in Figure 7.5.

Keep in mind that, while the use of LSI has considerable intuitive appeal, there are logistical challenges that can limit its applicability to certain settings. First, LSI is

Reflective Exercise #7
Many social skills interventions have resulted in only modest improvements and limited generalization across settings. What factors contribute to the poor showing of social skills teaching efforts? Can you think of strategies that can enhance our efforts to teach social behaviors that generalize and maintain over time?

At times of crisis the usual impenetrable defensive barriers to behavioral change among students with EBD are weakened and unusually open to intervention.

FIGURE 7.5

COMPONENTS OF THE LSI

The goals of the LSI are predicated on the psychodynamic assumption that intensive emotional life events and crises can be opportunities to influence a student's behavior. Developed by Fritz Redl and David Wineman (1957), these techniques have been applied in a range of educational and clinical settings serving students with EBD. The first goal—emotional first aid on the spot—is a series of short-term procedures designed to prevent excessive damage caused by delusional perceptions accompanying the crisis situation. Specific actions include the following:

- *Drain off frustration.* Encourage the student to vent anger and hostility in an acceptable way.
- *Support the management of panic, fury, and guilt.* Help the child put things back into perspective with a minimum of guilt over the outburst.
- *Communication maintenance.* Sustain meaningful interactions to prevent the child's withdrawal into a fantasy world.
- *Regulate behavioral and social traffic.* Remind the student that rules were broken and that there are consequences for such actions.
- *Provide umpire services.* Assist and reinforce the student's efforts at self-control and decision making.

The clinical exploitation of life events is the process of using the student's current outburst or crisis for the purpose of long-term therapeutic gain. Key techniques for exploiting these events include the following:

- *Reality rub-in.* Stress the facts surrounding the current behavioral situation and dispel the denial and/or delusional misinterpretation presented by the student.
- *Symptom estrangement.* Stress that inappropriate actions have limited secondary gain and that there are many negative consequences associated with the presenting behaviors.
- *Massaging numb value areas.* Reach out to seemingly dormant value areas in the student to develop a sensitivity to the feelings of others.
- *New tool salesmanship.* Assist the student to develop new coping skills to replace counterproductive inappropriate behaviors.
- *Manipulation of boundaries of self.* Help students see how their behaviors affect others in the immediate environment.

---

time-consuming and requires considerable coordination of efforts. Because it is essential that the LSI be conducted immediately at the time of the situation and be administered by a trained individual who is familiar with the student, staffing patterns must allow for flexibility in scheduling and coverage of classrooms. Second, teachers who conduct LSIs often uncover complex problems, many of which contain deep-seated psychological issues that are beyond the scope of school or classroom interventions and require clinical expertise.

Wraparound Services. Due to the extreme, pervasive, and multifaceted nature of problems faced by students with EBD, a highly structured, coordinated, and integrated system of service delivery is often necessary. As we noted in Chapter 5, the term *wraparound* is used to describe service coordination because it reflects that intervention plans are family- and child-centered. Wraparound is not a specific program or type of service but a definable planning process that results in a unique set of community services and supports designed to meet the unique needs of children and families (Burns & Goldman, 1998). Teachers involved in this process embrace families as full partners in the intervention process and stay involved with the range of service providers both within and outside of the school system.

What does it take to integrate wraparound services in schools? Eber, Sugai, Smith, and Scott (2002) recommend that school-based teams do the following:

- *Engage in initial conversations with family.* Family members discuss their ideas, values, views, frustrations, and dreams regarding their child. The

www.prenhall.com/rosenberg

information accessed assists in developing interventions that relate directly to the goals of the family.

- *Focus on student strengths and articulate a mission.* Develop a strength profile of the child across multiple life domains and construct a mission statement focusing on what the team is to accomplish.
- *Identify and prioritize needs.* Summarize the needs of student and family and develop goals that help the student function effectively in the school and community. Prioritize the goals, allowing those with greatest direct responsibility (e.g., teachers, family members) to have most impact on the list.
- *Develop an action plan and assign tasks.* List the steps to address the prioritized needs and note the persons responsible for implementing the task to completion.
- *Monitor, evaluate, and refine.* Review and evaluate actions proposed at previous meetings. If needs have not been met to the team's satisfaction, reexamine available data and revise the plan.

TRANSITION TO ADULT LIFE CONSIDERATIONS

Previously in this chapter we discussed the dismal postschool outcomes for students with EBD. When compared to peers with and without disabilities in longitudinal studies, these students underperform in nearly every important transition to adulthood variable. Initially, the employment outcomes experienced by young adults with EBD are comparable to those achieved by the general population of young adults leaving school. Both groups find relatively low-status, high-turnover jobs, and approximately 60% are employed at any given time. Four to five years after leaving school, however, the general population of young adults makes a significant shift to higher-status, family-wage jobs, an indicator of being on a stable career path. Young adults with EBD typically do not make this same upward shift. The following interventions can alter this situation and assist students to make a more successful transition to adulthood.

Vocational Education and Work Experience

Recent reviews of the research (Cheney & Bullis, 2004; Sample, 1998; Sitlington & Nuebert, 2004) indicate that vocational education and work experience, alone or in combination, are linked to positive postschool outcomes for students with EBD. Vocational education, one of the more common interventions for adolescents with EBD, is effective because it centers on the development of work-based competencies such as occupational skills, interpersonal skills, technological literacy, and employability skills associated with particular occupations. The impact of interpersonal skills in the workplace should not be underestimated: surveys of employers indicate that social skills, working as members of teams, and the absence of antisocial behaviors are major factors in the retention of employees (Heal & Rusch, 1995). Paid work experience during high school, particularly when combined with vocational education, decreases dropout rates and has a significant positive impact on postschool earnings. There is no substitute for the real-life experiences gained through placements in work settings (Bullis, 2001). In fact, students with EBD who work while in school continue to be workers once they leave school.

Supported Employment and Service Learning

Supported employment is a process in which a vocational specialist assists students in finding an appropriate job and then provides on-the-job coaching in the skills necessary for success in the work environment (Inge & Tilson, 1994). To meet the intensive needs of students with EBD, the role of the vocational specialist, or job coach, often goes beyond workplace issues and includes a full range of case-management activities. Specifically, the vocational specialist must have knowledge of and facilitate collaboration among social service agencies, juvenile justice personnel, schools, and potential employers. The ultimate goal of supported employment for students with

EBD is to help them succeed in paid employment and begin achieving personal goals that lead to success in the community (Lehman, 1992).

Another option for providing work experience is service learning. **Service learning** consists of (1) direct experience in working with communities or organizations that promote the public good and (2) lessons that allow for reflection of the experiences, with particular emphasis on how the service benefits both the community and the student. Because students with EBD have limited social skills, a high need for structure, and tendencies to think of self rather than others, service-learning projects need to be designed carefully. Activities need to be organized and well supervised as well as provide opportunities for students to develop and practice intrapersonal and interpersonal skills (Frey, 2003; Muscott, 2000).

Family and Demographic Factors

Keep in mind that, while the interventions just discussed are powerful, they do not alone account for successful transitions to adulthood. Students with EBD who have involved parents and families make the transition to adulthood with greater speed and effectiveness than do those whose parents are not active in the process. Also, demographic and socioeconomic characteristics such as family socioeconomic position, minority status, suburban living environment, low unemployment rate in the local labor market, and gender are also associated with success after high school (Wagner, D'Amico, Marder, Newman, & Blackorby, 1992).

PREVAILING ISSUES, CONTROVERSIES, AND IMPLICATIONS FOR THE TEACHER

Although great strides have been made in delivering services to those with EBD, some critical issues continue to challenge the field. Three of the more pressing issues—physical restraint, medication, and delivering on the national agenda—are discussed here.

PHYSICAL RESTRAINT

Reflective Exercise #8
How do you feel about the possibility of having to use physical restraint with one of your students? What preparation do you believe you would need to safely restrain a student who had lost control of himself or herself?

Should educators ever have to physically restrain a student? When working with students who engage in volatile, violent, and dangerous behaviors it may become necessary to keep a student from injuring himself or herself or others. Physical restraint is often regarded as a tool of restrictive placements such as psychiatric hospitals and residential treatment facilities, and many do not believe that its use has a place in general education settings. Nonetheless, the increase in the numbers of inclusive programs for students with EBD has thrust the issue of restraint into discussions of teaching. Although the research is limited, it is generally believed that physical restraint is commonly used with students with EBD.

Consequently, teachers working with violent and volatile students should be aware of guidelines regarding the safe and appropriate use of restraint. According to Ryan and Peterson (2004), restraint is only to be used by trained personnel who know how to apply it safely using the minimal amount of force. Moreover, procedures for reporting, data collection, and parent notification should be in place. Obviously, nonphysical options to diffuse crisis situations are available and can minimize the need for restraint.

MEDICATION

Drug or pharmacological treatment is one of the most frequently used and controversial methods for managing behavior problems. Consider the recent data: Approximately 2–4% of students in general education, 15–20% of children in special education, and 40–60% of students in residential settings receive medications for behavioral issues. Moreover, the rate of students using medications has tripled over the past 10 years, with increased use of stimulants and antidepressants leading the way (Konopasek & Forness, 2004). The popularity of psychotropic medications for students with behavioral issues is not surprising. For many students, medications work effectively with few if any side effects. Moreover, medications for all types of psychological diagnoses are advertised throughout the media, and we are arguably a society that demands fast, convenient solutions to problem situations. As educators, we have an important role in our students' medical interventions. We are well positioned to ensure that students receive their prescriptions on schedule as well as observe and report on the effects, both intended and unintended, of the medication (Quinn et al., 2000).

The frequent and increasing use of psychotropic medications, particularly among the preschool population, raises concerns regarding both the long-term health and the social impact of these controversial interventions (Barkley, 1981; Diller, 2000; Miller, 1999). Specifically:

- How ethical is it to treat children with medications of little-known long-term safety and efficacy?
- Are too many children being given drugs without appropriate management and supervision?
- Are physicians equipped with enough data to prescribe proper dosages of medications that are to be used in educational settings?
- Are children, parents, and policymakers viewing medications as an exclusive solution to social problems?

DELIVERING ON THE NATIONAL AGENDA FOR ACHIEVING BETTER RESULTS

Compared to students with other disabilities, students with EBD continue to be the most neglected and underserved group of students in our schools. Numerous national reports have documented how "we" in the educational and social service establishments have failed collectively to adequately address the needs of this challenging population (Rosenberg et al., 2004). To address these needs in a comprehensive fashion, the U.S. Department of Education has developed a comprehensive national agenda for achieving better results for students with EBD. The national agenda is unique in that it recognizes that, for school, work, and community outcomes to improve, the active involvement of many stakeholders is necessary. The agenda lists seven interdependent domains (see Figure 7.6) that focus on prevention, cultural sensitivity, hope, and accountability (Chesapeake Institute, 1994).

The national agenda, along with its strategic targets, is an admirable blueprint for engaging states, universities, local governments, schools, families, and social service agencies in efforts to improve services. Ironically, concurrent with this call for reform and increased services, there is a growing attitude of antipathy toward those who have behavior problems. Specifically, students with emotional and behavioral problems are particularly vulnerable to zero-tolerance policies that emphasize punishment and exclusion rather than increased opportunities for intervention (Webber & Scheuermann, 1997). How can reform elements such as the national agenda be implemented within such a sociopolitical context? According to Smith and Katsiyannis (2004), we need to "ask ourselves how we can contribute to an authentic and competent advocacy movement" (p. 298). Alliances of parents, educators, service providers, and researchers must lobby policymakers for adequate support of proactive agenda activities if positive outcomes are to occur.

Reflective Exercise #9
Although all of the interdependent strategic domains of the national agenda are important, which domains are most relevant to teachers of students with EBD? How might you contribute to ongoing advocacy activities to improve services for students with disabilities?

 To link to websites that support and extend the content of this chapter, go to the Web Links module of Chapter 7 at www.prenhall.com/rosenberg.

FIGURE 7.6

NATIONAL AGENDA GRAPHIC

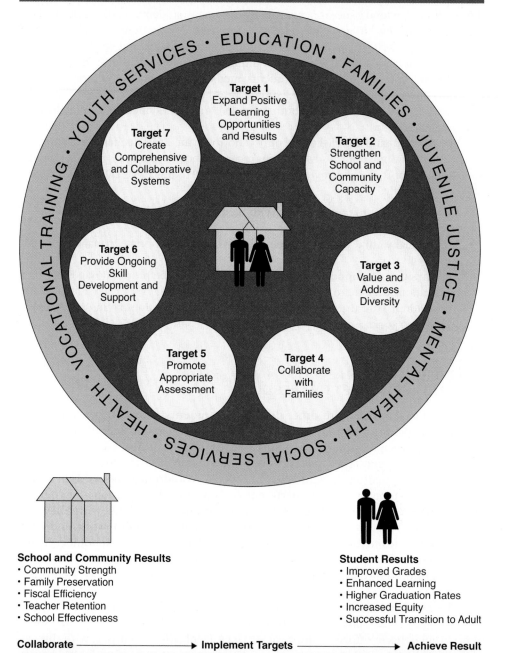

School and Community Results
- Community Strength
- Family Preservation
- Fiscal Efficiency
- Teacher Retention
- School Effectiveness

Student Results
- Improved Grades
- Enhanced Learning
- Higher Graduation Rates
- Increased Equity
- Successful Transition to Adult

Collaborate ⟶ **Implement Targets** ⟶ **Achieve Result**

Source: From Chesapeake Institute. (1994, September). *National agenda for achieving better results for children and youth with serious emotional disturbance.* Washington, DC: U.S. Department of Education.

SUMMARY

Students with EBD exhibit affect and behavior that differ significantly from those of age-related peers. The primary goal for teachers is to influence those behaviors that impede learning and improve student achievement.

Definitions and Classification Criteria for EBD

- There are two major definitions of EBD, each with its relative strengths and weaknesses.
- It is difficult, if not impossible, to develop an objective, fail-safe definition of EBD.
- Two classification systems—statistically derived and clinically derived—are used to categorize possible emotional and behavioral problems.

Primary Behavioral Characteristics of EBD

- Two broad classes of behavioral characteristics—externalizing and internalizing—typically indicate EBD.
- Common external behaviors are extreme rates of aggression and rule breaking; internalizing behaviors include pronounced social withdrawal, anxiety, and depression.
- Other behaviors associated with EBD include attention and social skills deficits.
- Students with EBD tend to have low average IQ scores, and earn low grades, and drop-out of school at alarmingly high rates.

Prevalence, Course, and Causal Factors

- The official prevalence of students with EBD is less than 1%, yet most believe that up to 6% of students require special education services.
- Students with EBD are underidentified, yet there is considerable concern that certain groups, particularly African American students, are overrepresented in the disability category.

- Students with EBD have dismal postschool outcomes, with almost 50% unemployed 3 to 5 years after leaving school.
- Many theories are used to explain EBD, including biophysical, psychodynamic, familial/home, societal, and even school factors. Still, EBD is more a function of interrelated, interacting factors rather than any single cause.

Identification and Assessment

- Students with EBD are identified using a series of objective and projective instruments, yet the most useful tool for instructional/behavioral planning is an FBA.
- FBAs help identify events, activities, and situations associated with a student's problem behaviors and guide environmental adjustments to alter such behaviors.

Educational Practices

- Typical interventions for students with EBD include behavioral techniques, instruction in self-control, and social skills, as well as life-space interviews.
- Students transitioning to the world of work often require vocational education, work experience, and supported employment. For students with extreme, pervasive, and multifaceted behavior problems community services and supports are coordinated and delivered in a "wraparound" fashion.

Prevailing Issues

- Although great strides have been made in how we teach students with EBD, prevailing issues include the use of physical restraint, the role of medications, and delivering on the National Agenda for Achieving Better Results.

 Council for Exceptional Children

ADDRESSING THE PROFESSIONAL STANDARDS

Council for Exceptional Children Knowledge Standards addressed in the chapter:

CC1K5, GC1K1, GC1K2, GC2K1, CC2K2, CC2K3, CC2K5, CC2K6, CC3K1, CC3K2

Appendix B: CEC Knowledge and Skill Standards Common Core has a full listing of the standards referenced here.

To learn more about Robert Hessels, his background, and his views on inclusion, collaboration, and high stakes testing, go to the Mr. Hessels module on the DVD-ROM.

much of the school day with peers in general education classrooms. He notes that these students gained many of the academic and social skills in general education classrooms that they would need for success in life. "They learned many things they would not have learned in a separate special education class." When these students were seniors, Robert worked with many of them to arrange transitions into work settings where they had "real paying jobs." Most of the students were successful in these work settings and continue to be successful to this day.

While Robert Hessels enjoys most things about his job, the bureaucracy that exists in schools frustrates him. This bureaucracy mandates tests and regulations that "are not always in the best interest of students." He notes that a special education teacher must use "artful end runs" at times to ensure that students "get what they need, in spite of the bureaucracy."

Robert's advice for those who are thinking about becoming special education teachers is to "carefully think about whether you want to be a special education teacher, then think about it again . . . and again." He goes on to note: "Liking kids is not enough. The rewards from teaching in special education do not come quickly. They accumulate slowly over time, often from unexpected sources." For example, he notes that the single greatest reward for him is getting a student out of a separate special education class and into an inclusive classroom.

Special education teachers must be "more creative than you imagined possible." He notes that an effective special education teacher is a person who can help students realize their potential and teach them so that they will become "life-long learners," continuing to gain skills that will allow them to be successful in life. He concludes: "We often focus on the trees and lose sight of the forest" when we're educating students with disabilities. "We need to concentrate on the long term and not just test scores." This prepares students not for next week or next year but for their lives.

Reflective Exercise #1

As we discussed in the "People-First Language" feature in Chapter 2, the words we use make a difference. Think of a word that has been used to describe you or some real or imagined characteristic you possess. This word may relate to your **race, ethnicity,** gender, body shape or type, hair color, religion, and so forth. How did you feel when this word was used? Is this word socially acceptable (or politically incorrect)?

If you have had direct contact over time with persons with **intellectual disabilities** (formerly called **mental retardation**). you know that these individuals vary dramatically in the characteristics they exhibit. This includes how they communicate and get along with others, how quickly they learn academic material, how much support they need in school, and a range of other variables.

To illustrate, consider for a moment the differences between students who have mild intellectual disabilities and those with severe intellectual disabilities. Most students with mild intellectual disabilities appear very similar to others in school, except for the fact that they learn academic material much more slowly than most other students. The President's Committee on Mental Retardation (1969) called these students the "**six hour retarded child**" because they were labeled as intellectually disabled during the school day but adapted well and were often not readily distinguishable as intellectually disabled at home or in the community. As our featured teacher, Robert Hessels, indicated, these are students who may need support as they transition from school to work settings but can often be successful in work settings with real paying jobs.

In contrast, students with severe intellectual disabilities are often readily distinguishable from other students in schools. These students have significant difficulties in communicating, learning, and interacting socially with others. Many students with severe disabilities also have significant weaknesses in sensory and physical development. As a result of these characteristics, limitations are placed on the level of independence of persons with severe disabilities, and they need supports (e.g., assistive technology, a paraeducator) in school and at home.

FAQ Sheet

STUDENTS WITH MILD INTELLECTUAL DISABILITIES

Who are they?	• Students with mild intellectual disabilities have a measured IQ that is lower than 98% of the school-age population (i.e., below approximately 70). • These students have adaptive behavior skills that are significantly below average. Adaptive behavior includes conceptual, social, and practical skills that people learn so that they can function in their everyday lives.
What are typical characteristics?	• Low achievement in all academic areas • Deficits in memory and motivation • Inattentive/distractible • Poor social skills • Deficits in adaptive behavior
What are the demographics?	• 0.84% of school-age students (approximately 555,000) are labeled with intellectual disabilities. • Approximately 470,000 students (0.71%) are labeled with mild intellectual disabilities. • The percentage of the school-age population identified with intellectual disabilities declined by approximately 10% between 1990 and 2004.
Where are students educated?	• 13% of students labeled with intellectual disabilities spend most of the day in general education classrooms, while 57% spend most of the school day segregated from typical peers. • The proportion of students with intellectual disabilities who are educated in general education classrooms for most of the school day increased by approximately 72% between 1990 and 2003, while the proportion of students educated in separate settings for most of the school day declined by 19%.
How are students identified and assessed for intervention?	• Primary criteria for identification are significantly subaverage intellectual functioning, existing concurrently with deficits in adaptive behavior and manifested during the developmental period, that adversely affects a child's educational performance. • A score of approximately 70 or below in an intelligence test is considered to be subaverage intellectual functioning. • A standardized test of adaptive behavior is used to determine if the child has deficits in conceptual, social, and practical skills that are significantly subaverage. • A standardized achievement test is used to determine if the child's educational performance is adversely affected (i.e., if the student's achievement is well below grade level).
What are the outcomes?	• Intellectual disabilities persist through the school years and into adulthood. • Adults with mild intellectual disabilities are often employed in occupations with low status and low pay. • Many students with mild intellectual disabilities continue to need support into adulthood in employment and independent living, although some of these students need no support.

Reflective Exercise #2
Have you ever used the word *retard* in casual conversation? Did others react negatively to your use of this word? Is this word considered politically incorrect? Have you heard others use it? How did you react? Why are reactions to the use of the words discussed in Reflective Exercise #1 so different from reactions to the word *retard*?

Perhaps in part due to the complexity of the category, intellectual disabilities are widely misunderstood. Many persons, especially those who have had little contact with individuals with intellectual disabilities, have narrow, stereotyped perspectives about the persons in this special education category. One thing that most professionals and the general public agree on is that intellectual disability is the most stigmatizing disability category. This stigma is vividly illustrated by the casual use of the word *retard* among school-age students and the frequent lack of reaction from teachers or parents when this term is used.

To address the complexity of the category of intellectual disabilities, we will primarily include information regarding students with mild intellectual disabilities in this chapter. Additional information regarding students with severe intellectual disabilities is provided in Chapter 12. For a quick overview of the category of intellectual disabilities, you might want to examine the critical information about these students that is included in the FAQ Sheet.

We struggled with choosing which terminology to use in this chapter. IDEA and most state education agencies currently use the term *mental retardation* to describe this category. But the term has become highly stigmatizing, as we note throughout the chapter. We made the decision to use the term *intellectual disabilities* in large part because of this stigma. While we do not believe that changing terminology will in the long term reduce the stigma attached to this category, it will help in the short term.

Also supporting our choice of this term was the decision by the leading professional association in this area, the American Association on Mental Retardation (AAMR), to change its name to the American Association on Intellectual and Developmental Disabilities in January 2007. It appears that the term *intellectual disability*, which is widely used in many European countries, is rapidly becoming the preferred term for the category. We discuss the controversy surrounding the use of the term *mental retardation* in more detail at the end of this chapter.

DEFINITIONS AND CLASSIFICATION CRITERIA

IDEA 2004 includes a general definition of intellectual disability (mental retardation is the term used in the law) but does not differentiate among students with mild and severe intellectual disabilities as we do in this text. Thus, in the following sections we discuss the full range of intellectual disabilities, including how intellectual disability is defined and what criteria are used to identify these students.

The definition of intellectual disability or **mental retardation** in IDEA 2004 stipulates that these students have "significantly subaverage general intellectual functioning, existing concurrently with deficits in **adaptive behavior** and manifested during the developmental period, that adversely affects a child's educational performance" (sec. 300.8[c][6]). Four criteria are used to identify students with intellectual disabilities based on this definition. First, these students must have a measured IQ that is significantly below average. This typically is defined as an IQ of approximately 70 or below, which means that the student scores lower than approximately 98% of all school-age students. Second, the student must have deficits in adaptive behavior. This criterion is used to ensure that intellectual functioning is not the exclusive criterion used to identify persons with intellectual disabilities. Thus, to be identified with an intellectual disability, students must also have significant limitations in adaptive behavior, which includes practical and social skills that students use to function effectively in their everyday lives (Hourcade, 2002). Third, the student must have manifested the intellectual disability during the developmental period, thus indicating that the disability is a long-term problem. This criterion is used to differentiate intellectual disabilities from other disabilities, such as traumatic brain injury, which may occur in adulthood. Finally, the intellectual disability must adversely affect the student's educational performance. This includes low levels of academic achievement, difficulty adapting to classroom or other school settings, poor social skills, and so forth.

TABLE 8.1

LEVELS OF INTELLECTUAL DISABILITY BASED ON IQ	
Label	**Range of IQ Scores**
Mild intellectual disability	50/55 to approximately 70
Moderate intellectual disability	35/40 to 50/55
Severe intellectual disability	20/25 to 35/40
Profound intellectual disability	Below 20/25
Source: APA, 2000.	

Levels of intellectual disability are often differentiated based on a student's IQ level (APA, 2000). For example, Table 8.1 provides IQ ranges for students with differing levels of intellectual disability. Students with mild intellectual disabilities typically have an IQ that ranges from 55 to 70. These are students who can attend to their personal needs, are largely independent in school settings, and in many cases can interact successfully with other students with limited assistance from teachers or other educators. In addition, the disability of students with mild intellectual disabilities is typically not readily noticeable and is only identified upon examining the student's learning and adaptive skills.

The needs of students with severe intellectual disabilities (including those who fall into the moderate, severe, and profound levels of intellectual functioning in Table 8.1) vary widely: Some can function relatively independently in performing daily living tasks, while others require a significant level of support. Overall, these students have disabilities that are often easily noticeable (Beirne-Smith, Patton, & Kim, 2006), and they have "significant weaknesses in learning abilities, personal and social skills, and/or sensory and physical development" (Westling & Fox, 2004, p. 3). In addition, students with severe intellectual disabilities often lack the skills to maintain themselves independently, and require support and assistance in school, at home, and in other settings (Westling & Fox, 2004). See Chapter 12 for a more extensive discussion of severe intellectual disabilities.

The **American Association on Intellectual and Developmental Disabilities** (formerly the **American Association on Mental Retardation [AAMR]**), the leading professional organization in the field of intellectual disabilities, has published a widely used definition of intellectual disability. This definition expands on some of the concepts provided in the IDEA definition (Luckasson et al., 2002): "[Intellectual disability] is . . . characterized by significant limitations in both intellectual functioning and in adaptive behavior as expressed in conceptual, social, and practical adaptive skills. This disability originates before age 18" (p. 13).

Luckasson and colleagues continue by noting five factors that should be considered when determining if a person should be identified with an intellectual disability:

1. Limitations in present functioning must be considered within the context of community environments typical of the individual's age peers and culture.
2. Valid assessment considers cultural and linguistic diversity as well as differences in communication, sensory, motor, and behavioral factors.
3. Within the individual, limitations often coexist with strengths.
4. The purpose of describing limitations is to develop a profile of needed supports.
5. With appropriate personalized supports over a sustained period, the life functioning of the person with mental retardation generally will improve. (p. 13)

FIGURE 8.1

ADAPTIVE BEHAVIOR SKILLS USED TO IDENTIFY PERSONS WITH INTELLECTUAL DISABILITIES

Conceptual Skills
Receptive and expressive language
Reading and writing
Money concepts
Self-directions

Social Skills
Interpersonal
Responsibility
Self-esteem
Gullibility (likelihood of being tricked or manipulated)
Naïveté
Following rules
Obeying laws
Avoiding victimization

Practical Skills
Personal activities of daily living such as eating, dressing, mobility, and toileting
Instrumental activities of daily living such as preparing meals, taking medication, using the
    telephone, managing money, using transportation, and doing housekeeping activities
Occupational skills
Maintaining a safe environment

Source: Adapted from AAMR, Definition of Mental Retardation: Fact Sheet of Frequently Asked Questions About Mental Retardation. 2005. Retrieved from http://www.aamr.org/policies/faq_mental_retardation.shtml.

This definition extends the IDEA definition in three noteworthy ways. First, it defines the developmental period as occurring before age 18. Thus, an intellectual disability should be manifested during the school years and is most often identified before school entry for students with more severe intellectual disabilities and early in elementary school for students with mild intellectual disabilities.

Second, the AAMR definition extends the concept of adaptive behavior to include conceptual, social, and practical skills that people use to function in their everyday lives. When these skills are significantly limited, a person's ability to respond to specific situations and the environment is affected (Luckasson et al., 2002). Areas in which adaptive behavior deficits occur are listed in Figure 8.1.

Third, and perhaps most significantly, rather than identifying students based on the severity of their disability (see Table 8.1), as currently occurs in most states, the AAMR recommends an emphasis on identifying students based on the **level of supports** needed to function effectively (see Figure 8.2). For example most students who have traditionally been identified with a mild intellectual disability would probably be identified using this approach as students needing intermittent support (episodic need), while perhaps a few would need limited support for specific periods of time. In contrast, the needs of students with severe disabilities would range from limited, to extensive, to pervasive support in most instances.

Most students with mild intellectual disabilities need intermittent supports.

www.prenhall.com/rosenberg

FIGURE 8.2

LEVELS OF SUPPORT FOR PERSONS WITH INTELLECTUAL DISABILITIES

Intermittent.   Supports on an "as needed basis." Characterized by episodic nature, person not always needing the support(s), or short-term supports needed during life-span transitions (e.g., job loss or acute medical crisis). Intermittent supports may be high or low intensity when needed.

Limited.   An intensity of support characterized by consistency over time, time-limited but not of an intermittent nature, may require fewer staff members and less cost than more intense levels of support (e.g., time-limited employment training or transitional supports provided during the school to adult period).

Extensive.   Supports characterized by regular involvement (e.g., daily) in at least some environments (such as work or home) and not time-limited (e.g., long-term support and long-term home living support).

Pervasive.   Supports characterized by their constancy and high intensity; provided across environments; potential life-sustaining nature. Pervasive supports typically involve more staff members and intrusiveness than do extensive or time-limited supports.

Source: **Luckasson et al., 2002,** *Mental retardation: Definition, classification, and systems of support* **(10th ed.), p. 152.**

Supports are defined as "the resources and individual strategies necessary to promote the development, education, interests, and personal well-being of a person with an intellectual disability. Supports can be provided by a parent, friend, teacher, psychologist, doctor or by any appropriate person or agency" (AAMR, 2005, p. 3). This approach to the identification of persons with intellectual disabilities is a radical departure from past practices and is intended as a first step in "forcing the field to think differently about mental retardation and how we intervene in the lives of people with that label" (Wehmeyer, 2003, p. 273).

More specifically, while past definitions have emphasized the student's deficits in intellectual development and adaptive behavior, the levels-of-support approach emphasizes how a person's needs can be met within a particular setting (e.g., school, home, work). Thus, rather than viewing an intellectual disability as solely a problem that resides within the student, this approach recognizes the need to consider how the environment can be altered so that the student receives appropriate supports and can be successful.

The extent to which professionals in the field of intellectual disabilities will accept this change in practice remains in question. While the levels-of-support approach to identification was originally proposed by AAMR in 1992 (Luckasson et al., 1992), by the late 1990s few states had adopted the definition (Polloway, Chamberlain, Denning, Smith, & Smith, 1999). While the levels-of-support approach to student identification is designed to reduce the stigma associated with the label *mental retardation* or *intellectual disability* and place more emphasis on the supports that students need to be successful, it will likely take many years to determine whether this approach can be successfully implemented in schools.

Reflective Exercise #3

Have you had contact with a person with an intellectual disability? How was this person different from others? How was he or she the same? Can you identify behaviors indicating that the person needs intermittent supports to function independently? Behaviors indicating that the person needs extensive or pervasive support?

PRIMARY CHARACTERISTICS OF STUDENTS WITH INTELLECTUAL DISABILITIES

In this section, we take a closer look at the characteristics of children and youth with mild intellectual disabilities. You should note that the characteristics of students with more severe intellectual disabilities are addressed in Chapter 12. In the following section, we describe these students based on key learning, cognitive, and social characteristics.

While we discuss several characteristics that are often seen when a student is identified with a mild intellectual disability, we do not mean to suggest that all students with this disability are alike. Indeed, as with any group of people, students with mild intellectual disabilities vary widely in their ability to do schoolwork and adjust to social situations in school and other locations. However, in contrast to most other disability categories, students with mild intellectual disabilities tend to have more general, delayed development in academic, social, and adaptive skills. This delayed development is reflected in low achievement across content and skill areas as well as significantly lower scores on measures of intelligence and adaptive behavior when compared with students who are not identified with intellectual disabilities.

ACADEMIC PERFORMANCE

Students who are identified with mild intellectual disabilities lag significantly behind grade-level peers in developing academic skills. Thus, students with mild intellectual disabilities are likely to be significantly delayed in learning to read and learning basic math skills (Taylor, Richards, & Brady, 2005). This delay in developing foundational skills in reading and math, coupled with delays in language skills, then results in delays in other academic areas that require the use of these skills (e.g., writing, spelling, science).

Students with intellectual disabilities continue to lag behind age-level peers in academic achievement throughout their school years. However, many students with mild intellectual disabilities develop basic literacy skills and functional mathematics skills. For example, most students with mild intellectual disabilities learn basic computational skills and functional arithmetic skills related to money, time, and measurement. However, most of these students continue to have difficulty with more advanced skills related to content, such as mathematical reasoning and applying concepts to solve problems (Beirne-Smith et al., 2006).

It is noteworthy that delayed language development, which is characteristic of students with mild intellectual disabilities, also has a negative influence on academic achievement. The academic area in which language delay has the most detrimental effect is reading (Torgesen, 2000). While students who are mildly intellectually disabled and who are poor readers share a deficit in phonological language skills similar to other students with disabilities (e.g., students with LD) (Fletcher, Scott, Blair, & Bolger, 2004), students with intellectual disabilities are also often significantly delayed in general oral language skills. Thus, even if students with mild intellectual disabilities develop the ability to read individual words and strategies for reading comprehension, they will have difficulty comprehending what they have read because of weak verbal skills in areas such as vocabulary. Therefore, teachers need to provide these students with instruction to address their phonological weaknesses as well as a broader range of language skills (e.g., vocabulary development) (Torgesen, 2000).

COGNITIVE PERFORMANCE

Students with mild intellectual disabilities are characterized by general delays in cognitive development that influence the acquisition of language and academic skills. Moreover, while these students can learn much information that is part of the general education curriculum, they learn more slowly than do typical students. Deficits in specific cognitive skill areas also contribute to this delay. Three of the most important cognitive skill deficits exhibited by students with mild intellectual disabilities are related to attention, memory, and generalization.

Attention

Students with mild intellectual disabilities have difficulty with different types of attention, including orienting to a task, selective attention, and sustaining attention to a task (Wenar & Kerig, 2006). Orienting to a task requires a student to look in the direction of the task (e.g., a teacher demonstrating how to solve a math problem on an overhead projector in the front of the room). Selective attention requires that the student attend to relevant aspects of the task and not to unimportant task components (e.g., attending to one type of math problem on a page and completing the appropriate operation). Finally, sustained attention requires that the student continue to attend to a task for a period of time.

The attentional difficulties of students with mild intellectual disabilities have several implications for how they may be more effectively taught (Beirne-Smith et al., 2006, p. 277). For example, teachers should

1. present initial stimuli that vary in only a few dimensions,
2. direct the individual's attention to these critical dimensions,
3. initially remove extraneous stimuli that may distract the individual from attending
4. increase the difficulty of the task over time, and
5. teach the student decision-making rules for discriminating relevant from irrelevant stimuli.

Memory

Students with mild intellectual disabilities also have difficulty remembering information (i.e., short-term memory). For example, these students may have difficulty remembering math facts or spelling words; or if they remember this information one day, they may forget it the next. To some degree, memory problems are influenced by attentional difficulties. That is, students will have difficulty remembering information if they do not orient to the information, select the information that needs to be remembered, and maintain attention to the important material for a period of time.

However, distinct from attentional problems, students with mild intellectual disabilities have difficulty generating and using strategies that help facilitate short-term memory. For example, when students attempt to remember information, many use a rehearsal strategy (repeating information over and over) to facilitate learning (Kirk, Gallagher, Anastasiow, & Coleman, 2006). Teaching approaches to addressing short-term memory deficits include focusing on meaningful content during instruction and instructing students about strategies that they might use to facilitate remembering information (e.g., rehearsal, clustering information, using mnemonic devices) (Smith, Polloway, Patton, & Dowdy, 2004). The use of mnemonic devices was discussed in Chapter 6.

Generalization

A final area in which many students with mild intellectual disabilities have difficulty relates to the generalization of information to other material or settings (Wenar & Kerig, 2006). For example, a student may learn operations for addition and subtraction but may then have difficulty generalizing this information to a division problem. Similarly, a student may learn a new word when reading material in one subject area but may have difficulty reading the same word in other reading material. Students with mild intellectual disabilities also have difficulty generalizing material learned in one setting to another (e.g., from school to the community). Teaching strategies that may be used to address difficulties with generalization include teaching material in relevant contexts, reinforcing students for generalizing information across material or settings, reminding students to apply information they have learned in one setting to another, and teaching information in multiple settings (Smith et al., 2004).

SOCIAL SKILLS PERFORMANCE

Many of the cognitive characteristics of students with mild intellectual disabilities may contribute to difficulty interacting socially. For example, a low level of cognitive development and delayed language development may cause a student with intellectual disability to have difficulty understanding the content of verbal interactions and understanding expectations (e.g., when to listen, when and how to respond) during verbal interactions. Similarly, difficulty with attention and memory impedes social interactions, as students with mild intellectual disabilities have difficulty attending to important aspects of social interactions, maintaining attention over time, and holding important aspects of what they observe in short-term memory.

Reflective Exercise #4
What skills do you and your friends need to get along socially? What characteristics of students with mild intellectual disabilities might negatively affect their ability to get along with others? What could a teacher do to reduce the effect of these characteristics and support students with mild intellectual disabilities in getting along with others?

Directly teaching social skills through activities such as role playing can be beneficial for many students.

In addition to social difficulties that result from general cognitive deficits, students with mild intellectual disabilities share many of the same social difficulties of students with learning disabilities (see Chapter 6), including the inability to read social cues and interact successfully in conversations, lack of affiliation in school activities, low social status, and negative self-concept.

As with students with LD, these characteristics often lead to lower social status in classrooms and, at times, alienation of students from teachers and peers and lack of affiliation or involvement in school. Moreover, social skills deficits may lead students with mild intellectual disabilities to feel that they are unimportant to peers and teachers and produce feelings that they are not involved in the social community of the school. These difficulties may lead students with mild intellectual disabilities to withdraw in social situations or seek attention in inappropriate ways. They may also behave inappropriately because they have difficulty distinguishing between acceptable and unacceptable standards of behavior (Beirne-Smith et al., 2006).

Directly teaching social skills is one approach that may be used to address the social skills deficits of students with mild intellectual disabilities. (See Chapter 7 for more information on this topic.) This may be necessary for many students with mild intellectual disabilities because their limited cognitive and language skills prevent them from developing these skills through spontaneous interactions with peers.

In addition, as you will see in a later section on placement practices for students with mild intellectual disabilities, most of these students have little opportunity to interact with age-level peers in school settings, due to the fact that they spend a large proportion of the school day in segregated school settings with other students with disabilities (Williamson, McLeskey, Hoppey, & Rentz, 2006). Extensive research evidence reveals that the social skills of students with mild intellectual disabilities tend to be improved when they are provided with appropriate supports and included in a general education classroom with age-appropriate peers for a large part of the school day (Freeman & Alkin, 2000).

PREVALENCE, COURSE, AND CAUSAL FACTORS

PREVALENCE

During the 2004–2005 school year, more than 555,000 U.S. students were classified as having intellectual disabilities, or 0.84% of the school-age population (U.S. Department of Education, 2006). Researchers have estimated that 70–85% of all children with intellectual disabilities have mild to moderate intellectual disabilities (Murphy, Yeargin-Allsopp, Decoufle, & Drews, 1995; Taylor et al., 2005). Our best estimate of the number of students with mild intellectual disabilities is about 470,000, resulting in a prevalence rate for these students of approximately 0.71%. Thus, when students with mild intellectual disabilities are included in general education classrooms, this results in approximately one student in every six general education classes.

It is important to note that the number of students in the intellectual disabilities category declined between 1990 and 2004 by approximately 10%. It is unclear why this decline occurred, although Beirne-Smith and colleagues (2006) have speculated that it could relate to factors such as (1) reticence to label students from culturally diverse backgrounds because of their overrepresentation in the mild intellectual dis-

www.prenhall.com/rosenberg

abilities category, (2) identifying high-functioning students with the less stigmatizing LD label; and (3) the positive effects of early intervention efforts that reduced the occurrence of mild intellectual disabilities.

A final consideration regarding the prevalence of students with intellectual disabilities is the extent to which students in this category represent the racial and ethnic population of students in the United States. Table 8.2 presents data from the 2004–2005 school year regarding the percentage of students from each of five racial groups who were identified with intellectual disabilities and the percentage of each of these groups in the population of school-age students in the United States. It is noteworthy that the group that is most significantly **overrepresented** in the intellectual disability category is African American students. Based on their representative proportion in the school-age population, these students are more than twice as likely to be identified with an intellectual disability as one would predict. Furthermore, African American students have been significantly overrepresented in the intellectual disability category for nearly 40 years (Hosp & Reschly, 2004).

Many professionals have expressed concern regarding the overrepresentation of African American students in the intellectual disability category because this category and the use of the label *mentally retarded* are viewed as very stigmatizing (Hosp & Reschly, 2004; Losen & Orfield, 2002). For example, research has shown that when students are given a negative label such as *mentally retarded,* teachers tend to focus on the students' negative behaviors, even though those behaviors may not differ significantly from other students' (Hosp & Reschly, 2004).

In addition to concerns regarding the stigma attached to the *intellectual disability* label, professionals have expressed concern because most students who are identified with intellectual disabilities are segregated from typical peers for much of the school day (Williamson et al., 2006). These segregated placements do not allow students with intellectual disabilities access to the general education curriculum and "often result in fewer opportunities for students to access postsecondary education and in fewer employment opportunities" (Zhang & Katsiyannis, 2002, p. 184). Furthermore, in some school districts, most students identified with intellectual disabilities

TABLE 8.2

PERCENTAGE OF ALL SCHOOL-AGE STUDENTS LABELED *INTELLECTUALLY DISABLED* BY RACE/ETHNICITY, 2004

Race/Ethnicity	Intellectually Disabled[1]	Total Population[2]
American Indian and Alaska Native	1.21	0.98
Asian and Pacific Islander	1.98	4.10
Black	33.36	15.08
Hispanic (not Black)	12.35	17.65
European American	51.00	62.19

Source: U.S. Department of Education, 2006.

1. These percentages represent the total percentage of students with disabilities who are labeled *intellectually disabled* for each race/ethnic group. Columns thus add to 100%.

2. These percentages reflect the percentage of the total school-age population that is represented by each racial/ethnic group. If students are proportionally represented, the percentage in each disability category should equal the percentage of the overall population in the third column. For example, 17.65% of Hispanic should be labeled *intellectually disabled* if they are proportionally represented in this category. The figure in the intellectually disabled column for these students is 12.35%, indicating that Hispanic students are proportionally underrepresented in this category.

are African American, resulting in racial segregation in separate classes for these students (Zhang & Katsiyannis, 2002).

A final concern that has been expressed regarding the overrepresentation of African American students in the intellectual disability category relates to the ineffectiveness of segregated special education placements for these students. As we have noted, extensive research evidence has revealed that students with mild intellectual disabilities tend to benefit academically and socially when they are provided with appropriate supports and included in general education classrooms with age-appropriate peers for much of the school day (Freeman & Alkin, 2000). Thus, not only is the label *mental retardation* or *intellectual disability* stigmatizing for African American students, but they are also often disadvantaged by being placed for much of the school day in highly segregated settings that limit their opportunities for academic and social growth as well as their long-term opportunities for success.

THE COURSE OF MILD INTELLECTUAL DISABILITIES

As students with mild intellectual disabilities progress through school, a performance gap widens between students with and without disabilities (Beirne-Smith et al., 2006; Patton et al., 1996). This occurs in reading and mathematics as well as across the rest of the curriculum. It also occurs with respect to the development of social and adaptive skills. In short, persons with mild intellectual disabilities enter adulthood at a significant disadvantage with respect to academic and social skills when compared to their peers who are not identified with intellectual disabilities.

Three outcomes are viewed as critically important for adults with mild intellectual disabilities (and other adults as well): productive employment, participating successfully in postsecondary education, and psychological well-being (Patton et al., 1996). While some persons with mild intellectual disabilities struggle greatly with each of these outcomes, others are relatively successful and are generally satisfied with their lives.

Productive Employment

Research has shown that persons with mild intellectual disabilities are typically employed in jobs requiring fewer skills with lower take-home pay than are typical peers and attain limited advancement in their employment (Seltzer et al., 2005). However,

Most adults with mild intellectual disabilities are employed but often in less skilled jobs.

some research has shown that adults with mild intellectual disabilities are "equally likely to be employed as their higher IQ siblings, [have] greater job stability, and [are] equally satisfied with their jobs" (Seltzer et al., 2005, p. 465). As our featured teacher, Robert Hessels, noted, careful transition planning is required, beginning early in adolescence, if students with mild intellectual disabilities are to be successful in obtaining and keeping real paying jobs after their school years. For additional information on transition planning, see Chapter 4.

Postsecondary Education

A major factor that impedes the success of many adults with intellectual disabilities is their lack of opportunity to participate in postsecondary education. Patton and colleagues (1996) note that a critical step toward successful involvement in postsecondary education for persons with mild intellectual disabilities is the extent to which they are welcomed into these settings and accommodations are provided for their disability. Until recently, postsecondary education was largely limited to persons without disabilities. This has changed dramatically in recent years, as large numbers of persons with disabilities, including those with mild to severe intellectual disabilities, have begun to attend postsecondary education institutions to network, learn social and academic skills, and obtain job skills (e.g., Pearman, Elliott, & Aborn, 2004; Zafft, Hart, & Zimbrich, 2004). As increasing numbers of adults with intellectual disabilities continue their education, it is likely that employment will improve as will other critical life outcomes.

Psychological Well-Being

Finally, some research indicates that adults with mild intellectual disabilities seem to be most at risk in the area of psychological well-being (Seltzer et al., 2005). More specifically, adults with mild intellectual disabilities often have less of a sense of purpose in life, fewer opportunities for personal growth, a higher rate of depressive symptoms, and less personal autonomy than do their peers without intellectual disabilities (Seltzer et al., 2005). This concern is currently being addressed, to some degree, by the growing use of approaches that provide persons with intellectual disabilities with the core skills needed for **self-determination** (Sands & Wehmeyer, 2005), which have been shown to correlate with "an improved quality of life for adults with disabilities, particularly those outcomes [such] as employment, community living, and postsecondary education" (Thoma & Getzel, 2005, p. 234). We provide further information regarding self-determination later in this chapter.

CAUSAL FACTORS

For almost all students identified with mild intellectual disabilities, we do not know the particular cause of the disability. However, we do know that many of these students come from families who are living in poverty and that a disproportionate number of such families are members of non–European American groups (Wenar & Kerig, 2006). Because of the strong family and cultural factors involved, this type of intellectual disability was originally called "cultural-familial" but now is referred to as "intellectual disability that results from psychosocial disadvantage" (Beirne-Smith et al., 2006, p. 162).

Before we address family and cultural factors that may put students at risk for being identified with a mild intellectual disability, it is important to note that most children who grow up in poor homes are not identified with mild intellectual disabilities, nor are most children from non–European American groups (often called "minority" groups) who grow up in these settings so identified. Moreover, most students who grow up in poor homes have measured IQs that fall within the normal range. However, there do seem to be family factors related to living in a low-socioeconomic-status home, especially for children from non–European American groups, which put a student at greater risk for being identified with a mild intellectual disability.

Many professionals have speculated that a combination of risk factors may exist in poor homes and contribute to the high incidence of mild intellectual disabilities in these settings. For example, Sameroff (1990) determined several risk factors based on previous research, including the amount of stress in the environment (e.g., inadequate housing, inadequate nutrition, inadequate health care), the family's resources for addressing this stress, the number of children in the family, the education level of the parent(s), head of household in an unskilled occupation, mental health and education level of the mother, and the family's flexibility in addressing children's needs. In a longitudinal study to examine these risk factors, Sameroff found that, as the number of risk factors increased, IQ scores for children tended to decrease. For example, in homes with multiple risk factors, children scored 30 points lower on IQ tests than did children in homes with no risk factors; and those children were much more likely to be identified with a mild intellectual disability.

In addition to family factors, cultural differences that exist in families living in poverty may contribute to the higher identification rate for students with mild intellectual disabilities. As we noted in Chapter 3, the number of students from non-middle-class,

Reflective Exercise #5
How will knowledge regarding the course of intellectual disabilities, especially adult outcomes, influence your expectations for these students in your classroom? How will this information influence what you teach these students? How will you guard against having expectations that are too low, which is difficult for any teacher to avoid?

Many factors during pregnancy, at birth, or during the early years of a child's life may contribute to the development of a mild intellectual disability.

Reflective Exercise #6
How does knowledge regarding the causes of mild intellectual disabilities influence how you perceive these students? Will this information influence how you interact with and teach these students in your classroom? What will you expect of these students?

non–European American families has increased dramatically over the past decade, while the number of teachers from these groups has declined (National Education Association, 2003). This leads to a demographic divide between students and teachers, as most teachers are female, European American, and from middle-class backgrounds that differ significantly from the backgrounds of their students. This divide may cause teachers to misunderstand or misinterpret the behavior of students from poor or different cultural backgrounds and lead them to have difficulty in effectively meeting the academic and behavior needs of these students.

With regard to this demographic divide, the identification of intellectual disabilities is often dependent on the extent to which a student varies from the social norms of a community (Murphy et al., 1995). A teacher determines these norms in her classroom, while teachers and administrators determine social norms for a school. Social norms relate to what a teacher expects as "normal" classroom behavior. For example, "normal" students might be those who are able to sit and listen for extended periods of time, complete pencil-and-paper tasks with minimal assistance, take turns speaking in class, use standard grammar, be deferential to adults, look teachers in the eye when reprimanded, ask questions when they don't understand, use a logical sequential communication style, and have parents who help them with homework and attend school events. Thus, a child who differs from these norms, as many students from low-socioeconomic-status homes and different cultural backgrounds do, is more likely to be referred and identified with a disability.

The issues of social norms and the demographic divide were addressed in Chapter 3, where you completed a personal demographic questionnaire and addressed differences that exist across cultural and socioeconomic settings. For more information regarding these topics and how they might be addressed in your classroom, see Chapter 3.

While family and cultural factors are the most widely studied cause of mild intellectual disabilities, several additional factors have been identified that may contribute to the development of these disabilities (The ARC, 2005; Wenar & Kerig, 2006). These factors include problems

- During pregnancy, such as use of alcohol or drugs, malnutrition, exposure to environmental toxins, or maternal illnesses such as rubella or syphilis
- At birth, such as prematurity and low birth weight, or difficulties during delivery, such as birth injuries or temporary oxygen deprivation
- After birth, such as infections (e.g., meningitis, encephalitis), injuries (e.g., a blow to the head), or exposure to environmental toxins (e.g., lead or mercury)

IDENTIFICATION AND ASSESSMENT

The primary criteria used to identify students with intellectual disabilities are subaverage scores on tests of intelligence and adaptive behavior. A school psychologist often administers a test of intelligence and interprets the results for the multidisciplinary team. The multidisciplinary team determines if the student's level of intelligence falls below the cutoff for an intellectual disability and, if the IQ score is below 70, which level of intellectual disability is indicated. (See Table 8.1 for cutoffs for different levels of intellectual disability.) Intelligence measures that are widely used to identify students with intellectual disabilities are the Stanford-Binet Intelligence Scale (5th ed.) (Roid, 2003) and the Wechsler Intelligence Scale for Children (4th ed.) (Wechsler, 2003). For more information regarding intelligence tests, see Chapter 4.

While an IQ score of 70 or below is a major criterion for identifying a student as intellectually disabled, it is not sufficient. The student also must have significant limitations in adaptive behavior. To make this determination, a team member administers a measure of adaptive behavior. Tests that are most often used in this area include the AAMR Adaptive Behavior Scale—School (Lambert, Nihira, & Leland, 1993), the Adaptive Behavior Assessment System (2nd ed.) (ABAS-II) (Harrison & Oakland, 2000), and the Vineland Adaptive Behavior Scales (2nd ed.) (Sparrow, Cicchetti, & Balla, 2005). See Figure 8.1 for a list of the adaptive behavior skills that are used to identify persons with intellectual disabilities.

Finally, if a student's IQ and adaptive behavior measures fall within the range that indicates significant limitations, the multidisciplinary team determines if the child's educational performance has been adversely affected. Measures of academic achievement, such as the Woodcock-Johnson Tests of Achievement (Woodcock, McGrew, & Mather, 2001) and the Wechsler Individual Achievement Test (2nd ed.) (WIAT-II) (Psychological Corporation, 2001), are typically administered to provide this information. These tests provide achievement scores in the areas of language, reading, writing, and mathematics.

Before we leave this topic, it is important to note that controversy has surrounded the identification of students with intellectual disabilities for several decades. Initially, this controversy related to the IQ cutoff that should be used to identify these students. In 1961 the IQ cutoff for intellectual disabilities was set at 85 (Heber, 1961). This meant that approximately 16% of the school-age population would theoretically meet this criterion. In 1973 the IQ cutoff was lowered to 70, reducing the proportion of the school-age population who would meet this criterion by 14% (i.e., to 2.28%) (Grossman, 1973). Some have suggested that this change in the definition "cured" 14% of the school-age population of intellectual disabilities. More recently, in 1992 the AAMR definition increased the IQ cutoff to 75 (Luckasson et al., 1992), doubling the number of students who would meet this criterion, but lowered it again to 70 in the most recent version (Luckasson et al., 2002).

Similarly, controversy has surrounded the extent to which adaptive behavior should be a criterion for identifying students with intellectual disabilities and how this construct should be defined. Adaptive behavior became a formal criterion for identifying students with intellectual disabilities in 1973 and has subsequently been redefined and refined.

It is important to note that these changes relate to issues surrounding the identification of students with mild intellectual disabilities (i.e., raising or lowering the upper limit on IQ changes the number of students with mild intellectual disabilities who are eligible for this category but has little or no influence on students with more severe disabilities). More specifically, the changes have been made, to a large extent, in response to concerns regarding the overrepresentation of students from non–European American groups in the intellectual disability category and the stigma that is often associated with this label (Dunn, 1968).

EDUCATIONAL PRACTICES

Extensive research has been conducted regarding evidence-based educational practices that are effective with students with mild intellectual disabilities. This evidence reveals that these students can learn far more than we anticipated in the past but need more time to learn and benefit from effective instructional practices. In the sections that follow, we review placement practices regarding students with intellectual disabilities and follow with a discussion of educational practices that are effective for these students as they progress through school and transition to adult life.

To see Robert Hessels discuss the topic of inclusion and how it relates to this population of students, go to the Mr. Hessels module on the DVD-ROM and click on clip 5: Inclusion.

SERVICE DELIVERY

While students with intellectual disabilities have been provided with an education in primarily segregated, separate settings for the past 100 years, researchers have questioned the effectiveness of these placements for more than 70 years (Bennett, 1932;

Carlberg & Kavale, 1980; Johnson, 1962; Polloway, 1984). Much of the research that has been conducted on this issue revealed that students with intellectual disabilities benefit from spending at least some—and, in many instances, a large—proportion of the school day in general education classrooms. For example, after reviewing research related to the effectiveness of **separate class placements** for students with intellectual disabilities, Freeman and Alkin (2000) concluded that "children with milder mental levels of intellectual disabilities achieve more positive results in the integrated classroom than do their counterparts in segregated settings." They go on to note that the placement of students "with mental retardation in general education classrooms tends to improve their social skills and competence" (p. 15).

In spite of the support from research to place these students in general education classes for at least part of the school day, many students with mild intellectual disabilities are taught in segregated, separate settings for most of the day (McLeskey, Henry, & Hodges, 1999; Williamson et al., 2006). For example, overall, 52% of students with disabilities spend 80% or more of the school day in general education classrooms, compared to only 13% of students with intellectual disabilities (see Table 8.3). Similarly, only 18% of all students with disabilities spend most of the school day (60% or more) segregated from peers, compared to 57% of students with intellectual disabilities.

It is important to note that changes have occurred over the past decade indicating that significant progress has been made in including increasing numbers of students with intellectual disabilities in general education classrooms (Williamson et al., 2006). For example, in 1989–1990, 7.6% of students with intellectual disabilities were educated in general education settings for most of the school day. By 2004–2005, this figure had increased to 13.1% (U.S. Department of Education, 2006). Similarly, in 1990–1991, 70% of students with intellectual disabilities were educated in settings where they were segregated for 60% or more of the school day. By 2004–2005, this figure had dropped to 57%.

As our featured teacher, Robert Hessels, noted, a highlight of his career has been including students with mild intellectual disabilities in high school general education classrooms. His comments suggest the difficulty of this task. If inclusive programs are to be developed for students with mild intellectual disabilities, several activities are needed to ensure that these students have the supports necessary to be successful academically and socially. Perhaps most important, these supports include well-prepared general and special education teachers who have the knowledge and skills

Reflective Exercise #7
In spite of evidence that students with mild intellectual disabilities benefit from placement in well-supported general education classrooms for much of the school day, few of these students are educated in such settings. Why do you think this is the case? What challenges would these students present for teachers? What types of support would teachers need to successfully include more students with intellectual disabilities?

TABLE 8.3

PERCENTAGE OF SCHOOL-AGE STUDENTS WITH INTELLECTUAL DISABILITIES AND ALL DISABILITIES TAUGHT IN DIFFERENT PLACEMENT SETTINGS, 2004–2005

Disability Category	Placement Settings			
	<21[1]	21–60[1]	>60[1]	Separate setting[2]
Mild intellectual disability	13.09	29.66	50.79	6.46
All disability	51.87	26.50	17.60	4.03

Source: U.S. Department of Education, 2006.
1. These percentages represent the time students spend outside of the general education classroom. Thus, the first category, <21%, indicates that these students spend less than 21% of the school day in a separate, special education setting and is thus the most inclusive settings.
2. Separate setting combines several categories reported by the U.S. Department of Education, including public separate facility, private separate facility, public residential facility, private residential facility, and home/hospital environment.

Site Visit:
Effective Practices in Action

THE INCLUSIVE SCHOOL PROGRAM (ISP)

As increasing numbers of students with mild disabilities are included in general education classrooms for much of the school day, it is important that inclusive programs be developed and validated that successfully include students in general education classrooms and ensure that these students make adequate yearly progress in core academic subjects (e.g., reading and mathematics). The purpose of the program developed by Waldron and McLeskey (1998) was to develop inclusive school programs in elementary schools that successfully met these goals for students with mild disabilities.

Waldron and McLeskey worked with teams of teachers from three elementary schools to develop inclusive school programs (ISPs). Teams of teachers and administrators from each of the three schools worked over the course of a semester to examine their school, plan an inclusive program that was tailored to meet the needs of students and teachers in their school, and plan professional development activities that were needed by teachers to implement the proposed program. They also read about and discussed the basic principles of school change (Fullan, 2001).

While ISPs across the three schools differed based on individual school needs, they shared several characteristics:

1. Separate classes for students with LD and mild intellectual disabilities were closed.
2. Special education teachers worked collaboratively with two or more general education teachers.
3. Programs for students with disabilities were built on the general education curriculum and ensured that effective instructional practices were used in the general education classroom.
4. Attempts were made to avoid disproportionate numbers of students with disabilities in any general education classroom.
5. School organization was examined and changed to ensure that students could be provided with instruction of appropriate intensity (e.g., small-group instruction in reading).
6. Instructional assistants were used to provide support and intensive instruction for students with disabilities.

As you will recognize, this program used many of the principles of effective instruction that have been discussed in this chapter and also adapted the general education classroom to include students with mild disabilities and ensure that they had access to the general education curriculum. While students with mild disabilities were included in general education classrooms for much of the school day, they were pulled out of general education classrooms, along with other students with similar instructional needs in reading or mathematics, for intensive instruction for short periods of time during the school day.

The results of research conducted by Waldron and McLeskey revealed that students with mild disabilities who were educated in these ISPs made more progress in reading and comparable progress in math to students who were educated in traditional special education resource programs.

related to classroom instruction and behavior management that are necessary to meet the needs of students with diverse needs. However, evidence also reveals that significant change in an entire school is needed if inclusive programs are to be successfully implemented (McLeskey & Waldron, 2000, 2006; Waldron & McLeskey, 1998). The "Site Visit" feature provides a description of an inclusive school program that has been successfully implemented in several schools (McLeskey & Waldron, 2006; Waldron & McLeskey, 1998).

EARLY INTERVENTION

Research has revealed that the early experiences of children have an important influence on their later development and that effective early intervention programs can have a significant positive influence on a student's intelligence level, academic achievement, and social competence (Taylor et al., 2005). For students with mild intellectual disabilities, evidence indicates that children of mothers with low IQs are at a particular risk for poor intellectual outcomes and possibly mild or moderate intellectual disabilities and thus would benefit from early intervention (Ramey & Ramey, 1992).

Ramey and Ramey (1992) examined the results of three early intervention programs for students who were at a particular risk for poor intellectual outcomes. Each program was designed to provide these students with intensive early intervention. Ramey and Ramey concluded that these children respond very favorably to intensive, systematic, early intervention. Based on this research, six essential types of experiences are recommended:

1. Children should be encouraged to explore the environment.
2. Children should be guided toward basic thinking skills in areas such as sorting and sequencing.
3. Accomplishments of children should be celebrated and reinforced.
4. Skills that are learned should be practiced and expanded upon.
5. Negative consequences should be avoided when children are engaged in trial-and-error learning.
6. Children should be provided with extensive oral and written language experiences.

It is noteworthy that long-term follow-up of children who were at risk and participated in programs that included these characteristics revealed very positive outcomes. For example, Campbell, Ramey, Pungello, Sparling, and Miller-Johnson (2002) found that reading and math gains persisted into adulthood and that, as adults, participants in these programs had more years of total education and were more likely to attend college.

CLASSROOM INTERVENTIONS

As you will recollect from the previous discussion of the characteristics of students with mild intellectual disabilities, these students tend to take longer to learn academic content than do other students and lag behind age-level peers in basic skills. They also do not automatically generate strategies for learning and remembering academic content, as many students do. Information that we have discussed regarding effective instruction (see Chapter 5), learning strategies (see Chapter 6), and principles to design effective curriculum and instruction (see Chapter 6) may be used to improve learning outcomes for students with mild intellectual disabilities. In addition, in the sections that follow we discuss the use of explicit instruction, peer tutoring, monitoring student progress, and technology to address the instructional needs of students with mild intellectual disabilities.

Well-designed early intervention programs are very beneficial for children with mild intellectual disabilities.

Explicit Instruction

In addition to these strategies, students with mild intellectual disabilities benefit from being provided with teacher-directed **explicit instruction.** While much research regarding this type of instruction has focused on students with mild intellectual disabilities, the instructional approaches that are sub-

www.prenhall.com/rosenberg

sequently described have also been proven effective for students with and without disabilities (Coyne, Kame'enui, & Carnine, 2007; Shuell, 1996).

If a student you are teaching does not gain proficiency in important curricular content, the most effective instructional strategies to ensure that this material is learned are built upon the principles of **mastery learning** (Bloom, 1971, 1976). Several assumptions underlie this approach to learning (Shuell, 1996):

- Instruction is organized into well-defined units.
- Mastery of each unit is expected of each student before proceeding to the next unit.
- Tests are administered to determine mastery.
- If a test reveals that mastery has not been achieved, supplemental materials and activities are used to teach the information again.
- Under appropriate conditions, all students can learn well or master most of the content.
- Time is used to individualize instruction. (Some students take more time to master content than others do and may have to repeat the instructional cycle more than once.)

Various programs and approaches to instruction have been developed based on mastery learning, and these programs have generally been proven effective (Shuell, 1996). The approach that has the strongest research to support its effectiveness and is the most widely used is **Direct Instruction (DI)** (Carnine, Silbert, Kame'enui, & Tarver, 2003; Coyne et al., 2007; Kame'enui & Carnine, 1998; Rosenshine & Stevens, 1986; Stein, Silbert, & Carnine, 1997; Swanson, Hoskyn, & Lee, 1999). Further information regarding this approach to teaching and learning is provided in the "Highly Effective Instructional Strategies" feature on Direct Instruction.

Peer Tutoring

Good and Brophy (2003) have noted that individualized tutoring is the optimal instructional method for meeting the needs of students who are struggling academically. Other researchers have reached a similar conclusion (Pinnell, Lyons, DeFord, Bryk, & Seltzer, 1994; Slavin et al., 1994; Spear-Swerling & Sternberg, 1996; Vaughn, Gersten, & Chard, 2000). This approach may be especially effective for students with mild intellectual disabilities, who need extra time and practice to learn academic material. Of course, the drawback to this method is that it is very expensive and needs to be targeted at students who will receive the maximum benefit.

Schools have engaged in a variety of activities to provide cost-effective individual tutoring. Most often, these programs have focused on young students experiencing difficulty learning to read, although programs have also been developed across age levels and content areas. To reduce costs, some schools have rearranged the school day to allow teachers to provide tutoring just before or after school. Others have trained tutors (e.g., parent volunteers, teacher education students from local universities) to work with students during or after school hours.

In addition to these approaches, peer-tutoring programs are widely used and cost-effective. These programs may involve after-school tutoring in subject areas for middle or high school students or tutoring in basic skills areas (e.g., reading and math) for elementary students. Peer tutoring is a group of strategies that use peers (either same-age or cross-age) as one-on-one teachers providing individualized instruction, practice, repetition, and clarification of concepts (Utley, Mortsweet, & Greenwood, 1997).

Extensive research has been conducted on the use of peer tutoring as a strategy for improving learning outcomes for both the student being tutored (the tutee) and the student doing the tutoring (the tutor). Research has revealed that well-designed tutoring programs result in improved educational outcomes for students with and without disabilities who are struggling to learn academic content (Elbaum, Vaughn, Hughes, & Moody, 1999; Fuchs, Fuchs, & Burish, 2000; Mathes, Howard, Babyak, & Allen, 2000; Vaughn et al., 2000). In addition, one of the unexpected findings of this research has been that the tutoring experience results in improved academic achievement for both the tutor and the tutee (Elbaum et al., 1999; Fuchs et al., 2000).

To learn more about explicit instruction, go to the Ms. Sprague module on the DVD-ROM and click on clip 7: Explicit Instruction.

Reflective Exercise #8
Based on what you have read in this chapter about the characteristics of students with mild intellectual disabilities, why do you think Direct Instruction has been so effective with these students? What characteristics of DI lead to this effectiveness?

FIGURE 9.1

DSM-IV-TR CRITERIA FOR IDENTIFYING ADHD

A. Either (1) or (2):

(1) six (or more) of the following symptoms of inattention have persisted for at least 6 months to a degree that is maladaptive and inconsistent with developmental level:

Inattention

(a) often fails to give close attention to details or makes careless mistakes in schoolwork, work, or other activities

(b) often has difficulty sustaining attention in tasks or play activities

(c) often does not seem to listen when spoken to directly

(d) often does not follow through on instructions and fails to finish schoolwork, chores, or duties in the workplace (not due to oppositional behavior or failure to understand instructions)

(e) often has difficulty organizing activities

(f) often avoids, dislikes, or is reluctant to engage in tasks that require sustained mental effort (such as schoolwork or homework)

(g) often loses things necessary for tasks or activities (e.g., toys, school assignments, pencils, books, or tools)

(h) is often easily distracted by extraneous stimuli

(i) is often forgetful in daily activities

(2) six (or more) of the following symptoms of hyperactivity-impulsivity have persisted for at least 6 months to a degree that is maladaptive and inconsistent with developmental level:

Hyperactivity

(a) often fidgets with hands or feet or squirms in seat

(b) often leaves seat in classroom or in other situations in which remaining seated is expected

(c) often runs about or climbs excessively in situations in which it is inappropriate (in adolescents or adults, may be limited to subjective feelings of restlessness)

(d) often has difficulty playing or engaging in leisure activities quietly

(e) is often "on the go" or often acts as if "driven by a motor"

(f) often talks excessively

Impulsivity

(a) often blurts out answers before questions have been completed

(b) often has difficulty awaiting turn

(c) often interrupts or intrudes on others (e.g., butts into conversations or games)

B. Some hyperactive-impulsive or inattentive symptoms that caused impairment were present before age 7 years.

C. Some impairment from the symptoms is present in two or more settings (e.g., at school [or work] and at home).

D. There must be clear evidence of clinically significant impairment in social, academic, or occupational functioning.

E. The symptoms do not occur exclusively during the course of a Pervasive Developmental Disorder, Schizophrenia, or other Psychotic Disorder and are not better accounted for by another mental disorder (e.g., Mood Disorder, Anxiety Disorder, Dissociative Disorder, or a Personality Disorder).

Code based on type:

314.01 Attention-Deficit/Hyperactivity Disorder, Combined Type: if both Criteria A1 and A2 are met for the past 6 months

314.00 Attention-Deficit/Hyperactivity Disorder, Predominantly Inattentive Type: if Criterion A1 is met but Criterion A2 is not met for the past 6 months

314.02 Attention-Deficit/Hyperactivity Disorder, Predominantly Hyperactive-Impulsive Type: if Criterion A2 is met but Criterion A1 is not met for the past 6 months

Source: Reprinted with permission from the *Diagnostic and Statistical Manual of Mental Disorders,* Fourth Edition, Text Revision, Copyright 2000. American Psychiatric Association.

> **Reflective Exercise #3**
> Think of times you have observed preschool children. Did many of these students exhibit characteristics similar to those used to identify students with ADHD? Have you observed a young child (e.g., in a grocery store, on a playground) who exhibited these behaviors at such an extreme level that you thought he or she might be identified with ADHD?

social adjustment (e.g., getting along with peers, making friends) and/or academic achievement.

As we have noted, ADHD is not a separate special education category that is included in federal legislation (i.e., IDEA 2004). In 1991, the U.S. Department of Education issued a "policy clarification" memorandum indicating that students with ADHD could be identified if they met the *other health impaired* (OHI) criteria in IDEA. (This category of disability is discussed further in Chapter 14.) However, this policy was not fully and effectively implemented (IDEA Law and Resources, 1999). This led to the formal inclusion of ADHD in the reauthorization of IDEA in 1997 as one of several disorders that could form the basis of identification for the OHI category. Thus, students with ADHD may receive services under IDEA if they meet criteria in the OHI category. *Other health impairments* are defined in IDEA as follows:

www.prenhall.com/rosenberg

Section 300.7 (c) (9) Other health impairment means having limited strength, vitality or alertness, including a heightened alertness to environmental stimuli, that results in limited alertness with respect to the educational environment, that—

(i) Is due to chronic or acute health problems such as asthma, attention deficit disorder or attention deficit hyperactivity disorder, diabetes, epilepsy, a heart condition, hemophilia, lead poisoning, leukemia, nephritis, rheumatic fever, and sickle cell anemia; and

(ii) Adversely affects a child's educational performance. (IDEA 1997, Sec. 300.7 [c] [9] [ii])

You will note that while **ADD** (an acronym formerly used to identify children with predominantly inattentive behaviors [ADHD-PI]) and ADHD are mentioned in Section (i) of this definition, a specific definition for ADHD is not provided. This is also the case (i.e., no definitions are provided) with the other medical conditions that are included in the OHI category because all of these conditions require a medical diagnosis. Thus, the medical definition and criteria for identification provided in DSM-IV-TR are used to determine if a student has ADHD, and a physician typically makes this determination.

Once a determination is made that a student has ADHD, the school-based multidisciplinary team addresses Section (ii) in the OHI definition and determines if this condition adversely affects the child's educational performance. If it is determined that this is the case, the student is then eligible for special education services as part of IDEA.

You should be aware that some students who have been identified with ADHD are not eligible for the OHI category, usually because they do not meet the criterion related to whether the condition adversely affects educational performance. This could occur because the ADHD condition is relatively mild or the symptoms of the ADHD may be controlled by medication. (We will provide more information about the use of medication as an intervention for ADHD later in this chapter.) Thus, the ADHD would thus not adversely affect educational performance. When this is the case, the student may still be eligible for accommodations in the general education classroom as part of **Section 504 of the Rehabilitation Act** of 1974.

As we discussed in Chapter 4, Section 504 is a civil rights act, not legislation that provides educational support for students (e.g., IDEA). Moreover, this law was enacted to prevent discrimination against persons with disabilities and ensure that these students receive reasonable accommodations (deBettencourt, 2002). Thus, a student who has been identified with ADHD and is eligible under Section 504 must receive reasonable accommodations in a general education classroom to ensure that he or she is not discriminated against because of the disability. Accommodations might include activities such as changing the location of the student's seat (e.g., nearer to a student who is a good role model or to a quiet area of the classroom); allowing the student to move about the room at appropriate times; allowing extended time for taking a test, with breaks as necessary; or providing support to the student to improve his organizational skills. For more information regarding eligibility for special education, see Chapter 4.

MAJOR CHARACTERISTICS OF STUDENTS WITH ADHD

A review of Figure 9.1 will provide you with a good overview of the major behaviors that characterize ADHD, the symptoms that are used to identify these behaviors, and the subtypes of this disorder. We will not discuss these characteristics further in this section but will address two major characteristics of students with ADHD: social and behavioral problems and academic difficulties. These difficulties often adversely affect educational performance and may result in eligibility for the OHI label. Moreover, when the academic or behavior problems are extreme, the student with ADHD may also be identified with a learning disability or emotional/behavioral disorder.

Social and Behavioral Disorders

If you consider the characteristics of ADHD that we have discussed to this point, it is apparent that students with this disorder will often have difficulty getting along with peers. Consider the behaviors that are used to identify these children that are included in Figure 9.1. As you can see, children with ADHD have difficulty sustaining attention during play activities, often do not listen when spoken to, run and climb excessively in situations where this behavior is inappropriate, have difficulty with turn taking, and often interrupt or intrude on others. These are behaviors that most do not want in friends and many find unacceptable and wish to avoid in others.

As you would expect, research has documented that many children with ADHD have difficulty getting along with others. Wenar and Kerig (2006) note that children with ADHD interact with peers in a more negative and unskilled manner than do other children. "Moreover, when introduced to a peer with ADHD, children take only minutes to notice and react negatively to the ADHD child's behavior" (p. 189). This is not to say that every child identified with ADHD has difficulty getting along with peers, but many children who are so identified have social problems.

Considering these social adjustment problems, a substantial proportion of students with ADHD are identified with emotional/behavioral disorders. Barkley (2003) found that, by age 7 or later, 54 to 67% of students with ADHD will be identified with oppositional-defiant disorder, while 20 to 50% of children and 44 to 50% of adolescents will be identified with conduct disorders. In addition to these disorders, 10 to 40% of children with ADHD will develop anxiety disorders, while 20 to 30% will develop mild to severe depression (Wenar & Kerig, 2006). (Emotional and behavioral disorders were discussed in Chapter 7.)

Academic Difficulties

As with social/behavioral disorders, many of the behaviors that are used to identify students with ADHD have the potential to have a negative influence on academic achievement. For example, symptoms of ADHD included in Figure 9.1 include inability to pay close attention to details, carelessness in schoolwork, difficulty sustaining attention, difficulty organizing tasks, and many additional behaviors that will likely lead to academic difficulties.

As you might expect, many children identified with ADHD have difficulty progressing academically in school. Research has revealed that 53 to 80% of children will probably have a learning problem in reading, arithmetic, or spelling by the time they reach the end of elementary school (Barkley, 2003; Reiff, 2004). A smaller but still substantial proportion of students with ADHD, ranging from 19 to 26%, are likely to have a learning disability in reading or mathematics (Barkley, 2003).

It has been suggested that there are two potential factors that contribute to academic problems among children with ADHD (Rapport, Scanlan, & Denney, 1999). First, as we have noted, the behaviors associated with ADHD increase the probability that students will have conduct problems, which contribute to lowered academic achievement. That is, students who are disruptive and inattentive frequently do not attend to and learn academic content that is addressed and reviewed in class. The second pathway connecting ADHD and academic problems is through cognitive deficits associated with ADHD. For these students, behaviors such as lack of organizational skills, lack of sustained attention to tasks, and problems with monitoring and controlling their behavior may lead to academic skills deficits.

PREVALENCE, COURSE, AND CAUSAL FACTORS

PREVALENCE

While there is general agreement that ADHD is the most common behavior disorder among children (Gureasko-Moore, DuPaul, & Power, 2005; Tsal, Shalev, & Mevorach, 2005), there are widely varying estimates of the prevalence of this disorder. The most frequently cited, and probably the most accurate estimate, of prevalence for ADHD is 3 to 7% of the school-age population (APA, 2000). Well-designed research by Costello et al. (2003) supports this estimate, although these researchers found that the prevalence rate for ADHD declined as children moved through school.

Reflective Exercise #4
Discuss how the symptoms of ADHD might lead to social problems for a student. How might a teacher address these behaviors to reduce the social adjustment problems?

Reflective Exercise #5
Students who are impulsive or inattentive to classroom activities are highly frustrating for some teachers. How can a teacher ensure that these student behaviors do not have a negative influence on how he or she interacts with or provides instruction to a student with ADHD?

What these prevalence rates mean is that anywhere from 2 to 4.5 million school-age students are identified with ADHD in the United States. The vast majority of these students are served in general education classrooms (Salend & Rohena, 2003), which means that general educators will see approximately one or two students with ADHD in their classrooms each year.

One aspect of prevalence that is clear is that boys are far more likely to be identified with ADHD than are girls. Barkley (2003) suggests that the average difference in identification rate is three boys to every one girl. There is also some evidence that ADHD is more common among children from low socioeconomic backgrounds; however, it is unclear whether differences exist across different racial groups (Wenar & Kerig, 2006).

A second aspect of prevalence that is important to note is that many of these students are also identified with another disability, most commonly learning disability or emotional/behavioral disorder. It has been estimated that between 50 and 60% of students with ADHD have a coexisting disability (Reiff, 2004). For example, up to 80% of children with ADHD have some type of academic difficulty in school and as many as one fourth of these problems are likely to be severe enough to result in identification of a learning disability (Barkley, 2003).

You should note that prevalence estimates for ADHD vary for several reasons. Perhaps the major reason is the difference among individuals, including well-trained professionals, in defining terms such as *sustained attention, inattention, impulsive,* and *hyperactive.* A second issue related to varying prevalence levels is the fact that the behavior of children with ADHD varies depending on the measurement procedures that are used to assess the existence of the condition. For example, lower prevalence rates result if parent reports are used to determine if a child meets the behavioral criteria for ADHD, while teacher reports result in higher prevalence rates (up to twice as high) (Barkley, 2003).

A final factor that contributes to variation in prevalence rates relates to the context within which the behaviors of concern occur. Barkley (2003) has reviewed research related to contextual factors that influence the ability of students with ADHD to sustain their attention, perform tasks, control impulses, regulate their activity level, and consistently produce work. He concludes that the performance of children with ADHD is worse

Later in the day
With greater task complexity
When restraint is needed
With tasks that are not highly stimulating
Under variable schedules of immediate task consequences
Under conditions with a long delay before reinforcement
In the absence of adult supervision during task performance

Thus, there is wide variation in the prevalence rates of children identified with ADHD. You will see the manifestation of these differences in schools: Some schools and school districts tend to have a high prevalence rate for students with ADHD, while others have a much lower rate. We will continue discussing these issues later in this chapter when we address controversies concerning ADHD.

THE COURSE OF ADHD

Parents often observe the first hint of ADHD when they note excessive motor activity as toddlers begin to walk and explore the world around them (APA, 2000). This is only a hint because the vast majority of very active toddlers are not later identified with ADHD. Moreover, only a few students with ADHD are identified before entering school. These students typically have very high levels of hyperactive and inattentive behavior as well as more negative temperaments and greater emotional reactivity to events (Barkley, 2003).

Most students with ADHD-C or ADHD-PHI are identified in early elementary school, as the demands placed on children to fit into the rules and structure of school

Some adolescents with ADHD exhibit inner feelings of restlessness.

create a context in which behaviors such as a high activity level and impulsiveness become apparent and result in teacher and parental concern about disruptive behavior and, for a substantial portion of these students, lack of academic progress. Students who are predominantly inattentive (ADHD-PI) are often identified later in elementary school; their inattentiveness may not be as obvious in the early school years and does not immediately produce academic problems or behaviors that disrupt classroom routines.

Most of the behaviors associated with ADHD are relatively stable through early adolescence (APA, 2000). However, for children with ADHD-C or ADHD-PHI, these behaviors are likely to contribute to behavior problems, with the result that some of these students are identified with emotional/behavioral disorders as they move through elementary school.

It is generally recognized that hyperactive and inattentive behaviors decline as students enter adolescence (APA, 2000; Barkley, 2003; Wenar & Kerig, 2006). However, these behaviors also decline in students without ADHD (i.e., typical students become more attentive and less active). The sum of these changes is that students with ADHD remain significantly more active and inattentive than do typical students in adolescence (Barkley, 2003). In addition, the manifestation of these behaviors may change in adolescence, as high levels of motor activity may be replaced by an inner feeling of restlessness, while reckless behavior on a bicycle may be replaced by reckless behavior while driving an automobile (Wenar & Kerig, 2006).

Overall, Barkley (2003) found that ADHD continued into adolescence for 50 to 80% of children who manifested this disorder in elementary school. ADHD is more likely to persist into adolescence for students with more extreme levels of hyperactive-impulsive behavior in elementary school, the existence of conduct or oppositional behavior, poor family relations, and maternal depression.

For a substantial portion of adolescents, ADHD persists into adulthood in a somewhat altered form. Symptoms related to hyperactivity seem to significantly decline or disappear for most adults, while inattentiveness and impulsive behavior decline both for adults with ADHD and those who are not so labeled (Barkley, Fischer, Smallish, & Fletcher, 2002). Overall, it has been estimated that, as adolescents with ADHD enter adulthood, 30% outgrow ADHD; 40% continue to have symptoms of restlessness, inattention, and impulsivity; while 30% develop additional problems (e.g., substance abuse, antisocial behavior) (Wenar & Kerig, 2006).

The extent to which the symptoms of ADHD persist into adulthood depends, to a large degree, on the severity of the hyperactive-impulsive behaviors in childhood, the coexistence of oppositional defiant behavior or conduct disorders, and the nature of the family relationship (Barkley, 2003). Students with ADHD who have the most difficulty adjusting as adults are those who are identified with conduct disorders or other major psychiatric disorders. Follow-up studies have revealed that, for approximately one-fourth of students with ADHD, conduct disorders persist into adulthood, while one-fourth of all students with ADHD develop a major depression as adults (Fischer, Barkley, Smallish, & Fletcher, 2002).

CAUSAL FACTORS

What causes the behavior of students with ADHD to develop as it does? Why do some preschool children have symptoms of ADHD that disappear as they grow older, while these behaviors persist in others? Are these behaviors a function of parents' childrearing practices, heredity, neurological anomalies, exposure to toxins, or intake of food additives? These are some of the questions that arise for parents and teachers regarding students with ADHD. The short answer to why students develop ADHD is, for the

Reflective Exercise #6
Have you observed an adult who might have been identified with ADHD? How did the behavior of this adult differ from the behavior of children with ADHD? Why do you suspect that the identification of adults with ADHD has grown rapidly in recent years?

vast majority of these students, "We don't know." It is apparent that ADHD is a function of a complex interaction of many factors that contribute to the development of this disorder, including brain injury, brain abnormalities, hereditary influences, and family issues.

Brain Injury

The one cause of ADHD that we can be sure of is brain injury. A long history of research, dating to the study of brain-injured World War I veterans, reveals that traumatic brain injury (this disability is discussed further in Chapter 14), especially to the frontal area of the brain, often results in hyperactive, impulsive, and inattentive behavior (Strauss & Lehtinen, 1947). You should note that most children with ADHD do not have brain damage. Only 5–10% of these children have documented brain damage that results from trauma (e.g., an auto accident or a fall), toxins, or disease (Barkley, 2000).

Brain Abnormalities

While 90 to 95% of students with ADHD do not have documented brain injury, a significant amount of evidence has accumulated suggesting that these students do have certain abnormalities in brain function that relate to ADHD. For example, the brain chemistry of children with ADHD is often different from those who do not have ADHD (DuPaul, Barkley, & Connor, 1998). In particular, research has shown that children with ADHD have a deficiency of the neurotransmitters dopamine and norepinephrine, which are chemicals in the brain that influence the transmission of signals between nerve cells. This relationship was initially recognized when researchers found that stimulant medications, which are effective in reducing the symptoms of ADHD, act by increasing the amount of these neurotransmitters in the brain (DuPaul et al., 1998).

Additional research has been conducted with neuropsychological tests and medical tests that measure brain activity, which have resulted in evidence that abnormalities primarily in the frontal areas of the brain contribute to ADHD (Barkley, 2000, 2003; Wenar & Kerig, 2006). These abnormalities are not brain damage but differences that exist when comparing children with ADHD with those who do not have this disorder.

Hereditary Influences

Compelling evidence supports the perspective that heredity plays a major role in ADHD. Research with families has shown that, if the mother, father, or a child has ADHD, the chances of another child having ADHD are five times as high as in a family with no previous evidence of ADHD (Biederman, Faraone, Keenan, & Tsuang, 1991). Studies of twins provide even more persuasive evidence. This research has revealed that, if one identical twin has ADHD, the odds that the other twin will have this disorder are between 67 and 81% (Barkley, 2003). This evidence suggests that heredity explains at least 80% of the range of behaviors related to ADHD, which is similar to the heritability of height (Barkley, 2003).

Parents play an important role in determining how the symptoms of ADHD will be manifested when the child is not in school.

Family Influences

Early theories regarding the causes of ADHD contended that poor parenting was a major cause of the disorder (Barkley, 2000). Research has not supported this perspective. While poor parent management skills can make the behaviors associated with ADHD worse, and extreme levels of stress in a family (e.g., an acrimonious divorce) can temporarily result in some of the symptoms of ADHD, there is no evidence that parenting practices or a dysfunctional family situation can cause the extreme behaviors that are associated with ADHD.

Reflective Exercise #7
Now that you have reviewed the range of causal influences associated with ADHD, comment on how useful knowledge of such factors would be in your planning of classroom-based instructional and behavioral interventions.

This is not to say that a parent's behavior isn't important in determining how the symptoms of ADHD will be manifested in the home and, to some degree, in school. Indeed, parents, siblings, teachers, and peers are all crucial in influencing the extent of negative behaviors exhibited by children with ADHD (APA, 2000). As we will discuss later in this chapter when we address interventions, well-managed programs to support these students, which often include well-designed instructional settings, use of good behavior-management practices, and, in many cases, the use of medication, can provide a very effective approach to treatment for these students.

IDENTIFICATION AND ASSESSMENT

The identification of a student with ADHD typically proceeds from (1) identification to (2) determination of eligibility based on IDEA or Section 504.

SCREENING

The first step in identifying a student with ADHD is screening (DuPaul, 2004). In a school, a teacher will typically be the first to observe that a student exhibits inattentiveness, hyperactivity, and/or impulsiveness at levels that are greater than peers' and that these behaviors interfere with the student's academic progress and/or social adjustment in the classroom. The Attention Deficit Hyperactivity Disorder Test (Gilliam, 1995) is a screening instrument that may be used by a teacher to evaluate students for possible ADHD (Venn, 2007). Once a teacher determines that a student may have ADHD, the teacher should seek the assistance of a psychologist to determine if further evaluation is needed. The psychologist will interview the teacher to screen for the severity and frequency of symptoms that might indicate ADHD.

It is important to note that a teacher should not recommend to a parent that a student be referred to a physician for evaluation for ADHD or that a student might be a good candidate for medication. The multidisciplinary team should be involved in any decision regarding whether a referral to a physician will be recommended to the parent. Moreover, the physician, in consultation with the psychologist, teachers, other relevant school professionals, and the child's parents, will make any decision regarding whether the student should be identified with ADHD and the use of any medical intervention that may be needed.

The criteria for determining whether a child has ADHD are included in Figure 9.1. As we've noted despite efforts to standardize the criteria for ADHD in DSM-IV-TR, these criteria "remain subjective and may be interpreted differently by different observers" (AAP, 2000, p. 1163). Because of this subjectivity in the identification process, multiple measures and multiple methods should be used to collect data regarding the student's behavior across a range of settings and sources (Salend & Rohena, 2003). These methods should include interviews with parents and teachers, behavior ratings scales completed by parents and/or teachers, observation of the child's behavior in multiple school settings (e.g., classroom, lunchroom, playground), and assessment of academic functioning (DuPaul, 2004). It is also useful to review the student's school records and medical history (OSEP, 2003).

Parent interviews are often an important aspect of the identification of students with ADHD.

The American Academy of Pediatrics (2000) has recommended the use of several behavior rating scales, questionnaires, and checklists that have been developed to

FIGURE 9.2

ADHD RATING SCALES, QUESTIONNAIRES, AND CHECKLISTS RECOMMENDED BY THE AMERICAN ACADEMY OF PEDIATRICS

Barkley's School Situations Questionnaire (Barkley & Murphy, 2005)

Child Behavior Checklist for Ages 6–18, Parent Form (Achenbach, 2001a)

Child Behavior Checklist for Ages 6–18, Teacher Report Form (Achenbach, 2001b)

Conners Parent Rating Scale—Revised Version: Long Form, ADHD Index Scale (Conners, 2002a)

Conners Teacher Rating Scale—Revised Version: Long Form, ADHD Index Scale (Conners, 2002b)

Devereux Scales of Mental Disorders (Naglieri, LeBuffe, & Pfeiffer, 1994)

Source: Adapted from American Academy of Pediatrics, 2000.

quantify the behavioral characteristics of students with ADHD. These rating scales are used to differentiate students who do and do not have ADHD (see Figure 9.2).

While a physician ultimately makes the decision regarding whether a student has ADHD, the multidisciplinary team has the responsibility for conducting an educational evaluation to determine the extent to which the behaviors associated with ADHD might have influenced the child's academic achievement and social adjustment. Both standardized norm-referenced tests and criterion-referenced measures of academic achievement may be used as well as curriculum-based measures that address progress that the child is making in the general education curriculum. In addition, observations of the student in the general education classroom, examination of test scores and report-card grades, and interviews with teachers and parents should be conducted to collect this information.

When the multidisciplinary team suspects that the student could have a coexisting disability, additional information should be collected. As we have noted, a substantial proportion of students with ADHD also have learning disabilities and emotional/behavioral disorders. More information regarding assessment of these disabilities is included in Chapters 6 (learning disabilities) and 7 (emotional/behavioral disorders).

DETERMINING ELIGIBILITY FOR SERVICES

Once the student has been identified as having ADHD and information has been collected from multiple sources regarding the student's academic progress and social adjustment, the multidisciplinary team examines and discusses these data to determine if the student is eligible for special education services. To be eligible for special education services, the student must be identified with ADHD, and the ADHD must adversely affect educational performance. It is important to note that the multidisciplinary team may decide the child has ADHD but is not eligible for special education services because the disability does not adversely affect educational performance.

A student who has ADHD but is not eligible for special education services may be appropriate for evaluation under Section 504. The same type of data is collected for making this determination. If the data collected demonstrate that the child's ADHD adversely affects his or her learning (which is a major life activity), the student may qualify under Section 504 for services (OSEP, 2003). Students who are eligible under Section 504 do not have an IEP but "must be provided regular or special education and related aids or services that are designed to meet their individual needs as adequately as the needs of non-disabled students are met" (p. 5).

EDUCATIONAL PRACTICES

In the past decade, extensive research has been conducted regarding practices that are effective in addressing the needs of students with ADHD. We begin with a review of placement practices regarding students with ADHD and then focus on the two major approaches that are used to address the needs of these students.

SERVICE DELIVERY

Based on all available data, it is clear that most students identified with ADHD spend the majority of the school day in a general education classroom. Separate data are not available from the U.S. Department of Education regarding placement settings for students with ADHD, as these students are included in the *other health impaired* category. However, data for the OHI category reveal that approximately 54% of these students spend the majority of the day (80% or more) in general education classrooms, while an additional 29% spend 40 to 79% of the school day in general education classes. These placements are similar to data for students with learning disabilities (U.S. Department of Education, 2005). Students who are identified as ADHD under Section 504 are also educated primarily in general education classrooms.

Of course, these data also reveal that some students with ADHD are educated in more restrictive settings (approximately 17% of students identified as other health impaired). Furthermore, students with ADHD who are identified with other disabilities, especially emotional/behavioral disorders, are likely to be educated in more restrictive settings for much of the school day. These students require more extensive interventions than those that can be effectively offered in the general education classroom. For more information regarding interventions that may be used to address the behavior and conduct problems manifested by students with ADHD, see Chapter 7.

What are the implications of these data? It is apparent that most students with ADHD have mild disabilities that are typically addressed in general education classrooms. The success that educators have in addressing the needs of these students depends on the use of effective interventions. Many of the interventions that have been developed for students with ADHD are effective in any setting.

EARLY INTERVENTION

The symptoms of ADHD are typically noted before the child enters school (i.e., before age 7) (APA, 2000). Furthermore, children who are identified with ADHD before entering school typically have more severe symptoms and are often identified with ADHD-PHI or ADHD-C. Many of these children present significant challenges for their parents and preschool teachers and are at a high risk for developing academic difficulties and oppositional and defiant behaviors (DuPaul & Stoner, 2003). This makes it especially important to intervene early to address current behavior difficulties as well as to prevent or reduce the severity of academic skill deficits, aggression, opposition, and defiance (DuPaul & Stoner, 2003).

One strategy that has been proven effective in addressing the needs of young children with ADHD is the use of parent-mediated interventions (DuPaul & Stoner, 2003). DuPaul and Stoner note that parent-mediated interventions that have proven effective include

1. Use of brief, direct commands
2. Positive parent attention to appropriate child behavior
3. Implementation of contingency management strategies in which children earn token reinforcers (e.g., poker chips) for compliance with parent directives
4. Use of response cost and time-out from positive reinforcement strategies to reduce noncompliant and aggressive behavior

If early intervention efforts are to succeed, it is important that home-school partnerships with families be developed. These partnerships are largely based on gaining trust of the family; addressing the diverse needs, backgrounds, and experiences of the family; and offering a range of usable, flexible services that address the changing needs of the family (Salend & Rohena, 2003). These partnerships also offer parents and teachers the opportunity to share information about the child, monitor the effective-

Reflective Exercise #8

Most students with ADHD are included in general education classrooms. What challenges might the impulsive and inattentive behaviors of these students present to classroom teachers? What types of support do classroom teachers need to ensure that these students are successful? **To hear and see students like you discuss this topic, go to the Students module on the DVD-ROM and click on clip 8: ADHD.**

ness of medications that may be administered, coordinate assignments, and develop behavior modification plans (Bos, Nahmias, & Urban, 1999).

Barkley (2000) has recommended the use of home-based reward programs as part of home-school partnerships in addressing the needs of students with ADHD. One such program is the behavior report card. The behavior report card consists of a structured form that the teacher completes daily as an evaluation of the student's behavior in targeted areas, such as class participation, performance of classwork, and following class rules. The parents then use this report card to give or take away rewards, depending on the child's behavior. Report cards are initially sent home daily; but as the child's behavior improves, the report cards are sent home less frequently.

In the case of young children with extreme hyperactive and impulsive behavior, it is likely that even with intensive interventions and close cooperation between home and school, the behaviors will continue to interfere with the child's development. Under these circumstances, medication will often be prescribed to control the child's behavior. When this occurs, it is especially important that teachers and families work together closely to monitor the effects of medication on the child's behavior and continue to use effective interventions to ensure the child's academic and social progress.

It is important that teachers and parents work together to ensure that early intervention efforts succeed for children with ADHD.

CLASSROOM INTERVENTIONS

Many of the classroom intervention strategies that are useful for students with emotional/behavioral disorders have proven effective for students with ADHD. In particular, the use of behavior modification, a token economy, social skills training/teaching replacement behaviors, functional behavior assessments, and teaching self-control (all described in Chapter 7) have been shown to be effective with students with ADHD (Duhaney, 2003; DuPaul & Stoner, 2003; Reid, Trout, & Schartz, 2005; Rosenberg, Wilson, Maheady, & Sindelar, 2004).

Similarly, effective instructional practices that are used to teach students who struggle to learn academic material may be used with students with ADHD. For example, the principles that guide effective curriculum design and instruction and the use of strategy instruction (described in Chapter 7) are useful for teachers of students with ADHD. Furthermore, instructional strategies described in Chapter 8, including Direct Instruction and classwide peer tutoring, may be used for students with ADHD.

An intervention that holds much promise for addressing the needs of students with ADHD is the use of strategies that help these students regulate their own behavior. **Self-regulation strategies** have been the topic of much research in recent years. Reid and colleagues (2005) reviewed this research and concluded that four self-regulation strategies have been proven effective for use with students with ADHD to decrease inappropriate behaviors, increase on-task behaviors, and increase academic accuracy and productivity. These strategies are described in the "Highly Effective Instructional Strategies" feature.

In addition to these interventions, Barkley (2000) has provided general principles for structuring and managing a classroom that are particularly important in addressing the needs of students with ADHD:

1. The presentation of rules and instructions should be brief, clear, and (whenever possible) presented visually in the form of charts, lists, and other visual reminders. Relying on a child's memory and verbal reminders will often be ineffective.
2. The approach to consequences must be well organized, thoroughly planned, and systematic. Feedback, rewards, and punishment used to manage a child's behavior must be delivered immediately.

Highly Effective Instructional Strategies

SELF-REGULATION STRATEGIES

Addressing the needs of students with ADHD in classrooms has typically taken the form of providing structure, consistency, and predictability; having the teacher closely monitor and respond to the student's behavior; and providing reinforcement for appropriate behavior. While these strategies are often successful in ameliorating the impact of the student's behavior in the classroom, they do not include strategies that allow the student to control his own behavior. Moreover, Barkley (2003) has suggested that the central difficulty faced by students with ADHD relates to problems with monitoring and regulating their behavior.

Barkley contends that several behaviors (he calls them *executive functions*) are used by children to control or manage their behavior. For example, one of the behaviors that Barkley has found to be lacking in students with ADHD is inner speech, which children use as a means of reflection to control their behavior. Inner speech is thus used to solve problems, follow instructions, abide by rules, and provide self-instruction. When inner speech is lacking, children tend to reflect less before speaking, talk excessively, have poor self-control, and have difficulty following rules.

Strategies have been developed and validated for children with ADHD that may be used to allow these children to regulate their own behavior (Reid et al., 2005). These self-regulation strategies are "used by students to manage, monitor, record, and/or assess their behavior or academic achievement" (p. 362). Two of these interventions are described here.

SELF-MONITORING

To use this intervention, the child self-monitors an academic task (such as practicing math facts), determines the amount of work completed and the accuracy of the work, and produces a graph that is used to monitor accuracy or work completion. Self-recording provides the student with an immediate consequence for his behavior and may be sufficient in some instances to result in improvement in the student's behavior.

For students whose behavior is more difficult to change, the child is provided with reinforcement for improving ac-

curacy or work completion to a predetermined level. The teacher may provide reinforcement, or the child may have this responsibility after meeting a predetermined level of performance.

It is important to note that self-monitoring can also be used with student behavior such as attention to task. When self-monitoring is used with attention to task, the teacher periodically provides the student with a reminder to record whether or not he or she is paying attention to a classroom task. These behaviors are then graphed, and reinforcement may be provided based on predetermined criteria.

SELF-MANAGEMENT

This intervention requires that a student "monitor, rate, and compare some aspect of his or her behavior to an external standard" (Reid et al., 2005, p. 363). While self-management is similar to self-monitoring, it adds a step that requires the student to evaluate accuracy, and the student's results are compared to an external evaluator (e.g., teacher, paraprofessional). Reinforcement is then provided based on the extent to which the student's self-evaluation closely matches the external evaluator.

Reid and colleagues point out several advantages of using self-regulation strategies with students with ADHD:

- The goal of these interventions is to teach students to self-regulate their behavior, a key difficulty for students with ADHD.
- These interventions have been shown to consistently improve behavior commonly exhibited by students with ADHD, including on-task behavior, amount of work completed, and accuracy of work.
- The interventions have also been shown to be effective in reducing inappropriate and disruptive behaviors.

TEACHER PREP

MERRILL PRENTICE HALL

Activity: Go to the Video Classroom section of the Teacher Prep website, click on Child Development and then module 11: Development of Motivation and Self-Regulation. Watch video 2 and answer the accompanying questions. Which of the four students featured in this video could benefit from the self-regulation strategies discussed here. Why?

3. Frequent feedback when the child follows rules is crucial for maintaining the child's compliance.
4. Children with ADHD are often less sensitive to social praise and reprimands. The consequences for good and bad behavior must be more powerful than those needed to manage the behavior of other children.
5. Rewards and incentives should be used before punishment is incorporated. More rewards should be used than punishments, by a ratio of at least three to one.

www.prenhall.com/rosenberg

TECHNOLOGY FOR ACCESS

USING COMPUTER-ASSISTED INSTRUCTION WITH STUDENTS IDENTIFIED WITH ADHD

Xu, Reid, and Steckelberg (2002) reviewed research regarding the use of technology with students with ADHD. They found only two studies that evaluated the effects of computer-assisted instruction (CAI) for these students. While both of these investigations resulted in positive outcomes, too few studies have been conducted to reach definitive conclusions regarding the use of CAI with students with ADHD. With this caveat in mind, Xu and colleagues reviewed the characteristics of many CAI software packages and suggest that many of the recommended strategies for effective teaching of students with ADHD (and other students, for that matter) are often built into CAI. Thus, this software may be especially beneficial for students with ADHD.

Xu and colleagues' review of research suggests that, as teachers choose software for computer-assisted instruction with students with ADHD, several considerations should guide selection to ensure student engagement and motivation. Software should have characteristics such as the following:

- Provide step-by-step instructions
- Wait for student responses, then provide immediate feedback and reinforcement following responses
- Allow students to work at their own pace
- Actively involve students in learning
- Organize content into small, manageable chunks of information
- Offer repeated trials using variable formats, as needed, when learning content
- Offer novel, attention-grabbing approaches when addressing critical content (e.g., introduce new material with graphics, words, and sounds within game formats, animation, or color, or use software to simulate real-world situations with images and sounds)

Source: Adapted from Xu, C., Reid, R., & Steckelberg, A. (2000). Technology applications for children with ADHD: Assessing the empirical support. *Education and Treatment of Children, 25*(2), 224–228.

6. Token reinforcement systems can be effective over an entire school year as long as rewards are changed frequently.
7. Anticipation is a key for students with ADHD, especially during classroom transitions. Ensure that students know rules and procedures that are used for transitions before the transition occurs.

Computer technology is a potentially useful approach for addressing the needs of students with ADHD. In spite of this great promise, surprisingly little research is available regarding the use of technology with these students. The "Technology for Access" feature provides information about this topic, including suggested characteristics of software to ensure engagement and motivation of students with ADHD.

INTERVENTIONS AND THE USE OF MEDICATION

Research on Medication

As we have mentioned, the use of medication to address the behaviors associated with ADHD has had a long and controversial history. You have probably seen or heard of some of the attacks in the media on the use of medication to control ADHD. Much of

Reflective Exercise #9
At the beginning of this chapter, Meridith Taylor-Strout describes several classroom strategies that are effective for meeting the needs of students with ADHD. Considering the behaviors frequently exhibited by students with ADHD, which of these strategies do you feel would be most effective? Why?

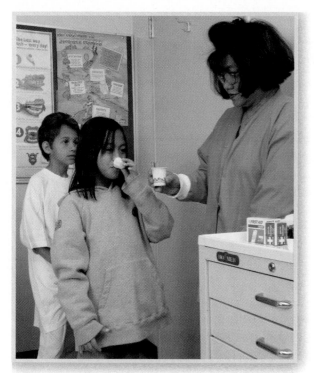

Medication is often highly effective in reducing the symptoms of ADHD.

Reflective Exercise #10

It is apparent that research strongly supports the effectiveness of medication for reducing the symptoms of ADHD. Given this research, why do you feel that some parents strongly oppose the use of medication for their children? How should you as a teacher respond to these parents?

the controversy has centered on the overidentification of students with ADHD and the increasing use of medication to address this disorder (Barkley, 2003; Stein, 1999; Zito et al., 2000). Given the subjectivity inherent in defining and determining if a child exhibits the behaviors that are used to identify ADHD, there is little doubt that some students are misidentified as having ADHD. However, with the appropriate use of assessment procedures and multidisciplinary team decision making, the overidentification of these students should be the exception rather than the rule.

The extreme behavior exhibited by some students with ADHD makes it very difficult for a teacher to manage their behavior and thus ensure that the children make adequate academic and social progress in school. The controversy surrounding ADHD and the use of medication has led to extensive research regarding the effectiveness of medication in reducing the symptoms of ADHD. The vast majority of this research has revealed that low to moderate doses of **stimulant medication** (e.g., methylphenidate [Ritalin or Concerta] or **amphetamine** (Dexedrine or Adderall) are the most effective treatments for children with ADHD (Kollins, Barkley, & DuPaul, 2001).

The largest study ever conducted regarding the effectiveness of medication and behavioral interventions with ADHD was sponsored by the National Institute of Mental Health and completed in the late 1990s. This study, called the Multimodal Treatment of ADHD (MTA) study (MTA Cooperative Group, 1999), compared the use of medication to behavioral interventions, community-based programs, and the combined use of medication and behavioral interventions. The results revealed that medication was the most effective intervention in reducing the symptoms of ADHD. However, the behavioral interventions and combined medication/behavioral interventions treatments were rated higher on parent satisfaction than other treatments, and the behavioral intervention was as effective as medication in addressing some behaviors of students with ADHD.

What this research reveals is that medication is a very effective treatment for reducing the symptoms for many students with ADHD. Some have suggested that from 70 to 96% of students with ADHD respond to medication with reduced symptoms (OSEP, 2003; Wenar & Kerig, 2006). However, it is important to recognize that medication controls negative behavioral symptoms of ADHD but does not directly address academic and social adjustment problems. Indeed, once medication is used to control negative student behavior, teachers find behavioral interventions to be most helpful in addressing academic needs and social adjustment of students with ADHD.

Considerations about Medication and ADHD

Stimulant medications are used by 2 to 4% of preschool and school-age students to treat the symptoms of ADHD (Gureasko-Moore et al., 2005; Zito et al., 2000). Table 9.1 provides information regarding the two major types of medications that are used to control the symptoms of ADHD.

Research has shown that methylphenidate is effective for most children and accounts for about 90% of prescribed medications for ADHD (Konopasek & Forness, 2004). However, the particular type of medication and dosage level that a student will respond to is unpredictable. Thus, it may be necessary to begin with one stimulant, closely monitor the effects (teachers may be asked to provide some of this feedback), and perhaps alter the dosage level or stimulant until an optimal response is achieved (Reiff, 2004).

Another consideration in selecting a medication relates to whether a short-acting or slow-release form of medication will be used. As Table 9.1 indicates, both methylphenidate and amphetamine come in short-acting, intermediate-acting, and extended-release forms. Some students respond more favorably to a sustained-release

TABLE 9.1

MEDICATION USED WITH ADHD		
Medication Name	**Dosage/Schedule**	**Duration**
Methylphenidate (generic name) Short-acting: Ritalin, Methylin, Focain	2 times per day, 2.5–20 mg.	3–5 hrs.
Intermediate-acting: Ritalin SR, Metadate ER, Methylin ER	1 or 2 times per day, 20–60 mg.	3–8 hrs.
Extended-release: Concerta, Metadate CD, Ritalin LA	1 time per day, 18–72 mg.	8–12 hrs.
Amphetamine (generic name) Short-acting: Dexedrine, Dextrostat	2–3 times per day, 5–15 mg.	4–6 hrs.
Intermediate-acting: Adderall, Dexedrine Spansule	1–2 times per day, 5–30 mg.	6–8 hrs.
Extended-release: Adderall-XR	1 time per day, 10–30 mg.	10 hrs.

Source: Austin, 2003; Kollins, Barkley, & DuPaul, 2001.

form of methylphenidate or amphetamine. Furthermore, longer-lasting forms of these medications reduce issues related to taking medication during the school day (e.g., forgetting to take the medication or interrupting school activities).

While stimulant medications are used to treat the vast majority of students with ADHD, other medications are used in some cases, including antidepressants or antianxiety medications. One of these medications, Strattera, is being used increasingly with school-age children and adults with ADHD. Strattera has side effects that are similar to stimulant medications, although they may be somewhat milder, and this medication lasts longer (up to 12 hours) than most stimulants.

When using medications to control the symptoms of ADHD, it also important that the child's parents and teacher closely monitor potential side effects. Educators are in a unique position because they can monitor the effects of medication on classroom behavior and academic achievement and also note how different dosage levels influence student behavior and achievement (Rosenberg et al., 2004). For example, in some instances when the level of the medication is too high, the child may behave "like a zombie" in class and be largely unresponsive to academic work and other school activities. Potential side effects of medications used to treat ADHD may include insomnia, decreased appetite, stomachache, headache, dizziness, and motor tics (Kollins et al., 2001).

In sum, a critical role for teachers and parents is to monitor the effect of medication on the child's behavior as well as any side effects that occur as a result of the use

Can You Help Me with This Student?

ADDRESSING THE NEEDS OF A STUDENT WITH ADHD— PREDOMINANTLY INATTENTIVE TYPE

Jerome transferred into Mr. Adams's eighth-grade math class at the beginning of January. Initially, Jerome seemed to adapt well and appeared to be making good progress in adjusting socially and academically, although he seemed a bit disorganized and forgetful about homework assignments. After a couple of weeks, Mr. Adams noticed that Jerome did not do well on pop quizzes that were used to determine students' understanding of material that had been covered during a class period. In preparation for an upcoming chapter exam, Mr. Adams worked with Jerome and several other students after school and was impressed with Jerome's grasp of the material. When the exam was administered and scored, Mr. Adams was disappointed to find that Jerome responded correctly to only 45% of the items. Mr. Adams reviewed the test with Jerome and found that Jerome had trouble with multiple items on a single page and seemed to have difficulty switching algorithms when moving from one math problem to the next. Over

the next several classes, Mr. Adams observed Jerome's on-task behavior and determined that he spent much of the class period off task, was easily distracted by unimportant activities, and had difficulty sustaining attention for more than a couple of minutes on a task.

Mr. Adams suspects that Jerome may have ADHD— Predominantly Inattentive Type. He will talk with the school psychologist about a possible referral for testing; but in the meantime, what can he as a teacher do to help this student?

The teacher in this scenario needs to address Jerome's attention in the classroom as well as his performance on exams and tests. While this behavior may result in a label of ADHD-PI, the teacher must immediately determine strategies for addressing Jerome's inattentive behavior. Strategies that may be used include the following (Zentall, 2006):

- *Use shorter, more frequent tasks or tests.* Determine if it is possible to break classwork down into smaller tasks

of medication. Moreover, the American Academy of Pediatrics (2001) in guidelines for the treatment of ADHD recommends that a sustained monitoring system be used to ensure that medication is effectively used. In particular, these guidelines recommend that parents and teachers gather information, monitor student outcomes, and track any adverse effects of medication. To ensure that these responsibilities are effectively addressed, teachers should have a basic understanding of the use of medications to control the symptoms of ADHD.

TRANSITION TO ADULT LIFE CONSIDERATIONS

As we have noted, the extent to which the symptoms of ADHD persist into adulthood depends, to a large degree, on the severity of the hyperactive-impulsive behaviors in childhood, the coexistence of oppositional-defiant behavior or conduct disorders, and the nature of the family relationship (Barkley, 2003). Up to 30% of students identified with ADHD have few or no symptoms of this disorder when they become adults (Wenar & Kerig, 2006).

Students with ADHD who have the most difficulty adjusting as adults are those who are identified with conduct disorders or other major psychiatric disorders. Up to 25% of adults with ADHD have conduct disorders that continue into adulthood, while 25% develop a major depression as an adult (Fischer et al., 2002).

For other students with ADHD, the transition to adulthood is much more promising. For these students, major barriers to success include overcoming continuing symptoms of ADHD, which include inattentiveness, poor inhibition, poor self-regulation or self-discipline, restlessness, and difficulty resisting distractions (Barkley, 2000). In addition, many of these students were identified with learning disabilities that are more manageable for Jerome. Similarly, administer an exam over a longer period of time (2–4 sessions), with fewer items per page and fewer types of problems per session.

- *Use distributed practice rather than massed practice.* As we noted in Chapter 5, practicing for short periods of time and spreading these sessions over several classes are more effective means of ensuring that students retain information. This strategy may be used with some material to benefit Jerome and other students in Mr. Adams's class.

- *Increase novelty.* Presenting information using novel means will help to ensure students' longer attention to tasks. This may include the use of technology, presenting real-world problems involving math, incorporating student interests in tasks, or alternating low- and high-interest tasks.

- *Increase opportunities for motor responding during or after task performance.* This may entail allowing students time to play with materials being used in class, providing opportunities for task-related talking, or allowing students to work in small groups using a method such as classwide peer tutoring.

- *Increase opportunities for self-monitoring and self-control.* Jerome may benefit from opportunities to monitor his own behavior. This may be done in collaboration with another student, or with Mr. Adams's assistance in developing a plan for self-monitoring. Self-monitoring consists of three components: self-assessment, goal setting, and self-determination of reinforcement (Polsgrove &

Smith, 2004). In self-assessment, Jerome will be asked to reflect on his behavior and recognize that the behavior of interest is inadequate or inappropriate. He will then recognize the behaviors required, set goals, and select strategies that help regulate behavior. Finally, Jerome will evaluate his performance and consider the nature and scope of reinforcement that should be received for performance of the target behavior.

For more information on strategies to address the needs of students with ADHD-PI, consult the following resource:

Zentall, S. (2006). *ADHD and education: Foundations, characteristics, methods, and collaboration.* Upper Saddle River, NJ: Merrill/Prentice Hall.

EXTEND AND APPLY

- If you were Jerome's teacher, how would you use the strategies just described or other strategies to ensure that Jerome had the opportunity to demonstrate what he had had learned in class on exams?
- How would you address the problem he has with pop quizzes?

TEACHER PREP
MERRILL
PRENTICE HALL

Activity: Go to the Video Classroom section of the Teacher Prep website, click on Special Education and then module 3: Curriculum and Instruction in the LRE/Inclusion. Watch video 2 and answer the accompanying questions. Think about how a lesson like the one presented in the video would be helpful for Jerome.

during their school years and will continue to have academic difficulties as adults. What interventions and supports are available to these students to improve the chances they will have a successful transition into adulthood?

Vocational Support

Many adults with ADHD can be successful with little or no support in job settings. However, those with more extreme manifestations of ADHD symptoms, such as distractibility and lack of self-regulation, will likely have difficulty with the demands of many work settings. In addition, many adults with ADHD have difficulty working independently, meeting deadlines, persisting in completing work, and/or getting along with co-workers (Barkley, 2000). These adults may need the support of a job coach (Inge & Tilson, 1994) to assist them in getting a job that is appropriate to their skills and abilities. For example, jobs demanding close attention to detail for sustained periods of time will not be appropriate for most adults with ADHD, while jobs requiring physical movement and frequent change in the focus of work may be a better fit for many of these adults.

In addition, the job coach may provide assistance on the job to ensure that the job demands and supervision are appropriate to the needs of the adult with ADHD. For example, Barkley (2000) has suggested that adults with ADHD may need a range of adjustments in the work settings, including (1) accountability to a supervisor on a more frequent and immediate basis than others, (2) work responsibilities that are broken down into smaller tasks, (3) a supervisor who states goals each day and provides close supervision to ensure goals are met, and (4) consequences that are contingent on meeting goals.

Site Visit: Effective Practices in Action

RECOMMENDATIONS FOR ADDRESSING ADHD IN COLLEGE

Students with ADHD who attend college often continue to have difficulty with inattention, impulsivity, and/or hyperactivity. Several strategies related to class scheduling and classroom organization and instruction may be used to reduce the effects of these behaviors on how students with ADHD perform in college classrooms.

Class Scheduling
1. Schedule classes at times when you feel you are most alert.
2. Avoid taking back-to-back classes whenever possible.
3. Avoid taking several classes with especially demanding reading or writing requirements during a single semester.
4. Do not take more than 12 hours of classes per semester.
5. Be aware of drop/add dates. Consider dropping a class if reasonable accommodations cannot be arranged.
6. If possible, plan to take especially difficult classes on a pass/fail basis.

Classroom Strategies
1. Do not sit by a window.
2. Tape-record class lectures or use notes from another dependable student or the professor.
3. Participate in class discussions as much as possible to enhance your concentration.
4. When unsure of the meaning of exam questions, ask the professor. Inform the professor of this possibility before your exam.
5. Seek accommodations (e.g., note takers, extended time for tests, support from the writing center).
6. Develop support strategies (e.g., get enough rest and exercise, learn ways to reduce stress).
7. Take medication as prescribed by a physician if it helps. Symptoms of ADHD do not disappear upon high school graduation, and medication can help.
8. Try to schedule the timing of medication doses to maximize your class performance.
9. Set appropriate goals and priorities.
10. Seek assistance with time management as needed.

Source: Adapted from Amenkhienan, C., 2003, Attention deficit disorder: Student handbook; National Resource Center on AD/HD, 2005. Retrieved from www.help4adhd.org.

Support in Higher Education

Many students with ADHD are quite capable of going to college or taking advantage of other appropriate postsecondary opportunities. Moreover, many colleges and universities have made accommodations for students with ADHD and LD to ensure that appropriate accommodations are made to maximize the opportunities these students have for success in higher education. Information on institutions of higher education that offer comprehensive programs for students with disabilities are described in *Peterson's Guide: Colleges with Programs for Students with Learning Disabilities or Attention Deficit Disorders* (Mangrum & Strichart, 2000).

In addition to this information, the National Resource Center on ADHD (2005) provides information for students with ADHD who are planning to attend college. The "Site Visit" feature contains recommendations for addressing ADHD symptoms in college classrooms that is taken from the National Resource Center as well as a college handbook for students with ADHD (Amenkhienan, 2003).

PREVAILING ISSUES, CONTROVERSIES, AND IMPLICATIONS FOR THE TEACHER

Although great progress has been made in developing interventions and delivering services for students with ADHD, controversial issues continue to challenge the field. Four of the most important of these issues are whether ADHD is a valid category, the overidentification of students with ADHD, the use of medication as an intervention, and the effectiveness of alternative interventions.

IS ADHD A VALID CATEGORY?

Critics of ADHD have long charged that professionals are too quick to label enthusiastic, energetic children, especially boys, as ADHD (Kohn, 1989; Schrag & Divoky, 1975). These critics have insisted that the symptoms of ADHD are part of the normal developmental pattern of many children and that many students are given this label because of poor behavior-management practices of parents and teachers or, in the worst cases, the desire of parents and teachers to have a child be quiet and docile.

There is little doubt that there is some truth to these accusations and that some children are identified with ADHD who are well within the normal range of typical child development. Poor behavior-management practices, coupled with parent expectations regarding the child's behavior, probably result in the identification of these children with ADHD; and there is no sound rationale for placing a disability label on such children.

Obviously the misidentification of students does not mean that the ADHD category is not viable. Moreover, there are children that almost all professionals and social critics agree have ADHD. These are typically students with ADHD-C or ADHD-PHI, who exhibit extreme hyperactive and impulsive behaviors across settings, produce significant challenges for teachers because of disruptive behavior, and require significant interventions if they are to make adequate academic progress and adjust socially in school.

In response to criticism of the category of ADHD and continuing questions about whether the category is real or simply a creation of U.S. educators, Barkley (2003) reviewed research studies of the prevalence of ADHD across several countries. This research reveals that the prevalence of ADHD varies from 3.8 to 20% across other countries, including Japan, Germany, China, Brazil, Columbia, the United Arab Emirates, and Ukraine. Moreover, Barkley found that ADHD is present in all countries where the category has been systematically studied.

Available evidence thus reveals that ADHD is a category that exists across cultures, and students with this label present behaviors in classrooms that result in significant difficulty for teachers and the student. While almost all professionals agree that ADHD does exist, the question that divides many is whether we identify too many students with this label.

ARE TOO MANY CHILDREN IDENTIFIED WITH ADHD?

A major concern of many professionals and advocates is the potential to significantly overidentify students with this disorder. The rapid growth of the OHI category over the past decade (a growth of almost 700%) has further fueled these fears. While criteria and evaluation procedures are in place that should largely prevent this problem (American Academy of Pediatrics, 2000; APA, 2000), evidence supports the perspective that some children are identified as having ADHD who should not be (Barbaresi et al., 2002; Dupaul & Stoner, 2003; Gureasko-Moore et al., 2005).

Reflective Exercise #11
Review the symptoms used to identify children with ADHD in Figure 9.1. What percentage of children in kindergarten and first grade exhibit many of these symptoms? Which symptoms are most common? Given these common symptoms and based on what you've learned in this chapter, how can professionals ensure that children with ADHD are not overidentified?

Research has confirmed that the application of recommended practices to identify children with ADHD that were described previously in this chapter will result in reliable identification and reduce the risk for overidentification (DuPaul & Stoner, 2003). However, research has also revealed that the people identifying students with ADHD often do not use these practices. For example, Wasserman and colleagues (1999) found that only 38.3% of physicians used the DSM-IV-TR standards to identify these students, while 36.9% used behavioral questionnaires as part of the identification process.

It is important to note that there is another side to this controversy. Some parents and advocates have reacted to the mis- or overidentification of children with ADHD by refusing to accept this label or refusing to use medication as a treatment (Carey, 2004; Leslie, 2004). This has led, in some areas, to the underidentification of children with ADHD and very limited use of medication as a treatment for these children (Barbaresi et al., 2002; Rowland et al., 2002).

Dr. Laurel Leslie (2004) eloquently addresses this issue of over- versus underidentification:

> My own experience mirrors these contradictory perspectives. Recently, I sat next to a teacher on a plane who commented that 9 children in her class of 30 in a suburb of New Jersey were taking a stimulant medication for ADHD. Yet, in my own community clinic setting, children and adolescents [who] present with blatant signs of ADHD and co-existing mental health disorders and learning disabilities have gone unrecognized by the medical and the educational professions. So is there an ADHD epidemic? Like many clinicians and researchers, I suspect that the truth falls somewhere in between. (p. 1)

We, too, suspect that this is the case. This controversy comes down to the particular child and the person or persons who are making the identification. Adherence to good practice will result, in the vast majority of cases, in the appropriate identification of children with ADHD (American Academy of Pediatrics, 2000; APA, 2000), and you as a teacher will play a central role in collecting data to ensure that this occurs.

SHOULD MEDICATION BE USED AS A MAJOR INTERVENTION FOR ADHD?

Another controversy regarding ADHD relates to the extent to which medication should be used to control symptoms of this disorder. It is clear that the use of medication to control symptoms of ADHD has increased dramatically in the past decade (Barbaresi et al., 2002; Jensen et al., 1999; Konopasek & Forness, 2004; Zito et al., 1999, 2000). Moreover, evidence reveals that approximately 75% of children identified with ADHD are treated with stimulant medication (Barbaresi et al., 2002; Hoagwood, Kelleher, Feil, & Comer, 2000).

Perhaps the major concern regarding the use of medication to treat ADHD relates to the previously described controversies. That is, parents are hesitant to use powerful medication to control the behavior of their child when so many questions and controversies swirl around the existence of the category and the overidentification of children with the disorder. Another issue that is frequently cited by those who oppose the use of medication for students with ADHD is the concern that its use may result in an increased risk for substance abuse later in life. Well-designed research that has been conducted to study this issue has revealed that the use of stimulant medication to treat ADHD does not increase the student's risk for substance abuse later in life (Barkley, Fischer, Smallish, & Fletcher, 2003; Wilens, Faraone, Biederman, & Gunawardene, 2003). Moreover, some evidence suggests there may be a reduced risk of substance abuse for some students who receive stimulant medication to treat ADHD during the school years (Wilens et al., 2003).

We contend that caution in using stimulant medication to treat ADHD is a good thing, very justifiable, and should help to reduce overidentification of this disorder. Indeed, parents, physicians, psychologists, and teachers (to the extent to which they are consulted about these decisions) should be very cautious in labeling a child with ADHD and using medication to treat the child's symptoms.

ARE ALTERNATIVE TREATMENTS FOR ADHD EFFECTIVE?

Given the previously discussed controversy regarding the use of medication to treat ADHD as well as the lack of effectiveness of medication with some students, many parents and professionals have sought alternative treatments. For example, one proposed treatment involves reducing the child's intake of food additives (particularly certain food colorings) and preservatives that are presumed to cause ADHD (Feingold, 1985). Many researchers have carefully studied this treatment, and results indicate that the modification of a child's diet is not an effective treatment for ADHD (Kavale, 2001).

Another proposed treatment for ADHD relates to problems with the child's vestibular system in the inner ear, which controls balance and movement. Levinson (2003), who developed this theory, contends that the vestibular system regulates the energy level of children; thus, problems with this system result in impulsive behavior and hyperactivity. Barkley (2000) notes that scientists do not agree with Levinson that energy levels are controlled by the vestibular system and that no research has been published or otherwise reported in support of this theory regarding the cause of ADHD or the recommended treatment.

Many other treatments for ADHD have been recommended, including giving children large doses of vitamins and minerals and reducing the intake of sugar. None of these alternative treatments of ADHD have been supported by research. Under these circumstances, it is important that professionals be aware of interventions that have been proven effective as well as interventions that lack such evidence. To this point, there is research to support the effectiveness of only two interventions related to ADHD: the use of medication and behavioral interventions, both discussed in this chapter. We encourage you to maintain caution regarding other interventions that are offered for ADHD and to ask for evidence that treatments work so that you remain well informed and can provide parents with advice regarding the effectiveness of interventions for ADHD.

 To link to websites that support and extend the content of this chapter, go to the Web Links module in Chapter 9 of the Companion Website, www.prenhall.com/rosenberg.

SUMMARY

Students with ADHD are often frustrating for parents and teachers. These students have some combination of impulsive, inattentive, and/or hyperactive behavior that often is difficult to control. Students with ADHD may or may not have behaviors that interfere with their educational performance.

Definition and Classification Criteria

- Students with ADHD are identified based on the extent to which they exhibit some combination of inattentive, hyperactive, and impulsive behaviors.
- Some students are predominantly hyperactive and impulsive (ADHD-PHI) and do not exhibit the other symptoms (i.e., inattentive behaviors), while some students are predominantly inattentive (ADHD-PI), and still others combine all three of the major characteristics (ADHD-C).
- These behaviors should last for at least 6 months and should occur across at least two settings (e.g., school and home).

Characteristics of Students

- The characteristics of students with ADHD often lead to difficulty getting along with others at school, and a significant proportion of these students develop behavior problems (e.g., oppositional-defiant disorder, anxiety disorder, conduct disorder).
- The symptoms of ADHD often influence the academic achievement of these students, as the impulsive, inattentive, and hyperactive behaviors cause difficulty in learning academic material, and may develop into a learning disability over time.

Prevalence, Course, and Causes

- ADHD is the most common behavior disorder. Its prevalence has been estimated as 3 to 7% of the school-age population.
- Significantly more boys than girls are identified with ADHD.

- Many students with ADHD are also identified with another disability, most commonly a learning disability or emotional/behavioral disorder.
- ADHD continues into adolescence for 50 to 80% of students with this disorder. For many of these students, ADHD persists into adulthood in somewhat altered form (e.g., as children with ADHD enter adolescence, the manifestation of their problem behaviors changes as the severity of symptoms declines).
- While we don't know what causes ADHD in most cases, contributing factors to this disorder may include brain injury, brain abnormalities, hereditary influences, and family issues.

Identification and Assessment

- It is difficult to identify students with ADHD because the criteria used for identification are somewhat subjective and many students exhibit at least some of these behaviors.
- To ensure that students are appropriately identified, multiple measures should be used across settings to ensure that the severity of the student's symptoms is sufficient to be identified as ADHD.

Educational Practices

- Extensive research has demonstrated that stimulant medication is the most effective intervention for reducing the symptoms of ADHD for most students.

- Medication should be closely monitored to ensure that the appropriate medication is used to reduce the symptoms of ADHD.
- Behavioral interventions, such as the use of behavior modification, a token economy, and teaching self-regulation, are effective interventions to support the students in learning appropriate classroom behaviors and make progress learning academic content.
- A combination of medication and behavioral interventions has proven the most effective approach for most students with ADHD.

Prevailing Issues

- Professionals and parents continue to debate whether ADHD is a valid category of disability.
- Many parents and professionals have expressed concern that students with ADHD are overidentified.
- The use of stimulant medications to control the symptoms of ADHD has led to controversy regarding whether students are overmedicated.
- Several treatments for ADHD have been recommended that have questionable effectiveness.

 Council for Exceptional Children

ADDRESSING THE PROFESSIONAL STANDARDS

Council for Exceptional Children (CEC) Knowledge Standards addressed in the chapter:

CC1K5, EC1K2, CC2K1, CC2K2, CC2K5, CC2K6, CC2K7, CC3K1, CC3K2, CC8K1, CC8K2.

Appendix B: CEC Knowledge and Skill Standards Core has a full listing of the standards referenced here.

TABLE 10.1

THE FIVE TYPES OF ASD

Type	Definition
Autistic disorder	Severe developmental disability characterized by an early age of onset, poor social development, impairments in language development, and rigidity in behavior
Asperger's disorder	Sustained and often lifelong impairments in social interactions and the development of restricted, repetitive patterns of behavior, interests, and activities
Rett's disorder	Following typical development during first year of life, a genetic deficit, almost exclusively affecting girls; characterized by rapid deterioration of behavior, language, and purposeful hand movements as well as mental retardation and seizures
Childhood disintegrative disorder	A rare condition in which a typically developing 3- to 15-year-old child experiences a rapid loss of language, social, motor, and toileting skills
Pervasive developmental disorder—not otherwise specified (PDD-NOS)	A vague designation used to describe children who resemble those with autistic disorder or Asperger's disorder but differ in a diagnostically significant way (e.g., age of onset)

Source: Adapted from Towbin, Mauk, & Batshaw, 2002; Van Acker, Loncola, & Van Acker, 2005; and Volkmar & Klin, 2005.

specified (PDD-NOS) (see Table 10.1). Because autistic and Asperger's disorders are by far the most prevalent, we focus our discussion on these two conditions.

AUTISTIC DISORDER

Autistic disorder, routinely referred to simply as autism, is a severe developmental disability characterized by an early age of onset, poor social development, impairments in language development, and rigidity in behavior (Phelps & Grabowski, 1991). Leo Kanner initially identified autism as a distinct diagnostic category in 1943. In his classic paper, "Autistic Disturbances of Affective Content," he presented detailed descriptions of 11 children "whose condition differs so markedly and uniquely from anything reported so far, that each case merits . . . a detailed consideration of its fascinating peculiarities" (Kanner, 1943, p. 217).

As with many other cognitive disabilities, clinicians rely on the definitions in the DSM-IV-TR (APA, 2000) to identify autistic disorder (Towbin, Mauk, & Batshaw, 2002). As Figure 10.1 illustrates, the diagnostic criteria that define the disorder include markedly abnormal or impaired development in social interaction and communication as well as rigidity in activities and interests. The definition and classification of autism, as it relates to eligibility for special education services, has changed. Earlier iterations of IDEA included it with physical and other health impairments (Rosenberg, Wilson, Maheady, & Sindelar, 2004). In more recent reauthorizations, autism received a category of its own and is defined as

> a developmental disability significantly affecting verbal and nonverbal communication and social interaction, generally evident before age 3, that adversely affects a child's educational performance. Other characteristics often associated with autism are engagement in repetitive activities and stereo-

FIGURE 10.1

Diagnostic criteria for 299.00 Autistic Disorder

A. A total of six (or more) items from (1), (2), and (3), with at least two from (1), and one each from (2) and (3):

(1) qualitative impairment in social interaction, as manifested by at least two of the following:

(a) marked impairment in the use of multiple nonverbal behaviors such as eye-to-eye gaze, facial expression, body postures, and gestures to regulate social interaction

(b) failure to develop peer relationships appropriate to developmental level

(c) a lack of spontaneous seeking to share enjoyment, interests, or achievements with other people (e.g., by a lack of showing, bringing, or pointing out objects of interest)

(d) lack of social or emotional reciprocity

(2) qualitative impairments in communication as manifested by at least one of the following:

(a) delay in, or total lack of, the development of spoken language (not accompanied by an attempt to compensate through alternative modes of communication such as gesture or mime)

(b) in individuals with adequate speech, marked impairment in the ability to initiate or sustain a conversation with others

(c) stereotyped and repetitive use of language or idiosyncratic language

(d) lack of varied, spontaneous make-believe play or social imitative play appropriate to developmental level

(3) restricted repetitive and stereotyped patterns of behavior, interests, and activities, as manifested by at least one of the following:

(a) encompassing preoccupation with one or more stereotyped and restricted patterns of interest that is abnormal either in intensity or focus

(b) apparently inflexible adherence to specific, nonfunctional routines or rituals

(c) stereotyped and repetitive motor mannerisms (e.g., hand or finger flapping or twisting, or complex whole-body movements)

(d) persistent preoccupation with parts of objects

B. Delays or abnormal functioning in at least one of the following areas, with onset prior to age 3 years: (1) social interaction, (2) language as used in social communication, or (3) symbolic or imaginative play.

C. The disturbance is not better accounted for by Rett's Disorder or Childhood Disintegrative Disorder.

Source: Reprinted with permission from the Diagnostic and Statistical Manual of Mental Disorders, Fourth Edition, Text Revision (Copyright 2000). American Psychiatric Association.

typed movements, resistance to environmental change or change in daily routines, and unusual responses to sensory experiences. The term does not apply if a child's educational performance is adversely affected primarily because the child has an emotional disturbance. (34 C.F.R., Part 300.7[c] [1][i][1997])

ASPERGER'S DISORDER

Asperger's disorder is characterized by severe, sustained, and often lifelong impairments in social interactions and the development of restricted, repetitive patterns of behavior, interests, and activities (APA, 2000). If you detect that these descriptors resemble those that define autism, you are correct. The presenting behaviors of Asperger's disorder are similar to high-functioning autism, except that people with Asperger's do not have the same intensity of impairment in language, cognition, and self-help skills. Hans Asperger, an Austrian pediatrician, documented the disorder 1 year after Kanner (1943) described autism. Although his research was based on investigations of more than 400 children, Asperger's efforts received little attention due fail to recognize their odd missteps and persist in their awkward, rigid, self-centered, and emotionally blunted modes of social engagement (APA, 2000; Sigman & Capps, 1997; Tager-Flusberg, Paul, & Lord, 2005).

DEFICIENCIES IN COMMUNICATION SKILLS

Deficits in communication skills are characteristic of all students with ASD, although, like deficits in social reciprocity, levels of severity vary considerably. For those with autistic disorder, impairments in communication skills are pervasive, involving most aspects of expressive and receptive language development. Approximately 50% of those with autistic disorder fail to acquire **functional language;** many, like Kim Thomas's students, are nonverbal or suffer **echolalia,** a response in which all or part of what is heard is repeated. Those who do speak often use speech in a monotonous tone accompanied by unusual pitch, rhythm, and syntax. Speech is not typically used for social communication. Consequently, gestures, body movements, and eye contact are infrequent; and verbalizations tend to be overly literal, filled with reversals, and lacking in abstract, metaphorical terms. Students with autistic disorder also have problems understanding spoken language. This is likely the result of their inability to process nonverbal cues when encountering verbal input.

For people with Asperger's disorder, deficits in communication are not as severe. Most have difficulty, however, in comprehending and making use of **figurative language**—idioms, metaphors, analogies, slang, and jokes that enhance and add emotion to communication. How important is figurative language? Review the examples of figurative language in Table 10.2 and consider how often figurative language is used in the media and during daily interactions with others.

As you have probably noted, the use of figurative language pervades most aspects of our lives. When people with Asperger's disorder encounter figurative phrases, they interpret words literally and have difficulty deciphering the communicative intent of the message. Along with difficulties in reading faces and understanding the interplay of voice (e.g., rhythm, intonation, stress, volume, and cadence), these students suffer other consequences from misunderstanding figurative language, especially when an immediate understanding of another person's motives and intentions is required. Impairments in communication are also evident when these individuals try to express themselves. Words and phrases are typically enunciated in an odd, robotic fashion accompanied by a limited range of gestures, facial expressions, and eye movements.

REPETITIVE, STEREOTYPICAL, AND RITUALISTIC BEHAVIORS

The most obvious behaviors observed among individuals with ASD are the repetitive, stereotypical, and ritualistic actions that typically interfere with everyday activities. Several of the more extreme motor behaviors—rocking, spinning, arm flapping, and finger flicking—are high-frequency actions typical of those with the most severe manifestations of the disability. Along with an unusual fascination with innocuous objects, people with ASD bring a rigidity and seemingly obsessive consistency to their actions. For example, while other children often have favorite dolls or blankets, students with autistic disorder may cling to pieces of string, repeatedly flush a toilet, or spend hours lining up toys in a carefully designed, elaborate pattern. Although less extreme, people with Asperger's disorder present their own unusual forms of ritualistic behavior (APA, 2000). Many have intense interests in weather systems, maps, or the telephone book as well as schedules for trains, airlines, and television shows (Loveland & Tunali-Kotoski, 2005). Teachers report that it is not unusual for such students to be preoccupied with obscure dialogue from movies and television shows and to be extremely anxious and upset when daily routines are changed due to unforeseen circumstances.

Many of the ritualistic and repetitive actions appear to be unpredictable, with little purpose. However, researchers suspect that these behaviors fulfill a specific need for people with ASD. Early theorists speculated that the ritualistic and repetitive be-

Reflective Exercise #2
Hyperbole, idioms, and metaphors are essential elements of satisfying social interactions. Try describing a favorite sports or entertainment event or a memorable meal without using abstract or figurative language.

www.prenhall.com/rosenberg

TABLE 10.2

EXAMPLES OF FIGURATIVE LANGUAGE

Form	Definition	Example	Meaning
Idiom	An expression whose meaning cannot be understood by analyzing its elements	A fine kettle of fish	A real mess; a really bad situation
Simile	An expression that compares two unlike things	As brave as a lion	To be brave
Metaphor	An expression that takes the attributes of one thing and transfers them to another in an implicit manner	To possess ideas is to gather flowers; to think is to weave them into garlands.	Thinking is composed of many ideas, just as a garland is woven from many flowers.
Allusion	Referring to a related thing or situation that requires prior knowledge	Pandora's box	A source of many problems, troubles
Analogy	A comparison of a like characteristic of two different things, generally one known and one less known	Food is to farming as laughing is to joking.	A person farms to produce food just as she tells jokes to produce laughter.
Understatement	An expression that intentionally de-emphasizes a thing in order to emphasize it	Hitler was not a nice person.	Of course
Hyperbole	An exaggeration or extravagant overstatement	I could eat a horse.	I could eat a lot.
Oxymoron	A figure of speech that combines two terms that normally contradict each other	Deafening silence	Complete silence
Slang	Language used by particular social groups to exclude others from the conversation; words may be standard but with encrypted meanings or may be unique	Fly right	To be honest and dependable

haviors were attempts to control episodes of **generalized anxiety** (Bettelheim, 1967; Kanner, 1943). Recently, researchers have hypothesized that the behaviors are mini-experiments conducted by the individual to figure out cause-and-effect relationships in the environment (Baron-Cohen, 2005). It is also possible that these behaviors may serve a range of functions that are specific to an individual, perhaps satisfying the person's perceived needs for attention, to engage in a particular activity, or to escape or avoid an unpleasant situation or task demand (Kennedy, Meyer, Knowles, & Shukla, 2000). As such, teachers need to be aware of how environmental events can influence the development, frequency, and intensity of repetitive and ritualistic behaviors.

Reflective Exercise #3
What would be your course of action to determine the functions of repetitive, stereotypical, and ritualistic behaviors?

SECONDARY BEHAVIORAL CORRELATES

Recall that when we speak of secondary behavioral correlates, we are referring to those characteristics that often occur in conjunction with the primary characteristics of a disability. Regarding ASD, three factors—age of onset, intellectual functioning, and self-injurious behavior—are of particular interest to teachers.

AGE OF ONSET

For a diagnosis of autistic disorder, there must be evidence of its universal and specific characteristics before a child reaches 3 years of age. Parents generally report concerns when their child is between 15 and 22 months of age, usually because of lack of speech and emergence of ritualistic and repetitive behaviors. However, retrospective videotape analysis studies have found that infants with autism can be distinguished from typical children as early as 6 to 8 months of age (Chawarska & Volkmar, 2005; Robins, Fein, Barton, & Green, 2001). Compared to their age mates, infants with autistic disorder exhibit diminished visual attention to people, are less likely to have early social communicative exchanges, and tend not to respond differentially to personal verbalizations such as the sound of their own names.

Compared to autistic disorder, Asperger's disorder tends to be diagnosed at a later age. Since most children with the disorder do not have clinically significant delays in language acquisition, cognitive development, or self-help skills, differences in functioning are not apparent until the child is in social situations with peers. In fact, compared to most children with autistic disorder who have diagnosis confirmed by about 5 years of age, children with Asperger's disorder are not typically diagnosed until they are 11 years of age (Howlin & Asgharian, 1999).

VARIABLE INTELLECTUAL FUNCTIONING

Although most children with ASD have below-average IQ scores, their measured intelligence ranges from superior to profound mental retardation (APA, 2000). Historically, estimates of intelligence of children with ASD indicated that only 15 to 30 % of those with the disability had IQ scores outside the range of intellectual impairment, a score of 70 or above. But measures of the intelligence of children with ASD have changed over time, and it appears that 38 to 48% have scores outside the intellectual impairment range. Consider two explanations for this change. First, there has been a sharp increase in the number of students with Asperger's disorder and higher-functioning autism included in epidemiological studies of those with ASD. Although these students have difficulty comprehending abstract materials, they typically have average intellectual abilities. Second, the increases in IQ scores may be a function of the increased frequency of beneficial early intervention efforts provided to students with ASD. Comprehensive and intensive programs have resulted in important positive outcomes in cognitive areas assessed by intelligence tests. For example, in an evaluation of a preschool educational and behavioral program, children with high-functioning autism had IQ scores increase by approximately 19 points after 1 year of participation (Harris, Handleman, Gordon, Kristoff, & Fuentes, 1991).

Keep in mind that increases in IQ scores do not mean that other challenging characteristics of ASD are no longer present. Increases in measured intelligence do not usually result in corresponding gains in adaptive skills and improvements in the social use of language. However, students with higher IQ scores are less likely to exhibit (1) gross deficits in social interaction and emotional expression, (2) inappropriate play, (3) self-injurious behavior, and (4) delays in motor and language development (Yirmiya, Sigman, Kasari, & Mundy, 1992).

SELF-INJURIOUS BEHAVIOR

Self-injurious behavior (SIB) is self-directed aggression manifested by severe head banging, punching, scratching, and/or biting. More common in children with autistic

Reflective Exercise #4
Why does it take so long to identify students with Asperger's disorder? Are there behavioral characteristics that parents and teachers can look for to secure early diagnosis and intervention?

www.prenhall.com/rosenberg

disorder than those with Asperger's disorder, self-injurious behavior can result in serious injury and, needless to say, elicit extreme levels of stress among those who love and care for these children. Not surprisingly, elimination of these behaviors is a priority for families and educators. In addition to the obvious health issues, self-injury precludes placement in the least restrictive environment and limits access to most learning, working, and leisure opportunities (Symons, 1995). Keep in mind that self-injurious behavior is not universal and specific to individuals with ASD. Approximately 10 to 20% of those with the disability do display it; however, a sizable proportion of individuals with severe developmental disabilities and psychiatric conditions also engage in these behaviors (Rosenberg et al., 2004).

Why would a person engage in behaviors that inflict pain and suffering on himself or herself? Intuition, common sense, and what we know about typical functions of behavior dictate that most people go to great lengths to avoid unpleasant physical stimuli. Although there are theories regarding the development and maintenance of self-injury, there are no definitive explanations. For example, from the biophysical perspective, it is believed to be a function of abnormal physiological development or impaired biological functioning (Filipek, 2005). The psychodynamic perspective views self-injurious behavior as the result of experiences in infancy and early childhood, when the child's attempts to reach out to others were blocked or frustrated. The child avoids danger by retreating from reality, not using language common to others, and refusing to react, preferring instead to turn aggression inward (Bettelheim, 1967; Bloch, 1978). Finally, from the behavioral perspective, self-injurious behavior is believed to be a learned response reinforced by positive and/or negative stimuli. Examples of positive reinforcement include others' attention and sensory gain; negative reinforcement takes the form of escape from demands or situations the individual with autism wishes to avoid.

For those in educational settings, the behavioral theory is most useful. There is considerable evidence that interventions based upon functional assessment or functional analysis of behaviors can reduce self-injury, and many behaviorally based techniques and programs have been developed to do so (Rosenberg et al., 2004).

PREVALENCE, COURSE OF DISABILITY, AND CAUSAL FACTORS

HOW MANY STUDENTS HAVE ASD?

Determining the number of students with autism spectrum disabilities is controversial and unfortunately inconclusive. Some have suggested that we are in the midst of an autism epidemic. According to the DSM-IV-TR (APA, 2000), the prevalence of autistic disorder ranges from 2 to 20 cases per 10,000 persons. However, recent epidemiological data suggest that the prevalence of ASD is 10 times higher than rates reported in the 1980s and early 1990s, a considerable 3.4 per 1,000 children (NAAR, 2005; Yeargin-Allsopp et al., 2003).

Are these sharp differences over time a function of some environmental threat, vaccine, or genetic agent, or can they be explained by methodological factors associated with the nature of the studies? Issues surrounding the increased prevalence rates remain controversial, and no one is certain. Nonetheless, several factors need to be considered when comparing prevalence rates of ASD over time. First, recent measures of prevalence have included all forms of ASD (e.g., Asperger's disorder), while previous studies employed a more narrow definition of autism. Second, in the past many students, because of their low IQ scores, were identified as having intellectual impairments. Currently, as a result of improved diagnostic systems and the increased competence of professionals who use them, many of these students are identified correctly as having ASD (Fombonne, 2003). Finally, as public awareness of ASD increases, parents and clinicians are probably looking earlier and more intensively for signs of the disability.

Consider other useful demographic information (Volkmar, Szatmari, & Sparrow, 1993; Yeargin-Allsopp et al., 2003): ASD occurs throughout the world and affects males four times more often than females. However, girls tend to be disabled more severely than boys (Tsai, Stewart, & August, 1981). Unlike several other disabilities in which certain racial groups are overrepresented, prevalence rates among African American and white students are comparable. Finally, if a family already has one child with autism, there is a 5 to 10% chance that they will have another with ASD.

COURSE OF ASD

Although the course of ASD is lifelong and chronic, outcomes vary depending on the level of severity of the disability. For example, the prognosis for students with autistic disorder is bleak. Identification of problems occurs in early childhood, and specialized treatments and supports are required through childhood and adolescence. Only a small percentage of people with autistic disorder are able to transition to work and living situations without support. Approximately one-third of those with the disability are able to sustain some level of supported or partial independence, and a full two-thirds remain severely disabled and fail to develop independent living skills (APA, 2000). Follow-up studies of people with the disability indicate that most have ongoing problems with social aspects of life, jobs, and independence (Howlin, Mawhood, & Rutter, 2000; Lotter, 1978). Those who achieve appropriate levels of adjustment and maintain the greatest amount of independence tend to have intelligence levels that are above the intellectual impairment range and have developed functional language skills.

Since they do not have significant delays in cognitive or language development, poeple with Asperger's disorder tend to have better outcomes than those with autistic disorder. Although many experience socialization and behavioral adjustment problems during their school years, many adults with Asperger's disorder obtain jobs that are related to their interests. Some students with the disability successfully complete college and pursue graduate studies. Still, their social problems persist: Rigidity, awkwardness, self-centeredness, and emotionally dulled social engagement continue to make interactions with others difficult. Not surprisingly, many require the services of mental health providers for depression and anxiety (Shea & Mesibov, 2005).

CAUSAL FACTORS

One of the many frustrations associated with the study and treatment of ASD is that we don't know for certain what causes these disorders. What is clear, however, it that the disabilities are probably the product of one or more nature-based factors such as genetic, neurochemical, and neurobiological abnormalities (Towbin et al., 2002). Nonetheless, nurture-based explanations from both behavioral and psychodynamic perspectives have also been forwarded as factors that contribute to the development and maintenance of ASD.

Nature-Based Factors

Increasingly, genetic influences are viewed as major contributors to the development of ASD. Studies on the occurrence of autism in twins and the presence of ASD-like behaviors in families suggest that there is a strong heritability of the traits associated with the entire autism spectrum (Gillberg & Cederlund, 2005; Segal, 2005). Unfortunately,

When provided with supports such as counseling, high-functioning students with ASD can have success in postsecondary environments such as college.

the specific genes susceptible to ASD have not been identified (Hu-Lince, Craig, Huentelman, & Stephan, 2005).

From the neurochemical perspective, abnormally high and low levels of certain chemicals in the brain and central nervous system have been linked to ASD. In particular, serotonin, an amino acid–based neurotransmitter that most likely contributes to the regulation of sleep, appetite, and mood, has been found to be elevated in a significant percentage of children with autistic disorder (Anderson & Hoshino, 2005). Irregular serotonin levels are associated with other conditions such as depression, anxiety, and obsessive-compulsive disorder. ASD has also been linked to certain physical aspects of brain development. The brains of some children with autistic disorder are larger and heavier than those of individuals without disabilities (Redcav & Courchesne, 2005). Moreover, recent research using magnetic resonance imaging (MRI) has found structural irregularities in sections of these brains that are responsible for language, facial recognition, and social cognition (Akshoomoff, Pierce, & Courchesne, 2002). The reasons for these structural problems remain the subject of considerable inquiry and speculation.

Nurture-Based Factors

Consider the feelings expressed by Catherine Maurice (1993), a parent of a child with ASD, in her memoir *Let Me Hear Your Voice:*

> It was I who had created this nightmare. I was sure of it. Either I had made Anne-Marie autistic by not giving her enough attention, or I had made everyone believe she was autistic by reading about it and talking about it too much. (p. 28)

Clearly, parents do not "cause" autism by their actions toward their child or by the child's perception of parental behavior. Nonetheless, you should be aware that parents of children with ASD question themselves regularly, from their selection of diet and lifestyle choices to their spirituality, the locations of their homes, and the vaccinations of their children.

Be aware that damaging generalizations of parent causality persist. Several prominent psychologists from both the psychodynamic and behavioral models have hypothesized that parents of children with ASD contribute to the development and maintenance of the disability (Rosenberg et al., 2004). Although now dismissed as being as misguided, fraudulent, and malicious, Bruno Bettleheim, a Freudian psychiatrist, claimed that autism was a child's response to extreme parental rejection. Based on initial positive responses to his book, *The Empty Fortress,* in 1967, generations of devastated mothers—actually referred to as "refrigerator mothers"—doubted their ability to bond with their children. Although Bettleheim's view has been disproved, it remains shocking that it took decades for the psychiatric community to disavow the counterproductive theory of maternal blame.

Interestingly, parent unresponsiveness is also part of the behavioral explanation of ASD. According to Ferster (1961), the child with autism fails to develop communicative language and appropriate social behaviors because early, unsophisticated attempts at such behaviors are not reinforced. Because parents either ignore or respond only intermittently to appropriate behavior, initial attempts of **prosocial behaviors** are extinguished, and the foundation for more complex skills do not have the opportunity to develop adequately. To secure the attention of others, the child engages in increasing bizarre behaviors. The result is that the attention actually serves to increase the frequency and intensity of the inappropriate behaviors. What are we to make of this seemingly logical explanation of ASD? Clearly, consideration of reinforcement contingencies when designing intervention strategies is essential. However, Ferster's use of basic stimulus-response explanations as an explanation for this pervasive spectrum of behaviors is a misguided overgeneralization of behavioral principles. More important, it is counterproductive for enlisting the essential support of parents and other primary caregivers.

Reflective Exercise #5
What are the ramifications of theories that implicate parents in the cause of their children's disabilities? How can such theories influence the outcomes of early intervention efforts that rely on intensive family involvement?

TABLE 10.3

SELECTED SCREENING AND IDENTIFICATION DIAGNOSTIC MEASURES

Type	Name	General Description
Screening	Checklist for Autism in Toddlers (CHAT) (Baird et al., 2000)	A general measure used to screen toddlers by gathering parent reports and measures of behaviors during interactions, particularly pretend play, gaze, and pointing
	Modified Checklist for Autism in Toddlers (M-CHAT) (Robins et al., 2001)	An extended parent report version of CHAT, with additional measures of symptoms not measured by CHAT, such as repetitive behaviors
	Screening for Autism in 2-Year-Olds (STAT) (Stone, Coonrod, & Ousley, 2000)	A measure designed particularly for early screening of ASD
Core deficit scales	Social Responsiveness Scale (SRS) (Constantino, 2002)	A measure that takes parents or teachers about 20 minutes to complete; a total of 65 items concerning communication, social interaction, and stereotypical behaviors
	Children's Social Behavior Questionnaire (CSBQ) (Luteijn, Luteijn, Jackson, Volkmar, & Minderaa, 2000)	A measure to be completed by parents or teachers; consisting of 96 items that measure such areas as acting out, social contact and insight, and anxious/rigid and stereotypical behaviors
	Pervasive Developmental Disorders Rating Scale (PDDRS)	A measure consisting of 51 items regarding arousal, affect, and cognition
Autism rating scales	Childhood Autism Rating Scale (CARS) (Schopler, Reichler, & Renner, 1986)	A 15-item behavioral rating scale that includes direct observation, parent report, and chart review to differentiate children with ASD from those with other disabilities
	Autism Behavior Checklist (ABC) (Krug, Arick, & Almond, 1980)	A 57-item behavior rating scale that assesses sensory, social, and repetitive behaviors and social, adaptive, communicative, and language skills
Diagnostic interviews	Autism Diagnostic Interview—Revised (ADI-R) (LeCouteur, Lord, & Rutter, 2003)	Interview administered to caregivers of children and adults with PDD, taking about 2 hours and consisting of 93 items
	Diagnostic Interview for Social and Communication Disorders (DISCO) (Wing, Leekam, Libby, Gould, & Larcombe, 2002)	A semi-structured interview that identifies behaviors associated with ASD
Direct observation scales	Autism Diagnostic Observation Schedule (ADOS) (Lord et al., 2000)	An observational measure of social and communicative behaviors of people with some language but who are not fluent and for high-functioning adolescents and adults
	Psychoeducational Profile—Revised (PEP-R) (Schopler, Reichler, Bashford, Lansing, & Marcus, 1990)	A measure of the severity of symptoms of autism that is used for children between ages 3 and 7
Instruments for Asperger's disorder	Asperger's Syndrome (and High-Functioning Autism) Diagnostic Interview (ASDI) (Gillberg, Gillberg, Rastam, & Wentz, 2001)	Designed for those who have Asperger's; measures behaviors, particularly social behaviors, interests, routines, verbal and speech abilities, and communication and motor skills

Source: Adapted from Coonrod & Stone, 2005; Lord & Corsello, 2005.

EDUCATIONAL PRACTICES

Evidence-based educational practices are recommended for students with autism spectrum disabilities—from specific instructional components and techniques to highly prescriptive comprehensive programs.

SERVICE DELIVERY

As with other students with disabilities, those with ASD should receive educational services in the least restrictive environment. For high-functioning students, such as those with Asperger's disorder, the least restrictive environment often includes inclusive programming in the general education classroom, typically with academic and behavioral supports. For those with more intensive instructional and behavior-management needs, such as Kim Thomas's students, programming is provided in more restrictive settings with supplemental opportunities for social inclusion.

What factors are considered in programming and placement decisions? According to Handleman, Harris, and Martins (2005), competence in social skills is an essential prerequisite for including students with ASD in general education classrooms. Because they are not affectionate, responsive to greetings, assertive in conversation and play, or purposeful when interacting with others, students with ASD stand out and are prone to rejection by classmates. However, meaningful contact with normally developing peers augments direct instruction in these social skills; peers serve as models of appropriate behavior and can be enlisted to initiate, prompt, and reinforce important social responses of students with ASD.

Do not underestimate the influence of those without disabilities on the success of inclusion efforts. Consider the results of a **naturalistic study** of 16 students with high-functioning autism included in general education classrooms (Ochs, Kremer-Sadlik, Solomon, & Sirota, 2001). Those who experienced negative experiences were in situations where teachers and classmates either disregarded or paid little attention to their special needs. Because peers were not made aware of the behavioral characteristics of ASD, the included students were often scorned, rejected, or simply left alone. In sharp contrast, students with ASD who had positive inclusion experiences had nondisabled classmates who were told explicitly about their peers' special needs. Armed with this awareness, nondisabled classmates were able to clarify instructional

Positive peer actions toward students with ASD can influence the success of inclusive programming.

requirements, correct inappropriate behaviors, minimize displays of certain symptoms, and include the students with ASD in social events.

A second component of successful inclusion involves academic benefit. Decisions regarding placement in the general education classroom should be based on the ability of the student with ASD to participate in academic activities with increasing independence with and without supports. Examples of participation include acquisition of new skills, generalization of acquired skills, and attention to group instructions (Simpson, de Boer-Ott, & Smith-Myles, 2003). Determining if there is a match between student and environmental characteristics requires careful observation and analysis in (1) curriculum delivery and reception; (2) environmental arrangements; (3) participation levels; (4) interaction types and amounts; and (5) attitudes of teachers, paraeducators, and peers.

EARLY INTERVENTION

Since early interventions usually result in better outcomes, they are essential (Woods & Wetherby, 2003). For students with ASD, early interventions typically focus upon (1) sensory issues—helping the young child process and integrate visual, auditory, touch, gustatory, olfactory, and kinesthetic input; (2) communication skills—developing functional communication, preverbal communication, and verbalizations; and (3) social behaviors—improving attention, initiation, and response frequency. **Applied behavior analysis (ABA)** techniques are most often used to improve young children's functioning in these areas. ABA (as we have noted throughout this text and review in subsequent sections) is the application of behavior change procedures involving functional relationships among antecedent events, specific behaviors, and actions that occur after behaviors of interest.

Infants and toddlers with ASD usually receive ABA interventions at home or in school- or center-based programs (Harris & Delmolino, 2002). In addition to working directly with the child, professionals involved in the home-based approach teach parents and family members the skills necessary to enhance and maintain the benefits of the behavioral techniques. Services delivered at home have the advantage of minimized time and effort when compared with travel to a center. Most important, the effects of interventions, because they are generated in the child's natural environment, have a higher probability of generalizing across family members and home activities. Unfortunately, the expectation that family members will, with fidelity, follow up with components of interventions is not always realistic. Time constraints and competing demands contribute to this slippage.

School- or center-based programs offer the advantage of easier access to a multidisciplinary team of professionals who can work together and coordinate services in a comprehensive, or wrap-around, fashion. Moreover, center-based programs give young children with ASD opportunities to interact with other children, situations that are critical for social development. Which of these approaches is best? According to Harris and Delmolino (2002), school- or center-based alternatives tend to be more cost-efficient than home-based methods because a range of specialists can see a child over the course of the day. However, when implemented properly, home-based interventions allow for the greatest intensity of treatment and generalization of benefits.

ACADEMIC AND SOCIAL/BEHAVIORAL INTERVENTIONS

The intensity and complexity of the academic and social challenges faced by students with ASD require comprehensive and programmatic interventions across a range of overlapping domains. Interventions are typically aligned with results of an individual student's assessment data and functional needs. However, due to the multiplicity of needs and limitation of time, interventions are commonly applied to improve academic performance, social/behavioral functioning, and language skills simultaneously.

Curriculum Content

Academic Content. There is no one particular academic curriculum for students with ASD. The standard school district curriculum, assessments of students' needs, and, to some degree, common sense dictate the individualized academic program for students with autistic and Asperger's disorders (Olley, 2005). Some students with ASD learn academic skills readily, while others struggle with basic pre-academic skills. Regardless of level of functioning, students with ASD have difficulty remembering and organizing information and do not always attend to all critical elements of a task. Consequently, students with ASD require supplemental cognitive and problem-solving strategies to learn academic concepts and skills. Higher-functioning students with Asperger's disorder included in general education settings also benefit from individualized supports and accommodations, particularly in content-rich areas that require large amounts of comprehension of verbal material and written expression. In many cases, the content-enhancement supports (e.g., graphic organizers, mnemonics, note taking, self-monitoring) are similar to those provided to students with learning disabilities. Keep in mind that strategies for teaching academics to students with ASD are similar to those that benefit students with learning disabilities and attention deficit disorder. Detailed information on academic supports and accommodations can be found in the "Educational Practices" section of Chapters 6 and 9.

To learn more about using graphic organizers and note taking to enhance instruction, go to the Ms. Biddle module on the DVD-ROM and click on clip 7: Graphic Organizer.

Social/Behavioral Content. Instruction in social/behavioral functioning typically focuses on age-appropriate behaviors that must be learned to survive and ultimately thrive in the real world. Although instruction is individualized and based on assessed strengths and needs, lesson content typically involves daily living skills, self-care skills, functional communication skills, and those intangible social graces that enable one to be integrated into the world at large. Many students with ASD require explicit instruction in how to play with peers and, as they get older, deal with the emotions and anxiety of being "different." Typically, instruction is needed in interpretative skills such as understanding facial expressions and gestures, comprehending nonliteral figurative language (i.e., idioms and metaphors), discriminating when others' intentions do not match their words, and understanding the implicit rules of social functioning—those ways of behaving that are not acquired through direct instruction (Smith-Myles & Simpson, 2001).

Language Content. The content of language instruction is determined by the student's ability to verbalize along with his or her corresponding intelligence level. Students who are nonverbal may be taught to communicate through the use of pictures, symbols, communication boards, sign language, and electronic devices that enable the child to press a button representing a symbol that is produced verbally. For those who are verbal, instruction often focuses on aspects of language production, including pragmatics, syntax, semantics, and articulation. *Pragmatics,* the social use of language, is the area that requires the greatest intensity of intervention for verbal, higher-functioning students with ASD. Specific instruction is typically required in recognizing the purpose of communication, speaking in a conversational manner, and understanding and being sensitive to the needs of the listener (Paul, 2005). Moreover, subtle skills such as beginning, sustaining, and ending conversations in a socially appropriate fashion are essential if students are to succeed among those without disabilities. Detailed information on the content of instruction in areas of language production is presented in Chapter 11.

Instructional Methods

Educational programs commonly used for improving the academic, social, and language skills of students with ASD include applied behavior analysis, **augmentative/alternative communication (AAC)** strategies, and **social skills instruction.**

Applied Behavior Analysis (ABA). At its most basic level, ABA is a highly structured behavior-change process that involves (1) conducting a baseline assessment of a targeted behavior, (2) implementing a behavior-change intervention, (3) collecting ongoing data on changes in the targeted behavior during intervention, (4) modifying the intervention based on the data, and (5) generalizing the effects of the intervention to untreated conditions and individuals (Arick, Krug, Fullerton, Loos, & Falco, 2005). Typically, a functional assessment of behaviors (FBA) guides the selection or development of the intervention plan.

in ways to integrate interests into social opportunities; and (3) coach explicit strategies in time management, independent living, speaking with professors, and stress management. Students with ASD who attend residential colleges should also have their own rooms—private places where they can reflect, decompress, and reduce the stress associated with managing their idiosyncratic behaviors (Baker & Welkowitz, 2005; Shea & Mesibov, 2005).

Living Arrangements

Without support and assistance, few adults with ASD are able to live independently. Accordingly, family members worry endlessly about how their relatives with special needs will live if, or when, family members are unable to take care of them. In the past, most adults with ASD were institutionalized; today there is a range of community-based, specialized, supported living facilities. Parents of children with ASD want to see an adult child live a rewarding life away from home. Consequently, transition planning and education, like the efforts of our featured master teacher, Kim Thomas, help shape independent living behaviors. Targeted education and training can help parents guide children in household maintenance, money management, and skills associated with **self-advocacy** and social self-protection. As adolescents approach early adulthood, opportunities for sampling or practicing independent living—in either group homes or supervised apartment complexes—should be provided (Marcus et al., 2005; Shea & Mesibov, 2005).

Emotional Supports

We all experience stress and anxiety as we grow into our adult roles, relationships, and responsibilities. However, when faced with these natural transitions, adolescents with ASD experience higher rates and greater intensities of anxiety and depression, often alone, without the benefit of peer or professional support. The pressure of having to do the correct things in social situations causes exhausting anxiety, much like a feeling of constant stage fright (Arick et al., 2005; Grandin, 1992). Moreover, the increasing opportunities for romantic and sexual relationships, brimming with subtle and implied communications, result in fear and confusion.

Unfortunately, the frequency and intensity of observable challenging behaviors masks the need for emotional support. Methods for providing emotional supports for people with ASD do not differ significantly from those provided to people without disabilities. First and foremost, students need a support person, perhaps a trained counselor, with whom they can discuss their fears and anxieties and plan a hopeful, socially appropriate course of action. Second, activities for diverting or reducing stress, including exercise, recreation, and relaxation techniques, must be available. Finally, students with ASD must be empowered with a mechanism for taking a self-directed time-out. After being taught to recognize when an anxiety or panic attack is near, students need an explicit procedure for regaining composure and emotional equilibrium (Arick et al., 2005).

PREVAILING ISSUES, CONTROVERSIES, AND IMPLICATIONS FOR THE TEACHER

As the incidence of children identified with autism spectrum disabilities increases and the interest in this mysterious group of disabilities heightens, controversies and critical issues continue to challenge the field. Following are three topical issues.

ROLE OF VACCINES IN ASD

Is Thimerosal, a mercury-based preservative used in vaccines, responsible for the considerable increase in the incidence of ASD and other neurological disorders? A number of organizations, independent physicians, and muckraking investigative journalists claim that scientific evidence indicates that there are cases of vaccine-induced autism, most likely caused by Thimerosal (National Vaccine Information Center, 2005). Moreover, some of these same sources suggest that government officials, conspiring with the pharmaceutical industry, are covering up damaging data that, if exposed, could dramatically reduce the profitability of the vaccine industry. Consider the evidence: In the

1990s, introduction of several new universal vaccines for infants, containing Thimerosal, was accompanied by dramatic increases in the incidence of ASD.

Responding to these indicators, researchers (e.g., Stehr-Green et al., 2003), employing a more controlled, empirical methodology, found no evidence of a relationship between vaccines and/or their mercury-based preservatives and the rise in incidence of ASD. Still, several states are taking no chances and have banned Thimerosal; scores of others are considering such action. Based on the available scientific evidence, the Centers for Disease Control and Prevention (CDC) do not support the hypothesis that vaccines cause autism. However, because of considerable public concern, particularly among parents who must decide if they should vaccinate their children, the CDC supports additional research on this issue. The fact that vaccines prevent measles, mumps, and rubella makes it inevitable that a cost-benefit debate will follow. Nonetheless, this debate does little to lessen the fears and uncertainty of those not wanting their child to be any part of the cost.

Reflective Exercise #7
What does "consideration of the cost-benefits of vaccination" mean? What levels of safety are required before an intervention should be approved for public consumption?

FACILITATED COMMUNICATION

Is it possible that trapped beneath the symptoms of ASD are individuals with hidden potential and creativity waiting to be heard? Facilitated communication (FC) is an emotionally charged technique that claims to assist individuals with ASD to express themselves. Originally developed by Rosemary Crossley in Australia in the 1970s, FC was touted as a method that assisted people with severe communication impairments to communicate and was eventually attempted with persons with autism. Due to compelling outcomes, interest in the technique spread (it is frequently highlighted when popular news periodicals focus on autism), and centers for the study and application of the process were developed across the world.

According to Biklen (1990), a founder of the Facilitated Communication Institute at Syracuse University, FC involves supporting the hand, typically at the wrist or forearm, and providing backward resistance to assist in the selection of letters from either a keyboard or a letter board. Proponents of FC claim that the technique allows many with ASD to communicate with complex language filled with abstract and emotional content. Based on these claims, FC has been used to administer intelligence tests and other standardized educational assessments. In some cases people previously found to function in the severe-profound range of mental retardation have been reclassified as having normal intelligence.

Unfortunately, the empirical evidence for FC does not match the excitement or enthusiasm expressed in anecdotal reports. Several independent reviews of the FC literature (e.g., Howlin, 1997; Mostert, 2001) have noted that facilitators influence responses of clients and that too many claims of communication remain unsubstantiated. Researchers have since labeled FC a fad (Frith, 2003), and some professional organizations have adopted a formal resolution opposing the technique as a valid mode of enhancing expression.

ONGOING PRESSURES AND DEMANDS ON FAMILIES

As we have noted throughout this chapter, developing and maintaining family involvement is critical in the education of students with ASD. Teachers facing their own ongoing classroom challenges and demands often overlook or underestimate the continual and sometimes exhausting social, emotional, and economic responsibilities associated with supporting a high-maintenance family member. Beyond the obvious physical demands, families perceive ASD as a confusing and frightening disability. They are often at a loss at how to engage their child, worry about ill-timed public displays of inappropriate behavior, and experience an almost constant roller coaster of hopefulness and frustration based on the uneven and often unusual developmental progress of their loved one. Moreover, they serve multiple roles: teachers, advocates, and loving (and sometimes resentful) family members (NRC, 2001).

How can families of students with ASD be supported and assisted? First, educators must demonstrate awareness and sensitivity to the developmental life cycle of the family and adjust their roles accordingly (Marcus et al., 2005). For example, during early childhood, assistance is best pointed toward direct assessment of functioning, emotional support for grieving family members, and parent counseling/training. As the child enters the elementary school years, the teacher should emphasize supports for maintaining home-school relationships, addressing learning problems, and providing strategies for improving adaptive behavior. During adolescence, efforts focus on independent living skills and work opportunities.

Other strategies for supporting parents and families include the following (Marcus et al., 2005):

For more information on the topics covered in this chapter, go to the Web Links module in Chapter 10 of the Companion Website at www.prenhall.com/rosenberg.

- Stressing that ASD is a long-term developmental disorder that is adapted to rather than removed
- Viewing inappropriate behaviors of the child as attempts to cope with the environment
- Assisting families to structure their environments by helping establish predictable routines and structured teaching processes
- Modeling mutual respect in the family-professional partnership
- Focusing on the needs of the total family

SUMMARY

Students with autism spectrum disabilities exhibit an extreme range of behaviors that separate them from activities and interactions that enrich everyone's quality of life.

Definition and Classification of ASD

- The two most common forms of ASD are autistic disorder and Asperger's disorder.
- Autistic disorder is characterized by an early age of onset, poor social development, impairments in receptive and expressive language development, and rigidity.
- Asperger's disorder is characterized by severe and sustained impairments in social interactions and restricted, repetitive patterns of behavior and interests.

Characteristics of ASD

- ASD students share three categories of characteristics: (1) impairments in social skills; (2) deficiencies in communication skills; and (3) stereotypical, ritualistic behavior.
- Many students with autistic disorder fail to acquire functional language, and students with Asperger's disorder have difficulty comprehending and making use of figurative language.
- Secondary behavioral correlates of ASD include early age of onset, variable intellectual functioning, and self-injurious behavior.

Prevalence Rates, Course, and Causal Factors

- Prevalence rates range from 2 to 20 cases per 10,000; and some have suggested that we are in the midst of an autism epidemic, with 3.4 per 1,000 children identified.
- The course of ASD is lifelong and chronic, with outcomes depending on the level of severity of the disability.
- The cause of ASD remains unknown, although it is generally accepted that the disorders are the result of one or more nature- or biophysically based factors.
- Damaging and counterproductive etiological theories implicating parents have been disavowed.

Identification and Assessment

- Identification and assessment of ASD requires measurement across disciplines.
- Initially, screening devices are used to determine if a child has either the specific or nonspecific behaviors suggesting risk for the disability.
- Children deemed at risk are referred to multidisciplinary teams that conduct intensive clinical evaluations.
- Once identified, the results of functional behavioral analyses (FBAs) are used for educational planning.

Educational Practices

- Factors used for making educational placement decisions include competence in social skills and ability to benefit from instruction.

- The focus of early educational efforts is on sensory issues, communication skills, and social behaviors. As students enter school, interventions focus on academic content, language, and social/functional material.
- Applied behavior analysis techniques, including discrete instruction (DTI), pivotal response training (PRT), and functional routine instruction (FRI) are frequently used practices for basic skills.

- Various techniques, including social stories and cartooning, are used to teach higher-functioning students.
- The need for supports and instruction does not go away once the student with ASD finishes school. Vocational training, supported employment, and help securing assisted living arrangements are essential.

 **ADDRESSING THE PROFESSIONAL STANDARDS**

Council for Exceptional Children (CEC) Knowledge Standards addressed in the chapter:

CC1K5, GC1K1, CC2K2, CC2K4, CC2K5, CCEK6, CC2K7, GC2K4, CC3K1, CC3K2, CC6K4, CC6S1,

Appendix B: CEC Knowledge and Skill Standards Common Core has a full listing of the standards referenced here.

speaker (a content problem), your ability to use the language to any degree at all was preferable to trying to communicate through gestures or drawing stick figures. This is because, whatever your limitation may have been, you could use the language well enough to meet a rudimentary need. So an important component of a person's language is the adequacy with which he can use the language—that is, how well he can apply language skills in daily social situations with others.

Language use disorders, which are also referred to as disorders in pragmatics, are characterized by individuals who do not use language that is appropriate for their current social context. A child that has a problem in pragmatics might have difficulties initiating conversations, taking turns with partners, engaging in extensive dialogues, or engaging in a wide range of other language uses in specific situations (e.g., greetings, making requests, or commenting). This person may have adequate language form and content but be deficient when using language for social purposes.

Manifestation of Language Disorders

Although we presented the different language disorders as discrete conditions, different types of disorders often occur together. In fact, children may exhibit combinations of language form, content, and use disorders, sometimes even with all three of the disorders occurring together. When this happens, the child is said to have a diffuse language disorder. What's more, the language disorders displayed by a child can change over time. Changes can occur because of maturation, speech/language intervention, or educational experiences. Additionally, a child may experience a particular type of language disorder at one time and another disorder at another time.

Appropriate use of language is a critical skill for toddlers and preschoolers to develop. Many young children who will ultimately be classified as having disabilities, such as learning disabilities or mild intellectual disabilities, will show problems in language use during the preschool years. These problems will also occur for other children, but many of them will develop adequate language skills as they get older. Any time you are in a program for toddlers or preschoolers, especially those who are developmentally at risk, you shouldn't be surprised to see the teachers placing a great deal of emphasis on children's appropriate language use.

SPEECH DISORDERS

Just as we can communicate without language, we can use language without speech. But just as language allows us to communicate easier, speech facilitates the use of language. Instead of speaking, we could use sign language or written language, and either would be perfectly acceptable. In fact, these forms of language production are very common. However, for most of us, neither signing nor writing is as efficient as speaking, which is why we opt to speak whenever possible.

In this section we will discuss speech disorders. Before we do, however, let's take a quick look at how speech is produced. This will help you appreciate the different ways in which speech may be adversely affected.

Building Blocks of Speech

Speech is undoubtedly the most complex activity that humans undertake. It relies on the coordinated use of four building blocks: **respiration, voice, articulation,** and **fluency.**

An essential need for speaking is being able to produce enough air pressure from our lungs. Our breathing, or respiration, produces a consistent and even breath stream that provides the power for speech. Just as air is used to produce sound in a pipe organ, it is the basic ingredient necessary for people to speak.

As air is exhaled, voice is used to create sound and to vary the sound in volume, pitch, and resonance. We use our **larynx** and **oral** and **nasal cavities** to modify the sounds we produce. The sounds are further refined into phonemes through articulation. (Remember that phonemes are consonant or vowel sounds that are combined in specific ways to form words.) Articulation is conducted by using our mouth parts, in-

Reflective Exercise #5
Have you ever been in a situation in which you had to communicate but could not speak? What did you do? Do you recall the extra effort required to get your message across?

www.prenhall.com/rosenberg

cluding our lips, tongue, teeth, jaws, and soft palate. These are referred to as the articulators. Finally, fluency is used to produce effortless and smooth speech so that the speaker's intention is easy to understand. Fluency allows us to speak hurriedly or slowly, transitioning smoothly from word to word and stopping and continuing at appropriate places in our speech. Justice (2006) provides this simple description to help us comprehend the complex process of speech:

> To better understand the processes involved with speech, say the word "eat" slowly and deliberately and think about the process as you do so. You will see that the speech process begins with the intake of a breath of air, which is then exhaled; this is the basic fuel needed for all speech. The exhalation travels up from the lungs through the windpipe (trachea) and over the vocal chords, which begin to vibrate and create the "eeeee" sound. This "eeeee" sound is then sent into the oral cavity, which is open and marked by a big toothy smile with the lips pulled wide. Notice that the upper and lower jaws are held fairly close together, but are not closed; the tongue sits low in the mouth, with the tip tucked behind the lower row of teeth and the middle rounded up on the sides to touch the upper teeth. Once the "eeeee" sound is in the oral cavity, a brief "ea" escapes and then the tongue comes quickly up behind the teeth to produce the "t" sound following the "ea." (p. 16)

When you understand that this is the process required for producing a *single* word, you have a good idea of what we mean when we say that speech is an extremely complex activity. Equally amazing is the fact that the mechanisms we use for speech did not evolve for the purpose of speaking but for breathing, eating, and drinking. Speech developed after these processes were already in place, although exactly when is the subject of scientific study and debate.

In the following sections, we will describe speech disorders that can sometimes occur. As you will see, these disorders can interfere significantly with the speaker's ability to say something that can be easily understood and comprehended. At the same time, the speech disorder can call attention to the speaker and sometimes cause personal discomfort. You should be able to see the relation between the building blocks of speech just described and how different disorders affect the normal functioning of these components.

Phonological and Articulation Disorders

If speech is to be an effective way to produce language, a speaker must generate speech sounds (specifically, phonemes) that a listener can understand and attach meaning to. Phonological and articulation disorders impair a person's ability to clearly create speech sounds. Instead of producing standard speech sounds, the speaker produces sounds that include distortions, substitutions, omissions, or additions. A distortion occurs when a nonstandard phoneme, like a lisp, is produced. A substitution is when one phoneme is replaced with another, such as "shair" for "chair." An omission is the deletion of a phoneme such as saying "chai" for "chair," and an addition is when an extra phoneme is added such as "chuh air" for "chair" (Owens et al., 2003).

You will recall from our discussion of language disorders that one type of form disorder was called a phonological disorder. As we explained, a phonological disorder is a language disorder that occurs when an individual has a faulty perceptual representation of a particular phoneme. This means that, although the person has the physical ability to produce the correct phoneme, he or she constantly produces an incorrect phoneme. The problem is attributed to having an inadequate mental representation of this aspect of the language sound. An example would be a person who can distinguish between a "ch" sound and an "sh" sound but doesn't make a distinction between the two sounds when speaking (Davis & Bedore, 2000).

Phonological disorders (a perceptual problem) produce what sounds like an articulation disorder that is actually a speech production problem. However, articulation problems can also be attributed to structural problems, such as a cleft palate, or faulty control of the articulators, such as incorrect placement of the tongue in relation to the

The pullout model is considered appropriate in many cases; but according to the American Speech-Language-Hearing Association (ASHA, 1999), the SLP has several other service-delivery options (see "Highly Effective Instructional Strategies" feature). According to ASHA (1999),

> Service delivery is a dynamic concept and changes as the needs of the students change. No one service delivery model is to be used exclusively during intervention. For all service delivery models, it is essential that time be made available in the weekly schedule for collaboration/consultation with parents, general educators, special educators and other service providers. (p. III–273)

COLLABORATION BETWEEN TEACHERS AND SLPS

More than ever, SLPs and teachers need to cooperate with each other in order to provide better services to students with communication disorders (Sunderland, 2004). The need for cooperation is based on effectiveness and efficiency. The SLP is not with the student as much as the teacher is. Therefore, the teacher has a much greater opportunity to reinforce a student's communication skills, which the SLP has targeted. In fact, authorities on communication disorders have proposed that collaboration with teachers, parents and other family members, and counselors is a critical part of service delivery for students with communication disorders and an important factor in the success of the intervention (Hampton, Whitney, & Schwartz, 2002; Santos, 2002). Teachers have the opportunity to collaborate in numerous ways with SLPs to improve students' communication skills. The second "Can You Help Me with This Student?" feature shows some ways in which this collaboration can occur.

PREVAILING ISSUES, CONTROVERSIES, AND IMPLICATIONS FOR THE TEACHER

School-based SLPs are likely to have very busy days, mixing their time among providing direct services to students, consulting with teachers on specific cases, and sometimes providing professional development information to teachers and other staff members. Not only are they concerned about providing remediation or developing compensatory skills, but they are also interested in preventing future communication disorders whenever possible.

A great number of parents of students with communication disorders feel that the best way for their child to be served is to receive direct therapy from the SLP. This is especially true when a student has a communication disorder existing as part of another disability, such as an intellectual and/or physical disability. In such cases parents often do battle with the SLP, the teacher, and the school administration to modify the IEP so that the direct contact time between the SLP and their child is increased.

There are two reasons why school personnel often resist this push from parents. First, as you have seen, there are various ways to provide services to individuals with communication disorders, and ASHA (1999) maintains that an SLP has a professional obligation to offer services suitable to the needs of the student. Sometimes this involves direct services, sometimes services of a less direct nature. Second, although not often discussed, there is a serious shortage of SLPs working in public schools. Therefore, their caseloads tend to be very heavy. From a practical point of view, then, most schools simply cannot provide the intensity of services that many parents would like. Unfortunately, the parents sometimes feel that the school isn't meeting their child's communication needs. In some cases it may be because the student will really benefit from collaborative consultation; in others it may be due to the lack of a sufficient supply of SLP services. In either case the parent may not be satisfied, and the special education teacher or the classroom teacher might get caught in the middle.

Can You Help Me with This Student?

WHAT A TEACHER SHOULD DO TO COLLABORATE WITH THE SLP

Charity was as pretty as a second grader could be and just as sweet, but her teacher noticed that she had a hard time saying what she wanted to say or asking and answering questions. When Mrs. Cates asked her what she had done over the weekend, Charity looked at her, looked down at her own feet, looked up again, and said, "My Mommy . . . my daddy . . . we had a . . . a . . . we went to the . . . " Mrs. Cates tried to give her extra time; but with 20 other children waiting to tell their stories, it was hard to wait. "Did you go to the beach?" "Yeah, but . . . we couldn't . . . there wasn't . . ." It was always difficult to figure out just what Charity was trying to say. If she wanted to ask for something, she had the same problem. "Miss Cates, can I . . . can you . . . Carl won't . . . I said . . . but he . . . "

Mrs. Cates decided that Charity's language might need some special intervention, but she had no idea what to do. She realized she should try to get Mrs. Graves, the school SLP, to help her out, so she decided to contact her.

How might teachers and SLPs cooperate? The following tips have been suggested by SLPs (Hampton et al., 2002; Reed & Spicer, 2003; Santos, 2002):

- Discuss with the SLP any students who appear to be having trouble communicating, whether the problem is with speech or with language. Ask for ways to screen students to help you find those whose communication difficulties might not be readily apparent.
- Ask the SLP to suggest ways to build speech and language exercises into your daily routine, both for students who are receiving SLP services and as ways to improve the communication skills of your entire class. Have her look at your lesson plans and offer suggestions, especially for students with communication disorders.

- Make sure you know the specific targeted skills the SLP is working on with individual students. Ask how you can help the students achieve these skills and generalize them. Know the specific do's and don'ts of how to intervene with students with communication disorders.
- Let the SLP know how students with communication disorders are progressing. You may even offer to help keep some type of data on their performance.
- Keep the SLP informed about behavioral challenges the students may exhibit and work with her to find effective communication skills for students who exhibit such behaviors.

For more information on collaboration among professionals, you may find one of the following books useful:

Cook, L., & Friend, M. P. (2002). *Interactions: Collaboration skills for school professionals* (4th ed.). Boston: Allyn & Bacon.
Pugach, M. C., & Johnson, L. J. (2002). *Collaborative practitioners, collaborative schools* (2nd ed.). Denver: Love.

EXTEND AND APPLY

- To be an effective professional, you must reflect on the challenges your students face and work collaboratively with others to address them. Besides those just suggested, what are some other ways in which teachers and SLPs can work together effectively?
- Do you believe that there are some personal characteristics that are necessary for collaboration? Do you have these characteristics, or do you believe you need to develop them?

Activity: Go to the Video Classroom section of the Teacher Prep website, click on Special Education and then module 8: Communication Disorders. Watch video 2 and answer the accompanying questions. How does this teacher seem to collaborate with the student's SLP and other support and caregivers?

A related critical issue is the ability of both special education teachers and classroom teachers to work in a collaborative relationship with SLPs. Many SLPs, like Kathleen Lance Morgan, express concern about the fact that some teachers don't really understand the role of the SLP and, worse, fail to realize that some children require active intervention to improve their communication skills. Without teachers' willingness and ability to work collaboratively with SLPs, the collaborative-consultation model will not be effective. Because of this concern, we encourage you to look at the suggestions in the "Can You Help Me with this Student" feature regarding ways for teachers and SLPs to work cooperatively and also suggest that you learn as much as possible about being a productive team member.

To link to websites that support and extend the content of this chapter, go to the Web Links module in Chapter 11 of the Companion Website at www.prenhall.com/rosenberg.

SUMMARY

Children with communication disorders are a relatively large group of students who receive services under IDEA. In this chapter we have included important facts about this group.

Definitions of Communication Disorders, Language Disorders, and Speech Disorders

- Communication disorders include both language disorders and speech disorders. Although a student may have both, they are not the same thing.
- A language disorder can be a disorder of form (including phonology, morphology, or syntax), content (also called semantics), or use (also called pragmatics). These can appear individually or in combination.
- Sometimes students with language disorders also have other disabilities.
- Speech disorders include articulation disorders, fluency disorders, voice disorders, and motor speech disorders.
- Like language disorders, speech disorders sometimes occur along with other disabilities, and sometimes they do not.
- It is important to be aware of the difference between a communication disorder and a communication difference. Some individuals may be erroneously assumed to have a communication disorder when actually their communication is appropriate within their own cultural milieu.

The Relation between Communication Disorders and Other Disabilities

- Students who have learning disabilities, intellectual disabilities, emotional/behavioral disabilities, physical disabilities, or traumatic brain injury often have communication disorders associated with their disabilities.

The Prevalence and Causes of Different Communication Disorders

- Almost one in five students served under IDEA is served because he or she exhibits a speech or language disorder.
- The cause for many communication disorders is unknown, and the causes that are known are usually associated with other disabilities such as intellectual disabilities, autism, or cerebral palsy.
- When the cause cannot be identified, we refer to the condition as a functional disorder.

Types of Assessment Used to Plan Interventions for Students with Communication Disorders

- SLPs use different types of assessment procedures to assess the nature of the communication and develop an intervention plan. These may include direct methods, such as taking a speech or language sample, and indirect methods, such as interviewing other persons about the student's communication characteristics.

Major Features of Interventions for Communication Disorders and Service-Delivery Options

- Using the diagnostic information, the SLP develops an intervention plan that includes long-term, short-term, and session goals.
- The SLP monitors the student's progress as the intervention is provided and continues providing services until the goals are achieved. If adequate progress is not occurring, the SLP modifies the intervention and continues observing the student's progress.
- An SLP may develop interventions based on different theoretical models or approaches. The most common include the behavioral approach, the linguistic-cognitive approach, the social-interactionist approach, and the information-processing model.
- Students whose needs are more severe may benefit from AAC devices. The nature of the AAC device must be based on unique student characteristics, such as intellectual and physical abilities, and his or her communicative context.
- The SLP can use different service-delivery options depending on the needs of the student. These range from providing direct therapy to offering consultation to teachers.
- The classroom teacher, the special education teacher, family members, and others can provide communication support for the student by collaborating with the SLP. For example, they may reinforce the intervention that is being provided and give the SLP feedback on the student's progress.

Major Issues in Providing Services to Students with Communication Disorders

- One major issue is how SLPs can deliver effective services when they often have many students in their caseload with different needs.
- Another is how teachers can work more collaboratively with SLPs to complement their services.

 Council for Exceptional Children

ADDRESSING THE PROFESSIONAL STANDARDS

Council for Exceptional Children (CEC) Knowledge Standards addressed in this chapter.

CC1K5, CC1K10, GC1K5, GC1K7, CC2K1, CC2K5, CC2K6, GC2K1, CC3K1, CC5K4, CC6K1, CC6K2, CC6K3, GC6K3, GC7K4, GC8K1, CC10K1, CC10K2, GC10K2, IC1K1, IC2K3, IC2K4, IC8K3

Appendix B: CEC Knowledge and Skill Standards Common Core has a full listing of the standards referenced here.

- A generic concept that includes traditional disability categories such as those pertaining to persons who have moderate, severe, or profound intellectual disabilities; those who fall on the autism spectrum; and those who have multiple disabilities, including intellectual disabilities
- Persons who exhibit relatively high rates of uncommon behaviors, such as self-stimulation, while at the same time lacking typical age-appropriate skills
- Persons who require extensive services to achieve their maximum potential

TASH, an organization supporting "equity, opportunity and inclusion for people with disabilities" (formerly called The Association for Persons with Severe Handicaps), defined the condition of severe disabilities in terms of necessary support, as suggested by the last meaning in the previous list:

> These people include individuals of all ages who require extensive ongoing support in more than one major life activity in order to participate in integrated community settings and to enjoy a quality of life that is available to citizens with fewer or no disabilities. Support may be required for life activities such as mobility, communication, self-care, and learning as necessary for independent living, employment and self-sufficiency. (Meyer, Peck, & Brown, 1991, p. 19)

As you may expect, persons who are considered to have severe disabilities constitute a very heterogeneous group. Although many people might be considered to have a severe disability, each is quite different from the other. If there is a common characteristic of the group, it is that individuals' ability to function on a day-to-day basis is very limited. As the TASH definition states, these individuals need a great deal of support to participate in various life activities. Here we outline some of the traditional categories of persons with severe disabilities.

INTELLECTUAL DISABILITIES CLASSIFICATIONS

As you may recall from Chapter 8, historically professional organizations and agencies have placed persons with intellectual disabilities in different subcategories based on IQ levels and functional abilities. These subcategories of intellectual disabilities and their approximate corresponding IQ levels included *mild* (55–70), *moderate* (40–55), *severe* (25–40), and *profound* (below 25).

Beginning in 1992, the American Association on Mental Retardation (AAMR, now the American Association on Intellectual and Developmental Disabilities) stopped using subcategories and instead developed a system in which it referred to individuals with intellectual disabilities based on *support needs* rather than disability levels (American Association on Mental Retardation, 2002). However, because classifications such as *moderate, severe,* and *profound* are still used by many organizations and agencies (such as public schools, human service agencies, and the American Psychiatric Association [1994]) when referring to people with intellectual disabilities, we think it is important that you have an accurate view of the ability of these individuals classified under these headings.

Persons with **moderate intellectual disabilities** score above 35 to 40 and below 50 to 55 on traditional intelligence tests. Generally, they are able to learn many basic skills in areas such as communication, self-help, functional academics, domestic skills, community functioning skills, and vocational skills. Many adults with a moderate intellectual disability are able to manage all of their own daily self-care needs, prepare food, participate in conversations, interact appropriately with others, use money correctly, and hold different kinds of jobs in the community (Westling & Fox, 2004).

If a person with **severe intellectual disabilities** has received a good education and has had adequate support, by adulthood he or she may have learned several useful skills. These could include being able to eat with a fork or spoon, dressing and bathing with some supervision, using the toilet independently, and washing hands and face without help (although he or she may have to be told or reminded to do so). The individual's physical ability will probably be fair to good, and he or she will probably be

Reflective Exercise #2
Based on certain concepts of severe disabilities, some persons who have a moderate intellectual disability would not be considered to have a severe disability. What's your opinion?

www.prenhall.com/rosenberg

able to walk, run, hop, skip, dance, and maybe skate, sled, or jump rope. The person with a severe intellectual disability probably will not learn many academic skills, such as reading, but may be able to recognize some words and common signs and enjoy books read aloud. The person may know that money is of value but may not be able to state the specific value of coins. Most adults with severe intellectual disability will be able to communicate using signs, symbols, or words (McLean, Brady, & McLean, 1996).

Often individuals with **profound intellectual disabilities** are referred to as having "the most severe" or "significant" disabilities. Their developmental levels will often be comparable to that of a child under 12 months of age. It is difficult to provide a typical profile of an individual at this functioning level because there is such an extreme degree of variability among them. Some are capable of near independent functioning in common self-care activities, such as eating and toileting, and may also possess functional skills in other domains such as vocational and domestic skills. Others may not speak, may have very limited sensory and motor abilities, might be nonambulatory, and may only minimally attend or respond to environmental stimuli. Still, many of these persons demonstrate the ability to learn and are capable of at least "partial participation" in normal daily activities (Westling & Fox, 2004).

INTELLECTUAL DISABILITIES SYNDROMES

Another way professionals categorize persons with severe disabilities is according to specific syndromes. A *syndrome* is a condition signified by a cluster of similar physical and behavioral characteristics having a common etiology or origin. Table 12.1 lists a few syndromes that might result in a "severe disability" classification. For additional information about these and other syndromes, you should refer to more complete references such as Batshaw (2002) or Dykens, Hodapp, and Finucane (2000).

MULTIPLE DISABILITIES

As we have said, the category of multiple disabilities usually includes a combination of some degree of intellectual disability as well as concomitant physical or sensory disabilities. The level of the intellectual disability is usually in the severe to profound range, but the individual's intellect may actually be higher than what is estimated. Because of how the person's physical condition limits his or her interaction with others, precisely determining how intelligent the person is may be very difficult.

People with multiple disabilities usually have various health problems that complicate and worsen their disabilities. They often develop diseases such as high blood pressure, obesity, brittle bones, depression, and general tiredness. Other conditions include cardiovascular (heart) diseases, respiratory diseases, eating disorders, and growth impairments (Heller, 2004; Thuppal & Sobsey, 2004).

Reflective Exercise #3
As you saw, for Pam Mims, a day as a teacher of students with severe and multiple disabilities included a great deal of time devoted to toileting, hygiene, and feeding. Do you suppose it is possible to do a good job at teaching when there are so many other needs you must address with these students?

CHARACTERISTICS OF STUDENTS WITH SEVERE INTELLECTUAL DISABILITIES AND MULTIPLE DISABILITIES

Considering the pool of students who can be classified as having severe disabilities, you will certainly agree that there are many differences among them. You might also agree that to speak in general about their characteristics is almost impossible. If you teach or work with any of these students, or if you do in the future, the best advice we can offer is to take your time to get to know each one. Having said that, though, we think it's fair to help you understand the very diverse population of these students by discussing in a limited way some things about them that seem to be generally true.

INTELLIGENCE

Quantitative measures of intellectual ability of persons with severe disabilities (i.e., IQ scores) as well as qualitative indicators (e.g., ability to demonstrate independent adaptive behavior) suggest that they function significantly below average. Individuals

TABLE 12.1

SYNDROMES ASSOCIATED WITH SEVERE INTELLECTUAL DISABILITIES

Name	Etiology	Key Features	Sources of Information
Down syndrome	Chromosomal anomaly (trisomy 21)	Mild to severe intellectual disabilities Physical characteristics: a flattening of the back of the head; slanting eyelids; small folds of skin at the inner corners of the eyes; depressed nasal bridge; small ears, mouth, hands, and feet; decreased muscle tone 60 to 80% have hearing impairments 40 to 45% have congenital heart disease A tendency toward obesity Hypothyroidism affects 15 to 20% Frequent skeletal problems, immunological concerns, leukemia, Alzheimer's disease, seizures, sleep disorders	National Down Syndrome Society (http://www.ndss.org/) National Association for Down Syndrome (http://www.nads.org/) Roizen (2001)
Fragile-X syndrome	X-linked transmission	Physical characteristics: a long, narrow face; large ears, jaw, and forehead Common characteristics: an unusual style of social interaction; may avoid direct eye contact; sometimes hand flapping or hand biting; may speak fast and repetitiously; can have short attention span and hyperactivity	National Fragile-X Foundation (http://www.fragilex.org/) Fragile X Research Foundation (http://www.fraxa.org/) Meyer & Batshaw (2001)
Fetal alcohol syndrome	Consumption of alcohol during pregnancy	General developmental delay, growth problems, and other physical problems Intellectual disabilities may range from mild to severe May have a small head, narrow eye slits, a flat midface, and a low nasal bridge Babies may have sleeping problems, be restless and irritable, and have sucking problems	FASlink (http://www.acbr.com/fas/) Wunsch, Conlon, & Scheidt (2001)
Prader-Willi syndrome	Chromosomal anomaly on chromosome 15	Often results in a moderate mental disability, but measured IQs have ranged from 40 to more than 100 Between ages 1 and 3, will develop insatiable appetites, become very preoccupied with food, want to eat continuously, and develop life-threatening obesity. Begin to show delayed psycho-motor activity, intellectual delay, and emotional/behavioral problems	Prader-Willi Syndrome Association (http://www.pwsausa.org/) Scott, Smith, Hendricks, & Polloway (1999)
Angelman syndrome	Chromosomal anomaly (a portion of chromosome 15 is missing)	Usually severe to profound intellectual disabilities Tend to have jerky body movements and stiff-legged walking Common facial features such as a wide smiling mouth, a thin upper lip, and deep-set eyes Often have fair hair and skin and light blue eyes About 80% of the time they will have epilepsy	Angelman Syndrome Foundation (http://www.angelman.org/angel/)

who are classified as having severe disabilities will generally have an IQ below 35 or 40, sometimes going so low that it cannot be reliably measured. From a developmental perspective, this means that these individuals, when they reach maturity, at best may have a mental age that ranges from below 1 year of age up to 3 or 4 years of age. This limited degree of development means that these persons will continue to need regular support from family, friends, and professionals throughout their lives.

www.prenhall.com/rosenberg

LEARNING

From an instructional point of view, teachers and others can expect that the learning abilities of students with severe disabilities will be very weak. In what is now considered a classic paper, Lou Brown and his colleagues (1983) made a strong case for providing the most functional education possible to students with severe disabilities based on the students' learning weaknesses. Brown et al. pointed out that, with regard to learning new skills, these students

- Require a greater amount of time to learn
- Have much difficulty in learning more complex skills
- Overall, learn fewer skills as compared to other students

Persons with severe disabilities will need support from family, friends, and professionals.

While it is possible for these students to learn many skills, the number and type of skills will not be comparable to those learned by most individuals. So those skills that we attempt to teach should be very functional and applicable to the individual's current and future needs.

You can see evidence of the limited learning abilities of students with severe disabilities in various ways. Psychological research on specific aspects of learning can help us understand some of the specific learning weaknesses of these students. Westling and Fox (2004) summarized some of the most significant learning difficulties of students with severe disabilities:

- *Attending to relevant environmental stimuli, dimensions of stimuli, and cues within the dimensions.* This means students may have difficulty learning what feature of an item or situation gives the information necessary for correct action.
- *Observational and incidental learning.* Observational learning is learning through watching and imitating a model (i.e., another person). Incidental learning is learning something that was not taught directly but that might be learned if attended to. Students with severe disabilities benefit from these forms of learning less well than do students who do not have disabilities.
- *Memory.* Major problems in this area are related to not being adequately exposed to the learning condition initially, having insufficient opportunity to practice or use the information or skill after it is initially learned, and then not using strategies adequately to pull the information from long-term memory for use when needed.
- *Skill synthesis.* Students with severe disabilities often fail to see the relation of different pieces of information to other information or to see how one area of knowledge or skill can be combined with another to produce a new skill set. Therefore, you usually cannot teach several separate skills and expect the student to organize them for application.
- *Generalization and discrimination.* With weak generalization skills, students have difficulty applying what was learned in one situation to other places, times, people, activities, and materials. Conversely, with weak discrimination skills, a student doesn't know when to do something and when not to do it. For example, a young man might know it is okay to hug his mom but not realize it is inappropriate to hug another woman.
- *Self-regulation.* In order to self-regulate, an individual must monitor her own behavior, evaluate it as being correct or incorrect, and then self-reinforce or withhold reinforcement. This is a sophisticated task, one that students with severe disabilities often have difficulty with. However, some research shows instructional methods might help students learn skills in this area (e.g., Agran, Fodor-Davis, Moore, & Martella, 1992; Hughes & Agran, 1993; Hughes, Hugo, & Blatt, 1996).

Can You Help Me with This Student?

TEACHING A STUDENT WITH SEVERE DISABILITIES TO COMMUNICATE

One of Pam Mims's middle schools students, Steve, was classified as having deaf-blindness and profound intellectual disabilities. He was nonambulatory and had few self-help skills. He could not reliably or appropriately seek attention, request assistance, or indicate pain or discomfort. He also did not respond to verbalization from others. Because he wore a body support jacket to counter his scoliosis, he was often thought to be uncomfortable or even in pain. It was also known that Steve did not sleep well at night. He was served in Pam Mims's full-time special classroom with six other students with severe disabilities and received related services in speech/language therapy, physical therapy, occupational therapy, and vision services.

Needless to say, Steve was a challenge for his teacher. This was primarily due to three reasons. First, because he had very limited skills and abilities, it was difficult to determine what to teach him. Second, his mother had very high expectations for him. She wanted Pam to work on phonics skills and teach him how to operate an electric wheelchair. Third, he would scream and hit his head with his fist for almost the entire school day.

The third problem caused the most stress, so Pam began by concentrating on this. At the same time she wanted to try to respect the mother's wishes and also teach something that Steve could benefit from.

Pam took the following steps:

- She conducted a functional behavioral assessment (FBA) to try to determine what affected Steve's behavior. She hypothesized that the screaming and self-hitting were related to his inability to communicate effectively about some need or desire.
- She developed an object-based communication system and taught Steve how to touch objects to indicate if he wanted something to eat or drink or if he wanted to get out of his body jacket and wheelchair and lie down on a mat.
- Pam also decided to try to get Steve into an electric wheelchair to see how well he could do in it.
- When Steve began to use his object schedule to indicate what he wanted, Pam responded immediately, presenting him with whatever he indicated.

SOCIAL BEHAVIOR

Many people with severe disabilities have full lives. They have friends, enjoy various leisure and recreational activities, and, as teenagers or adults, may have jobs in the community. However, these outcomes do not occur as easily as they do for persons without disabilities, and usually some intentional planning is necessary.

The learning weaknesses we have described can have an effect on the challenges that people with severe disabilities face when attempting to learn appropriate social skills. For example, they may not easily learn social skills simply by observing someone else and picking up the skills incidentally, they may not generalize skills that have been learned, or they may use social skills that are inappropriate for the time and place. As a result, it's common to see inappropriate social behaviors among persons with severe disabilities, especially when they have not received adequate instruction or had enough learning experiences.

On the other hand, persons with severe disabilities may develop positive relations with others when they have the opportunity to do so, when they are taught appropriate social behaviors, and when others have a little understanding about the nature of the person and how he is affected by his disabilities (Westling & Fox, 2004). Certainly this should be an important goal of instruction for these students.

Sometimes persons with severe disabilities have very challenging behavior. They may exhibit unusual, repetitive behaviors that are called **stereotyped behaviors,** or stereotypies. Or sometimes we may see episodes of aggression, self-injury, or noncompliance. The cause of these behaviors is often difficult to understand, but several theories have been developed in an attempt to explain them. Today, as we discussed

www.prenhall.com/rosenberg

- Steve indicated two desires very reliably: He wanted something to drink, and he wanted to get out of his chair and lie on his mat. When he did so and Pam responded, his screaming and self-hitting went way down. In fact, this behavior went from an average of more than 300 minutes a day to near zero!

As Steve's behavior began to improve, Pam was assisted by faculty members from Western Carolina University and its teacher support program. Through their efforts she located an electric wheelchair equipped with some special sensing-vibrating devices to let Steve try to propel himself.

- When Steve was placed in the wheelchair, Pam taught him how to press the joystick to go forward, backward, right, or left. The sensing devices were attached to vibrators in the seat of the chair to let Steve know when he was going to run into something.
- Pam used systematic instruction and was successful at teaching her student to go forward and to stop the chair. It was reported that Steve was always upright, smiling, and attentive in his electric wheelchair and never screamed or hit himself while using it!

The challenges Steve presented were certainly difficult but are not unlike those of many students who have severe or profound intellectual disabilities and multiple disabilities. Teachers of these students must be inquisitive and creative in order to seek and find answers that will lead to effective instructional approaches. There are many other students like Steve, and many more teachers like Pam Mims

are needed to provide them with the most effective instruction. Perhaps you would be interested in engaging in this very meaningful work.

For more information on intervening with students who exhibit challenging behaviors, you may find the following references useful:

Carr, E. G., Dunlap, G., Horner, R. H., Koegel, R. L., Turnbull, A. P., Sailor, W., Anderson, J. L., Albin, R. W., Koegel, L. K., & Fox, L. (2002). Positive behavior support: Evolution of an applied science. *Journal of Positive Behavior Interventions, 4,* 4–16, 20.

Carr, E. G., Horner, R. H., Turnbull, A. P., Marquis, J. G., McLaughlin, D. M., McAtee, M. L., Smith, C. E., Ryan, K. A., Ruef, M. B., & Doolabh, A. (1999). *Positive behavior support for people with developmental disabilities: A research synthesis.* Washington, DC: American Association on Mental Retardation.

EXTEND AND APPLY

- What was Pam's greatest challenge? Was it Steve's lack of skills? His challenging behavior? Or his mother's expectations?
- What personal characteristics do you have that might help you be an effective teacher of students like Steve?
- What particular strategy did Pam use that you would like to learn more about?

TEACHER PREP

MERRILL
PRENTICE HALL

Activity: Go to the Student and Teacher Artifacts section of the Teacher Prep website, click on Special Education and then module 16: Severe Disabilities. Read Artifact 1 and answer the accompanying questions. Think about what kind of assistive technology could be beneficial for Steve.

in Chapter 5, professionals often use functional behavior assessment and positive behavior support programs in an effort to improve challenging behaviors. A great deal of research has shown these procedures to generally be very effective (Carr et al., 1999; Hanley, Iwata, & McCord, 2003). In the "Can You Help Me with This Student?" feature we describe how a functional assessment and positive behavior supports were used to address Steve's very serious behavioral problem. (He is a student with deaf-blindness and profound intellectual disabilities.)

PHYSICAL CHARACTERISTICS

As we have stated in this chapter, individuals with severe intellectual disabilities and multiple disabilities often have serious medical or physical conditions. Cerebral palsy and epilepsy are two conditions that are often present (see Chapter 14). Other conditions can also limit normal physical development and activities. Common medical conditions include gastrointestinal disorders, inadequate ventilation of lungs, kidney and heart problems, sensory problems, and frequent infections (Thuppal & Sobsey, 2004).

In the classroom, teachers of students with severe disabilities will typically work with school nurses as well as physical and occupational therapists to address students' physical and medical needs. On a regular basis, students may have nutritional problems, **anemia,** dehydration, skin irritation and pressure sores, **respiratory infections,** asthma, ear infections, and **contractures** (Heller, 2004). These kinds of conditions led Pam Mims to think that part of Steve's problems might have been related to his discomfort (see the "Can You Help Me with This Student?" feature).

Reflective Exercise #4
How do you think students' physical and medical characteristics might affect their learning abilities? Do you think this would be a challenge to you as a teacher? How do you think a successful teacher would approach these students?

PREVALENCE AND TRENDS

It is difficult to pin down the exact number of public school–age students with severe disabilities. One problem is that there are no universal definition or accepted criteria. In our "FAQ Sheet," we reported an estimate of students with severe disabilities to be about 0.5 to 1% of all school-age children. This works out to roughly 10% of all students with disabilities. These figures are based on numbers reported by the U.S. Department of Education (2005) in certain disability categories, with a few adjustments to subtract students with milder disabilities.

What the numbers mean to you is based on what role you might play. Let's consider an elementary school with 400 students where inclusion is the norm. Of the 400, the school may provide special education services to 45 to 50 students. If they are proportionally represented, there may only be four or five students in the whole school with more severe disabilities. So if you are a special education teacher working with students with more severe disabilities in this school, you will have relatively few students. If you are a classroom teacher working in this school, you should not see more than two or three students with disabilities in your classroom and probably no more than one student with severe disabilities.

It is very hard to track the occurrence of disabilities and changes in occurrence across different times and places. Epidemiologists undertake this type of research. From their work, some conditions or syndromes have been recognized as occurring more often or being identified more often—for example, autism, **Fragile-X,** and **Angelman syndrome.** To better understand how such conditions appear within our society, the Centers for Disease Control (2004) have conducted an epidemiological study of birth anomalies and developmental disabilities in the Atlanta, Georgia, metropolitan area.

Reflective Exercise #5
If you are currently working in a school, can you describe the prevalence of students with severe intellectual disabilities and multiple disabilities? Do you see these students in inclusive schools? How many are in a classroom?

CAUSAL FACTORS

Severe disabilities can result from numerous etiological conditions. It is common to classify causes as occurring before birth (prenatal), around the time of birth (perinatal), or after birth (postnatal). The major causes, most of which are prenatal, are briefly explained in this section. For more detailed information, see Batshaw (2002); Dykens et al. (2000); Beirne-Smith, Patton, and Kim (2006); or Taylor, Richards, and Brady (2005).

PRENATAL CAUSES

Common prenatal causes of severe disabilities include genetic conditions, chromosomal anomalies, maternal infections, the ingestion of harmful substances, and radiation.

Genetic Conditions

Rare **genetic conditions** can lead to children being born with certain syndromes that are characterized by severe intellectual or multiple disabilities. These genetic conditions may be recessive or dominant. If they are **recessive,** both parents of the child must be carriers of the condition, and each of their offspring will have a 25% chance of inheriting the condition. If the condition is due to a **dominant** genetic condition, only one parent must have the genetic information, and each child will have a 50% chance of inheriting the condition. Recessive conditions cause severe disabilities more often than dominant conditions do. Syndromes that occur due to recessive genetic conditions include **Tay-Sachs disease.**

Some syndromes result from genetic material located on the **chromosomes** that determine the sex of an individual—that is, the 23rd pair of chromosomes in a human cell. These are called **X-linked** conditions, and in these cases the mother is the carrier of the genetic material but does not have the condition herself. The most common

X-linked condition is Fragile-X (see Table 12.1). Another is **Lesch-Nyhan syndrome,** a condition characterized by a high frequency of self-injurious behavior.

Chromosomal Anomalies

The genetic conditions just described occur because of specific genetic information that one or two parents pass on to the child. The genes are situated on specific strands of chromosomes. There are 23 chromosome pairs, including 22 **autosomes** and the 23rd pair of **sex chromosomes** that determine the sex of a person.

Sometimes a strand of chromosome may not join another during conception or a strand may break off and/or attach itself to another strand in an uncommon way. These chromosomal anomalies are not genetic inherited disorders in the sense that the parents transmit them to their children. However, they do affect the development of the offspring in an adverse way because of the change in the chromosomal patterns.

Several syndromes due to chromosomal anomalies are listed in Table 12.1, including **Down syndrome, Prader-Willi syndrome,** and Angelman syndrome. Websites with additional information about these syndromes are included in Table 12.1 and also on our Companion Website.

Some conditions, such as Down syndrome, are the result of a chromosomal anomaly.

Maternal Infections

Various viral or bacterial infections can occur during pregnancy that have little effect on the mother but may have more serious consequences for the developing fetus and result in severe disabilities. **Rubella, cytomegalovirus, herpes, syphilis,** and **toxoplasmosis** are common types of infections.

Most infections cause the greatest damage to the developing fetus during the first trimester of the pregnancy. At this time, the central nervous system is developing rapidly, and the infection can cause inflammation and damage brain tissue. The result is often severe intellectual disabilities and also physical and/or sensory disabilities.

Harmful Substances

If a mother consumes alcohol or takes drugs or ingests other chemicals during pregnancy, sometimes severe intellectual and multiple disabilities will occur. These substances can affect the development of the fetus by damaging the structure and functioning of cells. Physical growth, the developing brain, or both might be affected. For example, **thalidomide,** a drug developed in the 1950s to reduce morning sickness during pregnancy, results in impaired limb development; and alcohol can lead to brain damage. Anticonvulsant drugs and anticancer drugs are other agents that can lead to adverse development.

Radiation

If a woman is exposed to radiation during pregnancy (e.g., has an X ray for medical purposes), it is possible that the radiation may damage the baby's developing brain. This could result in severe intellectual disabilities. For the most part, the risk is small unless the X ray is directly targeted at the woman's stomach area.

Some have raised questions about the effects of being exposed to radiation *before* conception due to the possibility that the woman's ova or the man's sperm could be adversely affected by the radiation. **Radioiodine therapy** is often considered to create the greatest risk for this type of condition. A good discussion on this topic,

Reflective Exercise #6
Do you have an interest in a specific syndrome? Do you believe knowing the physiological etiology of a child's specific condition could help you as a teacher? Why or why not?

Reflective Exercise #7
Many mothers worry a lot about prenatal development, whereas others are less careful. How can you account for these differences? What might be done to help some mothers be more careful about prenatal development?

Employment and Adult Routines

Employment, or engaging in a meaningful adult routine, is a second concern for adults. Although too many adults with severe and multiple disabilities are still served in sheltered workshops or activities centers (Rusch & Braddock, 2004), many are employed in community-based jobs and given supports that help them to do those jobs. These supports include job coaches and natural supports often available in the job setting.

An important part of transition is to offer adolescents vocational training in real-world settings where they can learn essential job skills. Working in the community offers a chance to do meaningful work in exchange for fair wages in a natural context. Of course, it is more than work that is important; it is the chance to have a life that includes co-workers and friends and the social connections that come with them. Persons with severe disabilities have been able to learn a variety of jobs from groundskeeping and housecleaning to photocopying and data entry.

Quality of Life

Most important for any adult with severe disabilities, just as it is for you, is something that is hard to define: quality of life. The things we have talked about already—having a nice place to live and being employed or participating in a supportive environment—will contribute to this. Overall, though, quality of life for any adult is defined by being able to decide within reason what you want and then having a reasonable chance of getting it. Like everyone else, most adults with severe disabilities want to have some choices in daily routine, friends, social, and leisure activities, and a self-determined degree of participation in their community.

When school personnel develop transition plans, they tend to focus on supported employment or residential placements. But this isn't enough. Planning should also take into consideration the personal future of the person as well as the concerns of the family and look at ways to support a quality of life so that it can occur as it might for persons without disabilities (Kim & Turnbull, 2004).

PREVAILING ISSUES, CONTROVERSIES, AND IMPLICATIONS FOR THE TEACHER

From a historical perspective, students with severe intellectual and multiple disabilities were the last group to receive services under the special education umbrella. Until the mid-1970s they were excluded from most public schools. It took a federal law to give them the right to be taught in public schools. Even today, many issues continue to be discussed and debated:

- Should we spend so much on teaching students with severe disabilities when our educational budgets are always stretched?
- Can students with severe disabilities really be included in general education classrooms? How much can they learn? How will they affect the other students?
- Should students with severe disabilities be included in the general education curriculum? Is there any way they can participate meaningfully in the general education curriculum? Or should the focus be more on teaching functional skills and functional academics?
- Should these students be assessed at the end of the school year like students without disabilities and those with mild disabilities? Are the alternate assessment systems valid and reliable enough to get an accurate picture of their abilities? Should students' test scores be considered in evaluating schools and holding them accountable?

If you are employed as a special educator to teach students with severe disabilities or if they are a part of your general education classroom, these questions will probably always be on your mind. You will encounter people, including friends and colleagues, who will question the value of what you are doing with these students and

Reflective Exercise #11
Do you have or have you had your own transition plan? What is in it? Does it focus only on employment and living arrangements, or is quality of life also an issue?

whether or not they should really have the right to be in the public schools. There are many ways that you could respond to these challenges, but here is what we would say:

> In a society as rich in resources and human acceptance as ours, the greater error would be to reject someone from participation because they may not benefit as much as someone else. If we are to make an error, let's make it on the side of inclusion and acceptance rather than on the side of exclusion and rejection.

Of course, the answer that you give will have to be the one that makes most sense to you.

To link to websites that support and extend the content of this chapter, go to the Web Links module in Chapter 12 of the Companion Website at www.prenhall.com/rosenberg.

SUMMARY

Public schools in the United States have only served individuals with severe intellectual and multiple disabilities for about 30 years. In this chapter we have touched on some of the key points about this very heterogeneous population and how it is taught in public schools.

Definitions of Students with Severe Intellectual Disabilities and Multiple Disabilities and How They Are Related

- Persons with severe intellectual disabilities have been defined in different ways. Some people have defined them by their degree of intellectual disability (moderate, severe, or profound), by the syndromes they have, or by their limited abilities. Perhaps the most valid definition states that these individuals are likely to need some amount of support through life in order to have an adequate quality of life.
- Persons with multiple disabilities are those who, in addition to their intellectual disabilities, have physical or sensory disabilities.
- Many persons with severe to profound intellectual disabilities also have physical or sensory disabilities. Therefore, in reality these groups overlap a great deal. Persons in one or both groups are often referred to as having severe disabilities.

Significant Characteristics of Students with Severe Intellectual and/or Multiple Disabilities

- These individuals usually have reduced intellectual development; general learning weaknesses; and sometimes inappropriate, challenging behaviors.
- They often have medical problems associated with their intellectual and physical disabilities.

Prevalence of Students with Severe Disabilities and Causes of Severe Disabilities

- It is difficult to accurately state how many public school students are considered to have a severe

disability, but a safe estimate is about 0.5 to 1% of all students or about 10% of the students served in special education.
- The causes of severe disabilities are varied. Most are due to prenatal factors including genetic conditions, chromosomal anomalies, maternal infections, and the mother's ingestion of harmful substances. Different conditions that can occur at the time of birth or after birth can also lead to having severe disabilities.

Assessment and Planning Procedures Used with Students with Severe Intellectual Disabilities and Multiple Disabilities

- Different assessment and planning procedures can be very helpful in determining the instructional needs of students with severe disabilities. These can include adaptive behavior assessments, curriculum or activity guides, and ecological inventories.
- Person-centered planning may also be used. This procedure provides a very viable approach to developing meaningful instruction, daily activities, and other life conditions for students with severe disabilities.

Instructional Content, Instructional Methods, and Related Supports for Students with Severe Disabilities

- Traditionally, we have taught students with severe disabilities very functional skills, including functional academic skills.
- IDEA has directed schools to include these students in the general curriculum to the extent possible and to assess them at the end of the year using alternate assessment systems.
- Systematic instructional methods that involve identifying specific objectives, using prompting procedures such as the system of least prompts or constant time delay, and carefully measuring and monitoring student progress have been very

successful in helping students with severe disabilities learn new skills.

- Students with severe intellectual and multiple disabilities often have related physical and health care needs. Teachers can best address these needs by working collaboratively with parents and other school personnel such as the school nurse.

Major Issues and Controversies Related to Educating Students with Severe Intellectual Disabilities and Multiple Disabilities

- Controversies related to teaching students with severe disabilities revolve around cost-benefit issues, inclusion in general education, and participation in the general curriculum.

 **ADDRESSING THE PROFESSIONAL STANDARDS**

Council for Exceptional Children (CEC) Knowledge Standards addressed in the chapter:

CC1K: 1, 2, 4, 5, 7; IC1K: 1–8; CC2K: 2, 4, 5; IC2K: 1–4; CC3K: 1, 4; IC3K: 1, 3; IC4K: 2, 3, 4; IC5K: 5; CC7K: 1; IC7K: 1; CC8K: 1, 4; IC8K: 1; IC9K: 1, 2; CC10K: 1, 3

Appendix B: CEC Knowledge and Skill Standards Common Core has a full listing of the standards referenced here.

Many parents and deaf students frequently discard the idea of deafness as a disability, and embrace the notion of cultural and linguistic differences.

Reflective Exercise #2
Do you know a member of the Deaf community? How does this person view himself or herself within this community? Do you believe deaf people can be part of both their own community and the non-deaf community?

Acceptance of Deaf culture frequently has an impact on educational services. Parents who want their child to participate in this community will select educational settings in which ASL is used and where Deaf adults are prominent throughout the school. These parents and students frequently discard the idea of deafness as a disability and embrace the notion of cultural and linguistic differences. For these families, the concept of classification under IDEA may be considered offensive and demeaning.

BLIND OR VISUALLY IMPAIRED

Although many individuals believe the definition for legal blindness and the definition used for special education purposes are the same, this is not the case. "**Visual impairment including blindness** means an impairment in vision that, even with correction, adversely affects a child's educational performance. The term includes both partial sight and blindness" (U.S. Department of Education, 2006, sec. 300.8[c][13]). Legal blindness is a level of visual acuity that has been used to determine eligibility for various benefits, not for educational services. **Legal blindness** refers to a central acuity of 20/200 or less in the better eye with the best possible correction, as measured on a Snellen vision chart, or a visual field of 20 degrees or less.

When children participate in a vision screening in a physician's office, they are asked to stand 20 feet from a chart showing letters or shapes. With one eye covered at a time, the child is asked to read the letters or shapes on the smallest line she or he can see clearly. Based on responses, the child may be referred to an optometrist for further evaluation. The optometrist then uses a refraction test to determine the extent of vision loss. The refraction test and other evaluations conducted in the optometrist's office are designed to simulate the process of standing a distance away from the chart.

Visual acuity refers to how clearly a person sees at a specific distance and is expressed as a fraction. The top number refers to the distance you stand from the object. The bottom number indicates the distance at which a person with normal eyesight could see the same object. On a Snellen chart, acuity is measured using letters aligned in rows. For example, 20/20 is considered normal. 20/40 indicates that the line you correctly read at 20 feet can be read by a person with normal vision from 40 feet away. A person with 20/200 visual acuity would be standing 20 feet from a line that a person with normal vision could read from 200 feet away. To qualify as legally blind, this person is standing 20 feet from the sign and still wearing his glasses or contacts.

Visual field refers to the area in space around the head that can be seen without moving the head. Frequently this is also called peripheral vision. There are a variety of methods for measuring the visual field. A crude visual field test can be done by having

www.prenhall.com/rosenberg

FIGURE 13.2

PARTS OF THE EYE

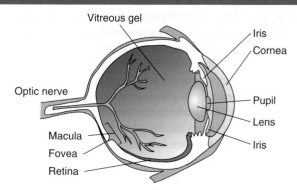

the patient look straight ahead and count the fingers shown by the examiner from the side. More typically, however, visual fields are measured by a computerized assessment in an optometrist's or ophthalmologist's office. For this procedure, one eye is covered, and the patient places his or her chin in a type of bowl. Then, when the patient sees lights of various intensities and at different locations, he or she pushes a button. This process produces a computerized map of the visual field. If the visual field is measured as 20 degrees or less, the individual is legally blind. Figure 13.2 is a diagram of the parts of the eye.

Typically, legal blindness has an adverse effect on students' educational performance; therefore, students who are blind qualify for special education services. In fact, the definition under IDEA is perceived as more broad than the definition of legally blind and frequently includes students with visual difficulties who do not meet the legal requirements of blindness. This is because the definition is focused on the educational impact of the vision loss rather than on a specific numerical target for the student to pass or fail.

Reflective Exercise #3
How do you think you would be able to support a child with visual disabilities in your classroom if you were a general education teacher? Do you think you might be able to work effectively with a visual disabilities teacher?

DEAF-BLIND

"**Deaf-blindness** means concomitant hearing and visual impairments, the combination of which causes such severe communication and other developmental and educational needs that they cannot be accommodated in special education programs solely for children with deafness or children with blindness" (U.S. Department of Education, 2006, sec. 300.8[c][2]). For most people, the term *deaf-blind* brings to mind the image of someone with no vision and no hearing, but this is not an accurate representation. Many students who are deaf-blind have some functional use of their vision or hearing or both.

In fact, only about 6% of children who are deaf-blind are totally deaf and totally blind (NTAC, 2004). Many children classified as deaf-blind have enough vision to be able to move about in their environments, recognize familiar people, see sign language at close distances, and perhaps read large print. Others have sufficient hearing to recognize familiar sounds, understand some speech, or develop speech themselves. Because deaf-blindness is a combination of vision and hearing losses, there are as many possible combinations as there are individuals. For this reason, no two children with deaf-blindness are alike, and educational programs for students who are deaf-blind are widely varied.

CHARACTERISTICS OF STUDENTS WITH SENSORY IMPAIRMENTS

INTELLIGENCE

Hearing or vision disabilities alone do not impact the cognitive skills of a child. For example, as a result of the Rubella epidemic of 1964–1965, a high number of children were born with sensory impairments, but relatively few had cognitive delays. As we've postsecondary education (English, 1997). As this information suggests, "far too many students leave school not prepared for the multidimensional demands of adulthood" (Luckner, 2002, p. 5).

With literacy being an area of critical focus, other necessary work skills are frequently left behind. The Laurent Clerc National Deaf Education Center recently sought feedback on the topic of transition services. The primary concern described by parents, caregivers, teachers, and other professionals was "the need for appropriate job behavior, opportunities for work-based learning, work exploration, and work experience including volunteer and paid work, prior to graduation from high school" (LeNard, 2001, p.13). These school-to-work experiences are necessary for students to learn the subtle social expectations of the workplace as well as specific job-related skills.

Blind/Visually Impaired

Postschool trends among students who are blind or visually impaired reflect low levels of self-determination. Only 42% of people who are blind and severely visually impaired are married (AFB, n.d.). When it comes to finding full-time work, only 46% of those with a visual impairment and 32% of those who are legally blind are employed (NCHS, 1998). Approximately 45% of students with severe visual impairment or blindness graduate with a high school diploma (NCHS, 1998). Among high school graduates, students are about as likely to attend college as those with no vision loss (24% compared to 27%) but are less likely to graduate (16% compared to 26%) (AFB, n.d.).

Career education activities for students with visual impairments should be directly tied to the school curriculum and integrated into family lives. Areas of instruction that will assist students as they prepare for the workplace include functional academics, work apprenticeships, cooperative education, and technology preparation. In addition to these skills, which are necessary for all students, Wolffe (1996) describes five areas that must be addressed for students who are blind or visually impaired: realistic feedback, high expectations, opportunities to work, compensatory skills, and exposure to visual input. In order to appropriately focus on career preparation, students with visual impairments and their families must begin early.

Deaf-Blind

Employment opportunities are often limited for young people who are deaf-blind for various reasons. Many parents and professionals fear that students with deaf-blindness are unable to work, partly because so many young adults who are deaf-blind also have other disabilities. Another reason for limited employment opportunities may be that children who are deaf-blind often have limited life experiences that have not allowed them to see and interact with a wide range of jobs.

How are children exposed to career options? Consider your average trip to the supermarket. During the trip to and from the store, a child will encounter bus and cab drivers, police and fire fighters, store clerks, stockers, managers, delivery people, and so on. Most children also have at least a basic understanding of what their parents, grandparents, and other family members do for a living. As they get older, children have opportunities to "practice" for future employment by doing chores around the house and providing services for others, including babysitting, lawn mowing, and selling lemonade at the corner. Many of these practice experiences are not available to children who are deaf-blind.

Starting as early as possible, the child who is deaf-blind must build a knowledge and experience base regarding employment. Teachers can begin by exposing the child to a variety of community experiences so they have opportunities for interaction. As the child moves into adolescence, providing opportunities for paid employment is a vital component of building that knowledge base. Formal programs have been established to help prepare students who are deaf-blind for the transition from work to school. See the "Site Visit" feature for an example of one of these programs.

Reflective Exercise #9
Can you think of some ways in which the postschool outcome for students who are deaf or who have hearing impairments might be improved?

www.prenhall.com/rosenberg

Site Visit:
Effective Practices in Action

The Helen Keller National Center for Deaf-Blind Youths and Adults (HKNC) in Long Island, New York, is the only national training center devoted exclusively to skills training for individuals who are deaf-blind. As part of their national outreach program, HKNC has regional representatives who provide consultations as well as assist students who attend on site in New York. The goal of HKNC is to offer intensive and comprehensive rehabilitation training to individuals who are deaf-blind. HKNC provides evaluation and training in communication skills, adaptive technology, orientation and mobility, independent living, work experience, and other support services.

Students who attend HKNC are given opportunities to practice work skills in both a separate training center and in real-world work environments. Students try several work experiences to help identify interests, strengths, weaknesses, and special considerations. In addition, HKNC staff provides comprehensive reports including "detailed suggestions for communication, mobility, residential supports, employment, recreation/leisure, environmental modifications and other areas" (Davis, 2003, p. 34).

Because the number of students who qualify for and receive services from HKNC is quite small, it is more appropriate to discuss the impact of the program on individual student lives than to seek statistical significance. HKNC has developed a reputation as a model program of the highest quality. In its 1999 annual progress report, HKNC indicated that nearly 50% of students gained employment in a less restrictive setting after leaving the program. For a group of students who enter with little expectation for postschool employment, these results are impressive. For more information, contact HKNC:

Helen Keller National Center for Deaf-Blind Youths and Adults
Technical Assistance Center
111 Middle Neck Road
Sands Point, NY 11050
Voice: (516) 944-8900
TTY: (516) 944-8637
Website: *www.helenkeller.org*

IMPLICATIONS FOR THE TEACHER

Teachers of students with sensory impairments have a rewarding and challenging career. These teachers experience several sources of stress in their jobs, including feelings of isolation, challenges to effective service delivery, and slow progress in some children (Hass, 1994). Although the main role of teachers of students with sensory impairments is to provide direct services to students, they also spend a considerable amount of time consulting with other teachers, adapting curricular materials, accommodating lesson plans, and completing paperwork. In spite of these challenges, teachers of students with sensory impairments frequently report on the joys and satisfactions of their jobs (Correa & Howell, 2004; Luckner & Howell, 2002). Generally, teachers of students with sensory impairments work with a wide variety of students who range in age, grade level, and ability level. They may work with the same students over several years, which often results in a strong relationship between the school and family.

There is a great need for professionals to continue learning throughout their careers as new information and techniques become available. Keeping up with technological advances is especially important. Aside from the specialized skills necessary to teach students with sensory impairments, teachers require expertise in overall teaching skills, communication, tact, and problem-solving ability (Correa & Howell, 2004; Luckner & Howell, 2002). If these challenges and rewards intrigue you, gather more information about becoming a specialized teacher of students with sensory impairments.

To link to websites that support and extend the content of this chapter, go to the Web Links module in Chapter 13 the Companion Website at www.prenhall.com/rosenberg.

SUMMARY

In this chapter, we have explored the education of students with sensory impairments and presented significant facts.

There Are Various Disability Classifications for Students with Various Sensory Impairments

- A student may be eligible for special education if he or she has sensory impairments that have an adverse impact on learning.
- Deafness means there is a hearing impairment "so severe that the child is impaired in processing linguistic information . . . with or without amplification that adversely affects a child's educational performance."
- Hearing impairment means an impairment "that adversely affects a child's educational performance but that is not included under the definition of deafness."
- There is also a cultural definition of deafness through which a person identifies himself or herself as part of the Deaf culture.
- Visual impairment including blindness means an impairment in vision that, even with correction, adversely affects a child's educational performance. The term includes both partial sight and blindness.
- Legal blindness refers to a central acuity of 20/200 or less in the better eye with the best possible correction as measured on a Snellen vision chart, or a visual field of 20 degrees or less.
- Deaf-blindness means concomitant hearing and visual impairments, the combination of which causes such severe communication and other developmental and educational needs that students cannot be accommodated in special education programs solely for children with deafness or children with blindness.

Key Characteristics of Students with Sensory Impairments and How They Differ from Other Students

- Hearing or vision disabilities alone do not impact cognitive skills of a child, but the mental processes required to learn new information is different for students with sensory impairments.
- A sensory impairment may be only one aspect of a student's educational needs. He or she may have other disabilities that affect learning ability. It can be difficult to distinguish between learning challenges caused by a lack of sensory input or by other conditions.
- It is very common for students with sensory impairments to have typical learning processes and learning modes: but their ability to access information may be restricted in some avenues, or the order in which they acquire new skills may vary.
- Social behavior of students with sensory impairments is impacted not because of an innate lack of social skills but because the sensory loss results in a loss of input.
- Physical development of students with sensory impairments is similar to that of all other children, unless the student has an additional disability.

Key Information about the Number and Distribution of Students with Sensory Impairments

- Students with sensory impairments fall into the category of students with low-incidence disabilities.
- According to the U.S. Department of Education about 78,000 school-age children have hearing impairments as their primary disability, and about 29,000 school-age students in special education have visual disabilities as their primary disability.

- The National Technical Assistance Consortium for Children and Young Adults Who Are Deaf-Blind reported 9,516 students with deaf-blindness between ages 0–21 in 2004.

Factors Relative to the Educational Experiences of Students with Sensory Impairments

- Early intervention and preschool services are critical to the later learning and development of children with sensory impairments.
- Different forms of educational services are used for students with sensory impairments, including consultation services, resource-room placements in regular schools, and residential schools. Sometimes students who are blind will go to residential schools for short periods of time to develop specific skills.
- Literacy skills of students who are deaf or have hearing impairments are often negatively affected; and both academic skills and functional living skills for students with visual impairments can be adversely affected.

What Areas of Curriculum Are Traditionally Addressed by Specialized Teachers of Students with Sensory Impairments?

- Teachers must address the needs of students that result from their sensory impairments as well as curricular areas in the general education curriculum.

 **ADDRESSING THE PROFESSIONAL STANDARDS**

Council for Exceptional Children (CEC) Knowledge Standards addressed in the chapter:

For teachers of students who are deaf and hard of hearing: DH1K1, DH1K4, DH2K1, DH2K2, DH3K1, DH3K2, DH6K2, DH6K3, DH6K5

For teachers of students who are blind or visually impaired: VI1K3, VI1K6, VI2K3, VI2K4, VI3K2, VI3K3, VI4K16, VI7K2

Appendix B: CEC Knowledge and Skill Standards Common Core has a full listing of the standards referenced here.

DEFINITION AND KEY CHARACTERISTICS OF STUDENTS WITH TRAUMATIC BRAIN INJURY

As we saw in the federal definition of TBI presented in Chapter 1 (see Table 1.2), the term applies to "open or closed head injuries resulting in impairments in one or more areas, such as cognition; language; memory; attention; reasoning; abstract thinking; judgment; problem-solving; sensory, perceptual, and motor abilities; psychosocial behavior; physical functions; information processing; and speech" (IDEA '97, sec. 300.7). As you will recall from our feature about Shannon Hunt and her student Josh, what struck her most about Josh was his immature social skills.

There are a variety of types of brain injury with different degrees of seriousness and potential harm to the student. Some you may hear about are these:

- *Skull fractures.* A linear fracture is a crack in the skull detectable by X ray that does not usually cause significant neurological damage. In contrast, a depressed fracture means the skull is broken and pressing against the brain and is often associated with significant brain damage.
- *Contusion.* This is a bruise to a part of the brain. The degree of damage will depend on how extensive the bruise is. The symptoms of the contusion may worsen for a few days after it occurs.
- *Hematoma.* A hematoma is a blood clot. An epidural hematoma is one that forms between the skull and the outer covering of the brain. A subdural hematoma forms directly on the brain itself and is usually more serious than an epidural hematoma.
- *Concussion.* Any injury that can cause a loss of consciousness or amnesia is a concussion. It is caused by a slight injury to nerve fibers in the brain.
- *Diffuse axonal injury.* This injury is similar to a concussion but much more severe. Nerve fibers (or axons) throughout the brain are injured through violent motion such as that caused by a car crash.

Although most head injuries are actually minor and do not result in long-term consequences, as a teacher, you should know that some signs should not be ignored. *If you see any of the following conditions following a head injury, you should seek emergency medical attention:*

- If there is a loss of consciousness, especially if it is for more than a few minutes
- If the student becomes lethargic, confused, or irritable
- If the student has a severe headache
- If there is an impairment in vision, speech, or movement
- If there is significant bleeding
- If there is repeated vomiting

Children or adolescents showing these signs should be taken to the emergency room for a neurological examination. If the student remains unconscious for more than a few minutes, you need to call for emergency medical service (Michaud, Semel-Concepción, Duhaime, & Lazar, 2002).

If serious brain injury occurs, the person will need both immediate and long-term care. Immediate care consists of addressing the injury through medical treatment, sometimes including neurosurgery. In some cases the child remains in a coma for an extensive amount of time—even days, weeks, or longer. During this time, doctors and health care professionals provide medical treatment to prevent or treat complications and seizures. A physical therapist will provide passive range of motion exercises to stimulate the muscles and to help prevent contractures and pressure sores. Other therapeutic provisions might include the use of casts or splints and sensory stimulation. People who recover from a coma often do so at an uneven pace, and doctors monitor their recovery in order to determine when more intensive post-coma treatments should be provided (Best, 2005b).

After medical treatment for the injury or when the person fully recovers from the coma, therapists provide rehabilitation to (1) counter conditions that can occur from immobilization and neurological dysfunction, (2) help the person regain abilities or teach him or her to adapt or compensate for any loss of function, and (3) help offset the effect of any form of chronic disability on learning or development.

Reflective Exercise #2
Have you or anyone you've known experienced a serious head injury? What type was it? What were the immediate and long-term effects?

www.prenhall.com/rosenberg

The student with TBI will very likely have problems concentrating and paying attention, remembering, carrying out complex cognitive tasks, and communicating (Keyser-Marcus et al., 2002). Reading and math are the most common academic problem areas, and students are likely to have weaknesses in specific skills in those subjects. Also, students may have behavioral issues such as being off task, increased or decreased activity levels, impulsivity, irritability, apathy, aggression, or social withdrawal. What sets apart students with TBI from students with learning disabilities, ADHD, or emotional/behavioral disorders is the variability that occurs in their performance and behavior and the changes that you may see over time. Flexible planning for these students is imperative (Keyser-Marcus et al., 2002; Michaud et al., 2002).

DEFINITIONS AND KEY CHARACTERISTICS OF STUDENTS WITH PHYSICAL DISABILITIES

Although we prefer the term *physical disabilities,* as you saw in Chapter 1 (see Table 1.2), the U.S. Department of Education uses the term *orthopedic impairment* for this category of students. According to the formal definition, "Orthopedic impairment means a severe orthopedic impairment that adversely affects a child's educational performance. The term includes impairments caused by congenital anomaly (e.g., clubfoot, absence of some member, etc.), impairments caused by disease (e.g., poliomyelitis, bone tuberculosis, etc.), and impairments from other causes (e.g., cerebral palsy, amputations, and fractures or burns that cause contractures)" (IDEA '97, sec. 300.7).

Note that the condition must negatively affect the student's educational performance in order for the student to qualify for an IEP and special education services. As we have mentioned, if this is not the case, the student may still qualify for a 504 plan.

Perhaps more important than the specific physical conditions of these students are the unique nonphysical characteristics of students with physical disabilities. Although you should never fall into the trap of stereotyping all persons with physical (or other) disabilities, you should know that their view of the world and their interactions with others are likely to be a bit different from those of people without physical disabilities. It is not that they are necessarily emotionally disturbed, but a person who has a physical disability, because of real experiences, often has a different reaction to life events.

For example, Doubt and McColl (2003) interviewed seven high schoolers with physical disabilities to learn what helped them to fit in versus what inhibited their interactions with other adolescents. The researchers found that there were two types of factors (what the authors called extrinsic and intrinsic factors) that either caused the students with disabilities to be left out or helped them be let in.

Intrinsic factors are those conditions that the person can control himself or herself. Based on what the students told the researchers, factors that helped the students be accepted included avoiding drawing attention to their disability; making fun of their own condition using self-deprecating humor; and finding a special niche among their peers, such as serving in a support role on a sports team. Sometimes students also found it helpful to educate their peers about their condition. On the other hand, certain intrinsic factors tended to isolate them, mainly their own physical limitations and self-exclusion. In some cases, simply keeping up was a problem. In others, students excluded themselves because they felt they would not be accepted by others.

Doubt and McColl (2003) also reported on extrinsic factors that limited integration. For example, the attitudes and behaviors of peers could be limitations for the students with disabilities. (Their peers sometimes treated them like they were younger or less competent individuals.) So could inaccessible extracurricular activities, especially athletics. Both intrinsic and extrinsic factors are unfortunate and suggest that one important teacher role is to try to reduce them. According to another study, however, the more that teachers integrate students with physical disabilities, the better the students' self-concept (Mrug & Wallander, 2002).

As you realize, we cannot address all of the different types of physical disabilities that you may encounter as a teacher. Therefore, we focus on those that are relatively common. In Table 14.1 we describe four types of physical disabilities that special

Reflective Exercise #3
Do you have intrinsic factors that you control that either allow you to be better accepted or lead to you being more isolated by your peers?

TABLE 14.1

PHYSICAL DISABILITIES TEACHERS ARE LIKELY TO ENCOUNTER

Condition	Cause	Classroom Considerations
Cerebral Palsy (CP) CP is a neuromuscular disorder that results in the brain's inability to control some or all of the body's muscles. It may affect the person's limbs, making them tense (hypertonic) or flaccid (hypotonic). The person's head, neck, and trunk may also be affected. It may impair the person's ability to walk, use her arms and hands, chew and swallow, sit upright, and other abilities. Some persons with CP have intellectual disabilities, but many do not. There are several different types of CP.	CP is caused by brain damage that occurs before, during, or after birth. It is a nonprogressive condition in that the damage does not worsen over time. The area of the brain that is damaged and the extensiveness of the damage determine the type of CP that will occur and how severe it is. There are several risk factors that increase the chance that CP will occur. Some include prematurity, low birth weight, and illness during pregnancy.	A student's ability to physically engage in class activities will depend on the severity and extent of the CP. Many can easily participate, but some will require adaptations or accommodations. The PT and OT can help teachers design ways to include the student with CP in various learning activities. Sometimes it is assumed that the student with CP also has a severe intellectual disability. While this may be true in some cases, it would be a mistake for teachers to approach the student with this assumption. The motor limitations of students with CP often mask their intellectual ability.
Muscular Dystrophy Muscular dystrophy is an inherited muscle disorder in which muscle tissue gradually degenerates. The most common type of the disease is Duchenne muscular dystrophy (DMD). Muscular dystrophy is a degenerative disease, meaning it gets worse over time. Fat tissue gradually replaces muscle tissue, and the child becomes weaker and weaker, with the weakness progressing from the legs upward. Ultimately the child loses the use of all muscles. Death usually occurs during adolescence or young adulthood.	Muscular dystrophy is an inherited muscle disorder. Mothers carry the gene but do not have the disease. Instead, they can transmit it to their sons. The disease first appears during early childhood, between about 2 and 6 years of age. DMD occurs about once in every 3,500 male births. Other forms of the disease are rarer. Becker muscular dystrophy occurs about once in every 20,000 births.	The child with muscular dystrophy becomes gradually weaker through the childhood years. His intellectual ability does not decrease, but about one-third of the boys with DMD have learning disabilities. Instructional activities have to take into consideration both physical and academic characteristics. The longer the child can remain upright, active, and mobile, the better. Teachers should maintain positive attitudes about the value of the student as a participating member of the class.

Spina Bifida

Spina bifida is a break in the spinal cord. There are different types of the condition, but the most severe form, called *myelomeningocele*, results in a loss of sensation and muscle control in parts of the body below where the lesion occurs. Persons with this condition aren't able to feel touch, temperature, pressure, or pain, and their lower body is very weak. They also do not have normal control over their bladder or bowels.

Spina bifida is a particular form of a neural tube defect (NTD). NTDs occur early in pregnancy when the vertebrae fail to fully grow around the spinal chord and instead leave a small opening in the protective bony structure. This opening, called a bifida, in some cases allows a part of the spinal cord and/or its covering, called the meninges, to pouch out of the vertebrae. The risk of spina bifida can be reduced if a woman takes folic acid before becoming pregnant.

The physical ability of the student with spina bifida varies based on where the lesion occurs, but most students require personal assistance to carry out daily activities. Adaptive devices are also commonly used. Many students with spina bifida are cognitively able but challenged by their physical limitations. Many students also experience social isolation from their peers, largely due to their bladder and bowel problems. Relations with the opposite sex can be especially trying.

Orthopedic and Musculoskeletal Conditions

Curvature of the spine (scoliosis), congenital hip dislocations, juvenile arthritis, osteogenesis imperfecta, and limb deficiencies are a few examples of orthopedic and musculoskeletal conditions. In these conditions, bodily structures involving the bones and muscles do not develop normally. Individuals may require surgery; may be fitted with prosthetic devices, such as artificial hands or legs; and usually have to use adapted approaches for accomplishing daily tasks.

There are various causes that lead to the different conditions in this category, but in many cases, the cause is idiopathic—that is, unknown. In some cases genetic conditions may be a factor; in other cases, drugs taken by the mother during pregnancy may be a factor (e.g., taking thalidomide resulted in limb deficiencies). Some conditions such as juvenile arthritis may result from a child's inefficient autoimmune system.

The biggest challenge for these students in the classroom, and for their teachers, is finding ways for them to be physically engaged and involved. Their prosthetic devices, body supports, wheelchairs, and other necessary supports may make it difficult for them to get close to instructional activities. OTs and PTs can help design classroom arrangements and conditions that increase physical closeness and participation. It is also important to address the discomfort that results from the devices so the student is not distracted from learning activities.

education teachers or classroom teachers are likely to encounter. We discuss two of the four conditions—cerebral palsy and muscular dystrophy—in more detail in the following sections.

CEREBRAL PALSY

Cerebral palsy (CP) is a neurological disorder caused by brain damage before, during, or after birth that affects a person's movement and posture. CP is considered a nonprogressive disability in that the brain damage does not continue to worsen. However, treatment is necessary to prevent the person's posture from declining and to improve movement ability and independence (Best & Bigge, 2005; Griffin, Fitch, & Griffin, 2002; Pellegrino, 2002).

CP is classified in three ways: (1) according to the part of the brain that is damaged, (2) based on the parts of the body affected and how they are affected, and (3) based on the severity of the functional impairment (i.e., mild, moderate, or severe). For information on the type and location of brain damage, we suggest that you refer to Pellegrino (2002). Here we briefly explain the other approaches used to classify CP.

Cerebral palsy is commonly defined by how it affects muscle tone. *Spastic CP* is the most common form of cerebral palsy. A student who has spastic CP has very stiff muscles, exhibits very labored movement, and has limited range of motion due to severe muscle contractures that can affect the hands, elbows, hips, knees, and feet. This individual is also likely to have a malformed spine and hip dislocation.

Athetoid CP is also referred to as *dyskinesia,* which means unwanted or involuntary movement. This form of CP is characterized by either slow, writhing movements or abrupt, jerky movements. These movements can occur in facial muscles, wrists and fingers, the trunk of the body, or one or more extremities. An uncommon type of cerebral palsy is *ataxic CP.* Ataxia is characterized by a lack of balance and uncoordinated movement (Best & Bigge, 2005).

Some persons have *mixed* cerebral palsy, meaning that more than one form of the condition occurs in the same person. Most often the mix includes spastic and athetoid CP. Spasticity and ataxia may also occur together. About one-third of the persons diagnosed with any particular form of cerebral palsy also show evidence of another form.

Doctors and other medical personnel also classify CP by the affected areas of the body. Hemiplegia means that one side of the body, such as the left leg and arm, are more affected than the other. Diplegia means the legs are more affected than the arms. Quadriplegia means that all four limbs are affected as well as the trunk and the muscles that control the neck, mouth, and the tongue. So you might see someone whose condition is described as *spastic hemiplegia, spastic diplegia, or spastic quadriplegia,* for example. These terms explain the characteristics of the muscle tone as well as the areas of the body that are affected.

As we have said, you can also classify CP by its functional impact. A person who has *mild* CP is able to walk and talk, control head and neck motion, have unimpaired or only slight limitations in their activities, and is independent with regard to daily activities. Someone with *moderate* CP has some impairment in speaking and walking abilities and head and neck control and has some limits with regard to what he or she can do. The person probably requires assistive technology devices, such as special controls for

Reflective Exercise #4
Do you know or have you had any experiences with a person with CP? What did you see as this person's strengths? What challenges did this individual face?

Cerebral palsy does not necessarily mean that a person has a cognitive limitation.

www.prenhall.com/rosenberg

an electric wheelchair or a special mechanism for computer input. Persons with a *severe* level of CP are very incapacitated, have little or no head and neck control, have contracted and malformed limbs, and need assistance to take part in most of their daily activities (Best & Bigge, 2005).

The brain damage that results in CP can sometimes lead to other problems as well. These may include visual impairments, hearing impairments, speech and language disorders, seizures, feeding problems, growth abnormalities, learning disabilities, emotional or behavioral disorders, and ADHD.

Although between 50 and 60% of persons with cerebral palsy may also have mild to profound intellectual disability (Pellegrino, 2002), it's very important to understand that CP does not necessarily mean that a person also has a cognitive deficit. In fact, it is often difficult to determine the actual degree of cognitive ability in persons with severe cerebral palsy. Standardized intelligence tests rely on a person's verbal and motor abilities; and because these are lacking in persons with severe CP, a precise determination of intelligence level is hard to ascertain (Best & Bigge, 2005; Willard-Holt, 1998).

MUSCULAR DYSTROPHY

Like CP, muscular dystrophy is a relatively visible disability in our society. Unfortunately, it is also a terminal condition, with death usually occurring during adolescence or early adulthood. When a child has muscular dystrophy, his muscle tissue gradually degenerates, turning into fatty tissue. The most common type of the disease is Duchenne muscular dystrophy (DMD), a disorder that is genetically transmitted by mothers to their sons. Although the mothers carry the disease, they do not themselves have any symptoms (Leet, Dormans, & Tosi, 2002).

Unlike CP, muscular dystrophy *is* a degenerative disease, meaning that it gets worse as time passes. Also, unlike CP, there is no central nervous system involvement. Muscular dystrophy first appears during early childhood, between about 2 and 6 years of age, when the child's calves seem to be growing larger. (This condition is called *pseudohypertrophy*.) Actually fat tissue is replacing muscle tissue in the legs. Gradually the child's legs become weaker and weaker. Unable to stand up in a typical manner, he has to push with his hands against his own legs to climb to a standing position. He is also less able to go up and down stairs or run and jump. When he walks, he may do so with a sway back to help compensate for the weakness in his legs.

Gradually the muscle weakness moves up the body, from the legs to the trunk and arms. Sooner or later, the child loses the ability to walk and has to use a wheelchair. Because of weak back muscles, scoliosis (curvature of the spine) is often a problem. To counter this, doctors may perform surgery to insert a metal rod to hold the back straight.

As he becomes weaker, the child will no longer be able to power a manual wheelchair, and an electric wheelchair may become necessary for mobility control. Even holding his head erect will be difficult. Ultimately early death occurs because of lung or heart failure (Leet et al., 2002).

With a student who has muscular dystrophy or any similar terminal condition, the teacher's most important job is to make sure that the value of his life is maintained. Mostly this means that you simply need to be a good teacher for this student, as you would be for any other student.

> It is important for teachers and others to maintain an attitude that the student is a valued, useful, and vital person. Demonstrating separate expectations for the student with DMD (e.g., altering classroom discipline or ignoring inappropriate behavior) heightens the risk of estranging the student from his peers and sends the undesirable message that he is not as important as others. Providing structure with the expectation of achievement to the best of one's ability provides good mental health. (Best, 2005b, p. 50)

Reflective Exercise #5
Have you had experience with the death of a child? What would you say to your students if one of their classmates died from a disease such as muscular dystrophy?

Reflective Exercise #6
Somewhat remarkably, many students with muscular dystrophy and similar degenerative diseases lead meaningful lives and maintain very positive attitudes. How do you suppose they maintain those positive attitudes?

DEFINITIONS AND KEY CHARACTERISTICS
OF STUDENTS WITH OTHER HEALTH IMPAIRMENTS

Like physical disabilities, certain chronic health impairments can seriously affect a student's ability to receive an appropriate education. Sometimes these conditions occur in combination with other conditions (as when a student with cerebral palsy has epilepsy), but in other cases, the health impairment is the primary disability. According to U.S. Department of Education (see Table 1.2 in Chapter 1),

> other health impairment means having limited strength, vitality or alertness, including a heightened alertness to environmental stimuli, that results in limited alertness with respect to the educational environment, that— (i) Is due to chronic or acute health problems such as asthma, attention deficit disorder or attention deficit hyperactivity disorder, diabetes, epilepsy, a heart condition, hemophilia, lead poisoning, leukemia, nephritis, rheumatic fever, and sickle cell anemia; and (ii) Adversely affects a child's educational performance.

Note that for the sake of receiving special education services, attention deficit hyperactivity disorder (ADHD) is considered a health impairment. However, because of its relatively high incidence, we have discussed it in a separate chapter.

As we said at the beginning of this chapter, sometimes health impairments are relatively minor and transitory, but more serious health impairments can be a significant detriment to a student's learning and can lead to the "other health impairment" classification. Even if this does not occur, the health impairment may still result in a Section 504 plan. With either situation, it becomes incumbent on the school and teachers such as Shannon Hunt to take the necessary steps to help the student achieve an adequate education despite the challenges caused by the health problem.

In the past 20 years there has been a significant increase in the number of students classified as having a health impairment (DePaepe et al., 2002). In Table 14.2 we list some of the more common chronic health conditions that teachers might encounter and explain their characteristics and causes. In the following sections, we describe three health conditions that may be of greatest concern for many teachers: asthma, epilepsy, and HIV/AIDS.

ASTHMA

Asthma is a chronic lung condition that affects millions of children in the United States and is on the rise worldwide, especially in inner cities and poor countries (American Lung Association, 2005). Because so many children have asthma, a teacher's chance of having one or more children with the disease is very high, especially in an urban area.

The signs of an asthma attack include difficult breathing, wheezing, coughing, excess mucus, sweating, and chest constriction. When a child is having an asthma attack, she is reacting to triggers in the environment. These triggers are antigens, or foreign bodies, that enter the lungs and cause the production of antibodies. As the antibodies respond to the antigens, they release chemicals that cause the lungs to swell, increase mucus secretion, and tighten the chest muscles. About half the people who have asthma have an allergic form of the disease and often have other allergies. The antigens that affect them can be tiny dust particles, cigarette smoke, or pet dander. The disease can also occur because of nonallergic conditions, with attacks triggered by cold, dry air, or exercise (AAAAI, 2005; Best, 2005a).

Besides being very dangerous, even potentially life-threatening, asthma can affect students' progress in school. According to the American Academy of Asthma Allergy and Immunology (AAAAI, 2005), in only one year, children with asthma have a total of 10 million absences, make 2.7 million doctor visits, and have 200,000 hospital admissions because of their condition. A big problem, of course, is lost instructional time and fewer opportunities for social and recreational activities.

Many people used to think that asthma was caused by emotional conditions. Now we know that the condition is caused by allergies or other physiological factors.

TABLE 14.2

CHRONIC HEALTH CONDITIONS TEACHERS ARE LIKELY TO ENCOUNTER

Condition	Cause	Classroom Considerations
Asthma Asthma is a chronic lung condition. Asthma attacks are characterized by difficult breathing, wheezing, coughing, excess mucus, sweating, and chest constriction. Attacks may result from different triggers, which may be allergens such as tiny dust particles, cigarette smoke, and pet dander or even cold, dry air, or physical exertion.	Asthma is caused by allergies or other physiological factors. Attacks do not occur as an emotional reaction, but a person may induce an attack by excessive crying or laughing. Approximately 5 to 10% of school-age children have asthma, with higher prevalence levels occurring in urban areas.	Teachers should try to keep the classroom free of any antigens that may cause an attack or at least keep the child away from the source. The teacher also needs to be aware of the child's medication and help manage its appropriate use based on home and school guidelines. The child may miss many school days, and the teacher needs to promote a supportive environment to help the child keep up with the other students.
HIV/AIDS Children who have HIV/AIDS become progressively more ill as time passes. They may show signs of motor and cognitive delay, have neurological problems, have seizures, and often be nauseous. Most die before they reach age 10, some much sooner.	HIV is transmitted through sexual contact; through exposure to infected blood, blood products, or tissue; and from mother to fetus or infant. Most children with HIV/AIDS have acquired the condition from their mothers before birth, at the time of birth, or through breastfeeding.	Some children with AIDS have learning disabilities, while others may have ADHD and poor language skills. Their instruction must be individualized to meet their needs. Teachers should follow universal precautions to avoid contact with *anyone's* bodily fluid, but acquiring the disease through casual contact is not known to occur.
Sickle-Cell Disease With this disease there is a block in normal blood flow. This results in pain episodes in the arms, legs, chest, and abdomen as well as priapism (painful prolonged erection). It also causes damage to most organs, including the spleen, kidneys, and liver. Young children with sickle-cell disease can be easily overwhelmed by certain bacterial infections.	Sickle-cell disease is an inherited blood disorder. When sickle-shaped cells block small blood vessels, less blood can reach that part of the body. Tissue that does not receive a normal blood flow eventually becomes damaged. This is what causes the complications of sickle-cell disease.	The student with sickle cell may be absent often because of pain episodes and hospitalization, so extra support and homework might help him keep up. Plenty of access to water and the restroom and avoidance of overheating and cold temperatures are important.
Epilepsy Epilepsy is a neurological condition that makes people prone to having seizures. Different types of seizures may occur. The most common type is a tonic-clonic seizure, referred to in the past as a grand mal seizure. When this seizure occurs, the person loses awareness, ceases to engage in any activity, and loses consciousness. She becomes stiff (tonic), and then jerking (clonic) movements begin.	Epilepsy occurs because of an underlying brain abnormality. This abnormality may occur at some time during the development of the brain or as the result of later trauma. When a seizure occurs, there is an abnormal hypersynchronous electrical discharge in the brain. Different conditions can cause a seizure, but only when the seizures recur is epilepsy diagnosed. Epilepsy is one of the most common disorders of the nervous system.	When a student has a seizure, the teacher should help her lie down, turn her to one side to prevent choking on saliva or vomit, loosen clothing around the neck, and place something soft under her head to prevent it from hitting a hard surface. The teacher should not insert anything into the mouth. If the seizure lasts for more than 5 minutes, the teacher should call for emergency assistance. He should also note when the seizure occurred and how long it lasted.

(continues)

385

TABLE 14.2 CONTINUED

CHRONIC HEALTH CONDITIONS TEACHERS ARE LIKELY TO ENCOUNTER

Condition	Cause	Classroom Considerations
Cancer	Cancer is the spread of abnormal cells. The most common types of cancer among children are leukemia and brain tumors. Cancer and its treatment by chemotherapy can lead to numerous side effects, including impairment of the student's learning ability. Nausea, weight loss or gain, and growth retardation can occur.	For the most part, the causes of cancer are unknown. It appears more often alongside Down syndrome and other chromosomal and genetically based disorders, and environmental factors are suspected but difficult to prove. Cancer causes about 1,500 deaths per year among children.	The child with cancer is often in pain and fatigued, which interferes with concentration and learning ability. Many are diagnosed as having learning disabilities. The immune system may be suppressed, and the child can be susceptible to infections from other children. Some days are better than others. Although as much participation as possible should be encouraged, reduced physical activities and shorter school days may be necessary.
Type 1 Diabetes	Type 1 diabetes, also called juvenile diabetes or insulin-dependent diabetes, is an autoimmune disease that destroys the cells in the pancreas that produce insulin. Type 1 diabetes develops often in children or young adults but can occur at any age. Children with Type 1 diabetes require insulin shots. Without medication, the student may become very thirsty, need to urinate often, lose weight, and be very weak.	Type 1 diabetes is less common than type 2 diabetes, accounting for 5 to 10% of all diagnosed diabetes. It is caused because the pancreas cannot produce insulin. Without insulin, the body can't use sugar and fat broken down from food. When sugar doesn't enter blood cells, blood sugar rises and causes damage to the body. Diabetes is genetically influenced but can be prevented or delayed through appropriate diet and exercise.	Students with diabetes can participate in most activities with other students but need a few special considerations. They may need privacy to test their blood sugar and inject insulin if necessary, may need access to the bathroom more frequently than others, and may need to have snacks more often than other students. In the case of hypoglycemia, there may be sweating, paleness, trembling, hunger, and weakness, indicating the need for emergency treatment.
Cystic Fibrosis	Cystic fibrosis (CF) is a disease that affects major body organs that secrete fluids. CF primarily affects the lungs, where airway passages become blocked, and the digestive system, where the mucus interferes with the release of digestive enzymes. The secretions of normal fluids are blocked by the mucus and cause cysts to develop, which become surrounded by scar tissue.	CF is a genetically transmitted disease that occurs in 1 out of every 2,000 live births. Both parents must be carriers of the condition for the child to inherit it, which occurs one out of four times. Boys and girls are equally affected. CF is a terminal condition, and death usually occurs between adolescence and early adulthood.	Students with CF undergo chest physiotherapy once or twice a day to loosen the mucus in their chests. This may occur before and after school; but while in school they need to take digestive enzymes and other medications. Problems with digestion affect bowel movements, and privacy at this time is an important issue. Steps may need to be taken to improve social inclusion.

However, there are important interactions between asthma and emotions. For example, extreme emotional reactions such as excessive laughing or crying can affect respiration sufficiently to precipitate an asthma attack. Additionally, fellow students may avoid students who experience frequent attacks, which may result in social isolation. Also, parents and teachers may limit play and recreational activities with the intention of protecting the child from too much activity in order to reduce the chance of an attack (Best, 2005a). So although we cannot say that emotions are the cause of asthma attacks, we do need to realize that having asthma might affect the emotional status of the student.

EPILEPSY

If you have never observed a person having a seizure, especially a very serious one such as a tonic-clonic seizure (what people used to call a grand mal seizure), when you first see one, it may frighten you. When a generalized tonic-clonic seizure occurs, usually the first visible sign is that the person appears to lose awareness. He then ceases to engage in the current activity, loses consciousness, and falls to the floor. He will become stiff (tonic), and then jerking (clonic) movements will begin. When this happens, the person becomes less rigid and shakes or jerks his arms, legs, or both. At some point during the seizure, the individual may lose control of his bowels or bladder, cry, or expel saliva from his mouth. After a few minutes, the person usually becomes drowsy and disoriented or falls into a deep sleep that may last from several minutes to several hours (Weinstein, 2002).

Asthma affects millions of children, especially those in inner cities and poor countries.

A seizure is an abnormal electrical discharge in the brain, a relatively uncommon occurrence. Several different conditions can cause a seizure, such as a fever or an acute insult to or infection of the brain; and in such cases, the seizure may occur once and never happen again. A good example is a febrile seizure. This occurs in about 5% of all children before they are 5 years old when they have temperatures near 102 degrees. More than 80% of the time, only one seizure occurs (Weinstein, 2002).

In contrast, epilepsy is a neurological condition that makes people prone to having seizures. With epilepsy, there is an underlying brain abnormality that periodically causes seizures to occur. Sometimes the seizures are the only apparent condition, but in other cases there are additional conditions such as cerebral palsy or intellectual disability. For most people with epilepsy, though, other conditions do not accompany their seizures, and their intellectual and physical abilities are normal. What's more, they probably take antiepileptic drugs, and their seizures are generally well controlled (Epilepsy Foundation, 2005; Weinstein, 2002).

When a seizure occurs, it may either originate in a specific part of the brain (this is called a partial onset) or involve the whole brain (this is called a generalized onset). Sometimes a partial onset remains in the part of the brain where it originates (a simple partial seizure), while in other cases it may spread to other parts of the brain (a complex partial). Although you don't need to recognize where in the brain the seizure is occurring, you should realize that the form of the seizure is a result of its origin; and because they may be seen in schools, you should be aware of three types of seizures: absence seizures, tonic-clonic seizures, and status epilepticus (Weinstein, 2002).

- *Absence seizures.* People used to call these petit mal ("little bad") seizures. They are generalized (i.e., they come from broad regions of the brain), but they are considered to be relatively harmless. They usually appear in children between the ages of 3 and 12. When an absence seizure occurs, the child loses consciousness for about 30 seconds. Sometimes the seizure is mistaken for daydreaming, but it is not possible to get the child to respond until the seizure is over. Sometimes the absence seizure evolves into a tonic-clonic seizure. Without treatment, a child might have hundreds of absence seizures a day.

- *Tonic-clonic seizures.* We described this type of seizure at the beginning of this section. They may be partial or generalized; but as you saw, they look very different from absence seizures. Many people still refer to them as grand mal ("big bad") seizures. If it is a partial seizure, only a part of the body may be affected; if it is generalized, the whole body will be affected. Sometimes the seizure starts in a particular area of the brain and then spreads to other parts. When this happens, the stiffness and jerking movements are spread throughout parts of the body that are next to each other. This is called a Jacksonian seizure. Tonic-clonic seizures are the most common types of seizures among children.

- *Status epilepticus.* Actually this is not a type of seizure but a condition in which a seizure continues to occur for a longer than usual amount of time. *It can require emergency action.* A tonic-clonic seizure usually ends after 2 or 3 minutes; and as we've said, an absence seizure is even briefer. But if a seizure does not end within a short time, status epilepticus is occurring, which may be life-threatening or lead to permanent brain damage. Any seizure that continues for longer than 5 minutes should be considered status epilepticus and be treated as a medical emergency.

As we have said, seizures can be scary; but once you know one may occur, dealing with it can become almost routine. If a student has a history of seizures, the teacher has three important roles: assist when the seizure occurs, help the student handle any stress that might result because of the seizure, and keep a record and report the seizure and any related information about its occurrence. In the "Can You Help Me with This Student?" feature we describe the appropriate actions to take when a seizure occurs.

HIV/AIDS

HIV/AIDS is a serious illness that we have certainly heard a lot about—and the medical community has learned a lot about—in the past 25 to 30 years. While we have made a great deal of progress in this country both in the prevention and treatment of HIV/AIDS, in poorer developing countries, programs to prevent the disease and provide effective medical treatment are lacking, and the illness remains a major cause of death (NIAID, 2004).

In fact, it has become a chronic illness among many children. You should also realize that most children with HIV/AIDS have acquired the condition from their mothers either before they were born, at the time of birth, or as infants through breastfeeding.

HIV can be transmitted from an infected person to another person in one of three ways: through sexual transmission; through exposure to infected blood, blood products, or tissue, which occurs when unclean needles are shared; and, as we have said, from mother to fetus or infant. Not all babies born to HIV-infected mothers will have the virus, especially if the mother is being actively treated using anti-AIDS medications and if the baby is delivered through a caesarian section. When doctors follow these medical precautions and when the baby is not breastfed, the baby's chances of getting HIV are much lower.

Generally, when a person becomes infected with the virus, it takes 6 to 12 weeks before the infection becomes detectable through blood tests. But according to the National Institute of Allergy and Infectious Diseases (NIAID, 2004), detecting HIV in babies can be difficult. The baby may show no signs of the diseases, and blood tests may be misleading because, for up to 18 months, the baby will have the mother's antibodies to HIV, which may lead to a false diagnosis. This means that it is possible for a test to come back positive even though the baby really does not have the virus. Recent scientific studies are leading to new approaches for more accurately testing a baby's blood for the virus.

Reflective Exercise #7
Do you think you would have an emotional reaction if you taught a child with HIV/AIDS? Would you worry about being infected by the disease?

www.prenhall.com/rosenberg

Can You Help Me with This Student?

WHAT A TEACHER SHOULD DO WHEN A SEIZURE OCCURS

It is not completely unlikely that at some time a teacher may need to assist a student who is having a major seizure. Although seizures are more likely to happen with students who have severe disabilities, they can also happen with students who have mild disabilities or no disabilities. Occasionally a student who has never had a seizure or any history of conditions related to seizures will have one. This can be very shocking, but usually there is no reason to panic. Unfortunately, too many people in society still have a great deal of fear and misunderstanding about seizures and why they sometimes occur. If, as a teacher, you must one day assist a student having a seizure, you should take the following actions.

STRATEGIES

- First, realize that there is nothing anyone can do to stop a seizure once it begins, so you shouldn't try. If it is an absence seizure (the person simply appears to lose contact with what is going on around him), there is not much to do unless the repeated seizures continue for more than 15 minutes. Then call for emergency medical assistance.
- For a tonic-clonic seizure (one in which the person loses consciousness, and falls to the floor and begins jerking and moving erratically), help the person to lie down and turn him to one side to prevent him from choking on excessive saliva or vomit. If possible, clothing around the neck should be loosened to make breathing easier, and a pillow or something soft should be placed under his head to keep him from banging it against the hard floor.
- During the seizure, the person will bite down hard. You *should not* insert anything into the person's mouth; he won't swallow his tongue! Just try to keep the head tilted to the side to prevent aspirating on saliva. Also, CPR is not necessary. You usually just need to let the seizure run its course.
- In some cases called status epilepticus, the seizure will continue to occur. If the seizure lasts for more than 5 minutes, you should call for emergency assistance (i.e., dial 911 or call the school office).
- After the seizure, let the student sleep in a quiet, private location. When he wakes up, comfort him and encourage him to resume normal activities.
- If the seizure and related effects (such as loss of bowel or bladder control) are embarrassing for the student, provide counseling. Explaining the nature of seizures to both the individual and classmates can help students understand the condition.
- Whenever a seizure occurs, you should keep a written record of it, including when it began and when it ended. Describe what happened as well as you can, including what preceded the seizure and what followed it. Give this information to the parents or directly to medical personnel.

For more information on what causes seizures and how to deal with them, the following two sources will be very helpful:

The Epilepsy Foundation at http://www.epilepsyfoundation.org/
The National Institute of Neurological Disorders and Stroke at http://www.ninds.nih.gov/disorders/epilepsy/epilepsy.htm

EXTEND AND APPLY

- If one of your students had a seizure, do you believe you could assist him calmly? Do you think you could keep your cool? Keep your emotions under control in order to act effectively?
- How would you like to be treated if YOU had a seizure?

Activity: Go to the Student and Teacher Artifacts section of the Teacher Prep website, click on Special Education and then module 14: OHI and TBI. Examine all of the artifacts and answer any accompanying questions. Think about the benefits and challenges of the Class Act Program for many students with chronic health impairments.

If it turns out that the child is positive, the virus may continue to grow for several years without having a noticeable effect on the child. The amount of time it takes for the virus to develop into AIDS varies, but there are two patterns. In the first, which affects about 20% of HIV-positive children, the child develops a serious illness in the first year of life and usually dies by the age of 4. In the second pattern, the disease progresses much more slowly, and the child continues to live into the school-age years (NIAID, 2004).

Slow physical growth and little weight gain are often the first indications of HIV in children. Delay may also occur in motor skills and cognitive development. Some children may have neurological problems as shown by difficulty in walking and coordination.

They may have seizures and perform poorly in their preschool or school activities. In school, some children with AIDS are classified as having learning disabilities, while others may have ADHD and poor language skills. The child is likely to often be nauseous, have episodes of vomiting, and be weak and in pain. During the final stage of the illness, when AIDS occurs, opportunistic infections such as pneumonia, certain types of cancer, or other diseases attack and cannot be rejected because of an ineffective immune system (Best, 2005a; NIAID, 2004).

The way in which HIV leads to AIDS is a complex process (see Figure 14.1), as is its treatment. However, as current and future progress makes clear, a diagnosis of HIV will not always necessarily mean that AIDS is inevitable. If you happen to become a teacher of a child with HIV/AIDS, it's better for you to think of it as a chronic illness rather than a terminal disease (Best, 2005a).

PREVALENCE AND TRENDS

During the 2001–2002 school year, within the population of school-age students, about 0.03% had TBI (3 out of every 10,000), about 0.11% had physical disabilities (11 out of every 1,000), and about 0.59% had other health impairments (6 out of every 1,000) (U.S. Department of Education, 2005). All together, the students we have been discussing in this chapter make up less than 1% of the total school population.

Keep in mind, however, that these percentages can be a little misleading. They are based on headcounts of students who were classified as having a disability in those specific categories for the purpose of receiving special education services. In other words, not included are students who (1) have various physical or medical needs but are classified within another disability area, such as a student with CP who is classified under intellectual disabilities, (2) have various physical or medical conditions but have 504 plans instead of special education classification; and (3) have a condition such as asthma or epilepsy but are able to manage it well enough without any special public school services.

FIGURE 14.1

HOW HIV BECOMES AIDS

Untreated HIV disease is characterized by a gradual deterioration of immune function. Notably, crucial immune cells called CD4 positive (CD4+) T cells are disabled and killed during the typical course of infection. These cells, sometimes called T-helper cells, play a central role in the immune response, signaling other cells in the immune system to perform their special functions. A healthy, uninfected person usually has 800 to 1,200 CD4+ T cells per cubic millimeter (mm^3) of blood. With untreated HIV infection, the number of these cells in a person's blood progressively declines. When the CD4+ T cell count falls below $200/mm^3$, a person becomes particularly vulnerable to the opportunistic infections and cancers that typify AIDS, the end stage of HIV disease. People with AIDS often suffer infections of the lungs, intestinal tract, brain, eyes, and other organs as well as debilitating weight loss, diarrhea, neurologic conditions, and cancers such as Kaposi's sarcoma and certain types of lymphomas.

Most scientists think that HIV causes AIDS by directly inducing the death of CD4+ T cells or interfering with their normal function and by triggering other events that weaken a person's immune function. For example, the network of signaling molecules that normally regulates a person's immune response is disrupted during HIV disease, impairing a person's ability to fight other infections. The HIV-mediated destruction of the lymph nodes and related immunologic organs also plays a major role in causing the immunosuppression seen in people with AIDS. Immunosuppression by HIV is confirmed by the fact that medicines that interfere with the HIV life cycle preserve CD4+ T cells and immune function as well as delay clinical illness.

www.prenhall.com/rosenberg

You may encounter students in any of these categories who have one or more of the conditions we have described. So it might be more useful to look at data about specific conditions.

TRAUMATIC BRAIN INJURY

Every year, about 1 out of 25 children is medically treated for head injuries, while about 1 out of 500 suffers TBI. This means that more than a million school-age students acquire brain injuries each year. The condition has been established as the most common cause of death and disability among children (Best, 2005b; Keyser-Marcus et al., 2002).

PHYSICAL DISABILITIES

Cerebral palsy affects 23 to 28 of every 10,000 children (0.28%). About 80% have the spastic form of CP, and 75% have at least one additional disability such as epilepsy or cognitive disabilities (National Center on Birth Defects and Disabilities, 2004). About 1 in every 3,500 live male births inherits the Duchenne type of muscular dystrophy, and about 1 in every 20,000 males inherits the Becker type (Batshaw, 2002). The most serious form of spina bifida, myelomeningocele, occurs in approximately 1 out of every 1,000 live births (National Dissemination Center for Children with Disabilities, 2004).

OTHER HEALTH IMPAIRMENTS

Asthma affects an estimated 5 to 6 million children in the United States and is especially prevalent in urban areas. Between 1 out of 10 to 1 out of 20 children in the United States has asthma (American Lung Association, 2005). More than 2.7 million Americans have epilepsy, and each year 181,000 Americans develop seizures and epilepsy for the first time (Epilepsy Foundation, 2005). At the end of 2003, an estimated 1,039,000 to 1,185,000 persons in the United States were living with HIV/AIDS. In 2003, the estimated number of diagnoses of AIDS in the United States was 43,171. Adult and adolescent AIDS cases totaled 43,112, but there were only 59 AIDS cases estimated in children under age 13 (Centers for Disease Control and Prevention, 2005a).

Over the past few years the prevalence of some of these conditions has changed, and further changes will occur in the future. Probably the greatest success has come with controlling HIV/AIDS in the United States. While poorer countries continue to be plagued by this virus, in the United States and other wealthier countries, prevention tactics have reduced the spread of HIV, and medical treatment has reduced AIDS fatalities. To fight HIV/AIDS, doctors use a "cocktail" of medications to support the patient and prolong health. These include **antiretroviral drugs** to slow the growth of the virus, **prophylactic antibiotics** to fight bacterial infections, and intravenous **immunoglobulin** to help the immune system. But the medications are expensive; thus, poorer countries have not been able to take advantage of them.

In contrast to HIV/AIDS, some physical disabilities and health impairments continue at the same rate of prevalence or have shown increases in recent years. Conditions such as spina bifida, cerebral palsy, epilepsy, and muscular dystrophy, for which the causes are either unknown or due to genetic influences, seem to continue to occur at about the same, albeit low, rates. On the other hand, conditions such as asthma seem to be increasing. Many blame this increase on worsening environmental conditions.

CAUSAL FACTORS

As you know, many different causes lead to the various conditions that we have discussed. We briefly describe some of the more common causes in following sections.

Reflective Exercise #8
If you are or will be a general education teacher, how many students with TBI, physical disabilities, or other health impairments would you expect to have in your class? Do you think there would be more or fewer of these students than you might have seen 20 years ago?

Serious accidents can lead to traumatic brain injury in children or adolescents.

TRAUMATIC BRAIN INJURY

A head injury is considered to cause trauma to the brain when it is harsh enough to change the child's level of consciousness and/or to change the normal structure of the brain (Michaud et al., 2002). TBI is most likely to occur at two critical times in a person's life: when a child is under 5, because that is when falls and child abuse are most common; and when he or she reaches adolescence, because that is when sports, recreation, driving, risk taking, and attempted suicide are most common (Best, 2005b).

Two kinds of forces can cause brain injuries: impact and inertial. An impact force occurs when something hits the head with enough force to fracture the skull, bruise parts of the brain, or cause bleeding in the skull. Inertial damage happens when the brain experiences rapid and severe motion that is violent enough to damage nerve fibers and blood vessels. In most cases of TBI, both forms of damage occur simultaneously (Michaud et al., 2002).

The location of the injury in the brain and how diffuse or widespread it is determine the amount of damage the person sustains. Generally the more localized the injury, the better the prognosis. When the damage is more diffuse, more areas of functioning are affected and often to a greater degree. The injured person will probably need medical treatment and therapy to aid rehabilitation in several areas. Brain injury may result in impaired motor functioning, feeding disorders, sensory impairments, communication impairments, cognitive disabilities, and emotional/behavioral disabilities (Best, 2005b; Keyser-Marcus et al., 2002; Michaud et al., 2002).

The challenges that persons with TBI face as children and adolescents will probably remain with them throughout their adult lives. They may have happy and successful lives, but this will depend on how well they are able to compensate for the TBI and the vocational and social demands they encounter as adults.

PHYSICAL DISABILITIES

Physical disabilities can result from different causes. They may be congenital (meaning the child is born with the condition) or acquired (meaning something causes the condition that happens immediately before, during, or after birth or even later in life). If they are congenital, they may be due to a genetically transmitted condition, such as Duchenne muscular dystrophy; to some nongenetic factor, such as the mother's ingestion of a harmful substance such as **thalidomide** during pregnancy; or to unknown causes, as in the case of spina bifida.

If they are acquired, they may be due to an event that occurs near the time of birth (which may be the case with cerebral palsy) or to an accident or illness (e.g., the loss of a limb or having polio). Some physical disabilities are linked to central nervous system damage, like CP or spina bifida; some are degenerative, like muscular dystrophy; and some are musculoskeletal and orthopedic conditions, such as arthritis, limb deficiencies, or scoliosis (Best, 2005b).

If the condition is due to neurological damage, like CP, it may take different forms (i.e., spasticity, athetosis, mixed). As with TBI, the specific type of CP that occurs will depend on which part of the brain was damaged and how extensive the damage is (Best & Bigge, 2005; Griffin et al., 2002; Pellegrino, 2002). If the condition is genetically transmitted, this means that it is inherited from one or both parents. For most genetic conditions, some of the children will inherit the condition, some may become carriers, and some will be unaffected. For example, Duchenne muscular dystrophy is an

www.prenhall.com/rosenberg

X-linked inherited condition. This means it is genetically transmitted by mothers to their male offspring (Leet et al., 2002).

People with physical disabilities continue to have the disabilities throughout their lives. For those with degenerative diseases, like muscular dystrophy, their lives are relatively short, and their conditions deteriorate until death occurs. For those whose conditions are nondegenerative, such as spina bifida or cerebral palsy, they will likely experience a typical span of life, but their disabilities will continue to present physical challenges that may affect their vocational prospects and lead to social and emotional issues, depending on their milieu and a variety of personal characteristics.

OTHER HEALTH IMPAIRMENTS

The causes of health impairments are as varied as the causes of physical disabilities. Some, such as HIV/AIDS, are transmitted through viruses. Others, such as sickle-cell disease and cystic fibrosis, are genetically transmitted. Similarly, diabetes has a genetic basis but can be environmentally influenced through diet and exercise. For others, like asthma, epilepsy, and cancer, experts do not clearly understand the cause. The expected life outcomes for those with different health impairments range from premature death to a long and normal life that requires management of the disease through medication, diet, and other medical treatments.

TRANSMISSION OF DISEASES TO TEACHERS

For many teachers and other human services professionals who deal with children or adults with health problems, a common question is "How likely am I to get this disease from a student?" For the most part, the answer is that you are not very susceptible. Diseases that have been genetically inherited by children pose no threat at all to you. You are not going to catch sickle cell, cystic fibrosis, or diabetes, for example. Nor are you likely to acquire asthma, epilepsy, or cancer from your students.

One situation that many teachers worry a great deal about is the possibility of getting HIV/AIDS from a student. But this is not likely. As we have discussed, HIV/AIDS is transmitted through the exchange of bodily fluids or from mother to child. And except in the most extraordinary circumstances, most teachers will not be at risk for any of these occurrences with their students.

On the other hand, teachers should be concerned about contracting contagious diseases, such as cytomegalovirus (CMV) and hepatitis B. CMV actually poses little danger to you unless you are pregnant. A person who catches CMV has the symptoms of a cold or the flu for a couple of weeks. But if a woman is pregnant, the child may be born with severe, multiple disabilities. Hepatitis B is a serious disease caused by a virus that attacks the liver. The virus can cause lifelong infection, cirrhosis of the liver, liver cancer, liver failure, and death.

The best approach to protecting yourself against all contagious diseases is to use universal precautions. Universal precautions were developed by the Centers for Disease Control and Prevention in 1987 in order to help control the spread of disease (Best, 2005a, Centers for Disease Control and Prevention, 2005b; DePaepe et al., 2002). They are referred to as "universal" because they should be used in any situation where the transmission of disease is possible, no matter how remote. Additionally, when there is even the smallest chance, you should assume that a contagious disease is present in all individuals with whom you work and apply the precautions to all.

Universal precautions include proper handwashing (see Figure 14.2); use of personal protective equipment; safe methods for getting rid of waste, cleaning up spills, and handling laundry; and procedures for dealing with accidental contact to potentially infectious materials. You should use these precautions whenever you have contact with blood, semen, vaginal secretions, or other body fluids that may contain blood (Best, 2005a; DePaepe et al., 2002).

Reflective Exercise #9
Have you thought about the classroom as a place where contagious diseases can be transmitted? Does this concern you?

FIGURE 14.2

HANDWASHING PROCEDURE WHEN USING UNIVERSAL PRECAUTIONS

1. Inspect your hands for any visible soiling, breaks, or cuts in the skin or cuticles.
2. Remove any jewelry. If you have a watch on, push it up your arm as high as possible. Also push up the sleeves of your blouse or jacket so that they are well above the wrist.
3. Turn on the water and adjust water flow and temperature to ensure that it is not too hot or has too much flow. Warm water is needed to ensure proper action of the soap. Use cold water only if warm water is not available. Water that is too hot will remove the protective oils of the skin and will dry the skin, making it vulnerable to damage. Water that comes out of the tap with too much force is more likely to splash onto the floors and walls, possibly spreading the microorganisms.
4. With the water running, wet your hands and wrists. Ensure that your hands are lower than your elbows so that the water flows from the least contaminated areas (i.e., the wrists) to the most contaminated areas (i.e., the hands). Lather hands with soap. Liquid soap is preferable to bar soap, which can be a reservoir for bacteria. Use bar soap only when dispensed soap is not available.
5. Wash thoroughly for at least 30 seconds. If you have just handled a contaminated object (e.g., a dirty glass), wash for 1 minute. If you have been in direct contact with any type of bodily fluid (e.g., you have just changed a diaper), you should wash for up to 2 minutes. Use a firm, circular motion and friction and ensure that you wash the back of hands, palms, and wrists. Wash each finger individually, making sure that you wash between fingers and knuckles (i.e., interlace fingers and thumbs and move hands back and forth) as well as around the cuticles. Do not use too much pressure, as this may result in skin damage.
6. Rinse thoroughly with warm water. Use a fingernail file or orange stick and clean under each fingernail while the water is still running. If a file or stick is not available, use the fingernails of the opposite hand.
7. Shake hands to remove excess water. Dry your hands thoroughly using a paper towel, working upward from fingertips, to hands, to wrists, and finally to forearms. When drying, rather than rub vigorously, it is best to pat the skin. It is important that the hands be dried well to prevent chapping.
8. Turn off the taps using the paper towel you used to dry your hands. Use the paper towel to wipe the surfaces surrounding the sink. Dispose of the paper towel in a covered childproof receptacle with a disposable plastic liner.
9. Apply lotion, if desired, to keep skin soft, reduce the risk of chapping, and act as a barrier for invasion of microorganisms.

IDENTIFICATION AND ASSESSMENT

Different professionals will evaluate students who sustain brain injuries or who have physical disabilities or health impairments for different reasons. Besides educational evaluations, medical and therapeutic evaluations will also be conducted.

MEDICAL EVALUATION

Typically, physicians are the first to conduct evaluations of students with TBI, physical disabilities, or other health impairments. They assess the physical status of the individual and determine their medical needs. The result of this process is to prescribe medications or medical interventions to improve the person's physical status.

Although we cannot cover the medical procedures used to evaluate all of the conditions discussed in this chapter, let's consider briefly how a child with CP is identified. The pediatrician or family physician is usually the professional who recognizes and diagnoses the condition. He or she usually observes that the child's **primitive reflexes** are not disappearing according to a normal developmental timeline. These reflexes, including **asymmetric tonic neck reflex, tonic labyrinthine reflex, and positive support reflex** are present in all newborns but usually disappear in the first year. When they don't disappear, they interfere with normal motor development and impede the child's ability to sit, stand, and walk. This is often the first symptom that the child has CP. When this condition is recognized, the physician continues to follow the child's development for a period of time. Ultimately a medical diagnosis is made and subsequent treatment prescribed. The treatment may include medication, surgery, or physical therapy. These children are often served in early intervention programs.

EDUCATIONAL EVALUATION

After a medical professional has determined the child's medical status and a diagnosis has been established, educational personnel must determine if the condition has a significant negative impact on the student's educability. If it does, then they evaluate the student for early intervention services or special education services, depending on the child's age, and develop an IFSP or an IEP (see Chapter 4). Schools serve most children with TBI, physical disabilities, and other health impairments in the general education classroom most of the time, but students with TBI are also often placed in separate special classes (U.S. Department of Education, 2005).

One issue that always presents a challenge for schools is accurately assessing the intellectual capacity of students with severe physical disabilities. Consider, for example, a nonverbal student with quadriplegic spastic cerebral palsy. Because of the student's severe verbal and motor limitations, it is often difficult to accurately gauge his intelligence and therefore what type of instruction he should receive. Many times, these students are placed in programs for students with severe intellectual disabilities.

Because of this problem, Colleen Willard-Holt (1998) attempted to identify key characteristics of students with CP who were also gifted. She studied two students with severe CP who showed extraordinary intellectual abilities. The students did not verbally communicate and had extremely limited mobility, so Willard-Holt spent 3 years observing, recording, and learning about them to identify their gifted characteristics. She found ample evidence that, even though they did not communicate in a typical fashion, they were gifted in terms of their academic abilities in most areas. In the "Can You Help Me with This Student?" feature we share some of Willard-Holt's suggestions for identifying students with severe CP who also have above-average intellectual abilities.

Reflective Exercise #10
Have you ever worried about an individual who may have had her intellectual potential underestimated because of a physical or health-related disability?

THERAPEUTIC AND HEALTH CARE EVALUATION

As part of public school services for students with disabilities, the school must consider if related services are necessary so that the student may benefit from public education. For the student with physical disabilities, this means that physical and occupational therapists conduct evaluations and, if necessary, create intervention programs to meet a student's needs. In the case of CP, for example, the physical therapist assesses and develops interventions for positioning the student to better align the spine, legs, and feet; fits and monitors orthotic devices for the student; and performs range-of-motion and postoperative exercises. The occupational therapist evaluates and works on areas such as eye-hand control, facilitating the use of hands and arms, fitting the child with hand splints to offset contractures, improving perceptual skills, evaluating sensory integration, and improving various daily skills (Best & Bigge, 2005).

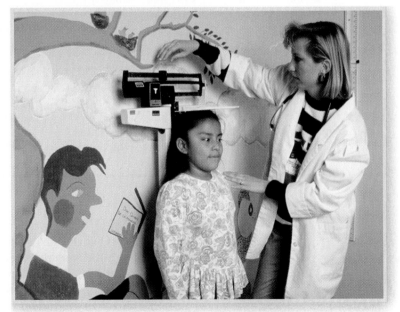

For students with health care needs, the school nurse will play a critical role.

Can You Help Me with This Student?

DETERMINING ABOVE-AVERAGE INTELLECTUAL ABILITIES IN STUDENTS WITH SEVERE CEREBRAL PALSY (CP)

Jan is a 6-year-old child with severe athetoid and spastic CP that greatly limit his ability to control movement throughout his body. He is nonverbal and communicates through body motion and a communication board. He is served in a regular first-grade classroom. You have heard some people refer to him as having a "severe disability," but you're not sure. In fact, you think he might really be very bright (Willard-Holt, 1998), like a genius trapped inside a body that doesn't work very well. He seems to understand a great deal of what you say, he often appears very attentive, and he laughs at your dry sense of humor—something that the other children usually miss. How can you figure out for sure if Jan is really smart? You don't want to underestimate his abilities.

Colleen Willard-Holt studied children like the one described above and recommended several things that could be done to uncover such a student's real ability.

- To begin, there are nonverbal tests, such as the Peabody Picture Vocabulary Test, that will give you a good estimate of intellectual ability. The child only has to look at or point to the picture that you name on the page. Many people, including some school psychologists, are not very familiar with nonverbal tests, but these offer a good chance to find out in a systematic way how much the student knows.

There are also other sources of evidence. Willard-Holt (1998, p. 48) suggests doing the following:

- "Be willing to look beyond the disability for talent. . . ." It is easy to overlook a student's abilities if you concentrate too much on his disabilities. Try to see if the student has a special knack for any academic areas or any artistic abilities.
- "Carefully observe the child's reaction to people and occurrences in his or her environment. . . . A child who grins at humorous comments or puns is showing mature verbal comprehension. A child at an early age who, for ex-

ample, watches the clock when told the time of an event shows understanding of cause and effect relationships."
- "Gather information from parents about their child's capabilities in the home setting." Parents know their children best and will be happy to share with you their knowledge of their child's unique gifts and talents.
- "Look for evidence of learning ability and memory. During testing situations, gifted students with disabilities often indicate knowledge that surprises their parents, indicating that the information has not been taught directly. This demonstrates easy acquisition and recall of information. A sign of superior memory is the child's ability to recall appointment times and medication schedules often better than his or her parents."

You can find more information about evaluating nonverbal students in Overton (2006) or Venn (2007). Also, for more information on students with CP see Best and Bigge (2005) or Pellegrino (2002).

EXTEND AND APPLY

- Teaching students like the one described here can present one of the greatest rewards for teachers as well as one of the greatest challenges. Imagine being a very intelligent person and yet not being able to communicate in a way that people can easily understand you. Although it could be challenging, can you imagine how rewarding it could be to contribute to the education of a student with such disabilities and gifts?

Activity: Go to the Video Classroom section of the Teacher Prep website and click on Child Development and then module 6: Intelligence. Watch video 2 and think about how you might do this type of activity with Jan.

For students with health care needs, the school nurse plays a critical role. This person works with the student, parents, teachers and other school staff, the student's physician, and other health care professionals to develop medical supports for the student while she is in school. The nurse seeks information from parents and medical personnel so that an *individual health care plan* can be developed for the student. This plan includes medical care information for both ongoing needs and emergency

FIGURE 14.3

SAMPLE STUDENT HEALTH CARE PLAN

Student Individualized Health Care Plan

☐ 504
☐ Special Education

Student's Name _____   Birth Date _____
Student's Teacher _____   School _____
Grade _____   School Year _____

Physician's Name _____
Address _____   Telephone Number _____
Parents/Guardians _____   Home Phone _____
Work Phone (Mother) _____   Emergency Phone _____
Work Phone (Father) _____   Emergency Phone _____
Work Phone (Guardian) _____   Emergency Phone _____
Hospital Health Care Coordinator _____   Phone _____
School Health Care Coordinator _____   Phone _____
Education Coordinator _____   Phone _____

MEDICAL OVERVIEW
Brief Medical History _____
_____
_____
_____

Known Allergies _____
_____
_____

Medications _____

Medication Authorization Form Attached for Each Medication   Yes ☐   No ☐
Specific Health Care Needs _____
_____
_____

Procedure Authorization Form Attached for Each Procedure   Yes ☐   No ☐

ADDITIONAL NEEDS/PLANS
Emergency Plan Attached   Yes ☐   No ☐
Recreational Activity Permission Form Attached   Yes ☐   No ☐

Transportation Plan Attached   Yes ☐   No ☐
Personnel Training Plan Attached   Yes ☐   No ☐
Entry/Reentry Checklist Completed   Yes ☐   No ☐
Other: _____

ADDITIONAL INFORMATION
Special Diet _____
_____
_____

Additional Information Attached   Yes ☐   No ☐
Special Safety Measures _____

Source: From Best, S. (2005). Health impairments and infectious diseases. In S. J. Best, K. W. Heller, & J. L. Bigge (Eds.), *Teaching individuals with physical or multiple disabilities* (5th ed., pp. 59–85). Upper Saddle River, NJ: Merrill/Prentice Hall.

medical treatment. The student's health care plan should be attached to the IEP and include information such as how medication should be delivered, skin care, catheterization procedures, gastronomy and respiratory care, and what to do in the case of an asthma attack or a seizure (DePaepe et al., 2002). Figure 14.3 shows an example of an individualized health care plan.

EFFECTIVE INSTRUCTIONAL PRACTICES

To effectively educate students with TBI, physical disabilities, or other health impairments, teachers and school personnel must address several important questions. Where should they serve the student, and what accommodations must they provide? What are the student's individual goals, and what is the appropriate curriculum for the student? What instructional methods will best meet the student's needs? Should adaptive devices be used; and, if so, what devices? How can they make sure the student's physical and health care needs are addressed as outlined in the individual health care plan? How can they interact most effectively with parents, families, and health care professionals? Let's look at how some of these issues are addressed at different stages of the student's school life.

PRESCHOOL YEARS

Physical or medical conditions that occur relatively early in life may allow the child to be served in early intervention programs before the age of 3 or in public schools when he reaches the age of 3. As you know, the earlier interventions can start for children, the more effective the interventions can be. Consider the importance of preschool programs for two conditions we have addressed in this chapter, CP and HIV/AIDS.

During the years of early physical growth, it is very important to maximize physical functioning while decreasing the impact of the disability. To do this, therapeutic intervention by pediatric PTs and OTs is essential. **Orthotic devices** can be applied to a very young child's body to provide support for weak muscles, improve posture, help prevent contractures in the arms and the legs, and help reduce tone in the hands. The devices also help to increase or maintain the **range of motion** of the limbs, improve stability, and reduce involuntary movements. The rehabilitation engineers and orthopedic specialists who work with the PTs and OTs must individually design all orthotic devices for the child and modify or exchange the devices as she grows older and larger and as different needs develop.

PTs and OTs have another important job: consulting with parents so that they can carry through with exercises at home. Ketelaar, Vermeer, Helders, and Hart (1998) reviewed 13 research studies on the involvement of parents in intervention programs for their children with CP. They found that overall, when parents participate in intervention programs for their children, greater gains are generally made. In a related study, Lin (2000) found that, although many families had difficulty adapting to the disability of their child with CP, some were better able to cope than others. The important factors included having "positive family appraisal," "support from concerned others," "spiritual support," "personal growth and advocacy," and "positive social interaction."

Preschool programs can also serve young children with HIV/AIDS, which benefits both the child and his family. One important outcome of being in a preschool is that program personnel may play an important role in helping the child take the required medication. This may seem like a minor issue, but children's need to take different medications is often a problem that requires careful monitoring. If a drug is missed, not only will it be less effective, but the child may develop dosage resistance (Best, 2005a).

Besides directly helping the child, preschool programs might also work with other community agencies to help facilitate stability in the home. Most young children with AIDS either have one or two parents who are infected with the disease—or have lost one or both parents—and may also have infected siblings. For certain, life at home will be stressful. In the United States, most children who have HIV/AIDS are poor and live in inner cities. Their lives are complicated not only by their illness but by high rates of crime and violence, poor housing, and limited access to health care and social services. In order to have any success with these children, school personnel, health care providers, social workers, and other mental health professionals and community agencies must work together closely (Spiegel & Bonwit, 2002).

Reflective Exercise #11
Do you think it is possible for personnel from different agencies to work together effectively on behalf of a student with HIV/AIDS? What do you think would facilitate or inhibit this process?

ACADEMIC AND FUNCTIONAL INSTRUCTION

As the child moves into the school years, the services just described as well as others continue to be significant. During the school years, there are three issues of concern when educating students with TBI, physical disabilities, or other health impairments: curriculum and instruction, classroom considerations, and assistive technology devices and services. We address each of these here.

Curriculum and Instruction

Determining the most appropriate individual goals for a student and placing her in the curriculum that best meets her needs are very important decisions. According to IDEA, to the extent possible, all students with disabilities are to participate in the general curriculum. Many of the students we have been discussing in this chapter should be able to do this with little difficulty. However, there are a few relevant issues for you to consider.

Many students with TBI, physical disabilities, and especially health impairments miss an inordinate number of school days. They may not get enough sleep the night before, they may be too weak or in too much pain, or they may be hospitalized for a period of time. Therefore, although cognitively they are able to participate in the general curriculum, teachers and parents have to work together to help the student catch up when he falls behind.

Additionally, when in school, a student may miss some class time because of her condition. For example, a child may have to leave the class if an asthma attack occurs, if she is in too much pain to participate due to sickle-cell disease or HIV/AIDS, or if she has to go to the bathroom frequently or leave to check her blood sugar because she is diabetic. So again, there must be as much opportunity as possible for her to catch up on different learning activities.

Finally, we need to realize that some of the students we have discussed have cognitive or learning disabilities occurring along with their physical or health challenges. When this is the case, we must carefully consider both their individual learning needs and the overall curriculum in which they should be placed. Stump and Bigge (2005) suggest we consider four curricular options:

- *The general education curriculum.* Students in this curriculum work on the same learning activities as other students do. As we have said, many of the students we have been discussing perform well using the standard curriculum.
- *The general education curriculum with modifications.* Modifications might include changes in the content, desired outcomes, or levels of complexity. This curriculum may be appropriate for a student whose condition impedes success in the general curriculum without modifications—for example, a student with cerebral palsy who cannot maintain the same pace as the rest of the class.
- *Life skills curriculum.* If a student needs skills necessary for succeeding in life, this is the appropriate curriculum. Participation in a life skills curriculum may either complement or supplement participation in the general curriculum with or without modifications. This curriculum is appropriate for a student who is not acquiring sufficient life skills without specific instruction or for a student who needs to learn to use adaptive devices to participate in different activities.
- *Curriculum modified in communication and task performance.* Those who need explicit instruction in communication skills in order to participate in home, school, and community life participate in learning activities in this curriculum. These students have relatively severe physical disabilities that may exist with or without concurrent intellectual disabilities.

Reflective Exercise #12
Based on what you have read about the different conditions that may affect students, how do you see some of the students fitting into the different curricula?

Success within a curriculum often depends on the use of unique instructional strategies and tactics and how the teacher interacts with the student. Although we can't cover all of these for the many different students we have discussed in this chapter, the "Highly Effective Instructional Strategies" feature offers examples of some of the focused, highly structured instructional strategies that teachers of students with TBI need to use.

needs. The person who has not learned to do these tasks, or cannot do them, may have difficulties.

- *Limited social experiences.* Most important, people expect that an acceptable level of social ability be demonstrated by those in a working environment. Persons who have not learned these important skills are at a disadvantage.

If persons with TBI, physical disabilities, or chronic health impairments are to be successful in jobs or careers, they must be able to overcome these barriers or find situations in which their limitations are not a factor. Part of the way in which this can be done is by preparing for life career opportunities through a career education program.

The career education model has been used effectively for many years in preparing persons with different types of disabilities for the future (Clark & Bigge, 2005). It has four stages:

- Career awareness begins during early childhood education. At this level children learn that there are many important roles that they might fill as adults and that, by having a particular role, they can be an important part of society.
- Career exploration occurs during the elementary school years and continues into the middle school. During this stage, students explore specific jobs and career areas and the requirements of workers who take these positions.
- Career preparation is emphasized at the high school level, particularly for students who will not be going into postsecondary education. Students may enroll in regular or special vocational preparation classes or attend vocational or technical training schools. For some students, training at this level may consist of community-based instruction in order to achieve a competitive or a supported employment position.
- Career placement involves follow-up and continuing education. After training, students are placed on a job and support is provided as long as necessary to make sure they can be successful. As part of this stage, some students may be able to continue training in a postsecondary education setting.

PREVAILING ISSUES, CONTROVERSIES, AND IMPLICATIONS FOR THE TEACHER

Although most of us clearly accept the right of school attendance for students with disabilities, some of the students we have discussed in this chapter (and others who have not been discussed) require rather extensive supports in order to attend school. According to DePaepe et al. (2002), the lines have been blurred between what constitutes a related educational service (i.e., a service that supports students so they can participate meaningfully in school) and what is actually a medical service. For example, in an early court case (*Irving Independent School District* v. *Tatro,* 1984), the Supreme Court ruled that a process called clean intermittent catheterization was a school health service that schools had to provide. The court noted that this was necessary for the child to attend school and that the school nurse or another qualified person could do it. (In fact, this procedure is now performed by many special education teachers.)

But in other cases, courts have ruled that the cost of procedures and safety issues needs to be considered when deciding whether or not a specific service should be provided. The issue, then, is what should schools be required to do for students with physical or health-related disabilities, and how much should they be required to spend on an individual student? There are those who say that, with our limited educational budgets, we should invest in programs that will benefit the most students, especially those who are likely to gain the most from the intervention. On the other hand, isn't our treatment of those with great needs an important indicator of our quality as a nation?

There is a parallel topic to this issue directly related to the teacher. If we believe that all children have a right to a free and appropriate education in the least restrictive environment, do we as individuals place any limitations on what *we* are willing to do or with whom we are willing to work to support this value?

SUMMARY

In this chapter we discussed three special education disability categories identified by the U.S. Department of Education: traumatic brain injury, orthopedic handicaps (which we refer to as physical disabilities), and other health impairments. These categories include some specific conditions that were described in the chapter. Because of the nature of the conditions, we focused on the physical and medical aspects of the conditions.

Definitions of Traumatic Brain Injury, Physical Disabilities, and Other Health Impairments As Used in Special Education

- Traumatic brain injury refers to "open or closed head injuries resulting in impairments in one or more areas, such as cognition; language; memory; attention; reasoning; abstract thinking; judgment; problem-solving; sensory, perceptual, and motor abilities; psychosocial behavior; physical functions; information processing; and speech."
- Physical disabilities are referred to in special education law as "orthopedic impairments," which "includes impairments caused by congenital anomaly (e.g., clubfoot, absence of some member, etc.), impairments caused by disease (e.g., poliomyelitis, bone tuberculosis, etc.), and impairments from other causes (e.g., cerebral palsy, amputations, and fractures or burns that cause contractures)."
- Health impairment means having "limited strength, vitality or alertness, including a heightened alertness to environmental stimuli, that results in limited alertness with respect to the educational environment, that is due to chronic or acute health problems such as asthma, attention deficit disorder or attention deficit hyperactivity disorder, diabetes, epilepsy, a heart condition, hemophilia, lead poisoning, leukemia, nephritis, rheumatic fever, and sickle cell anemia; and . . . adversely affects a child's educational performance."
- Not only is it necessary to exhibit physical or health limitations in order to be served in special education, but these conditions must interfere with the student's ability to receive an appropriate education.

Major Characteristics of Students with TBI, Physical Disabilities, and Other Health Impairments

- Students with TBI may have problems concentrating and paying attention, remembering, carrying out complex cognitive tasks, and communicating. Reading and math will be their most common academic problem areas. They may have behavioral issues such as being off task, increased or decreased activity levels, impulsivity, irritability, apathy, aggression, or social withdrawal. There is likely to be variability in their performance and behavior over time.
- The physical characteristics of students with physical disabilities vary according to their specific disabilities. However, as we noted, persons with physical disabilities often have different reactions to life events. To help fit in, they may do things such as try to avoid calling attention to their disability, make fun of their own condition, or find a special niche among their peers. They may also try to educate their peers about their conditions.
- Students with health impairments can be affected by their lack of learning and socialization opportunities caused by missed time in school, limited play and recreational opportunities, isolation by peers, and family challenges that might result from their ongoing medical conditions.

Prevalence of TBI, Physical Disabilities, and Other Health Impairments

- Students with TBI, physical disabilities, and other health impairments, as categories in special education, make up less than 1% of the total school population. About 0.03% of public school students have TBI, about 0.11% have physical disabilities, and about 0.59% have other health impairments.

Areas of Assessment and Planning for Students with TBI, Physical Disabilities, and Health Impairments

- Assessment first occurs in the medical arena in which the condition of the student is initially diagnosed and medical interventions developed.
- Second, within schools, eligibility for special education must be determined based on the extent to which the condition affects the student's learning ability. If the child meets criteria, an IFSP may be developed if he or she is served in an early intervention program, or an IEP if served in a public school.
- Third, as a part of these plans, related services such as PT or OT may be offered. In this case, additional

assessments will be conducted and plans will be developed to meet a student's needs.

- If a student is not eligible for special education services, it is still possible that a section 504 plan may be developed in order that the student can participate in school.

Special Considerations for Students with TBI, Physical Disabilities and Health Impairments with Regard to Instruction and Related Services

- Students with TBI, physical disabilities, and health impairments may receive special education and related services at the preschool level, during school years, and as they transition into the adult years.
- Variations of the general curriculum may be provided to students based on their unique needs, but most will participate in the general curriculum.
- Most students with TBI, physical disabilities, and health impairments will be in the general education classroom. Special considerations for their physical and health care needs will be necessary for them to participate, and some modifications in the physical structure of the classroom may be necessary. It may be particularly helpful for an OT or PT to evaluate the classroom in order to better accommodate students.

- Teachers should especially be attuned to classroom situations that might endanger the health of some students. For example, chalk dust may trigger an asthma attack.
- Assistive technology devices can help students participate in the general education classroom and the general curriculum.
- Students will need supports as they transition into adolescence and adulthood. Their unique physical and health care needs will need to be considered when further educational and career possibilities are discussed.

Major Issues Related to Teaching and Providing Services to Students with Traumatic Brain Injury, Physical Disabilities, or Other Health Impairments

- The major issue related to serving students with TBI, physical disabilities, and health impairments is determining the divide between the responsibilities of the educational system and educators and the medical field and health care professionals. What are appropriate responsibilities for teachers? What areas of student care should be left to health care professionals? To some extent this debate has been addressed in the courts, but there is still much that has not been resolved.

 Council for Exceptional Children **ADDRESSING THE PROFESSIONAL STANDARDS**

Council for Exceptional Children (CEC) Knowledge Standards addressed in the chapter:

CC1K: 1,2,4,5,7; PH1K: 1,3; CC2K: 1–7; PH2K: 1–4; CC3K: 1,2; PH3K: 1; PH4K: 1,2; CC5K: 1–4; PH5K: 1–3; CC6K: 3; CC7K: 1; CC8K: 1; PH8K: 1,2; PH9K: 1; PH10K: 1–3

Appendix B: CEC Knowledge and Skill Standards Common Core has a full listing of the standards referenced here.

15

Academically Gifted and Talented

REFLECT UPON

- How is giftedness defined and classified?

- What are the primary behavioral characteristics of students with gifts and talents?

- How prevalent are students with gifts and talents, and what causal factors are associated with these characteristics?

- How are students with gifts and talents identified and assessed?

- What educational practices are used for early intervention, academic enhancements, and transitions to adult life for students with gifts and talents?

- What are the major issues confronting the education of students with gifts and talents?

by Eric Jones and W. Thomas Southern

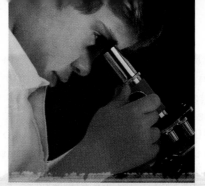

My Profession, My Story: Julie Lenner

Julie Lenner is a teacher of students identified as gifted in the Sandusky city schools in northwestern Ohio. She has been on the job for 5 years. She has completed a master's degree in gifted education and has recently become a part-time instructor in gifted education at a local university.

Julie became interested in these children almost by chance. As an undergraduate elementary education major, she frequently sought out opportunities to volunteer in a wide variety of educational settings, including summer camps and community programs. During the summer following her junior year, Julie was hired to serve as a counselor in a summer program for students with gifts and talents. Her curiosity was piqued by the enthusiasm of the students and the range of the challenges they pursued. During the following summer, she not only participated in the same program (this time as a residential director) but also took graduate classes in the field of gifted education. At the same time she was looking for a job. Jobs in elementary education turned out to be highly competitive. However, she noticed a posted opening in Sandusky. While she had not completed her licensure in gifted education (required under state of Ohio law), she applied. Julie had student-taught in this district, and staff members had already expressed interest in her.

Julie's initial appointment was wide-ranging and intense. She met with students identified as gifted. In addition, she was expected to develop curricula for the program in language arts and mathematics, provide counseling for students and consultation with students' general classroom teachers, meet with and counsel parents, develop individual written plans for each student, and assist in identifying students for the following year. Julie describes her first group of students as "great." She was concerned about some identified students who were experiencing difficulty and worried about whether or not she was providing appropriate experiences. Since her district has a culturally diverse student body, she struggled with the issues of identifying students with inappropriate instruments and dealing with students who might be missed by the district's policy. And there were other challenges. Some students seemed unconnected to the curriculum, even when their abilities and precocities were evident in nonacademic exchanges. Some were confrontational; others were too quietly compliant or behaviorally difficult (challenging her initial assumptions that gifted students would accept and rise to challenges). She also noted that classroom teachers were often unaware of the kinds of difficulties gifted students experienced in educational settings. They seemed to feel that these kids could make it on their own with little problem and that the services they received were not as essential as those provided in the general classroom.

FIGURE 15.2

GARDNER'S MULTIPLE INTELLIGENCES

1. Linguistic (sensitivity to the meaning and order of words)
2. Logical-mathematical (ability in numbering/reasoning and other logical systems)
3. Musical (ability to understand and create music)
4. Spatial (ability to perceive the visual world accurately and re-create or alter it)
5. Bodily-kinesthetic (ability to use one's body in a skilled way—e.g., a dancer)
6. Interpersonal (ability to perceive and understand other individuals)
7. Intrapersonal (ability to understand one's own emotions; self-knowledge)
8. Naturalist (ability to discriminate among elements of natural world; knowledge of nature)

Also see http://www.infed.org/thinkers/gardner.htm for a summary of Dr. Howard Gardner's research; discussions of multiple intelligences, including additional intelligences that he has considered; references, and links to related sources.
Source: From Gardner, H. (1999). *Intelligence reframed. Multiple intelligences for the 21st century.* New York: Basic Books.

Gardner's Definition Using Multiple Intelligences

Gardner and colleagues (e.g., Gardner, 1983; Gardner & Hatch, 1989; Walters & Gardner, 1986; Ramos-Ford & Gardner, 1991) believe that intelligence and giftedness are not general traits and therefore should not be viewed as the general factors that IQ tests purport to measure. Consequently, they developed a theory of multiple types of intelligences in which intelligence is defined as "the capacity to solve problems or to fashion products that are valued in one or more cultural settings" (Gardner & Hatch, 1989, p. 5). In their view there are eight areas of intelligence: logical mathematical, linguistic, musical, spatial, bodily kinesthetic, interpersonal, intrapersonal, and naturalistic. Figure 15.2 lists the eight intelligences with examples of roles and abilities generally associated with each. Gardner (1983) allowed that the list may not be exhaustive and that other intelligences could be identified. However, it does include a set of competencies that, although they may usually operate in combination, are capable of functioning individually. Thus, each talent may be studied, identified, and developed apart from the others.

Reflective Exercise #3

What is your opinion of the theory of multiple intelligences? Do you believe these specific areas exist? Do you believe that intelligence can be reduced to eight specific areas? Explain.

CLASSIFICATION CRITERIA FOR IDENTIFYING GIFTEDNESS

The two most frequently used classification systems in the education of the students with gifts and talents are (1) types of gifts and (2) levels of giftedness.

Types of Gifts and Talents

When students are classified by type of gift or talent, criteria from the Marland (1972) federal definition are used. For example, general intellectual ability refers to scores on IQ tests, and specific academic aptitude refers to high abilities in content-specific areas (most frequently mathematics, science, social studies, reading, and writing). Creativity describes students who have numerous, useful, and original ideas. Leadership describes students who are natural or developing leaders. Students with talents in visual and performing arts excel in instrumental or local performance, two- or three-dimensional arts, dance, or theater.

Some students with gifts and talents excel in the visual and performing arts.

www.prenhall.com/rosenberg

Another distinction among the types is what some researchers characterize as gifts versus talents. Intellectual and academic performances were often referred to as gifts, while the others were labeled talents. Many theorists view this distinction as invalid (all observed behaviors are manifestations of gifts) and portray the talent areas as less important or remarkable. For example, Gagné (1999) suggests that initial gifts in the individual become recognized talents after opportunity, instruction, environment, and chance factors contribute to their development and exposure. This more ecological view appears to be winning approval in the field.

Levels of Giftedness

The notion that giftedness should be sorted into levels arose with the study of individuals with high IQ scores. Hollingsworth (1940) suggested that individuals with IQs higher than 180 are very different than those with lower IQs still in the gifted range. Other researchers attempted to determine if bands of intelligence might have different characteristics and needs. This led to a designation of levels of giftedness:

IQ 130–145: Gifted
IQ 145–160: Highly gifted
Above IQ 160: Profoundly gifted

Still, many are not pleased with this classification system. They feel that IQ alone is an inadequate measure to accurately classify types of giftedness and that the performance of students at each level is not that dissimilar. Nonetheless, there are still references to such a system in gifted texts, and research into the profoundly gifted is still being conducted (e.g., Gross, 2004; Silverman, 1990).

Reflective Exercise #4
How much influence should IQ test scores have in the determination of giftedness? What other factors should be part of the classification system?

PRIMARY BEHAVIORAL CHARACTERISTICS OF STUDENTS WITH GIFTS AND TALENTS

As we have seen, the term *giftedness* suggests a range of different patterns of behavior. We first consider some of the early stereotypes of students with gifts and then identify empirically derived characteristics.

EARLY CONCEPTUALIZATIONS

Early written accounts of students with gifts and talents presented a variety of physical, cognitive, and affective characteristics. Lombroso (1891), a 19th-century writer, described them as being near-sighted, physically weak, and oversensitive. He claimed that genius was a force that burned the body's substance and put sanity at risk. The cliché that "genius is separated from madness by a fine line" was originally one of Lombroso's assertions.

Terman (1925) conducted a study of the characteristics of more than 1,500 students with IQs above 140 in order to investigate Lombroso's characterizations. He concluded that students identified as gifted were physically larger and healthier, more likely to mature into adults who were also highly productive, and had superior mental health compared to their average peers. Terman's and Lombroso's characterizations are contradictory, but they are both represented in current stereotypes of giftedness. Neither characterization is adequately supported. Terman's more scientific study was flawed because it was based primarily on white middle-class students from advantaged backgrounds. The characteristics he found might not be typical of students who demonstrate exceptional abilities in today's diverse multicultural communities.

CURRENT VIEWS

Students with gifts and talents vary greatly in physical, cognitive, and affective characteristics. Some students exhibit traits that can be viewed quite positively. For example, some students show high degrees of empathy for others, task commitment, motivation to excel, or desire to fulfill teacher expectations. On the other hand, high-ability students may exhibit behaviors that are viewed negatively. They may display impatience with

Questioning rules and authority, a trait associated with creative students, may alienate some teachers and peers.

peers' inability to rapidly learn information, question authority and become rebellious, or express distaste for tasks that require drill and repetition.

Some students with gifts and talents are disorganized and appear flighty and unfocused. Ironically, some traits associated with creative students may actually interfere with their being selected to participate in gifted education programs (Richert, Alvino, & McDonnel, 1982). Unusual responses may be considered flaky and off-the-wall. Questioning rules and authority may be viewed as rudeness or sarcasm. A high degree of risk-taking behavior may result in the adoption of attitudes and behaviors that ostracize the student from peers and teachers.

Developmental Factors

The characteristics of students who are gifted also vary according to developmental age. As these children go through school, more and more specific sorts of talent develop. Young children may be well developed in all the school tasks. They may be able to accomplish most of the learning in early grades with apparent ease. However, by the time a student reaches middle grades, preferences, strengths, and comparative weaknesses become more apparent. Some students excel in mathematics or science, while others express high achievement in writing or history. Some of these differences arise because, in later grades, content becomes more specific and directed.

Cognitive, affective, and physical development is not uniform. For example, young children may display very large vocabularies or advanced problem-solving skills. They may also engage in temper tantrums and emotional displays common to other children their age. When students with gifts and talents enter school, their school-related fine-motor skills may not match their cognitive development. Faced with tasks such as handwriting and coloring, they may experience frustration. Young boys often express impatience with the cumbersome process of handwriting, even developing strong dislike for the entire writing process. Students who enter school early or skip grades are not as apt to participate in varsity athletics as their chronological-age peers. While they may continue to participate in sports, lower levels of physical maturation may disadvantage young students if they have to compete with grade-level peers. Many students will pursue other interests and choose not to compete or participate in interscholastic sports (Olenchak & Hebert, 2002).

Adolescence

Adolescence is perhaps the most challenging period of development for high-ability students. Buescher (1991) describes adolescence as a time of personal redefinition for all youth. The role of "good student" and "high achiever" may be questioned in the

www.prenhall.com/rosenberg

Can You Help Me with This Student?

ADDRESSING THE NEEDS OF A GIFTED CHILD

Wes's mother was annoyed. Once more the 3-year-old had pulled volumes of the World Book Encyclopedia *from the shelf and was paging through them. He never seemed to harm them, but it was an irritation for her to have to continually replace them. As she walked over to him, he looked up, pointed at a picture caption, and asked, "What's this word, Mommy?" She told him and then asked why he wanted to know. He replied, "Because I can read all the other words." Without instruction, Wes had taught himself to read at the age of 3.*

When he entered school, achievement tests indicated that he was reading above the sixth-grade level. Some of the school officials wanted him to skip kindergarten, but the kindergarten teacher was adamant that he would miss valuable skills and that gaps in instruction would later limit his progress. The parents and school officials opted for a 6-week trial in kindergarten with a review of placement at the end of that time. At the review, the kindergarten teacher still opposed acceleration to first grade, citing immaturity and poor foundations in reading. "He can't even do letter cards [matching capital and lower case letters]," she stated. The coordinator for gifted education and the curriculum director conducted an observation during which Wes appeared silent and a bit resentful of various tasks. At one point the teacher passed out a worksheet with

a picture of a dinosaur and asked students to name the initial sound of the object in the picture. When one of his class-mates responded with a "d" sound, for dinosaur, *Wes suddenly became animated. He shook his head vigorously and raised his hand frantically. The teacher with one raised eyebrow at the observers called on him.*

"No!" he cried. "It's a 't' sound, for Trachodon. *That's what it says right here," indicating the fine print below the picture.*

EXTEND AND APPLY

- There are a large number of children like Wes in American schools. If you were Wes's teacher, how would you have handled this situation to avoid the initial confrontation? What advice would you have given the kindergarten teacher to help her avoid the period of increasing hostility?
- What should happen next for Wes? What kind of follow-up and monitoring needs to be done in the future?

Activity: Go to the Video Classroom section of the Teacher Prep website, click on Special Education and then module 5: Families and Special Education. Watch video 1 and answer the accompanying questions. Think about how Wes's family could advocate for him with his teacher and the school.

---

light of the intense physical and emotional changes occurring during this period. Some students begin to distrust their ability and question whether they really have gifts and talents. Others may change priorities and acquire greater preferences for relations with peers that conflict with goals for advanced achievement. For females, this can sometimes include rejection of mathematics and science as a course of study (Reis & Graham, 2005). For males, it may result in adopting more rebellious and noncompliant roles. It is important that teachers remember that these changes are more a function of adolescence than of giftedness (Buescher, 1991) (see "Can You Help Me with This Student?").

As students with gifts and talents progress further in school, a major task facing them is the selection of training and career options. For many students, interests and abilities have been channeled for some time. They have identified career choices (or an area of knowledge to pursue) early and clearly. For others, these choices are more difficult. Some students with gifts, particularly those with multiple talents, experience difficulties making decisions about which options to pursue (Berger, 1994).

Postsecondary education is the time when students redefine themselves, this time as young adults with different responsibilities. At this point they may, and frequently do, change career aspirations and goals. For instance, students who might have identified a long graduate educational course may change their minds and choose a more direct career path.

Reflective Exercise #5
What were your initial thoughts regarding the characteristics of students with gifts and talents? How do the empirically derived characteristics compare with your initial thoughts?

Adulthood

Studies of adults with gifts and talents tend to take the form of biographical surveys, usually of the famous and the eminent (e.g., Goertzel & Goertzel, 1962; Roe, 1952). While these life histories provide insight into some of the later development of individuals with gifts and talents, the sample is biased. Studies that have identified and followed groups of "typical" individuals with gifts and talents through adulthood are scarce. Terman (1925) completed the most noteworthy longitudinal study. Although that study relied on the IQ data of a very narrow sample, it provides a glimpse of how highly capable students progress into adulthood. The group, as a whole, was stable, in both personal and professional relationships. The males in Terman's group were generally satisfied with their life achievements. Some members of the group were near the top of their professions. Females told a different story. Few of the women identified in the group had engaged in careers. When they were interviewed as adults, the women expressed disappointment that they had not fulfilled their academic potential. Given the societal roles and expectations for women at the time of the study, that result is not surprising. More recent studies (e.g., Arnold, 1993) have indicated that high-achieving women do not find it easy to resolve professional and family options (Tomlinson-Keasey & Keasey, 1993).

PREVALENCE AND CAUSAL FACTORS

PREVALENCE

Estimates of the numbers of students who are gifted and talented vary so widely that it is difficult to find consensus among them. The estimates differ as a function of three variables: (1) the prevailing conceptualizations of giftedness, (2) services offered for gifted students, and (3) the quality of the general education program. Gagné (1991) reported that most prevalence estimates are based on IQs of 130 or on academic achievement at the 95th percentile. Accordingly, we would expect to find that about 5% of the school-age population is gifted, but actual numbers vary considerably from that estimate. Renzulli (1986) argued that performances on standardized, norm-referenced tests do not provide adequate bases for the identification of giftedness and talent. More liberal criteria would allow for the identification of 15 to 20% of the school's population as potentially gifted. It seems that the general public shares the liberal criteria. Gagné, Bélanger, and Motard (1993) surveyed noneducators regarding their estimates of the prevalence of school-age children with gifts and talents. They found that estimates varied widely for both labels. An average of 19% of school-age children were estimated to be gifted, while the average estimate of talented students was 36%.

From these data we can draw three conclusions. First, estimates of prevalence vary widely depending on how closely you adhere to the IQ model of giftedness. Second, professionals offer lower estimates than nonprofessionals do. Third, estimates vary if the notion of high ability is broadened from cognitive or academic abilities to include artistic, creative, social, and psychomotor talents. Also keep in mind that the demand for special education for students with gifts and talents increases if the general curriculum is inadequate to meet their instructional needs. Schools with high academic demands, well-designed curricula, and good instruction experience less pressure for special services. Thus, variations in local education programs are accompanied by variations in demands for educational services.

CAUSAL FACTORS

Where does giftedness come from? Answers to that question rarely seem adequate. To many, the term **gifted** suggests something mystical. However, most of the professional discussion on causality centers on inheritance and environment. While the debate has waxed and waned, most theorists believe that both genetic and environmental factors are important in the development of intellectual gifts. Gagné (1993) and Feldhusen (1992) offer models of talent development that describe a genetic and environmental interaction. In Gagné's model, for example, giftedness is a predisposed set of inborn abilities that allows a range of development in the child. These abilities, however, interact with environmental factors such as guidance from other significant people, appropriate early instruction, and even chance. The environment also impacts motivational and personality traits important for the development of talent.

While innate abilities may provide the bases for giftedness, the preponderance of relatively advantaged students in programs for gifted students clearly suggests that the socioeconomics of communities, schools, and families also play critical causal roles. Specifically, where you live and the school you attend can influence the development of giftedness. More affluent communities, schools, and families tend to have more opportunities for intellectual and creative efforts. Gifted education programs are only sporadically available in rural and low-income school districts (Southern & Jones, 1992).

IDENTIFICATION AND ASSESSMENT

There is a wide assortment of evaluation procedures used to identify students for gifted education programs. These varied procedures contribute to the diverse characteristics and different numbers of students who are identified as gifted. Test-driven identification systems tend to be based on rather simple conceptualizations that identify only 2 to 5% of the school population as gifted. The major problem is that tests alone do not identify many students who consistently demonstrate significant talent and capabilities. Standardized tests only offer general predictions and are not very useful in identifying students for programs that provide for diverse opportunities for individual enrichment. Currently, the most useful identification processes are based on the use of multiple criteria (Davis & Rimm, 2003), including intelligence tests, achievement tests, creativity tests, teacher nominations, peer nominations, parent nominations, product sampling, and self-nominations.

INTELLIGENCE TESTS

Intelligence tests provide information that is often useful for predicting future school performance. Scores are highly reliable and relatively stable. Critics, however, argue that there are several limitations to IQ tests. First, they are based on limited conceptualizations of intelligence because they only test convergent and analytical reasoning. Second, IQ tests do not adequately identify students from special populations. Third, IQ tests become less useful in determining specific abilities and talents as students grow older.

ACHIEVEMENT TESTS

Achievement tests offer more specific information about student learning and also provide norm-referenced comparative data. Achievement tests are generally organized into subtests that provide information on academic strengths and weaknesses. For this reason achievement test batteries are often used to identify specific academic abilities. However, these tests have potential drawbacks.

The content of standardized achievement tests is made up of samples of items that test what is taught, or what should be taught, in schools. However, there are great variations in the contents of local curricula among school districts. Frequently, what is tested is not what is taught, so norm-referenced comparisons may not be valid. Moreover, achievement tests may lack sufficient numbers of difficult questions to reliably measure the achievement of very capable students. The tests are fairly easy; and although the students earn high scores, their achievement is not thoroughly tested.

CREATIVITY TESTS

During the 1950s, researchers developed instruments to assess divergent thinking and creativity. Many tests of creativity measure traits such as creative fluency, or the ability to produce large numbers of responses; flexibility, or the ability to produce responses in a large number of categories; elaboration, or the ability to link words or symbols together to make new ideas; and originality, or the ability to generate responses that are unusual or unique. Research with creativity tests has shown some lower correlation with IQ testing. Proponents therefore claim that the instruments are measuring a construct different from intelligence. Nonetheless, links among creativity-test performance and adult productivity have not been clearly established, and some research claiming that creativity is linked to school achievement has been called into question (Piirto, 1992).

TEACHER NOMINATIONS

Teachers often participate in the process of identifying students who may benefit from specialized programs. Usually they are asked to either supply ratings of students' strengths and weaknesses or nominate students who they think would benefit from special services. Teachers do not rate and nominate only students who appear to be academically precocious. They are frequently asked to provide ratings on different abilities or aptitudes, such as creativity, content ability, artistic aptitude, and motivation. The importance of teachers' participation should not be ignored. Teachers directly observe students' academic performance. They also observe the performances of their students in comparison to one another in academic and relevant nonacademic settings. Teacher ratings/nominations are also inexpensive and easily collected.

Still, teachers' judgments should be used cautiously. Some researchers have found that teachers are relatively poor at identifying both students with high IQs and students with specific academic aptitudes (Pegnato & Birch, 1959; Terman & Oden, 1947). Some teachers orient to indicators that are not highly related to gifted behaviors. For example, they might view neatness, grammatical speech, or exact compliance with assignments as highly related to student ability when, in fact, such traits may be irrelevant. The literature on the use of teacher evaluations suggests several guidelines. First, teacher ratings are perhaps most useful if they are used to indicate talents and abilities that may be missed in formal testing. Second, since some teachers may have dramatically high rates of nominations while others nominate relatively few students, teachers should be trained in rating and nominating students. Third, even if training is provided, teachers' evaluations should be used cautiously because differences do not disappear with training. Fourth, teachers should provide capable students with instruction that requires the students to use abstract reasoning, creativity, or problem solving. If students do not have opportunities to show their cognitive abilities, teachers will not be able to observe them.

PEER NOMINATIONS

When observing their fellow students, peers see a wider variety of behaviors than do teachers. Consequently, peers can be asked questions that help identify giftedness. There can, however, be difficulties with peer nomination. First, young students may be overly influenced by teacher praise of student peers. Peer judgment may reflect the teacher's judgments. Second, older peers tend to be less informative because they are reluctant or they take the process less seriously than younger students do. Third, peer judgments are frequently influenced by behaviors that have little to do with aptitudes or abilities of their peers. For example, students who irritate others or belittle their peers will probably not be selected as frequently as other students will. Fourth, the number of nominations that are needed to identify a student is open to question. Given some of the factors that cause students to undernominate certain students, peer nominations should be used cautiously.

PARENT NOMINATIONS

Arguably, parents are the greatest source of nominations of students (Jones & Southern, 1991). Parents know a great deal about their child's behavior. Thus, they are often asked to participate in assessments by filling out forms or rating scales or are simply asked if their son or daughter should be a part of a program for the gifted and talented.

Parents can provide extensive information about current habits, skills, leisure activities, and preferred learning tasks. However, it can be difficult to determine the value of some types of parental information. Unless they have kept accurate records, questions about milestone events in a child's life (e.g., the age at which speech began or the age at which an interest in books emerged) are difficult to interpret and recall. Unlike teachers, parents are apt to lack a comparative frame of reference. For example, questions about the size of their child's vocabulary or the relative sophistication of the child's sense of humor are difficult for many parents to answer accurately.

PRODUCT SAMPLING

Products provide information about how students perform in terms of critical and creative thinking in various content areas or provide information about prior achievements or awards. Products collected over time have the advantage of showing a profile of student growth and learning, but they also have limitations. First, it can be difficult to assess the relative performance of students with product samples because evaluation criteria frequently are not clear and well defined. Second, using multiple judges and holistic scoring can increase the cost of the assessment process. Third, teachers and program administrators do not often have access to products and achievements of students outside school (or outside the teacher's classroom), and important information may be missing.

SELF-NOMINATION

Perhaps the most direct method of assessment involves self-nomination by the student for various programs. Though many would guess that such a procedure would result in massive amounts of overreferral, there is evidence that self-nomination is as effective as other nomination methods. Shore and Tsiamis (1986) conducted a study in which they selected students for a university-based summer program in two ways. One group was required to submit standardized achievement test data and teacher checklists. The other group was asked only to submit a letter from a teacher saying the student might benefit from the program. In fact, the letters were never examined and were used only to ensure a minimal amount of student interest. When the two groups of students were compared, the researchers discovered that they were equivalent in aptitude and achievement. Students who had selected themselves actually had the same characteristics as those who underwent external review.

There are several limitations on the value of self-referrals. First, young children may not be aware of their abilities to perform in novel settings. Descriptions that emphasize the fun and exciting elements of programs and underplay the difficulty of the academic demands may be so appealing that they attract students who are more hopeful than accurate about their abilities to perform adequately. Self-nomination does, however, provide the benefit of opening involvement in programs and can help students identify interests that school personnel may not have witnessed.

INTERPRETING DATA COLLECTED DURING ASSESSMENT

There are three basic approaches to analyzing assessment data and determining which students are eligible for services in gifted education. The first approach is to gather several measures on relevant traits and set acceptable minimum criteria or thresholds for each measure. Students who do not meet the minimum criteria on any individual measures are then eliminated from the selection process. The second approach is to organize the data into matrices. This involves assigning values to various levels of performance for each of the instruments. Results are then summed, and students are selected for participation based on their overall scores.

A third approach is to create profiles of students' abilities. Profiles are visual representations of the information collected in the assessment. They can illustrate the relative ability levels within individual students as well characterize the patterns of talent of the group of students that is participating in or seeking service from an existing program. Profile analysis has three advantages over the other two methods. First, it allows for consideration of data that are not drawn from test scores (e.g., student awards and achievements, whether the student has participated in gifted programs in the past). Second, it allows for comparisons of the patterns of talents and interests that may go beyond the specific focus of the program, thus letting educators, students, and parents make judgments about the appropriateness of a special program or academic option (Southern, Spicker, Kierouz, & Kelly, 1990).

None of the selection processes are without potential problems, and errors in selection will occasionally occur. Students may be erroneously excluded from or placed in programs. It is therefore good practice to develop and expect to use an appeals process. Appeals may be made by teachers, parents, or students. The process should allow new information to be introduced that might be relevant to reconsiderations of initial selection decisions.

EDUCATIONAL PRACTICES

Evidence-based educational practices are recommended for addressing the instructional and social needs of students with gifts and talents. We first address the thorny issue of early intervention and then focus on strategies for providing academic and social support.

EARLY INTERVENTION

Early intervention for students with gifts and talents is not mandated by law as it is for students with disabilities. Early identifications are usually made when a young child demonstrates very atypical performances that alert or even alarm their parents. Parents often seek interventions when children learn to read without instruction at 3 or 4 years of age, when they are able to solve problems adults do not expect them to perform, or when they have rapidly expanding and astonishing supplies of knowledge. Keep in mind that the absence of these kinds of behaviors doesn't mean a child is not gifted. However, when such evidence is observed, it is a signal to parents and educators that some unusual and rather immediate efforts may be needed. Early intervention for students with gifts and talents, however, is rare. Schools in most states are not required to provide services, and parents are generally unaware of potential need and benefit. Hence, most instances of these services revolve around prodigious achievement. Many districts actively discourage parents from pursuing any service. When suggestions are made, they generally revolve around some form of acceleration (e.g., early admission or grade skipping).

As students progress though school, the pressure for services generally increases for those who have mastered the curriculum or for those who are not adapting to school-related provisions. These students are mismatched with the curriculum (see the "Site Visit" feature). Various other issues may come into consideration, but choices of whether to offer accelerative options or enrichment options generally revolve around the following five factors.

1. *Adequacy of general education curriculum.* In some cases there may be serious questions about whether or not the curriculum is too "dumbed down" (Renzulli, 2002) to be of significant value even if the student could proceed through it rapidly.
2. *Ability of student to handle the demands of more rapid presentation of content or placement in higher-level classes.* Determine if the student can adapt to the rapid pace of instruction and the increasing complexity of the material being presented.
3. *Separation from age-level peers.* If parents or educators think that there is too much risk to social/emotional adjustment, accelerative options such as grade skipping and early entrance are rejected in favor of options that allow the student to remain with age-level peers.

Reflective Exercise #6
Describe an evaluation system that you believe would result in more equitable identifications among economically disadvantaged and ethnically diverse students.

www.prenhall.com/rosenberg

Site Visit:
Effective Practices in Action

One of the most consistently troubling issues in the education of the gifted is the disappearing culturally diverse learner—disappearing, that is, from advanced level programs at middle and high school levels. This is particularly true in mathematics and the sciences. Project EXCITE is a collaborative project involving Northwestern University's Center for Talent Development, Evanston/Skokie School District 65, and Evanston Township High School District 202. The goal of the project is to address the problem of underrepresentation in advanced programs that accelerate learning and provide stimulating instruction (Olszewski-Kubilius, Lee, Ngoi, & Ngoi, 2004).

The first cohort of Project EXCITE third graders was selected during the 2000–2001 school year; these students are now in their sixth and final year of the program as eighth graders. The project is designed to provide a two-tiered intervention program for 20 to 25 students per year. During the first year of the cohort, students attend enrichment classes at their home school after the regular school day. These include science and math enrichment taught by district teachers. Students also attend a two-week summer program on the Northwestern University campus where classes are taught by faculty from local high schools and colleges. Elementary school children extract DNA from strawberries, do Lego math, and visit the high school's nature center. Activities such as measuring their own heart rates, calculating horsepower, dissecting pigs, and mixing two clear chemicals to make a bright yellow one motivate students to come back. In subsequent years, the cohort participates in Saturday enrichment classes on topics such as robotics, neuroscience, advanced math, and solving math-contest problems. They continue to attend summer programs with gifted students who are participating in one of the national academic talent searches from the midwest region and students who have taken and excelled at the Explore eighth-grade achievement test, the SAT, or the ACT as fourth through eighth graders. The program includes the opportunity to enroll in nationally accredited coursework in math and science at the high school level and to achieve appropriate recognition for academic attainment.

Parent involvement is a critical component. Meetings are scheduled throughout the year to provide information and support to the project EXCITE parents as well as to give them an opportunity to meet and network with other Project EXCITE parents. Prior to the meetings, parents are notified by mail regarding the time, date, and place. They also receive agendas. Coordinators also call parents prior to the meetings to stress the importance of attendance. Those parents unable to attend, however, are subsequently mailed any information distributed at the meetings. Northwestern University students are recruited to serve as volunteer tutors for the project. For those EXCITE students who may need extra help, particularly in mathematics, this provides an additional support system.

The results have been gratifying. Attrition rate across the six-year program is low and mainly attributable to mobility of students. For the first cohort of 17 students, 15 were placed in algebra, honors algebra, or honors geometry. They represent some of the first and only culturally diverse students in these classes, and the number is twice the historic average in the district before EXCITE. The program has been described as a preventative to the low expectations these students frequently experience as well as a "rocket launcher" for attainment. The project's heavy commitment to accelerative options has resulted in diverse students' enrollment in some of these advanced courses for the first time. During the 2006–2007 school year, one student in the eighth grade has been recommended for participation in honors trigonometry and as a sophomore will be on track for honors calculus. He will be the first African American in the district participate in these classes at such an early age.

4. *Skepticism about accelerating the curriculum.* If school personnel are opposed to acceleration, they may consciously or unconsciously place road blocks in the way of the intervention.
5. *Missing important instruction.* Not having certain instruction could disadvantage the student during future learning activities (Shore, Cornell, Robinson, & Ward, 1991).

ACADEMIC INTERVENTIONS

For students with gifts and talents, academic interventions center on six dimensions: *content, complexity, abstraction, pacing, documenting achievement,* and *choice and independence* (Maker & Nielson, 1996).

Content

Students who are identified as gifted require advanced content instruction either because they have generally mastered content at earlier ages or because they can master content at a faster pace. Perhaps the most easily identifiable characteristic of such students is their vast store of information. It is critical that a teacher offer greater and more varied academic content to such learners.

Complexity

The content for students with gifts and talents should be more complex. It should include multiple perspectives, multiple implications, and advanced demands on the learner to see interactions with other areas of study. Compared to students with more typical academic capacities, students with gifts and talents are capable of considering more variables as they contemplate problems. They are also capable of understanding abstractions to a greater degree than other children of the same chronological age. In fact, most gifted children relish this capacity. Unlike children with cognitive deficits, they are capable of intuitive leaps. However, without providing gifted students with access to opportunities to demonstrate their capacities, their teachers will not be able to observe the facility with which they can learn. Limits to opportunities will be repaid with limits in achievement.

Abstraction

For many children with exceptionalities, a major challenge for educators is to provide concrete instruction that avoids ambiguities and abstractions. With children who have gifts, differentiation of instruction requires efforts to allow increased abstraction of principles, ideas, and examples. These students ask a great many more questions, such as

What if the events in history did not happen?
Why were the outcomes of the War of 1812 so beneficial to the status quo?
What would have occurred if steam had become the predominant motorcar fuel in the 1920s?

Pacing

If the most apparent trait of children identified as gifted is their ability to learn quickly and easily, then the most important implication is that they should be provided a rapid or accelerated pace of instruction. Teachers must be aware of the need to quickly and efficiently assess the current state of learning for their students. They also need to adequately assess this learning and to document it for the next levels of instruction.

Documenting Achievement

The teacher has to prove that the student has met achievement criteria. In our age of accountability, this is difficult. In order for a third-grade teacher to assure a fourth-grade teacher (or a fifth- or sixth-grade teacher) that a student is truly competent, he must provide very thorough documentation of curriculum compacting and must participate in consultations during the process. It can sometimes be a challenge to collaborate and to document achievement across grade levels.

www.prenhall.com/rosenberg

Choice and Independence

Nearly every theorist in gifted education suggests that student choice is extremely important. Four variables are key in exercising choice (Treffinger & Barton, 1988):

- Content, or the area of interest to be studied
- Process, or the way one should pursue the investigation
- Product, or the way one will show the results of the investigation
- Evaluation, or the way one will view the success of the investigation

Treffinger and Barton (1988) note that students are not generally encouraged to make choices. Teachers generally provide the content to be studied, the media for learning, and the product to be delivered. Students with gifts and talents, however, should be given these choices (see the "Highly Effective Instructional Strategies" feature).

TRANSITION TO ADULT LIFE

Very little research has been done on the transition to adulthood among those with gifts and talents. What we do know comes from longitudinal studies of very specific populations of students (e.g., Noble, Subotnik, & Arnold, 1999). Individuals identified as gifted often choose career paths and academic interests early and concentrate on achieving career goals. Others, however, seem paralyzed by the multiplicity of options available, even to the point where they cannot choose. As adults, these individuals often express regret for choices made and options not selected (Berger, 1991).

If we are to assist these students, we need to make them aware of the implications of choices they are making along the way in school and of the fact that as adults they may pursue multiple careers and pathways. A major goal of counseling students with gifts and talents about adulthood is to prepare them for careers and career change.

Facilitating transitions to higher levels of academic demand and social expectation can be facilitated through counseling that focuses on (1) early academic guidance, (2) awareness of self-perception, and (3) dealing with transition stages.

Early Academic Guidance

Students with gifts and talents, especially those who are exceptionally capable, benefit from early guidance that points out ways to access the academic pathways open to them. Casey and Shore (2000) noted that these students are often unaware of potential careers and may have choices pressed on them by family or caregivers that are not consistent with their temperament and/or their abilities. Any discussions of accelerative options should also be accompanied by counseling on curricular and adjustment issues. Such guidance and counseling are appropriate considerations for students in upper elementary programs on through early entrants to college and university. Students intending to access more advanced studies will need advice on what preliminary or related coursework to take. They will also benefit from considerations of the potential repercussions of their decisions. Early on, advisors are able to help easily. As the student becomes more advanced, however, helping becomes more difficult. For example, if a child is doing fourth-grade work in the second grade, the curricular issues and personal challenges are fairly easy to predict. If the student is doing 11th-grade work in middle school, it is more difficult to readily anticipate issues or concerns. A freshman taking graduate courses may baffle the most informed counselor.

As students with gifts and talents advance through the school curriculum and the established grades, it is very important to have a well-written plan that both documents progress and provides a mentor to help navigate each level of schooling. The more these students diverge from "normal" development, the greater the need for explicit planning statements.

Providing choices in content as well as how it is studied, represented, and evaluated are critical variables in instruction for students with gifts and talents.

Reflective Exercise #7
How can teachers provide choices to students without giving up control over the curriculum? **To hear and see students like you discuss this topic, go to the Students to Students module on the DVD-ROM and click on clip 9: Gifted & Talented.**

Highly Effective Instructional Strategies

CURRICULAR RESPONSIVENESS FOR INCREASING CULTURAL DIVERSITY

Most students in academic programs for students with gifts and talents are white and from fairly affluent homes where English is the primary if not the only language. Our nation is, however, increasingly multicultural, and an important policy issue is to include students from diverse cultures in academic programs for gifted students. In pursuit of greater inclusiveness, three issues are of particular importance: identification, retention, and curriculum.

The most important components of these efforts include

- Training teachers to be thoughtful, fair, and watchful in looking for performances that indicate precocious learning or potential for achievement or talent in all populations
- Considering which characteristics tend to hide students in various populations from identification for gifted programs

- Identifying instruments that are the most representative for local populations and curricular offerings
- Frequently analyzing local outcomes of evaluations that include gender, ethnicity and race, as well as socioeconomic status representations in the identified gifted population
- Examining the degree to which transportation and other financial demands disenfranchise various culturally and economically diverse groups
- Considering inequities of opportunities for culturally diverse students to access the logistics and resources of gifted programs

Once these students are identified, we need to make greater efforts to retain them in programs. Culturally diverse students leave programs at higher rates than do middle-class Caucasian students. Many students from cul-

Like students with other exceptionalities, students with gifts and talents who are transitioning to adulthood often require instruction and counseling in essential life skills.

Awareness of Self-Perception

We know that there are several predictable transition stages for gifted individuals. We also know that the students may choose dysfunctional ways to redefine themselves. To assist in the transitions, it is important to help students know that changes are coming, to arm them with awareness of pitfalls, and to help them select constructive ways of dealing with new academic and societal expectations. Counseling for successful transitions for gifted children involves life skills, just as it does for other exceptionalities.

www.prenhall.com/rosenberg

turally diverse backgrounds perceive gifted programs as culturally alien places. When they are included in gifted programs, culturally diverse students often see fewer (if any) students like themselves. It is difficult for them to not have feelings of alienation from more typically identified gifted students. They also may feel pressured to avoid acculturation into white, middle-class expectations and values (Ford & Harris, 2000). As a consequence, ethnically diverse students leave these programs at rates that accelerate with age. Clearly, if culturally diverse students don't feel welcome, they will not stay.

One way to make culturally diverse students feel welcome is to make the curriculum responsive to their presence and to represent their interests and strengths in programming. Too often, the curricular demands and content of gifted students have oriented to traditional middle-class, Eurocentric values. The following suggestions can contribute to a better fit between student and curriculum:

1. Be inclusive of the groups targeted for differential identification and retention.
2. Ensure that the curriculum samples from experiences of culturally diverse groups.
3. Avoid materials, texts, and activities that are culturally biased.

4. Program appropriate opportunities to express and explore cultural differences among names, experiences, holidays, and literature.
5. Be aware of how cultural differences are related to performance expectations. For example, some groups of children do not feel comfortable in competitive situations, and others may shy away from face-to-face confrontation.
6. Recognize accomplishment but remember that, within some cultures, individual praise may not be perceived as rewarding.

Experience with and sensitivity to diverse cultural perspectives yields many benefits and is essential to providing adequate services for students who show evidence of high aptitude. For gifted students from culturally diverse backgrounds, careful and open-minded planning and the selection of relevant curriculum are especially important issues.

Activity: Go to the Video Classroom section of the Teacher Prep website, click on Multicultural Education and then module 3: Ethnicity and Race. Watch videos 1 and 2 and answer the accompanying questions. Think about the importance of appropriate materials selection for students.

PREVAILING ISSUES, CONTROVERSIES, AND IMPLICATIONS FOR THE TEACHER

The most important issues affecting gifted education are related to the difficulties of defining intelligence, creativity, and giftedness. These concepts are critical to defining the nature of giftedness, but there is little substantive agreement on what they mean. On the other hand, debates about the nature and varieties of intelligence have been constructive. We now have a broader appreciation for the nature of intelligence and a broader view of student needs. There has not been enough discussion about the concepts of talent or creativity. As a result, those issues are even more ill-defined than intelligence and giftedness are. Unfortunately, the imprecision makes advocacy and programming difficult.

Other factors linked directly to policies concerning gifted students include (1) declining quality of education and reform, (2) underrepresented groups of students, (3) accountability, and (4) updating standards.

DECLINING QUALITY OF EDUCATION AND REFORM

There are increased demands on schools to be accessible to and successful for all students. These demands often lead to simplification of curriculum materials for general education (Renzulli & Reis, 1991). The issue is important because high-quality educational programs are at the core of the best gifted education.

The most recent round of educational reform efforts began more than a decade ago in response to general and growing dissatisfaction with public education. While the reforms raise possibilities for improving education for students with gifts and talents, reforms also pose threats. Gallagher (1993) argues that school failure is not only rooted in educational problems. It is also likely to be the result of societal problems. Renzulli and Reis (1991) observe that reform proposals consistently address goals of excellence in achievement for the most promising students and/or goals of equal opportunity and access for disadvantaged and at-risk students. These may be viewed as competing goals. For the teacher, this may cause anxiety or a rejection of one or the other general goals. It does not need to be so. Schools can pursue excellence and rigor for all students.

Teachers are bombarded by reformist calls for the elimination of ability grouping, implementation of cooperative learning, adoption of middle school student/teacher teaming, establishment of master or mentor teachers, institution of site-based management, accountability, and adoption of inclusion policies. Each of these elements of reform has important merits; but unfortunately, as policy initiatives, many are based on misinterpretations and misapplications of the research.

UNDERREPRESENTED GROUPS OF STUDENTS

Students who are challenged by economic disadvantage are not only hard to identify as having gifts and talents but also difficult to retain in specialized programs. Economically disadvantaged students face disruptions, pressures, and distractions that threaten their educational careers (Maker, 1989). They face greater demands to work in order to support their own financial needs and perhaps the needs of their families. It is important for teachers to be aware of these problems and to encourage and assist in retention.

Students with gifts and talents who also have disabilities represent another group that is seriously underserved. These students can be difficult to identify, and their unique programming needs can be difficult to meet in gifted programs. The disability need not result in a decrease in ability or aptitude, but it may necessitate alternate approaches to assessment and instruction. All teachers need to separate the disability from the underlying gifts. Some children actually use their gifts and talents to mask their disabilities in other areas.

ACCOUNTABILITY

Providing for the special educational needs of students with gifts and talents requires expenditures of time and resources. It is important that gifted education programs be based on defensible service models. Local implementations of gifted education programs should also be evaluated to determine their effectiveness. It is important to evaluate instructional arrangements that involve high-ability students but are not specifically designed for their benefit—particularly if the application is potentially controversial. For example, cooperative learning is a widely recommended practice in general education classrooms (Slavin, 1990a), but discussions in the literature suggest that it is a controversial arrangement for gifted students (Robinson, 1990; Slavin, 1990b). The fact is that cooperative learning arrangements are applied in general education programs, and high-achieving students are included. The challenge for teachers is to make data-based decisions about implementing any educational option.

UPDATING STANDARDS

As in other areas of special education, the education of students with gifts and talents has a set of standards for teachers entering the field. The standards were developed under the auspices of the Council for Exceptional Children (CEC) with the participation of The Association for the Gifted (TAG, a division of CEC). The resulting standards were designed to provide uniform language for all special education teachers entering the field. In many instances, the language was not entirely appropriate for teachers of the gifted. During the most recent revision of teacher standards, two professional organizations, the National Association for Gifted Children and TAG, collaborated to produce a set of draft standards that will serve as the base for National Council for Accreditation of Teacher Education (NCATE) and Interstate New Teacher Assessment and Support Consortium (INTASC) standards. One major feature of the revision going on throughout NCATE is a move from identifying coursework that is supposed to provide the knowledge and skills that pre-service teachers need to have to be qualified to teach gifted students.

In many areas of special education, national examinations are required before certification/licensure. To date, there are no specific national examinations to demonstrate knowledge and skills in gifted education. For states that require endorsement, certification, or licensure (currently 21), requirements usually list courses or competencies.

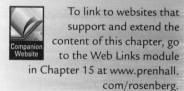
To link to websites that support and extend the content of this chapter, go to the Web Links module in Chapter 15 at www.prenhall. com/rosenberg.

www.prenhall.com/rosenberg

SUMMARY

Students with gifts and talents have demonstrated or show potential for achieving knowledge and skills at significantly higher levels and at faster rates than their age-level peers. The tasks for teachers are the same as the tasks of educators of students with other special learning needs. Gifted children must be identified; decisions must be made about what and how they should be taught. Their progress needs to be evaluated and planned for.

Definitions and Classification Criteria

- Three common definitions of giftedness are the Marland federal definition, Renzulli's three-ring conceptualization, and Gardner's multiple intelligences approach.
- Giftedness is usually classified by (1) types of gifts and talents and (2) level of giftedness.

Primary Behavioral Characteristics

- Early conceptualizations of giftedness were flawed and perpetuated mistaken stereotypes of individuals with superior mental health or of people who were physically weak, oversensitive, and highly productive.
- Current studies have found that students with gifts and talents vary greatly and have a range of positive and negative traits and patterns of behavior.
- As students with gifts progress in school, a major challenge is redefining their life roles, clarifying aspirations, and selecting careers.

Prevalence and Causal Factors

- Prevalence rates of students with gifts and talents vary widely and typically range from 5 to 20% of the school-age population.
- Although speculations as to where giftedness comes from remain controversial, most believe that it is rooted in a genetic/environmental interaction.

Identification and Assessment

- Standardized intelligence tests alone are not useful for identifying students who could benefit from gifted programming.

- The most useful identification processes use multiple criteria that supplement intelligence tests with achievement tests, creativity tests, teacher nominations, peer nominations, parent nominations, student self-nominations, and product samples.

Educational Practices

- Early intervention for students with gifts and talents is rare and usually provided to those with prodigious achievement.
- The decision to offer accelerative or enrichment options for students in school revolves around five factors: adequacy of the general education curriculum, ability of students to handle demands, risk of separation from age-related peers, skepticism about acceleration, and the risk of missing instruction.
- Successful academic interventions for students with gifts and talents focus on content, complexity, abstraction, pacing, documenting achievement, and choice and independence.
- Transitions to higher levels of academic demand are facilitated by counseling that focuses on early academic guidance, awareness of self-perception, and strategies for dealing with change.

Prevailing Issues

- The most important issues affecting the education of students with gifts and talents relate to the difficulties inherent in defining intelligence and creativity.
- Factors influencing policies toward the education of students with gifts and talents include the declining quality of general education and school reform efforts, underrepresentation of certain groups among those identified as having gifts and talents, accountability, and the need to update standards.

 Council for Exceptional Children **ADDRESSING THE PROFESSIONAL STANDARDS**

Council for Exceptional Children (CEC) Knowledge Standards addressed in the chapter:

CC1K5, GC1K1, GC4K5, CC4S3, CC5K4, GC7S2, CC10S2

Appendix B: CEC Knowledge and Skill Standards Common Core has a full listing of the standards referenced here.

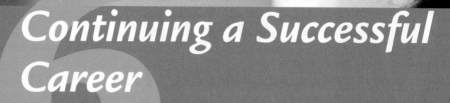

Continuing a Successful Career

Professionalism, Collaborative Support, and Professional Development

REFLECT UPON

- What activities and actions help beginning teachers develop into special education professionals?

- What key elements of support help new special education teachers navigate early career development?

- What actions can new teachers of students with disabilities take to contribute, maintain, and represent ongoing personal and professional growth?

- What strategies help keep special educators invigorated and committed to their students and profession?

James McLeskey

"The most effective special education teachers are those who can effectively manage the educational system so that the needs of students with disabilities are met using effective practices. This is often a very difficult task which is unique for each student and requires teachers to continually learn and grow as professionals. Professional educators engage in this work for one reason—they care so deeply for each child they serve."

David L. Westling

"Being an effective professional is a life style, not a life outcome. To become an effective professional, a teacher needs to view learning as an ongoing process. One of the most interesting things about teaching students with special needs is that one student's needs can be very different than those of another. This requires you to seek out new opportunities to learn so that you can be an effective educator for all of the students you teach. Undoubtedly, your experience will give you an invaluable set of tools to be successful in the classroom, but you also need to take advantage of more formal opportunities to learn."

Michael S. Rosenberg

"Highly effective special education teachers recognize that their training is just the start of their professional development. Reading the current literature, attending conferences sponsored by professional organizations, and interacting with other experienced educators are all opportunities for beginning teachers to hone their craft and better serve their students."

Many beginning teachers experience difficulties due to feelings of isolation, confusion about role expectations, and excessive paperwork.

As we begin this final chapter of the text, we would like you to reflect back to several of the more personal topics presented in Chapter 1. Recall that we asked you to consider whether a career spent teaching students with disabilities was for you. We presented what is special about special education and highlighted the roles, responsibilities, and work settings typical of special education teachers. Most important, we shared personal qualities—attributes, **dispositions,** and characteristics—that are prerequisites for a successful teaching career. For example, we emphasized that effective teachers value diversity and recognize that it is their responsibility to teach all students regardless of needs or challenging conditions. We concluded the chapter by asking you if providing service to others, helping influence the lives of young people, and improving society could provide you with the personal satisfaction you might want in a career.

In the subsequent chapters of the text, we introduced you to exceptional special educators. Our intent was to illustrate how individuals with the appropriate personal qualities find their roles and experience the rewards of teaching students with various disabilities. Our goal was to encourage those of you with the appropriate dispositions to consider a career in special education. Our hope was that you may continue pursuing this career path, taking more content-specific courses, participating in a variety of field experiences, engaging in relevant professional development, and eventually entering the classroom as a teacher. For those already teaching, perhaps we were able to provide you with some information on how to better serve your students and navigate through the demanding situations typical of a quick start in the classroom.

Whatever your situation, you know or will soon realize that the first years of teaching students with special education needs is challenging. Many preservice and beginning teachers have difficulties because of (1) feelings of isolation, (2) confusion regarding roles and responsibilities, and (3) work-related issues such as excessive paperwork and limited planning time (see Billingsley, 2005; Gersten, Keating, Yovanoff, & Harniss, 2001; Kozleski, Mainzer, & Deshler, 2000). Some people—in fact, far too many—leave the profession completely, but you do not have to be part of this group. Those considering or beginning a career in special education help themselves by participating actively in their own professional growth and well-being. Those who thrive in the classroom understand what it means to be a professional, are aware of the supports available to help them succeed, take charge of their ongoing growth and development, and use proactive strategies to remain invigorated and enthusiastic.

BECOMING A SPECIAL EDUCATION PROFESSIONAL

Broadly defined, **professionalism** is an inclusive pattern of behavior that includes respect, responsibility, communication, leadership, risk taking, ongoing development, and a positive attitude (see Grouse, 2003; Kramer, 2003; Phelps, 2006). Professional behavior involves persevering in the face of intermittent successes and remaining poised when encountering frustrating situations. Let's consider the variety of ways in which one develops as a professional.

Reflective Exercise #1

Put yourself into the role of a committee member seeking to fill several special education teaching positions in your school district. What essential qualities, characteristics, and dispositions are you looking for in applicants? **To hear and see students like you discuss this topic, go to the Students to Students module on the DVD-ROM and click on clip 4: Attitudes & Dispositions.**

DEVELOPING PROFICIENCY

Professions are knowledge-based occupations requiring specialized expertise. Professionals recognize that initial preparation alone is not sufficient for professional success. Teachers develop professionally by consistently enhancing their content expertise and instructional delivery skills. Areas in which teachers regularly seek to improve their proficiency include

- Assessing for diversity of learning styles and levels of competence among students
- Developing meaningful learning activities that bring curricular objectives, concepts, and learning principles to life
- Providing adaptations, supports, and **assistive technology** to learners who require specialized accommodations
- Managing the learning environment in a positive manner, ensuring that all students have an opportunity to access instruction
- Delivering instruction in a culturally responsive fashion

"My colleagues tell me that my students tend to take on certain parts of my personality. If true, this is quite satisfying. I present a very strong work ethic, and my students reflect this in their work and when they advocate for themselves."

Monique Green, Prince Georges County, Maryland

CARING FOR STUDENTS AND FAMILIES

Professional special educators demonstrate explicitly that they care for their students. Caring—responding regularly to the physical and emotional needs of children—facilitates and complements instruction. Caring teachers remain vigilant about in-school and out-of-school factors that impede student success. This awareness is as simple as recognizing the best time to provide a mid-morning break from reading activities to more complicated and diplomatic matters such as alerting families to free breakfast and lunch programs. On rare occasions, caring teachers have the troubling task of reporting instances of child abuse and neglect. Caring also involves advocacy for the legal rights of students with disabilities, ensuring that due process protections are honored and mandated services delivered.

When it comes to caring interactions with families, teachers communicate "more in attitude than, hours" (Rosenberg, O'Shea, & O'Shea, 2006, p. 311). Connecting successfully with parents requires a host of interpersonal communication skills such as effective listening, nonjudgmental questioning, flexibility, and compromise. Through open, honest, and positive discussions designed to promote school-home coordination, professional teachers dispel the often-held perception that only appreciative, flattering, uncritical, and noninterfering interactions are welcome at school.

Reflective Exercise #2
How can you distinguish a teacher who cares for students from one who does not? Can caring be taught in a teacher preparation program, or do you believe it is a disposition or character trait that one must have before entering teaching?

Students need to know that their teachers care for them and respect them as individuals. I try to speak informally with each of my students throughout the day, seeking to build positive relationships. I have found that these brief interactions are an important precondition for motivation, achievement, and appropriate behavior.

Bobby Biddle, science teacher, Herndon Middle School, Fairfax County, Virginia

Communicating effectively with parents requires effective listening, flexibility, and nonjudgmental questioning.

BEING A PUBLIC FIGURE

Inherent in developing professionally is recognizing that teachers are always in the public eye. What you do and how you act, both inside and outside the classroom, are topics of discussion around countless family dinner tables and community social events. Teachers are positive ambassadors to the public, highlighting the accomplishments of the school-based learning team, being responsive to parent and community concerns, and serving as sources of information (Feiman-Nemser & Floden, 1986; Kauchak & Eggen, 2005). Never underestimate the value and trust that the public places on teacher communication. Polls indicate that 88% of American parents consider their child's teacher the most credible source of information on educational issues, well ahead of clergy and members of the media (Richardson, 1999). Moreover, parents in crisis over the care and safety of their children depend on the responsiveness of well-informed educators.

ADDRESSING PAPERWORK AND LEGAL RESPONSIBILITIES

Most educators agree that the paperwork requirements associated with teaching students with disabilities are excessive and burdensome. In fact, many report that they spend more time on legal and compliance paperwork than on directly teaching students with disabilities (President's Commission on Excellence in Special Education, 2002). Teachers are typically responsible for (1) screening and prereferral documentation, (2) documentation of student progress, (3) formal and informal assessments, (4) eligibility and placement information, (5) IEPs, and (6) FBAs. These are useful documents that contribute to the creation of effective learning environments for students and an organized workplace for adults (Rosenberg et al., 2006). Since the completion of important documentation requires attention, patience, and effort, a professional approach to paperwork management is warranted (Billingsley, 2005; Kozleski et al., 2000; Rosenberg et al., 2006):

- Remain aware of required paperwork and frequently updated forms.
- Develop a plan for handling paperwork. Organize and review due dates and multiple requests to ensure necessity, clarify requirements, and eliminate redundancy.
- Delegate, whenever possible, routine clerical tasks to support personnel.
- Use technology and data-based software to organize relevant student data and facilitate report preparation. Electronic case-management tools can assist with record keeping, data analysis, and the monitoring of instructional accommodations.
- Develop and use standardized tools and universal design to record and document student performance.

Reflective Exercise #3
Special education teachers often cite the considerable paperwork as one reason for leaving the profession. What aspects of documentation can be reduced without endangering legal compliance? What specific time-management strategies can be used to minimize the impact of paperwork and documentation on instructional time?

www.prenhall.com/rosenberg

Teachers are legally responsible for their students. **In loco parentis**—the same judgment and care exercised by parents in protecting their children—is the legal principle used to assess the extent of a teacher's professional responsibility for students' well-being. If teachers fail to protect students from injury, they are considered negligent and, with their school districts, subject to legal actions (Kauchak & Eggen, 2005). Accidents happen whenever groups of active children share a common space. However, because of their behavioral profiles, students with disabilities have an increased probability of mishaps. In addition to purchasing liability insurance (which is recommended and often offered by professional teaching associations; see Figure 16.1), teachers can take several precautions to minimize risk (Kauchak & Eggen, 2005; Westling & Korland, 1988). First and foremost, try to anticipate troubling and dangerous circumstances and make every effort to protect students from such situations. One way is to establish and reinforce concrete rules and procedures that prompt students about potentially dangerous situations. Second, professionalism involves delivering a standard of care that corresponds to the environment, situation, and characteristics

"I'm scrappy. I like a good fight, and special education provides that. I'm also on the side of the underdog, and that makes it difficult to be successful. It's a challenge. I don't mind losing many of the battles as long as I win the war. Special education provides an opportunity to work for human rights. Inclusion is obviously a human right. The more we can work to enhance the inclusion of people with disabilities, the better place the world will be."

Robert Hessels, middle school special education teacher, Howard Bishop Middle School, Gainesville, Florida

FIGURE 16.1

IS THERE A NEED FOR LIABILITY INSURANCE?

Accidents and mistakes will happen, and working with challenging students can increase the probability that things may go wrong. For better or worse, there is little doubt that we live in an increasingly litigious society. From formal courtrooms to reality-based television shows, large numbers of citizens are seeking legal restitution for actions perceived as offensive, wrongful, and injurious. Regardless of how we feel about the role of malpractice lawsuits in public schools, teachers are liable for the care of their students and may be subject to legal action if students are injured. Recent data suggest that the number of lawsuits against educators has increased more than 270% in the past decade; in fact, more than 1/3 of all high school principals report having been involved in a lawsuit. Parents, students, and even colleagues may use the legal system if they feel they have been injured because of another educator's actions.

Although most school districts have liability insurance, many professional organizations, education law experts, and, not surprisingly, insurance vendors recommend that all educators consider obtaining additional liability insurance (Educators Protection Group, 2005; Henderson, Gullatt, Hardin, Jannik, & Tollett, 1999). Without individual coverage, a teacher would have no choice but to rely on the district's policies and procedures for dealing with liability and could be personally liable if the district's policy is not comprehensive. Determine your need for liability insurance:

- Review the extent of coverage provided by your districts and teacher's association.
- Determine the extent of the school's policy to provide legal representation.
- Assess your exposure to risk. For example, consider the extent of your responsibilities for supervision of challenging students who are prone to injury due to reckless behavior.
- Review the nature of your supervisory responsibilities.
- Determine how much your clinical judgment and decision making may be challenged by others.
- Assess your own emotional reactions to risk and possible legal exposure.

Keep in mind that most liability insurance plans provide up to 2 million dollars in coverage for relatively small premiums. However, most plans do not include criminal actions and corporal punishment where forbidden by law.

To minimize accidents, teachers should anticipate troubling and dangerous circumstances and make every effort to protect students from such situations.

Reflective Exercise #4

In Chapter 7 we discussed why wraparound programming is an essential feature of school programs for students with EBD. How can viewing the neighborhood school as an integrated system of care promote the delivery of wraparound services to all students? How can teachers ensure that involvement in the coordination of services does not cut into instructional time?

of your students. For example, taking students with severe developmental disabilities on a field trip to the mall food court requires structures, support, and supervision of much greater intensity than would be provided to typical high school students eating in their school's cafeteria.

SEEING SCHOOLS AS INTEGRATED SYSTEMS OF CARE

We have emphasized throughout this text that educating students with disabilities (and many without disabilities) requires more than effective academic instruction. To benefit from their education, many students require related services. Consequently, some schools have established school-based, cross-agency systems designed to deliver a comprehensive spectrum of health, mental health, and other necessary services in a coordinated fashion. These activities require teachers to collaborate professionally with other stakeholders who deliver services to students with disabilities, including school-based mental health clinicians, social workers, juvenile justice personnel, and medical professionals. The ancillary activities provided by these specialists are essential for students, and schools are a logical location for coordinating service delivery (Woodruff et al., 1998). These additional responsibilities increase already heavy teacher workloads and reduce time for planning, instruction, and recharging one's batteries. Professional teachers recognize the necessity of these additional demands and account for them within their time-management activities.

BEING AN EDUCATED CONSUMER OF RESEARCH-BASED PRACTICES

As you have read this text, we trust you have noticed that the knowledge base for addressing learning and behavioral difficulties is substantial and useful. Unfortunately, far too few teachers apply what is known with consistency and regularity. Educational research is not viewed as trustworthy, readily accessible, or relevant to many teachers' daily experiences (Kauffman, 1996; Kennedy, 1997). Consequently, empirical evidence is often ignored, and anecdote and appearance influence the selection of instructional practices. When research-based practices are employed, they are too often adapted rather than adopted. Steps in instructional protocols are modified to fit an individual teacher's values, beliefs, and situations rather than being applied as intended. Unfortunately, these changes often alter components of the intervention that make it successful.

Putting research into practice can be challenging. However, increased knowledge and use of validated practices are signs of increased professionalism and occur when teachers do the following (Abbott et al., 1999; Fuchs & Fuchs, 1998):

- Keep up with the relevant literature and participate in educational research activities
- Are educated and skeptical consumers of proposed curricular materials and content-area programs
- Advocate for data-based decision making when making curricular decisions
- Recognize that teaching is both an art and a science, requiring a balance between creativity and fidelity to research-based practices
- Develop action research activities that allow for the data-based evaluation of classroom techniques and interventions

COLLABORATIVE SUPPORT FOR BEGINNING TEACHERS

Even the most enthusiastic, idealistic, and well-prepared teachers of students with disabilities experience pressure, frustration, and periods of disillusionment. These feelings are natural. Students present a wide range of complex academic and behavioral challenges, the roles and responsibilities of addressing student needs are not always well defined, and there is seldom enough time for adequate planning or coordination. You will undoubtedly hear from many veteran teachers that early career challenges shaped their future attitudes, practices, and path to professionalism. How can you survive the mental bumps, bruises, peaks, and valleys typical of early career development? What support systems are available to assist beginning teachers? How can you access this support?

SUPPORT THROUGH LEARNING COMMUNITIES

In past years, teaching was a career characterized by rugged individualism: one knowledgeable adult responsible for the development of students in his or her charge. Isolated teachers were expected to handle their own classrooms and address learning and behavior problems with little assistance from others. Recent research on effective schools has found that individual teacher effectiveness is dependent on a collaborative, supportive, and encouraging professional learning community (Louis, Marks, & Kruse, 1996). Not surprisingly, there is a greater emphasis on educators working together in purposeful groupings or communities.

Professional learning communities share five characteristics: supportive and shared leadership, collective learning, shared values and vision, supportive conditions in human and physical resources, and shared practice (Hord, 1997). Rather than feeling isolated, misunderstood, or not valued—reasons why many teachers leave the field—teachers in professional learning communities have a shared sense of empowerment and purpose. Members of the community believe they are useful and valued contributors to efforts that lead to student achievement.

To learn more about learning communities, go to the Ms. Sprague module on the DVD-ROM and click on clip 4: Learning Community and clip 5: Professional Dev.

Keep in mind, however, that learning communities have their costs. Participation requires time, commitment, diplomacy, and patience. As members of a learning community, teachers are expected to serve on committees, observe their colleagues, be observed by others, as well as participate in functional behavioral assessments (FBAs) and behavior intervention plans (BIPs). Nonetheless, the benefits of having a professional learning community are usually worth the effort and energy. Schools that are challenging, satisfying, empowering, creative, and growth-oriented for adults achieve good outcomes for students (Saphier, 1995).

SUPPORT THROUGH INDUCTION AND MENTORING

Knowing that beginning teachers are both a valuable and fragile resource, many school district administrators have enhanced their induction activities and programs, which are support mechanisms geared to the needs of those new to the field. Characteristics of high-quality **induction** activities include (1) a supportive school culture in which veteran educators are committed to socializing new teachers; (2) frequent opportunities for interactions, including mentoring, between new and experienced teachers; (3) targeted professional development opportunities aimed at improving new teacher performance; and (4) graduated adjustments in the complexity and difficulty of tasks assigned to the beginning teacher (Billingsley, 2005; Griffin, Winn, Otis-Wilborn, & Kilgore, 2003).

The most powerful component in an induction program is the direct contact new teachers have with colleagues. New teachers crave purposeful contact with both experienced teachers and other beginners in similar situations. These opportunities can be a formal, comprehensive, one-to-one mentorship arrangement or part of an overall school- or peer-support team. Effective mentorship and peer-support programs share certain elements. First, there are ample opportunities to take part in problem solving and conflict resolution team activities. Integrated into these activities is an ethic of care, characterized by frequent opportunities for dialogue, reflection, cooperation, questioning, and validation, ingredients essential in effective teams.

> "Early in my career I came to the realization that I didn't have all of the answers and that I needed a lot more help. Thankfully, I worked with a mentor and co-teacher who was knowledgeable and patient. I learned so much from her."
>
> Carol Sprague, Thomas County, Georgia

Second, adequate attention is given to the emotional needs of the new teacher. Novice teachers require trusted guides and confidants, successful mentors who are supportive and empathetic rather than evaluative. Effective mentors and peers create a welcoming school environment, make frequent use of informal meetings, and provide a safe zone for beginning teachers to deal with stress, vent frustrations, and secure emotional first-aid. Finally, effective mentorship activities allow novice teachers to acquire system information, the nuts and bolts of responding to school and district responsibilities and securing resources and materials (Whitaker, 2000).

You can make the most of available induction and mentoring activities by doing the following (Billingsley, 2005; Rosenberg, Griffin, Kilgore, & Carpenter, 1997; Rosenberg et al., 2006):

- **Attend all district, school, and department orientation meetings.**
  These meetings focus on general and special education policies and procedures and provide a forum for understanding the roles and responsibilities of key personnel in the school.

The most powerful component in a new teacher induction program is direct, purposeful contact among experienced teachers and beginning teachers.

www.prenhall.com/rosenberg

- **Recognize the competence of colleagues.** New teachers discover quickly that many of their colleagues—teachers, administrators, and related-service personnel—have their own ways of doing things. In some cases they contradict what you believe or how you were taught. Remain diplomatic. Rather than shutting these individuals out, recognize that much can be learned by understanding why certain professionals act in the manner that they do.
- **Communicate willingness for consultative services.** Consider all forms of assistance as a benefit provided by your school. Be aware that input from colleagues and related-service professionals will help you and your students. For example, veteran teachers and behavior specialists provide useful suggestions about discipline plans, and speech/language pathologists suggest ways to integrate communication strategies into instruction.
- **Reflect on feedback constructively.** It is difficult to avoid being defensive when presented with alternative ways of approaching your job. Nonetheless, when presented with constructive criticism, open your mind to new ideas by listening carefully and reflecting on the information being conveyed. No one expects perfection during the beginning years of a teaching career, and improvements in practice require feedback, reflection, and change.
- **Understand and respect school culture.** Schools are microcosms of society; and appropriately or not, people socialized to the school's existing culture make value judgments about newcomers, sometimes superficially. Remain patient with those who seek to overwhelm you with advice about how to reach your challenging students and avoid flaunting your own knowledge of innovative practices, especially when no one asks your advice. Focus on the positive aspects of school culture and avoid being soured by cynics who appear disillusioned, apathetic, and worn out.

See Figure 16.2 for more suggestions:

FIGURE 16.2

BEGINNING TEACHER SUPPORT IN ACTION: BTSA-SE

The Beginning Teacher Support and Assessment Program for Special Education (BTSA-SE) was designed to support first- and second-year special education teachers in the Los Angeles Unified School District (Kennedy & Burstein, 2004). Unlike generic induction programs, BTSA-SE focuses on the unique responsibilities and challenges faced by teachers of students with disabilities. Specific goals of the program are to ease the transition into teaching for new teachers; improve the educational performance of students through new teacher development; provide information and assistance to new teachers; facilitate retention in urban schools; and enhance collegiality and heighten new teacher confidence.

Several program features form the core of the BTSA-SE program:
- A mentorship component in which nonevaluative support is provided through classroom visitations, after-school meetings, telephone conferences, and e-mail
- Completing new teacher activities as part of California's program for assessing and supporting beginning teachers
- Up to five professional release days for new special educators to observe experienced teachers and/or exemplary programs
- Monthly professional development workshops that focus on the expressed needs of the beginning teachers
- Stipends available for beginning teachers to access conferences and materials

In its first 4 years, 190 beginning special education participated in the program. Beginning teachers accessed most of the activities offered, although workshop attendance was much greater than attendance at professional conferences. However, the most powerful measure of program impact was teacher retention. Among those who participated during the first 3 years of the program, 95% remained on the job. Kennedy and Burstein attribute the success of BTSA-SE to the statewide funding of the program, the range of activities and supports focusing on the expressed needs of beginning special education teachers, and the close collaboration among participating school districts and the university.

SUPPORT THROUGH COLLABORATIVE CONSULTATION AND TEAMING

Collaborative consultation is another structured opportunity to learn from other professionals engaged in work similar to your own. Collaborative practices may take many forms but most often occur through teacher-to-teacher consultation or in collaborative groups.

Teacher-to-Teacher Consultation

Support through teacher-to-teacher consultation typically focuses on everyday classroom concerns (e.g., managing the behavior of disruptive students, developing alternative methods of teaching a child long division, best practices for assessing academic content of resistant students). Collaborative consultation is more than casually talking with another teacher in the hallway or teachers' lounge. It is a formal process that includes (1) specific problem identification and goal setting, (2) analysis of factors contributing to the problem and brainstorming possible problem-solving interventions, (3) planning an intervention, and (4) evaluating the outcomes (Salend, 2005).

Teacher-to-teacher consultation appears direct and straightforward. However, for the process to work, those involved must employ effective interpersonal communication skills. By interpersonal communication skills, we are referring to the processes of active listening, picking up nonverbal signals, effective and appropriate questioning, talking in nonthreatening ways, and expressing ideas clearly (Friend & Cook, 2003). Keep in mind that attitudinal factors contribute greatly to interpersonal communication (Rogers, 1965). For example, positive regard for others—typically demonstrated through the delivery of honest feedback and specific, descriptive encouragement—should be conveyed during all facets of the process. Second, empathy (understanding and concern about what the other person is going through) is an essential part of the process. Finally, effective interpersonal communication requires frequent efforts to monitor congruence—the degree to which a collaborator's perceptions actually correspond to the situation being experienced by the other person. When stakeholders agree upon the patterns of troublesome situations, there is a greater opportunity for honest, sincere, and productive discussions (Rosenberg et al., 2006).

Collaborative Teaming

Collaboration also occurs as part of teacher-assistance problem-solving teams (Chalfant & Pysh, 1989). These teams follow steps similar to those used in teacher-to-teacher collaboration but involve groups of professionals with different types of expertise. This process provides the teacher with possible interventions for a given student situation, allowing increased opportunities for supportive activities such as classroom observations and group brainstorming.

Collaborative teams, often used to address schoolwide issues such as discipline and inclusion, ensure that the shared expertise of multiple professionals is integrated into the important everyday activities of the school and classroom (McLeskey & Waldron, 2000, 2002; Rosenberg & Jackman, 2003). Friend and Bursuck (2006) characterize effective collaborative teams as formal work groups that "have clear goals, active and committed members, and leaders; they practice to achieve their results; and they do not let personal issues interfere with the accomplishment of their goals" (p. 90). Successful teams share the same goal: ensuring that teachers (and other professionals) share their expertise to develop the best possible educational system that effectively meets the needs of all students.

SUPPORT FROM PARAPROFESSIONALS

Many teachers of students with disabilities have the benefit of paraprofessional assistance. Paraprofessionals (1) assist teachers in delivering effective educational programs, (2) provide opportunities for flexible grouping by increasing the adult-student ratio in the classroom, (3) provide additional pairs of eyes to monitor behavior and academic performance, (4) contribute to completion of data-collection and accounta-

Reflective Exercise #5
Why has teaching evolved from an isolated endeavor to a collaborative enterprise? How are the steps involved in collaborative consultation similar to other group problem-solving tasks, such as the development of functional behavior analyses?

bility requirements, and (5) perform numerous important and time-consuming noninstructional tasks. In the teacher-paraprofessional relationship, the teacher is responsible for supervising and managing the paraprofessional, a role that few teachers are formally prepared to undertake (French, 2001).

How can you maximize the effectiveness of paraprofessional support? Most experts (Doyle, 2002; French & Pickett, 1997; Wallace, Bernhardt, & Utermarck, 1999; Warger, 2002; Westling & Korland, 1988) agree that a productive teacher-paraprofessional relationship involves the following:

- Understanding and respecting the roles and responsibilities of paraprofessionals
- Clearly articulating expectations and providing guidance, mentoring, and support
- Being diplomatic; modeling and maintaining effective communication and providing positive feedback for tasks completed appropriately
- Assigning tasks in a fair and reasonable manner; modeling how the task is to be completed
- Sharing relevant information about students with the paraprofessional
- Treating the individual as a valued member of the educational team by encouraging the sharing of observations, suggestions, and concerns
- Scheduling private opportunities to provide formal feedback of paraprofessional performance and never criticizing the paraprofessional in front of students or colleagues

Effective teachers treat paraprofessionals as valued members of the educational team and assign tasks in a fair and respectful manner.

PROFESSIONAL GROWTH AND PERSONAL DEVELOPMENT

The pursuit of success and satisfaction in teaching is a marathon rather than sprint, and those pursuing long-term careers take an active role in their own progress. How can you support yourself and facilitate your own personal and professional growth? Four areas typically require ongoing attention: being resilient, recognizing and managing stress, maintaining highly qualified status, and monitoring and documenting professional growth.

BEING RESILIENT: MANAGING THE UPS AND DOWNS OF TEACHING

When you work with students with special needs, there are going to be days when you feel ineffectual and question your decision to become a teacher. During these down times, you may doubt that you have any positive influence on your students and focus on the negative aspects of your career choice. Fortunately, there are other days when you feel on top of the world, confident in your abilities to meet the social and academic needs of your students. At these times, you will experience **self-efficacy,** the belief that your professional decisions, actions, and choices result in positive outcomes in your students' lives.

Early in your career the down days may seem to outnumber the high self-efficacy days. Consequently, it is important to remember two factors. First, events unrelated to job performance often influence a teacher's attitudes and feelings. Second, days of doubt and unease are part of the human condition. Elements such as health, family circumstances, current world events, and even the weather affect our moods and dispositions (Knowles, Cole, & Presswood, 1994). Although these pressures are always

"One of the most rewarding experiences I had was having a student from a center school for severely emotionally disturbed students where I taught go on to enter a traditional high school and become the student body president. Also satisfying is when former students come back to see me and say, 'You were tough and I thought you were mean but now I get it; look what I'm doing with my life!'"

Suzy
Clary Wilson,
Gainesville, Florida

Reflective Exercise #6

Knowing the importance of navigating through the ups and downs of teaching students with disabilities, how would you advise a colleague who wants to improve his or her level of resiliency? **To hear and see students like you discuss this topic, go to the Students to Students module on the DVD-ROM and click on clip 2: Ups and Downs.**

present in one form or another, the extreme emotional ups and downs will diminish over time. As teachers gain experience and learn from missteps, the frequency and intensity of hardships fade, and instances of success take their place.

Resiliency is the process of adjusting to varied situations and increasing competence in the face of adverse conditions (Gordon & Coscarelli, 1996). Strategies that contribute to the development of resiliency in teachers include the following (Billingsley, 2005; Bobek, 2002):

- Developing and maintaining significant relationships with others who value teaching, communicating honestly and openly, understanding the challenges associated with teaching, and offering tangible suggestions for dealing with problem situations
- Referring back, reflecting upon, and making use of content and pedagogical skills acquired during professional training
- Acknowledging your distinct contributions to your students' success, recognizing that external recognitions of effort are infrequent, and reminding yourself that your actions are instrumental in promoting positive student outcomes
- Establishing realistic expectations for yourself and your students; being aware that the rewards of teaching students with disabilities are often small and incremental
- Working at a reasonable pace, employing time-management strategies, and celebrating all of the little victories associated with your work
- Maintaining a sense of humor; recognizing that humor diffuses tense situations in the classroom and serves as a method for venting frustrations during and after challenging situations

RECOGNIZING AND MANAGING STRESS

As resiliency promotes performance during adverse circumstances, excessive stress produces a series of psychological and physiological responses that inhibits effective actions. All classrooms, regardless of the number of special, at-risk, or typically achieving students, produce organizational pressures that heighten the stress level of teachers. Doyle (1986) has characterized the classroom as a public forum where the teacher is always on stage, responding with limited resources to multiple, immediate, simultaneous, and sometimes unpredictable demands. Although early recognition of the organizational pressures of the classroom can minimize stress, many teachers who work in special education have reported additional pressures—work assignment problems, role definition, feelings of isolation, minimal support—as persistent sources of stress.

There are specific signs and signals of stress, some obvious and others so subtle they may be unrecognizable (see Figure 16.3). How can teachers minimize the stress associated with working with students with disabilities? The keys are maintaining flexibility and taking care of your physical and mental health. First and foremost, expect the unexpected. Westling and Korland (1988) note that, in busy classrooms, events requiring immediate action and attention are going to happen; and unfortunately, they occur when you least think they will. Second, prepare in advance for stressful events by employing time-management strategies. This is done by planning time for specific assignments, not overcommitting, monitoring how your time is spent, and making sure that periods of rest and reflection are built into your day. Finally, maintain a balanced and healthy lifestyle. Physically, stress can be managed through exercise, adequate amounts of sleep, a healthy diet, and self-verbalizations that emphasize the positive side of situations and events.

www.prenhall.com/rosenberg

FIGURE 16.3

OBVIOUS AND SUBTLE SIGNS OF STRESS

Obvious Indicators
  • Avoidance of work
  • Apathy toward students and responsibilities
  • Withdrawal from colleagues
  • High rate of negative self-statements regarding work and self-efficacy
  • Lack of effort and perfunctory performance
  • Frequent physical ailments (headaches, stomachaches, etc.)
Subtle Indicators
  • Irritability with family and colleagues
  • Inability to concentrate for sustained periods of time
  • Decreased productivity
  • Increased eating, smoking, and drinking
  • Feeling bored and exhausted
  • Appearing rigid and angry

BECOMING AND REMAINING HIGHLY QUALIFIED

The requirements of the No Child Left Behind Act have many special education teachers asking a clear and direct question: What does it take to become and remain a highly qualified teacher? Unfortunately, the answer is not nearly as straightforward as the question. In past years, teachers completed an approved course of study, obtained state certification and licensure in their area of expertise, and maintained their skills and knowledge through various forms of ongoing professional development. For the most part, professional development activities were based on standards, guidelines, and requirements set by professional organizations, state education agencies, and local boards of education. Teachers' self-reflection also influenced the selection of activities. Today, the legal definition of what it means to be a highly qualified teacher drives many teachers' thoughts of professional development. Becoming and remaining highly qualified requires an understanding of teaching standards, tests, the high objective uniform state standard of evaluation (HOUSSE), and professional development alternatives (see Figure 16.4).

Professional Teaching Standards

When we speak of professional teaching standards, we are referring to what a teacher should know and what he or she should be able to do (Galluzzo, 1999). Few in the educational establishment disagree with the need for professional teaching standards; they represent tangible benchmarks for initial and continual professional development. Four sets of performance standards are most relevant for those who teach students with disabilities (Dudzinski, Roszmann-Millican, & Shank, 2000):

1. **Interstate New Teacher Assessment and Support Consortium (INTASC).** INTASC standards specify the knowledge, dispositions, and performance indicators for all beginning teachers regardless of content area or grade level. Adopted in 33 states, the core elements of the 10 principles of the standards include subject-matter knowledge, child development, varied instructional strategies, assessment, reflective teaching, and lifelong development.
2. **National Board for Professional Teaching Standards (NBPTS).** NBPTS seeks to advance the quality of teaching by maintaining standards for what accomplished teachers should know and do as well as having a voluntary system for certifying teachers who meet these standards. Five core propositions serve as the foundation for the standards: (a) being committed to students and their learning, (b) knowing the subject matter one teaches and how to teach that subject to students, (c) managing and monitoring student learning, (d) thinking systematically about practice, and (e) being a member of a learning community. Certification involves a

FIGURE 16.4

BECOMING A HIGHLY QUALIFIED SPECIAL EDUCATION TEACHER

Concurrent with the passage of NCLB and the most recent reauthorization of IDEA, there has been an increase in confusion as to what constitutes a highly qualified special education teacher. Although some professional organizations (e.g., National Education Association, National Association of State Directors of Special Education) have advocated that a special educator should be considered highly qualified if licensed or certified, special education is not recognized as a core academic subject area. Consequently, additional requirements must be met for a special educator to be considered highly qualified. How can a teacher determine his or her highly qualified status? Consider the following guidelines developed by NEA and NASDSE (2004):

- The highly qualified requirements apply only to those teachers who provide instruction in core academic subjects; those who provide consultative services (e.g., adapt materials, develop academic and behavioral supports and accommodations) to other highly qualified subject-area teachers do not need subject-matter competency.
- Elementary special education teachers who provide content-area instruction must either pass a state test of subject knowledge and teaching skills in reading, writing, math, and other areas of the basic elementary school curriculum or demonstrate competence in core subject areas by completing a state's HOUSSE.
- Secondary special education teachers who teach subject-area content such as math, science, history, etc., must have had an academic major of coursework equivalent to a major in each of the subjects taught, pass a test determined by their state in each of the areas, or complete HOUSSE requirements within a state-approved time period.

series of performance-based assessments, including portfolios, student work samples, and videotapes of teaching.

3. **Council for Exceptional Children (CEC).** Through its work as the national leader in special education advocacy, CEC has developed a series of performance-based standards that address both categorical and noncategorical licensure and preparation frameworks. In its most recent iteration of *What Every Special Educator Must Know* (2003), CEC details (a) a code of ethics, principles to be applied when meeting day-to-day responsibilities (see Appendix C); (b) a common core of knowledge and skills in 10 areas, including foundations, characteristics, learning differences, instructional strategies, social interactions, language, planning, assessment, professional practice, and collaboration; (c) specialized knowledge and skills to meet the needs of students with specific disabilities (see Appendix B); and (d) tools and strategies for using the standards in the development of professional development plans. (Note that we have keyed the content of this text to these standards at the end of every chapter.)

4. **State standards.** Because certification and licensure are state functions, states have unique standards for initial and ongoing licensure and professional development. In many cases states augment nationally recognized professional standards with additional requirements.

Teacher Tests

To ensure that each of its teachers is highly qualified, many states require a passing score on standardized pencil-and-paper tests of basic academic skills, principles of learning and teaching, and specific subject areas. Among states that require tests, most utilize THE PRAXIS SERIES™ (www.ets.org/praxis), a product of the Educational Testing Service (ETS), to assess various facets of teacher competence. Teaching students with disabilities often requires would-be teachers to pass several Praxis tests. First, it is necessary to pass the Praxis I: Pre-Professional Skills Tests, three separate assessments that tap basic skills in reading, math, and writing. These tests are typically taken early in a student's college career and are often used as a component of admission to the teacher education program.

www.prenhall.com/rosenberg

Second, teachers must take the Praxis II: Subject Assessments, which tests general and specific-subject teaching skills and knowledge (see Appendix A). For special educators, the required tests vary as a function of the ages of the students one intends to teach, the intensity of service delivery in which these students are educated, the types of disabilities they possess, and the nature (i.e., categorical or noncategorical) of certification structure in your state. For example, a resource teacher of elementary students integrated in general education for most of her school day who resides in a noncategorical licensure state is likely to be required to pass (1) Education of Exceptional Students: Core Content Knowledge, (2) Special Education: Application of Core Principles across Categories of Disability, and (3) Principles of Learning and Teaching: Grades K–6. However, a science teacher assigned to a self-contained classroom for secondary students who resides in a categorical licensure state is required to pass (1) Education of Exceptional Students: Core Content Knowledge, (2) Special Education: Teaching Students with Behavioral Disorders/Emotional Disturbances, and (3) a subject assessment in the specific area of science expertise.

Finally, some teachers may be assessed for licensure using the Praxis III, an on-site classroom performance measure that includes direct observation of classroom practice, reviews of documentation prepared by the teacher, and interviews with teacher and relevant colleagues. The emphases of these multiple data sources are on four interrelated domains: planning to teach, the classroom environment, instruction, and professional responsibilities.

HOUSSE Procedures

Veteran teachers demonstrate that they are highly qualified in a variety of ways. HOUSSE, the high objective uniform state standard of evaluation, is a procedure used by states to assess an existing teacher's subject-matter competency in place of a test, coursework, degree, or certification. Although HOUSSE systems vary across states, several general categories of documentation are used to document highly qualified status (Azordegan, 2004):

- **Professional development:** Participation in set amounts of professional development related to the subject taught
- **Performance evaluation:** Observations of teaching by peers or supervisors focusing on content knowledge and instructional skills
- **Portfolio:** A collection of evidence reflecting teacher practice in the subject area (we outline methods for portfolio development later in this chapter)
- **Student achievement data:** An assessment of a teacher's effect on student achievement through test scores
- **Point systems:** Teacher-accumulated points for various professional activities associated with the subject taught, including coursework, professional development activities, awards, recognitions, and student performance data

Ongoing Professional Development

No matter how lengthy or comprehensive an initial preparation program, teachers of students with disabilities recognize quickly that they need more strategies if they are to remain successful. Professional development activities allow teachers to improve their skills by keeping pace with the many innovative changes that impact the field. Effective professional development is not a passive or time-limited undertaking. A common misconception is that professional development activities are contractually mandated presentations, usually directed by school administrators and delivered during one or two inservice days throughout the school year. However, professional development is most useful and effective when individual teachers take an active role in the process. Teachers take this responsibility by (1) recognizing that careers require a lifelong commitment to self-improvement, (2) reflecting on and articulating strengths and needs, (3) developing a development plan, (4) selecting activities that best meet their objectives, and (5) evaluating the effectiveness of selected activities.

As you plan your own activities, keep in mind that professional development is most effective when activities are school-based, embedded in daily routines, balanced between the priorities of the school and teachers, linked directly to student outcomes, delivered in a supportive working environment, and structured in ways that allow teachers

Reflective Exercise #7
Although common in most states, the use of tests to determine teacher licensure remains controversial. Do you believe that a passing score on a test is predictive of success as a teacher of students with disabilities? Would you suggest consideration of any other measures to ensure that teachers are highly qualified?

Reflective Exercise #8
What types of professional development do you find most appealing and beneficial? What activities are particularly rewarding? Identify activities that you find aversive. Given the opportunity, how would you plan and deliver professional development for yourself and your peers?

> "It is incredibly satisfying helping kids transition from being dependent on staff to becoming the most independent person they can become. No one knows everything, so I attend all professional development activities to learn better ways to help my kids."
>
> Kim Thomas

to share their expertise with each other (Dudzinski et al., 2000; Public Education Network, 2004). You can also contribute to your own professional development by becoming active in professional organizations, reading the professional literature, pursuing advanced degrees, and assuming leadership positions.

Professional Organizations. Professional organizations provide a wealth of formal and informal mechanisms for teachers to develop professionally. Most organizations set up conferences with nationally recognized speakers, sponsor staff development activities, and publish periodicals that focus on current issues and innovations in research and development. In addition to providing a wealth of instructional strategies, attendance at profession meetings serves as a source of rejuvenation—a jolt of motivation and a tangible reminder of the challenges and rewards of special education. Those who assume an active role in the governance and activities of an organization—assisting with the planning of conferences or editing newsletters—find that informal networking activities provide a sense of purpose, a source of new ideas, and a new avenue for giving and receiving emotional support.

Reading the Professional Literature. The professional literature—journals, monographs, texts—is the lifeblood of any profession. The most current validated information on issues associated with the teaching of students with disabilities is found in special education journals. Typically, journals present a variety of formats including (1) how-to articles that focus on the application of specific methods and techniques, (2) commentary and opinion pieces on controversial issues in the field, (3) program descriptions and evaluations, and (4) reports of quantitative and qualitative research efforts. While print copies of most of these journals are housed in district professional development centers, regional resource centers, and university libraries, most articles are also available online in electronic form through ERIC, Wilson Web, and other databases.

Although the Internet has made physical access to professional journals instantaneous, finding time and energy to read the relevant information remains a challenge. Clearly, the most desirable method for putting research into practice would be for teachers to have assigned professional development time at school for reading, applying, and discussing journal content (Westling & Korland, 1988). Unfortunately, most time on the job is committed to instructional activities, and teachers must find other sources of time for professional reading. Here are some suggestions. First, set aside a fixed, reasonable amount of time for journal reading. Second, be selective in your reading; read the abstract to assess the applicability of the article to your needs. Finally, infuse a social component into your reading. Try to interest peers in forming a weekly lunchtime journal discussion group.

Pursuing Advanced Degrees and Certificates. Most institutions of higher education offer degree and certificate programs that focus on specific aspects of the subject matter and skills associated with teaching students with disabilities. In addition to traditional full-time options, most graduate programs offer advanced degree programs that address the needs of working teachers, offering courses at convenient times and locations. For those who do not wish to pursue an advanced degree, focused certificate programs are often available. In many cases these programs allow for in-depth analyses of topical issues (e.g., inclusion, comprehensive behavior management) or specialized techniques that can be used with particular populations of students with disabilities (e.g., autism spectrum disorder). Partnership programs between school districts and universities are becoming quite common, and it may be possible to secure academic credits for courses sponsored by and completed in your local school district. Sources are available that describe advanced degree programs in special education. Links to these sources are easily accessed through centers such as the National Center for Special Education Personnel and Related Service Providers (http://www.personnelcenter.org/).

Assuming Leadership Positions.   Perhaps the most natural form of professional development is assuming leadership positions within your department, school, or district. Teacher-leadership activities include serving as a mentor, participating in curriculum review and development, facilitating parent groups, and chairing committees that govern activities and events in the school or district. Be aware that there are leadership development programs that combine staff development activities with internships and often lead to positions of increased responsibility, status, and compensation.

MONITORING YOUR GROWTH: THE PROFESSIONAL PORTFOLIO

Professionals in many disciplines rely on portfolios as a way of displaying their best work. For example, artists and architects collect samples of their many creations, and even lawyers and physicians (particularly plastic surgeons) maintain attractive displays to showcase their efforts. For teachers, portfolios are mechanisms to record evidence of development as well as to showcase creative efforts and achievements. This documentation is quite useful when interviewing for teaching and leadership positions or for advanced graduate study. A well-presented portfolio demonstrates that you have what it takes—the knowledge, skills, creativity, and dispositions—to advance to the next level (Rosenberg et al., 2006).

Still, for teachers, portfolios serve an even greater personal and professional development purpose: Portfolios are a vehicle for allowing teachers to reflect on their own growth and development, both as educators and learners. In some cases they are used to measure progress in meeting advanced professional standards (e.g., National Board for Professional Teaching Standards Certification). For those experiencing a particularly frustrating day, portfolios provide comfort in that they are a tangible way to reflect upon previous successes and experience feelings of self-efficacy. Be aware that each professional teaching portfolio is unique to the individual who creates it. Consequently, portfolios vary in content, form, and emphasis, reflecting an individual's philosophy, values, and viewpoints (Hurst, Wilson, & Cramer, 1998).

Although there are no hard and fast rules as to what should be included in a portfolio, several generic considerations are helpful when using the portfolio as a tool for both reflection and demonstration (Hurst et al., 1998; Reese, 2004; Rosenberg et al., 2006; Van Wagenen & Hibbard, 1998):

- Include evidence and artifacts that reflect who you are, what you are about, and your goals and aspirations.
- Present evidence of your achievements and indicate how they are tied to your goals and aspirations.
- Provide actual samples of assessment, instructional, and behavioral materials that you have developed, implemented, and evaluated.
- Show evidence of student work, family involvement, and community-outreach activities.
- Align your accomplishments with professional standards that are meaningful to you and your school district.
- Maintain representations of your degrees, teaching credentials, letters of reference, and awards.
- Integrate what you have learned from your experiences and articulate these insights into professional goals.
- Ensure that the material in the portfolio is presented in an organized and attractive manner.
- Consider the use of an electronic portfolio, a vehicle that integrates paper-based and video-based evidence in a format that is easy to access, expand upon, and transport.

A professional portfolio is a personal statement of who you are, why you selected a career in special education, and what you hope to accomplish as a professional.

A final note on completing a professional portfolio: Try not to consider this activity as an additional dull paperwork responsibility. The portfolio is your personal statement, a tangible representation of who you are, why you selected a career in special education, and what you hope to accomplish as a professional. It is your running narrative of growth and, with minimal nurturance, serves as a reliable resource to reflect on your teaching career.

FINAL THOUGHTS: STAYING INVIGORATED AND COMMITTED

In this chapter we highlighted how supports and professional development can facilitate the development of a successful and professional special education career. In concluding this chapter we offer a few final suggestions for remaining invigorated and committed to teaching students with disabilities.

First, remember why you had chosen a career involving the education of students with disabilities. As you discovered in Chapter 1, a number of factors entered into your decision to pursue this challenging and rewarding career. It is likely you were committed to helping others succeed or had a desire to give back to the community. Perhaps you believed that you had a special gift or disposition for reaching children and youth from troubling backgrounds. Difficult and frustrating days may result in serious questioning of your assumptions. This is natural and healthy. As you consider your chosen career, recognize that teaching is a tough job, requiring not only specific knowledge but also a commitment of physical and mental energy and breadth of character demanded of precious few other careers. Along with having high expectations, remain patient with your students. As Banner and Cannon (1997) have observed, "patience enables teachers to suspend disappointment and frustration out of an understanding of the difficulties students have in catching on [to] what their teachers already know" (p. 96).

Second, build upon your professional and creative disposition. As we discussed at the start of this chapter, professionalism is a pattern of behaviors (e.g., Grouse, 2003; Kramer, 2003; Phelps, 2006) that includes respect, ethics, responsibility, communication, leadership, risk taking, and a positive attitude. Persevere in the face of intermittent successes and remain poised when encountering frustrating situations. Do not let the important technical and methodical aspects of teaching overshadow artistic and inventive activities. Although scientific and research-based practices inform the selection of specific instructional methods, materials, and processes, teaching is in large part a creative act in which you share elements of your own personality, spirit, experience, and humanity. By revealing aspects of your personality and value system, you become a central figure in the lives of students. Meaningful learning occurs not only through the effective presentation of subject matter but by the thoughtful modeling of care, honor, and integrity. Regardless of the subject matter being taught, the creative force of a trusted and principled teacher facilitates life-changing learning.

Third, don't take the politics of education personally. Educational decisions, like other social policy issues requiring taxpayer contributions, are often based on practical matters such as the limited availability of resources rather than merit. Politics is the process of trying to influence the direction of decisions being made as well as urging how much and where resources should be allocated (Goor, 1995). Rather than ignoring or fearing them, recognize the energizing role of politics in teaching and special education. Be aware of changes in educational policies and trends at the national, state, and local levels and know how such changes affect the delivery of educational programs. Whenever possible and appropriate, participate in community discussions on how best to educate students with disabilities. Participation in political-action activities of professional groups, disability-advocacy organizations, teacher associations, and local parent groups are among the most effective methods of advocating for policies and funding to enhance educational services.

"In my seventh year of teaching, I witnessed some of my first students graduate from high school. I know that I cried more than most parents. The feeling that in some small way I had impacted their lives was unbelievable."

Bill Addison, Baltimore County, Maryland

"I think you can know every research-based reading program out there; but if you don't respect your students as individuals, they won't grow as individuals."

Meridith Taylor-Strout, Gainsville, Florida

www.prenhall.com/rosenberg

Finally, take pleasure in teaching. Most of us have chosen to teach because we enjoy it. Trust your instincts. We get satisfaction in seeing our students acquire skills, master complex concepts, and grow emotionally. How can teachers maximize their pleasure in teaching? Banner and Cannon (1997) recommend (1) creating an atmosphere where students enjoy learning, (2) letting others' wit shine, (3) modeling an enduring love of learning, (4) acknowledging the challenges as well as the joys of learning, and (5) recognizing and celebrating when students learn as a result of your efforts.

Plan well, work hard, have compassion, take care, and enjoy the many pleasures in teaching students with disabilities!

 To link to websites that support and extend the content of this chapter, go to the Web Links module in Chapter 16 of the Companion Website at www.prenhall.com/rosenberg.

SUMMARY

Those who seek a successful, long-term career in special education recognize the importance of developing as a professional, are aware of the supports available to help them grow, and take charge of their ongoing personal and professional growth.

Developing into a Special Education Professional

- Teachers are typically expected to deliver instructional content in an effective manner, differentiate instruction for individual students in a culturally responsive manner, provide supports and adaptations, manage the learning environment, evaluate student performance, care for students, and communicate effectively with colleagues and parents.
- Expectations have expanded and include knowledge of testing accommodations, awareness and management of paperwork and legal responsibilities, and participation in schools that are both integrated systems of care and professional learning communities.

Key Elements of Collaborative Professional Support

- Early in a teacher's career, support is provided through induction, mentoring, and peer coaching, activities that allow novice teachers to acquire important school-system information as well as provide critical emotional support.
- Throughout their career, teachers give and receive assistance through professional learning

communities, collaborative consultation, collaborative teaming, and assistance from paraprofessionals.

Successful Teachers Take an Active Role in Their Own Personal Growth and Professional Development

- Successful teachers are resilient, adjusting to situations and developing competence in the face of adverse conditions.
- Professional growth is predicated on recognizing and managing stress.
- Professional growth requires highly qualified status, a process that is facilitated by knowledge of standards, tests, and professional development alternatives.
- Professional growth is documented by a well-organized portfolio.

Special Educators Remain Invigorated and Committed to Their Students and Profession

- Motivated teachers remember why they have chosen this challenging and rewarding career.
- Creative teachers do not allow the technical and political aspects of the job to overshadow the inventive aspects of teaching.
- Professionals take time to enjoy the pleasure of teaching.

 Council for Exceptional Children **ADDRESSING THE PROFESSIONAL STANDARDS**

Council for Exceptional Children (CEC) Knowledge Standards addressed in the chapter:

CC1K3, CC1S1, CC9K2, CC9K3, CC9K4, CC9S1, CC9S2, CC9S3, CC9S4, CC9S8, CC9S10, CC9S11, CC9S12, CC10S3, CC10S11

Appendix B: CEC Knowledge and Skill Standards Common Core has a full listing of the standards referenced here.

As we noted in Chapter 16, most states that require tests for certification and licensure utilize THE PRAXIS SERIES™ developed by the Educational Testing Service (ETS). For special educators, a central element in the test series is the Special Education Core Principles: Content Knowledge Assessment. This "core knowledge" centers on three areas: Understanding Exceptionalities, Legal and Societal Issues, and Delivery of Services to Students with Disabilities.

In the following grid we reference where the relevant material associated with the Praxis content areas are located in each chapter (chapter number is followed by chapter sections). We anticipate that this content will be helpful as you prepare for the test. *However,* keep in mind that success on PRAXIS™ exams (as well as success teaching students with and without disabilities) requires greater in-depth study and application than any broad-based introductory textbook can provide. We urge you to utilize the foundational material found in the chapters to anchor and organize future coursework and field experiences.

I. Understanding Exceptionalities

PRAXIS™ Content Area	Relevant Chapter Content
Human development and behavior as related to students with disabilities	• **Chapter 4:** Indicators of Disabilities from Infancy Through School Ages • **Chapter 6:** Defining Learning Disabilities; Course and Causal Factors of LD • **Chapter 7:** Defining Emotional and Behavioral Disabilities; Course and Causal Factors EBD • **Chapter 8:** Defining Mild Intellectual Disabilities; Course and Causal Factors of Mild Intellectual Disabilities • **Chapter 9:** Defining ADHD; Course and Causal Factors of ADHD • **Chapter 10:** Defining Autism Spectrum Disabilities; Course and Causal Factors ASD • **Chapter 11:** Defining Communication Disorders; Causes of Communication Disorders; Types of Language Disorders and Speech Disorders • **Chapter 12:** Definitions and Classification Criteria for Students with Severe Intellectual Disabilities and Multiple Disabilities • **Chapter 13:** Definitions and Classification Criteria for Sensory Disabilities

(continues)

PRAXIS™ Content Area	Relevant Chapter Content
	• **Chapter 14:** Definitions and Classification Criteria of Traumatic Brain Injury, Physical Disabilities, and Health Impairments • **Chapter 15:** Defining Giftedness
Characteristics of students with disabilities	• **Chapter 3:** Influence of Cultural and Linguistic Factors on Disabilities • **Chapter 4:** Characteristics of Infants, Toddlers, and Preschoolers • **Chapter 6:** Primary Behavioral Characteristics of Students with LD • **Chapter 7:** Primary Behavioral Characteristics of EBD • **Chapter 8:** Primary Behavioral Characteristics of Students with Mild Intellectual Disabilities • **Chapter 9:** Primary Behavioral Characteristics of Students with ADHD • **Chapter 10:** Primary Behavioral Characteristics of ASD • **Chapter 11:** Types of Language Disorders and Speech Disorders; Relationship Between Communication Disorders and Other Disabilities; Prevalence of Communication Disorders • **Chapter 12:** Learning Characteristics and Challenging Behavior Associated with Severe and Multiple Disabilities; Physical and Medical Problems Associated with Severe and Multiple Disabilities • **Chapter 13:** Learning, Academic, and Social Characteristics of Students with Vision or Hearing Losses • **Chapter 14:** Characteristics of Students with Traumatic Brain Injury, Physical Disabilities, and Health Impairments
Basic concepts in special education	• **Chapter 1:** Meaning of Special Education; Roles of Special Education Teachers and Other Professionals and Paraeducators; Importance of Evidence-based Instruction; Rewards and Challenges of Being a Special Education Teacher; Reasons for Choosing Special Education as a Career; Dispositions and Attitudes Appropriate for Special Education Teachers • **Chapter 2:** Social History of Special Education • **Chapter 4:** Ways Students with Disabilities are Recognized, Referred, and Evaluated; Types of Plans that Schools Develop; Parents' Rights; Prereferrals; Early Intervening Services; Response to Intervention (RTI) • **Chapter 5:** Communicating Instruction and Behavior Management • **Chapter 12:** School Programs and Related Services • **Chapter 13:** Special Education Eligibility Requirements for Students with Visual or Hearing Loss; Legal Definition of Blindness; Criteria for Deaf-blindness • **Chapter 14:** Special Education Eligibility Requirements for Students with Traumatic Brain Injury, Physical Disabilities, and Health Impairments • **Chapter 16:** Professionalism; Collaboration, Consultation, and Teaming; Professional Growth and Development

II. Legal and Societal Issues

PRAXIS™ Content Area	Relevant Chapter Content
Federal laws and legal issues related to special education	• **Chapter 2:** IDEA: Legal Basis for IDEA; Major Components of IDEA; IDEA Outcomes and Improvements; NCLB: Major Components of NCLB; NCLB Outcomes; Section 504; Americans with Disabilities Act • **Chapter 3:** Cultural and Community Influences on Attitudes Toward Disabilities • **Chapter 4:** Eligibility Requirements for Special Education; Prereferral and Referral Procedures; IEP and Section 504 Requirements; IFSP Requirements; IEP Team Members; Transition Plans • **Chapter 8:** Developing Student Self Advocacy • **Chapter 9:** Section 504 • **Chapter 12:** Prevailing Issues, Controversies, and Implications for the Teacher • **Chapter 14:** Eligibility Requirements for Students with Traumatic Brain Injury, Physical Disabilities, and Health Impairments
The school's connections with the families, prospective and actual employers, and communities of students with disabilities	• **Chapter 6:** Early Intervention for Students with LD; Transition to Adult Life Considerations for Students with LD • **Chapter 7:** Early Intervention EBD; Transition to Adult Life Considerations EBD • **Chapter 8:** Early Intervention for Students with Mild Intellectual Disabilities; Transition to Adult Life Considerations for Students with Mild Intellectual Disabilities • **Chapter 9:** Early Intervention for Students with ADHD; Transition to Adult Life Considerations for Students with ADHD • **Chapter 10:** Early Intervention ASD; Transition to Adult Life Considerations ASD • **Chapter 11:** Roles of families in supporting students with communication disorders • **Chapter 12:** Prevailing Issues, Controversies, and Implications for the Teacher • **Chapter 13:** Deaf People as a Culture

III. Delivery of Services to Students with Disabilities

PRAXIS™ Content Area	Relevant Chapter Content
Background knowledge	• **Chapter 3:** Cultural and Linguistic Considerations Regarding Curriculum and Instruction • **Chapter 6:** Service Delivery for Students with LD • **Chapter 7:** Service Delivery EBD • **Chapter 8:** Service Delivery for Students with Mild Intellectual Disabilities • **Chapter 9:** Service Delivery for Students with ADHD • **Chapter 10:** Service Delivery ASD • **Chapter 11:** Service Delivery for Students with Communication Disorders • **Chapter 12:** School Programs and Related Services • **Chapter 14:** Academic and Functional Instruction

(continues)

III. Delivery of Services to Students with Disabilities—*continued*

PRAXIS™ Content Area	Relevant Chapter Content
Curriculum and instruction and their implementation across the continuum of educational placements	• **Chapter 5:** Curriculum and Students with Special Needs; Approaches to Teaching; Systematic Teaching; Managing Student Behavior; Proactive Behavior Management • **Chapter 6:** Academic Interventions for Students with LD • **Chapter 7:** Academic and Social/Behavioral Interventions EBD • **Chapter 8:** Academic Interventions for Students with Mild Intellectual Disabilities • **Chapter 9:** Academic and Social/Behavioral Interventions for Students with ADHD • **Chapter 10:** Academic and Social/Behavioral Interventions ASD • **Chapter 11:** Intervention Procedures; Supporting Students Using AAC Devices; Service Delivery Models • **Chapter 12:** School Programs and Related Services • **Chapter 13:** Academic Interventions for Students with Visual or Hearing Impairments • **Chapter 14:** Academic and Functional Instruction
Assessment	• **Chapter 4:** Identification Procedures for Infants and Toddlers; Preschoolers and School-Age Students; Overview of Assessment Instruments for Identification and Planning • **Chapter 6:** Identification and Assessment of Students with LD • **Chapter 8:** Identification and Assessment of Students with Mild Intellectual Disabilities • **Chapter 9:** Identification and Assessment of Students with ADHD • **Chapter 7:** Identification and Assessment of Students with EBD • **Chapter 10:** Identification and Assessment of Students with ASD • **Chapter 11:** Identification and Assessment of Students with Communication Disorders • **Chapter 12:** Identification and Assessment of Students with Severe and Multiple Disabilities • **Chapter 13:** Identification and Assessment for Students with Visual or Hearing Impairments • **Chapter 14:** Identification and Assessment of Students with Traumatic Brain Injury, Physical Disabilities, and Health Impairments

Standard I: Foundations

CC1K1: Models, theories, and philosophies that form the basis for special education practice.

CC1K2: Laws, policies, and ethical principles regarding behavior management, planning, and implementation.

CC1K3: Relationship of special education to the organization and function of educational agencies.

CC1K4: Rights and responsibilities of students, parents, teachers, and other professionals, and schools related to exceptional learning needs.

CC1K5: Issues in definition and identification of individuals with exceptional learning needs, including those from culturally and linguistically diverse backgrounds.

CC1K6: Issues, assurances, and due process rights related to assessment, eligibility, and placement within a continuum of services.

CC1K7: Family systems and the role of families in the educational process.

CC1K8: Historical points of view and contributions of culturally diverse groups.

CC1K9: Impact of the dominant culture on shaping schools and the individuals who study and work in them.

CC1K10: Potential impact of differences in values, languages, and customs that can exist between the home and school.

CC1S1: Articulate personal philosophy of special education.

Standard II: Development and Characteristics of Learners

CC2K1: Typical and atypical human growth and development.

CC2K2: Educational implications of characteristics of various exceptionalities.

CC2K3: Characteristics and effects of the cultural and environmental milieu of the individual with exceptional learning needs and the family.

CC2K4: Family systems and the role of families in supporting development.

CC2K5: Similarities and differences of individuals with and without exceptional learning needs.

CC2K6: Similarities and differences among individuals with exceptional learning needs.

CC2K7: Effects of various medications on individuals with exceptional learning needs.

Standard III: Individual Learning Differences

CC3K1: Effects an exceptional condition(s) can have on an individual's life.

CC3K2: Impact of learner's academic and social abilities, attitudes, interests, and values on instruction and career development.

CC3K3: Variations in beliefs, traditions, and values across and within cultures and their effects on relationships among individuals with exceptional learning needs, family, and schooling.

CC3K4: Cultural perspectives influencing the relationships among families, schools, and communities as related to instruction.

CC3K5:   Differing ways of learning of individuals with exceptional learning needs including those from culturally diverse backgrounds and strategies for addressing these differences.

Standard IV: Instructional Strategies

CC4S1:   Use strategies to facilitate integration into various settings.
CC4S2:   Teach individuals to use self-assessment, problem-solving, and other cognitive strategies to meet their needs.
CC4S3:   Select, adapt, and use instructional strategies and materials according to characteristics of the individual with exceptional learning needs.
CC4S4:   Use strategies to facilitate maintenance and generalization of skills across environments.
CC4S5:   Use procedures to increase the individual's self-awareness, self-management, self-control, self-reliance, and self-esteem.
CC4S6:   Use strategies that promote successful transitions for individuals with exceptional learning needs.

Standard V: Learning Environments and Social Interactions

CC5K1:   Demands of learning environments.
CC5K2:   Basic classroom management theories and strategies for individuals with exceptional learning needs.
CC5K3:   Effective management of teaching and learning.
CC5K4:   Teacher attitudes and behaviors that influence behavior of individuals with exceptional learning needs.
CC5K5:   Social skills needed for educational and other environments.
CC5K6:   Strategies for crisis prevention and intervention.
CC5K7:   Strategies for preparing individuals to live harmoniously and productively in a culturally diverse world.
CC5K8:   Ways to create learning environments that allow individuals to retain and appreciate their own and each other's respective language and cultural heritage.
CC5K9:   Ways specific cultures are negatively stereotyped.
CC5K10: Strategies used by diverse populations to cope with a legacy of former and continuing racism.
CC5S1:   Create a safe, equitable, positive, and supporting learning environment in which diversities are valued.
CC5S2:   Identify realistic expectations for personal and social behavior in various settings.
CC5S3:   Identify supports needed for integration into various program placements.
CC5S4:   Design learning environments that encourage active participation in individual and group settings.
CC5S5:   Modify the learning environment to manage behaviors.
CC5S6:   Use performance data and information from all stakeholders to make or suggest modifications in learning environments.
CC5S7:   Establish and maintain rapport with individuals with and without exceptional learning needs.
CC5S8:   Teach self-advocacy.
CC5S9:   Create an environment that encourages self-advocacy and increased independence.
CC5S10: Use effective and varied behavior management strategies.
CC5S11: Use the least intensive behavior management strategy consistent with the needs of the individual with exceptional learning needs.
CC5S12: Design and manage daily routines.
CC5S13: Organize, develop, and sustain learning environments that support positive intracultural and intercultural experiences.

CC5S14:   Mediate controversial intercultural issues among students within the
           learning environment in ways that enhance any culture, group, or
           person.
CC5S15:   Structure, direct, and support the activities of paraeducators, volunteers,
           and tutors.
CC5S16:   Use universal precautions.

Standard VI: Language

CC6K1:   Effects of cultural and linguistic differences on growth and development.
CC6K2:   Characteristics of one's own culture and use of language and the ways in
          which these can differ from other cultures and uses of languages.
CC6K3:   Ways of behaving and communicating among cultures that can lead to
          misinterpretation and misunderstanding.
CC6K4:   Augmentative and assistive communication strategies.
CC6S1:   Use strategies to support and enhance communication skills of
          individuals with exceptional learning needs.
CC6S2:   Use communication strategies and resources to facilitate understanding
          of subject matter for students whose primary language is not the
          dominant language.

Standard VII: Instructional Planning

CC7K1:   Theories and research that form the basis of curriculum development
          and instructional practice.
CC7K2:   Scope and sequences of general and special curricula.
CC7K3:   National, state or provincial, and local curricula standards.
CC7K4:   Technology for planning and managing the teaching and learning
          environment.
CC7K5:   Roles and responsibilities of the paraeducator related to instruction,
          intervention, and direct service.
CC7S1:   Identify and prioritize areas of the general curriculum and
          accommodations for individuals with exceptional learning needs.
CC7S2:   Develop and implement comprehensive, longitudinal individualized
          programs in collaboration with team members.
CC7S3:   Involve the individual and family in setting instructional goals and
          monitoring progress.
CC7S4:   Use functional assessments to develop intervention plans.
CC7S5:   Use task analysis.
CC7S6:   Sequence, implement, and evaluate individualized learning objectives.
CC7S7:   Integrate affective, social, and life skills with academic curricula.
CC7S8:   Develop and select instructional content, resources, and strategies that
          respond to cultural, linguistic, and gender differences.
CC7S9:   Incorporate and implement instructional and assistive technology into
          the educational program.
CC7S10:   Prepare lesson plans.
CC7S11:   Prepare and organize materials to implement daily lesson plans.
CC7S12:   Use instructional time effectively.
CC7S13:   Make responsive adjustments to instruction based on continued
          observations.
CC7S14:   Prepare individuals to exhibit self-enhancing behavior in response to
          societal attitudes and actions.

Standard VIII: Assessment

CC8K1:   Basic terminology used in assessment.
CC8K2:   Legal provisions and ethical principles regarding assessment of individuals.
CC8K3:   Screening, prereferral, referral, and classification procedures.
CC8K4:   Use and limitations of assessment instruments.

CC8K5: National, state or provincial, and local accommodations and modifications.
CC8S1: Gather relevant background information.
CC8S2: Administer nonbiased formal and informal assessments.
CC8S3: Use technology to conduct assessments.
CC8S4: Develop or modify individualized assessment strategies.
CC8S5: Interpret information from formal and informal assessments.
CC8S6: Use assessment information in making eligibility, program, and placement decisions for individuals with exceptional learning needs, including those from culturally and/or linguistically diverse backgrounds.
CC8S7: Report assessment results to all stakeholders using effective communication skills.
CC8S8: Evaluate instruction and monitor progress of individuals with exceptional learning needs.
CC8S9: Develop or modify individualized assessment strategies.
CC8S10: Create and maintain records.

Standard IX: Professional and Ethical Practice

CC9K1: Personal cultural biases and differences that affect one's teaching.
CC9K2: Importance of the teacher serving as a model for individuals with exceptional learning needs.
CC9K3: Continuum of lifelong professional development.
CC9K4: Methods to remain current regarding research-validated practice.
CC9S1: Practice within the CEC Code of Ethics and other standards of the profession.
CC9S2: Uphold high standards of competence and integrity and exercise sound judgment in the practice of the professional.
CC9S3: Act ethically in advocating for appropriate services.
CC9S4: Conduct professional activities in compliance with applicable laws and policies.
CC9S5: Demonstrate commitment to developing the highest education and quality-of-life potential of individuals with exceptional learning needs.
CC9S6: Demonstrate sensitivity for the culture, language, religion, gender, disability, socioeconomic status, and sexual orientation of individuals.
CC9S7: Practice within one's skill limit and obtain assistance as needed.
CC9S8: Use verbal, nonverbal, and written language effectively.
CC9S9: Conduct self-evaluation of instruction.
CC9S10: Access information on exceptionalities.
CC9S11: Reflect on one's practice to improve instruction and guide professional growth.
CC9S12: Engage in professional activities that benefit individuals with exceptional learning needs, their families, and one's colleagues.

Standard X: Collaboration

CC10K1: Models and strategies of consultation and collaboration.
CC10K2: Roles of individuals with exceptional learning needs, families, and school and community personnel in planning of an individualized program.
CC10K3: Concerns of families of individuals with exceptional learning needs and strategies to help address these concerns.
CC10K4: Culturally responsive factors that promote effective communication and collaboration with individuals with exceptional learning needs, families, school personnel, and community members.
CC10S1: Maintain confidential communication about individuals with exceptional learning needs.
CC10S2: Collaborate with families and others in assessment of individuals with exceptional learning needs.

CC10S3: Foster respectful and beneficial relationships between families and professionals.

CC10S4: Assist individuals with exceptional learning needs and their families in becoming active participants in the educational team.

CC10S5: Plan and conduct collaborative conferences with individuals with exceptional learning needs and their families.

CC10S6: Collaborate with school personnel and community members in integrating individuals with exceptional learning needs into various settings.

CC10S7: Use group problem-solving skills to develop, implement, and evaluate collaborative activities.

CC10S8: Model techniques and coach others in the use of instructional methods and accommodations.

CC10S9: Communicate with school personnel about the characteristics and needs of individuals with exceptional learning needs.

CC10S10: Communicate effectively with families of individuals with exceptional learning needs from diverse backgrounds.

CC10S11: Observe, evaluate, and provide feedback to paraeducators.

Appendix C
CEC Code of Ethics and Standards
for Professional Practice for Special Educators

CEC CODE OF ETHICS FOR EDUCATORS OF PERSONS WITH EXCEPTIONALITIES

We declare the following principles to be the Code of Ethics for educators of persons with exceptionalities. Members for the special education profession are responsible for upholding and advancing these principles. Members of the Council for Exceptional Children agree to judge and be judged by them in accordance with the spirit and provisions of this Code.

A. Special education professionals are committed to developing the highest educational and quality of life potential of individuals with exceptionalities.
B. Special education professionals promote and maintain a high level of competence and integrity in practicing their profession.
C. Special education professionals engage in professional activities which benefit individuals with exceptionalities, their families, other colleagues, students, or research subjects.
D. Special education professionals exercise objective professional judgment in the practice of their profession.
E. Special education professionals strive to advance their knowledge and skills regarding the education of individuals with exceptionalities.
F. Special education professionals work within the standards and policies of their profession.
G. Special education professionals seek to uphold and improve where necessary the laws, regulations, and policies governing the delivery of special education and related services and the practice of their profession.
H. Special education professionals do not condone or participate in unethical or illegal acts, nor violate professional standards adopted by the Delegate Assembly of CEC.

CEC STANDARDS FOR PROFESSIONAL PRACTICE

PROFESSIONALS IN RELATION TO PERSONS WITH EXCEPTIONALITIES AND THEIR FAMILIES

Instructional Responsibilities

Special education personnel are committed to the application of professional expertise to ensure the provision of quality education for all individuals with exceptionalities. Professionals strive to

1. Identify and use instructional methods and curricula that are appropriate to their area of professional practice and effective in meeting the individual needs of persons with exceptionalities.
2. Participate in the selection and use of appropriate instructional materials, equipment, supplies, and other resources needed in the effective practice of their profession.

3. Create safe and effective learning environments, which contribute to fulfillment of needs, stimulation of learning, and self concept.
4. Maintain class size and caseloads that are conducive to meeting the individual instructional needs of individuals with exceptionalities.
5. Use assessment instruments and procedures that do not discriminate against persons with exceptionalities on the basis of race, color, creed, sex, national origin, age, political practices, family or social background, sexual orientation, or exceptionality.
6. Base grading, promotion, graduation, and/or movement out of the program on the individual goals and objectives for individuals with exceptionalities.
7. Provide accurate program data to administrators, colleagues, and parents, based on efficient and objective record keeping practices, for the purpose of decision making.
8. Maintain confidentiality of information except when information is released under specific conditions of written consent and statutory confidentiality requirements.

Management of Behavior

Special education professionals participate with other professionals and with parents in an interdisciplinary effort in the management of behavior. Professionals

1. Apply only those disciplinary methods and behavioral procedures, which they have been instructed to use and which do not undermine the dignity of the individual or the basic human rights of persons with exceptionalities, such as corporal punishment.
2. Clearly specify the goals and objectives for behavior management practices in the persons with exceptionalities individualized education program.
3. Conform to policies, statutes, and rules established by state/provincial and local agencies relating to judicious application of disciplinary methods and behavioral procedures.
4. Take adequate measures to discourage, prevent, and intervene when a colleague's behavior is perceived as being detrimental to exceptional students.
5. Refrain from aversive techniques unless repeated trials of other methods have failed and only after consultation with parents and appropriate agency officials.

Support Procedures

Professionals
1. Seek adequate instruction and supervision before they are required to perform support services for which they have not been prepared previously.
2. May administer medication, where state/provincial policies do not preclude such action, if qualified to do so or if written instructions are on file which state the purpose of the medication, the conditions under which it may be administered, possible side effects, the physician's name and phone number, and the professional liability if a mistake is made. The professional will not be required to administer medication.
3. Note and report to those concerned whenever changes in behavior occur in conjunction with the administration of medication or at any other time.

Parent Relationships

Professionals seek to develop relationships with parents based on mutual respect for their roles in achieving benefits for the exceptional persons. Special education professionals

1. Develop effective communication with parents, avoiding technical terminology, using the primary language of the home, and other modes of communication when appropriate.
2. Seek and use parents' knowledge and expertise in planning, conducting, and evaluating special education and related services for persons with exceptionalities.

3. Maintain communications between parents and professionals with appropriate respect for privacy and confidentiality.
4. Extend opportunities for parent education utilizing accurate information and professional methods.
5. Inform parents of the educational rights of their children and of any proposed or actual practices, which violate those rights.
6. Recognize and respect cultural diversities which exist in some families with persons with exceptionalities.
7. Recognize that the relationship of home and community environmental conditions affects the behavior and outlook of the exceptional person.

Advocacy

Special education professionals serve as advocates for exceptional students by speaking, writing, and acting in a variety of situations on their behalf. They

1. Continually seek to improve government provisions for the education of persons with exceptionalities while ensuring that public statements by professionals as individuals are not construed to represent official policy statements of the agency that employs them.
2. Work cooperatively with and encourage other professionals to improve the provision of special education and related services to persons with exceptionalities.
3. Document and objectively report to one's supervisors or administrators inadequacies in resources and promote appropriate corrective action.
4. Monitor for inappropriate placements in special education and intervene at appropriate levels to correct the condition when such inappropriate placements exist.
5. Follow local, state/provincial, and federal laws and regulations which mandate a free appropriate public education to exceptional students and the protection of the rights of persons with exceptionalities to equal opportunities in our society.

PROFESSIONALS IN RELATION TO EMPLOYMENT

Certification and Qualification

Professionals ensure that only persons deemed qualified by having met state/provincial minimum standards are employed as teachers, administrators, and related service providers for individuals with exceptionalities.

Employment

1. Professionals do not discriminate in hiring on the basis of race, color, creed, sex, national origin, age, political practices, family or social background, sexual orientation, or exceptionality.
2. Professionals represent themselves in an ethical and legal manner in regard to their training and experience when seeking new employment.
3. Professionals give notice consistent with local education agency policies when intending to leave employment.
4. Professionals adhere to the conditions of a contract or terms of an appointment in the setting where they practice.
5. Professionals released from employment are entitled to a written explanation of reasons for termination and to fair and impartial due process procedures.
6. Special education professionals share equitably in the opportunities and benefits (salary, working conditions, facilities, and other resources) of other professionals in the school system.
7. Professionals seek assistance, including the services of other professionals in instances where personal problems threaten to interfere with their job performance.
8. Professionals respond objectively when requested to evaluate applicants seeking employment.

9. Professionals have the right and responsibility to resolve professional problems by utilizing established procedures, including grievance procedures, when appropriate.

Assignment and Role

1. Professionals should receive clear written communication of all duties and responsibilities, including those which are prescribed as conditions of their employment.
2. Professionals promote educational quality and intra- and interprofessional cooperation through active participation in the planning, policy development, management, and evaluation of the special education program and the education program at large so that programs remain responsive to the changing needs of persons with exceptionalities.
3. Professionals practice only in areas of exceptionality, at age levels, and in program models for which they are prepared by their training and/or experience.
4. Adequate supervision of and support for special education professionals is provided by other professionals qualified by their training and experience in the area of concern.
5. The administration and supervision of special education professionals provides for clear lines of accountability.
6. The unavailability of substitute teachers or support personnel, including aides, does not result in the denial of special education services to a greater degree than to that of other educational programs.

Professional Development

1. Special education professionals systematically advance their knowledge and skills in order to maintain a high level of competence and response to the changing needs of persons with exceptionalities by pursuing a program of continuing education including but not limited to participation in such activities as inservice training, professional conferences/workshops, professional meetings, continuing education courses, and the reading of professional literature.
2. Professionals participate in the objective and systematic evaluation of themselves, colleagues, services, and programs for the purpose of continuous improvement of professional performance.
3. Professionals in administrative positions support and facilitate professional development.

PROFESSIONALS IN RELATION TO THE PROFESSION AND TO OTHER PROFESSIONALS

The Profession

1. Special education professionals assume responsibility for participating in professional organizations and adherence to the standards and codes of ethics of those organizations.
2. Special education professionals have a responsibility to provide varied and exemplary supervised field experiences for persons in undergraduate and graduate preparation programs.
3. Special education professionals refrain from using professional relationships with students and parents for personal advantage.
4. Special education professionals take an active position in the regulation of the profession through use of appropriate procedures for bringing about changes.
5. Special education professionals initiate, support, and/or participate in research related to the education of persons with exceptionalities with the aim of improving the quality of educational services, increasing the accountability of programs, and generally benefiting persons with exceptionalities. They
   • Adopt procedures that protect the rights and welfare of subjects participating in the research.

- Interpret and publish research results with accuracy and a high quality of scholarship.
- Support a cessation of the use of any research procedure that may result in undesirable consequences for the participant.
- Exercise all possible precautions to prevent misapplication or misutilization of a research effort, by self or others.

Other Professionals

Special education professionals function as members of interdisciplinary teams, and the reputation of the profession rides with them. They

1. Recognize and acknowledge the competencies and expertise of members representing other disciplines as well as those of members in their own disciplines.
2. Strive to develop positive attitudes among other professionals toward persons with exceptionalities, representing them with an objective regard for their possibilities and their limitations as persons in a democratic society.
3. Cooperate with other agencies involved in serving persons with exceptionalities through such activities as the planning and coordination of information exchanges, service delivery, evaluation, and training, so that duplication or loss in quality of services may not occur.
4. Provide consultation and assistance, where appropriate, to both general and special educators as well as other school personnel serving persons with exceptionalities.
5. Provide consultation and assistance, where appropriate, to professionals in non-school settings serving persons with exceptionalities.
6. Maintain effective interpersonal relations with colleagues and other professionals, helping them to develop and maintain positive and accurate perceptions about the special education profession.

Glossary

5p or cri-du-chat (cry of the cat) syndrome: A rare condition in which a portion of the fifth chromosome is missing. The condition usually results in severe intellectual disabilities. The children with this condition are characterized by a high-pitched, cat-like cry.

AAMR/AAIDD: *See* American Association on Mental Retardation

Ability grouping: An instructional arrangement that allows students with common learning characteristics to benefit from targeted teaching.

Abstraction: The ability to understand particular applications of principles, ideas, and examples in a more theoretical way.

Accelerative options: Instructional options such as skipping grades, early admissions, or increasing the pace of work.

Achievement tests: Assessments that are used to identify specific academic abilities, strengths, and weaknesses.

Adaptive behavior: Part of most definitions of intellectual disability. Adaptive behavior includes the practical and social skills that students use to function effectively in their everyday lives.

ADD: An acronym that was formerly used to identify students with ADHD who exhibit primarily inattentive behaviors.

Adequate yearly progress (AYP): The No Child Left Behind Act mandates that all students make adequate yearly progress. AYP is defined by each state, and is intended to measure student progress and ensure that all students experience continuous and substantial growth in academic achievement.

ADHD: *See* Attention deficit hyperactivity disorder.

ADHD-C: *See* Combined type

ADHD-PHI: *See* Predominantly hyperactive-impulsive type

ADHD-PI: *See* Predominantly inattentive type

Advance organizer: An explicit introduction to a lesson that shows students how current activities fit contextually with past and future activities, heightening motivation/anticipation.

Alternative or augmentative communication (AAC) devices: A variety of techniques and devices used to supplement a person's oral speech.

American Association on Mental Retardation (AAMR): The leading professional organization that addresses intellectual disabilities. The name of AAMR was changed in January 2007 to the **American Association on Intellectual and Developmental Disabilities (AAIDD).**

Americans with Disabilities Act (ADA): An act that requires nondiscriminatory protection of civil rights and accessibility to physical facilities and applies to all segments of society with the exception of private schools and religious organizations.

Amphetamine: A type of stimulant medication used to treat the symptoms of ADHD. Amphetamines include Adderall and Dexedrine.

Anemia: A blood disorder characterized by a low level of healthy red blood cells.

Angelman syndrome: A syndrome due to a chromosomal anomaly in which a portion of chromosome 15 is missing.

Antiretroviral drugs: Medications for the treatment of infection by retroviruses, primarily HIV.

Applied behavior analysis (ABA): The application of the scientific method and behavioral principles to the observation, study, and modification of behavior.

Articulation: The movement of mouth, lips, tongue, and voice box to produce speech sounds.

Asperger's syndrome: This syndrome is part of the autism spectrum. It is a disorder characterized by qualitative impairments in nonverbal behaviors, social relationships, interests, and social and emotional reciprocity but, unlike autism, involves no delays in language or cognitive development.

Assistive technology (AT): Any item or piece of equipment, whether available commercially, modified, or customized, that is used to increase, maintain, or improve the functional capabilities of a student with a disability.

Asymmetric tonic neck reflex: A postural reaction that occurs while a baby is lying on his back. The head turns to one side causing the arm and leg on the side that he is looking toward to extend or straighten, while his other arm and leg will flex.

Attention deficit hyperactivity disorder (ADHD): A persistent pattern of inattention and/or hyperactivity/impulsivity that is more frequently displayed and more severe than is typically observed in individuals at a comparable level of development.

Augmentative/alternative communication (AAC): Simple or technologically advanced methods that support or enhance oral and mechanical modes of communication.

Autism: A neurological disorder that appears during the first 3 years of life. It adversely affects development in the areas of social interaction and communication skills. Individuals with autism typically show difficulties in verbal and nonverbal communication, social interactions, and leisure or play activities.

Autism rating scales: Instruments that measure specific characteristics, abilities, and behaviors associated with autism.

Autism spectrum disorders (ASD): ASD, also referred to as pervasive developmental disorders (PDD), are a group of developmental disorders that share common social, communicative, and stereotyped and ritualistic behavioral similarities, varying in age of onset and severity of symptoms. The group includes autism, Asperger's syndrome, pervasive developmental disorder—not otherwise specified (PDD-NOS), Rett syndrome, and childhood disintegrative disorder (CDD).

Autistic disorder: Sometimes referred to as early infantile autism, childhood autism, or Kanner's autism, it is characterized by marked impairments in social interactions and communication, and restrictions in activities or interests.

Autosomes: The first 22 pairs of chromosomes that normally are in human cells.

Bilingualism: The ability to speak two languages. Multilingualism refers to the ability to speak more than two languages.

Bloom's taxonomy: A useful planning tool developed by Benjamin Bloom based on the assumptions that most content can be learned at different conceptual levels and that all students can benefit from well-planned lessons.

Braille: A code used to present text in a tactile format, represented in a rectangular cell with six dots.

Brain injury: Any injury or damage to the brain or central nervous system resulting in problems. The damage can be in one area or diffused throughout the brain and can affect mood, the ability to focus, memory, sleep, and physical functioning.

Brown v. Board of Education, 1954: The landmark case that struck down racial segregation in public schools based upon the equal protection provisions guaranteed by the 14th Amendment of the Constitution.

Child Find: An IDEA requirement that says states must identify, locate, and evaluate all children with disabilities, aged birth to 21, who are in need of early intervention or special education services.

Childhood disintegrative disorder: Following 2 years of relatively normal development, the individual develops a severe loss of functioning.

Chromosomal anomalies: This condition is one in which strands of chromosomal material within cells are not arranged in their normal pattern. Anomalies often result in syndromes such as Down syndrome.

Chromosomes: The carriers of the genetic material within cells. The human cell normally has 23 pairs of chromosomes.

Civil rights movement: A particularly active period from the late 1950s to the early 1990s that advocated for the application of the Bill of Rights to all disenfranchised persons, whether by race, gender, or disability.

Collaborative consultation: A formal process that includes (a) specific problem identification and goal setting; (b) analysis of factors contributing to the problem and brainstorming possible problem-solving interventions; (c) planning an intervention; and (d) evaluating the outcomes.

Collectivist culture: A culture in which working for the common good is more highly valued than individual achievement.

Combined type (ADHD-C): A subtype of students with ADHD who exhibit inattentive, hyperactive, and impulsive behaviors.

Comorbidity: The co-occurrence of two or more disorders or diseases that are not caused by each other.

Complexity: Consideration of multiple perspectives, multiple implications, and advanced demands for a learner to see interactions with other disciplines.

Conceptual framework: An organizational structure that guides beliefs and understandings about a subject of inquiry.

Configuration of hearing loss: Describes qualitative aspects of hearing, such as whether both ears are affected or whether different frequencies are affected differently.

Contractures: A physical development in which normally elastic connective tissue is replaced by inelastic fibrous tissue, making the affected area resistant to stretching and preventing normal movement.

Core deficit scales: Assessments that allow for the precise measurement of specific symptoms and functioning.

Cornelia de Lange: This syndrome is characterized by several distinctive facial features such as arched, well-defined eyebrows and curly eyelashes, small (microcephalic) heads, and other features. These children may have intellectual disabilities ranging from mild to profound.

Criterion-referenced test: A student's performance on a criterion-referenced test is evaluated in terms of how well he or she performs on specific standards or criteria.

Culturally and linguistically diverse (CLD): Students from backgrounds that are non-European American and, in some instances, non-English speaking, including African American, Hispanic, American Indian/Alaskan Native, and Asian/Pacific Islander.

Culturally responsive teaching and management: Classroom instruction and management that is based upon a consideration of students' cultural backgrounds.

Culture: The values, beliefs, traditions, and behaviors associated with a particular group of people who share a common history.

Curriculum-based measurement: An efficient method of monitoring student performance through the collection and monitoring of academic progress over time.

Cytomegalovirus (CMV): A common virus that infects many people. The infection is usually harmless and rarely causes illness unless a person's immune system is seriously weakened. The virus remains alive but dormant in the body for life.

Deaf: With a capital *D*, used to describe a particular group of people who share a language (American Sign Language) and a culture (Deaf culture).

Deaf-blindness: Concomitant hearing and visual impairments, the combination of which causes such severe communication and other developmental and educational needs that they cannot be accommodated in special education programs solely for children with deafness or children with blindness.

Deafness: A hearing impairment that is so severe that the child is impaired in processing linguistic information through hearing with or without amplification which adversely affects the child's educational performance.

Decibel (dB): A unit of measurement of the intensity or loudness of sound.

Degree of hearing loss: A measure of the degree of severity of hearing loss expressed in decibels (dB).

Deinstitutionalization: The policy of releasing people, particularly those with disabilities of the mind, from institutions and into community settings.

Developmental aphasia: A language impairment that is assumed to be the result of some type of neurological dysfunction.

Developmental assessments: These assessments are intended to judge a child's development in relation to other children. They are based on the children's achievement of developmental milestones.

***Diagnostic and Statistical Manual* (4th ed.) DSM-IV TR:** A manual produced by the American Psychiatric Association that includes definitions and identification criteria used to identify persons with psychiatric and other related disorders.

Diagnostic interviews: Semistructured narrative methods of gathering information on patterns of development and behavior.

Direct Instruction (DI): Systematic, explicit instruction, often based on scripted instructional materials.

Direct observation scales: A structured method for observing characteristics and abilities.

Dispositions: One's temperament or tendency, generally learned over time, to act or respond in a certain way given a certain situation.

Down syndrome: A condition due to chromosomal anomaly in which there are three chromosome strands (instead of two) at pair 21 (trisomy 21). Children with Down syndrome are usually smaller than average and have slower physical, motor, language, and mental development.

Due process: Found in the 14th Amendment of the Constitution of the United States, it is the assurance of open and fair legal and procedural processes in which certain rights are inviolable.

Dyscalculia: A disability in the area of mathematics that is assumed to be the result of some type of neurological dysfunction. This disability may be manifested by difficulty in learning basic math facts, mathematical operations, and/or abstract mathematical concepts.

Dysgraphia: A disability in the area of writing that is assumed to be the result of some type of neurological dysfunction. This disability may be manifested by difficulty with handwriting, spelling, and/or written expression.

Dyslexia: A reading disability that is assumed to be the result of some type of neurological dysfunction.

Early intervening services: Early intervening services are intensive interventions provided to students who are having difficulties in general education but who have not yet been referred to special education. The purpose of these services is to try to keep children from being placed in special education unless absolutely necessary.

Echolalia: Repeating words and parts of or whole sentences spoken by other people, with little understanding.

Emotional disturbance/behavior disorders: A classification used in special education for students who exhibit inappropriate personal or social behavior that interferes with learning.

English-language learner (ELL): A person whose birth language is not English and who is learning English.

Enrichment: An increase in the quality of academics and the learning experience designed to enhance creativity and critical thinking ability.

Entrepreneurial supports: Supportive, self-sustaining, for-profit corporations built upon the skills and interests of those with disabilities.

Equal protection: A clause of the 14th Amendment to the Constitution of the United States that prohibits the denial of equal protection of the laws. As such, discrimination by race, gender, or disability is prohibited.

Ethnic: A group in which individual members identify with one another, usually based on ancestry. Ethnic groups often share common practices related to factors such as culture, religion, and language.

Eugenics: The study and policy of "improving" the human race through selective reproductive practices.

Evidence-based educational practices: Scientifically based practices founded on well-conducted research, which therefore have proven in some manner their efficacy.

Evidenced-based instructional practices: Teaching approaches that have been repeatedly demonstrated through research to result in student learning.

Exclusion clause: This clause is included in the definition of LD to ensure that the primary reason for a student's academic difficulty is a learning disability, and not another disability (e.g., intellectual disability or emotional/behavior disorder) or environmental conditions (e.g., poor teaching).

Explicit instruction: When instructional content is explicitly taught using systematic instructional methods, often based on behavioral theory.

Figurative language: A variety of figures of speech such as idioms, metaphors, analogies, similes, hyperbole, understatement, jokes, allusions, and slang.

Fluency: The rate and smoothness of speech.

Fragile-X syndrome: A genetically transmitted condition that is the most common cause of genetically transmitted intellectual disabilities. It is transmitted mostly from mothers to their sons. When inherited by boys, about 80% will have intellectual disabilities ranging from mild to severe.

Frequency (or pitch): How high or low a voice is.

Functional behavioral assessment (FBA): A systematic, highly structured method of gathering information to determine the purpose or function of observed behaviors.

Functional language: Communicating with a purpose, such as being able to communicate basic wants and needs.

Gastroesophageal reflux: This condition occurs when the lower esophageal sphincter does not close properly and stomach contents leak back, or reflux, into the esophagus.

Generalized anxiety: A state of fear, worry, and tension that is continuous and often accompanied by a variety of physical symptoms such as headaches, irritability, sweating, and nausea.

Genetic condition (dominant): A genetic condition that may be inherited if only one parent has the condition. If one parent has the condition, there is a 50% chance that the child will inherit it.

Genetic condition (recessive): A genetic condition that can only be inherited if both parents have the condition or if both parents are carriers. If both parents are carriers, there is a 25% chance that the child will inherit both abnormal genes and manifest the condition, and a 50% chance that the child will become a carrier but not manifest the condition.

Genetic condition (X-linked): A genetic condition that is carried on the X sex chromosome of the mother and is usually transmitted from a mother to a son.

Gift: Intellectual and academic ability/performance.

Giftedness: With no single definition, giftedness is usually defined by one of three conceptualizations (the Marland federal definition, Renzulli's three ring conceptualization, and Gardner's multiple intelligences), each of which refers generally to enhanced talents and cognitive ability.

Guided practice: Closely supervised practice activities designed to reinforce appropriate practices and correct errors.

Hearing impairment: An impairment in hearing, whether permanent or fluctuating, that adversely affects a child's educational performance but that is not included under the IDEA definition of deafness.

Herpes: A common viral infection that causes oral herpes (cold sores or fever blisters) and genital herpes (genital sores or sores below the waist).

Highly qualified teachers: NCLB requirement that teachers be appropriately licensed and have the requisite qualifications in core academic subject areas. Special education teachers must be highly qualified in special education as well as in each of the core subject areas they teach.

HOUSSE: The high objective uniform state standard of evaluation is a procedure used by states to assess an existing teacher's subject-matter competency in place of a test, coursework, degree, or certification.

Hyperactivity: A characteristic used to identify students with ADHD. Students who are hyperactive exhibit a high level of activity that is not appropriate in a particular setting and is not age-appropriate.

IEP team: This group of persons is responsible for writing a student's IEP. It must include professionals from the school and the school district, the student's parents, and, if appropriate, the student.

Immunoglobulin: An antibody used by the immune system to identify and neutralize foreign objects like bacteria and viruses.

Impulsivity: A characteristic used to identify students with ADHD. Students who are impulsive respond without thinking at a level that is not age-appropriate.

Inattention: A characteristic used to identify students with ADHD. Students who are inattentive cannot sustain attention for age-appropriate periods of time.

Independent practice: Practice activities designed to build fluency such as seatwork and homework typically completed independently.

Individualist culture: A culture in which individual achievement and initiative are valued and self-realization is promoted.

Individualized education plan (IEP): A detailed, structured plan of action required by IDEA that informs and guides the delivery of instruction and related services.

Individualized family service plan (IFSP): This document is used to plan services for infants and toddlers. The plan can include services for both the child and the family.

Individuals with Disabilities Education Improvement Act of 2004 (IDEA 2004): Landmark legislation, originally enacted in 1975 as the Education for All Handicapped Children Act, that guides how states and school districts must educate children with disabilities.

Induction: Introductory experiences novice teachers have that expose them to experienced teachers and mentors, professional activities that improve performance, more and more complex tasks, and the overall culture surrounding teaching.

In loco parentis: Teachers are entrusted by parents to exercise responsibility toward their children in the parents' place, and with that responsibility come associated privileges and liabilities.

Instructional technology: A general term that refers to the hardware and software used to enhance teaching and learning.

Intellectual disability: A widely used term in many European countries, which is emerging in the United States as the preferred term for students who are currently labeled *mentally retarded.*

Intensity (of sound): The loudness of sound, which is measured in decibels.

Intraindividual differences: Varying strengths and weaknesses that exist within individual profiles of performance and functioning.

Laryngeal tension: A chronic voice condition due to vocal abuse and misuse.

Larynx: A valve structure between the trachea (windpipe) and the pharynx (the upper throat) that is the primary organ of voice production.

Learning disabilities: A classification used in special education for students who exhibit significant problems in academic areas (such as reading) that cannot be explained by other disabilities. Under IDEA, the term "specific learning disabilities" is used for this condition.

Least restrictive environment (LRE): Services and the setting in which a free and appropriate education meets a child's individual needs while being educated with children without disabilities to the greatest extent possible.

Legal blindness: Central acuity of 20/200 or less in the better eye with the best possible corrections as measured on a Snellen vision chart, or a visual field of 20 degrees or less.

Legislation: Proposed or enacted law or set of laws.

Lesch-Nyhan syndrome: An X-linked recessive disease. The gene is carried by the mother and passed on to her son. A characteristic of this syndrome is self-injurious behavior, primarily lip and finger biting.

Levels of support: A criterion used to identify students with intellectual disabilities based on the level of support the student needs to function effectively. Levels of support may be intermittent, limited, or extensive.

Life-space interview (LSI): An intervention that occurs after an extreme behavioral event. Assumes that verbal mediation following this problematic event can result in lasting behavioral changes.

Litigation: A lawsuit or other action in the courts that seeks to settle a legal disagreement or issue.

Marland federal definition of giftedness: Giftedness is identified by performance or potential in intellectual, academic, productivity, leadership, visual and performing arts and psychomotor ability, and calls for special education services for students who cannot be adequately served by general education programs.

Mastery learning: A systematic approach to instruction that assumes that all students can learn, if given sufficient time and effective instruction. Students must master one level of instruction before they advance to the next instructional level.

Meningitis: An inflammation of the meninges (the membranes that cover the brain and spinal cord) caused by bacteria or viruses.

Mental retardation: Subaverage general intellectual functioning, existing concurrently with deficits in adaptive behavior and manifested during the developmental period, that adversely affects a child's educational performance.

Mentorship: The process through which veteran teachers help novices by modeling, demonstrating, guiding, and instructing effective methods, by explaining underlying theories, and by motivating them to be persistent in educating students.

Metacognition: An awareness of thinking processes and how these processes are monitored.

Mild intellectual disability: Also referred to as mild mental retardation, this is a developmental disability characterized by a low intelligence quotient (IQ) that is between about 55 to 70 points and poor adaptive behavior.

Moderate intellectual disability: Also referred to as moderate mental retardation, this is a developmental disability characterized by a low intelligence quotient (IQ) that is between about 40 to 55 points and poor adaptive behavior.

Morpheme: The smallest unit of language that has meaning.

Morphology: How sounds and words are put together to form meaning.

Multiple disabilities: Multiple disabilities means concomitant impairments (such as mental retardation and blindness, or mental retardation and an orthopedic impairment) that are usually very severe and require educational provisions that are different than if the student had only one of the conditions.

Multiple intelligences: The ability to solve problems of value to the culture at large by using eight areas of intelligence: logical mathematical, linguistic, musical, spatial, bodily kinesthetic, interpersonal, intrapersonal, and naturalistic.

Musculoskeletal disorders: These are disorders of the bones, connective tissue, and muscles. Examples include polio, arthritis, bone fractures or tumors, malformed bones, and joint disorders.

Nasal cavity: A large, air-filled space above and behind the nose in the middle of the face.

Naturalistic study: Research conducted in real-life situations, such as in the classroom or the school.

No Child Left Behind Act (NCLB): Federal legislation that requires states to (1) assess student performance in reading, math, and science; (2) ensure that all students have highly qualified teachers; and (3) provide public school choice and supplemental services to students unable to meet adequate yearly progress (AYP) for 2 years.

Nondiscriminatory assessment: Assessments that are not biased against or harmful toward students who are being tested.

Norm-referenced test: A student's performance on a norm-referenced test is evaluated in terms of how well he or she performs in comparison to other students of the same age or grade who were included in the standardization process or test development.

Obsessive-compulsive disorder (OCD): An anxiety disorder characterized by an inordinate fear or worry in the form of frequent problematic thoughts and the belief that these thoughts can be managed by the performance of repetitive actions and rituals.

Oral cavity: Opening or hollow part of the mouth.

Orthotic devices: Braces and similar devices used to support feet and ankles.

Overrepresentation: For certain demographic groups, the proportion of students identified for special education services is higher than the proportion of that group in the general population.

Pacing: The speed at which one is presented and ultimately learns material being taught.

Paraeducator: Also called a paraprofessional, teacher assistant, or teacher's aide, this is a person who assists a teacher in a special education or general education classroom.

Peer tutoring: A series of grouping alternatives that allow same-age or cross-age peers to assist classmates who are struggling with specific academic content.

Pervasive developmental disorder—not otherwise specified (PDD-NOS): Individuals who do not meet the criteria or the degree of severity that characterizes the four other disorders in the PDD group but who still show a pattern of impairments in social interaction, verbal and nonverbal communication skills, and stereotypical or restricted interests.

Phonatory quality (of sound): The quality of sound in a person's voice.

Phoneme: A meaningful unit in the sound system of a language.

Phonological processing: The ability to use sound-symbol correspondences to sound out words. Many students with reading disabilities have problems with phonological processing.

Phonology: The sound system of language, including speech sounds, speech patterns, and rules that apply to those sounds.

Picture Exchange Communication System (PECS): An augmentative/alternative communication system that uses pictures to systematically teach people to initiate communication.

Positive support reflex: A reaction that occurs when holding a baby under his arms and allowing his feet to bounce on a flat surface, he will extend (straighten) his legs

for about 20–30 seconds to support himself, before he flexes his legs again and goes to a sitting position.

Posttraumatic stress: The reexperiencing of fear that resulted originally from an extremely threatening or an actual terrible event or threat. Feelings of helplessness, terror, and horror accompany any reexperience of like events, and energy is spent avoiding like occurrences.

Prader-Willi syndrome: A genetic disorder that includes short stature, intellectual disabilities or learning disabilities, incomplete sexual development, behavior problems, low muscle tone, and an involuntary urge to eat constantly that leads to obesity.

Pragmatics: The rules that govern and describe how language is used in different contexts and environments.

Predominantly hyperactive-impulsive type (ADHD-PHI): A subtype of students with ADHD who are primarily hyperactive and impulsive.

Predominantly inattentive type (ADHD-PI): A subtype of students with ADHD who are primarily inattentive.

Prelinguistic communication: These are communication efforts that occur before the development of formal language. They include eye gaze, affective expressions, gestures, and vocalizations.

Prereferral intervention: Before a child is formally referred and evaluated for eligibility for special education services, prereferral intervention will be tried in the regular classroom in an attempt to improve the child's academic or behavioral functioning.

Primitive reflexes: Reflexes that occur in infants but disappear as they grow older.

Product sampling: The systematic collection of work done by students that demonstrates critical and creative thinking as well as other achievements.

Professionalism: The conduct, qualities, and purposes one has that reflect one's profession. It is an inclusive pattern of behavior that includes respect, responsibility, communication, leadership, risk taking, ongoing development, and a positive attitude.

Professional learning communities: Collaborative groups that share five characteristics: supportive and shared leadership, collective learning, shared values and vision, supportive conditions in human and physical resources, and shared practice.

Professional teaching standards: Tangible performance-based benchmarks for the initial and continuous development of professional teaching career.

Profound intellectual disabilities: Also referred to as profound mental retardation, this is the most severe form of a developmental disability characterized by a low intelligence quotient (IQ) that is b
elow 25 and extremely poor adaptive behavior.

Prophylactic antibiotics: Antibiotics used to prevent infections.

Prosocial behaviors: A series of behaviors, such as helping, sharing, or showing empathy, intended to benefit others or to evoke a meaningful interactive response from others.

Race: Often considered a socially constructed approach to grouping people based on visible characteristics such as skin color, hair texture, and hair color.

Radioiodine therapy: Treatment of an overactive thyroid gland using a form of iodine that is radioactive.

Range of motion: Joint flexibility usually measured by the number of degrees from the starting position of a segment to its position at the end of its full range of the movement.

Replacement behaviors: A series of positive actions that help the child achieve the same functions as do the challenging behaviors of concern.

Resilience: Successful adaptation in school or other settings, despite challenging or threatening life circumstances; a capacity that is available to all students and is bolstered by supportive factors.

Resiliency: The process of adjusting to varied situations and increasing competence in the face of adverse conditions.

Respiration: Breathing.

Respiratory infections: Multiple conditions including the common cold, viral respiratory infections, and bacterial respiratory infections.

Response-to-intervention (RTI): A new approach to the identification of special education needs that is based on the assumption that students who struggle academically should only be identified with a learning disability if they do not respond to effective and intensive levels of instruction.

Rett's disorder: A neurodevelopmental disorder characterized by seizures and mental retardation as well as a loss of functional or purposeful use of hands.

Routines and procedures: Activities or structures that help teachers organize and orchestrate everyday events with effectiveness and efficiency.

Rubella: A condition (commonly known as German measles) caused by the rubella virus that primarily affects the skin and lymph nodes.

Savant: A person who exhibits an exceptional skill or ability in one area, more than expected given intelligence or level of functioning.

Scaffolding: The temporary support that teachers give students as they learn academic content.

Schizophrenia: A severe mental illness characterized by bizarre behaviors, disorganized thinking and speech, decreased ability to express emotions, diminished or loss of contact with reality, and withdrawal from social relationships.

Screening: Determining whether a child has a broad set of behavioral characteristics that suggest the possibility of a disability and the need for further assessments.

Screening tests: These tests are used to evaluate all students during the early school years to determine if they might potentially need special services.

Section 504 of the Rehabilitation Act: Civil rights legislation that provides protections for those whose disabilities do not match the definitions under IDEA, including communicable diseases; temporary disabilities; and allergies, asthma, or illnesses due to the environment. It considers the child as having a disability if that child functions as though disabled and extends protections against discrimination beyond schools to employment and social and health services.

Self-advocacy: A principle and set of practices that allow people with disabilities to assume responsibility and advocate for their own lives and interests.

Self-determination: When persons act as the primary decision makers in their lives and make choices free from undue influence.

Self-efficacy: The belief that one's professional decisions, actions, and choices result in positive outcomes in students' lives.

Self-fulfilling prophecy: When someone behaves in ways that meet or go further below one's communicated low expectations, or when someone is unable to meet unreasonably high expectations and then becomes frustrated or depressed.

Self-injurious behaviors (SIBs): These are behaviors such as hitting your own head or biting your own hand that can be potentially dangerous. They are sometimes exhibited by students with severe and profound intellectual disabilities.

Self-management: A range of behaviors, such as self-instructing, monitoring, evaluation, reinforcement, graphing, and advocacy, by which a student can increase independence by increasing positive behaviors and skills.

Self-regulation strategies: Strategies that may be used by students with disabilities to decrease inappropriate behaviors, increase appropriate behaviors, and increase academic accuracy and productivity.

Semantics: The study of the meaning of language, including meaning at the word, sentence, and conversational level.

Separate class placement: A class placement setting in which a student with a disability is educated with other students with disabilities for 60% or more of the school day.

Separation anxiety: Inordinate fear, worry, and distress of being away from persons to whom a child is attached.

Service learning: An activity that combines educational and community service goals, which, by promoting self-reflection with reflection upon the experience, results in positive changes to both the person engaged in service learning activities and the persons being helped.

Severe discrepancy: The primary criterion currently used to identify students with LD in most states. Results when there is a severe discrepancy between expected achievement (typically based on an IQ score) and actual achievement.

Severe intellectual disabilities: Also referred to as severe mental retardation, this is developmental disability characterized by a low intelligence quotient (IQ) that is between about 25 to 40 points and poor adaptive behavior.

Sex chromosomes: The 23rd pair of chromosomes that are normally within a human cell.

Sheltered workshops: Segregated facilities that provide noncompetitive training and employment opportunities for individuals with disabilities.

Situational specificity: The ability to adjust behaviors to conform to varying circumstances, including social circumstances involving verbal and nonverbal exchanges.

Six hour retarded child: A phrase that was initially used by the President's Committee on Mental Retardation in 1969. Refers to the perspective that mild intellectual disabilities are more obvious during the school day than when students are at home or in the community.

Smith-Magenis: This syndrome is a chromosomal disorder with a recognizable pattern of physical, behavioral, and developmental features. It is characterized by infant feeding problems, low muscle tone, developmental delay, variable levels of intellectual disability, speech/language delay, middle-ear problems, skeletal anomalies, and decreased sensitivity to pain.

Social reciprocity: An exchange of meaningful communication that begins in infancy and continues throughout life.

Social skills instruction: The teaching of social interactive skills, including attending, affective, and pragmatic interaction.

Special schools: These are separate schools that only serve students with disabilities, usually students with more severe disabilities.

Specific language impairment (SLI): Difficulty with language in the absence of problems such as intellectual disabilities, hearing loss, or emotional disorders.

Standard American English (SAE): The dialect of English most common in the United States; most authorities believe it is best represented by a Midwestern accent.

Standard English: A controversial term that is most often used to refer to the dialect of English that is spoken by educated people.

Standardization process: This refers to the process used to develop standardized, norm-referenced tests. It involves creating the test and administering it to a large sample of students in a very systematic way in order to determine the norms or the performance levels of students at different ages or grade levels.

Stereotyped behaviors: Repetitive behaviors such as hand flapping that are seen among some individuals with disabilities.

Stimulant medication: Medications that are frequently used to treat students with ADHD. These medications have been found to be highly effective for many students with ADHD because they increase attention and reduce restlessness. Stimulant medications include Ritalin and Concerta.

Strategies Intervention Model (SIM): A combined cognitive and behavioral method of instruction that explicitly teaches a series of learning strategies that guide students in the acquisition, integration, and generalization of content.

Stuttering: An interruption in the smooth, easy flow of speech that includes repetitions, prolongations, interjections, and silent pauses.

Supported employment: A range of supports that enable people with disabilities to work in natural environments.

Surface management techniques: A series of teacher-based actions that address minor instances of misbehavior with little disruption to the instructional environment.

Syntax: The order of language, especially the way in which words are put together in phrases or sentences to produce meaning.

Syphilis: A sexually transmitted infection. The infection can also be passed from mother to infant during pregnancy, causing congenital syphilis.

Talent: An ability that is not intellectual or academic.

Targeted interventions: Powerful school-based actions directed toward the chronic and persistent problem behaviors of those students who do not respond to school-wide methods of discipline and behavior management.

Tests of creativity: Assessments that measure traits such as creative fluency, flexibility, elaboration, and originality.

Tay-Sachs disease: An inherited disease of the central nervous system that leads to death by age 5.

Thalidomide: A drug chiefly sold and prescribed during the late 1950s and 1960s to pregnant women to combat morning sickness and as a sleeping aid. The drug resulted in children born with limb deficiencies.

Three ring conception of giftedness: Interlocking factors that characterize giftedness as well above average ability, task commitment (motivation), and creativity.

Token economy: A common behavioral technique in which criteria are set for the exchanges of tokens for the display of positive behaviors. The tokens can be exchanged for items or activities a child finds meaningful.

Tonic labyrinthine reflex: A primitive reflex found in newborns in which tilting the head back while lying on the back causes the back to stiffen and even arch backwards, causes the legs to straighten, stiffen, and push together, causes the toes to point, causes the arms to bend at the elbows and wrists, and causes the hands to become fisted or the fingers to curl.

Toxemia: Also called preeclampsia, this is a disorder associated with pregnancy that consists of hypertension, which occurs most often after the 20th week of pregnancy.

Toxoplasmosis: An infection caused by a microscopic parasite that lives inside the cells of humans and animals, which is passed from animals, especially cats, to humans.

Type of hearing loss: The point in the auditory system where the hearing loss is occurring.

Universal design for learning: A method of making curriculum and instructional activities accessible to all students by including supports and accommodations into the original design rather than making alterations after the fact.

Videostroboscopy: A technique for recording and observing the motion of the vocal chords that allows for examination of the vibration of the vocal chords during speaking.

Visual acuity: How clearly a person sees at a specific distance. Expressed as a fraction. The numerator refers to the distance from the object; the denominator indicates the distance at which a person with normal eyesight could see the same object.

Visual field: The area in space around the head that can be seen without moving the head. Frequently this is also called peripheral vision.

Visual impairment including blindness: An impairment in vision that, even with correction, adversely affects a child's educational performance. The term includes both partial sight and blindness.

Vocal chords (or vocal folds): Muscular folds of mucous membrane that extend from the larynx wall.

Vocal folds: *See* Vocal chords

Vocal nodules: Benign growths on both vocal folds that are caused by vocal abuse.

Voice: Sound produced by air passing out through the larynx and upper respiratory tract.

Voice output communication aids (VOCA): Devices that are portable and allow people with difficulty in speech to communicate through the use of graphic symbols and words on computerized displays.

Working memory: Memory that is used to temporarily store and use information. Working memory allows an individual to see something, think about it, and then act on this information.

Wraparound interventions: Intensive interventions that are grounded in values of family empowerment and cultural competence, which typically require the coordinated and integrated efforts of teams of professional service providers.

Zero reject: The policy that prevents the exclusion of any child with a disability from receiving an education in the least restrictive environment.

References

Abbott, M., Walton, C., Tapia, Y., & Greenwood, C. (1999). Research to practice: A blueprint for closing the gap in local schools. *Exceptional Children, 65,* 339-354.

Abeson, A., Bolick, N., & Hass, J. (1976). Due process of law: Background and intent. In F. J. Weintraub, A. Abeson, J. Ballard, & M. L. LaVor (Eds.), *Public policy and the education of exceptional children.* (pp. 22-32). Reston, VA: The Council for Exceptional Children.

Achenbach, T. (2001a). *Child behavior checklist: Parent form.* Burlington, VT: Achenbach System of Empirically Based Assessment.

Achenbach, T. (2001b). *Child behavior checklist: Teacher report form.* Burlington, VT: Achenbach System of Empirically Based Assessment.

Achenbach, T. M., & Rescorla, L. (2001). *Manual for the ASEBA school-age forms and profiles.* Burlington: University of Vermont, Research Center for Children, Youth, and Families.

Adams, L., Gouvousis, A., VanLue, M., & Waldron, C. (2004). Social story intervention: Improving communication skills in a child with an autism spectrum disorder, *Focus on Autism and Other Developmental Disabilities, 19*(2), 87-94.

Agency for Healthcare Research and Quality. (2003). *Criteria for determining disability in infants and children: Low birth weight.* Retrieved October 14, 2005, from http://www.ahrq.gov/clinic/epcsums/lbwdissum.htm

Agran, M., Alper, S., & Wehmeyer, M. (2002). Access to the general curriculum for students with significant disabilities: What it means to teachers. *Education and Training in Mental Retardation and Developmental Disabilities, 37*(2), 123-133.

Agran, M., Fodor-Davis, J., Moore, S. C., & Martella, R. C. (1992). Effects of peer-delivered self-instructional training on a lunch-making work task for students with severe disabilities. *Education and Training in Mental Retardation, 27,* 230-240.

Ahearn, E. (2003). *Specific learning disability: Current approaches to identification and proposals for change.* Alexandria, VA: National Association of State Directors of Special Education.

Akshoomoff, N., Pierce, K., & Courchesne, E. (2002). The neurobiological basis of autism from a developmental perspective. *Development and Psychopathology, 14,* 613-634.

Albert, L. (2003). *Cooperative discipline: A teacher's handbook.* Circle Pines, MN: AGS.

Algozinne, B., Ysseldyke, J., & Elliot, J. (1998). *Strategies and tactics for effective instruction.* Longmont, CO: Sopris West.

Allbritten, D., Mainzer, R., & Ziegler, D. (2004). Will students with disabilities be scapegoats for school failure? *TEACHING Exceptional Children, 36*(3), 74-75.

Allsopp, D., Minskoff, E., & Bolt, L. (2005). Individualized course-specific strategy instruction for college students with learning disabilities and ADHD: Lessons learned from a model demonstration project. *Learning Disabilities Research and Practice, 20*(2), 103-118.

Amenkhienan, C. (2003). *Attention deficit disorder: Student handbook.* Blacksburg: Virginia Tech, Cook Counseling Center.

American Academy of Asthma Allergy and Immunology (AAAAI). (2005). *Pediatric asthma: Feature article.* http://www.aaaai.org/

American Academy of Pediatrics. (2000). Clinical practice guideline: Diagnosis and evaluation of the child with attention-deficit/hyperactivity disorder. *Pediatrics, 105*(5), 1158-1170.

American Academy of Pediatrics. (2001). Clinical practice guideline: Treatment of school-age children with attention-deficit/hyperactivity disorder. *Pediatrics, 108*(4), 1033-1044.

American Association of Colleges for Teacher Education, Committee on Multicultural Education. (2002). *Educators' preparation for cultural and linguistic diversity: A call to action.* Retrieved December 1, 2005, from http://www.aacte.org/Programs/Multicultural/culturallinguistic.pdf

American Association on Mental Retardation. (2002). *Mental retardation: Definition, classification, and systems of supports* (10th ed.). Washington, DC: Author.

American Association on Mental Retardation (AAMR). (2005). *Definition of mental retardation.* Retrieved June 12, 2006, from http://www.aamr.org/Policies/faq_mental_retardation.shtml

American Foundation for the Blind (AFB). (n.d.). *Quick facts and figures on blindness and low vision.* Retrieved August 30, 2005, from http://www.afb.org/Section.asp?SectionID=42&DocumentID=1374

American Lung Association. (2005). *Asthma and children fact sheet.* Retrieved August 11, 2005, from www.lungusa.org

American Printing House for the Blind (APH). (2003). *APH field services and federal quota info: An overview of federal quota.* Retrieved December 6, 2006, from http://www.aph.org/fedquotpgm/fedquota.htm

American Psychiatric Association. (1994). *Diagnostic and statistical manual of mental disorders* (3rd ed.). Washington, DC: Author.

American Psychiatric Association. (2000). *Diagnostic and statistical manual of mental disorders* (4th ed.). Washington, DC: Author.

American Psychological Association (APA). (2003). *Guidelines for non-handicapping language in APA journals.* Retrieved August 5, 2006, from www.apastyle.org/disabilities.html

American Speech-Language-Hearing Association (ASHA). (1999). *Guidelines for the roles and responsibilities of the school-based speech-language pathologist.* Retrieved January 11, 2006, from http://search.asha.org/query.html?col=asha&qt=scope+of+practice

American Speech-Language-Hearing Association (ASHA). (n.d.). *Hearing assessment.* Retrieved September 30, 2005, from http://www.asha.org/public/hearing/testing/assess.htm

Anderson, G. M., & Hoshino, Y. (2005). Neurochemical studies of autism. In F. R. Volkmar, R. Paul, A. Klin, & D. Cohen (Eds.), *Handbook of autism and pervasive developmental disorders: Vol. 2. Assessment, interventions, and policy* (4th ed., pp. 453-472). Hoboken, NJ: Wiley.

Anderson, L., & Krathwohl, D. (Eds.). (2001). *A taxonomy for learning, teaching, and assessing.* New York: Longman.

Arick, J. R., Krug, D. A., Fullerton, A., Loos, L., & Falco, R. (2005). School-based programs. In F. R. Volkmar, R. Paul, A. Klin, & D. Cohen (Eds.), *Handbook of autism and pervasive developmental disorders: Vol. 2.*

Assessment, interventions, and policy (4th ed., pp. 1003-1028). Hoboken, NJ: Wiley.

Arnold, K. D. (1993). Academically talented women in the 1930s: The Illinois valedictorian project. In K. D. Hulbert & D. T. Schuster (Eds.), *Women's lives through time* (pp. 393-414). San Francisco: Jossey-Bass.

Assistive Technology Act of 1998. Retrieved December 11, 2006, from www.section508.gov/docs/AT1998.html

Azordegan, J. (2004, January). *Initial findings and major questions about HOUSSE.* Retrieved November 3, 2005, from http://www.ecs.org/topnav_NEW.htm

Babbidge Committee Report. (1965). *Education of the deaf in the United States: Report of the advisory committee on the education of the deaf.* Washington, DC: U.S. Government Printing Office.

Baca, L. M., & Cervantes, H. T. (2004). *The bilingual special education interface.* Upper Saddle River, NJ: Merrill/Prentice Hall.

Baglieri, S., & Knopf, J. H. (2004). Normalizing difference in inclusive teaching. *Journal of Learning Disabilities, 37*(6), 525-529.

Bailey, D. B., McWilliam, R. A., Darkes, L. A., Hebbeler, K., Simeonsson, R. J., Spiker, D., et al. (1998). Family outcomes in early intervention: A framework for program evaluation and efficacy research. *Exceptional Children, 64,* 313-328.

Baird, G., et al. (2000). A screening instrument for autism at 18 months of age: A 6-year follow-up. *Journal of the American Academy of Child and Adolescent Psychiatry, 29,* 694-702.

Bali, V., & Alvarez, M. (2004). The race gap in student achievement scores: Longitudinal evidence from a racially diverse school district. *Policies Studies Journal, 32*(3), 393-417.

Bandura, A. (1977). Self-efficacy: Toward a unifying theory of behavioral change. *Psychological Review, 84,* 191-215.

Bangert, A. W., & Cooch, C. G. (2001). Facilitating teacher assistance teams: Key questions. *Bulletin, 85*(626). Retrieved December 2, 2004, from http://www.principals.org/news/bltn_tchr_asst901.cfm

Banks, J., Cochran-Smith, M., Moll, L., Richert, A., Zeichner, K., LePage, P., et al. with McDonald, M. (2005). Teaching diverse learners. In L. Darling-Hammond & J. Bransford (Eds.), *Preparing teachers for a changing world: What teachers should learn and be able to do* (pp. 232-273). San Francisco: Jossey-Bass.

Banner, J. M., & Cannon, H. C. (1997). *The elements of teaching.* New Haven, CT: Yale University Press.

Barbaresi, W., Katusic, S., Colligan, R., et al. (2002). How common is attention-deficit/hyperactivity disorder? *Archives of Pediatric Adolescent Medicine, 156,* 217-224.

Barkley, R. (2000). *Taking charge of ADHD.* New York: Guilford.

Barkley, R. (2003). Attention-deficit/hyperactivity disorder. In E. J. Mash & R. Barkley (Eds.), *Child psychopathology* (2nd ed., pp. 75-143). New York: Guilford.

Barkley, R., Fischer, M., Smallish, L., & Fletcher, K. (2002). The persistence of attention-deficit/hyperactivity disorder into young adulthood as a function of reporting source and definition of disorder. *Journal of Abnormal Psychology, 111*(2), 279-289.

Barkley, R., Fischer, M., Smallish, L., & Fletcher, K. (2003). Does the treatment of attention-deficit/hyperactivity disorder with stimulants contribute to drug use/abuse? A 13-year prospective study. *Pediatrics, 111,* 97-109.

Barkley, R., & Murphy, K. (2005). *Attention deficit hyperactivity disorder: A clinical workbook* (3rd ed.). New York: Guilford.

Barkley, R. A. (1981). *Hyperactive children: A handbook for diagnosis and treatment.* New York: Guilford.

Bartoli, J. S. (2001). *Celebrating city teachers: How to make a difference in urban schools.* Portsmouth, NH: Heinemann.

Batshaw, M. L. (2002). *Children with disabilities* (5th ed.). Baltimore: Brookes.

Beirne-Smith, M., Patton, J., & Kim, S. (2006). *Mental retardation: An introduction to intellectual disabilities* (7th ed.). Upper Saddle River, NJ: Merrill/Prentice Hall.

Bell, L. I. (2003). Strategies that close the gap. *Educational Leadership, 60*(4), 32-34.

Bempechat, J. (1998). *Against the odds.* San Francisco: Jossey-Bass.

Benard, B. (2004). *Resiliency: What we have learned.* San Francisco: WestEd.

Bender, W. (1999). Learning disabilities in the classroom. In W. Bender (Ed.), *Professional issues in learning disabilities* (pp. 3-26). Austin, TX: PRO-ED.

Benner, G. J., Nelson, J. R., & Epstein, M. H. (2002). Language skills of children with EBD: A literature review. *Journal of Emotional and Behavioral Disorders, 10,* 43-59.

Bennett, A. (1932). *A comparative study of subnormal children in the elementary grades.* New York: Columbia University, Teachers College, Bureau of Publication.

Bennett, C. (2003). *Comprehensive multicultural education: Theory and practice.* New York: Allyn & Bacon.

Berger, S. L. (1994). *College planning for gifted students* (2nd ed.). Reston, VA: Council for Exceptional Children.

Bernas-Pierce, J., & Miller, T. (2005). *Natural environments: Service and advocacy for children who are visually impaired or deafblind* [Monograph 1]. Watertown, MA: Perkins School for the Blind.

Best, S. (2005a). Health impairments and infectious diseases. In S. J. Best, K. W. Heller, & J. L. Bigge (Eds.), *Teaching individuals with physical or multiple disabilities* (5th ed., pp. 59-85). Upper Saddle River, NJ: Merrill/Prentice Hall.

Best, S. (2005b). Physical disabilities. In S. J. Best, K. W. Heller, & J. L. Bigge (Eds.), *Teaching individuals with physical or multiple disabilities* (5th ed., pp. 31-58). Upper Saddle River, NJ: Merrill/Prentice Hall.

Best, S. J., & Bigge, J. L. (2005). Cerebral palsy. In S. J. Best, K. W. Heller, & J. L. Bigge (Eds.), *Teaching individuals with physical or multiple disabilities* (5th ed., pp. 87-109). Upper Saddle River, NJ: Merrill/Prentice Hall.

Bettelheim, B. (1967). *The empty fortress: Infantile autism and the birth of the self.* New York: Free Press.

Bhanpuri, H., & Sexton, S. (2006). *A look at the hidden costs of high school exit exams: CEP policy brief.* Washington, DC: Center on Education Policy. Retrieved October 20, 2006, from http://www.cep-dc.org/pubs/hseepolicybriefSep2006/

Biederman, J., Faraone, S., Keenan, K., & Tsuang, M. (1991). Evidence of a familial association between attention deficit disorder and major affective disorders. *Archives of General Psychiatry, 48,* 633-642.

Biklen, D. (1990). Communication unbound: Autism and praxis. *Harvard Educational Review, 60,* 291-314.

Billingsley, B. (2005). *Cultivating and keeping committed special educators: What principals and district administrators can do.* Thousand Oaks, CA: Corwin.

Billingsley, B. S., & Tomchin, E. M. (1992). Four beginning LD teachers: What their experiences suggest for trainers and employers. *Learning Disabilities Research and Practice, 7,* 104-112.

Blatt, B. (1970). *Exodus from pandemonium: Human abuse and a reformation of public policy.* Boston: Allyn & Bacon.

Blatt, B. (1976). *Revolt of the idiots: A story.* Glen Ridge, NJ: Exceptional Press.

Blatt, B., & Kaplan, F. (1966). *Christmas in Purgatory: A photographic essay on mental retardation* (2nd ed.). Boston: Allyn & Bacon.

Bloch, D. (1978). *"So the witch won't eat me": Fantasy and the child's fear of infanticide.* Boston: Houghton Mifflin.

Bloom, B. (1971). Mastery learning. In H. H. Block (Ed.), *Mastery learning: Theory and practice* (pp. 47-63). New York: Holt, Rinehart, and Winston.

Bloom, B. (1976). *Human characteristics and school learning.* New York: McGraw-Hill.

Bobeck, B. L. (2002, March/April). Teacher resiliency: A key to career longevity. *Clearing House, 75*(4), 202-205.

Bogdan, R., & Biklen, D., (1977). Handicapism. *Social Policy, 7*(5), 59-63.

Bondy, E., Ross, D. D., Gallingane, C., & Hambacher, E. (2006, April). *Creating environments of success and resilience: Culturally responsive classroom management and more.* Paper presented at the annual meeting of the American Educational Research Association, San Francisco.

Books, S. (2004). *Poverty and schooling in the U.S.* Mahwah, NJ: Erlbaum.

Bos, C., Nahmias, M., & Urban, M. (1999). Targeting home school collaboration for students with ADHD. *Teaching Exceptional Children, 31*(6), 4-11.

Bricker, D. (1978). A rationale for the integration of handicapped and non-handicapped preschool children. In M. Guralnick (Ed.), *Early intervention and the integration of handicapped and non-handicapped children* (pp. 3-26). Baltimore: University Park Press.

Bricker, D., & Squires, J. (1999). *Ages & stages questionnaries: A parent completed child-monitoring system.* Baltimore: Brookes.

Brigance, A. (1991). *The Brigance screens.* North Billerica, MA: Curriculum Associates.

Brigham, F. J., Scruggs, T. E., & Mastropieri, M. A. (1992). Teacher enthusiasm in learning disabilities classrooms: Effects on learning and behavior. *Learning Disabilities Research and Practice, 7,* 68-73.

Brilliant, R. L., & Graboyes, M. (1999). Historical overview of low vision: Classifications and perceptions. In R. L. Brilliant (Ed.), *Essentials of low vision practice* (pp. 2-9). Boston: Butterworth Heinemann.

Brophy, J. E. (1998). *Motivating students to learn.* Boston: McGraw-Hill.

Browder, D. M. (2001). *Curriculum and assessment for students with moderate and severe disabilities.* New York: Guilford.

Browder, D. M., & Spooner, F. (2003). Understanding the purpose and process of alternate assessment. In D. L. Ryndak & S. Alper (Eds.), *Curriculum and instruction for students with significant special needs in inclusive settings* (2nd ed., pp. 51-72). Boston: Allyn & Bacon.

Brown v. Board of Education. (1954). 348 U.S. 886, 72 S. Ct. 120.

Brown, D. F. (2004). Urban teachers' professed classroom management strategies: Reflections of culturally responsive teaching. *Urban Education, 39,* 266-289.

Brown, L., Branston-McLean, M. B., Baumgart, D., Vincent, L., Falvey, M., & Schroeder, J. (1979). Using the characteristics of current and subsequent least restrictive environments as factors in the development of curricular content for severely handicapped students. *AAESPH Review, 4,* 407-424.

Brown, L., Nietupski, J., & Hamre-Nietupski, S. (1976). Criterion of ultimate functioning. In A. Thomas (Ed.), *Hey, don't forget about me!* Reston, VA: CEC Information Center.

Brown, L., Nisbet, J., Ford, A., Sweet, M., Shiraga, B., York, J., & Loomis, R. (1983). The critical need for nonschool instruction in educational programs for severely handicapped students. *Journal of The Association of the Severely Handicapped, 8,* 71-77.

Brownell, M. (1997). Coping with stress in the special education classroom. *Teaching Exceptional Children, 30*(1), 76-79.

Bruininks, R. H., Woodcock, R. W., Weatherman, R. F., & Hill, B. K. (1996). *The scales of independent behavior—revised.* Itasca, IL: Riverside.

Bryant, D., & Dix, J. (1999). Mathematics interventions for students with learning disabilities. In W. Bender (Ed.), *Professional issues in learning disabilities* (pp. 219-259). Austin, TX: PRO-ED.

Buck, G. H., Polloway, E. A., Smith-Thomas, A., & Cook, K. W. (2003). Prereferral intervention processes: A survey of state practices. *Exceptional Children, 69,* 349-360.

Buescher, T. M. (1991). Gifted adolescents. In N. Colangelo & G. A. Davis (Eds.), *Handbook of gifted education* (pp. 382-401). Needham Heights, MA: Allyn & Bacon.

Bulgren, J., Hock, M., Schumaker, J., & Deshler, D. (1995). The effects of instruction in a paired-associates strategy on the information mastery performance of students with learning disabilities. *Learning Disabilities Research and Practice, 10,* 22-37.

Bullis, M. (2001). Job placement and support considerations in transition programs for adolescents with emotional disabilities. In L. M. Bullock & R. A. Gable (Eds.), *Addressing the social, academic, and behavioral needs of students with challenging behavior in inclusive and alternative settings* (pp. 31-41). Arlington, VA: Council for Exceptional Children.

Burns, B. J., & Goldman, S. K. (1998). *Promising practices in wraparound for children with serious emotional disturbance and their families:* Vol. 4. *Systems of care: promising practices in children's mental health 1998 series.* Washington, DC: Georgetown University, Child Development Center, National Technical Assistance Center for Children's Mental Health.

Buros Institute of Mental Measurements. Retrieved December 28, 2004, from http://www.unl.edu/buros/

Busch, T. W., Pederson, K., Espin, C. A., & Weissenburger, J. W. (2001). Teaching students with learning disabilities: Perceptions of a first year teacher. *Journal of Special Education, 35,* 92-99.

Cafiero, J. M. (1998). Communication power for individuals with autism. *Focus on Autism and Other Developmental Disabilities, 13*(2), 113-122.

Campbell, F., Ramey, C., Pungello, E., Sparling, J., & Miller-Johnson, S. (2002). Early childhood education: Young adult outcomes from the Abecedarian Project. *Applied Developmental Science, 6*(1), 42-57.

Carey, K. (2004a, Fall). The funding gap 2004: Many states still shortchange low-income and minority students. *Education Trust.* Retrieved October 20, 2006, from http://www2.edtrust.org/edtrust/Product+Catalog/special+reports

Carey, K. (2004b). The real value of teachers: Using new information about teacher effectiveness to close the achievement gap. *Education Trust, 8*(1).

Carey, W. (2004). ADHD: An epidemic. *Developmental Behavioral Pediatrics Online.* Retrieved September 28, 2005, from http://www.dbpeds.org/articles/detail.cfm?TextID=128

Carlberg, C., & Kavale, K. (1980). The efficacy of special versus regular class placement for exceptional children: A meta-analysis. *Journal of Special Education 14*(3), 295-309.

Carlson, E., Lee, H., & Schroll, K. (2004). Identifying attributes of high quality special education teachers. *Teacher Education and Special Education, 27,* 350-359.

Carnine, D., Engelmann, S., & Steely, D. (1999). *Corrective math.* Columbus, OH: SRA.

Carnine, D., Silbert, J., Kame'enui, E., & Tarver, S. (2003). *Direct instruction reading* (4th ed.). Upper Saddle River, NJ: Merrill/Prentice Hall.

Carr, E. G., Horner, R. H., Turnbull, A. P., Marquis, J. G., McLaughlin, D. M., McAtee, M. L., et al. (1999). *Positive behavior support for people with developmental disabilities: A research synthesis.* Washington, DC: American Association on Mental Retardation.

Carter, J., & Sugai, G. (1989). Survey on prereferral practices: Response from state departments of education. *Exceptional Children, 55,* 298-302.

Casey, K. M. A., & Shore, B. M. (2000). Mentors' contributions to gifted adolescents' affective, social, and vocational development. *Roeper Review, 22,* 227-230.

Center for Effective Collaboration and Practice. (1998). *Functional behavioral assessment.* Retrieved November 10, 2005, from http://cecp.air.org/fba/problembehavior/main.htm

Center on Education Policy. (2004). *State high school exit exams: A maturing reform.* Washington, DC. Retrieved October 20, 2006, from http://www.cep-dc.org/highschoolexit/statematuringAug2004.cfm

Center on Education Policy. (2006). *State high school exit exams: A challenging year: Summary and methods.* Washington, DC. Retrieved October 20, 2006, from http://www.cep-dc.org/pubs/hseeAugust2006/

Centers for Disease Control. (2003). *Meningococcal disease.* Retrieved June 28, 2005, from http://www.cdc.gov/ncidod/dbmd/diseaseinfo/meningococcal_g.htm

Centers for Disease Control. (2004). *The Metropolitan Atlanta Developmental Disabilities Surveillance Program (MADDSP).* Retrieved June 27, 2005, from http://www.cdc.gov/ncbddd/dd/ddsurv.htm#mr

Centers for Disease Control and Prevention. (2005a). *HIV estimate.* Retrieved September 27, 2005, from http://www.cdc.gov/hiv/stats.htm#hivest

Centers for Disease Control and Prevention. (2005b). *Universal precautions for prevention of transmission of HIV and other bloodborne infections.* Retrieved August 28, 2006, from http://www.cdc.gov/ncidod/dhqp/bp_universal_precautions.html

Chalfant, J. C. (1998). Why Kirk stands alone. *Learning Disabilities Research and Practice, 13*(1), 2-7.

Chalfant, J. C., & Pysh, M. (1989). Teacher assistance teams: Five descriptive studies on 96 teams. *Remedial and Special Education, 10,* 49-58.

Chalfant, J. C., Pysh, M. V., & Moultrie, R. (1979). Teacher assistance teams: A model for within—Building problem solving. *Learning Disability Quarterly, 2,* 85-96.

Chandler, L. K., & Dahlquist, C. M. (2002). *Functional assessment: Strategies to prevent and remediate challenging behaviors in school settings.* Upper Saddle River, NJ: Merrill/Prentice Hall.

Chawarska, K., & Volkmar, F. R. (2005). Autism in infancy and early childhood. In F. R. Volkmar, R. Paul, A. Klin, & D. Cohen (Eds.), *Handbook of autism and pervasive developmental disorders: Vol. 1. Diagnosis, development, neurobiology, and behavior.* (4th ed., pp. 223-246). Hoboken, NJ: Wiley.

Chen, D., Alsop, L., & Minor, L. (2000). Lessons from Project PLAI in California and Utah: Implications for early intervention services to infants who are deaf-blind and their families. *Deaf-Blind Perspectives, 7*(3), 1-5.

Cheney, D., & Bullis, M. (2004). The school-to-community transition of adolescents with emotional and behavioral disorders. In R. B. Rutherford, Jr., M. M. Quinn, & A. R. Mathur (Eds.), *Handbook of research in emotional and behavioral disorders* (pp. 369-384). New York: Guilford.

Chesapeake Institute. (1994, September). *National agenda for achieving better results for children and youth with serious emotional disturbance.* Washington, DC: U.S. Department of Education.

Cimera, R. E. (2003). *The truth about special education: A guide for parents and teachers.* Lanham, MD: Scarecrow Press.

Clarizo, H. F. (1994). *Assessment and treatment of depression in children and adolescents* (2nd ed.). Brandon, VT: Clinical Psychology.

Clark, G. M., & Bigge, J. L. (2005). Transition and self-determination. In S. J. Best, K. W. Heller, & J. L. Bigge (Eds.), *Teaching individuals with physical or multiple disabilities* (5th ed., pp. 367-398). Upper Saddle River, NJ: Merrill/Prentice Hall.

Codell, E.R. (2001). *Educating Esme.* Chapel Hill, NC: Algonquin.

Cole, C., Horvath, B., Chapman, C., Deschenes, C., Ebeling, D., & Sprague, J. (2000). *Adapting curriculum & instruction in inclusive classrooms: A teachers' desk reference* (2nd ed.). Bloomington: Indiana Institute on Disability and Community.

Coleman, M., & Vaughn, S. (2000). Reading interventions for students with emotional/behavioral disorders. *Behavioral Disorders, 25*(2), 93-104.

Conners, K. (2002a). *Conners parent rating scale—Revised version: Long form, ADHD index scale.* North Tonawanda, NY: Multi-Health Systems.

Conners, K. (2002b). *Conners teacher rating scale—Revised version: Long form, ADHD index scale.* North Tonawanda, NY: Multi-Health Systems.

Connor, M. H., & Boskin, J. (2001). Overrepresentation of bilingual and poor children in special education classes: A continuing problem. *Journal of Children and Poverty, 7*(1), 23-32.

Conroy, M. A., Hendrickson, J. M., & Hester, P. P. (2004). Early identification and prevention of emotional and behavioral disorders. In R. B. Rutherford, Jr., M. M. Quinn, & A. R. Mathur (Eds.), *Handbook of research in emotional and behavioral disorders* (pp. 199-215). New York: Guilford.

Coonrod, E. E., & Stone, W. L. (2005). Screening for autism in young children. In F. R. Volkmar, R. Paul, A. Klin, & D. Cohen (Eds.), *Handbook of autism and pervasive developmental disorders: Vol. 2. Assessment, interventions, and policy* (4th ed., pp. 707-729). Hoboken, NJ: Wiley.

Cooper, H. (2001). *The battle over homework* (2nd ed.). Thousand Oaks, CA: Corwin.

Cooper H., & Nye, B. (1994). Homework for students with learning disabilities: The implications for policy and practice. *Journal of Learning Disabilities, 27*(8), 470-479.

Coping.org. (2006). *Tools for coping with life's stressors.* Retrieved July 14, 2006, from http://www.coping.org/specialneeds/assistech/aacdev.htm

Coplan, J. (1987). Deafness: Ever heard of it? *Pediatrics, 79*(2), 202-213.

Corbett, D., Wilson, B., & Williams, B. (2002). *Effort and excellence in urban classrooms.* New York: TC Press.

Corbett, W. P., Clark, H. B., & Blank, W. (2002). Employment and social outcomes associated with vocational programming for youths with emotional or behavioral disorders. *Behavioral Disorders, 27,* 358-370.

Correa, S. C., & Howell, J. J. (2004). Facing the challenges of itinerant teaching: Perspectives and suggestions from the field. *Journal of Visual Impairment and Blindness, 98,* 420-433.

Correa, V., & Tulbert, B. (1993). Collaboration between school personnel in special education and Hispanic families. *Journal of Educational and Psychological Consultation, 4*(3), 253-265.

Correa, V. I., Fazzi, D. L., & Pogrund, R. L. (2002). Team focus: Current trends, service delivery, and advocacy. In R. L. Pogrund & D. L. Fazzi (Eds.), *Early focus: Working with young children who are blind or visually impaired and their families* (2nd ed., pp. 405-441). New York: AFB Press.

Corwin, M. (2001). *And still we rise: Trials and triumphs of twelve gifted inner city high school students.* New York: HarperCollins.

Costello, J., Mustillo, S., Erkanli, A., et al. (2003). Prevalence and development of psychiatric disorders in childhood and adolescence. *Archives of General Psychiatry, 60,* 837-844.

Council for Exceptional Children (CEC). (2003). *What every special educator must know: Ethics, standards, and guidelines for special educators* (5th ed.). Arlington, VA: Author.

Coutinho, M. J., & Oswald, D. P. (2000). Disproportionate representation in special education: A synthesis and recommendations. *Journal of Child and Family Studies, 9*(2), 135-156.

Coutinho, M. J., Oswald, D. P., & Forness, S. R. (2002). Gender and sociodemographic factors and the disproportionate identification of culturally and linguistically diverse students with emotional disturbance. *Behavioral Disorders, 27*(2), 109-125.

Coyne, M., Kame'enui, E., & Carnine, D. (2007). *Effective teaching strategies that accommodate diverse learners* (3rd ed.). Upper Saddle River, NJ: Merrill/Prentice Hall.

Crawford, J. (2002). *Census 2000: A guide for the perplexed.* Retrieved November 27, 2005, from http://ourworld.compuserve.com/homepages/JWCRAWFORD/census02.htm

Crozier, S., & Tincani, M. J. (2005). Using a modified social story to decrease disruptive behavior of a child with autism. *Focus on Autism and Other Developmental Disabilities, 20*(3), 150-157.

Cullinan, D. (2002). *Students with emotional and behavior disorders: An introduction for teachers and other helping professionals.* Upper Saddle River, NJ: Pearson Education.

Cullinan, D. (2004). Classification and definition of emotional and behavioral disorders. In R. B. Rutherford, Jr., M. M. Quinn, & A. R. Mathur (Eds.), *Handbook of research in emotional and behavioral disorders* (pp. 32-53). New York: Guilford.

Cullinan, D., & Sabornie, E. J. (2004). Characteristics of emotional disturbance in middle and high school students. *Journal of Emotional and Behavioral Disorders, 12,* 157-167.

Cummins, J. (1984). *Bilingualism and special education: Issues in assessment and pedagogy.* Clevedon, UK: Multilingual Matters.

Cummins, J. (2001). Assessment and intervention with culturally and linguistically diverse learners. In S. Hurley & J. Tinajero (Eds.), *Literacy assessment of bilingual learners* (pp. 115-129). Boston: Allyn & Bacon.

Curwin, R. L., & Mendler, A. N. (1988). Packaged discipline programs: Let the buyer beware. *Educational Leadership, 46,* 68-71.

Curwin, R. L., & Mendler, A. N. (1999). *Discipline with dignity* (2nd ed.). Alexandria, VA: ASCD.

Dalston, R. M. (2000). Voice disorders. In R. B. Gillam, T. P. Marquardt, & F. N. Martin (Eds.), *Communication sciences and disorders: From science to clinical practice* (pp. 283-312). San Diego: Singular.

Daniel R. R. v. State Board of Education. (1989). 874 F.2d 1036 (5th Cir.).

Darling-Hammond, L. (1998). Equal opportunity race and education: The nature of educational inequality. *Brookings Review, 16*(2), 28-32.

Davenport, C. (1910). *Eugenics: The science of human improvement by better breeding.* Retrieved February 5, 2005, from http://www.eugenicsarchive.org/html/eugenics/static/themes/28.html

Davis, B. L., & Bedore, L. M. (2000). Articulatory and phonological disorders. In R. B. Gillam, T. P. Marquardt, & F. N. Martin (Eds.), *Communication sciences and disorders: From science to clinical practice* (pp. 233-254). San Diego: Singular.

Davis, C. C. (2003, August). Transition: It's all about collaboration. *See/Hear Newsletter.* pp. 34-36.

Davis, G. A., & Rimm, S. B. (2003). *Education of the gifted and talented* (5th ed.). Upper Saddle River, NJ: Prentice Hall.

Deaf Culture Information. (2005). *Deaf history.* Retrieved February 5, 2005, from http://members.aol.com/deafcultureinfo/deaf_history.htm

deBettencourt, L. (2002). Understanding the differences between IDEA and Section 504. *Teaching Exceptional Children, 34*(3), 16-23.

Delpit, L. (1995). *Other people's children.* New York: New Press.

Delpit, L. (2002). No kinda' sense. In L. Delpit & J. K. Dowdy (Eds.), *The skin we speak: Thoughts on language and culture in the classroom* (pp. 31-48). New York: New Press.

Deno, S. (1985). Curriculum-based measurement: The emerging alternative. *Exceptional Children, 52,* 219-232.

Deno, S. (2003). Developments in curriculum-based measurement. *Journal of Special Education, 37*(3), 184-192.

DePaepe, P., Garrison-Kane, L., & Doelling J. (2002). Supporting students with health needs in schools: An overview of selected health conditions. *Focus on Exceptional Children, 35*(1), 1-24.

Deshler, D. (2005). Adolescents with learning disabilities: Unique challenges and reasons for hope. *Learning Disability Quarterly, 28,* 122-124.

Deshler, D., & Schumaker, J. (Eds.). (2006). *Teaching adolescents with disabilities: Accessing the general education curriculum.* Thousand Oaks, CA: Corwin.

Deshler, D., Schumaker, J., Lenz, K., Bulgren, J., Hock, M., Knight, J., et al. (2001). Ensuring content-area learning by secondary students with learning disabilities. *Learning Disabilities Research and Practice, 16*(2), 96-108.

Dever, R. B. (1988). *Community living skills: A taxonomy.* Washington, DC: American Association on Mental Retardation.

Dickens, C. (1842). *American notes.* Retrieved February 9, 2005, from http://xroads.virginia.edu/~hyper/detoc/fem/dickens.htm

Diller, L. H. (2000). The Ritalin wars continue. *Western Journal of Medicine, 173,* 366-367.

Doubt, L., & McColl, M. A. (2003). A secondary guy: Physically disabled teenagers in secondary schools. *Canadian Journal of Occupational Therapy, 70*(3), 139-151.

Doyle, M. B. (2002). *The paraprofessional's guide to the inclusive classroom* (2nd ed.). Baltimore: Brookes.

Doyle, W. (1986). Classroom organization and management. In Merlin C. Wittrock (Ed.), *Handbook of research on teaching* (3rd ed.). New York: Macmillan.

Drotar, D. (2002). Behavioral and emotional problems in infants and young children: Challenges of clinical assessment and intervention. *Infants and Young Children, 14*(4), 1-5.

Dubowitz, H. (Ed.). (1999). *Neglected children: Research, policy, and practice.* Thousand Oaks, CA: Sage.

Dudzinski, M., Roszmann-Millican, M., & Shank, K. (2000). Continuing professional development for special educators: Reforms and implications for university programs. *Teacher Education and Special Education, 23*(2), 109-124.

Duhaney, L. (2003). A practical approach to managing the behaviors of students with ADHD. *Intervention in School and Clinic, 38*(5), 267-279.

Dunn, L. M. (1968). Special education for the mildly retarded—Is much of it justifiable? *Exceptional Children, 35,* 5-22.

DuPaul, G. (2004). *ADHD identification and assessment: Basic guidelines for educators.* Bethesda, MD: National Association for School Psychologists.

DuPaul, G., Barkley, R., & Connor, D. (1998). Stimulants. In R. Barkley (Ed.), *Attention deficit hyperactivity disorder: A handbook for diagnosis and treatment* (2nd ed., pp. 510-551). New York: Guilford.

DuPaul, G., & Stoner, G. (2003). *ADHD in the schools: Assessment and intervention strategies* (2nd ed.). New York: Guilford.

Dwyer, K., & Osher, D. (2000). *Safeguarding our children: An action guide.* Washington, DC: U.S. Department of Education and Justice, American Institutes for Research.

Dwyer, K., Osher, D., & Warger, C. (1998). *Early warning, timely response: A guide to safe schools.* Washington, DC: U.S. Department of Education.

Dykens, E. M., Hodapp, R. M., & Finucane, B. M. (2000). *Genetics and mental retardation syndromes: A new look at behavior and interventions.* Baltimore: Brookes.

Eber, L., Sugai, G., Smith, C. R., & Scott, T. M. (2002). Wraparound and positive behavioral interventions and supports in the schools. *Journal of Emotional and Behavioral Disorders, 10*(3), 171-180.

Eckenrode, J., Laird, M., & Doris, J. (1993). School performance and disciplinary problems among abused and neglected children. *Developmental Psychology, 29,* 53-62.

Education Alliance (2002). *The Diversity Kit.* Providence, RI: Author. Retrieved December 1, 2005, from http://www.alliance.brown.edu/tdl/diversitykitpdfs/dk_culture.pdf

Education Trust. (2004). *The ABCs of AYP.* Retrieved April 5, 2005, from www2.edtrust.org/nr/rdonlyres/37b8652d-84f4-4fa1-aa8d-319ead5a6d89/0/abcayp.pdf

Edyburn, D. (2000). Assistive technology and students with mild disabilities. *Focus on Exceptional Children, 32*(9), 1-23.

Edyburn, D. (2002). *What every teacher should know about assistive technology.* Boston: Allyn & Bacon.

Elbaum, B., Vaughn, S., Hughes, M., & Moody, S. (1999). Grouping practices and reading outcomes for students with disabilities. *Exceptional Children, 65*(3), 399-415.

Elliott, S. N., & Busse, R. T. (2004). Assessment and evaluation of students' behavior and intervention outcomes: The utility of rating scale methods. In R. B. Rutherford, Jr., M. M. Quinn, & A. R. Mathur (Eds.), *Handbook of research in emotional and behavioral disorders* (pp. 54-77). New York: Guilford.

Emmer, E. T., Everton, C. M., & Anderson, L. M. (1980). Effective classroom management at the beginning of the school year. *Elementary School Journal, 80,* 219-231.

Engelmann, S., & Bruner, E. (1995). *Reading mastery.* Columbus, OH: SRA.

Engelmann, S., Carnine, D., Bernadette, K., & Engelmann, O. (1997). *Connecting math concepts.* Columbus, OH: SRA.

Engelmann, S., Hanner, S., & Johnson, G. (1999). *Corrective reading.* Columbus, OH: SRA.

Englert, C. S., Wu, X., & Zhao, Y. (2005). Cognitive tools for writing: Scaffolding the performance of students through technology. *Learning Disabilities Research and Practice, 20*(3), 184-198.

English, K. M. (1997). *Self advocacy for students who are deaf or hard of hearing.* Austin, TX: PRO-ED.

Epilepsy Foundation. (2005). *Epilepsy: An introduction.* Retrieved August 1, 2005, from http://www.epilepsyfoundation.org/

Epstein, J. L. (2001). *School, family, and community partnerships: Preparing educators and improving schools.* Boulder, CO: Westview.

Epstein, M. H., & Sharma, J. M. (1998). *Behavioral and emotional rating scale.* Austin, TX: PRO-ED.

Escamilla, K., & Coady, M. (2001). Assessing the writing of Spanish speaking students: Issues and suggestions. In S. Hurley & J. Tinajero (Eds.), *Literacy assessment of bilingual learners* (pp. 43-63). Boston: Allyn & Bacon.

Esquith, R. (2004). *There are no shortcuts.* New York: Knopf.

Evertson, C., Emmer, E., & Worsham, M. (2005). *Classroom management for elementary teachers* (7th ed.). Boston: Allyn & Bacon.

Evertson, C. M., Emmer, E. T., Sanford, J. P., & Clements, B. S. (1983). Improving classroom management: An experiment in elementary school classrooms. *Elementary School Journal, 84,* 172-188.

Farel, A. M., Meyer, R. E., Hicken, M., & Edmonds, L. (2003). Registry to referral: A promising means for identifying and referring infants and toddlers for early intervention services. *Infants and Young Children, 16,* 99-105.

Federal Register. (1993, February 10). Washington, DC: U.S. Government Printing Office.

Feiman-Nemser, S., & Floden, R. E. (1986). The cultures of teaching. In Merlin C. Wittrock (Ed.), *Handbook of research on teaching* (3rd ed.). New York: Macmillan.

Feingold, B. (1985). *Why your child is hyperactive.* New York: Random House.

Feldhusen, J. F. (1992). *Talent identification and development in education (TIDE).* Sarasota, FL: Center for Creative Learning.

Feldman, R. S. (2000). *Development across the life span* (2nd ed.). Upper Saddle River, NJ: Prentice Hall.

Ferrell, K. (n.d.). *Issues in the field of blindness and low vision.* Retrieved July 22, 2005, from http://nclid.unco.edu/newnclid/foreword.php?itemid=77&blogid=33

Ferrell, K. A. (1997). *Reach out and teach.* New York: American Foundation for the Blind.

Ferrell, K. A. (1998). *Project PRISM: A longitudinal study of developmental patterns of children who are visually impaired* [Final report]. Greeley: University of Northern Colorado.

Ferster, C. B. (1961). Positive reinforcement and behavioral deficits of autistic children. *Child Development, 61,* 437-456.

Filipek, P. (2005). Medical aspects of autism. In F. R. Volkmar, R. Paul, A. Klin, & D. Cohen (Eds.), *Handbook of autism and pervasive developmental disorders: Vol. 1. Diagnosis, development, neurobiology, and behavior.* (4th ed., pp. 534-578). Hoboken, NJ: Wiley.

Fischer, M., Barkley, R., Smallish, L., & Fletcher, K. (2002). Young adult follow-up of hyperactive children. *Journal of Abnormal Child Psychology, 30*(5), 463-475.

Fisher, M., & Meyer, L. H. (2002). Development and social competence after two years for students enrolled in inclusive and self-contained educational programs. *Research and Practice for Persons with Severe Disabilities, 27*(3), 165-174.

Fletcher, J., Lyon, R., Barnes, M., Stuebing, K., Francis, D., Olson, R., et al. (2002). Classification of learning disabilities: An evidence-based evaluation. In R. Bradley, L. Danielson, & D. Hallahan (Eds.), *Identification of learning disabilities: Research to practice* (pp. 185-250). Mahwah, NJ: Erlbaum.

Fletcher, J., Morris, R., & Lyon, R. (2003). Classification and definition of learning disabilities: An integrative perspective. In L. Swanson, K. Harris, & S. Graham (Eds.). *Handbook of learning disabilities* (pp. 30-56). New York: Guilford.

Fletcher, K., Scott, M., Blair, C., & Bolger, K. (2004). Specific patterns of cognitive abilities in young children with mild mental retardation. *Education and Training in Developmental Disabilities, 39*(3), 270-278.

Fletcher, T. V., & Navarrete, L. A. (2003). Learning disabilities or difference: A critical look at issues associated with misidentification and placement of Hispanic students in special education. *Rural Special Education Quarterly, 22*(4), 37-45.

Fombonne, E. (2003, January). The prevalence of autism. *Journal of the American Medical Association, 289*(1), 87-89.

Foorman, B., & Torgesen, J. (2001). Critical elements of classroom and small-group instruction promote reading success in all

children. *Learning Disabilities Research and Practice, 16*(4), 203-212.

Ford, A., Schnorr, R., Meyer, L., Davern, L., Black, J., & Dempsey, P. (Eds.). (1989). *The Syracuse community-referenced curriculum guide for students with moderate and severe disabilities.* Baltimore: Brookes.

Ford, D. Y., & Harris, J. J. (2000). A framework for infusing multicultural curriculum into gifted education. *Roeper Review, 23,* 4-10.

Foreman, P., Arthur-Kelly, M., Pascoe, S., & King, B. S. (2004). Evaluating the educational experiences of students with profound and multiple disabilities in inclusive and segregated classroom settings: An Australian perspective. *Research and Practice for Persons with Severe Disabilities, 29,* 183-193.

Forest, M., & Lusthaus, E. (1987). The kaleidoscope. Challenge to the cascade. In M. Forest (Ed.), *More education/integration* (pp. 1-16). Downsview, Ontario: Roeher Institute.

Forness, S. R., & Kavale, K. A. (2000). Emotional or behavioral disorders: Background and current status of the E/BD terminology and definition. *Behavioral Disorders, 25*(3), 264-269.

Forni, P. M. (2002). *Choosing civility: Twenty-five rules of considerate conduct.* New York: St. Martin's/Griffin.

Foshay, J., & Ludlow, B. (2005). Implementing computer-mediated supports and assistive technology. In M. Wehmeyer & M. Agran (Eds.), *Mental retardation and intellectual disabilities: Teaching students using innovative and research-based strategies* (pp. 101-124). Washington, DC: AAMR.

Fox, J., & Gable, R. A. (2004). Functional behavioral assessment. In R. Rutherford, M. Quinn, & S. Mathur (Eds.), *Handbook of research in emotional and behavioral disorders* (pp. 142-163). New York: Guilford.

Frankenburg, W., et al. (1990). *Denver developmental screening test—II.* Denver: Denver Developmental Materials.

Freeman, S. F. N., & Alkin, M. C. (2000). Academic and social attainments of children with mental retardation in general and special education settings. *Remedial and Special Education, 21,* 2-18.

French, N. (2001). Supervising paraprofessionals: A survey of teacher practices. *Journal of Special Education, 35*(1), 41-53.

French, N., & Pickett, A. L. (1997). Paraprofessionals in special education: Issues for teacher educators. *Teacher Education and Special Education, 20*(1), 61-73.

Frey, L. M. (2003). Abundant beautification: An effective service-learning project for students with emotional or behavioral disorders. *Teaching Exceptional Children, 35*(5), 66-75.

Friend, M., & Bursuck, W. (2006). *Including students with special needs: A practical guide for classroom teachers* (4th ed.). Boston: Allyn & Bacon.

Friend, M., & Cook, L. (2003). *Interactions: Collaboration skills for school professionals* (4th ed.). Boston: Allyn & Bacon.

Frith, U. (2003). *Autism: Explaining the enigma* (2nd ed.). Malden, MA: Blackwell.

Frost, L., & Bondy, A. (2000). *The picture exchange communication system (PECS).* Newark, DE: Pyramid Products.

Fuchs, D., & Fuchs, L. S. (1994). Inclusive school movement and the radicalization of special education reform. *Exceptional Children, 60*(4), 294-309.

Fuchs, D., & Fuchs, L. (1998). Researchers and teachers working together to adopt instruction for diverse learners. *Learning Disabilities Research and Practice, 13*(3), 126-137.

Fuchs, D., Fuchs, L., & Burish, P. (2000). Peer-assisted learning strategies: An evidence-based practice to promote reading achievement. *Learning Disabilities Research and Practice, 15*(2), 85-91.

Fuchs, D., Fuchs, L., & Compton, D. (2004). Identifying reading disabilities by responsiveness-to-instruction: Specifying measures and criteria. *Learning Disability Quarterly, 27*(4), 216-227.

Fuchs, D., Fuchs, L., Mathes, P., Lipsey, M., & Roberts, H. (2002). Is "learning disabilities" just a fancy term for low achievement? A meta-analysis of reading differences between low achievers with and without the label. In R. Bradley, L. Danielson, & D. Hallahan (Eds.).

Identification of learning disabilities: Research to practice (pp. 737-762). Mahwah, NJ: Erlbaum.

Fuchs, D., Mock, D., Morgan, P., & Young, C. (2003). Responsiveness-to-intervention: Definitions, evidence, and implications for the learning disabilities construct. *Learning Disabilities Research and Practice, 18*(3), 157-171.

Fuchs, D., Mock, D., Morgan, P. L., & Young, C. L. (2003). Responsiveness to intervention: Definitions, evidence, and implications for the learning special needs construct. *Learning Special Needs Research and Practice, 18,* 157-171.

Fuchs, L. (2003). Assessing intervention responsiveness: Conceptual and technical issues. *Learning Disabilities Research and Practice, 18*(3), 172-186.

Fuchs, L. (2004). The past, present, and future of curriculum-based measurement research. *School Psychology Review, 33*(2), 188-192.

Fuchs, L., Compton, D., Fuchs, D., Paulsen, K., Bryant, J., & Hamlett, C. (2005). Responsiveness to intervention: Preventing and identifying mathematics disability. *Teaching Exceptional Children, 37*(4), 60-63.

Fuchs, L., Fuchs, D., & Speece, D. (2002). Treatment validity as a unifying construct for identifying learning disabilities. *Learning Disability Quarterly, 25,* 33-45.

Fullan, M. (2001). *The new meaning of educational change* (3rd ed.). New York: Teachers College Press.

Gable, R. A., Hendrickson, J. M., & Van Acker, R. (2001). Maintaining the integrity of FBA-based interventions in schools. *Education and Treatment of Children, 24*(3), 248-260.

Gaffney, J. S. (1987). *Seatwork: Current practices and research implications.* Paper presented at the 64th meeting of the Council for Exceptional Children, Chicago.

Gagné, F. (1991). Toward a differentiated model of giftedness and talent. In N. Colangelo & G. A. Davis (Eds.), *Handbook of gifted education* (pp. 65-80). Needham Heights, MA: Allyn & Bacon.

Gagné, F. (1993). Constructs and models pertaining to exceptional human abilities. In K. A. Heller, F. J. Monks, & A. H. Passow (Eds.), *International handbook of research and development of giftedness and talent* (pp. 69-87). Oxford, England: Pergamon.

Gagné, F. (1999). My convictions about the nature of abilities, gifts, and talents. *Journal for the Education of the Gifted, 22,* 109-136.

Gagné, F., Bélanger, J. & Motard, D. (1993). Popular estimates of the prevalence of giftedness and talent. *Roeper Review, 16,* 96-98.

Gallagher, J. J. (1993). Current status of gifted education in the United States. In K. A. Heller, F. J. Monks, & A. H. Passow (Eds.), *International handbook of research and development of giftedness and talent* (pp. 755-770). Oxford, England: Pergamon.

Gallagher, J. J. (1998). The public policy legacy of Samuel A. Kirk. *Learning Disabilities Research and Practice, 13*(1), 11-14.

Gallaudet Research Institute. (2005). *Regional and national summary report of data from the 2003-2004 annual survey of deaf and hard of hearing children and youth.* Washington, DC: Author.

Galluzzo, G. (1999). *Aligning standards to improve teacher preparation and practice.* Washington, DC: National Council for Accreditation of Teacher Education.

Garcia, S. B., Perez, A. M., & Ortiz, A. A. (2000). Mexican American mothers' beliefs about disabilities. *Remedial and Special Education, 21*(2), 90-100.

Gardner, H. (1983). *Frames of mind: A theory of multiple intelligences.* New York: Basic Books.

Gardner, H., & Hatch, T. (1989). Multiple intelligences go to school: Educational implications of the theory of multiple intelligences. *Educational Researcher, 18*(8), 4-9.

Gaylord-Ross, R., & Peck, C. A. (1985). Integration efforts for students with severe mental retardation. In D. Bricker & J. Fuller (Eds.), *Severe mental retardation: From theory to practice* (pp. 185-207). Reston, VA: Council for Exceptional Children, Division on Mental Retardation.

Geertz, C. (1973). *The interpretation of culture.* New York: Basic.

Gerber, M. (2005). Teachers are still the test: Limitations to response to intervention strategies for identifying children with learning disabilities. *Journal of Learning Disabilities, 38*(6), 516-524.

Gerhardt, P. F., & Holmes, D. L. (2005). Employment: Options and issues for adolescents and adults with autism spectrum disorders. In F. R. Volkmar, R. Paul, A. Klin, & D. Cohen (Eds.), *Handbook of autism and pervasive development disorders: Vol. 2. Assessment, interventions, and policy* (4th ed., pp. 1087-1101). Hoboken, NJ: Wiley.

Gersten, R., Keating, T., Yovanoff, P., & Harniss, M. K. (2001). Working in special education: Factors that enhance special educators' intent to stay. *Exceptional Children, 67*(4), 549-567.

Giangreco, M. F., Broer, S. M., & Edelman, S. W. (1999). The tip of the iceberg: Determining whether paraprofessional support is needed for students with disabilities in general education settings. *Journal of the Association for Persons with Severe Handicaps, 24,* 281-291.

Giangreco, M. F., Cloninger, C. J., & Iverson, V. S. (1998). *Choosing options and accommodations for children: A guide to planning inclusive education* (2nd ed.). Baltimore: Brookes.

Giangreco, M. F., & Doyle, M. B. (2002). Students with disabilities and paraeducator supports: Benefits, balance, and Band-Aids. *Focus on Exceptional Children, 34*(7), 1-12.

Giangreco, M. F., Edelman, S. W., Broer, S. M., & Doyle, M. B. (2001). Paraeducator support of students with disabilities: Literature from the past decade. *Exceptional Children, 68,* 45-63.

Gillam, R. B. (2000a). Fluency disorders. In R. B. Gillam, T. P. Marquardt, & F. N. Martin (Eds.), *Communication sciences and disorders: From science to clinical practice* (pp. 313-339). San Diego: Singular.

Gillam, R. B. (2000b). Language disorders in school-age children. In R. B. Gillam, T. P. Marquardt, & F. N. Martin (Eds.), *Communication sciences and disorders: From science to clinical practice* (pp. 437-459). San Diego: Singular.

Gillberg, C., & Cederlund, M. (2005). Asperger syndrome: Familial and pre- and perinatal factors. *Journal of Autism and Developmental Disorders, 35*(2), 159-166.

Gillberg, C., Gillberg, C., Rastam, M., & Wentz, E. (2001). The Asperger syndrome (and high-functioning autism) diagnostic interview (ASDI): A preliminary study of a new structured clinical interview [Special issue]. *Autism, 5*(1), 57-66.

Gilliam, J. (1995). *Attention deficit/hyperactivity disorder test.* Austin, TX: PRO-ED.

Goertzel, V., & Goertzel, M. G. (1962). *Cradles of eminence.* London: Constable.

Goldstein, A. P., & McGinnis, E. (1997). *Skillstreaming the adolescent: New strategies and perspectives for teaching prosocial skills.* Champaign, IL: Research Press.

Goldstein, D., Murray, C., & Edgar, E. (1998). Employment earnings and hours of high-school graduates with learning disabilities through the first decade after graduation. *Learning Disabilities Research and Practice, 13*(1), 53-64.

Gonzalez, N., Moll, L., & Amanti, C. (2005). *Funds of knowledge: Theorizing practices in households and classrooms.* Mahwah, NJ: Erlbaum.

Good, T., & Brophy, J. (2003). *Looking in classrooms* (9th ed.). Boston: Allyn & Bacon.

Goode, D. (1998). *The history of the Association for the Help of Retarded Children.* Retrieved March 2, 2005, from http://www.ahrcnyc.org/index.htm

Goor, M. B. (1995). *Leadership for special education administration: A case-based approach.* Fort Worth, TX: Harcourt Brace.

Gordon, K. A., & Coscarelli, W. C. (1996). Recognizing and fostering resilience. *Performance Improvement, 35*(9), 14-17.

Graham, S., & Harris, K. R. (2003). Students with learning disabilities and the process of writing: A meta-analysis of SRSD studies. In H. L. Swanson, K. R. Harris, & S. Graham (Eds.), *Handbook of learning disabilities* (pp. 323-344). New York: Guilford.

Grandin, T. (1992). An inside view of autism. In E. Schopler & G. B. Mesibov (Eds.), *High functioning individuals with autism* (pp. 105-126). New York: Plenum.

Gray, C. A. (2000). *The new social story book.* Arlington, TX: Future Horizons.

Gray, C. A., & Garand, J. D. (1993). Social stories: Improving responses of students with autism with accurate social information. *Focus on Autistic Behavior, 8*(1), 1-10.

Greenfield, P. M., Raeff, C., & Quiroz, B. (1996). Cultural values in learning and education. In B. Williams (Ed.), *Closing the achievement gap: A vision for changing beliefs and practices* (pp. 37-55). Alexandria, VA: Association for Supervision and Curriculum Development.

Gresham, F. (2002). Responsiveness to intervention: An alternative approach to the identification of learning disabilities. In R. Bradley, L. Danielson, & D. Hallahan (Eds.), *Identification of learning disabilities: Research to practice* (pp. 467-519). Mahwah, NJ: Erlbaum.

Gresham, F. M. (1988). Social competence and motivational characteristics of learning disabled students. In M. C. Wang, M. C. Reynolds, & H. J. Walberg (Eds.), *Handbook of special education: Research and practice: Vol. 2. Mildly handicapped conditions.* Oxford, UK: Pergamon.

Gresham, F. M., Beebe-Frankenberger, M. E., & MacMillan, D. L. (1999). A selective review of treatments for children with autism: Description and methodological considerations. *School Psychology Review, 28*(4), 559-575.

Gresham, F. M., & Elliott, S. N. (1990). *The social skills rating system (SSRS).* Circle Pines, MN: American Guidance Service.

Gresham, F. M., & Gansle, K. (1992). Misguided assumptions in *DSM-III-R:* Implications for school psychological practice. *School Psychology Quarterly, 7,* 79-95.

Gresham, F. M., & Kern, L. (2004). Internalizing behavior problems in children and adolescents. In R. B. Rutherford, Jr., M. M. Quinn, & A. R. Mathur (Eds.), *Handbook of research in emotional and behavioral disorders* (pp. 54-77). New York: Guilford.

Gresham, F. M., Lane, K. L., MacMillan, D. L., & Bocian, K. M. (1999). Social and academic profiles of externalizing and internalizing groups: Risk factors for emotional and behavioral disorders. *Behavioral Disorders, 24,* 231-245.

Gresham, F. M., Sugai, G., & Horner, R. H. (2001). Interpreting outcomes of social skills training for students with high-incidence disabilities. *Exceptional Children, 67,* 331-344.

Griffin, C. C., Winn, J. A., Otis-Wilborn, A., & Kilgore, K. L. (2003, September). *New teacher induction in special education* (COPSSE Document No. RS-5). Gainesville: University of Florida, Center on Personnel Studies in Special Education.

Griffin, H. C., Fitch, C. L., & Griffin, L. W. (2002). Causes and interventions in the area of cerebral palsy. *Infants and Young Children, 14*(3), 18-23.

Gross, M. U. M. (2004). *The use of radical acceleration in cases of extreme intellectual precocity.* Thousand Oaks, CA: Corwin.

Grossman, H. (Ed.). (1973). *Manual on terminology and classification in mental retardation* (rev. ed.). Washington, DC: AAMR.

Grouse, W. F. (2003). Reflecting on teacher professionalism: A student perspective. *Kappa Delta Pi Record, 40,* 17-37.

Gudykunst, W. B., & Kim, Y. Y. (2003). *Communicating with strangers: An approach to intercultural communication.* New York: McGraw-Hill.

Guetzloe, E. (1999). Inclusion: The broken promise. *Preventing School Failure, 43*(3), 92-98.

Gureasko-Moore, D., DuPaul, G., & Power, T. (2005). Stimulant treatment for attention-deficit/hyperactivity disorder: Medication monitoring practices of school psychologists. *School Psychology Review, 34*(2), 232-245.

Gutiérrez, K., & Rogoff, B. (2003). Cultural ways of learning: Individual traits or repertoires of practice. *Educational Researcher, 32*(5), 19-25.

Hahn, H. (1985). Toward a politics of disability: Definitions, disciplines and policies. *Social Science Journal, 22*(4), 87-105.

Hall, D., Wiener, R., & Carey, K. (2003). What new "AYP" information tells us about schools, states, and public education. *Education Trust, 2003,* pp. 1-10.

Hampton, E. O., Whitney, D. W., & Schwartz, I. S. (2002). Weaving assessment information into intervention ideas: Planning communication interventions for young children with disabilities. *Assessment for Effective Intervention, 27,* 49-59.

Handleman, J. S., Harris, S. L., & Martins, M. P. (2005). Helping children with autism enter the mainstream. In F. R. Volkmar, R. Paul, A. Klin, & D. Cohen (Eds.), *Handbook of autism and pervasive developmental disorders: Vol. 2. Assessment, interventions, and policy* (4th ed., pp. 1029-1042). Hoboken, NJ: Wiley.

Hanley, G. P., Iwata, B. A., & McCord, B. E. (2003). Functional analysis of problem behavior: A review. *Journal of Applied Behavior Analysis, 36,* 147-185.

Hardman, M. L., & Mulder, M. (2004). Federal education reform: Critical issues in public education and their impact on students with disabilities. In L. M. Bullock & R. A. Gable (Eds.), *Quality personnel preparation in emotional/behavioral disorders: Current perspectives and future directions.* Denton, TX: Institute for Behavioral and Learning Differences at the University of North Texas.

Hardman, M. L., & Nagle, K. (2004). Public policy: From access to accountability in special education. In A. McCray Sorrells, H. J. Rieth, & P. T. Sindelar (Eds.), *Critical issues in special education: Access, diversity, and accountability.* Boston: Pearson Education.

Harris, S. L., & Delmolino, L. (2002, January). Applied behavior analysis: Its application in the treatment of autism and related disorders in young children. *Infants and Young Children, 14*(3), 11-17.

Harris, S. L., Handleman, J. S., & Jennett, H. K. (2005). Models of educational intervention for students with autism: Home, center, and school-based programming. In F. R. Volkmar, R. Paul, A. Klin, & D. Cohen (Eds.), *Handbook of autism and pervasive developmental disorders: Vol. 2. Assessment, interventions, and policy* (4th ed., pp. 1043-1054). Hoboken, NJ: Wiley.

Harris, S. L., Handleman, J. S., Gordon, R., Kristoff, B., & Fuentes, F. (1991). Changes in cognitive and language functioning of preschool children with autism. *Journal of Autism and Developmental Disabilities, 21,* 281-290.

Harrison, P., & Oakland, T. (2000). *Adaptive behavior assessment system* (2nd ed.). San Antonio, TX: Psychological Corporation.

Hart, D., Mele-McCarthy, J., Pasternack, R., Zimbrich, K., & Parker, D. (2004). Community college: A pathway to success for youth with learning, cognitive, and intellectual disabilities in secondary settings. *Education and Training in Developmental Disabilities, 39*(1), 54-66.

Hass, J. (1994). Role determinants of teachers of the visually impaired. *B. C. Journal of Special Education, 18,* 140-148.

Hasselbring, T. S., & Glaser, C. H. W. (2000). Use of computer technology to help students with special needs. *Future of Children, 10*(2), 102-122.

Hatton, D. D. (2001). Model registry of early childhood visual impairment: First-year results. *Journal of Visual Impairment and Blindness, 95,* 418-433.

Heal, L. W., & Rusch, F. R. (1995). Predicting employment for students who leave special education high school programs. *Exceptional Children, 61*(5), 472-487.

Health Physics Society. (2005). *Pregnancy and radiation exposure.* Retrieved June 28, 2005, from http://hps.org/

Heath, S. B. (1982). Questioning at home and at school: A comparative study. In G. D. Spindler (Ed.), *Doing the ethnography of schooling* (pp. 102-131). New York: Holt, Rinehart & Winston.

Heber, R. (1961). A manual on terminology and classification in mental retardation (rev. ed.). *American Journal of Mental Deficiency, 64.* [Monograph Supplement].

Heller, K. W. (2004). Integrating health care and educational programs. In F. P. Orelove, D. Sobsey, & R. K. Silberman (Eds.), *Educating children with multiple disabilities: A collaborative approach* (2nd ed., pp. 379-424). Baltimore: Brookes.

Heller, K. W., & Kennedy, C. (1994). *Etiologies and characteristics of deaf-blindness.* Monmouth, OR: Teaching Research Publications.

Henderson, K., & Bradley, R. (2004). A national perspective on mental health and children with disabilities: Emotional disturbances in children. *Emotional and Behavioral Disorders in Youth, 4*(3), 67-74.

Henderson, M. V., Gullatt, D. E., Hardin, D. T., Jannik, C., & Tollett, J. R. (1999). *Preventative law curriculum guide* (ED437366). Baton Rouge: Louisiana State Board of Regents.

Hendrick, I. G., & MacMillan, D. L. (1989). Selecting children for special education in New York City: William Maxwell, Elizabeth Farrell, and the development of ungraded classes, 1900-1920. *Journal of Special Education, 22*(4), 395-417.

Henley, M., Ramsey, R., & Algozzine, R. (2006). *Teaching students with mild disabilities* (5th ed). Boston: Pearson Education.

Herr, S. (1995). A humanist's legacy: Burton Blatt and the origins of the disability rights movement. *Mental Retardation, 33*(5), 328-331.

Heward, W. L. (2003). Ten faulty notions about teaching and learning that hinder the effectiveness of special education. *Journal of Special Education, 36*(4), 186-205.

Higgins, K., Boone, R., & Williams, D. (2000). Evaluating educational software for special education. *Intervention in School and Clinic, 36*(2), 109-115.

Hitchcock, C., Meyer, A., Rose, D., & Jackson, R. (2002). Providing new access to the general curriculum: Universal design for learning. *Teaching Exceptional Children, 35*(2), 8-17.

Hoagwood, K., Kelleher, K., Feil, M., & Comer, D. (2000). Treatment services for children with ADHD: A national perspective. *Journal of the American Academy of Child and Adolescent Psychiatry, 39*(2), 198-206.

Hodgkinson, H. (2000). *Secondary schools in a new millennium: Demographic certainties, social realities.* Reston, VA: National Association of Secondary School Principals.

Hollins, E. R. (1996). *Culture in school learning: Revealing the deep meaning.* Mahwah, NJ: Erlbaum.

Hollinsworth, L.S (1940). Intelligence as an element of personality. *Yearbook of the National Society of Education, 39,* 271-275.

Holt, J. (1993). Stanford achievement test—8th edition: Reading comprehension subgroup results. *American Annals of the Deaf, 138,* 172-175.

Hoover, D. H., Dunbar, S. B., & Frisbie, D. A. (2001). *Iowa test of basic skills.* Itasca, IL: Riverside.

Hord, S. M. (1997). *Professional learning communities: Communities of continuing improvement.* Austin, TX: Southwest Educational Development Laboratory.

Hosp, J., & Reschly, D. (2004). Disproportionate representation of minority students in special education: Academic, demographic, and economic predictors. *Exceptional Children, 70*(2), 185-199.

Hourcade, J. (2002). *Mental retardation update: Overview and definition.* Retrieved December 28, 2005, from http://ericec.org/digests/e637.html

Howell, J. J. (2003). An examination of literacy instruction by teachers of adolescents who are deaf or hard of hearing. *Dissertation Abstracts International, 64*(7), 2445A. (UMI No. 3099710).

Howlin, P. (1997). *Autism: Preparing for adulthood.* London: Routledge.

Howlin, P., & Asgharian, A. (1999). The diagnosis of autism and Asperger syndrome: Findings from a survey of 770 families. *Developmental Medicine and Child Neurology, 41,* 834-839.

Howlin, P., Mawhood, L., & Rutter, M. (2000). Autism and developmental receptive language disorder—A follow-up comparison in early adult life. II: Social, behavioural, and psychiatric outcomes. *Journal of Child Psychology and Psychiatry, 41,* 561-578.

Huebner, K. M., Merk-Adam, B., Stryker, D., & Wolffe, K. E. (2004). *The national agenda for the education of children and youths with visual impairments, including those with multiple disabilities—Revised.* New York: AFB Press.

Hughes, C., & Agran, M. (1993). Teaching persons with severe disabilities to use self-instruction in community settings: An analysis of the applications. *Journal of The Association for Persons with Severe Handicaps, 18,* 261-274.

Hughes, C., Hugo, K., & Blatt, J. (1996). Self-instructional intervention for teaching generalized problem-solving within a functional task sequence. *American Journal on Mental Retardation, 100,* 565-579.

Hughes, C., Ruhl, K., Schumaker, J., & Deshler, D. (2002). Effects of instruction in an assignment completion strategy on the homework performance of students with learning disabilities in general education classes. *Learning Disabilities Research and Practice, 17,* 1-18.

Hu-Lince, D., Craig, D. W., Huentelman, M. J., & Stephan, D. A. (2005). The autism genome project: Goals and strategies. *American Journal of Pharmacogenomics, 5*(4), 233-246.

Humphrey, G. (1962). Introduction. In J. M. G. Itard, *The wild boy of Aveyron.* New York: Appleton-Century-Crofts.

Humphries, T., & Padden, C. (1988). *Deaf in America: Voices from a culture.* Cambridge, MA: Harvard University Press.

Hunt, P., & Goetz, L. (1997). Research on inclusive educational programs, practices, and outcomes for students with severe disabilities. *Journal of Special Education, 31,* 3-29.

Hurst, B., Wilson, C., & Cramer, G. (1998). Professional teaching portfolios. *Phi Delta Kappan, 79*(8), 578-582.

Hussar, W. J. (2005). *Projections of education statistics to 2014.* Washington, DC: National Center for Education Statistics.

IDEA Law and Resources. (1999). *Law & regulations: IDEA '97 Law and regs.* Retrieved October 13, 2005, from http://www.cec.sped.org/law_res/doc/law/index.php

Indiana Department of Education. (2005). *2004-2005 special education statistical report.* Indianapolis: Division of Exceptional Learners. Retrieved on December 2, 2005, from http://ideanet.doe.state.in.us/exceptional/speced/welcome.html

Individuals with Disabilities Education Act (IDEA), Public Law 105-17. (1997). Retrieved November 21, 2006, from http://www.ed.gov/offices/OSERS/Policy/IDEA/index.html

Individual with Disabilities Education Improvement Act. (2004). 20 U.S.C. § 1400 et seq.

Individuals with Disabilities Education Improvement Act (IDEA), Public Law 108-446 (2004). Retrieved November 7, 2006, from http://frwebgate. access.gpo.gov/cgi-bin/getdoc.cgi?dbname=108 cong.public. laws&docid=f:pub1446.108

Inge, K. J., & Tilson, G. (1994). Supported employment: Issues and applications for individuals with learning disabilities. In P. J. Gerber & H. B. Reiff (Eds.), *Learning disabilities in adulthood: Persisting problems and evolving issues* (pp. 179-193). Boston: Andover Medical Publishers.

Interstate New Teacher Assessment and Support Consortium. (1992). *Model standards for beginning teacher licensing, assessment and development: A resource for state dialogue.* Retrieved June 7, 2004, from http://www.ccsso.org/content/pdfs/corestrd.pdf

Irvine, J. J. (2002). *In search of wholeness: African American teachers and their culturally specific practices.* New York: Palgrave/St. Martin's Press.

Irvine, J. J. (2003) *Educating teachers for diversity: Seeing with a cultural eye.* New York: Teachers College Press.

Janney, R. E., Snell, M. E., Beers, M. K., & Raynes, M. (1995). Integrating students with moderate and severe disabilities into general education classes. *Exceptional Children, 61,* 425-439.

Jensen, P., Kettle, L., Roper, M., et al. (1999). Are stimulants over-prescribed? Treatment of ADHD in four U.S. communities. *Journal of the American Academy of Child and Adolescent Psychiatry, 38*(7), 797-804.

Jewell, E. J., & Abate, F. (Eds.). (2001). *The new Oxford American dictionary.* New York: Oxford University Press.

Johns, B. H., & Carr, V. G. (1995). *Techniques of managing: Verbally and physically aggressive students.* Denver: Love.

Johnson, D., Johnson, R., & Holubec, E. (1993). *Circles of learning: Cooperation in the classroom.* Edina, MN: Interaction Book Company.

Johnson, D., & Thurlow, M. (2003). *A national study on graduation requirements and diploma options for youth with disabilities* (Technical Report 36). Minneapolis: University of Minnesota, National Center on Educational Outcomes.

Johnson, G. O. (1962). Special education for the mentally handicapped: A paradox. *Exceptional Children, 29,* 62-69.

Johnson, R. A. (1976). Renewal of school placement systems for the handicapped. In F. J. Weintraub, A. Abeson, J. Ballard, & M. L. LaVor (Eds.), *Public policy and the education of exceptional children* (pp. 47-61). Reston, VA: Council for Exceptional Children.

Jolivette, K., Jung, L. A., McCormick, K. M., & Lingo, A. S. (2004). Making choices—Improving behavior—Engaging in learning. *Teaching Exceptional Children, 34,* 24-29.

Jolivette, K., McCormick, K. M., & Lingo, A. S. (2004). Embedding choices into the daily routines of young children with behavior problems: Eight reasons to build social competence. *Beyond Behavior, 13*(3), 21-26.

Jones, E. D., & Southern, W. T. (1991). Objections to early entrance and grade skipping. In W. T. Southern & E. D. Jones (Eds.), *The academic acceleration of gifted children* (pp. 51-74). New York: Teachers College Press.

Jones, V., & Jones, L. (2004). *Comprehensive classroom management: Creating communities of support and solving problems* (7th ed.). Boston: Pearson.

Jorgensen, C. M. (1998). *Restructuring high schools for all students: Taking inclusion to the next level.* Baltimore: Brookes.

Justice, L. M. (2006). *Communication sciences and disorders: An introduction.* Upper Saddle River, NJ: Merrill/Prentice Hall.

Kame'enui, E., & Carnine, D. (1998). *Effective teaching strategies that accommodate diverse learners.* Upper Saddle River, NJ: Merrill/Prentice Hall.

Kame'enui, E., & Simmons, D. (1999). *Toward successful inclusion of students with disabilities: The architecture of instruction.* Reston, VA: Council for Exceptional Children.

Kanner, L. (1943). Autistic disturbances of affective contact. *Nervous Child, 2,* 217-250.

Kaplan, S. G., & Cornell, D. G. (2005). Threats of violence by students in special education. *Behavioral Disorders, 31,* 107-119.

Kasari, C., & Wong, C. (2002). Five early signs of autism. *Exceptional Parent, 32*(11), 60-62.

Kauchak, D., & Eggen, P. (2005). *Introduction to teaching: Becoming a professional* (2nd ed.). Upper Saddle River, NJ: Merrill/Prentice Hall.

Kauchak, D., Eggen, P., & Carter, C. (2002). *Introduction to teaching: Becoming a professional.* Upper Saddle River, NJ: Merrill/Prentice Hall.

Kauffman, J. M. (1981). Introduction: Historical trends and contemporary issues in special education in the United States. In J. M. Kauffman & D. P. Hallahan (Eds.), *Handbook of special education* (pp. 3-23). Upper Saddle River, NJ: Prentice Hall.

Kauffman, J. M. (1996). Research to practice issues. *Behavioral Disorders, 22,* 55-60.

Kauffman, J. M. (2001). *Characteristics of emotional and behavioral disorders of children and youth* (7th ed.). Upper Saddle River, NJ: Merrill/Prentice Hall.

Kauffman J. M., Bantz, J., & McCullough, J. (2002). Separate and better: A special public school class for students with emotional and behavioral disorders. *Exceptionality, 10*(3), 149-170.

Kauffman, J. M., & Hallahan, D. P. (2005). *Special education: What it is and why we need it.* Boston: Pearson Education.

Kauffman, J. M., Mostert, M. P., Trent, S. C., & Hallahan, D. P. (2002). *Managing classroom behavior: A reflective case-based approach* (3rd ed.). Boston: Allyn & Bacon.

Kaufman, A. S., & Kaufman, N. L. (1998). *Kaufman test of educational achievement/normative update.* Circle Pines, MN: American Guidance Service.

Kaufman, A. S., & Kaufman, N. L. (2004). *The Kaufman brief intelligence test* (2nd ed.). Upper Saddle River, NJ: Pearson Assessments.

Kavale, K. (2001). Decision making in special education. The function of meta-analysis. *Exceptionality, 9*(4), 245-268.

Kavale, K., & Forness, S. (1995). *The nature of learning disabilities: Critical elements of diagnosis and classification.* Mahwah, NJ: Erlbaum.

Kavale, K., Holdnack, J., & Mostert, M. (2005). Responsiveness to intervention and the identification of specific learning disability: A critique and alternative proposal. *Learning Disability Quarterly, 28*(1), 2-16.

Kavale, K. A., Mathur, S. R., & Mostert, M. P. (2004). Social skills training and teaching social behavior to students with emotional and behavioral disorders. In R. B. Rutherford, Jr., M. M. Quinn, & A. R. Mathur (Eds.), *Handbook of research in emotional and behavioral disorders* (pp. 446-461). New York: Guilford.

Kendziora, K. T. (2004). Early intervention for emotional and behavioral disorders. In R. B. Rutherford, Jr., M. M. Quinn, & A. R. Mathur (Eds.), *Handbook of research in emotional and behavioral disorders* (pp. 327-351). New York: Guilford.

Kennedy, C. H., Meyer, K. A., Knowles, T., & Shukla, S. (2000). Analyzing the multiple functions of stereotypical behavior for students with autism: Implications for assessment and treatment. *Journal of Applied Behavioral Analysis, 33,* 559-571.

Kennedy, C. H., & Shukla, S. (1995). Social interaction research for people with autism as a set of past, current, and emerging propositions. *Behavioral Disorders, 21,* 21-35.

Kennedy, M. M. (1997). The connection between research and practice. *Educational Researcher, 26*(7), 4-12.

Kennedy, V., & Burstein, N. (2004). An induction program for special education teachers. *Teacher Education and Special Education, 27*(4), 444-447.

Ketelaar, M., Vermeer, A., Helders, P. J. M., & Hart, H. (1998). Parental participation in intervention programs for children with cerebral palsy: A review of research. *Topics in Early Childhood Special Education, 18*(2), 108-117.

Keyser-Marcus, L., Briel, L., Sherron-Targett, P., Yasuda, S., Johnson, S., & Wehman, P. (2002). Enhancing the schooling of students with traumatic brain injury. *Teaching Exceptional Children, 34*(4), 62-67.

Kidsource. (2000). *What do parents need to know about children's television viewing?* Retrieved January 20, 2005, from http://www.kidsource.com/kidsource/content/TV.viewing.html

Kilgore, K., & Griffin, C. C. (1998). Beginning special education teachers: Problems of practice and the influence of school context. *Teacher Education and Special Education, 21,* 155-173.

Kilgore, K., Griffin, C., Otis-Wilborn, A., & Winn, J. (2003). The problems of beginning special education teachers: Exploring the contextual factors influencing their work. *Action in Teacher Education, 25,* 38-47.

Kim, K., & Turnbull, A. (2004). Transition to adulthood for students with severe intellectual disabilities: Shifting toward person-family interdependent training. *Research and Practice for Persons with Severe Disabilities, 29,* 53-57.

Kirk, S., Gallagher, J., Anastasiow, N., & Coleman, M. (2006). *Educating exceptional children* (11th ed.). Boston: Houghton Mifflin.

Kliewer, C., & Biklen, D. (2001). "School's not really a place for reading": A research synthesis of literate lives of students with severe disabilities. *Journal of The Association for Persons with Severe Handicaps, 26,* 1-12.

Klin, A., McPartland, J., & Volkmar, F. R. (2005). Asperger syndrome. In F. R. Volkmar, R. Paul, A. Klin, & D. Cohen (Eds.), *Handbook of autism and pervasive developmental disorders: Vol. 1. Diagnosis, development, neurobiology, and behavior* (4th ed., pp. 88-125). Hoboken, NJ: Wiley.

Klingner, J., & Artiles, A. (2003). When should bilingual students be in special education? *Educational Leadership, 61*(2), 66-71.

Knowles, J. G., Cole, A. L., & Presswood, C. S. (1994). *Through preservice teachers' eyes: Exploring field experience through narrative and inquiry.* New York: Macmillan.

Koenig, L. (2000). *Smart discipline for the classroom: Respect and cooperation restored* (3rd ed.). Thousand Oaks, CA: Corwin.

Kohn, A. (1989, November). Suffer the restless children. *Atlantic Monthly,* pp. 90-100.

Kollins, S., Barkley, R., & DuPaul, G. (2001). Use and management of medications for children diagnosed with attention deficit hyperactivity disorder (ADHD). *Focus on Exceptional Children, 33*(5), 1-24.

Konopasek, D., & Forness, S. (2004). Psychopharmacology in the treatment of emotional and behavioral disorders. In R. B. Rutherford, Jr., M. M. Quinn, & A. R. Mathur (Eds.), *Handbook of research in emotional and behavioral disorders* (pp. 352-368). New York: Guilford.

Kortering, L., Braziel, P. M., & Tompkins, J. R. (2002). The challenge of school completion among youth with behavioral disorders: Another side of the story. *Behavioral Disorders, 27*(2), 142-154.

Kottler, J. A. (2002). *Students who drive you crazy: Succeeding with resistant, unmotivated, and otherwise difficult young people.* Thousand Oaks, CA: Corwin.

Kozleski, E., Mainzer, R., & Deshler, D. (2000). *Bright futures for exceptional learners: An agenda to achieve quality conditions for teaching & learning.* Arlington, VA: Council for Exceptional Children.

Kramer, C. (2004). *The effects of a self-management device on the acquisition of social skills in adolescent males with SED.* Unpublished doctoral dissertation, Johns Hopkins University, Baltimore.

Kramer, P. A. (2003). The ABC's of professionalism. *Kappa Delta Pi Record, 40,* 22-25.

Krashen, S. (1985). *The input hypothesis: Issues and implications.* London: Longman.

Krashen, S. D. (2006). *Bilingual education accelerates English language development.* Retrieved June 1, 2006, from http://www.sdkrashen.com/articles/krashen_intro.pdf

Krug, D. A., Arick, J. R. & Almond, P. J. (1980). Behavior checklist for identifying severely handicapped individuals with high levels of autistic behavior. *Journal of Child Psychology and Psychiatry and Allied Disciplines, 21*(3), 221-229.

Kyle, D., McIntyre, E., Miller, K., & Moore, G. (2006). *Bridging school & home through family nights.* Thousand Oaks, CA: Corwin.

Ladson-Billings, G. (1994). *The dreamkeepers: Successful teachers of African American children.* San Francisco: Jossey-Bass.

Laing, R. D. (1967). *The politics of experience.* New York: Ballantine.

Lambert, N., Nihira, K., & Leland, H. (1993). *AAMR adaptive behavior scale—School* (2nd ed.). Austin, TX: PRO-ED.

Lambros, K. M., Ward, S. L., Bocian, K. M., MacMillan, D. L., & Gresham, F. M. (1998). Behavioral profiles of children at-risk for emotional and behavioral disorders: Implications for assessment and classification. *Focus on Exceptional Children, 30*(5), 1-16.

Lane, K. L. (2004). Academic instruction and tutoring interventions for students with emotional and behavioral disorders: 1990 to the present. In R. B. Rutherford, Jr., M. M. Quinn, & A. R. Mathur (Eds.), *Handbook of research in emotional and behavioral disorders* (pp. 462-486). New York: Guilford.

Langdon, C. (1999). The fifth Phi Delta Kappa poll of teachers' attitudes toward public schools. *Phi Delta Kappan, 80*(8), 611-618.

Langer, J. A. (2000). Excellence in English in middle and high school: How teachers' professional lives support student achievement. *American Educational Research Journal, 37,* 397-439.

La Paro, K. M., Olsen, K., & Pianta, R. C. (2002). Special education eligibility: Developmental precursors over the first three years of life. *Exceptional Children, 69,* 55-66.

Larson, E. J. (2002). The meaning of human gene testing for disability rights. *University of Cincinnati Law Review, 70,* 1-26.

LeCouteur, A., Lord, C., & Rutter, M. (2003). *The autism diagnostic interview: Revised (ADI-R).* Los Angles: Western Psychological Services.

Leet, A. I., Dormans, J. P., & Tosi, L. L. (2002). Muscles, bones, and nerves: The body's framework. In M. L. Batshaw (Ed.), *Children with disabilities* (5th ed., pp. 263-284). Baltimore: Brookes.

Lehman, C. (1992, July). Job designs: A community based program for students with emotional and behavioral disorders. *Teaching Research Newsletter,* pp. 1-7.

LeNard, J. M. (2001). *How public input shapes the Clerc Center's priorities: Identifying critical needs in transition from school to postsecondary education and employment.* Washington, DC: Laurent Clerc National Center on Deaf Education.

Lerner, J., & Kline, F. (2006). *Learning disabilities and related disorders.* Boston: Houghton Mifflin.

Leslie, L. (2004). ADHD: An epidemic. *Developmental Behavioral Pediatrics Online.* Retrieved September 28, 2005, from http://www.dbpeds.org/articles/detail.cfm?TextID=129

Levine, P., & Edgar, E. (1995). An analysis by gender of long-term postschool outcomes for youth with and without disabilities. *Exceptional Children, 61*(3), 282-300.

Levinson, H. (2003). *Smart but feeling dumb: New research on dyslexia—and how it may help you.* New York: Warner.

Lewis, T. J., & Sugai, G. (1999). Effective behavior support: A systems approach to proactive school-wide management. *Focus on Exceptional Children, 31*(6), 1-24.

Lin, S. L. (2000). Coping and adaptation in families of children with cerebral palsy. *Exceptional Children, 66,* 201-218.

Linn, A., & Smith-Myles, B. (2004). Asperger syndrome and six strategies for success. *Beyond Behavior, 14*(1), 3-9.

Loewen, J. W. (1995). *Lies my teacher told me.* New York: Touchstone.

Lombroso, C. (1891). *The men of genius.* London: Scott.

Lord, C., & Corsello, C. (2005). Diagnostic instruments in autistic spectrum disorders. In F. R. Volkmar, R. Paul, A. Klin, & D. Cohen (Eds.), *Handbook of autism and pervasive developmental disorders: Vol. 2. Assessment, interventions, and policy* (4th ed., pp. 730-771). Hoboken, NJ: Wiley.

Lord, C., Risi, S., Lambrecht, L., Cook, E. H., Jr., Leventhal, B. L., & DiLavore, P. C. (2000). The autism diagnostic observation schedule generic: A standard measure of social and communication deficits associated with spectrum of autism. *Journal of Autism and Developmental Disorders, 30*(3), 205-223.

Losen, D., & Orfield, G. (Eds.). (2002). *Racial inequity in special education.* Cambridge, MA: Harvard Educational Publishing Group.

Lotter, V. (1978). Follow-up studies. In M. Rutter & E. Schopler (Eds.), *Autism: A reappraisal of concepts and treatment* (pp. 475-596). New York: Plenum.

Louis, K. S., Marks, H. M., & Kruse, S. D. (1996). Teachers' professional community in restructuring schools. *American Educational Research Journal, 33,* 757-798.

Loveland, K. A., & Tunali-Kotoski, B. (2005). The school-age child with an autistic spectrum disorder. In F. R. Volkmar, R. Paul, A. Klin, & D. Cohen (Eds.), *Handbook of autism and pervasive developmental disorders: Vol. 1. Diagnosis, development, neurobiology, and behavior* (4th ed., pp. 247-287). Hoboken, NJ: Wiley.

Luckasson, R., Borthwick-Duffy, S., Buntinx, W. H. E., Coulter, D. L., Craig, E. M., Reeve, A., et al. (2002). *Mental retardation: Definition, classification, and systems of supports* (10th ed.). Washington, DC: AAMR.

Luckasson R., Coulter, D., Polloway, E., Reiss, S., Schalock, R., Snell, N., et al. (1992). *Mental retardation: Definition, classification, and systems of support* (9th ed.). Washington, DC: AAMR.

Luckner, J. L. (2002). *Facilitating the transition of students who are deaf or hard of hearing.* Austin, TX: PRO ED.

Luckner, J. L., & Howell, J. J. (2002). Suggestions for preparing itinerant teachers: A qualitative analysis. *American Annals of the Deaf, 147*(3), 54-61.

Luteijn, E., Luteijn, F., Jackson, S., Volkmar, F., & Minderaa, R. (2000). The children's social behavior questionnaire for milder variants of PDD problems: Evaluation of the psychometric characteristics. *Journal of Autism and Developmental Disorders, 30,* 317-330.

Lyon, R., Fletcher, J., Shaywitz, S., Shaywitz, B., Torgesen, J., Wood, F., et al. (2001). Rethinking learning disabilities. In C. Finn, A. Rotherham, & C. Hokanson (Eds.), *Rethinking special education for a new century* (pp. 259-287). Retrieved on December 28, 2005, from http://www.edexcellence.net/foundation/publication/index.cfm

Maag, J. (2002). A contextually based approach for treating depression in school-age children. *Intervention in School and Clinic, 37*(3), 149-155.

Maas, E., & Robin, D. A. (2006). Motor speech disorders: Apraxia and dysarthria. In L. M. Justice, *Communication sciences and disorders: An introduction* (pp. 180-211). Upper Saddle River, NJ: Merrill/ Prentice Hall.

Mace, A. L., Wallace, K. L., Whan, M. Q., & Steimachowicz, P. G. (1991). Relevant factors in the identification of hearing loss. *Ear and Hearing, 12*(4), 287-293.

MacLean, W. E., & Symons, F. (2002). Self-injurious behavior in infancy and young childhood. *Infants and Young Children, 14*(4), 31-41.

MacMillan, D., & Siperstein, G. (2002). Learning disabilities as operationalized by schools. In R. Bradley, L. Danielson, & D. Hallahan (Eds.), *Identification of learning disabilities: Research to practice* (pp. 287-333). Mahwah, NJ: Erlbaum.

Maker, C. J. (1989). *Critical issues in gifted education: Defensible programs for cultural and ethnic minorities.* Austin, TX: PRO-ED.

Maker, C. J., & Nielson, A. B. (1996). *Curriculum development and teaching strategies for gifted learners* (2nd ed.). Austin, TX: PRO-ED.

Mangrum, C., & Strichart, S. (Eds.). (2000). *Peterson's guide: Colleges with programs for students with learning disabilities or attention deficit disorders.* Stamford, CT: Thomson Learning.

Mann, V. (2003). Language processes: Keys to reading disability. In H. L. Swanson, K. R. Harris, & S. Graham (Eds.), *Handbook of learning disabilities* (pp. 213-228). New York: Guilford.

Marcus, L. M., Kunce, L. J., & Schopler, E. (2005). Working with families. In F. R. Volkmar, R. Paul, A. Klin, & D. Cohen (Eds.), *Handbook of autism and pervasive developmental disorders: Vol. 2. Assessment, interventions, and policy* (4th ed., pp. 1055-1086). Hoboken, NJ: Wiley.

Mardell-Czudnowski, C. D., & Goldenberg, D. S. (1998). *Developmental indicators for the assessment of learning* (3rd ed.). Circle Pines, MN: American Guidance Service.

Marks, D. (2005). *Culture and classroom management: Grounded theory from a high poverty predominately African American elementary school.* Unpublished doctoral dissertation. Gainesville: University of Florida.

Markwardt, F. C. (1998). *Peabody individual achievement test, revised/ normative update.* Circle Pines, MN: American Guidance Service.

Marland, S. P. (1972). *Education of the gifted and talented: Report to the Congress of the United States by the U.S. Commissioner of Education.* Washington, DC: U.S. Government Printing Office.

Marzano, R., Pickering, D., & Pollock, J. (2001). *Classroom instruction that works.* Alexandria, VA: ASCD.

Masten, A. S., Best, K. M., & Garmezy, N. (1990). Resilience and development: Contributions from the study of children who overcome adversity. *Development and Psychopathology, 2,* 425-444.

Mastropieri, M., & Scruggs, T. (2005). Feasibility and consequences of response to intervention: Examination of the issues and scientific evidence as a model for the identification of individuals with learning disabilities. *Journal of Learning Disabilities, 38*(6), 525-531.

Mastropieri, M., & Scruggs, T. (2007). *The inclusive classroom: Strategies for effective instruction* (3rd ed.). Upper Saddle River, NJ: Prentice Hall.

Mastropieri, M. A. (2001). Introduction to the special issue: Is the glass half full or half empty? Challenges encountered by first year special education teachers. *Journal of Special Education, 35,* 66-74.

Mastropieri, M. A., & Scruggs, T. E. (2000). *The inclusive classroom: Strategies for effective instruction.* Upper Saddle River, NJ: Merrill/Prentice Hall.

Mather, M., & Rivers, K. (2002). *State profiles of child well-being: Results from the 2000 census.* Retrieved November 4, 2006, from http://www.aecf.org/kidscount/census_2000_march_03.pdf

Mathes, P., Howard, J., Babyak, A., & Allen, S. (2000). Peer-assisted learning strategies for first-grade readers: A tool for preventing early reading failure. *Learning Disabilities Research and Practice, 14*(1), 50-60.

Mattison, R. E. (2004). Psychiatric and psychological assessment of emotional and behavioral disorders during school mental health consultation. In R. B. Rutherford, Jr., M. M. Quinn, & A. R. Mathur (Eds.), *Handbook of research in emotional and behavioral disorders* (pp. 54-77). New York: Guilford.

Maurice, C. (1993). *Let me hear your voice.* New York: Knopf.

Maxwell, J. C. (2002). *The 17 essential qualities of a team player: Becoming the kind of person every team wants.* Nashville, TN: Nelson.

Mayer, G. R. (2001). Antisocial behavior: Its causes and prevention within our schools. *Education and Treatment of Children, 24*(4), 414-429.

McConnell, M. E., Hilvitz, P. B., & Cox, C. J. (1998). Functional assessment: A systematic approach for assessment and intervention in general and special education classrooms. *Intervention in School and Clinic, 34,* 10-20.

McDonnell, A., & Hardman, M. L. (1989). The desegregation of America's special schools: Strategies for change. *Journal of The Association for Persons with Severe Handicaps, 14,* 68-74.

McGinnis, E., & Goldstein, A. P. (1997). *Skillstreaming in early childhood: New strategies and perspectives for teaching prosocial skills.* Champaign, IL: Research Press.

McLean, L. K., Brady, N. C., & McLean, J. E. (1996). Reported communication abilities of individuals with severe mental retardation. *American Journal on Mental Retardation, 100,* 580-591.

McLean, M. (2004). Assessment and its importance in early intervention/early childhood special education. In M. McLean, M. Wolery, & D. B. Bailey, Jr. (Eds.), *Assessing infants and preschoolers with special needs* (3rd ed., pp. 1-21). Upper Saddle River, NJ: Merrill/Prentice Hall.

McLeskey, J., Henry, D., & Axelrod, M. (1999). Inclusion of students with LD: An examination of data from *Reports to Congress. Exceptional Children, 65,* 55-66.

McLeskey, J., Henry, D., & Hodges, D. (1999). Inclusion: What progress is being made across disability categories? *Teaching Exceptional Children, 31*(3), 60-64.

McLeskey, J., Hoppey, D., Williamson, P., & Rentz, T. (2004). Is inclusion an illusion? An examination of national and state trends toward the education of students with learning disabilities in general education classrooms. *Learning Disabilities Research and Practice, 19*(2), 109-115.

McLeskey, J., & Pacchiano, D. (1994). Mainstreaming students with LD: Are we making progress? *Exceptional Children, 60,* 508-517.

McLeskey, J., & Waldron, N. (1996). Responses to questions teachers and administrators frequently ask about inclusion. *Phi Delta Kappan, 78,* 150-156.

McLeskey, J., & Waldron, N. (2000). *Inclusive education in action: Making differences ordinary.* Alexandria, VA: ASCD.

McLeskey, J., & Waldron, N. (2002, September). School change and inclusive schools: Lessons learned from practice. *Phi Delta Kappan, 84*(1), 65-72.

McLeskey, J., & Waldron, N. (in press). Comprehensive school reform and inclusive schools: Improving schools for all students. *Theory into Practice.*

Meadows, N. B., & Stevens, K. B. (2004). Teaching alternative behaviors to students with emotional and behavioral disorders. In R. B. Rutherford, Jr., M. M. Quinn, & A. R. Mathur (Eds.), *Handbook of research in emotional and behavioral disorders* (pp. 385-398). New York: Guilford.

Mellard, D., & Lancaster, P. (2003). Incorporating adult community services in students' transition planning. *Remedial and Special Education, 24*(6), 359-368.

Mercer, C., & Pullen, P. (2005). *Students with learning disabilities* (6th ed.). Upper Saddle River, NJ: Prentice Hall.

Meyer, G. A., & Batshaw, M. L. (2001). Fragile X syndrome. In M. L. Batshaw (Ed.), *Children with disabilities* (5th ed., pp. 321-331). Baltimore: Brookes.

Meyer, L. H., Peck, C. A., & Brown, L. (Eds.). (1991). *Critical issues in the lives of people with severe disabilities.* Baltimore: Brookes.

Michaud, L. J., Semel-Concepción, J., Duhaime, A., & Lazar, M. F. (2002). Traumatic brain injury. In M. L. Batshaw (Ed.), *Children with disabilities* (5th ed., pp. 525-545). Baltimore: Brookes.

Miller, A. (1999). Appropriateness of psychostimulant prescriptions to children: Theoretical and empirical perspectives. *Canadian Journal of Psychiatry, 44,* 1017-1024.

Miller, C. J., Sanchez, J., & Hynd, G. W. (2003). Neurological correlates of reading disabilities. In H. L. Swanson, K. R. Harris, & S. Graham (Eds.), *Handbook of learning disabilities* (pp. 242-255). New York: Guilford.

Minskoff, E. H. (1998). Sam Kirk: The man who made special education special. *Learning Disabilities Research and Practice, 13*(1), 15-21.

Mitchell, R. (2004). *How many people use ASL? And other good questions without good answers.* Retrieved December 12, 2005, from http://gri.gallaudet.edu/Presentations/2004-04-07-1.pdf

Mitchell, R. (2005). *A brief summary of estimates for the size of the deaf population in the USA based on available federal data and published research.* Retrieved August 2, 2005, from http://gri.gallaudet.edu/Demographics/deaf-US.php

Mooney, J., & Cole, D. (2000). *Learning outside the lines.* New York: Simon & Shuster.

Mostert, M. (2001). Facilitated communication since 1995: A review of published studies. *Journal of Autism and Developmental Disorders, 31,* 287-313.

Mostert, M. P., & Crockett, J. B. (2000). Reclaiming the history of special education for more effective practice. *Exceptionality, 8*(2), 133-143.

Mount, B., & Zwernik, K. (1988). *It's never too early, it's never too late.* St. Paul, MN: Metropolitan Council.

Mrug, S., & Wallander, J. L. (2002). Young people with physical disabilities: Does integration play a role? *International Journal of Disabilities, 49*(3), 267-280.

MTA Cooperative Group. (1999). A 14-month randomized clinical trial of treatment strategies for attention-deficit/hyperactivity disorder. *Archives of General Psychiatry, 56,* 1073-1086.

Murdick, N., Gartin, B., & Crabtree, T. (2002). *Special education law.* Upper Saddle River, NJ: Merrill/Prentice Hall.

Murphy, C., Yeargin-Allsopp, M., Decoufle, P., & Drews, C. (1995). The administrative prevalence of mental retardation in 10-year-old children in metropolitan Atlanta. *American Journal of Public Health, 85*(3), 319-323.

Muscott, H. S. (2000). A review and analysis of service learning programs involving students with emotional/behavioral disorders. *Education and Treatment of Children, 23*(3), 346-368.

Naglieri, J., LeBuffe, P., & Pfeiffer, S. (1994). *Devereux scales of mental disorders.* San Antonio, TX: Harcourt Assessment.

Naglieri, J. A., LeBuffe, P. A., & Pfeiffer, S. I. (1993). *Devereux behavior rating scale—school form.* San Antonio, TX: Psychological Corporation.

National Alliance for Autism Research (NAAR). (2005). *What is autism: An overview.* Retrieved November 5, 2005, from http://www.autismspeaks.org/whatisit/index.php

National Association of the Deaf (NAD). (2000). *Cochlear implants: Position statement.* Retrieved December 16, 2005, from http://www.nad.org/site/pp.asp?c=foINKQMBF&b=138140

National Association of the Deaf (NAD). (n.d.) *What is the difference between a deaf and hard of hearing person?* Retrieved November 22, 2005, from http://www.nad.org/site/pp.asp?c=foINKQMBF&b=180410

National Center for Education Statistics (NCES). (2005). *NAEP 2004 trends in academic progress: Three decades of student performance in reading and mathematics: Findings in brief.* Retrieved December 14, 2005, from http://nces.ed.gov/pubsearch/pubsinfo.asp?pubid=2005463

National Center for Educational Statistics (NCES). (2002). *The condition of education.* Retrieved March 23, 2005, from http://nces.ed.gov/ pubsearch/pubsinfo.asp?pubid=2002025

National Center for Health Statistics (NCHS). (1998). *National health interview survey—Disability supplement, 1994-95.* Hyattsville, MD: Author.

National Center for Hearing Assessment and Management. (2004). *2004 state EHDI survey: Screening.* Retrieved August 8, 2006, from http://www.infanthearing.org/survey/2004statesurvey/results_screening.html

National Center on Birth Defects and Disabilities. (2004). *Cerebral palsy.* Retrieved September 27, 2005, from http://www.cdc.gov/ncbddd/dd/ddcp.htm

National Clearinghouse on Child Abuse and Neglect. (2006). *Child maltreatment 2004: Summary and key findings.* Retrieved May 25, 2006, from http://nccanch.acf.hhs.gov/general/stats/index.cfm

National Commission on Teaching and America's Future. (2003). *No dream denied: A pledge to America's children.* Retrieved December 13, 2005, from http://www.nea.org/goodnews/citation.html

National Council for Accreditation of Teacher Education. (2002). *Professional standards for the accreditation of schools, colleges, and departments of education.* Retrieved June 1, 2004, from http://www.ncate.org/2000/unit_stnds_2002.pdf

National Dissemination Center for Children with Disabilities. (2004). *Spina bifida.* Retrieved September 27, 2005, from http://www.nichcy.org/pubs/factshe/fs12txt.htm

National Education Association (NEA). (2003). *The status of the American public school teacher 2000-2001.* Retrieved December 13, 2005, from http://www.nea.org/newsreleases/2003/nr030827.html

National Institute of Allergy and Infectious Diseases (NIAID). (2004). *HIV infection in infants and children.* Retrieved August 30, 2005, from http://www.niaid.nih.gov/factsheets/hivchildren.htm

National Institute on Deafness and Other Communication Disorders (NIDCD). (2002). *Cochlear implants: Who gets a cochlear implant?* Retrieved December 8, 2005, from http://www.nidcd.nih.gov/health/hearing/coch.asp

National Institute on Deafness and Other Communication Disorders (NIDCD). (2004). *Statistics on voice, speech, and language.* Retrieved January 2, 2006, from http://www.nidcd.nih.gov/health/statistics/ vsl.asp#2

National Research Council (NRC). (2001). *Educating children with autism.* Washington, DC: National Academy Press.

National Resource Center on AD/HD. (2005). *College issues for students with ADHD.* Retrieved October 13, 2005, from http://www.help4adhd.org/en/education/college/collegeissues

National Technical Assistance Consortium for Children and Young Adults Who Are Deaf-Blind (NTAC). (2004). *National deaf-blind child count.* Retrieved August 16, 2006, from http://www.tr.wou.edu/ntac/documents/census/2004-Census-Tables.pdf

National Vaccine Information Center. (2005). *Autism and vaccines: A new look at an old story.* Retrieved December 7, 2005, from http://www.909shot.com/Diseases/autismsp.htm

NEA and NASDSE. (2004). The path to "highly qualified" special education teacher under the Individuals with Disabilities Education Improvement Act of 2004. Retrieved May 8, 2005 from http://www.nea.org/specialed/hqspecial.html

Neel, R. S., & Cessna, K. K. (1990). Behavioral intent: Instructional content for students with behavior disorders. In K. K. Cessna (Ed.), *Instructionally differentiated programming* (pp. 31-40). Denver: Colorado Department of Education.

Nelson, J. R. (1996). Designing schools to meet the needs of students who exhibit disruptive behavior. *Journal of Emotional and Behavioral Disorders, 4*(3), 147-161.

Nelson, J. R., Martella, R. M., & Machand-Martella, N. (2002). Maximizing student learning: The effects of a comprehensive school-based program for preventing problem behaviors. *Journal of Emotional and Behavioral Disorders, 10*(3), 136-148.

Newcomer, P. L., Barenbaum, E., & Pearson, N. (1995). Depression and anxiety in children and adolescents with learning disabilities, conduct disorders, and no disability. *Journal of Emotional and Behavioral Disorders, 3*(1), 27-39.

Nieto, S. (2004). *Affirming diversity: The sociopolitical context of multicultural education* (4th ed.). Boston: Allyn & Bacon.

Nihira, K., Leland, H., & Lambert, N. (1993). *AAMR adaptive behavior scale—residential and community* (2nd ed.). Austin, TX: PRO-ED.

Noble, K. D., Subotnik, R. F. & Arnold, K. D. (1999). To thine own self be true: A new model of female talent development. *Gifted Child Quarterly, 43,* 140-149.

No Child Left Behind Act. (2001). 20 U.S.C. § 6301 et seq.

Noddings, N. (1988, December 7). Schools face crisis in caring. *Education Week,* p. 32.

Oakes, J. (1992). Can tracking research inform practice? Technical, normative, and political considerations. *Educational Researcher, 21*(4), 12-21.

Ochs, E., Kremer-Sadlik, T., Solomon, O., & Sirota, K. G. (2001). Inclusion as social practice: Views of children with autism. *Social Development, 10*(3), 399-419.

Odom, S. L., Brantlinger, E., Gersten, R., Horner, R. H., Thompson, B., & Harris, K. R. (2005). Research in special education: Scientific methods and evidenced-based practices. *Exceptional Children, 71,* 137-148.

Odom, S. L., & DeKlyen, M. (1986). *Social withdrawal in childhood.* Unpublished manuscript.

Office of Special Education Programs (OSEP). (2003). *Identifying and treating attention deficit hyperactivity disorder: A resource for school and home.* Washington, DC: Author.

O'Leary, K., & Becker, W. (1967). Behavior modification of an adjustment class: A token reinforcement program. *Exceptional Children, 9,* 637-642.

Olenchak, F. R., & Hebert, T. P. (2002). Endangered academic talent: Lessons learned from gifted first generation college males. *Journal of College Student Development, 28,* 195-212.

Olley, G. J. (2005). Curriculum and classroom structure. In F. R. Volkmar, R. Paul, A. Klin, & D. Cohen (Eds.), *Handbook of autism and pervasive developmental disorders: Vol. 2. Assessment, interventions, and policy* (4th ed., pp. 863-881). Hoboken, NJ: Wiley.

Olszewski-Kubilius, P., Lee, S. Y., Ngoi, M., & Ngoi, D. (2004). Addressing the achievement gap between minority and non-minority children by increasing access to gifted programs. *Journal for the Education of the Gifted, 28*(2), 127-158.

O'Neil, P. (2001). Special education and high stakes testing for high school graduation: An analysis of current law and policy. *Journal of Law and Education, 30*(2), 185-222.

Orkwis, R., & McLane, K. (1998). *A curriculum every student can use: Design principles for student access.* Reston, VA: Council for Exceptional Children, ERIC Clearinghouse on Disabilities and Gifted Education.

Osher, D., Morrison, G., & Bailey, W. (2003). Exploring the relationship between student mobility and dropout among students with emotional and behavioral disorder. *Journal of Negro Education, 72,* 79-96.

Overton, T. (2003). *Assessing learners with special needs: An applied approach* (4th ed.). Upper Saddle River, NJ: Merrill/Prentice Hall.

Overton, T. (2006). *Assessing learners with special needs: An applied approach* (5th ed.). Upper Saddle River, NJ: Merrill/Prentice Hall.

Owens, R. E., Metz, D. E., & Haas, A. (2003). *Introduction to communication disorders: A life span perspective* (2nd ed.). Boston: Allyn & Bacon.

Paine, S. C., Radicci, J., Rosellini, L. C., Deutchman, L., & Darch, C. B. (1983). *Structuring your classroom for academic success.* Champaign, IL: Research Press Company.

Paley, V. G. (2000). *White teacher.* Cambridge, MA: Harvard University Press.

Patrick, H., Turner, J., Meyer, D. K., & Midgley, C. (2003). How teachers establish psychological environments during the first days of school: Associations with avoidance in mathematics. *Teachers College Record, 105,* 1521-1558.

Patterson, G. R., Reid, J. B., Jones, R. R., & Conger, R. E. (1975). *A social learning approach to family intervention: Vol. 1. Families with aggressive children.* Eugene, OR: Castalia.

Patton, J., Polloway, E., & Smith, T. (1996). Individuals with mild mental retardation: Postsecondary outcomes and implications for educational policy. *Education and Training in Mental Retardation and Developmental Disabilities, 31,* 75-85.

Patton, J., Polloway, E., Smith, T., Edgar, E., Clark, G., & Lee, S. (1996). Individuals with mild mental retardation: Postsecondary outcomes and implications for educational policy. *Education and Training in Mental Retardation and Developmental Disabilities, 31,* 77-85.

Paul, R. (2005). Assessing communication in autism spectrum disorders. In F. R. Volkmar, R. Paul, A. Klin, & D. Cohen (Eds.), *Handbook of autism and pervasive developmental disorders: Vol. 2. Assessment, interventions, and policy* (4th ed., pp. 799-816). Hoboken, NJ: Wiley.

Payne, R. K. (2003). *Framework for understanding poverty* (rev. ed.). Highlands, TX: aha! Process.

Pearman, E., Elliott, T., & Aborn, L. (2004). Transition services model: Partnership for student success. *Education and Training in Developmental Disabilities, 39,* 26-34.

Pegnato, C. W., & Birch, J. W. (1959). Locating gifted children in junior high schools—A comparison of methods. *Exceptional Children, 25,* 300-304.

Pellegrino, L. (2002). Cerebral palsy. In M. L. Batshaw (Ed.), *Children with disabilities* (5th ed., pp. 443-466). Baltimore: Brookes.

Pelo, A., & Davidson, F. (2000). *That's not fair! A teacher's guide to activism with young children.* St. Paul, MN: Redleaf.

Peña, E. D., & Davis, B. L. (2000). Language disorders in infants, toddlers, and preschoolers. In R. B. Gillam, T. P. Marquardt, & F. N. Martin (Eds.), *Communication sciences and disorders: From science to clinical practice* (pp. 409-436). San Diego: Singular.

Penno, D. A., Frank, A. R., & Wacker, D. P. (2000). Instructional accommodations for adolescent students with severe emotional or behavioral disorders. *Behavioral Disorders, 25,* 325-343.

Peterson's Guide. (2003). *Colleges with programs for students with learning disabilities or attention deficit disorders* (7th ed.). Lawrenceville, NJ: Thomson Learning.

Phelps, L., & Grabowski, J. (1991). Autism: Etiology, differential diagnosis, and behavioral assessment update. *Journal of Psychopathology and Behavioral Assessment, 13*(2), 107-125.

Phelps, P. (2006). The three Rs of professionalism. *Kappa Delta Pi Record, 42,* 69-71.

Pierce, C. D., Reid, R., & Epstein, M. H. (2004). Teacher mediated interventions for children with EBD and their academic outcomes. *Remedial and Special Education, 25*(3), 175-188.

Piers, E., & Harris, D. (1984). *The Piers-Harris children's self-concept scale.* Nashville, TN: Counselor Recordings and Tests.

Piirto, J. N. (1992). *Understanding those who create.* Dayton: Ohio Psychology Press.

Pinnell, G., Lyons, C., DeFord, D., Bryk, A., & Seltzer, M. (1994). Comparing instructional models for the literacy education of high-risk first graders. *Reading Research Quarterly, 29,* 9-39.

Platt, J. M. (1987). Substitute teachers can do more than just keep the lid on. *Teaching Exceptional Children, 19*(2), 28-31.

Polloway, E. (1984). The integration of mildly retarded students in the schools: A historical review. *Remedial and Special Education, 5*(4), 18-28.

Polloway, E., Chamberlain, J., Denning, C., Smith, J., & Smith, T. (1999). Levels of deficits or supports in the classification of mental retardation: Implementation practices. *Education and Training in Mental Retardation and Developmental Disabilities, 34,* 200-206.

Polsgrove, L., & Smith, A. W. (2004). Informed practice in teaching self-control to children with emotional and behavioral disorders. In R. B.

Rutherford, Jr., M. M. Quinn, & A. R. Mathur (Eds.), *Handbook of research in emotional and behavioral disorders* (pp. 399-425). New York: Guilford.

Postman, N., & Weingartner, C. (1969). *Teaching as a subversive activity.* New York: Delta.

President's Commission on Excellence in Special Education. (2002). *A new era: Revitalizing special education for children and their families.* Jessup, MD: Education Publications Center, U.S. Department of Education.

President's Committee on Mental Retardation. (1969). *The six-hour retarded child.* Washington, DC: U.S. Government Printing Office.

Psychological Corporation. (2001). *Wechsler individual achievement test* (2nd ed.). San Antonio, TX: Author.

Public Education Network. (2004). *Teacher professional development: A primer for parents & community members.* Washington, DC: Author.

Public Schools of North Carolina State Board of Education. (2004). *ABCs 2004 accountability report background packet.* Raleigh: North Carolina Department of Public Instruction. Retrieved January 10, 2005, from http://abcs.ncpublicschools.org/abcs/

Putnam, J. (1998). *Cooperative learning and strategies for inclusion* (2nd ed.). Baltimore: Brookes.

Quay, H. C., & Peterson, D. R. (1993). *The revised behavior problem checklist: Manual.* Odessa, FL: Psychological Assessment Resources.

Quinn, M. M., & Poirier, J. M. (2004). Linking prevention research with policy: Examining the costs and outcomes of the failure to prevent emotional and behavioral disorders. In R. B. Rutherford, Jr., M. M. Quinn, & A. R. Mathur (Eds.), *Handbook of research in emotional and behavioral disorders* (pp. 54-77). New York: Guilford.

Quinn, M. M., Osher, D., Warger, C., Hanley, T., Bader, B. D., Tate, R., et al. (2000). *Educational strategies for children with emotional and behavioral problems.* Washington, DC: Center for Effective Collaboration and Practice, American Institutes for Research.

Racino, J. A. (1995). Community living for adults with developmental disabilities: A housing and support approach. *Journal of The Association for Persons with Severe Handicaps, 20,* 300-310.

Ramey, C., & Ramey, S. (1992). Effective early intervention. *Mental Retardation, 30*(6), 337-345.

Ramey, S. L., & Ramey, C. T. (1998). The transition to school: Opportunities and challenges for children, families, educators, and communities. *Elementary School Journal, 98*(4), 293-295.

Ramos-Ford, V., & Gardner, H. (1991). Giftedness from a multiple intelligences perspective. In N. Colangelo & G. A. Davis (Eds.), *Handbook of gifted education* (pp. 55-64). Needham Heights, MA: Allyn & Bacon.

Rapport, M., Scanlan, S., & Denney, C. (1999). Attention deficit/hyperactivity disorder and scholastic achievement: A model of dual developmental pathways. *Journal of Child Psychology and Psychiatry and Applied Disciplines, 40*(8), 1169-1183.

Raver, C. C., & Knitze, J. (2002). *Ready to enter: What research tells policymakers about strategies to promote social and emotional school readiness among three- and four-year-olds* (Policy Paper No. 3). Columbia University: National Center for Children in Poverty.

Redcav, E., & Courchesne, E. (2005). When is the brain enlarged in autism? A meta-analysis of all brain size reports. *Biological Psychiatry, 58*(1), 1-9.

Redl, F., & Wineman, D. (1957). *The aggressive child.* New York: Free Press.

Reed, V. A., & Spicer, L. (2003). The relative importance of selected communication skills for adolescents' interactions with their teachers: High school teachers' opinions. *Language, Speech, and Hearing Services in Schools, 34,* 343-357.

Reese, S. (2004, May). Teacher portfolios: Displaying the art of teaching. *Techniques, 79*(5), 18-21.

Regenbogen, L., & Coscas, G. (1985). *Oculo-auditory syndromes.* New York: Masson.

Rehabilitation Research and Training Center on Independent Living Management. (2002). *Disability history timeline.* Retrieved July 7, 2005, from http://courses.temple.edu/neighbor/ds/disabilityrightstimeline.htm

Reid, R., Trout, A., & Schartz, M. (2005). Self-regulation interventions for children with attention deficit/hyperactivity disorder. *Exceptional Children, 71*(4), 361-377.

Reiff, M. (2004). *ADHD: A complete and authoritative guide.* Elk Grove Village, IL: American Academy of Pediatrics.

Reis, S. M., & Graham, C. (2005). Needed: Teachers to encourage girls in math, science, and technology. *Gifted Child Today, 28,* 14-21.

Renzulli, J. S. (1977). *The enrichment triad model: A guide for developing defensible programs for the gifted and talented.* Mansfield, CT: Creative Learning Press.

Renzulli, J. S. (1986). The three ring conception of giftedness: A developmental model for creative productivity. In R. Sternberg & J. E. Davidson (Eds.), *Conceptions of giftedness* (pp. 53-92). New York: Cambridge University Press.

Renzulli, J. S. (2002). Emerging conceptions of giftedness: Building a bridge to the new century. *Exceptionality, 10,* 67-75.

Renzulli, J. S., & Reis, S. M. (1991). The reform movement and the quiet crisis in gifted education. *Gifted Child Quarterly, 35*(1), 26-35.

Reschly, D. (2005). Learning disabilities identification: Primary intervention, secondary intervention, and then what? *Journal of Learning Disabilities, 38*(6), 510-515.

Reutzel, R. (2003). Organizing effective literacy instruction: Grouping strategies and instructional routines. In L. M. Morrow, L. B. Gambrell, & M. Pressley (Eds.), *Best practices in literacy instruction* (2nd ed., pp. 241-267). New York: Guilford.

Rhode, G., Jenson, W., & Reavis, K. (1998). *The tough kid book: Practical classroom management strategies.* Longmont, CO: Sopris West.

Rhodes, W. C. (1967). The disturbing child: A problem in ecological management. *Exceptional Children, 33,* 449-455.

Richards, D. (2003). *The top Section 504 errors: Expert guidance to avoid 25 common compliance mistakes.* Horsham, PA: LRP.

Richardson, J. (1999, February/March). Engaging the public builds support for schools. *Tools for Schools.* Retrieved October 5, 2005, from http://www.nsdc.org/library/publications/tools/tools2-99rich.cfm

Richert, E. S., Alvino, J., & McDonnel, R. (1982). *The national report on identification of gifted and talented youth: Assessment and recommendations for comprehensive identification of gifted and talented youth.* Sewell, NJ: Educational Improvement Center South.

Rivera, G. (2004). *Early biography.* Retrieved June 27, 2005, from http://www.geraldo.com/index.php?/archives/14_EARLY_BIO.html

Rivkin, S., Hanushek, E., & Kain, J. (2001). *Teachers, schools, and academic achievement.* Political Economy Working Paper 09/01. Richardson: University of Texas at Dallas.

Robins D., Fein, D., Barton, M., & Green, J. (2001). The modified checklist for autism in toddlers. *Journal of Autism and Developmental Disorders, 31*(2), 131-144.

Robinson, A. (1990). Cooperation or exploitation? The argument against cooperative learning for talented students. *Journal for the Education of the Gifted, 14,* 9-27.

Rock, E. E., Fessler, M. A., & Church, R. P. (1997). The concomitance of learning disabilities and emotional/behavioral disorders: A conceptual model. *Journal of Learning Disabilities, 30*(3), 245-263.

Rock, E., Fessler, M., & Church, R. (1999). Co-occurring disorders and learning disabilities. In W. Bender (Ed.), *Professional issues in learning disabilities* (pp. 347-384). Austin, TX: PRO-ED.

Rodgers, C. (1965). *Client centered therapy.* Boston: Houghton Mifflin.

Roe, A. (1952). A psychologist examines 64 eminent scientists. *Scientific American, 187,* 21-25.

Rogan, J. (2000). Learning strategies: Recipes for success. *Beyond Behavior, 10*(1), 18-22.

Roid, G. (2003). *Stanford-Binet intelligence test* (5th ed.). Itasca, IL: Riverside.

Roizen, N. J. (2001). Down syndrome. In M. L. Batshaw (Ed.), *Children with disabilities* (5th ed., pp. 307-320). Baltimore: Brookes.

Rorschach, H. (1932). *Psychodiagnostic: Methodik und Ergebnisse eines Wahrnehmungs-diagnostischen Experiments* (2nd ed.). Bern, Switzerland: Huber.

Rosenberg, M. S., & Jackman, L. A. (1997). Addressing student and staff behavior: The PAR model. *Fourth R, 79,* 1-12.

Rosenberg, M. S., & Jackman, L. A. (2000, May). *Up to PAR: Development, implementation, and maintenance of comprehensive school-wide behavior management systems.* Paper presented at Comprehensive Systems of Personnel Development, Alexandria, VA.

Rosenberg, M. S., & Jackman, L. A. (2003). Development, implementation, and sustainability of comprehensive school-wide behavior management systems. *Intervention in School and Clinic, 39*(1), 10-21.

Rosenberg, M. S., Griffin, C., Kilgore, K., & Carpenter, S. L. (1997). Beginning teachers in special education: A model for providing individualized support. *Teacher Education and Special Education, 20*(4), 301-321.

Rosenberg, M. S., O'Shea, L., & O'Shea, D. J. (2006). *Student teacher to master teacher: A practical guide for educating students with special needs* (4th ed.). Upper Saddle River, NJ: Merrill/Prentice Hall.

Rosenberg, M. S., Wilson, R. J., Maheady, L., & Sindelar, P. T. (2004). *Educating students with behavior disorders* (3rd ed.). Boston: Pearson Education.

Rosenfeld, J. S. (2005). Section 504 and IDEA: Basic similarities and differences. *Learning Disabilities OnLine.* Retrieved November 29, 2005, from http://www.ldonline.org/ld_indepth/legal_legislative/edlaw504.html

Rosenshine, B., & Stevens, R. (1986). Teaching functions. In M. C. Wittrock (Ed.), *Handbook of research on teaching* (3rd ed., pp. 376-391). New York: Macmillan.

Ross, J. A. (1994). The impact of an inservice to promote cooperative learning on the stability of teacher efficacy. *Canadian Journal of Education, 17,* 51-65.

Roth, F. P., & Worthington, C. K. (1996). *Treatment resource manual for speech-language pathology.* San Diego: Singular.

Rothstein, R. (2002). *Class and schools.* Washington, DC: Economic Policy Institute.

Rotter, J. B. (1966). Generalized expectancies for internalized versus externalized control of reinforcement. *Psychological Monographs, 80,* 1-28.

Rowland, A., Umback, D., Stallone, L., et al. (2002). Prevalence of medication treatment for attention deficit-hyperactivity disorder among elementary school children in Johnston County, North Carolina. *American Journal of Public Health, 92,* 231-234.

Ruiz, R. (1988). Orientations in language planning. In S. L. McKay & S. C. Wong (Eds.), *Language diversity: Problem or resource?* (pp. 3-26). New York: Newbury House.

Rusch, F. R. & Braddock, D. (2004). Adult day programs versus supported employment (1988-2002): Spending and service practices of mental retardation and developmental disabilities' state agencies. *Research and Practice for Persons with Severe Disabilities, 29,* 237-242.

Rutter, M. (1978). Diagnosis and definition. In M. Rutter & E. Schopler (Eds.), *Autism: A reappraisal of concepts and treatment* (pp. 1-26). New York: Plenum.

Ryan, A., Halsey H., & Matthews, W. (2003). Using functional assessment to promote desirable student behavior in schools. *Teaching Exceptional Children, 35,* 8-15.

Ryan, J. B., & Peterson, R. L. (2004). Physical restraint in school. *Behavioral Disorders, 29*(2), 154-168.

Safford, P. J., & Safford, E. J. (1996). *A history of childhood and disability.* New York: Teachers College Press.

Safran, J. S. (2002). Supporting students with Asperger's syndrome in general education. *TEACHING Exceptional Children, 34*(5), 60-66.

Salend, S. (2005). *Creating inclusive classrooms: Effective and reflective practices for all students* (5th ed.). Upper Saddle River, NJ: Merrill/Prentice Hall.

Salend, S., & Duhaney, L. (1999). The impact of inclusion on students with and without disabilities and their educators. *Remedial and Special Education, 20,* 114-126.

Salend, S., & Rohena, E. (2003). Students with attention deficit disorders: An overview. *Intervention in School and Clinic, 38*(5), 259-266.

Salisbury, C. L., & Smith, B. J. (1993). *Effective practices for preparing young children with special needs for school.* ERIC Digest #E519. Reston VA: ERIC Clearinghouse on Special Needs and Gifted Education. (ED358675).

Sameroff, A. (1990). Neo-environmental perspectives on developmental theory. In R. Hodapp, J. Burack, & E. Zigler (Eds.), *Issues in the developmental approach to mental retardation* (pp. 93-113). New York: Cambridge University Press.

Sample, P. (1998). Postschool outcomes for students with significant emotional disturbance following best-practice transition services. *Behavioral Disorders, 23*(4), 231-242.

Sanders, W., & Horn, S. (1998). Research findings from the Tennessee Value-Added Assessment System (TVAAS) database: Implications for educational evaluation and research. *Journal of Personnel Evaluation in Education, 12*(3), 247-256.

Sands, D., & Wehmeyer, M. (2005). Teaching goal setting and decision making to students with developmental disabilities. In M. Wehmeyer & M. Agran (Eds.), *Mental retardation and intellectual disabilities: Teaching students using innovation and research-based strategies* (pp. 273-296). Washington, DC: AAMR.

Sansosti, F. J., Powell-Smith, K. A., & Kincaid, D. (2004). A research synthesis of social story interventions for children with autism spectrum disorders. *Focus on Autism and Other Developmental Disabilities, 19*(4), 194-204.

Santos, M. (2002). From mystery to mainstream: Today's school-based speech-language pathologist. *Educational Horizons, 80,* 93-96.

Saphier, J. D. (1995). *Bonfires and magic bullets. Making teaching a true profession: The step without which other reforms will neither take nor endure.* Carlisle, MA: Research for Better Teaching.

Scheff, T. (1966). *Being mentally ill: A sociological theory.* Chicago: Aldine.

Schirmer, B. R. (2000). *Language and literacy development in children who are deaf* (2nd ed.). Needham Heights, MA: Allyn & Bacon.

Schirmer, B. R. (2001a). *Psychological, social, and educational dimensions of deafness.* Boston: Allyn & Bacon.

Schirmer, B. R. (2001b). Using research to improve literacy practice and practice to improve literacy research. *Journal of Deaf Studies and Deaf Education, 6*(2), 83-91.

Schoenbrodt, L., Kumin, L., & Sloan, J. M. (1997). Learning disabilities existing concomitantly with language disorder. *Journal of Learning Disabilities, 30,* 264-281.

Schopler, E. (2005). Cross-cultural program priorities and reclassification of outcome research methods. In F. R. Volkmar, R. Paul, A. Klin, & D. Cohen (Eds.), *Handbook of autism and pervasive developmental disorders: Vol. 2. Assessment, interventions, and policy* (4th ed., pp. 1174-1192). Hoboken, NJ: Wiley.

Schopler, E., Reichler, R. J., Bashford, A., Lansing, M. D., & Marcus, L. M. (1990). *Psychoeducational profile—Revised.* Austin, TX: PRO-ED.

Schopler, E., Reichler, R. J., & Renner, B. R. (1986). *The childhood autism rating scale (CARS) for diagnostic screening and classification of autism.* Irvington, NY: Irvington.

Schrag, P., & Divoky, D. (1975). *The myth of the hyperactive child.* New York: Pantheon.

Schreibman, L., & Ingersoll, B. (2005). Behavioral interventions to promote learning in individuals with autism. In F. R. Volkmar, R. Paul, A. Klin, & D. Cohen (Eds.), *Handbook of autism and pervasive developmental disorders: Vol. 2. Assessment, interventions, and policy* (4th ed., pp. 882-896). Hoboken, NJ: Wiley.

Schumaker, J., & Deshler, D. (2003). Can students with LD become competent writers? *Learning Disability Quarterly, 26,* 129-141.

Schumaker, J., & Deshler, D. (2006). Teaching adolescents to be strategic learners. In D. Deshler & J. Schumaker (Eds.), *Teaching adolescents with disabilities* (pp. 121-156). Thousand Oaks, CA: Corwin.

Schumaker, J., Deshler, D., Alley, G., Warner, M., & Denton, P. (1982). A learning strategy for improving reading comprehension. *Learning Disability Quarterly, 5,* 295-305.

Schumm, J. (1999) *Adapting reading and math materials for the inclusive classroom.* Reston, VA: Council for Exceptional Children.

Schumm, J., Vaughn, S., & Leavell, A. (1994). Planning pyramid: A framework for planning for diverse student needs during content area instruction. *Reading Teacher, 47*(8), 608-615.

Schwab Foundation for Learning. (1999). *Learning special needs: Common warning signs.* Retrieved November 1, 2004, from http://www.schwablearning.org/index.asp

Schworm, R., & Birnbaum, R. (1989). Symptom expression in hyperactive children: An analysis of observation. *Journal of Learning Disabilities, 22,* 35-40.

Scott, E. M., Smith, T. E. C., Hendricks, M. D., & Polloway, E. A. (1999). Prader-Willi syndrome: A review and implications for educational intervention. *Education and Training in Mental Retardation and Developmental Disabilities, 34,* 110-116.

Scott, K. (1999). Cognitive instructional strategies. In W. Bender (Ed.), *Professional issues in learning disabilities* (pp. 55-82). Austin, TX: PRO-ED.

Scruggs, T., & Mastropieri, M. (2002). On babies and bathwater: Addressing the problems of identification of learning disabilities. *Learning Disability Quarterly, 25*(3), 155-168.

Scruggs, T. E., & Mastropieri, M. A. (1996). Teacher perceptions of mainstream/inclusion, 1958-1995: A research synthesis. *Exceptional Children, 63,* 59-74.

Segal, N. L. (2005). Twin study summaries. *Twin Research and Human Genetics, 8*(4), 411-2, 413-4.

Selig, R. A. (2005). *The Revolution's black soldiers.* Retrieved November 27, 2005, from http://www.americanrevolution.org

Seltzer, M., Floyd, F., Greenberg, J., Lounds, J., Lindstron, M., & Hong, J. (2005). Life course impacts of mild intellectual deficits. *American Journal of Mental Retardation, 110,* 451-468.

Shackelford, J. (2006). *State and jurisdictional eligibility definitions for infants and toddlers with special needs under IDEA* (NECTAC Notes No. 20). Chapel Hill: University of North Carolina, FPG Child Development Institute, National Early Childhood Technical Assistance Center. Retrieved June 22, 2006, from http://www.nectac.org/%7Epdfs/pubs/nnotes20.pdf

Shapiro, D. A. (1999). *Stuttering intervention: A collaborative journey to fluency freedom.* Austin, TX: PRO-ED.

Shapiro, E. S., Miller, D. N., Sawka, K., Gardill, M. C., & Handler, M. W. (1999). Facilitating the inclusion of students with EBD into general education classrooms. *Journal of Emotional and Behavioral Disorders, 7*(2), 83-93.

Shaywitz, B., Shaywitz, S., Blachman, B., Pugh, K., Fulbright, R., Skudlarski, P., et al. (2004). Development of left occipito-temporal systems for skilled reading in children after a phonologically-based intervention. *Biological Psychiatry, 55,* 926-933.

Shea, V., & Mesibov, G. B. (2005). Adolescents and adults with autism. In F. R. Volkmar, R. Paul, A. Klin, & D. Cohen (Eds.), *Handbook of autism and pervasive developmental disorders: Vol. 1. Diagnosis, development, neurobiology, and behavior* (4th ed., pp. 288-311). Hoboken, NJ: Wiley.

Shippen, M. E., Simpson, R. G., & Crites, S. A. (2003). A practical guide to functional behavioral assessment. *Teaching Exceptional Children, 35,* 36-44.

Shore, B. M., Cornell, D. G., Robinson, A., & Ward, V. S. (1991). *Recommended practices in gifted education.* New York: Teachers College Press.

Shore, B. M., & Tsiamis, A. (1986). Identification by provision: Limited field test of a radical alternative for identifying gifted students. In K. A. Heller & J. F. Feldhusen (Eds.), *Identifying and nurturing the gifted: An international perspective* (pp. 93-109). Toronto: Huber.

Shuell, T. (1996). Teaching and learning in a classroom context. In D. Berliner & R. Calfee (Eds.), *Handbook of educational psychology* (pp. 726-764). New York: Macmillan.

Siegel, L. (2001). The educational and communication needs of deaf and hard of hearing children: A statement of principal regarding fundamental systemic educational changes. *American Annals of the Deaf, 145*(2), 64-77.

Siegel, L. S. (2003). Basic cognitive processes and reading disabilities. In H. L. Swanson, K. R. Harris, & S. Graham (Eds.), *Handbook of learning disabilities* (pp. 158-181). New York: Guilford.

Sigman, M., & Capps, L. (1997). *Children with autism: A developmental perspective.* Cambridge, MA: Harvard University Press.

Silverman, L. K. (1990). Social and emotional education of the gifted: The discoveries of Leta Hollingworth. *Roper Review, 12,* 171-178.

Simonsen, C. E., & Gordon, M. S. (1982). *Juvenile justice in America.* New York: Macmillan.

Simonsen, C. E., & Vito, G. F. (2003). *Juvenile justice today* (4th ed). Englewood Cliffs, NJ: Prentice Hall.

Simpson, R. L., de Boer-Ott, S. R., & Smith-Myles, B. (2003). Inclusion of learners with autism spectrum disorders in general education settings. *Topics in Language Disorders, 23*(2), 116-133.

Simpson, R. L., & Myles, B. S. (1998). Aggression among children and youth who have Asperger's syndrome: A different population requiring different strategies. *Preventing School Failure, 42*(4), 149-153.

Sindelar, P. T., Griffin, C. C., Smith, S. W., & Watanabe, A. K. (1992). Pre-referral intervention: Encouraging notes on preliminary findings. *Elementary School Journal, 92,* 245-259.

Sitlington, P. L., & Nuebert, D. A. (2004). Preparing youths with emotional or behavioral disorders for transition to adult life: Can it be done within the standards-based reform movement? *Behavioral Disorders, 29*(3), 279-288.

Skiba, R., Poloni-Staudinger, L., Gallini, S., Simmons, A., & Feggins-Azziz, R. (2006). Disparage access: The disproportionality of African American students with disabilities across educational environments. *Exceptional Children, 72*(4), 411-424.

Skinner, R., & Staresina, L. (2004). State of the states. In *Education Week* [special issue]: *Special education in an era of standards: Count me in,* pp. 97-123.

Slavin, R. (2004). Built to last: Long-term maintenance of success for all. *Remedial and Special Education, 25*(1), 61-66.

Slavin, R., Madden, N., Dolan, L., Wasik, B., Ross, S., & Smith, L. (1994). Whenever and wherever we choose: The replication of "success for all." *Phi Delta Kappan, 75,* 639-647.

Slavin, R. E. (1990a). Ability grouping, cooperative learning and the gifted. *Journal for the Education of the Gifted, 14,* 3-8.

Slavin, R. E. (1990b). *Cooperative learning: Theory, research, and practice.* Upper Saddle River, NJ: Prentice Hall.

Sleeter, C. (1995). Radical structuralist perspectives on the creation and use of learning disabilities. In T. Skrtic (Ed.), *Disability & democracy: Reconstructing (special) education for postmodernity* (pp. 153-165). New York: Teachers College Press.

Smith, C. R., & Katsiyannis, A. (2004). Behavior, discipline, and students with emotional or behavioral disorders: Promises to keep . . . miles to go. *Behavioral Disorders, 29*(3), 289-299.

Smith, D. D., & Rivera, D. P. (1995). Discipline in special education and general education settings. *Focus on Exceptional Children, 27*(5), 1-14.

Smith, D. J. (1998). Histories of special education: Stories from our past, insights for our future. *Remedial and Special Education, 19*(4), 196-200.

Smith, J. D. (2003). *In search of better angels: Stories of disability in the human family.* Thousand Oaks, CA: Corwin.

Smith, T., Polloway, E., Patton, J., & Dowdy, C. (2004). *Teaching students with special needs in inclusive settings* (4th ed.). Boston: Allyn & Bacon.

Smith, T. E. C. (2001). Section 504, the ADA, and public schools. *Remedial and Special Education, 22*(6), 335-343.

Smith-Myles, B., & Simpson, R. L. (2001). Effective practices for students with Asperger's syndrome. *Focus on Exceptional Children, 34,* 1-16.

Snell, M. E., & Brown, F. (Eds.). (2005). *Instruction of students with severe disabilities* (6th ed.). Upper Saddle River, NJ: Merrill/Prentice Hall.

Snell, M. E., & Eichner, S. J. (1989). Integration for students with profound disabilities. In F. Brown & D. H. Lehr (Eds.), *Persons with profound disabilities: Issues and practices* (pp. 109-138), Baltimore: Brookes.

Snow, K. (2006). *People first language.* Retrieved August 1, 2006, from http://www.disabilityisnatural.com/peoplefirstlanguage.htm

Soto, G., & Goetz, L. (1998). Self-efficacy beliefs and the education of students with severe disabilities. *Journal of the Association for Persons with Severe Handicaps, 23,* 134-143.

Southern, W. T., & Jones, E. D. (1992). Programming, grouping, and acceleration in rural school districts: A survey of attitudes and practices. *Gifted Child Quarterly, 36,* 172-117.

Southern, W. T., Spicker H. H., Kierouz, K., & Kelly, K. (1990). *The Indiana guide for the identification of the gifted and talented* (K. Kierouz, Ed.). Indianapolis: Indiana Department of Education.

Sparrow, S. S., Cicchetti, D. V., & Balla, D. A. (2005). *Vineland adaptive behavior scales* (2nd ed.). Circle Pines, MN: American Guidance Service.

Spear-Swerling, L., & Sternberg, R. (1996). *Off track: When poor readers become "learning disabled."* Boulder, CO: Westview.

Spiegel, H. M. L., & Bonwit, A. M. (2002). HIV infection in children. In M. L. Batshaw (Ed.), *Children with disabilities* (5th ed., pp. 123-139). Baltimore: Brookes.

Sprague, J. R., & Walker, H. M. (2005). *Safe and healthy schools: Practical prevention strategies.* New York: Guilford.

Stainback, W., & Stainback, S. (1989). Practical organizational strategies. In S. Stainback, W. Stainback, & M. Forest (Eds.), *Educating all students in the mainstream of regular education* (pp. 71-87). Baltimore: Brookes.

Stehr-Green P., et al. (2003). Autism and Thimerosal-containing vaccines: Lack of consistent evidence for an association. *American Journal of Preventive Medicine, 25*(2), 101-106.

Stein, D. (1999). *Ritalin is not the answer: A drug-free, practical program for children diagnosed with ADD or ADHD.* San Francisco: Jossey-Bass.

Stein, M., Silbert, J., & Carnine, D. (1997). *Designing effective mathematics instruction: A Direct Instruction approach* (3rd ed.). Upper Saddle River, NJ: Merrill/Prentice Hall.

Stone, W. L., Coonrod, E. E., & Ousley, O. Y. (2000). Screening tool for two-year olds (STAT): Development and preliminary data. *Journal of Autism and Developmental Disorders, 30,* 607-612.

Stronge, J. H. (2002). *Qualities of effective teachers.* Alexandria, VA: Association for Supervision and Curriculum Development.

Stump, C. S., & Bigge, J. (2005). Curricular options for individuals with physical, health, or multiple disabilities. In S. J. Best, K. W. Heller, & J. L. Bigge (Eds.), *Teaching individuals with physical or multiple disabilities* (5th ed., pp. 278-318). Upper Saddle River, NJ: Merrill/Prentice Hall.

Sugai, G., & Horner, R. H. (2002). Introduction to special series on positive behavior supports in schools. *Journal of Emotional and Behavioral Disorders, 10*(3), 130-135.

Sugai, G., & Lewis, T. J. (1996). Preferred and promising practices for social skills instruction. *Focus on Exceptional Children, 29*(4), 1-16.

Sunderland, L. C. (2004). Speech, language, and audiology services in public schools. *Intervention in School and Clinic, 39,* 209-217.

Swaggart, F. L., & Gagnon, E. (1995). Using social stories to teach social and behavioral skills to children with autism. *Focus on Autistic Behavior, 10*(1), 1-16.

Swanson, L., Hoskyn, M. & Lee, C. (1999). *Interventions for students with learning disabilities: A meta-analysis of treatment outcomes.* New York: Guilford.

Swanson, L., & Saez, L. (2003). Memory difficulties in children and adults with learning disabilities. In H. L. Swanson, K. R. Harris, & S. Graham (Eds.), *Handbook of learning disabilities* (pp. 182-198). New York: Guilford.

Symons, F. J. (1995). Self-injurious behavior: A brief review of theories and current treatment perspectives. *Developmental Disabilities Bulletin, 23,* 91-104.

Tager-Flusberg, H., Paul, R., & Lord, C. (2005). Language and communication in autism. In F. R. Volkmar, R. Paul, A. Klin, & D. Cohen (Eds.), *Handbook of autism and pervasive developmental disorders: Vol. 1. Diagnosis, development, neurobiology, and behavior.* (4th ed., pp. 335-364). Hoboken, NJ: Wiley.

Tashie, C., Jorgensen, C., Shapiro-Barnard, S., Martin, J., & Schuh, M. (1996). High school inclusion. *TASH Newsletter, 22*(9), 19-22.

Tatum, B. D. (1997). *Why are all the black kids sitting together in the cafeteria?* New York: Basic Books.

Taylor, R., Richards, S. B., & Brady, M. (2005). *Mental retardation: Historical perspectives, current practices, and future directions.* Boston: Pearson/Allyn & Bacon.

Taylor-Greene, S., Brown, D., Nelson, L. A., Longton, J., Gassman, T., Cohen, J., et al. (1997). School-wide behavior support: Starting the year off right. *Journal of Behavioral Education, 7*(1), 99-112.

Teicher, M. H. (2002). Scars that won't heal: The neurobiology of child abuse. *Scientific American, 286*(3), 68-75.

Terman, L. M. (1925). *Mental and physical traits of a thousand gifted children.* Vol. 1 of L. M. Terman (Ed.), *Genetic studies of genius.* Stanford, CA: Stanford University Press.

Terman, L. M., & Oden, M. H. (1947). *The gifted child grows up: Twenty-five years' follow-up of a superior group.* Stanford, CA: Stanford University Press.

The ARC. (2005). *Causes and prevention of mental retardation.* Retrieved October 17, 2006, from http://www.thearc.org/causes.html#

The Individuals with Disabilities Education Improvement Act (IDEA), P. L. 108-446. (2004). Retrieved November 7, 2006, from http://frwebgate.access.gpo.gov/cgi-bin/getdoc.cgi?dbname=108 cong public laws&docid=f:publ446.108

Thoma, C., & Getzel, E. (2005). "Self-determination is what it's all about": What post-secondary students with disabilities tell us are important considerations for success. *Education and Training in Developmental Disabilities, 40,* 234-242.

Thompson, G. L. (2004). *Through ebony eyes: What teachers need to know but are afraid to ask about African American students.* San Francisco: Jossey-Bass.

Thomson, J., & Raskind, W. (2003). Genetic influences on reading and writing disabilities. In H. L. Swanson, K. R. Harris, & S. Graham (Eds.), *Handbook of learning disabilities* (pp. 256-270). New York: Guilford.

Thorndike, R. L., Hagen, E., & Sattler, J. (1986). *Stanford-Binet intelligence scale* (4th Ed.). Itasca, IL: Riverside.

Thuppal, M., & Sobsey, D. (2004). Children with special health care needs. In F. P. Orelove, D. Sobsey, & R. K. Silberman (Eds.), *Educating children with multiple disabilities: A collaborative approach* (2nd ed., pp. 311-377). Baltimore: Brookes.

Thurlow, M. L., Elliott, J. L., & Ysseldyke, J. E. (2003). *Testing students with disabilities: Practical strategies for complying with district and state requirements* (2nd ed.). Thousand Oaks, CA: Corwin.

Tobin, T., Sugai, G., & Colvin, G. (1996). Patterns in middle school discipline records. *Journal of Emotional and Behavioral Disorders, 4*(2), 82-94.

Tomlinson-Keasey, C., & Keasey, C. B. (1993). Graduating from college in the 1930's: The Terman genetic studies of genius. In K. D. Hulbert & D. T. Schuster (Eds.), *Women's lives through time* (pp. 63-92). San Francisco: Jossey-Bass.

Torgesen, J. (2000). Individual differences in response to early interventions in reading: The lingering problem of treatment resisters. *Learning Disabilities Research and Practice, 15*(1), 55-64.

Torgesen, J. (2002). Empirical and theoretical support for direct diagnosis of learning disabilities by assessment of intrinsic processing weakness. In R. Bradley, L. Danielson, & D. Hallahan (Eds.), *Identification of learning disabilities: Research to practice* (pp. 565-613). Mahwah, NJ: Erlbaum.

Torgesen, J., Alexander, A., Wagner, R., Rashotte, C., Voeller, K., & Conway, T. (2001). Intensive remedial instruction for children with severe reading disabilities: Immediate and long-term outcomes from two instructional approaches. *Journal of Learning Disabilities, 34*(1), 33-58, 78.

Torgesen, J., & Wagner, R. (1998). Alternative diagnostic approaches for specific developmental reading disabilities. *Learning Disabilities Research and Practice, 13,* 220-232.

Towbin, K. E., Mauk, J. E., & Batshaw, M. L. (2002). Pervasive developmental disorders. In M. L. Batshaw (Ed.), *Children with disabilities* (5th ed.). Baltimore: Brooks.

Traxler, C. B. (2000). The Stanford achievement test, 9th edition: National norming and performance for deaf and hard-of-hearing students. *Journal of Deaf Studies and Deaf Education, 5*(4), 337-348.

Treffinger, D. J., & Barton, B. L. (1988). Fostering independent learning. *Gifted Child Today, 11,* 28-30.

Trumbull, E., Rothstein-Fisch, C., & Greenfield, P. M. (2000). *Bridging cultures in our schools: New approaches that work.* San Francisco: WestEd.

Tsai, L. Y., Stewart, M. A., & August, G. (1981). Implications of sex differences in the familial transmission of infantile autism. *Journal of Autism and Developmental Disorders, 11,* 165-173.

Tsal, Y., Shalev, L., & Mevorach, C. (2005). The diversity of attention deficits in ADHD. *Journal of Learning Disabilities, 38*(2), 142-157.

Tschannen-Moran, M., Woolfolk Hoy, A., & Hoy, W. K. (1998). Teacher efficacy: Its meaning and measure. *Review of Educational Research, 68,* 202-248.

Turnbull, H. R., Stowe, M., & Huerta, N. E. (2007). *Free appropriate public education: The law and children with disabilities.* Denver: Love.

Tyler, N., Yzquierdo, Z., Lopez-Reyna, N., & Flippin, S. (2004). Cultural and linguistic diversity and the special education workforce: A critical overview. *Journal of Special Education, 38*(1), 22-38.

U.S. Census Bureau. (2006). *State and county quick facts.* Retrieved October 18, 2006, from http://quickfacts.census.gov/qfd/

U.S. Department of Education. (1991). *Clarification of policy to address the needs of children with attention deficit disorders within general and/or special education.* Retrieved November 21, 2006, from http://www.wrightslaw.com/law/code_regs/ OSEP_Memorandum_ADD_1991.html

U.S. Department of Education. (2003). *25th annual report to Congress on the implementation of the Individuals with Disabilities Education Act: To assure the free appropriate public education of all children with disabilities.* Washington, DC: Author.

U.S. Department of Education. (2004). *26th annual report to Congress on the implementation of the Individuals with Disabilities Education Act.* Retrieved March 5, 2005, from http://www.ed.gov/ about/ reports/annual/osep/2004/index.html

U.S. Department of Education. (2005). *IDEA 2004 resources.* Retrieved June 11, 2006, from http://www.ed.gov/policy/speced/guid/idea/ idea2004.html

U.S. Department of Education. (2005). *26th annual report to Congress on the implementation of the Individuals with Disabilities Education Act* (Vol. 1). Washington, DC: Author.

U.S. Department of Education. (2005). Assistance to states for the education of children with disabilities. *Federal Register, 70*(118), 34 CFR, parts 300, 301, amend. 304, sec. 300.8.

U.S. Department of Education. (2005). *Individuals with Disabilities Education Act (IDEA) data.* Retrieved October 13, 2005, from http://www.ideadata.org/

U.S. Department of Education. (2006). *Assistance to states for the education of children with disabilities and preschool grants for children with disabilities.* [34 CFR Parts 300 and 301]. Washington, DC: Author.

U.S. Department of Education. (2006a). *Individuals with Disabilities Education Act data.* Retrieved June 11, 2006, from https://www.ideadata.org/index.html

U.S. Department of Education. (2006b). *IDEA regulations: Identification of specific learning disabilities.* Retrieved November 15, 2006, from http://idea.ed.gov/explore/home

U.S. Department of Education. (n.d.). *History: 25 years of progress in educating children with disabilities through IDEA.* Retrieved March, 10, 2005, http://www.ed.gov/policy/speced/leg/idea/ history.html

U.S. Department of Education, Office for Civil Rights. (n.d.). Retrieved January 10, 2005, from http://www.ed.gov/about/offices/list/ocr/

Utley, C., Mortsweet, S., & Greenwood, C. (1997). Peer mediated instruction and interventions. *Focus on Exceptional Children, 29*(5), 1-23.

Uzgiris, I. C. (1970). Sociocultural factors in cognitive development. In H. C. Haywood (Ed.), *Social-cultural aspects of mental retardation* (pp. 7-58). New York: Appleton-Century-Crofts.

Valdés, G. (1996). *Con respeto: Bridging the distance between culturally diverse families and schools.* New York: Teachers College Press.

Van Acker, R., Loncola, J. A., & Van Acker E. Y. (2005). Rett syndrome: A pervasive developmental disorder. In F. R. Volkmar, R. Paul, A. Klin, & D. Cohen (Eds.), *Handbook of autism and pervasive developmental disorders: Vol. 1. Diagnosis, development, neurobiology, and behavior* (4th ed., pp. 126-164). Hoboken, NJ: Wiley.

Vandercook, T., York, J., & Forest, M. (1989). The McGill Action Planning System (MAPS): A strategy for building the vision. *Journal of The Association for Persons with Severe Handicaps, 14,* 205-215.

Van Wagenen, L., & Hibbard, K. M. (1998, February). Building teacher portfolios. *Educational Leadership, 55*(5), 26-29.

Vaughn, S., Bos, C., & Schumm, J. (2007). *Teaching exceptional, diverse, and at-risk students in the general education classroom* (4th ed.). Boston: Allyn & Bacon.

Vaughn, S., & Fuchs, L. (2003). Redefining learning disabilities as inadequate response to instruction: The promise and potential problems. *Learning Disabilities Research and Practice, 18*(3), 137-146.

Vaughn, S., Gersten, R., & Chard, D. (2000). The underlying message in LD intervention research: Findings from research syntheses. *Exceptional Children, 67*(1), 99-114.

Vaughn, S., LaGreca, A., & Kuttler, A. (1999). The why, who, and how of social skills. In W. Bender (Ed.), *Professional issues in learning disabilities* (pp. 187-217). Austin, TX: PRO-ED.

Vellutino, F., Scanlon, D., Sipay, E., Small, S., Pratt, A., Chen, R., et al. (1996). Cognitive profiles of difficult-to-remediate and readily remediated poor readers: Early intervention as a vehicle for distinguishing between cognitive and experiential deficits as a basic cause of specific reading disability. *Journal of Educational Psychology, 88,* 601-638.

Venn, J. J. (2004). *Assessing students with special needs* (3rd ed.). Upper Saddle River, NJ: Merrill/Prentice Hall.

Venn, J. J. (2007). *Assessing students with special needs* (4th ed.). Upper Saddle River, NJ: Merrill/Prentice Hall.

Villa, R. A., & Thousand, J. S. (2000). *Restructuring for caring and effective education: Piecing the puzzle together.* Baltimore: Brookes.

Vogel, S., & Adelman, P. (2000). Adults with learning disabilities 8-15 years after college. *Learning Disabilities: A Multidisciplinary Journal, 10,* 165-182.

Volkmar, F. R., & Klin, A. (2005). Issues in the classification of autism and related conditions. In F. R. Volkmar, R. Paul, A. Klin, & D. Cohen (Eds.), *Handbook of autism and pervasive developmental disorders: Vol. 1. Diagnosis, development, neurobiology, and behavior* (4th ed., pp. 5-41). Hoboken, NJ: Wiley.

Volkmar, F. R., Szatmari, P., & Sparrow, S. S. (1993). Sex differences in pervasive developmental disorders. *Journal of Autism and Developmental Disorders, 23,* 579-591.

Wadsworth, D. E. D., & Knight, D. (1999). Preparing the inclusion classroom for students with special physical and health needs. *Intervention in School and Clinic, 34,* 170-175.

Wagner, M., Blackorby, J., Cameto, R., Hebbeler, K., & Newman, L. (1993). *The transition experiences of young people with disabilities: A summary of findings from the national longitudinal transition study of special education students.* Menlo Park, CA: SRI International.

Wagner, M., D'Amico, R., Marder, C., Newman, L., & Blackorby, J. (1992). *What happens next? Trends in postschool outcomes of youth with disabilities. The second comprehensive report from the National Longitudinal Transition Study of Special Education Students.* Menlo Park, CA: SRI International.

Wagner, M. M., & Blackorby, J. (1996). Transition from high school to work or college: How special education students fare. *Special Education for Students with Disabilities, 6*(1), 103–120.

Wagner, M. M., Kutash, K., Duchnowski. A. J., Epstein, M. H., & Sumi, W. C. (2005). The children and youth we serve: A national picture of the characteristics of students with emotional disturbances receiving special education. *Journal of Emotional and Behavioral Disorders, 13*(2), 79–96.

Waldron, N., & McLeskey, J. (1998). The impact of a full-time inclusive school program (ISP) on the academic achievement of students with mild and severe learning disabilities. *Exceptional Children, 64,* 395–405.

Walker, H., Colvin, G., & Ramsey, E. (1995). *Antisocial behavior in school: Strategies and best practices.* Pacific Grove, CA: Brooks/Cole.

Walker, H. M. (1983). *Walker problem behavior identification checklist.* Los Angeles: Western Psychological Services.

Walker, H. M., Horner, R. H., Sugai, G., Bullis, M., Sprague, J. R., Bricker, M., et al. (1996). Integrated approaches to preventing antisocial behavior patterns among school-age children and youth. *Journal of Emotional and Behavioral Disorders, 4*(4), 194–209.

Walker, H. M., Kavanagh, K., Stiller, B., Golly, A., Severson, H. H., & Feil, E. G. (1998). First step to success: An early intervention approach for preventing school antisocial behavior. *Journal of Emotional and Behavioral Disorders, 6*(2), 66–80.

Walker, H. M., McConnell, S. R., Holmes, D., Todis, B., Walker, J., & Golden, N. (1983). *ACCEPTS: A children's curriculum for effective peer and teacher skills.* Austin, TX: PRO-ED.

Walker, H. M., & Severson, H. H. (1992). *Systematic screening for behavior disorder (SSBD): User's guide and technical manual* (2nd ed.). Longmont, CO: Sopris West.

Walker, H. M., Severson, H. H., & Feil, E. G. (1995). *The early screening project: A proven child-find process.* Longmont, CO: Sopris West.

Walker, H. M., & Walker, J. E. (1991). *Coping with noncompliance in the classroom: A positive approach for teachers.* Austin, TX: PRO-ED.

Wallace, T., Bernhardt, J., & Utermarck, J. (1999). *Minnesota paraprofessional guide.* Minneapolis: University of Minnesota, Institute on Community Integration, Minnesota Paraprofessional Project.

Walters, J. M., & Gardner, H. M. (1986). The theory of multiple intelligences: Some issues and answers. In R. J. Sternberg & R. K. Wagner (Eds.), *Practical intelligence: Origins and nature of competence in the everyday world* (pp. 161–182). New York: Cambridge University Press.

Warger, C. (2002). *Supporting paraeducators: A summary of current practices* (ED475383). Arlington, VA: ERIC Clearinghouse on Disabilities and Gifted Education.

Wasserman, R., Kelleher, K., Bocian, A., et al. (1999). Identification of attentional and hyperactivity problems in primary care: A report from pediatric research in office settings and the ambulatory sentinel practice network. *Pediatrics, 103*(3), 661.

Waters, G., & Doehring, D. (1990). Reading acquisition in congenitally deaf children who communicate orally: Insights from an analysis of competent reading, language, and memory skills. In T. Carr & B. A. Levy (Eds.), *Reading and its development* (pp. 323–368). San Diego: Academic.

Watkins, S. (1987). Long term effects of home intervention with hearing-impaired children. *American Annals of the Deaf, 132,* 267–271.

Webber, J., & Scheuermann, B. (1997). A challenging future: Current barriers and recommended action for our field. *Behavioral Disorders, 22*(3), 167–178.

Webster, R. E., & Matthews, A. (2000). *Pre-kindergarten screen.* East Aurora, NY: Slosson Educational Publications.

Wechsler, D. (1991). *Wechsler intelligence scale for children* (3rd ed.). San Antonio, TX: Psychological Corporation.

Wechsler, D. (2003). *Wechsler intelligence scale for children* (4th ed.). San Antonio, TX: Psychological Corporation.

Wehby, J. H., Lane, K. L., & Falk, K. B. (2003). Academic instruction for students with emotional and behavioral disorders. *Journal of Emotional and Behavioral Disorders, 11*(4), 194–197.

Wehmeyer, M. (1996). Self-determination as an educational outcome: Why is it important to children, youth, and adults with disabilities? In D. Sands & M. Wehmeyer (Eds.), *Self-determination across the life span: Independence and choice for people with disabilities* (pp. 15–34). Baltimore: Brookes.

Wehmeyer, M. (2003). Defining mental retardation and ensuring access to the general curriculum. *Education and Training of Developmental Disabilities, 38,* 271–277.

Wehmeyer, M., & Schwartz, M. (1997). Self-determination and positive adult outcomes: A follow-up study of youth with mental retardation or learning disabilities. *Exceptional Children, 63*(2), 245–255.

Wehmeyer, M. L., Lance, G. D., & Bashinski, S. (2002). Promoting access to the general curriculum for students with mental retardation: A multi-level model. *Education and Training in Mental Retardation and Developmental Disabilities, 37*(3), 223–234.

Weinstein, R. (2002). *Reaching higher: The power of expectations in schooling.* Cambridge, MA: Harvard University Press.

Weinstein, S. (2002). Epilepsy. In M. L. Batshaw (Ed.), *Children with disabilities* (5th ed., pp. 493–523). Baltimore: Brookes.

Weintraub, F. J., & Abeson, A. (1976). New education policies for the handicapped: The quiet revolution. In F. J. Weintraub, A. Abeson, J. Ballard, & M. L. LaVor (Eds.), *Public policy and the education of exceptional children* (pp. 7–13). Reston, VA: Council for Exceptional Children.

Wenar, C., & Kerig, P. (2006). *Developmental psychopathology: From infancy through adolescence.* Boston: McGraw-Hill.

Westling, D. L., & Fox, L. (2004). *Teaching students with severe disabilities* (3rd ed.). Upper Saddle River, NJ: Merrill/Prentice Hall.

Westling, D. L., & Korland, M. A. (1988). *The special educator's handbook.* Boston: Allyn & Bacon.

Wetherby, A. M., Goldstein, H., Cleary, J., Allen, L., & Kublin, K. (2003). Early identification of children with communication disorders: Concurrent and predictive validity of the CSBS developmental profile. *Infants and Young Children, 16,* 161–174.

White, R. (1996). Unified discipline. In B. Algozzine (Ed.), *Problem behavior management: An educator's resource service* (pp. 11:28–11:36). Gaithersburg, MD: Aspen.

White, R., Algozzine, B., Audette, R., Marr, M. B., & Ellis, E. D. (2001). Unified discipline: A schoolwide approach for managing problem behavior. *Intervention in School and Clinic, 37*(1), 3–8.

Wilcox, B., & Bellamy, T. G. (1987). *The activities catalog: An alternative curriculum for youth and adults with severe disabilities.* Baltimore: Brookes.

Wilder, L. K., Taylor Dyches, T., Obiakor, F. E., & Algozzine, B. (2004). Multicultural perspectives on teaching students with autism. *Focus on Autism and Other Developmental Disabilities, 19*(2), 105–113.

Wilens, T., Faraone, S., Biederman, J., & Gunawardene, S. (2003). Does stimulant therapy of attention deficit hyperactivity disorder beget later substance abuse? Meta-analytic review of the literature. *Pediatrics, 111,* 179–185.

Willard-Holt, C. (1998). Academic and personality characteristics of gifted students with cerebral palsy: A multiple case study. *Exceptional Children, 65,* 37–50.

Williamson, P., McLeskey, J., Hoppey, D., & Rentz, T. (2006). Educating students with mental retardation in general education classrooms. *Exceptional Children, 72,* 347–361.

Willis, S. M. (1996). *Childhood depression in school age children* (ERIC Document Reproduction Service No. ED415973).

Wilson, B. L., & Corbett, H. D. (2001). *Listening to urban kids.* Albany: SUNY Press.

Wing, L. (1981). Asperger's syndrome: A clinical account. *Psychological Medicine, 11,* 115-129.

Wing, L., Leekam, S. R., Libby, S. J., Gould, J., & Larcombe, M. (2002). The diagnostic interview for social and communication disorders: Background, inter-rater reliability and clinical use. *Journal of Child Psychology and Psychiatry and Allied Disciplines, 43*(3), 307-325.

Winzer, M. A. (1998). A tale often told: The early progression of special education. *Remedial and Special Education, 19*(4), 212-218.

Wisniewski, L., & Gargiulo, R. M. (1997). Occupational stress and burnout among special educators: A review of the literature. *Journal of Special Education, 31,* 325-346.

Witt, J., VanDerHeyden, A., & Gilbertson, D. (2004). Troubleshooting behavioral interventions: A systematic process for finding and eliminating problems. *School Psychology Review, 33,* 363-383.

Wolery, M., Ault, M. J., & Doyle, P. M. (1992). *Teaching students with moderate to severe disabilities: Use of response prompting strategies.* New York: Longman.

Wolery, M., & Bailey, D. B. (2002). Early childhood special education research. *Journal of Early Intervention, 25,* 88-99.

Wolfensberger, W. (1985). An overview of social role valorization and some reflections on elderly mentally retarded persons. In M. Janicki & H. Wisniewski (Eds.), *Expanding systems of service delivery for persons with developmental disabilities* (pp. 127-148). Baltimore: Brookes.

Wolffe, K. (1996). Career education for students with visual impairments. *RE:view, 28*(2), 89-93.

Wolk, S., & Allen, T. E. (1984). A 5-year follow-up of reading comprehension achievement of hearing-impaired students in special education programs. *Journal of Special Education, 18,* 161-176.

Woodcock, R., McGrew, K., & Mather, N. (2001). *Woodcock-Johnson tests of achievement.* Itasca, IL: Riverside.

Woodcock, R., McGrew, K., & Mather, N. (2001). *Woodcock-Johnson III.* Itasca, IL: Riverside.

Woodcock, R. W., McGrew, K. S., & Mather, N. (2001). *Woodcock-Johnson III tests of cognitive abilities.* Itasca, IL: Riverside.

Woodruff, D. W., Osher, D., Hoffman, C. C., Gruner, A., King, M. A., et al. (1998). *Systems of care: Promising practices in children's mental health. 1998 series: Vol. 3. The role of education in a system of care: Effectively serving children with emotional or behavioral disorders.* Washington, DC: Center for Effective Collaboration and Practice, American Institute for Research.

Woods, J. J., & Wetherby, A. M. (2003, July). Early identification of and early intervention for infants and toddlers who are at risk for autism spectrum disorder. *Language, Speech, and Hearing Services in Schools, 34,* 180-193.

Wright-Strawderman, C., & Lindsay, P. (1996). Depression in students with disabilities: Recognition and intervention strategies. *Intervention in School and Clinic, 31*(5), 261-265.

Wunsch, M. J., Conlon, C. J., & Scheidt, P. C. (2001). Substance abuse: A preventable threat to development. In M. L. Batshaw (Ed.), *Children with disabilities* (5th ed., pp. 107-122). Baltimore: Brookes.

Xu, C., Reid, R., & Steckelberg, A. (2002). Technology applications for children with ADHD: Assessing the empirical support. *Education and Treatment of Children, 25*(2), 224-248.

Yeargin-Allsopp, M., Rice, C., Karapurkar, T., Doernberg, N., Boyle, C., & Murphy, C. (2003). Prevalence of autism in a U.S. metropolitan area. *Journal of the American Medical Association, 289*(1), 49-55.

Yell, M. L., & Drasgow, E. (2005). *No child left behind: A guide for professionals.* Upper Saddle River, NJ: Pearson.

Yirmiya, N., Sigman, M. D., Kasari, C., & Mundy, P. (1992). Empathy and cognition in high-functioning children with autism. *Child Development, 63*(1), 150-160.

Yoshinaga-Itano, C. (1987). Aural habilitation: A key to the acquisition of knowledge, language, and speech. *Seminars in Hearing, 8*(2), 169-174.

Yoshinaga-Itano, C., Coulter, D., & Thomson, V. (2000). Infant hearing impairment and universal hearing screening. The Colorado Newborn Hearing Screening Project: Effects on speech and language development for children with hearing loss. *Journal of Perinatology, 20,* S131-S136.

Ysseldyke, J., Dennison, A., & Nelson, R. (2004). *Large-scale assessment and accountability systems: Positive consequences for students with disabilities* (Technical Report 51). Minneapolis: University of Minnesota, National Center on Educational Outcomes.

Zafft, C., Hart, D., & Zimbrich, K. (2004). College career connection: A study of youth with intellectual disabilities and the impact of postsecondary education. *Education and Training in Developmental Disabilities, 39,* 45-53.

Zentall, S. (2006). *ADHD and education: Foundations, characteristics, methods, and collaboration.* Upper Saddle River, NJ: Prentice Hall.

Zhang, D., & Katsiyannis, A. (2002). Minority representation in special education: A persistent challenge. *Remedial and Special Education, 23*(3), 180-187.

Zito, J., Safer, D., dosReis, S., et al. (1999). Psychotherapeutic medication patterns for youth with attention deficit hyperactivity disorder. *Archives of Pediatric and Adolescent Medicine, 153*(12), 1257-1263.

Zito, J., Safer, D., dosReis, S., et al. (2000). Trends in the prescribing of psychotropic medications in preschoolers. *Journal of the American Medical Association, 283*(8), 1025-1030.

Name Index

Abate, F., 80
Abbott, M., 439
Abeson, A., 32, 34
Aborn, L., 213
Achenbach, T., 245
Achenbach, T. M., 173, 184, 185
Adams, L., 283
Adelman, P., 150
Agency for Healthcare Research and Quality, 354
Agran, M., 327, 336
Ahearn, E., 143
Akshoomoff, N., 273
Albert, L., 130
Albin, R. W., 329
Algozinne, B., 123
Algozzine, B., 69
Algozzine, R., 178
Alkin, M. C., 117, 210, 212, 216, 228
Allbritten, D., 45
Allen, L., 88, 89
Allen, S., 118, 219
Allen, T. E., 355
Alley, G., 158
Allsopp, D., 164
Almond, P. J., 276
Alper, S., 336
Alsop, L., 364
Alvarez, M., 59
Alvino, J., 416
Amanti, C., 75
Amenkhienan, C., 254, 255
American Academy of Asthma Allergy and
    Immunology (AAAAI), 384
American Academy of Pediatrics (AAP), 244, 245,
    252, 255, 256
American Association of Colleges for Teacher
    Education, 59
American Association on Mental Retardation
    (AAMR), 206, 207, 324
American Foundation for the Blind, 358, 370
American Lung Association, 384, 391
American Printing House for the Blind, 358
American Psychiatric Association (APA), 173, 174,
    177, 205, 236, 237, 238, 240, 241, 242, 244,
    246, 255, 256, 262, 264, 265, 266, 268, 270,
    271, 272, 324
American Speech-Language-Hearing Association
    (ASHA), 315, 316, 350
Anastasiow, N., 209
Anderson, G. M., 273
Anderson, J. L., 329
Anderson, L., 113
Anderson, L. M., 75
Angelman Syndrome Foundation, 326
ARC, 214
Arick, J. R., 276, 279, 286
Arnold, K. D., 418, 425

Arthur-Kelly, M., 336
Artiles, A., 66
Asgharian, A., 270
August, G., 272
Ault, M. J., 338
Austin, G. W., 251
Axelrod, M., 152
Azordegan, J., 447

Babbidge Committee Report, 369
Babyak, A., 118, 219
Baca, L. M., 66
Baglieri, S., 61
Bailey, D., 154
Bailey, D. B., 87, 335
Bailey, W., 179
Baird, G., 275, 276
Baker, L. J., 286
Bali, V., 59
Balla, D. A., 104, 215
Bandura, A., 18
Bangert, A. W., 93
Banks, J., 72, 75, 76, 77
Banner, J. M., 450, 451
Bantz, J., 188
Barbaresi, W., 255, 256
Barenbaum, E., 177
Barkley, R., 240, 241, 242, 243, 245, 247, 248, 250,
    251, 252, 253, 255, 256, 257
Barkley, R. A., 197
Baron-Cohen, S., 269
Barry, M., 89
Bartoli, J. S., 79
Barton, B. L., 425
Barton, M., 270
Bashford, A., 276
Bashinski, S., 337
Batshaw, M. L., 264, 325, 326, 330
Becker, W., 190
Bedore, L. M., 299, 300
Beebe-Frankenberger, M. E., 285
Beers, M. K., 13
Beirne-Smith, M., 154, 205, 208, 209, 210, 212,
    213, 228, 229, 330
Belanger, J., 418
Bell, L. I., 17
Bellamy, T. G., 333
Bempechat, J., 70
Benard, B., 70, 74, 75
Bender, W., 148
Benner, G. J., 308
Bennett, A., 215
Bennett, C., 64
Berger, S. L., 417, 425
Bernadette, K., 221
Bernas-Pierce, J., 363
Bernhardt, J., 443

Best, K. M., 70
Best, S., 378, 383, 384, 387, 390, 391, 392, 393,
    397, 398
Best, S. J., 382, 383, 392, 396
Bettelheim, B., 269, 271
Bhanpuri, H., 69
Biederman, J., 243, 256
Bigge, J., 399
Bigge, J. L., 382, 383, 392, 396, 397, 402, 404
Biklen, D., 229, 287, 336
Billingsley, B. S., 20, 47, 434, 436, 440, 444
Birch, J. W., 420
Birnbaum, R., 178
Blackorby, J., 179, 180, 196
Blair, C., 208
Blank, W., 180
Blatt, J., 327
Bloch, D., 271
Bloom, B., 219
Bobeck, B. L., 444
Bocian, K. M., 173, 176
Bogdan, R., 229
Bolger, K., 208
Bolick, N., 34
Bolt, L., 164
Bondy, A., 280
Bondy, E., 65, 75
Bonwit, A. M., 398
Books, S., 68
Boone, R., 120
Bos, C., 114, 115, 247
Boskin, J., 66, 67
Braddock, D., 342
Bradley, R., 180, 187
Brady, M., 208, 330
Brady, N. C., 325
Braziel, P. M., 179
Bricker, D., 275, 336
Brigance, A., 275
Brigham, F. J., 17
Brilliant, R. L., 358
Broer, S. M., 14
Brophy, J., 117, 219, 220
Brophy, J. E., 17
Browder, D. M., 105, 332
Brown, D. F., 65, 75
Brown, F., 335, 340
Brown, L., 324, 327, 333, 337
Bruininks, R. H., 104
Bruner, E., 221
Bryant, D., 147
Bryant, J., 144
Bryk, A., 118
Buck, G. H., 93
Buescher, T. M., 416, 417
Bulgren, J., 159
Bullis, M., 180, 195

Forness, S., 71, 146, 147
Forness, S. R., 172, 180, 181, 197, 250, 256
Forni, P. M., 133
Foshay, J., 223
Fox, J., 187
Fox, L., 121, 205, 223, 226, 323, 324, 325, 327, 328, 329, 335, 337, 339, 340
Frank, A. R., 190
Frankenburg, W., 102
Fránquiz, M., 67
Freeman, S. F. N., 117, 210, 212, 216, 228
French, N., 443
Frey, L. M., 196
Friend, M., 442
Friend, M. P., 317
Frisbie, D. A., 102
Frith, U., 287
Frost, L., 280
Fuchs, D., 33, 93, 94, 104, 118, 141, 144, 145, 165, 166, 219, 439
Fuchs, L., 33, 118, 120, 141, 144, 145, 150, 151, 165, 166, 219, 439
Fuentes, F., 270
Fullan, M., 217
Fullerton, A., 279

Gable, R. A., 186, 187
Gaffney, J. S., 119
Gagné, F., 415, 418, 419
Gagnon, E., 283
Gallagher, J., 209
Gallagher, J. J., 33, 427
Gallaudet Research Institute, 357, 365
Gallingane, C., 65
Gallini, S., 227
Galluzzo, G., 445
Gansle, K., 173
Garcia, S. B., 68
Gardill, M. C., 188
Gardner, H., 414
Gardner, H. M., 414
Gargiulo, R. M., 21
Garmezy, N., 70
Garrison-Kane, L., 376
Gartin, B., 32
Gaylord-Ross, R., 336
Geertz, C., 62
Gerand, J. D., 282
Gerber, M., 165
Gerhardt, P. F., 284
Gersten, R., 21, 118, 219, 434
Getzel, E., 213, 225
Giangreco, M. F., 14, 333, 337
Gibbons, P., 67
Gilbertson, D., 127
Gillam, R. B., 301, 307, 309
Gillberg, C., 272, 276
Gilliam, J., 244
Glaser, C. H. W., 402, 403
Goertzel, M. G., 418
Goertzel, V., 418
Goetz, L., 18, 336
Goldenberg, D. S., 102
Goldman, S. K., 194
Goldstein, A. P., 193
Goldstein, D., 162, 163
Goldstein, H., 88
Gonzalez, N., 75, 79
Good, T., 117, 219, 220
Goode, D., 33
Goor, M. B., 450
Gordon, K. A., 444
Gordon, M. S., 175
Gordon, R., 270
Gouvousis, A., 283

Grabowski, J., 264
Graboyes, M., 358
Graham, S., 147
Grandlin, T., 286
Gray, C. A., 282
Green, J., 270
Greenfield, P. M., 62, 63
Greenwood, C., 219
Gresham, F., 143
Gresham, F. M., 104, 173, 175, 176, 178, 184, 285
Griffin, C., 20, 440
Griffin, C. C., 20, 94, 392, 440
Griffin, H. C., 382
Griffin, L. W., 382
Gross, M. U. M., 415
Grossman, H., 215
Grouse, W. F., 434, 450
Gudykunst, W. B., 62, 63
Guetzloe, E., 188
Gullat, D. E., 437
Gunawardene, S., 256
Gureasko-Moore, D., 240, 250, 255
Gutiérrez, K., 64

Haas, A., 296
Haas, J., 34
Hagen, E., 103
Hahn, H., 71
Hall, D., 45
Hallahan, D. P., 5, 6, 133
Halsey, H., 186
Hambacher, E., 65
Hamlett, C., 144
Hampton, E. O., 316, 317
Hamre-Nietupski, S., 337
Handleman, J. S., 270, 277, 282
Handler, M. W., 188
Hanley, G. P., 329
Hanner, S., 221
Hanushek, E., 110
Hardin, D. T., 437
Hardman, M. L., 42, 45, 336
Haring, N., 184
Harniss, M. K., 21, 434
Harris, D., 185
Harris, J. J., 427
Harris, K. R., 147
Harris, S. L., 270, 277, 278, 280, 282
Harrison, P., 215
Hart, D., 213, 226
Hart, H., 398
Hass, J., 371
Hasselbring, T. S., 402, 403
Hatch, T., 414
Hatton, D. D., 363
Heal, L. W., 195
Heath, S. B., 68
Hebbeler, K., 180
Heber, R., 215, 229
Hebert, T. P., 416
Helders, P. J. M., 398
Heller, K. W., 325, 329, 339, 359, 397
Henderson, K., 180, 187
Henderson, M. V., 437
Hendrick, I. G., 31
Hendricks, M. D., 326
Hendrickson, J. M., 186, 188
Henley, M., 178
Henry, D., 152, 216
Herr, S., 32
Hester, P. P., 188
Heward, W. L., 5
Hibbard, K. M., 449
Hicken, M., 87
Higgins, K., 120

Hill, B. K., 104
Hilvitz, P. B., 186
Hitchcock, C., 113, 114, 224
Hitchings, W. E., 99
Hoagwood, K., 256
Hock, M., 159
Hodapp, R. M., 325
Hodges, D., 216
Hodgkinson, H., 56
Hollins, E. R., 77, 79
Hollinsworth, L. S., 415
Holmes, D. L., 284
Holt, J., 369
Holubec, E., 118
Hoover, D. H., 102
Hoppey, D., 152, 210
Hord, S. M., 439
Horn, S., 110
Horner, R. H., 122, 178, 329
Horvath, M., 99
Hoshino, Y., 273
Hoskyn, M., 219
Hosp, J., 57, 211, 228
Hourcade, J., 204
Howard, J., 118, 219
Howell, J. J., 365, 366, 372
Howlin, P., 270, 272, 284, 287
Hoy, W. K., 18
Huebner, K. M., 368
Huentelman, M. J., 272
Huerta, N. E., 35
Hughes, C., 159, 327
Hughes, M., 118, 219
Hugo, K., 327
Hu-Lince, D., 272
Hulsey, D., 39
Humphrey, G., 30
Humphries, T., 351
Hunt, P., 336
Hurst, B., 449
Hussar, W. J., 56
Hynd, G. W., 150

Igoa, C., 67
Indiana Department of Education, 149
Individuals with Disabilities Education Act (IDEA), 24, 34, 86, 95, 97, 98, 100, 121, 141, 145, 221, 235, 238, 378, 379
Inge, K. J., 195, 253
Ingersoll, B., 280
Interstate New Teacher Assessment and Support Consortium, 16
Irvine, J. J., 70, 79
Iverson, V. S., 333
Iwata, B. A., 329

Jackman, L. A., 122, 123, 124, 127, 131, 442
Jackson, R., 113, 224
Jackson, S., 276
Janney, R. E., 13
Jannik, C., 437
Jennet, H. K., 282
Jensen, P., 256
Jewell, E. J., 80
Johns, B. H., 130
Johnson, D., 69, 118
Johnson, G., 221
Johnson, G. O., 216
Johnson, L. J., 317
Johnson, R., 118
Johnson, R. A., 40
Jolivette, K., 191
Jones, E. D., 419, 420
Jones, L., 121, 130
Jones, R. R., 174

www.prenhall.com/rosenberg

Subject Index

507

Replacement behaviors, 193
Research and Demonstration Projects in Education
    of Handicapped Students Act (1964), 36
Research-based practices, 438–439
Residential services, 341, 349, 365–368
Resilience
    defined, 70
    fostering of, 71
    professionalism and, 443–444
Resource rooms
    blindness and, 367
    deafness and, 365
    special education teachers and, 11
    students with gifts and talents, 411
Resources, access to, 59–60
Respect
    communication and, 111, 133
    special education teachers and, 20
    teacher attitudes and, 17
Respiration, 298
Respiratory infections, 329, 339
Response to intervention (RTI)
    identification and, 85, 93, 94, 95
    students with learning disabilities and, 42, 143,
        144–145, 150, 151, 154, 165
Rett's disorder, 263, 264
Revised Behavior Problem Checklist, 102
Reynolds, Maynard, 39
Rhode Island, 143
Right to education movement, 26
Ritualistic behaviors, 268–269
Rivera, Geraldo, 32–33
Rodgers, Roy, 32
Routines
    behavior management and, 124, 126
    explicit teaching of, 75–76
Routines and procedures, 124, 126
RTI. See Response to intervention (RTI)
Rubella, 331, 353, 359
Rules
    explicit teaching of, 75–76
    inclusive behavior management and, 123
    students with attention deficit hyperactivity
        disorder and, 247
    students with emotional and behavioral
        disorders, 175
    tangible management plan and, 127
    teacher insistence and, 76

Safeguarding Our Children (Dwyer and Osher), 122
Savants, 262
Scaffolding, students with learning disabilities,
    157–159, 160
Scales of Independent Behavior-Revised, 104
Schaffer v. Weist, Montgomery County Schools
    (2005), 37
Schizophrenia, 266
School influences, students with emotional and
    behavioral disorders, 182–183
School population, changes in, 55–57
School psychologists, as related-services
    professionals, 14, 15
School to Work Opportunities Act (1994), 36
Screening for Autism in 2-Year-Olds (STAT), 376
Screening tests
    administration of, 102
    identification and, 93
    initial evaluation and, 94
    students with attention deficit hyperactivity
        disorder, 244–245
    students with autism spectrum disabilities,
        274–275, 276
    students with emotional and behavioral
        disorders, 183, 188
Secondary behavioral correlates, 270

Section 504 of the Rehabilitation Act
    criteria for disability, 376
    evolution of IDEA 2004 and, 36
    504 plans and, 98
    and interactional model of disabilities, 71
    provisions of, 27, 45–46
    students with attention deficit hyperactivity
        disorder and, 239, 245, 246
Seizures, 387–388
Self-advocacy, 286
Self-contained special classrooms, special
    education teachers, 12
Self-control, students with emotional and
    behavioral disorders, 192–193
Self-determination, students with mild intellectual
    disabilities, 225–226
Self-fulfilling prophecy, 183
Self-injurious behaviors (SIBs), 90, 270–271, 328
Self-management
    students with attention deficit hyperactivity
        disorder and, 248
    students with emotional and behavioral
        disorders and, 188
Self-monitoring
    students with attention deficit hyperactivity
        disorder and, 248
    students with emotional and behavioral
        disorders and, 192
Self-nomination, students with gifts and talents, 421
Self-regulation strategies
    students with attention deficit hyperactivity
        disorder and, 247
    students with severe intellectual disabilities
        and, 327
Semantics, 296
Separate class placements
    students with mild intellectual disabilities and,
        203, 211, 216
    students with sensory impairments, 349
    students with severe intellectual disabilities,
        336–337
Separation anxiety, 177
Service delivery
    special education history and, 27, 33
    students with attention deficit hyperactivity
        disorder and, 246
    students with autism spectrum disabilities and,
        277–278
    students with communication disorders and,
        312, 316
    students with emotional and behavioral
        disorders and, 186–188
    students with learning disabilities and, 152–153
    students with mild intellectual disabilities and,
        215–217
Service learning, students with emotional and
    behavioral disorders, 196
Severe discrepancy criterion, 143–144, 151, 152, 165
Severe intellectual disabilities
    accountability and, 43
    classification of, 324–325
    general education classroom and, 11
    identifying preschoolers with special needs
        and, 88
Sex chromosomes, 331
Sheltered workshops, 284
Short-term services, 368
SIBs (self-injurious behaviors), 90, 270–271, 328
Sickle-cell disease, 385
SIM (strategies intervention model), 117
Site Visits
    Asheville City Schools Preschool Program, 92
    First Steps to Success, 189
    Helen Keller National Center for Deaf-Blind
        Youths and Adults, 371

inclusive school programs, 217
    Multiliteracy Project, 78
    Project EXCITE, 423
    schoolwide behavior-management programs, 122
    students with attention deficit hyperactivity
        disorder in college, 254
    students with learning disabilities and, 164
    TEACCH program, 285
Situational specificity, 267
Situation-options-consequences-choices-strategies-
    stimulation (SOCCSS), 280–281
Six hour retarded child, 202
SLPs. *See* Speech/language pathologists (SLPs)
Smith-Magenis syndrome, 90
Snellen charts, 102
SOCCSS (situation-options-consequences-choices-
    strategies-stimulation), 280–281
Social anxiety, 177
Social behavior
    students with communication disorders and,
        307–308
    students with severe intellectual disabilities and,
        328–329
Social justice, culturally relevant curriculum and,
    79–80
Social reciprocity, 266–268
Social Responsiveness Scale (SRS), 276
Social services, Section 504 and, 46
Social skills
    students with attention deficit hyperactivity
        disorder and, 239–240
    students with autism spectrum disabilities and,
        277, 279, 280
    students with emotional and behavioral
        disorders and, 178, 193
    students with learning disabilities and, 148–149
    students with mild intellectual disabilities and,
        209–210
    students with sensory impairments and,
        356–357
Social Skills Rating System (SSRS), 104, 184
Social stories, 282–283
Social withdrawal, students with emotional and
    behavioral disorders, 175–176
Social workers, as related-services professionals,
    14, 15
Sociocultural factors, preschoolers with special
    needs, 90
Socioeconomic status
    academic achievement and, 59
    in school population, 56–57
    of students with disabilities, 54
    students with emotional and behavioral
        disorders and, 182
    students with gifts and talents, 428
    students with learning disabilities and, 144
    students with mild intellectual disabilities and,
        213–214
Spastic CP, 382
Special education
    conceptual framework of, 26
    continuum of services in, 9, 10
    diversity in, 57
    evidence-based teaching approaches and, 18–19
    historical overview of, 29
    personal reflections, 3, 5, 7, 11, 12, 13, 14,
        16, 17, 19, 433, 435, 437, 438, 440, 444,
        448, 450
    professionalism in, 434–439
    social history of, 26, 27–34
    "special" aspects of, 4–5, 6
    tests used in, 102–105
Special education curriculum
    general education curriculum compared to, 5
    history of, 31